PORTRAIT OF GEORGE WASHINGTON AS A VIRGINIA
COLONEL OF MILITIA.

(Painted by C. W. Peale at Mount Vernon, 1772.)

GEORGE WASHINGTON

The Human Being and the Hero
1732-1762

GEORGE
WASHINGTON
The Human Being & The Hero
1732–1762

RUPERT
HUGHES

1926

NEW YORK

WILLIAM MORROW & COMPANY

COPYRIGHT, 1926, BY
WILLIAM MORROW AND COMPANY, INC.

Published, October, 1926
Second Printing, October 15, 1926
Third Printing, November 10, 1926
Fourth Printing, December 20, 1926
Fifth Printing, February, 1928

PRINTED IN THE U S. A. BY
QUINN & BODEN COMPANY, INC.
RAHWAY, N. J.

"A nation's attitude toward its own history is like a window into its own soul and the men and women of such a nation cannot be expected to meet the great obligations of the present if they refuse to exhibit honesty, charity, open-mindedness, and a free and growing intelligence toward the past that has made them what they are."

CHARLES MCLEAN ANDREWS.
From *The Colonial Background of the American Revolution.*

CONTENTS

ILLUSTRATIONS

ix

ILLUSTRATIONS

I

HIS NATIVE SCENE AND HIS ANCESTRY

"& the pursuit of happiness."

HAPPINESS as an inalienable right! Happiness as a decent thing to pursue! as an ideal, indeed! as an object worthy of a revolution!

Who but a Virginian, at that period of American history, would have put such a word into the Declaration of Independence? Where else in America was happiness so completely and frankly an art and an ambition?

Virginia was Paradise or Purgatory according to the point of view of the visitor. One wrote of "Virginia Richly Valued"; another of "Virginia Unmasked." The author of *A Perfect Description*[1] esteemed it an Eden, though he said of New England, "there is not much in that land," and found it such a desert that "except a Herring be put into the hole you set the Corne or Maize in, it will not come up."

Corn, or maize, was much neglected in Virginia. Tobacco was the breath of its life, and there was an old saying that "The story of Virginia is but the story of tobacco." John Rolfe, who married Pocahontas, began the cultivation of it in 1612, and seven years later he described the arrival of "a Dutch man of warre that sold us twenty Negars."[2] These first slaves were not sold into lifetime bondage, but for only a term of years; and it was not until 1625 that a lawsuit made the negro a property.

Tobacco soon subordinated "all other interests, agricultural as well as manufacturing. This influence permeated

[1] For all footnote references, etc., see Appendix I, pages 495-551.

I

the entire social fabric of the colony, directed its laws, was an element in all its political and religious disturbances, and became the direct instigation of its curse of African slavery." [3] In early Virginia, tobacco was money. The clergymen's salaries were paid in it. The imported white slaves were bought with it.

For the Virginia settlers soon found it profitable to bring over indentured servants by the thousands. England was in a state of dreadful unemployment and America was convenient as a cure for "the plurisy of people." The poor sold themselves for a term of years long enough to pay their passage money of six pounds sterling. The stolen ones were known as "Kids." They were respectable but poor, and vastly outnumbered the criminals whom England dumped into Virginia. In fact, the indentured servants outnumbered all other classes.

"It is probable," says Beard,[4] "that the number of bondservants exceeded the original twenty thousand Puritans, the yeomen, the Virginia gentlemen, and the Huguenots combined. . . . The story of this traffic in white servants is one of the most striking things in the history of labor."

There has been much satire on the convict origin of the First Families of Virginia, and genealogists have been invited to turn their attention to the records of Newgate Prison. James Davie Butler said that Bancroft told him he dared not publish the enormous number of felons and lesser criminals sent to Virginia.

Though New England offered a bounty for convicts and bought numberless Irishmen, Virginia protested incessantly. Benjamin Franklin, it was said, sent to Sir Robert Walpole a number of rattlesnakes, as an ornament to the King's gardens at Kew "in return for the curious venomous reptiles the ministers had been pleased to present to Virginia." [5]

But crime seeks its own level and this element could have

exerted no more influence on the social or official life of Virginia than on that of England. They had no more political power than the slaves, except in the case of those who were only criminals through political shifts of opinion. Many of these were noble souls in disgrace because of their resistance to tyranny.

Numbers of cavaliers were driven over by the Puritans. After the Restoration, the Puritan partisans of Cromwell were shipped across in such numbers as to clog the tobacco fields and furnish an element strong enough to threaten a Puritan insurrection. It cannot, therefore, be said that Virginia was overwhelmingly Cavalier in its origins, though the Puritan spirit lasted but a little while in that atmosphere.

The tobacco boom and the insatiable need for hands to work in the fields led to wholesale kidnapping or "spiriting" of helpless victims, young and old. It became a regular business, in which ladies of the court took part. At one time as many as ten thousand persons were kidnapped annually and shipped to various parts of the British Empire.

The indentured servants, being permitted to marry and acquire property, and freedom in seven years, became so numerous as small landholders of tracts ranging from fifty to five hundred acres that they soon filled the bulk of the cultivated territory. The rest was held by men of aristocratic origin, many of whom held vast domains of almost incredible magnitude.

But toil was hard, tobacco uncertain, and the increasing importation of slaves greatly checked the importation of indentured servants, utterly altered the character of the Virginians. The indentured servants who had gained their freedom, and other immigrants of moderate means, could not withstand the competition with slaves, and a mighty exodus began. Thousands fled from Virginia to escape the black flood.

Those who remained tried for a time to maintain themselves by raising a leaf of better grade than the stupid slaves could produce. But by the time the negroes had learned to raise tobacco, the poor whites had learned to buy slaves, and raise them. Virginia became a slave-breeding, slave-selling community.

All but the very poorest whites had slaves and grew haughty. They forgot how to toil and learned to enjoy the virtues and vices of leisurely elegance. They had time and money to spend.

This social revolution is compared by Wertenbaker [6] to the profound alteration of Rome when "in the third and second centuries before Christ the glory of the republic lay in its peasantry. . . . Thrown into competition with slave labor the peasant proprietor found it impossible to sustain himself. . . . Thus Italy was transformed from the land of the little farmer into the land of big estates cultivated by slaves."

John Spencer Bassett [7] has explained why conditions prevented the growth of large towns in Virginia, and how inconvenient this was for the planters. Yet it made each plantation more or less self-sustaining.

The settlers of Virginia were described with wide variance. Peter Collinson, in 1737, wrote to a friend about to visit them:

"For these Virginians are a very gentle, well-dressed people, and look, perhaps, more at a man's outside than his inside. For these and other reasons, pray go very clean, neat and handsomely dressed in Virginia."

On the other hand, an unlucky anonymous English officer [8] wrote home from Virginia:

"I reckon the Day I bought my Commission the most unhappy in my Life, excepting that in which I landed in this Country." After berating the climate of all four seasons, he says: "What is excessively disagreeable here is, that the Wealth of the Country consists in Slaves, so that all one eats rises out of driving and whipping these poor Wretches; this Kind of Authority so Corrupts the Minds of the Masters, and makes them so overbearing, that they are the most troublesome Company upon Earth. . . . With respect to public Diversions, the worst English Country Town exceeds all they have in the whole Province . . . their only tolerable Drink is Rum Punch, which they swill Morning, Noon, and Night.   Their Produce is Tobacco; they are so attached to that, and their Avarice to raise it, makes them neglect every Comfort of Life."

The Marquis de Chastellux was also shocked by what he saw and complained "that the indolence and dissipation of the middling and lower classes of white inhabitants of Virginia is such as to give pain to every reflecting mind." [9]

The Virginians had indeed become a separate people when Englishmen found them haughty and Frenchmen found them dissolute.

Their educational standards were low as they were everywhere, though the aristocratic element sent its children to be educated at Oxford and elsewhere "back home." "Back home" meant England, of course.   But, as in Europe, the common herd were illiterate to a degree undreamed of in our times.

When in 1671, the Royal Governor, Sir William Berkeley [10] answered a number of questions sent out by the Commissioners of Plantations, he answered Query 23: "What course is taken about the instructing the people, within your government in the christian religion?" in these immortal words:

"The same course that is taken in England out of towns; every man according to his ability instructing his children. We have fforty eight parishes, and our ministers are well paid, and by my consent should be better *if they would pray oftener and preach less.* But of all other commodities, so of this, *the worst are sent us,* and we had few that we could boast of, since the persication in *Cromwell's* tiranny drove divers worthy men hither. But, I thank God, *there are no free schools* nor *printing,* and I hope we shall not have these hundred years; for *learning* has brought disobedience, and heresy, and sects into the world, and *printing* has divulged them, and libels against the best government. God keep us from both!"

It was during Berkeley's administration that the first American ancestors of Washington arrived in Virginia. They came out neither as indentured servants, nor as convicts. They were educated gentlemen, royalists, nephews of knights, sons of an Oxford man, a clergyman; yet they might have been transported involuntarily if they had not come of their own accord to escape the cruelty of a sect that is more advertised as persecuted than persecuting.

Among the many things America owes to the Puritans is the birth on these shores of the least Puritan of great Americans.

Had it not been for the Puritan persecution of his great-great-grandfather, the Reverend Lawrence Washington, in England, his great-grandfather, John Washington, would probably never have come overseas.

It was only when he was perhaps the most eminent man in the world that Washington either knew or cared much about his origins abroad. In 1792, Sir Isaac Heard, the Garter King of Arms, sent him an incomplete genealogical table and asked him to fill it up. Washington replied that "this is a subject to which I confess I have paid very little attention."

But he wrote to his nephew, William Augustine Washington, for help, saying, "The enquiry is in my opinion of very little moment, but as Sir Isaac has interested himself in the matter . . . I wish to give him as correct information of it—as I am able to procure."

Then he compiled a table beginning: "In the year 1657, or thereabouts . . . John and Lawrence Washington, brothers, emigrated from the North of England, and settled at Bridges' Creek, on the Potomac River, in the County of Westmoreland. But from whom they descended, the sub-scriber is possessed of no document to ascertain." [11]

An affliction of the eyes prevented Sir Isaac from finishing his researches and Washington died without knowing whence he came. But the hunt went on, and none of the lies, tricks and forgeries that make genealogy one of the most un-reliable of sports were wanting in the pursuit; nor was there lack of the indefatigable search of musty documents and tombstones.

The line seems now to be established with almost com-plete certainty to John Washington of Whitfield, Lancaster county, or perhaps Northampton, in the fifteenth century. From this John followed two more Johns, then a Lawrence, who, on the dissolution of the monasteries by Henry VIII, received a parcel of the priory of St. Andrew—the manor of Sulgrave, about seventy-five miles northwest of London as the crow flies.

He died in 1584, and in his will he bequeathed to a poor widow Compton a cottage, "so as she well and honestly be-have herself . . . without paying any rent therefor, other than one red rose at the feast of Saint John Baptist yearly, if the same be demanded. And my further meaning and intent is that the said Robert and his heirs shall from time to time forever appoint some honest aged or impotent person to inhabit the same cottage for term of life . . . and not pay to my heirs any manner of rent therefor . . . other than a red rose." [12]

This gracious gentleman left a son Robert, who left a

son Lawrence, called "Lawrence of Sulgrave and Brington."

This Lawrence sold Sulgrave and retired to Brington. He begot eight boys in succession and then eight girls. Two of his sons were knighted, Sir William, and Sir John; one went to Spain as a page to Prince Charles and died there, one was the Reverend Lawrence Washington, the last of Washington's direct ancestors to live and die in England.

He was born about 1602, entered Brasenose College at Oxford in 1619, took his B.A. in 1623, became Fellow the next year, and was presented to the valuable living of Purleigh in Essex County in 1632, in which year he married Amphillis Roades, believed to have been the daughter of one of the servants of Sir Edmund Verney.

Civil war flared up in England, beginning with the clash between King Charles I and his Parliament, of which Macaulay said, "Their meeting was one of the great eras in the history of the civilized world. Whatever of political freedom exists either in Europe or America has sprung directly or indirectly from those institutions which they secured and reformed. We never turn to the annals of those times without feeling increased admiration of the patriotism, the energy, the decision, the consummate wisdom, which marked the measures of that great parliament."

The bishops, undaunted by the wrath of Parliament, passed resolutions supporting the unlimited power and divine right of the King, and granted him money. Parliament promptly annihilated the authority of the bishops, fined them from £5,000 to £20,000 apiece, abolished kneeling, removed crosses and pictures and denounced idolatry, and finally threw the bishops into the Tower. A brewer's wife, in the name of many gentlewomen, presented a petition against the bloody papists and prelates, and it was received with respect. Parliament ousted the bishops from the House of Lords and from civil offices.

The King finally revolted against the revolt and set up a standard bearing the words, "Render unto Cæsar the things that are Cæsar's." A wind threw it down and a gale carried away the crown and the King's head with it.

In came grim Noll Cromwell. Down from Scotland stalked the dour Presbyterians, with more rigid ideas of conformity and sanctity than the weaker tyrants they had deposed. They began ejecting Anglican clergymen from their livings by the wholesale. The Puritan historian, Neal, says that only sixteen hundred were thrown out of their churches. Walker, the author of the *Sufferings of the Clergy*, set the number at eight thousand. The truth was probably somewhere between the two, but among the throng was the Reverend Lawrence Washington, he who was almost certainly the great-great-grandfather of George Washington.

A book published by order of Parliament in 1643 puts him ninth on the list of "The First Century of Scandalous, Malignant Priests,"—"for that he is a common frequenter of Ale-houses, not onlly himselfe sitting dayly tippling there, but also incouraging others in that beastly vice, and hath been oft drunk, and hath said, *That the Parliament have more Papists belonging to them in their Armies than the King had about him or in his Army, and that the Parliaments Armie did more hurt than the Cavaliers, and that they did none at all;* and hath published them to be Traitours, that lend to or assist the Parliament."

John Walker, in his *Sufferings of the Clergy*, defended the Reverend Lawrence Washington from the charges of "that Infamous Pamphlet," as "a Worthy, Pious . . . very Modest, Sober Person, and . . . withal a Loyal Person, and had one of the best Benefices in these Parts, and this was the ONLY Cause of his Expulsion. . . . Mr. Washington was afterwards permitted to Have, and Continue upon a Living in these Parts, but it was such a Poor and Miserable

one, that it was always with Difficulty that anyone was persuaded to Accept of it."

By a coincidence, in the very year of 1643 when the
Puritans expelled John's father from his living, the Virginians expelled all Puritan pastors from the boundaries
of Virginia. The year before, the Bostonian Puritans had
sent a supply of pastors to Virginia at the request of a
number of dissenters who had seeped in among the Cavaliers. The Anglican clergymen, being paid in tobacco,
would not preach where the tobacco was poor, and Puritans
and Quakers crept into such regions, since they would not
have known what to do with luxury and so accounted it a
sin.[13]

Lawrence was buried in 1652, and two years later
Amphillis was laid alongside him. They had had three
sons and four daughters, one, Martha Washington, who
emigrated to America and died there in 1697 as the wife
of Nicholas Hayward. Her will has been discovered and
it includes legacies to the two of her brothers, John and
Lawrence, who were apparently driven by the poverty of
their father and the harshness of the Puritans to the shelter
of Virginia.

The Reverend Lawrence Washington's son John seems
to have gone first to Barbados, in 1655, then to have returned to England and sailed thence to Virginia about
1658, acting as supercargo and first mate of a ship in whose
profits from tobacco he was to share equally with one
Edward Prescott.

Prescott absconded and Washington sued him in Maryland, had him arrested and put in bond of 40,000 pounds
of tobacco. Incidentally, he made a complaint "accusing ye
s'd Prescott of ffelony . . . alleging how that hee ye s'd
Prescott hanged a witch on his ship, as hee was outward
bound from England."

Prescott had not even given her the respectable water test, by which a supposed witch was thrown into the water: if she drowned, she was innocent; if she floated, it must be by the devil's aid, so she was guilty and must hang or burn. Prescott had simply strung her up, and John Washington flatly charged him with murder.

That was refreshing and does the Washingtons eternal honor, for it was as far back in the dark as 1659, and the Spanish Inquisition was burning an old witch in Seville in 1782, and one was burned in Peru as late as 1788.

But when the time for trying embezzler Prescott arrived, his accuser, John Washington, begged to be excused from making the long journey to Maryland from Westmoreland, because he had married, as his second wife, Ann Pope, (daughter of the lieutenant-governor, and widow of William Broadhurst), and because then, "God willing, I intend to gett my young Sonne baptized. All ye company and Gossips being already invited."

This "young Sonne" was George Washington's grandfather, Lawrence.

In 1661, John Washington was made a vestryman at Appomattox, but not the place where, two hundred and four years later, the argument about slavery was to come to an end.

John Washington, whose two uncles were knights and whose mother was a servant, foreshadowed his great grandson, George, by becoming a member of the house of Burgesses, a colonel of militia and a fierce Indian-fighter. In a desperate campaign of his against a bloody uprising of the savages, five Indian chiefs, who came into his camp to discuss peace terms, were butchered. Maryland witnesses averred that Colonel Washington would listen to no parleys, but gave an order for the five envoys "to be knocked on the head."

It is curious that he should have been accused of violating the laws of war, just as Colonel George Washington was charged with assassinating an envoy eighty years later. The Maryland allies of Virginia denounced Colonel John Washington's act as barbarous, and Governor Berkeley of Virginia held an investigation, in which Virginia witnesses averred that the Maryland commander had ordered the butchery; so the matter was dropped, as it was later in the case of Colonel George. But the Indians gave John the name of Conotocarius, "Destroyer of Villages," as they later gave George the same name, and still later the name of "Destroyer of Orchards."

Colonel John married three times, and acquired by his own energies, three children, many servants (slaves and indentured bondfolk were both called servants) and much other cattle, as well as large landholdings before he died in about 1677, leaving two sons and a daughter. The eldest son, Lawrence, was named after John's beloved brother Lawrence, who fled from England with him but of whom little is known. The wills of the brothers prove them both men of much property, very fond of each other, and very pious. John says: "Being hartily sorry from the bottome of my hart for my sins past, most humbly desireing forgiveness of the same from the Almighty god (my saviour) & redeimer in whome & by the merrits of Jesus Christ, I trust & believe assuredly to be saved . . . & inherit the Kingdom of heaven, prepared for his ellect & Chossen." [14]

Lawrence said much the same thing. Their wills make a sharp contrast with the will of George Washington, in which there is no religious reference at all beyond the opening phrase, "In the name of God, Amen," which was a legal formality.

The two brothers, John and Lawrence, who were the first to come to America, had numerous marriages, and numerous children, who displayed the same fertility and facility for remarriage and thus scattered Washingtons all over Virginia.

Our interest is with John's son, Lawrence, who was born at Bridges' Creek. He married only once, leaving two sons, John and Augustine. They were young when their father died, and the widow, remarrying promptly, took the children to England, where she died. She was George Washington's grandmother.

Her boy, Augustine (born in 1694), grew up in England, but returned to America in ample time to prepare for his destiny as the father of the Father of his Country. He married Jane Butler, who gave him two sons, Lawrence and Augustine, and died in 1726. Two years later he tried again, selecting as his bride Mary Ball, whose firstborn was the immortal George.

After this triumph, she gave the world three other sons and two daughters, Betty (1733-1797); Samuel (1734-1781); John Augustine (1735/6-1787); Charles (1738-1799); Mildred (1739-1740).

The greedy genealogists have prepared for Mary Ball an impressive ancestry, some tracing her back to mad John Ball, "the crazy preacher of Kent," whose imprisonment in 1381 by the Archbishop of Canterbury was partly responsible for the rebellion of Wat Tyler.[15]

A more modest claim takes her only to 1480.[16] We are more certain that William Ball, son of a London attorney, settled in Virginia in 1650, and had a son Joseph, who married for his second wife a Widow Johnson (born Montague), who was probably his housekeeper. Among their children was Mary, born in 1708. Her father died and her mother remarried a Captain Richard Hewes in 1713. He promptly left her thrice-widowed and she did not marry again, but died in 1721.

Mary Ball was thus left motherless at thirteen, receiving

among other things in the will, "one young likely negro woman, one young mare, two gold rings, two Diaper Table clothes, one good young paceing horse, together with a good silk plush side saddle."

Letters discovered during the Civil War by a Union soldier in an abandoned house at Yorktown, delighted the world by seeming to describe the mother of Washington as having hair like unto flax, and "chekes like May blossoms," and the letters were put in her monument. But after forty years, a will was found that proved the beauty to be some other Mary Ball.[17] The letters are still in the monument—whose story is in itself a strange, sordid, pitiful thing, for telling in its place.

Mary's guardian and girlhood benefactor was Major George Eskridge, after whom she named her oldest son.

She was twenty-two when she married Augustine Washington, March 6, 1730/1.

Her son Samuel married five times and had more children than money. It was of him that George Washington once wrote to his brother John Augustine:

"In God's name, how did my brother Samuel contrive to get himself so enormously in debt?"

Mary had two great fears, one of war, the other of lightning—"in early life a female friend had been killed at her side, while sitting at the table, the knife and fork in the hands of the unfortunate being melted by the electric fluid. The matron never recovered from the shock." [18]

While she has been the victim of almost as much deification as George—she has been set next to the mother of Christ—she seems to have been a terrifyingly strict mother, and not to have shared George's ideals of rebellion. But he shared with her a gift for bad spelling and a passion for dancing.

In a letter written by Mary Washington to her brother

in England in 1760, she says: "You Seem to blam me for not writing to you butt I doe a Shour you it is Note for wante of a very great Regard for you & the family butt as I Dont Ship tobacco the Captins Never Calls on me Soe that I Never knows when tha Come or when tha goe."

Few women have ever had such rhetoric of adulation heaped upon them, and Washington is quoted as saying that he owed all he was to his mother. But it is a cruel truth that she was chiefly remarkable as a very human, cantankerous old lady, who, from being a fond taskmaster in her early motherhood, evolved into a trial to everybody. She seems to have smoked a pipe incessantly. George never smoked at all. This was not the only point in which she and her son were at a constant clash of interests. She had little to do with his upbringing, far less than his half-brothers; she could not understand and never aided his ambitions; she dragged his pride into the dust by seeking a pension during his lifetime, by wheedlings and borrowings and complaints among the neighbors.

He did his duty by her devotedly, but on occasion he switched her with his own high temper as soundly as she had switched him in his youth with that bundle of peach branches she is said to have carried always in her pocket for her children's correction. The last letter Washington wrote to her is as drastic a trouncing as a parent ever had from a child.

These are the abundantly supported facts, and there is no excuse for the maudlin perversion of the truth; yet the picturesque little old woman struggling with unusual hardships and her own traits should have all the sympathy in the world. It cannot be comfortable to be the mother of an arch-rebel.

II

HIS CHILDHOOD

FABLES, legends, fairy-stories, historical riddles, envelop nearly all the circumstances of the birth of George Washington.

According to one account, his father married his mother in England, whither the lovelorn suitor had followed her; the boy was born there and brought back overseas in the arms of a devoted aunt. It is known that Washington's father was a seafaring man, he got his title, "Captain," thence. He went to England at least once to fetch a shipload of convicts.

According to other histories, nobody knows where George was born or baptized.

In his mother's Bible there is this entry, which some say he wrote himself at the age of seventeen, though Conway [1] says it was written in after his celebrity, and it is not certainly in his hand:

"George Washington Son to Augustine & Mary his Wife was Born ye 11th Day of February 1731/2 about 10 in the Morning & was Baptiz'd on the 3:th of April following. Mr. Beverley Whiting & Capt. Christopher Brooks Godfathers and Mrs. Mildred Gregory Godmother."

The blur after the 3 is doubtless a cipher. His wilful mother broke the rule that gave to children the names of their fathers, grandfathers or uncles, and immortalized her gratitude to her devoted guardian, George Eskridge. [2]

PORTRAIT OF MARY WASHINGTON.

(Supposed to be the one by Middleton.)

It is fairly safe to say that he was born in Westmoreland
County on a plantation bordered by Pope's Creek on one
side and Bridges' Creek on the other. Many years after
his father moved away, the plantation was given the name
of Wakefield. Consequently, during his lifetime Washington was said to have been born at Pope's Creek or at
Bridges' Creek; while later works say that he was born at
Wakefield. They were all the same place.

The plantation of Washington's nativity was a mile wide,
comprising a thousand acres of fine wood and bottom land;
the house faced the Potomac, the lawn sloping to the bank.
The river loafed along three or four hundred yards from
the porch, and doubtless kept the mother and the baby's
black mammy fluttering like hens to prevent their duckling
from entering the water before he could swim.

The house burned down in 1779,[3] and no picture of it
was ever made. A monument stands there now, an obelisk
like a miniature of the great shaft in Washington City.
Owing to a blunder, the monument was set over what was
probably an outhouse.

In order to get everything wrong, we celebrate Washington's birthday on the twenty-second of February, instead of the eleventh. Wise men had long known the in-
accuracy of the popular opinion that a year is always $365\frac{1}{4}$
days long, and, as far back as 1582, Pope Gregory had lent
his authority to a revision of the old calendar. But anti-
Catholic England did not accept the Gregorian correction
until 1752, by which time it was necessary to add eleven
days to all Old Style dates to bring them up to the sun.
New Year's day was simultaneously changed from the 25th
of March (the Day of the Annunciation) to the first of January. Hence we find the date of Washington's birth put
with an ambiguous double numeral, as February 11, 1731/2.

During the Revolutionary War, the French allies celebrated his birthday on the eleventh of February. President Ezra Stiles of Yale speaks of it as February 11th, in 1779.[4] And to his dying day he thought of himself as born on February eleventh. In the last two Februaries of his life he wrote in his Diary[5] under February 11th, that he went up to Alexandria to attend "an elegant Ball and Supper at Night," "in commemmoration" of his birthday.

He doubtless caused his little mother a heavy travail, for he was probably a big and lusty child, since he was so big and lusty a man.

But he probably did not cry much, since his voice was never strong, and he was subject to colds. He must have been a blue-eyed babe, for his eyes were almost white in later years.

Unlike Abraham Lincoln, whose birthday is a day later, February twelfth, Washington was no scion of poverty. He came of high aristocratic lineage and was christened in a baptismal robe of silk, a little mantle that was shown in 1850, and may still be cherished in some collection.[6]

The church where he was baptized is unknown and the record perished, though it may have been at Pope's Creek Church, which has also perished. But even without the Bible entry, it would have been certain that he was baptized, as his parents were pious and, had they not been, they would hardly have dared to brave the law, for it was a crime in Virginia then to omit the rite of baptism, and the child could be taken away from its evil parents. Almost worse yet, the law of 1662 imposed a fine of 2000 pounds of tobacco for failure to have a child baptized.[7]

It was a crime also for man or woman to stay away from the various church services. Virginia passed in 1610 the earliest Sunday law in America; the penalties being, for staying away the first time, a fine; for the second, a whipping, "and for the third to suffer death." In 1623 the penalty was reduced to one pound of tobacco for one absence, or 50 pounds a month.[8]

The people were taxed to support the clergy. By the law of 1696, "all and every minister and ministers . . . shall have and receive, for his or their maintenance, the sum of sixteen thousand pounds of tobacco, besides their lawful perquisites." [9]

The clergy of the time were so unreliable that laws had to be passed to force them to attend to their duties, but they would brook no delinquency in the payment of the taxes levied on believers and unbelievers, dissenters and all alike for the support of the Anglican establishment—whose disestablishment and ruination for half a century would one day be largely due to the very George Washington whose infant bulk weighed down the arms of his father's sister, Widow Gregory, at the christening.

Perhaps, indeed, the baby George, who became so fervid a lover of the dance, was baptized to dance-music! Many other children were. We cannot be sure that the minister who christened him was sober.

"Nothing was more common, even with the better portion of them," says Bishop Meade [10] of the Virginia clergy, "than to celebrate the holy ordinance of Baptism, not amidst the prayers of the congregation, but the festivities of the feast and the dance, the minister sometimes taking a full share in all that was going on."

So much emphasis has been so often laid on the intensely religious atmosphere in which George Washington was reared that it is important to realize just what that atmosphere was. The picture of the times has been painted in infinite detail by one whose information and religious fervor are beyond cavil, by no less an authority than Bishop

Meade of Virginia, whose father was Colonel Richard Meade, the "friend Dick" and military aide of Washington.

His conscience forced him to describe with fidelity "the unworthy and hireling clergy of the Colony. . . . There was at this time not only defective preaching but most evil living among the clergy . . . many of them had been addicted to the race-field, the card-table, the ball-room, the theatre—nay, more, to the drunken revel. One of them had been for years the president of a jockey-club.

"Another preached against the four sins of atheism, gambling, horse-racing, and swearing, while he practiced all of the vices himself. When he died, in the midst of his ravings he was heard hallooing the hounds to the chase . . .

"There was no such thing as family prayers at that day. . . . Infidelity became rife in Virginia, perhaps beyond any other portion of the land. The clergy, for the most part, were a laughing-stock or objects of disgust . . . almost all men thought and spoke ill of our clergy and communicants. . . . I have from time to time become acquainted with the state of things at Ripon Lodge and Mount Vernon as to the clergy . . . at Dumfries and Pohick . . . in order to conceal the shame of the clergy from the younger ones and to prevent their loss of attachment to religion and the Church, the elder ones sometimes had to hurry them away to bed or take them away from the presence of these ministers when indulging too freely in the intoxicating cup."

There arose so much dispute as to the point at which a clergyman's "excitement from intoxicating liquors has reached that point which must be regarded as the sin of drunkenness" that a report was made to the Bishop of London a few years before Washington's birth, in which the tests of clerical intoxication in Virginia were given, including these: "Striking, challenging, or threatening to fight, staggering, reeling, vomiting; incoherent, impertinent, obscene, or rude talking." [11]

When George Washington was three years old his father moved away from Bridges' Creek and settled in Prince William County, where he became a vestryman in Truro parish in 1735. He also represented the county in the House of Burgesses.[12]

Captain Washington was a man of increasing consequence. He had sent his eldest son, Lawrence, to England for his education. In 1737 the Captain went over again himself and brought back a shipload of convicts. In the batch he probably included a teacher for his five-year-old boy. For, according to the Reverend Jonathan Boucher,[13] an English clergyman who was later a tutor to Jacky Custis:

"George, like most people thereabouts at that time, had no other education than reading, writing and accounts, which he was taught by a convict servant whom his father bought for a schoolmaster."

The convicts of those wild and cruel times, when little children were hanged for stealing a shillingsworth, must have been of a better class than now, or an indulgent father would never have entrusted his son to one. The sexton of Truro parish was a convict, William Grove, and many of the transported exiles were well-educated gentlemen whose disgrace was their glory.[14]

There were two other teachers, Mr. Williams and Rev. James Marye, of Fredericksburg, to whose environs Captain Washington had moved when George was seven. Fredericksburg, founded in 1727, was only five years older than the boy and was hardly so much as a hamlet, for Colonel Byrd [15] described it as it was in 1732:

"Besides Colo. Willis, who is top man of the place, there are only one Merchant, a Taylor, a Smith and an Ordinary keeper; though I must not forget Mrs. Levinstone, who

Acts here in the Double Capacity of a Doctress and Coffee Woman."

But then Virginia had no large towns at that time. Nor had any colony, but Virginia was peculiarly rural. Captain Washington, the mariner-farmer, was speculating now in the iron mines of the Principio Company, which were distinct from those developed by Spotswood in Virginia and Maryland.[16]

The region all about was sprinkled with Washingtons of all degrees of kinship. On the wooded shores of the Rappahannock the child Washington grew up like a young Indian prince with a slave to wait upon him. But the life was one of almost primeval savagery, mitigated with luxuries imported from England and enlivened with all the sports of the English country squiredom.

The Indians were still everywhere about them, though they were being crowded out by the felling of their sheltering forests and the ever-widening areas of the fenced tobacco fields where the stolen citizens of Africa were swarming as they came in from the ocean or from the yet more mysterious realm where the pickaninnies waited the summons of their fertile race.

From the far west of the Blue Ridge mountains the Rappahannock River slanted down in a winding parallel with the Potomac on the north and the Pamunkey and the James on the south to the great arm of the Atlantic called Chesapeake Bay.

The ebb and flow of the ocean throbbed up and down these rivers and gave them such a character that the whole region was called Tide-Water Virginia. The very name Rappahannock meant in the Indian language, "the stream that comes and goes." "Tidewater Virginia," says Homer C. Hockett,[17] "was almost as large as England."

At that time, the people lived a life of utter confusion

between the pioneer and the voluptuary. In Colonel Byrd's account [18] of his visit to the iron-maker, Colonel Spotswood, in 1732, he pictures a home differing in degree but not in kind of luxury from that of Washington. He describes both the "Room elegantly set off with Pier Glasses," and the tame deer that ran about the house, and "unluckily Spying his own Figure in the Glass, made a spring over the Tea Table that stood under it, and shatter'd the Glass to pieces, and falling back upon the Tea Table, made a terrible Fracas among the China. This Exploit was so sudden, and accompany'd with such a Noise, that it surpriz'd me, and perfectly frighten'd Mrs. Spotswood. But twas worth all the Damage to shew the Moderation and good humour with which she bore this disaster. . . .

"At night the Colo. and I quitted the threadbare Subject of Iron, and changed the Scene to Politicks. He told me the Ministry had receded from their demand upon New England, to raise a standing Salary for all succeeding Governors, for fear some curious Members of the House of Commons shou'd enquire How the Money was dispos'd of, that had been rais'd in the other American Colonys for the Support of their Governors. . . ."

Already there was omen of conflict between England and her colonies, and the children must have overheard incessant grievances against the gluttonous far-off mother country, which George Washington was never to see.

Of George's early boyhood and education, such as it was, little is known and much imagined. It was this gap that Parson Weems filled up with such slush of plagiarism and piety. The story of the apple orchard, of the cherry tree, of the floral initials, are included among these things which the public seems unable to forget and will never willingly let die, however often they are denied. And this is strange, for the only result of these anecdotes is to make George Washington almost as much of an odious prig as it makes the sea captain who fathered him.

Everybody remembers the story of the cherry tree—it had to be a favorite cherry tree—and the little hatchet whose edge tempted the child to use it, and his sturdy refusal, or rather his inability, to tell a lie—a disability he outgrew in good time. But few people recall the actual lines of the original author, Parson Weems,[19] who gives the entire dialogue with no suggestion that he made it up.

According to him, following the dramatic discovery and the paternal voice sounding like Jehovah's over Eden after the apple incident, George did not imitate Adam, but "bravely cried out, 'I can't tell a lie, Pa; you know I can't tell a lie. I did cut it with my hatchet.'—'Run to my arms, you dearest boy,' cried his father in transports, 'run to my arms; glad am I, George, that you killed my tree; for you have paid me for it a thousand fold. Such an act of heroism in my son is more worth than a thousand trees, though blossomed with silver, and their fruits of purest gold.' It was in this way, by interesting at once both his heart and head, that Mr. Washington conducted George with great ease and pleasure along the happy paths of virtue."

Later, "to startle George into a lively sense of his Maker, he fell upon the following very curious, but impressive experiment." Then Weems tells how the father secretly planted seeds in furrows that spelled "George Washington." When they grew up, the deceptive old man allowed George to happen upon them and to toy a while with the truth before he led the boy by Socratic questioning into a realization that God Almighty did everything and gave him everything.

Though the cherry tree anecdote has never been traced, the flower-story is a plain theft on the part of Parson Weems from Dr. James Beattie.[20] The sentimentalism and crudity of Weems' version was carried on with the logical result that his young George became a mawkish spoil-sport and tattle-tale.

Weems tells us next that when George quitted his school, he left the boys in tears, "for he had ever lived among them in the spirit of a brother. He was never guilty of so brutish a practice as fighting himself; or would he, when able to prevent it, allow them to fight one another. If he could not disarm their savage passions by his arguments, he would instantly go to the master, and inform him of their barbarous intentions.

"The boys were often angry with George for this. But he used to say, 'angry or not angry, you shall never, boys, have my consent to a practice so shocking! shocking even in slaves and dogs; then how utterly scandalous in little boys at school, who ought to look on one another as brothers. And what must be the feelings of our tender parents, when, instead of seeing us come home smiling and lovely, as the JOY OF THEIR HEARTS! they see us creeping in like young blackguards, with our heads bound up, black eyes, and bloody clothes.' "

The name of the stenographer who took down these exact words and kept them for over sixty years is not given, but surely such words as "blackguards" and "bloody" must be mistaken. The George who said the rest could never have used them.

The extreme popularity in a boys' school of a big boy who ran to the teacher with stories of playground quarrels, can be imagined. The most puzzling thing about it all is that such a George grew up to be a soldier instead of another parson like Weems.

Yet there is something joyous about the hilarious Parson's style. He wielded the pen as lightly as the bow of that fiddle of his, with which he redeemed the mawkish-ness of his sermons. He goes on: "Some of his historians have said, and many believe, that Washington was a Latin scholar! But 'tis an error. He never learned a syllable of Latin. His second and last teacher, Mr. Williams, was indeed a capital hand—but not at Latin; for of that he understood perhaps as little as Balaam's ass. But at reading, spelling, English grammar, arithmetic, surveying, bookkeeping, and geography, he was indeed famous. And in these useful arts, 'tis said he often boasted that he had made young George Washington as great a scholar as himself."

He boasted indeed, for while Washington was a master of arithmetic, surveying, and bookkeeping, his spelling and his English grammar were atrocious in his early years, and faulty to the end. Wherever we have Washington's own writings to consult, they give the lie to the fables and reveal the man behind the mist. Weems says he never had a syllable of Latin, yet there exists a bit of Latin in his own autograph written in a copy of Patrick's Latin Translation of Homer, published in 1742, and pleading for the return of the book by anyone who may have it:

> Hunc mihi quaeso (bone Vir) Libellum
> Redde, si forsan tenues repertum,
> Ut scias qui sum sine fraude scriptum.
> Est mihi nomen
> Georgio Washington
> George Washington.

But that is as far as his Latin probably ever went, and no doubt he copied that from the book of some other boy, as he probably copied those famous "Rules of Civility" of his fourteenth year, which are so much praised by such dismal persons. It is not certainly known who wrote the originals, though they have a certain kinship with a Jesuit work in

Latin, as well as with a very popular English translation by Hawkins of a French book on Conduct.[21] Even on the improbable assumption that Washington composed them himself, there is nothing in them that any ordinarily decent and well-bred thirteen-year-old boy might not have compiled from memory and imagination.

Besides, Washington was always one of the most considerate, tactful and courteous men that ever lived, and his extreme dread of giving offence may well have been prefigured in the admirable boy he must have been.

There are a hundred and ten of the maxims, including such doleful preachments as:

"Let your Recreations be Manfull not Sinfull."

"Labor to keep alive in your Breast that Little Spark of Celestial fire called Conscience."

These are the ones that are most celebrated and praised in their carefully corrected form, but there are also reminders to be respectful, attentive, sympathetic, receptive, meek, modest; not to hum or drum, flatter, annoy, look at people who are writing, argue, mock, "break jests that are sharp-biting," curse, scoff, intrude, not to prompt people who hesitate in their speech, make comparisons; "if any of the company be commended for a brave act of virtue, commend not another for the same"—in short, a long array of admonitions to be tactful and decent, and courteous to the finest detail—an especially Virginian ideal.

For the most vivid and realistic of them one must read the exact transcription of them by Dr. Toner. Here one finds homely realism, genuine consideration and fine tactfulness:

"EVERY Action done in Company, ought to be with Some Sign of Respect, to those that are Present.

"When in Company, put not your Hands to any Part of the Body, not usualy Discovered.

Shew Nothing to your Friend that may affright him.

In the Presence of Others sing not to yourself with a humming Noise, nor Drum, with your Fingers or Feet.

IF YOU Cough, Sneeze, Sigh, or Yawn, do it not Loud, but Privately; and Speak not in your Yawning, but put Your handkerchief or Hand before your face and turn aside.

AT PLAY and at Fire its Good manners to give Place to the last Commer, and affect not to Speak Louder than ordenary.

SPIT not in the Fire, nor Stoop low before it neither Put your Hands into the Flames to warm them, nor Set your Feet upon the Fire especially if there be meat before it.

SHIFT not yourself in the Sight of others nor Gnaw your nails.

SHAKE not the head, Feet, or Legs rowl not the Eys, lift not one eyebrow higher than the other wry not the mouth, and bedew no mans face with your Spittle.

KILL no Vermin as Fleas, lice ticks &c in the Sight of Others, if you See any filth or thick Spittle put your foot Dexteriously upon it if it be upon the Cloths of your Companions, Put it off privately, and if it be upon your own Cloths return Thanks to him who puts it off.

KEEP your Nails clean and Short, also your Hands and Teeth Clean, yet without Shewing any great Concern for them.

When you see a Crime punished, you may be inwardly Pleased; but always shew Pity to the Suffering Offender.

IN PULLING off your Hat to Persons of Distinction, as Noblemen, Justices, Churchmen &c make a Reverence, bowing more or less according to the Custom of the Better Bred, and Quality of the Persons Amongst your equals expect not always that they Should begin with you first, but to Pull off the Hat when there is no need is Affectation, in the Manner of Saluting and resaluting in words keep to the most usual Custom.

TIS ill manners to bid one more eminent than yourself be covered as well as not to do it to whom it's due Likewise he that makes too much haste to Put on his hat does not well, yet he ought to Put it on at the first, or at most the Second time of being ask'd; now what is herein Spoken, of Qualification in behaviour in Saluting, ought also to be observed in taking of Place, and Sitting down for ceremonies without Bounds is troublesome.

TO one that is your equal, or not much inferior you are to give the chief Place in your Lodging and he to who 'tis offered ought at the first to refuse it but at the Second to accept though not without acknowledging his own unworthiness.

IN visiting the Sick, do not Presently play the Physician if you be not Knowing therein.

When a man does all he can though it Succeeds not well blame not him that did it.

BEING to advise or reprehend any one, consider whether it ought to be in publick or in Private; presently, or at Some other time in what terms to do it & in reproving Shew no Signs of Cholar but do it with all Sweetness and Mildness.

MOCK not nor Jest at anything of Importance break no Jest that are Sharp Biting and if you Deliver anything witty and Pleasent abstain from Laughing thereat yourself.

WEAR not your Cloths, foul, unript or Dusty but See they be Brush'd once every day at least and take heed that you approach not to any Uncleaness.

PLAY not the Peacock, looking everywhere about you, to See if you be well Deck't, if your Shoes fit well if your Stockings Sit neatly, and Cloths handsomely.

UTTER not base and frivolous things amongst grave and Learn'd Men nor very Difficult Questions or Subjects, among the Ignorant or things hard to be believed, Stuff not your Discourse with Sentences amongst your Betters nor Equals.

BEING Set at meat Scratch not neither Spit Cough or blow your Nose except there's a Necessity for it.

TAKE no Salt or cut Bread with your Knife Greasy.

IF you Soak bread in the Sauce let it be no more than what you put in your Mouth at a time and blow not your broth at Table but Stay till Cools of it Self.

PUT not your meat to your Mouth with your Knife in your hand neither Spit forth the Stones of any fruit Pye upon a Dish nor cast anything under the table.

CLEANSE not your teeth with the Table Cloth Napkin Fork or Knife but if Others do it let it be done wt. a Pick Tooth."

Some of these counsels are still needed; others give a glimpse of the times that surprises; for instance, the following, which gives a boy advice that Greek lads were trained to remember:

"When you Sit down, Keep your Feet firm and Even, without putting one on the other or Crossing them."

This looks odd in days when even the women cross their manifest knees all the time.

The old anecdote that Washington once doffed his hat to a slave and explained that he would not be outdone in good manners by a servant, seems to have a justification in these:

"IF ANY one come to Speak to you while you are Sitting Stand up tho he be your Inferiour, and when you Present Seats let it be to every one according to his Degree.

ARTIFICERS & Persons of low Degree ought not to use many ceremonies to Lords, or Others of high Degree but Respect and highly Honour them, and those of high Degree ought to treat them with affibility & Courtesie, without Arrogancy."

As a boy, Washington, like all other boys, was the victim of the usual dosage of copybook morality. No child escapes it; most children try to digest it, and with the solemnity of childhood, to parrot it.

In after-years, these early sentiments are pointed to with pride if the child turns out well. If he does not, they are forgotten. It is strange how few historians dwell on the moralizing strain and pious ejaculations of Benedict Arnold; how much is made of Washington's juvenile exercises in penmanship and platitude.

Far more precious and significant is the reminiscence that mingles his characteristic studiousness with his characteristic and pathetic hankering after the companionship of women:

"Whilst his brother and other boys at playtime were at bandy or other games he was behind the door ciphering. But one youthful ebullition is handed down while at that school, and that was romping with one of the largest girls." [22]

He began to love early and often, and with passion, but with a bewildering accumulation of rejections. He dabbled in poetry and we have old copy-books of his, in which crude faces and birds litter the margins, and lines of mournful verse break in on the exercises in penmanship of various styles, copies of legal forms, problems in surveying, navigation, physics, what not.

He was especially determined to write a good hand, and soon acquired a steel-plate clarity that makes his manuscripts as legible as his character.

While he was perfecting his penmanship he was developing his great body to heroic power and skill; schooling his extraordinarily big feet to dance, to leap with the long pole, and to outrun all the other boys; training freakishly huge hands to pitch quoits, toss bars and hurl weights. Tradition has hallowed a spot near the lower ferry of old Fredericksburg where his playmate and kinsman, Lewis Willis,[23] often said that he had often seen him throw a stone (some say a dollar) to the incredibly distant opposite bank of the Rappahannock. It was probably a stone, for while certain coins had long been called dollars, it was not characteristic of George Washington to throw money away. He had always some poor dependent to give it to, if no other use for it.

He became an excellent wrestler, and was astounding at the lifting of weights. Weems describes him as interested in playing soldier and fighting mock battles, with a lad named William Bustle commanding the "French," while George led the "Americans." They had "Corn-stalks for muskets and calabashes for drums."

He must have begun horsemanship very early, too, for he became marvellous at it, and there is reason to believe the story that Custis[24] tells of his killing a colt by literally breaking its heart:

It was a blooded horse, a sorrel of fierce and ungovernable nature; and had reached his fullest size and vigor, un-

conscious of a rider, though many had tried to mount him
but been frightened off. The young Washington persuaded
his companions to help him bridle "this terror of the
parish," and then "sprang to his unenvied seat." The
struggle was terrific, but Washington "clung to the furious
steed, till centaur like, he appeared to make part of the
animal itself." At last "the gallant horse, summoning all
his powers to one mighty effort, reared, and plunged with
tremendous violence, burst his noble heart, and died in an
instant. . . . From distended nostrils gushed in torrents
the life-blood."

In the Custis version, the boy had to confess his deed
with grandiloquence to his mother, and she had to deliver
a sermon on the supreme delight of having a truthful son.

But the legend at least presents Washington in action.
He is almost always presented as a marble snob on a con-
ceited marble horse. He should be remembered as the most
graceful rider of his time, and one of the most tireless,
riding sixty miles a day if need be, dashing across the scene
on a fleet steed with wind-blown mane, leaping fences,
ditches, running down the fox, charging among the soldiers
in an ecstasy of living, a fury of power.

George might have been sent "back home" to England
to finish his education as his half-brother Lawrence was, at
the age of fifteen; but his father's finances had not pros-
pered—perhaps because of the iron-mines. George was
only eleven when his father died of "gout of the stomach,"
April 12, 1743, at the age of forty-nine. For some reason,
he willed the bulk of his land to the two surviving sons of
his first marriage, leaving his widow not much property and
five living children, the oldest eleven. She had a hard
struggle and was driven to sharp measures of discipline.

But the half-brothers were generous, especially to George,
in whom both of them took a special interest.

Lawrence, who was fourteen years older than George, had returned from England but gone away again at the age of twenty-two as an officer with the Virginia volunteers in the war with Spain. Spotswood, appointed general, died at Annapolis, and Colonel Gooch replaced him, with Lawrence Washington second in command.[25]

He served with the land-troops under Admiral Vernon and in 1741 took part in the famous siege of Cartagena on the South American coast of Colombia. The British were repulsed with heavy slaughter by the Spanish.

The historians usually say that Lawrence covered himself with honor, but Reverend Jonathan Boucher says that while at Cartagena, "getting into some scrape with a brother officer, it was said he did not acquit himself quite so well as he ought, and so sold out."

In any case, he lost his health, and gave up his plans to go on with his soldiery. Returning home in 1742, he was elected to the House of Burgesses for seven years. He also paid court to Anne Fairfax, daughter of William Fairfax, of the King's Council, one of Virginia's foremost men, land agent and cousin to Lord Fairfax, and owner of a fine estate called Belvoir, close to a 2500-acre tract of land which Lawrence inherited from his father. This had been known as "Hunting Creek," but Lawrence named it Mount Vernon, after the Admiral he had served under. In case Lawrence should die without issue, this tract had been willed to George by their father, on account of whose untimely death Lawrence had postponed his marriage with Anne Fairfax till three months after the funeral.

In 1746, George was invited to spend a week at Belvoir, and there he apparently had some adventure, for William Fairfax wrote to Lawrence that George had promised to be "steady" thereafter. Conway [26] takes this as indicating "some youthful declaration of independence," which is one way of referring to a scrape. It was then that George went back to his mother's house and, casting about for a career, was tempted to try the sea.

The only story of Washington and his mother that everybody knows is the story of how he had been offered a post as middy on one of Admiral Vernon's battleships, and had all his things packed, and—but let Parson Weems [27] tell it in his own inimitable words:

"It was in his 15th year, according to the best of my information, that Washington first felt the kindlings of his soul for war. The cause was this— In those days the people of Virginia looked on Great Britain as the *mother country;* and to go thither was, in common phrase, *'to go home.'* The name of OLD ENGLAND was music in their ears: and the bare mention of a blow meditated against her, never failed to rouse a something at the heart, which instantly flamed on the cheek, and flashed in the eye. Washington had his full share of these virtuous feelings: on hearing, therefore, that France and Spain were mustering a black cloud over his MOTHER COUNTRY, his youthful blood took fire; and he instantly tendered what aid *his little arm* could afford. The rank of midshipman was procured for him on board a British ship of war, then lying in our waters; and his trunk and clothes were actually sent on board. But when he came to take leave of his mother, she wept bitterly, and told him, *she felt that her heart would break if he left her.* George immediately got his trunk ashore! as he could not, for a moment, bear the idea of inflicting a wound on that dear life which had so long and so fondly sustained his own."

This anecdote, like that of the cherry tree, has been dinned into children's souls for over a hundred years to make them tell the truth and obey their mothers "as Washington always did."

But like nearly everything else that nearly everybody knows, especially about Washington, the story is probably false, even though one can see at the Masonic Museum in Alexandria, Va., a little penknife that his mother is said to have sent to England for, as his reward. People actually approve the motto on it, "Always obey your superiors," as if that were good advice.

In any case, where should we have been if Washington had always followed it? Fortunately, he knew when to obey and when to rebel.[28]

The sea-going legend has two plausible elements. There was some talk of Washington's going into the tobacco-trade on one of the tobacco-ships that use to come up the river, but though Lawrence Washington encouraged the idea in a letter that he advised George not to show to his mother, she seems to have appealed to her own brother, who lived in England, Joseph Ball. He strongly advised against the commercial promise and dignity of the sea in a letter dated at a place made famous by Chaucer, Stratford-by-Bow, 19th of May, 1747:

"I understand that you are advised and have some thoughts of putting your son George to sea. I think he had better be put apprentice to a tinker, for a common sailor before the mast has by no means the common liberty of the subject; for they will press him from a ship where he has fifty shillings a month and make him take twenty-three, and cut and slash and use him like a negro, or rather like a dog. And, as to any considerable preferment in the navy, it is not to be expected, as there are always so many gaping for it here who have interest, and he has none. And if he should get to be master of a Virginia ship (which it is very difficult to do,) a planter that has three or four hundred acres of land and three or four slaves, if he be industrious, may live more comfortably, and leave his family in better bread, than such a master of a ship can. . . . He must not be too hasty to be rich, but go on gently and with patience, as things will naturally go. This method, without aiming at being a fine gentleman before his time, will carry a man more comfortably and surely through the world than going to sea, unless it be a great chance indeed. I pray God keep you and yours.

"Your loving brother,

"JOSEPH BALL."

The second note of plausibility is Mother Mary Washington's reluctance to let her children risk their lives in any venture. As Weems [29] says, truly for once:

"Where George got his great military talents, is a question which none but the happy believers in a *particular Providence* can solve: certain it is, his earthly parents had no hand in it. For of his father, tradition says nothing, save that he was a most amiable old gentleman; one who made good crops, and scorned to give his name to the quill-drivers of a counting-room. And as to his mother, it is well known that she was none of Bellona's fiery race. For as some of the Virginia officers, just after the splendid actions of Trenton and Princeton, were complimenting her on the generalship and *rising glory* of her son, instead of shewing the exultation of a Spartan dame, she replied, with all the sang-froid of a good old Friend, *'Ah, dear me! This fighting and killing is a sad thing! I wish George would come home and look after his plantation! !'*

"Nor does it appear that nature had mixed much of gunpowder in the composition of any of his brothers: for when one of them, in the time of Braddock's war, wrote him a letter, signifying something like a wish to *enter into the service;* George, it is said, gave him this short reply: *'Brother, stay at home, and comfort your wife.'* "

Most certain of all is that George Washington is about the poorest example that could be chosen as a model of filial obedience. If he obeyed his mother in the matter of quitting the sea, he felt that he had done enough for her. For we have no other record of his ever yielding to her commands, her prayers, or her tears. But we have several records of his disobeying her, scolding her, and preaching at her.

Yet one ought not to love her any the less for loving her son above all his fantastic ideals, even above her country, if the Virginians of that day really had a country. Fact was, they had to imagine one until they could make one for themselves.

George left the Rappahannock for the Potomac, left his mother to manage the other children, and went to live with his half-brother Lawrence at Mount Vernon. He got into society with a vengeance.

It was an inconceivably important day for the history of America, its liberty, its union, its development of the Western Wilderness and its Westward spread, when George Washington resigned the quest of wealth or fame as a tarry-thumbed mariner and became a polished country gentleman, a fanatic farmer, and a future millionaire in real estate. He studied surveying with a passionate enthusiasm that glowed to the last of his days, and kept his diaries full of references to the countless occasions when he would "run of" a few lots for exercise.

The Father of his Country was a swell from his sixteenth year on. He consorted with English lords, rode to hounds, learned to love foppery and all the elegancies, became a past master of dancing, of gambling, polite drinking and exquisite flirtation. He shone in everything but the successful making of love.

The question of sending George abroad to school must have come up, judging from a letter said to have been written by Lord Fairfax to the anxious mother:

HONOURED MADAM: You are so good as to ask what I think of a temporary residence for your son George in England. It is a country for which I myself have no inclination, and the gentlemen you mention are certainly renowned gamblers and rakes, which I should be sorry your son were exposed to, even if his means easily admitted of a residence in England. He is strong and hardy, and as good a master of a horse as any could desire. His education might have been bettered, but what he has is accurate and inclines him to much life out of doors. He is very grave for one of his age, and reserved in his intercourse; not a great talker at any time. His mind appears to me to act slowly, but, on the whole, to reach just conclusions, and he has an ardent wish to see the right of questions—what my friend Mr. Addison was pleased to call "the intellectual conscience." Method and exactness seem to be natural to George. He is, I suspect, beginning to feel the sap rising, being in the spring of life, and is getting ready to be the prey of your sex, wherefore may the Lord help him, and deliver him from the nets those spiders, called women, will cast for his ruin. I presume him to be truthful because he is exact. I wish I could say that he governs his temper. He is subject to attacks of anger on provocation, and sometimes without just cause; but as he is a reasonable person, time will cure him of this vice of nature, and in fact he is, in my judgment, a man who will go to school all his life and profit thereby.

I hope, madam, that you will find pleasure in what I have written, and will rest assured that I shall continue to interest myself in his fortunes.

Much honoured by your appeal to my judgment, I am, my dear madam, your obedient humble servant.

To Mrs. Mary Washington.

FAIRFAX.[30]

As a character study of Washington the youth this is a speaking likeness. As counsel it is finely reasoned. If George had been sent to Oxford and the Continent to be "finished," he might well have been just that.

III

HE BEGINS TO SURVEY THE WORLD

WHEN Lawrence (who was fourteen years older than George and tried to take the place of their dead father) fetched the sixteen-year-old George from his mother's side to live with him at Mount Vernon, the young and impressionable lad fell into a whole nest of Fairfaxes.

First, there was old Lord Fairfax, who had inherited from his mother the Culpeper grant of six million acres known as the Northern Neck.[1] It lay between the Potomac and the Rappahannock and he had sent his cousin, William, to Virginia to act as his agent. This William had a fine estate near Mount Vernon. It was spelled "Belvoir," and therefore pronounced "Beaver." William's daughter married Lawrence Washington and they lived for a time with her parents at Belvoir.

William's son, George William Fairfax, after finishing his education in England, came to America and proved himself an expert surveyor and pathfinder. He was eight years older than George, but the two young men struck up a lifelong friendship that survived many peculiar strains. To this Fairfax, George owed much of his own remarkable ability as a surveyor.

Eventually, George William became a Colonel of Militia, a member of the House of Burgesses, and later of the Council. These two bodies made up the legislature of Virginia, the council being appointed by the royal governor, the burgesses elected by the people of the various counties as their representatives.

Young George became a mighty fox hunter, the boon companion of the old peer, sixty-year-old Lord Fairfax, who had recently come over to visit his cousin William, in an effort to drown an amorous sorrow in the wilderness. A lady that he loved in England had preferred to marry a duke. Even Lords suffer from their lowly station!

In addition to his vast holdings in the Northern Neck, Lord Fairfax owned immense tracts of land beyond the Blue Ridge Mountains—almost the whole Shenandoah Valley, indeed. Squatters had squatted there in great numbers. The first group of fourteen families came down from Pennsylvania in the year of George Washington's birth, but neglected to secure their titles and were easy victims of Lord Fairfax's alleged "insatiable disposition for the monopoly of wealth." Joist Hite, however, fought for his claims and began in 1736 a lawsuit that was not settled till 1786, and then in his favor, though both he and Lord Fairfax were dead.

In 1748 Lord Fairfax decided to mulct all intruders, after having his lands parcelled off into building lots and manor estates. He sent out a surveying party in March, 1748, under George William Fairfax; and George Washington went along as an assistant surveyor to James Genn. His wages varied from a doubloon a day to six pistoles. A doubloon was then worth $7.20, and a pistole half of that, so that George's first earnings, at the age of sixteen, ran from twenty to fifty dollars a week. He was always a good hand at making money.

The seventeen-year-old lad kept a diary of his first great adventures: "A Journal of my Journey over the Mountains began Fryday the 11th of March 1747/8." [2]

It is an uncouth schoolboyish story enlivened by amused

and amusing accounts of midnight battles for sleep under "but only one thread Bear blanket with double its Weight of Vermin such as Lice Fleas &c." The next day at Frederick Town, "we cleaned ourselves (to get Rid of y. Game we had catched y. Night before) and took a Review of y. Town . . . had a good Dinner prepar'd for us Wine and Rum Punch in Plenty and a good Feather Bed with clean Sheets which was a very agreeable regale."

He could always endure hardships when he had to, but he never despised the luxuries and he was very clean in an age none too sanitary.

On the morrow was "nothing Remarkable . . . but that we had a Tolerable good Bed to lay on." A few days later "we were agreeably surpris'd at y. sight of thirty odd Indians coming from War with only one Scalp We had some Liquor with us of which we gave them Part it elevating there Spirits put them in y. Humour of Dauncing of whom we had a War Daunce there manner of Dauncing is as follows Viz They clear a Large Circle and make a Great Fire in y. middle then seats themselves around it y. Speaker makes a grand speech telling them in what Manner they are to Daunce after he has finished y. best Dauncer jumps up as one awaked out of a Sleep and runs and Jumps about y. Ring in a most comical Manner he is followed by y. Rest then begins there Musicians to Play ye. Musick is a Pot half [full] of Water with a Deerskin Streched over it as tight as it can and a Goard with some Shott in it to Rattle and a Piece of an horses Tail tied to it to make it look fine y. one keeps Rattling and y. other Drumming all y. while y. others is Dauncing."

On "Fryday" they decided to "slip it" and moved on. On "Sonday, 20th" they broke the Virginia laws against travel on the Sabbath, and swam their horses across a stream. They were drenched with rain, surveyed much territory, shot wild turkeys, and had an exciting Saturday night when "our Straw catch'd a Fire yt. we were laying upon and was luckily Preserv'd by one of our Mens awaking." The next night was "much more blostering than ye. former we had our Tent Carried Quite of with ye. Wind and was obliged to Lie ye. Latter part of ye. night without covering."

Monday "we did two Lots and was attended by a great Company of People Men Women and Children that attended us through ye. Woods as we went Showing there Antick tricks I really think they seemed to be as Ignorant a Set of People as the Indians they would never speak English but when spoken to they speak all Dutch."

These were German emigrants who had slipped down from Pennsylvania into the Shenandoah Valley, and established homesteads on Lord Fairfax's property.

On Thursday the 7th one of the men "Killed a Wild Turkie that weight 20 Pounds we went and Survey'd 15 Hundred Acres." That night they slept in a house for the first time since they had come to the Branch. The next night they spent under a haystack. "We pull'd out our Knapsack in order to Recruit ourselves every was his own Cook our Spits was Forked Sticks our Plates was a Large Chip as for Dishes we had none."

On Sunday the 10th they took their "farewell of ye Branch." On Tuesday the 12th "after Riding about 20 Miles we had 20 to go for we had lost ourselves. . . . This day see a Rattled Snake ye first we had seen in all our Journey.

"Wednesday ye. 13th of April 1748 Mr Fairfax got safe home and I myself safe to my Brothers which concludes my Journal."

In the meanwhile, his half-brothers, Lawrence and Augustine, had joined in a great land-development scheme called the Ohio Company, to which the King of England

had graciously granted half a million acres along the Ohio
River, on certain difficult conditions, including the building
of a fort and its upkeep.

The Indians occupied this land and the French claimed
it for their King by right of discovery, but that did not
check the generosity of the English King. The Ohio Company sent out surveyors, traders and builders of forts, but
the French prepared to gobble them up and enforce their
"rights." Each nation was eager to avoid war but unwilling to lose any advantages in the race for the West.
The Indians, of course, were fair prey for both sides.

Lawrence Washington was active in the affairs of the
company, and became its President. But his health was
breaking rapidly, and George began to look upon the French
as nothing more than squatters on his family preserves.

With the aid of Lord Fairfax, he secured a post as public
surveyor at a salary of £100 a year, and he was kept busy.
His work was so exquisitely exact that his surveys are found
faultless to this day. By its charter, the College of William
and Mary (says Dr. Lyon Gardiner Tyler, president of the
college) "had the right to appoint all the county surveyors,
and in 1749 George Washington received the appointment
for Fairfax County. The original bond executed by Washington for the faithful performance of his duties provided
that he should pay to the college treasurer one-sixth part of
all his 'fees and profits for surveying.' . . . Though not an
alumnus, he received from the college his first public office
of surveyor, and his last as chancellor of the institution." [3]

Though it is generally stated that Washington was surveyor for Fairfax County, Mr. Fairfax Harrison, who has
made immense research in this period, states that Washington was surveyor only for Culpepex County.

Lord Fairfax moved over into the Shenandoah Valley,
and built a log house there in a ten-thousand-acre estate

called Greenway Court, after the estate in England. He stocked it with books, and Washington, visiting him from time to time, spent many an evening browsing about. It has been assumed that he looked at nothing but the noblest literature, and some of his surveying memoranda include references to his progress. But they also include sighs of love, and as Charles Moore [4] points out, the library of the gay old Fairfax also contained such books as *Joseph Andrews*, *Tom Jones*, and others, edifying, indeed, but in the history of love.

Joseph Andrews was published when Washington was ten years old. That it had great vogue in Virginia is known. Startling as it was in its frank and hilarious indecencies, it was read by young girls. Sally Wister included *Joe Andrews* in her "Charming Collection." She was fifteen years old.

Of love stories, George was writing no little on his own. He must have gone at this time on a visit to the Lowland, or Tide-water, country, where he lost his heart, or thought he did.

At the same time, his friend, George William Fairfax, going down to the Assembly at the capital, Williamsburg, was courting one of the daughters of the rich and important Colonel Wilson Cary, whose mansion on the James River was called Ceelys. He singled out for his attentions a most remarkable girl, Sarah, or Sally, Cary, who, in becoming his wife, became also, eventually, the lifelong love of his best friend, George Washington.

Either the self-control or the lukewarmness of Fairfax is revealed in the letter he wrote announcing his engagement:

"Attending here on the general assembly, I have had several opportunities of visiting Miss Cary, a daughter of Colonel Wilson Cary, and finding her amiable person to answer all the favorable reports made, I addressed myself

PORTRAIT OF MARY CARY.

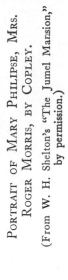

PORTRAIT OF MARY PHILIPSE, MRS.
ROGER MORRIS, BY COPLEY.

(From W. H. Shelton's "The Jumel Mansion,"
by permission.)

and having obtained the young lady's and her parents' consent, we are to be married on the 17th instant. Col. Cary wears the same coat-of-arms as Lord Hunsden."

George William Fairfax expected to become Lord Fairfax some day, though the expectation was never realized, and Sally Cary never became Lady Fairfax; but there seems to have been more wisdom than passion in the match, and Mrs. Sally Nelson Robins,[5] historian of the Colonial Dames, is moved to sneer at Fairfax as "a deliberate unemotional gentleman . . . Arms and amiable person, forsooth! For marriages of 'convenance' and neat calculation commend me to these Colonial Virginians; Miss Cary's beauty and fortune and George William Fairfax's position and expectations, plus the arms of Lord Hunsden, equals matrimony!"

When Fairfax brought his bride to Belvoir, her pretty sister, Mary Cary, came along. George Washington also returned, with his heart broken by a heartless Lowland lady. Belvoir must have been a crowded house at that time, for it had only two stories, with four rooms on the first floor and five on the second.[6]

Across a little stretch of water Mount Vernon was visible, but George Washington spent most of his time at Belvoir making a noble effort to fight off despair. Mary Cary gave him excellent help.

They formed a strange community, those old Virginians with their stately mansions rising here and there in a wilderness yet unconquered; with their arms and their titles and their carriages, their slaves and their aristocracy set in a jungle of pioneering crudities: with their dances, intrigues, love-affairs, and their bad spelling.[7]

In the dancing, the love-making and the bad spelling, none of them exceeded George Washington.

But he went on with his work as a public surveyor, toiling industriously in the wilderness. That it was not all toil is evident from the high spirits shown in his Diary; and that rum was always with him there is evidence enough. There may be reason, therefore, to believe the legend still cherished in West Virginia, then a part of Lord Fairfax's estate, and first settled by Germans from whom he collected quit rents. The story was told during the Washington's Birthday Celebration, February 22, 1926, at Martinsburg, West Virginia, and may well have startled the citizens as much as the newspaper account indicated. The speaker was a prominent attorney, A. C. Nadenbousch, and his speech was thus reported in the Washington *Post* of February 23, 1926:

"Pointing to a near-by corner, the speaker said the Yellow Tavern, popular with early settlers, once stood there and that one day George Washington, then a young surveyor in the employ of Lord Fairfax, tramped into the tavern and demanded a dram of whisky.

"The liquor was placed before the future leader of the revolution. He drank it down. When he went to pay for it, he found he had no money. Undismayed, young George drew from his bag a coonskin. This was accepted in payment for the drink and the innkeeper returned 158 rabbit skins as change.

"Whether it was the quality of the liquor or the great heap of small 'change' before him, I do not know. But history records that young George felt so elated that he proceeded to treat the crowd, and kept on treating until the last rabbit skin had been returned over the bar.

"Mr. Nadenbousch praised Washington, declaring he was the greatest man this or any other country ever produced, but added that he took no faith in those who tried to picture Washington as a mollycoddle."

IV

HIS "LOWLAND BEAUTY"

NO youth of such after fame ever took his puppy-loves more seriously, or was more inconstant or more unlucky than George Washington. They drove him as far as the writing of poetry, which was, if possible, worse even than the verses of Abraham Lincoln.[1]

His own confessions are the authority for most of them. And the list of his hapless loves is long.

It begins with the big girl he romped with in school. She might have been Jane Strother,[2] with whom and her sister Alice, the Washington children and their relatives, Lawrence and Robin Washington, played.[3] Other neighbors were the Alexanders, and this juvenile acrostic to "Frances Alexa" might have been written to one of that family:[4]

"From your bright sparkling Eyes I was undone;
Rays, you have; more transperent than the Sun,
Amidst its glory in the rising day
None can you equal in your bright array;
Constant in your calm and unspotted Mind;
Equal to all, but will to none Prove kind,
So knowing, seldom one so Young, you'l Find.

Ah! woe's me, that I should Love and conceal
Long have I wish'd, but never dare reveal,
Even though severely Loves Pains I feel;
Xerxes that great, was't free from Cupids Dart,
And all the greatest Heroes, felt the smart."

The worse it is as poetry the better it is as humanity, and one may well be glad that it was not even so good as mediocrity. Washington did enough great things greatly; it would have been too much to have him a Byron as well.

Washington's puerile verse is included in a little book that contains also his first entry of a survey, March 11th, 1747/8, when he was sixteen years old. This contains such items as these:

> "Read to the Reign of K: John.
> "In the Spectator Read to 143
> "M. The regulator of my watch now is 4m: and over the fifth from the Slow end.
> "'Twas perfect Love before } S. Young M: A
> But now I do adore }
> "Whats the noblest Passion of the Mind. Qy."

Here also is a most doleful elegy of twelve lines and a fine frenzy of grammar and prosody:

> "Oh Ye Gods why should my Poor Resistless Heart
> Stand to oppose thy might and Power
> At Last surrender to cupids feather'd Dart
> And now lays Bleeding every Hour
> For her that's Pityless of my grief and Woes,
> And will not on me Pity take.
> I'll sleep amongst my most inveterate Foes
> And with gladness never wish to wake,
> In deluding sleepings let my Eyelids close
> That in an enraptured Dream I may
> In a soft lulling sleep and gentle repose
> Possess those joys denied by Day."

This is a poem that can be read over and over with delight. One always discovers some new quirk in it. The protestations of abysmal gloom are pure rhetoric—or rather most impure rhetoric. The only thing that reassures us as to its author's sanity is that it was as insincere as it was bombastic.

For in the same batch of prose, doggerel, and surveying exercises were found three letters invaluable as character-exposure and revealing a heart as hopelessly tangled as his syntax.

It is from these letters that we learn of the girl concealed, perhaps forever, under the haunting phrase, "the Lowland Beauty." Nobody knows who she was, though "half a dozen Virginia families still claim that their ancestress was the lowland beauty." [5] And none of them can prove it.

He had evidently made ardent love to the anonymous girl and been sharply rebuffed, as he was by the girl in the acrostic and the other girl, who would not on him "pity take." But it was always hard for George to give up anything that was dear to him, and he was a glutton for defeat.

He was still smarting with the loss of the Lowland Beauty and the humiliation which must have been conspicuously well known to his friends, and still tingling with desire for her conquest when he went up into Fairfax county to be with his brother Lawrence and the Fairfaxes at Belvoir. Here he was beguiled but not at first consoled by Mary Cary.

He had to put his highly important emotions on paper, and when his delighted pen happened on a phrase that sounded grandiloquent, he felt it too good to use once and throw away; so he repeated it.

By some whim of good luck we have his own copies of three letters he wrote at this time, misspelled, awkward, but exceedingly human and juvenile. There was a certain pomposity in his phraseology, but it was the laughable, loveable monkey-pomposity of a young ape, deliciously but hopelessly perplexed and too headlong for punctuation.

It was unfortunate for the world's knowledge of the real Washington that these and other letters of his were either suppressed or corrected insufferably by the early historians who created the Washington tradition. His first biographer was a canting sentimentalist, Parson Weems, his next was the stern and rock-bound New Englander, Jared Sparks,[6] who labored indefatigably to find out all he could about Washington and then labored quite as indefatigably to doctor the documents so as to make him out a cross between Cotton Mather and Cromwell. Washington Irving[7] was overawed by Sparks, in whose editions he trusted too implicitly. John Marshall hardly counts.

If Washington had been first crystallized by a typical Virginian, perhaps he would have been realized as the romantic, amorous, love- and laughter-loving, fickle, restless adventurer that he was until national tragedies solemnized him and scared him into a self-protective pomposity.

Nobody else could open Washington's young heart with such revelation as he gives in these letters. In the first, to Robin Washington of Chotank, he strings together one of the longest and most chaotic sentences in the literature of love:

"DEAR FRIEND ROBIN:

"As it's the greatest mark of friendship and esteem, absent Friends can show each other, in writing and often communicating their thoughts, to his fellow companions, I make one endeavor to signalize myself in acquainting you, from time to time, and at all times, my situation and employments of life, and could wish you would take half the pains of contriving me a letter by any opportunity, as you may be well assured of its meeting with a very welcome reception.

"My place of Residence is at present at His Lordships where I might was my heart disengag'd pass my time very pleasantly as theres a very agreeable Young Lady Lives in the same house (Colo George Fairfax's Wife's Sister) but as thats only adding Fuel to fire it makes me the more uneasy for by often and unavoidably

being in Company with her revives my former Passion for your
Low Land Beauty whereas was I to live more retired from young
Women I might in some measure eliviate my .sorrows by burying
that chast and troublesome Passion in the grave of oblivion or
etarnall forgetfulness for as I am very well assured thats the only
antidote or remedy that I shall be releivd by or only recess that can
administer any cure or help to me as I am well convinced was I ever
to attempt anything I should only get a denial which would be only
adding grief to uneasiness." [8]

The letter to "Dear Friend John" reveals the same absolute welter of sentiment and grammar:

"DEAR FRIEND JOHN:
   "As it is the greatest mark of friendship and esteem you can
show to an absent Friend In often writing to him so hope youl not
deny me that Favour as its so ardently wish't and desired by me.
its the greatest pleasure I can yet forsee of having in fairfax to
hear from my friends   Particularly yourself was my affections
disengaged I might perhaps form some pleasures in the conversa-
sion of an agreeable young Lady as theres one now lives in the
same house with me but as that's only nourishment to my former
affec't for by often seeing her brings the other into my remembrance
whereas perhaps was she not often (unavoidably) presenting herself to my view I might in some measure eleviate my sorrows by
burying the other in the grave of oblivion.   I am well convinced
my heart stands in defiance of all others but only she thats given it
cause enough to dread a second assault and from a different Quarter tho I well know let it have as many attacks as it will from
others they cant be more fierce than it has been   I could wish to
know whether you have taken your intended trip downwards or
not if you with what success as also to know how my friend Lawrence drives on in the art of courtship as I fancy you both nearly
guess how it will respectively go with each of you."

The last of this batch was addressed to a "dear Sally," [9]
who, like all the rest, treated him with indifference, having
failed to answer three preceding letters.   In this he is
strangely tactless, for him, since he commits the decidedly

indiscreet blunder of describing one woman's fascinations to another. It is surprising to find how illiterate a boy he really was at that time. Indeed, to his dying day, the English language always whipped him:

"DEAR SALLY:
This comes to Fredericksburg fair in hopes of meeting with a speedy Passage to you if your not there which hope youl get shortly altho I am almost discouraged from writing to you as this is my fourth to you since I receivd any from yourself. I hope youl not make the Old Proverb good out of sight out of Mind as its one of the greatest Pleasures I can yet foresee of having in Fairfax in often hearing from you hope you'l not deny it me.

"I pass the time of much more agreable than what I imagined I should as there's a very agrewable young Lady lives in the said house where I reside (Colo. George Fairfax's wife's sister) which in a great measure chears my sorrow and dejectedness tho' not so as to draw my thoughts altogether from your Parts   I could wish to be with you down there with all my heart but as it is a thing almost Impractakable shall rest myself where I am with hopes of shortly having some Minutes of your transactions in your Parts which will be very welcomely receiv'd by your" [10]

These three letters are so vital as they stand (or run) that it is hard to imagine any one either disprizing them or daring to alter an iota of their darling errors. Yet General B. T. Johnson [11] speaks of the letters as "unfortunately preserved," and Jared Sparks suppresses all but part of the one to Robin, profanes that with the emendations of a school teacher and calls them "imperfect and of very little importance." As if the imperfection were not of the utmost importance!

As if it were not important for us to know that the unsurpassed patriot was once a lovesick swain mangling prose and sweating out poetry.

But who was his Lowland Beauty?

Nobody knows. She is as mysterious a ghost as the

"unsterbliche Geliebte" of the three love letters found in Beethoven's desk after his death.

Mary Bland of Westmoreland is one of the candidates for the glory of being the scornful Lowland Beauty and the target of his poems. She married a Henry Lee.

Lucy Grymes has more support for the honor. She lived in Richmond County on the estate called "Morattico." Her father, Charles Grymes, was the son of John Grymes of Grymesby "on the Piankatank where the bullfrog leaps from bank to bank." [12] She threw away the chance to marry the Father of his Country and married another Henry Lee (of Stratford). She became a famous mother and grandmother, numbering among her children Lighthorse Harry Lee, who was a favorite of Washington's, and among her grandchildren, Robert E. Lee. And Robert E. Lee married Mary Custis, the daughter of Martha Custis' grandson, whom George adopted as his son. Thus Washington was mystically and really involved in the career of the perfect hero who led Virginia out of the Union into which Washington had led her with so much difficulty.

A still more likely Lowland Beauty was the girl who rejoiced in the pretty name of Betsy Fauntleroy. We know that she rejected Washington at least once, for he says so himself, and she was a Lowland beauty, even if she were not the Lowland Beauty he referred to in the letters to Robin and John.

She was descended from the famous cavalier Moore Faunt Le Roy, a Huguenot who was the proprietor of a great tract on the Rappahannock.[13] It bore the name of Naylor's Hole, or Hold. Betsy (or Elizabeth) was the daughter of William Fauntleroy by his first wife. She was the only child of that marriage; he had ten children by his second wife.

Betsy was beautiful, of course, and her hand much sought

in marriage. But she was coquettish and kept a number of swains in suspense. She kept Washington hoping for three years after she rejected him. She must have been hard to forget.

A portrait of her hangs in the Washington Museum of the Masonic Lodge at Alexandria.[14] It probably does her little justice. She stands plump and pleasing with a low-cut short-sleeved gown. Her right hand rests at her waist, her left stiffly upholds a flower. The pose is so much like Sally Fairfax's in the portrait at Belvoir that there is reason for suspecting the same painter of libelling them both.

But if Betsy were fickle, so was Washington, for even while he was pouring out his grief for the Lowland Beauty his versatile heart is accused of falling deeper and deeper in love with Mary Cary, whom he had spoken of as "the very agreeable Young Lady Lives in the same house."

Mary was only fourteen at the time when she visited her sister Sally, the wife of Colonel George William Fairfax, but some of the girls married young in Virginia then, as now. Twelve-year-old girls thought and wrote earnestly then of being "not so eager to tye a Knot which Death alone can Dissolve." It was noted of a sixteen-year-old girl that she "never swears, which is here a distinguished virtue." Thomas Jefferson, who was also an earnest dancer, also jilted by his "Belinda," once bet a pair of garters with Alice Corbin.[15]

It is affirmed and denied that Washington went so far at last as to propose to Mary's father for her hand. Whether he went down to Ceelys or Colonel Wilson Cary came up to Belvoir, it is claimed and disclaimed, George decided to brave the haughty old man before he asked the more terrible young girl.

He had no sooner made his errand clear than the Colonel growled at him:

"If that is your business here, sir, I wish you to leave the house, for my daughter has been accustomed to ride in her own coach." [16]

After that, of course, it would have been futile for George to propose to Mary herself. Elopements of unmarried girls in that wilderness were unknown. There was no place to elope to.

Furthermore, the famous "urbanity and breeding" of Colonel Cary "forbid belief that he could have been guilty of such a breach of good manners," says a descendant, Captain Wilson Cary.[17]

George's heart had a busy youth. All of these flames had leapt and lapsed and he was not yet twenty. The strange thing to us, seeing him in the clouds of glory, is that none of these women would even be engaged to him, or promise to wait until he grew up and won a competence. They must have laughed at him. Why?

They could not see what time would make of him, nor could he have dreamed of the day when all those delicious belles would be remembered only because they scorned him. He had no prophetic second sight to console him. He was only an overgrown lout of a young surveyor, who could not spell, who had never made the Grand Tour through Europe, who had never been sent "back home" to study, who had no great prospects and no immediate fascination.

Troubled by the mystery, Bishop Meade guesses that "he may have been too modest and diffident a young man to interest the ladies, or he was too poor at that time, or he had not received a college or university education in England or Virginia, or, as is most probable, God had reserved him for greater things . . . an early marriage might have been injurious to his future usefulness."

But to poor George Washington no such divine assurance

was vouchsafed. He was a failure at everything in his own eyes, disaster following upon disaster.

And now he was called away from his courtships to make his first and only voyage at sea. The errand was melancholy enough: his devoted brother Lawrence was so ill that the only hope of saving him was to get him away to the tropical sun of the West Indies. His wife was not able to go with him and he took George along as his companion, with the result that Lawrence did not save his life and George nearly lost his own.

Late in 1925 a picturesque incident of this period was brought to light by Mrs. A. B. Fothergill of Richmond, who dug it out of the records of Spotsylvania County under the date of December 3, 1751.

It seems that during the summer of that year, Washington went swimming in the Rappahannock near his mother's home, and while he disported in the waves, two women stole his clothes, or at least stole any valuables he may have had in them. They were simply charged with robbing his clothes.

For this they were arrested and tried; one of them turned state's evidence and the other received fifteen lashes on her bare back.

The case is thus recorded in the Order book of 1749-55, William Hunter being one of the county justices:

"3 Dec. 1751. Ann Carrol and Mary McDaniel Senr. of Frederickburgh, being Committed to the Goal of this County by William Hunter Gent, on Suspicion of Felony & Charged with robing the Cloaths of Mr. George Washington when he was washing in the River some time last Summer, the Court having heard Several Evidences Are of Oppinion that the said Ann Carroll be discharged & Admitted an Evidence for our Lord the King against the said Mary McDaniel.

"And Upon Considering the whole Evidences & the prisoners defence, The Court are of Oppinion that the said Mary McDaniel is guilty of petty Larceny, whereupon the said Mary desired immediate punishment for the sd Crime & relied on the Mercy of the Court, therefore it is ordered that the Sheriff carry her to the Whipping post & inflict fifteen lashes on her bare back, And then she be discharged." [18]

Fortunately for our effete sensibilities, Washington was not in the country during the trial and the punishment. He had sailed for Barbados in September.

V

HIS FIRST AND LAST SEA-VOYAGE

GEORGE had to leave behind him all those lovely girls and become indefinitely the male nurse of a heart-broken man dying of tuberculosis. But gratitude would have constrained him if affection had not, and he must have been fond of the step-brother who had been a father to him.

He had made some study of navigation years before, and he kept a record of this voyage, imitating, as far as possible, a log-book and writing down the details of the ship's course, the incidents of each day, and the fish as well as the vessels sighted. He kept, also, an account of the weather with that amazing fidelity that fills all his diaries. He often omits the mention of world-shaking events, but almost never fails to record the state of the sky.

The manuscript of his Journal [1] has been badly preserved, with many pages missing, and others tattered and frayed till only a few words or letters remain.

Barbados is a small island of a hundred thousand acres, and the name of Washington is often found in its records. The progenitor of George is believed to have gone there before he went to Virginia.

The coastwise voyage is, even in our days and ships, a test of a sea-stomach, and George was not immune to the churning motion, though it was not until his return voyage that he confessed his surrender in an entry: "Met with a brisk Trade Wind and pretty large Swell wch made the Ship rowl much and me very sick."

58

It was a long cruise in a small boat, within three days of as long as Noah's incarceration. He and Lawrence left the Potomac river on September 28, 1751, and arrived at Bridgetown, November 3rd. The name of the vessel is lost with the first pages.

Nothing could show less literary ability or important observation than the diary George kept. His spelling is as bad as ever, and in his confusion he now writes "Breese," now "breeze"; either "Sail" or "sale"; "Dolphin," or "Dalphin." "Rigging" is "riggan"; "Schooner," "Chooner." "News" is "knews," "indifferent" is "indiferent," and "seperated" has the fatal "e." On a Sunday he "dressed in order for Church but got to town two Late." "We was" is frequent, and he has his usual trouble with proper names like "Philiadelphia."

And yet it is human and at times humorous. It has the convincing quality of something real, the actual Washington tossing about on the waves and hurrying to record what he saw in his little book. He tries to write like an old seadog, with latitude, longitude, knots, course, and sails sighted, religiously indicated, along with such events as: "Catched a Dolphin at 8 P. M., a Shark at 11 and a one of his pilot fish; the Dolphin and pilot was dressed for Dinner."

On the 17th of October there was "a disturb'd and large Sea which iminently endanger'd our masts roling away." On the 19th and 20th there was "a fomented [?] Sea jostling in heaps occasioned by Wavering wind. . . . The Seamen seemed disheartned confessing they never had seen such weather before. . . . A Constant succession of hard Winds, Squals of Rain, and Calms was the remarkable attendants of this day which was so sudden and flighty we durst not go under any but reef'd Sails."

When the sun at length came out over the "large tumbling Sea running many ways by the Various winds," they got out the bread and sunned it over, it was "almost Eaten up by Weavel and Maggots."

(30th) "This Morning arose with agreeable assurances of a certain and steady trade Wind which after near five Weeks buffiting and being toss'd by a fickle and Merciless ocean was glad'ening knews: the preceeding night we seperated from sloop abe mentioned."

On November 2nd they were alarmed by the cry of land at 4 A. M., and were surprised to find they were only "3 leauges distance" when by their reckoning they should have been "150 Leauges to the Windward." A few more leagues and they would have missed the island altogether and probable not have discovered the error in time to regain the land for three weeks or more.

On shore, a physician gave Lawrence assurance of a cure, and they were "perfectly ravished by the beautiful prospects which on every side presented to our view the fields of Cain, Corn, Fruit Trees, &c in a delightful Green."

Then began a series of dinners. They found their lodgings 'extravagently dear. . . . £15 pr. Month . . . exclusive of Liquors and washing which we find."

They dined at a "Club call'd the Beefstake and tripe." They dined everywhere; once "with some Ladys" at the fort which mounted "36 Gunes."

Now he went to the theatre and saw the *Tragedy of George Barnwell.* It was perhaps his first taste of the drama for which he acquired so great a passion, but his criticism is probably the least profound on record. Yet it is becomingly modest; he never pretended to knowledge or experience he did not have.

"The character of Barnwell and several others was said to be well perform'd there was Musick a Dapted and regularly conducted by Mr. ———."

On November 17th he was "strongly attacked with the

small Pox: sent for Dr. Lanahan whose attendance was very constant till my recovery, and going out which was not 'till thursday the 12th of December."

When one imagines what a difference it meant to the world whether or not that long young Virginian, gasping in the remote little island, should join the throng hurried graveward, or should recover, the name of Dr. Lanahan should not be ignored as it has been. He had vast interests at stake upon his skill, but how can a physician know what evil or good he is doing to the future when he lets any young man or woman slip through his hands, or wins the battle?

Washington survived, and the immunity to further attacks of smallpox was of infinite value to him all his life.[2] But his face was thereafter pitted, as at least a third of the faces were in those ante-vaccination days; yet Weems,[3] who knew him, assures us that the smallpox "marked him rather agreeably than otherwise."

On the first entry after his illness, he condensed a good deal of drama into a small room:

"On Munday last began the Grand sessions and this Day brought on the Tryal of Colo. Chaunack a Man of oppulent fortune and infamous Character he was dicted for commiting a Rape on his servant Maid and was brought in Guiltless and sav'd by one single Evidence on . . . was generally reckone[d] suborn'd."

There are six entries stating nothing but where he dined. On the 21st, simply this: "At my Lodgings . . . my Brother." On the next day, "Took my leave of my Br. Majr Clarke &ca and Imbar[ked] . . . wai'd anchor and got out of Carlile Bay." The name of the boat was the *Industry*. She sailed December 22d and reached the mouth of the York river on January 26th.

There is no mention of the fact that poor Lawrence gave

up hope of recovery in Barbados and was advised to try Bermuda, for which he sailed, while he sent George back to Virginia to fetch Mrs. Lawrence to him.

Of this dismal history there is no word, probably because George felt no need to write it in a book. Instead, he occupied the day of his sailing by a long review of his impressions of Barbados.

In the following lines he writes of something that he was to encounter himself in his latest years:

"The Governor of Barbados seem[s] to keep a proper State: Lives very retired and at Little expence it is said he is a Gentleman of good Sence As he avoids the Errors of his predecessor he gives no handle for complaint but at the same time by declining much familiarity is not over zealously beloved."

The farmer was perhaps stronger in Washington's soul than ever the soldier was. He shows already, at nineteen, a keen curiosity about all forms of produce and the art of production, and an earnest reverence for the farmer's best friend, manure. He describes the fruits, the "Avagado pair," the rich black earth, the fruitfulness, and the "extraordinary Sail" of ginger, yet—"How wonderful that such people shou'd be in debt!"

"Their dung they are very careful in saving, and curious in makg. which they do by throughing up large heaps of Earth and a number of Stakes drove there in Sufficient for Sixteen head of Cattle to Stand seperately tied too which they are three months together tramplg. all the trash &ca. than . . . and then its fit to manu . . . the Ground. Provisions in Genl. are very indeferent but much better than the same quantity of pasturage wou'd afford in Virginia.

"Taverns they have none but in their Towns so that Travellers is oblig'd to go to private houses however the Island being but abt. 22 Miles in length and 14 in width preven[ts] their being much infested with ym. The Ladys Generally are very agreeable but by ill custom or wt . . . affect the Negro Style."

"Agreeable" was a strong word for George. Mary Cary was "very agreeable."

On Christmas the ship's company dined on an Irish goose and drank a health to absent friends. The next day there was no breeze "to paliate the heat of the Sun," which was "very permament and troublesome."

On January 9th "At 2 A:M came on excessive hard Wind at No. Wt; Rain Lightning and some thunder the Wind increased so violently and had raiz'd so Mountanous a Sea that oblig'd the hauling all her Sails and driving with bear Masts."

He was apparently flung about and made "a criple" by the ship's tossing. The ship "lay too" day after day on account of the high wind. But at last they were able to sail on. On the 23rd of January there is this lively note:

"This day inticed the Mate to c[rawl] from his Cabbin (as a snail enlivened by the genial heat of the Sun) who since the third or four[th] day after leaving Barbados has been coop'd up with a fashionable disorder contracted there." He had evidently caught the large form of the also fashionable disorder that George contracted there.

When he landed he presented letters to the new Governor of Virginia, Robert Dinwiddie, "and was received Graceously." This was the beginning of a long and close relationship. The old Scotsman, who has been much abused for annoying Washington, really discovered him.

On the last of January Washington attended a cockfight in Yorktown—the very Yorktown where a still greater cockfight was one day to be held. He records this one as "A Great Main . . . tween Glouster and York for 5 pistoles each battle and 100 ye odd I left it with Colo. Lewis before it was decided and had part of his chariot to his house."

A few tatters and the Journal is over. He went to Pope's Creek, thence to Fredericksburg and on to Mount Vernon, where he delivered his letters to Lawrence's wife. For some reason, she and George did not sail to Bermuda, but waited at Mount Vernon until Lawrence gave up the battle a year later and wrote to his wife, "I shall hurry home to my grave."

He arrived in 1752, died on July 26th, and was buried in a vault that he had built. George joined him there half a century later.

Lawrence willed a life-interest in Mount Vernon to his wife, with reversion to his infant daughter Sarah, if she outlived him; but in the event of her death without issue, the estate was to go to "his beloved brother George." This had been his father's wish and will.

Anne Fairfax Washington had borne her husband four children, none of whom survived infancy. Sarah, the last, lived only a few weeks after her father's death. Naturally, she had no issue. The widow remained one for only five months, then married George Lee, uncle to Lighthorse Harry Lee. Her new husband wanted to live in Westmoreland County, so George came into the estate whose name is immortally linked with his. He had to pay his brother's widow's husband an annual rent of fifteen thousand pounds of tobacco, which amounted to about eighty pounds in Virginia money. He paid it for nine years, and there was a good deal of litigation over it until George Lee and his wife died within a few months of each other, leaving George's title clear.

On his return to Virginia, George had returned to the torments of love. Two months before Lawrence's death, he has resolved to have another try at that Lowland Beauty,

Betsy Fauntleroy. All that we know about it is that he wrote to her grandfather on May, 1752, referring to his previous rejection and announcing that as soon as he got well enough for the journey, he would ride down and see if she had changed her mind. This is the letter:

To Wm. Fauntleroy, sr.

"Sir: I should have been down long before this, but my business in Frederick detained me somewhat longer than I expected, and immediately upon my return from thence I was taken with a violent pleurise, which has reduced me very low; but purpose, as soon as I recover my strength, to wait on Miss Betsy, in hopes of a revocation of the former cruel sentence, and see if I can meet with any alteration in my favor. I have enclosed a letter to her, which should be much obliged to you for the delivery of it. I have nothing to add but my best respects to your good lady and family."

There is no record that he ever went down into the Lowlands, but if he did, she refused him again.

There was no authenticated writing of Washington's to fill the gap between his letter to Betsy Fauntleroy's grandfather, dated May 20th, 1752, and the publication of the journal of his remarkable journey to the Ohio River in 1753. Discussion of a manuscript of certain prayers wrongly attributed to Washington and assigned to this period is given in the Appendix.

Betsy married a lover named Bowler Cocke. Whereupon another lover, Thomas Adams, was so upset that he fled to England to drown his love, as Lord Fairfax had fled to America to drown his.

Bowler Cocke lived long enough to make Betsy a mother more than once, but he died at last and Thomas Adams, who had evidently found nobody in London so fascinating as Betsy, hurried back to Virginia and won the widow to wife.[4] She bore him a son, called after his father, Thomas Adams.

The story was told that when she saw young Colonel Washington ride by some years later she fainted.

And that is all we know of the Lowland Beauty, if, indeed, the name belongs to Betsy and not to another even less unknown.

When he failed to win Betsy Fauntleroy, Washington found that Mary Cary was no longer so available as an antidote to despondency.

Mary had a new lover,[5] one who had the advantage of foreign polish, the son of Richard Ambler, collector of the port at Yorktown, who had married Elizabeth Jaqueline, of Huguenot stock, and had nine children, all of whom died at an early age except three sons, Edward, John and Jaqueline. The youngest of these married early a girl named Rebecca Burwell, who had been vainly courted by a young Virginian named Thomas Jefferson. Jaqueline also became a very distinguished Virginian. Edward and John were sent abroad as children and educated in England. They graduated at Cambridge with high honors, toured the continent for the finishing touches, and returned home.

Edward, then a little over twenty-one, at once came courting Mary Cary, and in the face of such competition, Washington was an illiterate boor. Mary became Mrs. Ambler in 1752,[6] and her husband succeeded his father in the lucrative post of collector of the port of York. He fell heir soon to the noble estate of Jamestown Island and represented the county in the House of Burgesses till his death in 1767. He was very wealthy and Washington had his fortune yet to make. The military career was rather an expense than a livelihood.

Mary Cary's grandson, Edward Ambler,[7] tells this story of his grandmother:

"It was an anecdote of the day, that this lady, many years after she had become the wife of Edward Ambler, hap-

pened to be in Williamsburg when General Washington
passed through that city at the head of the American army,
crowned with never-fading laurels and adored by his countrymen.   Having distinguished her among the crowd, his
sword waved toward her a military salute, whereupon
she is said to have fainted.   But this wants confirmation, for her whole life tended to show that she never for
a moment regretted the choice she had made."

The story of Mary Cary's fainting at the sight of George
Washington riding by on his way home from his great victory at Yorktown "wants confirmation" indeed, for there is
no reason why he should have passed through Williamsburg after Yorktown, and no evidence of it.   And Mary
Ambler's tombstone at Jamestown shows that she died the
Spring before Cornwallis surrendered.[8]

So legends rise and grow.   First, Betsy Fauntleroy faints
at seeing Washington ride by as a colonel.   Then Mary
Cary faints (posthumously) at seeing him ride by as the victorious general who had taken Cornwallis prisoner.

A note of grim tragedy is added to Mary Cary's fate, for
her grandson tells of the desecration of her grave by British troops who came to ransack and to plunder.   Convinced
that the missing family plate was buried in the graveyard,
"they proceeded to the grave of my grandmother and actually opened it before they would be satisfied that the
object of their search was not there."

So ended the story of poor Molly Cary Ambler, whose
elder sister, Mrs. Sally Fairfax, certainly knew the love of
Washington.

Perhaps his love for Sally Fairfax came upon him when
he was much in need of consolation, seeing that Betsy
Fauntleroy had rejected him for good, Mary Cary had
married a more cultured gentleman, and Lucy Grymes was
yielding to the suasion of Henry Lee.

In any case, the dark love for Sally was a man's love, for Washington was no longer a cub. He was a young giant of twenty-one, an Adjutant-General with the rank of Major. He had already been accepted as a Mason on November 4th, 1752, in the lodge at Fredericksburg[9] and was studying the manual of tactics and the art of war with Adjutant Muse, of Virginia, also the art of fencing with Jacob Van Braam, a Dutchman. Both of these men had been comrades of Lawrence Washington's Carthagena days and had been engaged by him to teach George the rudiments of soldiery, of which he knew absolutely nothing when he was appointed Adjutant-General.

Lawrence had been a good step-brother. He had introduced George to the high world of fashionable amusement, had enabled him to learn surveying and practice it, taught him, and had him taught the military arts, and secured him the high favor of the new governor of the colony.

He was not commissioned at the age of nineteen as has been stated in perhaps all of the biographies of Washington. Sparks, making a deduction from John Marshall, announced that Washington was made an Adjutant General before he was twenty, and the story has been repeated ever since.

The error was discovered by Mr. Fairfax Harrison. In an article called "George Washington's First Commission," (published in the *Virginia Magazine of History and Biography* for July, 1923) he quotes from the records of the Executive Council of Virginia proof that Washington was not commissioned until four months after Lawrence Washington died, and within two months of his own twenty-second birthday.

His commission was voted November 6th, 1752, when he was appointed one of four adjutants-general, being assigned to the Southern District comprising several counties. In November, 1753, he was transferred to the Northern Neck.

Though the legendary nineteen-year-old Adjutant-General thus vanishes, there was still scandal at the time about entrusting such a post to a young man with no military knowledge whatsoever. The other three Adjutants-General, though older and more experienced, were hard-drinkers and not gentlemen, while Washington was of the aristocracy, and, though he was always drinking, carried his liquor well.

Still, the protest at his youth was insistent, though George Fairfax was amused to answer: "All Washingtons are born old."

Besides, the chief business of the militia at that time was said to be getting gloriously drunk on training days and searching negro cabins for weapons; so military scholarship was not expected. Yet Governor Dinwiddie foresaw trouble and sighed: "Our Militia, under God, is our chief Dependance, for the Protection of our Lives and Fortunes; (our Country being very extensive and without Fortifications)." [10]

At any rate, Washington now had a commission with the rank of Major and a salary of £100 a year.[11] And he was in uniform. Washington was about to begin being Washington.

VI

HE PIERCES THE WILDERNESS

NOTHING was easier, more gracious or more graceful for the King of England than to sign a paper giving away a million acres or a continent to the first man who said he saw it, or to the courtier who wheedled best.

The geography of America back of the coast was largely a matter of imagination, rumor and the mistranslation of signs and grunts made by ignorant Indians. Consequently the King's munificent gifts often overlapped or contradicted one another and generally contained more or less territory claimed by some rival monarch.

Young Washington arrived on the scene as a soldier a little after high noon in the Second Hundred Years War between France and England, which, in the words of Randolph G. Adams,[1] "began with William of Orange and ended with Napoleon. It was a series of wars, each of which was a general European War. . . . In every case from 1689 to 1815, there was not a single great European War (and there were seven of them) in which American lives were not lost, American property was not destroyed, and in which American soldiers and sailors were not involved."

It is only now coming to be realized how largely history has been a matter of land speculation. The settlement of America and other continents was enormously vitalized by just what we call real estate booms and homestead rushes guided by astute salesmen and attended with incredible corruption and disaster to the poor deluded victims of swindling, exploitation, lying advertisement, and hysterical propaganda.

The original colonization of Virginia, as of other provinces, was to a disgraceful degree a matter of stock-jobbing corporations unloading their more or less fraudulent properties on pitiful souls called pioneers. Legitimate ambition, honest dealing and high courage were not lacking, but the great waves of migration, the wild bull-panics in land and the after-collapses of our day are mere imitations of what has gone on since time began.

Many patriots hate to hear these facts, but the truth must out. And it is an undeniable truth that in the settlement of the West, the opening of the Mississippi Valley and of the Ohio River, which was part of it, land speculation led the way.

Two of the leaders were men whom the average American never dreams of as business-men and speculators, Benjamin Franklin and George Washington.

The realization of this truth should not diminish the prestige of those exceedingly great men. Rather, should their glory enhance other business men and speculators who in times past have revealed, and are today revealing, prophetic vision, indomitable courage and heroic perseverance.

It has been overlong the custom to assume that epic poetry flies out of the window the moment business comes in at the door. We should realize the truer truth that all great business men and business triumphs have been, when understood, epic in virtues, epic in sins, aglow with poetic imaginations both of horror and beauty, tragedy and triumph.

In his fine work, *The Mississippi Valley in British Politics*, Clarence W. Alvord wrote:

"In the unbroken wilderness across the mountain the speculators were in advance of the actual home maker. The historic muse has always delighted in singing of the daring deeds of the explorer wandering through the dark forest or paddling his canoe on unknown rivers; and even the homesteader, with family goods packed in his prairie schooner, has had his exploits chanted in majestic measures; but few have noted the fact that both explorer and homesteader were frequently only the advance agents of the speculator who dreamed of large enterprises in land exploitation—that the Daniel Boones of the wilderness were only the pawns of some Richard Henderson. From that distant date when Joliet and La Salle first found their way into the heart of the great West, up to the present day when far-off Alaska is in the throes of development, 'big business' has been engaged in western speculation. The Mississippi Valley has been explored, cleared, and settled in large measure through the enterprise and financial boldness of moneyed men who have staked fortunes in opening up the successive lines of the American frontier.

"In the American colonies the speculative enterprise of the mother country naturally had its influence, and the men of America allied themselves with the British moneyed classes in business operations which were practically limited by conditions and colonial laws to the sale of merchandise and land speculation—in the West to land speculation and the fur trade.

"The earliest attempts to form settlements in the West were due entirely to this speculative enterprise."

"The original grant to the Virginia Company included a large part of the present area of the United States," says Latané. The western border was the Mississippi river, wherever that might be. The Forks of the Ohio (where Pittsburgh now is) were in Virginia's territory, and also in Pennsylvania's, with consequent mutual wrath. Later the King gave Maryland to Lord Baltimore, and when the Virginians understood that this grant came bodily out of the

Virginia grant, there was vain opposition and prolonged bitterness, exacerbated by the fact that the Baltimore people were Catholics, and all Catholics were criminals by the law. Quaker Pennsylvania also disputed Maryland's borders, as well as Virginia's.

The Virginians, the Marylanders and Pennsylvanians henceforth hated one another so heartily that they could never be induced to co-operate effectively in protecting settlers from Indian massacre, or even from the French claims, since the French King was also graceful with the pen, and carefree as to boundaries.

The colonies vied with one another in their greed for the lands in the "far west," which was then what is now Ohio. As they pushed their Indian traders like feelers into the fog of woods, mountains and streams, they soon penetrated the invisible barrier set up by the French, who planned a chain of forts to connect their colonies in Canada and Louisiana.

The French claim was supported by the "right" of discovery. But discovery usually means that there was somebody already in the discovered territory. Still, the French had made arrangements with the Indians, whom they treated with far more justice and friendliness than the English.

But what did the colonists care for the French or their King? He was only the ridiculous pretender to the land divinely established by a Protestant God for the benefit of Virginia—or Maryland—or Pennsylvania, as the case might be.

Who was the French King anyway?—nothing but an impudent papist who could always be fought on the loftiest religious grounds without mentioning the base uses of commerce or land-lust.

The Indians, of course, being heathen, had no rights to

anything but conversion and salvation. If their souls were saved, or if the opportunity to have them saved were offered them, enough had been done for them.

It has been estimated that there were only 40,000 Indians of all tribes east of the Mississippi. The Ohio tribes had been whipped to a standstill by the Six Nations (otherwise known as the Iroquois or Mingoes), and they fought one another now for such lesser honors as the Iroquois despised. Benjamin Franklin gazed with amazement at the firm confederation of six savage tribes while a dozen English colonies could not agree. The Indians gazed with amazement at both French and English, who called them brothers, made themselves at home on the Indian soil and disputed rival claims as if the Indian had never been there at all.

An old Delaware chief asked the Virginia surveyor, Gist, this riddle:

"The French claim all the land on one side of the Ohio, the English claim all the land on the other side. Just where is the Indian's land?"

American history has answered the riddle with an epitaph: "The only good Indian is a dead Indian. The Indian's land lies in the Happy Hunting Grounds overhead somewhere."

As for the poor beasts of the fields, woods and streams, they had no rights that even the Indians respected. The fur-trade was the cause of wars disguised with resounding purposes. The Ohio Company was after the pelts of animals and incidentally the scalps of either Indians or whites who interfered with the hope of profits. If man had been a fur-bearing animal instead of a fur-wearing one, human history would have been less crowded with the slaughter of men as well as the incomputable butchery and unspeakable cruelty of trapping poor wretches for their pelts.

In North America, Europe had found a vast game-preserve thronged with precious quadrupeds. It was thinly sprinkled with bipeds, also, who had evolved but little further than the cunning and the ferocity necessary to the pursuit of their food and clothing.

Here was a Golconda that surpassed the ancient peltries of Russia and China. The hunt for furs and hides was more tempting, easier, and more profitable than the search for gold or spices or precious gems, more tempting far than the slow and uncertain profits of agriculture or manufacture. Underneath all the talk of persecution, "rights" and religions was the great necessity for easier money and more of it, for land and the privilege of spreading out on it or selling it at a profit.

France and England began the great North American Fur-War about thirty years before Washington's birth, and it lasted till about thirty years later, till 1763. He came to his majority just in time to seize an opportunity that was the making of him, though his fame as a pathfinder and Westward-looking prophet has been overshadowed by his fame for other deeds looking Eastward and toward the centralizing union of the colonies.

Even thus, his glory has swallowed up the credit of earlier and more forward men who were less lucky in historians. They were frankly trappers, Indian traders and explorers, and their motives were hence suspect. But Washington, while his motives were equally adventurous, mercenary and immediate, has been seen in the rosy afterglow of his later fame as solely actuated by patriotism and the love of mankind. No man was ever a purer patriot than he, but the necessary alloy was not lacking. He fought also for the sacred and inalienable right to make money—a right which the theologists and the anarchists alike revile, but one that is none the less admirable and essential.

Among the colonies, Pennsylvania, lying nearest to the Ohio River, had taken the lead away from Albany in the westering push. Her traders went farther than any others. By 1750 they were out on the Wabash and the Maumee, and Paul Pierce was "bringing in 4000 weight of summer skins taken on the Wabasha." [2] The English were edging toward the Mississippi itself, and riddling the French line.

From about the time of Washington's birth, the English trade was handled mainly from Philadelphia, then by far the largest town in America. Canny Benjamin Franklin was at the head of its activities, and his devotion to the opening of the West has been blurred, like Washington's, by the splendor of his other fame, as Franklin's fame in many directions has been dimmed by Washington's. The forty-eight-year-old Franklin was at Albany proposing his draft of a Plan of Union for the colonies in June, 1754, at a time when the twenty-two-year-old Washington had just led forty men against thirty-two in his first skirmish.

Too little fame has been the portion of George Croghan, a Dublin Irishman who came to America when George Washington was only ten years old. He was called a papist, being Irish, but was an Episcopalian, in fact. [3]

By 1741 he had a twelve-hundred-acre farm on the border of Pennsylvania, and his house was a landmark on the map where whites and Indians met to trade. He had a tanyard, too, for the deerskins. He had his employees out as far as Lake Erie, and his packhorse trains established stations for the Ohio trade.

The French began to complain of his far-flung energies, especially as he was as perfectly willing to stir the Indians to attack or betray the French as any other good American was at that time. Croghan knew the Indians, spoke two of their languages, and treated Indians as human beings. The French believed that if they could get rid of Croghan, they

could win over the Ohio Indians.   They called him George
"Crocquen" and offered a thousand dollars for his scalp.[4]

He had many rival traders, but Virginians did not com-
pete with him much until the founding of the Ohio Company, which was organized to end Pennsylvania's monopoly
of the fur-trade.   "A bitter cutthroat competition" was
threatened between the colonies, and actual civil war was
prevented only by the greater hatred of the French.

The extreme rancor of commercial rivalry between the
colonies can only be appreciated when it is made clear that it
was inter-colonial jealousy rather than French enterprise
that first stirred the French and Indians to advance upon the
Ohio Company and the hopes of the Washingtons.   For
this astounding statement Alvord [5] is the authority:

"The preparations of Virginia to extend her dominion
over the rich western territory by actual occupation were
watched with increasing jealousy by the men of other colonies, who were far from being satisfied with a policy that
would place in the control of any one province the exploitation of such a vast and valuable region.   It is therefore not
strange that any plans promoted by them should assume the
form of a limitation of the territory of Virginia by the erection of independent colonies.   The city of Philadelphia in
particular was very much interested in the disposition of the
West, which was well known there from the accounts of her
merchants who at an early date had sent their fur-trading
representatives across the mountains.   These traders, it was
said, were so hostile to Virginia that they were the chief
agents in arousing among the Indians fears of the threatened
encroachments on their hunting-grounds and were therefore
the real instigators of the war, because the French were induced to enter the valley of the Ohio by the clamor of their
Indian allies."

The Ohio Company, in which the Washingtons were eminent from first to last, enfuriated not only the French, not only the other colonies, but even the Virginians who were outside the corporation. As Alvord emphasizes:

"The company from the first found itself beset with difficulties, arising not only from that lack of knowledge and experience to be expected in a new undertaking but also from the jealousies of local politics, for the government of Virginia, always fearful of some infringement on its western rights by the imperial government, threw all the obstacles it could in the way of the enterprise.

"Moreover, Virginia had already begun on her own account to make land cessions in this western region . . . and by 1757 Virginia had granted about two million acres in this region."

Lawrence Washington, who had turned from iron to fur and gained the leadership of the Ohio Company, would perhaps have long overshadowed George if he had kept his health and lived through the great events that were shaping and being shaped by all mankind. Lawrence was both tolerant enough and good businessman enough to see that the Ohio Company would lose many of its most desirable customers if religion were allowed to throttle business; if the Established Church should compel the Pennsylvania German and Dutch settlers to pay tithes and attend the sermons of the clergy of a church from which they dissented. He pleaded, therefore, for liberty of conscience, and referred enviously to Pennsylvania, "which has flourished under that delightful liberty, so as to become the admiration of every man who considers the short time it has been settled . . . We have increased by slow degrees, except negroes and convicts." [6]

Religious tolerance has usually had its birth and preservation in commercial interests. When zealots find that their devotion is driving off trade and reducing profits, they almost always grow liberal for a time.

Fortunately for mankind, bigotry is bad business, and Lawrence Washington realized it. It was from him, perhaps, that George learned such indifference to other men's religious views as once to say that he cared not whether a man were Mohammedan, Jew, or atheist, provided he did his work well.

The warfare in the colonies between creeds was checked, but general toleration by no means hastened, from dread of France, for French success meant Catholic success, the loss of the whole project and the annihilation of the Ohio Company. Already the English traders were being pushed back, captured and killed and the French invisible barrier was becoming an advancing wall of steel.

The French commander, Bienville de Céloron, sent the Governor of Pennsylvania a message saying how "surprised" he was to find Englishmen in the French domain, and a warning to keep his traders out of French territory, since "our Commandant-General would be very sorry to be forced to use violence." [7] Croghan was sent out to reconnoitre, and he reported that the French had a thousand men advancing to the Ohio.

From New York came word of another French advance. Croghan was sent out again with an order to the French to keep out of English territory.

There was need of prompt action on Pennsylvania's part. The settlers must have a fort to fly to. The friendly Indians demanded a stronghold on the Ohio for the shelter of their wives and children. Croghan said the right place was at the Forks of the Ohio. But Governor Hamilton of Pennsylvania could not persuade his Quakers to build a fort.

So Pennsylvania lost her prestige as the leader of English defence against the French. [8] The honor fell to Virginia,

and the new Governor Dinwiddie was willing to assume it,
especially as the French were reported to have their eye
on the Forks of the Ohio, the very heart of the lands in
which Dinwiddie was a shareholder.

The charter of the Ohio Company stipulated that it must
establish a fort and at least a hundred families there.[9] A
path to the tract had already been mapped out by a trader,
Thomas Cresap, and an Indian named Nemacolin. A surveyor, Christopher Gist, had also gone out and come back
with rosy reports.

The next thing to do was to build the fort and garrison it.
Dinwiddie called for recruits and offered to divide among
them two hundred thousand of the company's acres. If
he did not settle the land and maintain the fort, the Ohio
Company would lose the royal grant and the extra three
hundred thousand acres to be assigned in compliance with
the conditions.

Immediately the Pennsylvanians roared that this Virginian was giving away their property. They would not
defend it, but they would not permit anyone else to enjoy
it except the French. Dinwiddie tried to quiet them by
saying that he would give them all the quit rent money
until a boundary line could be drawn. Quit rent money
was the tribute paid on all land to the King or the proprietary company. The boundary line was not drawn till
1779: by which time many unforeseen things had happened
and Governor Dinwiddie was no longer with us.

In 1753, however, Dinwiddie was exceedingly active,
battling with the languid Virginians, bombarding the governors of the other colonies with information and vain
appeals for co-operation, and pouring out letters to the
English government, berating the inconceivable indolence
and equal insolence of the colonies and begging for help
from overseas.

The pressure of the French threatened not only his shares in the Ohio Company, but the integrity of Virginia and the whole colonial empire of his majesty the King. He had every inducement to fight for his flag, his Protestant creed, and his investments.

He felt that a war with France was inevitable, and while crying aloud for preparedness, was willing to strike the first blow if necessary. But he must give a polite warning to the French before the blow was struck.

He hired William Trent, who knew the Ohio region and was a partner of Benjamin Franklin's, to go out and warn the French squatters away, gave him a writ of eviction to deliver to the French commander.

Trent set out, but at Logstown (near the present Pittsburgh), he learned that, while the French commander was a hundred and fifty miles away, the French troops had been active and had routed the Miami, or Twightwee, Indians, who were trying, at their own expense, to be friendly to the English. Trent, therefore, turned back and won an undeserved reputation for cowardice.

Dinwiddie sent him out again with gifts for the Ohio tribes, and a hundred Indians later came down to call on Dinwiddie at Winchester and secure guns and ammunition. The Virginians dreaded to give them enough weapons to fight the French lest they turn on the English. The disgruntled Indians went on to Pennsylvania and met the same timidity, which chilled their friendship. The English made blunder after blunder in their efforts to bribe the Indians. They tried everything but trust, and were repaid with ruination.

Dinwiddie was set on sending somebody out to inform the French commander how deeply it grieved the gracious King of England to learn that certain stupid subjects of his beloved cousin, the most Christian King of France, had blundered in upon the private property of the English King. The French commander would politely answer, of course, that all Dinwiddie said was perfectly true if the terms were exactly reversed. Whereupon war would probably follow.

But fair warning must be given for the sake of the record. Also, Dinwiddie wanted his sacred messenger to do a bit of spying on the way, note what forts the French had built, and where and how strong they were, and the best place for the English to build their fort. He found a reluctance among the first he approached. What more natural than that his eye should light on his stalwart young friend, George Washington, the ward of one of the founders of the Ohio Company?

Early in 1752, George Washington, as he says in his Barbados journal, had waited upon the Governor with letters, and had been "received Graceously he enquired kindly after the health of my Br. and invited me to stay and dine."

He saw Dinwiddie again at the capital, Williamsburg, when the Governor gave him his commission as Adjutant-General of the Northern Division, though he was only twenty-one. This, of course, was due to the pressure of Lord Fairfax and the memory of Lawrence Washington. There was never a time when "pull" had more power, or an instance in which it was more justified.

A final argument in Washington's favor was undoubtedly the social grace he had acquired. The Indian traders were rough woodsmen and nothing more. Washington was not only a woodsman of great experience in his three years as a surveyor, but also a gentleman, a cavalier, an aristocrat able to exchange delicate courtesies with any French officer he might encounter. Nobody ever found him maladroit in the drawing-room, the ballroom or the problems of exquisite military etiquette.

What more natural than that Washington should accept the commission—ask for it indeed? He was ambitious, fearless, skilled in forest-craft. He had been studying military tactics, fortification. If the French stayed where they were, the Ohio Company would be wiped out, and with it his dreams of enormous riches and countless acres.

There may have been a further reason for his eagerness to plunge into the wilderness. It is known that he had once loved Lucy Grymes, and had not won her. Some have supposed that she was the Lowland Beauty. Mrs. Pryor thought so, and believed that Washington had been "for him—very faithful to her." A month after he dashed off into the jungle, Miss Grymes became Mrs. Henry Lee. Mrs. Pryor [10] imagined that it was grief over her loss that led Washington to offer his services to Dinwiddie, that he might retreat gracefully and hide his broken heart and wounded pride in the solitudes.

But whether driven by disprized love or by prized real estate, he volunteered to go, and Dinwiddie gave him a letter written with all the delicacy of insult at his command.

In this, his first great adventure, as in the Barbados voyage, Washington is his own biographer; but unfortunately his manuscript has been lost and we must take his delightful awkwardness as they were revised, punctuated and re-spelled by the editor and proofreader, some unknown Jared Sparks, who cut out most of the blunders that humanize Washington's own young solemnities. [11]

When Washington rode out of Williamsburg, October 1st, 1753, he took with him his Dutch fencing-teacher, Van Braam, who pretended to understand French well enough to serve as an interpreter. His ability was soon shown, for when the Indians used the word "Illinois," he understood it as *"Isle Noire."* He translated this "Black Islands!" and Washington gravely transcribed it so. Later, Van Braam's

bad French would be blamed for casting a permanent stain
on Washington's reputation.

Picking up provisions, guns and blankets and horses as
he went, he reached a branch of the Potomac called Will's
Creek (now Cumberland, Maryland), where he engaged
Christopher Gist as "pilot." Gist had already covered the
ground without a guide. Two "servitors" and two traders
went along. The party, seven in all, left Fort Cumberland November 15th in "excessive Rains and vast Quantity
of Snow," through which it worried to one of the cabins
of the trader Frazier, at the mouth of Turtle Creek on
the Monongahela, near the fatal spot afterwards known as
Braddock's Field.

Here it was learned that the French had retired to Winter
Quarters, and that death had removed their commander,
General Marin, who had been sent from Canada by the new
governor Du Quesne to build a fort at the junction of the
Allegheny and Monongahela rivers, just where the two
rivers flow into one and merge both their names and their
waters in the one stream known as the Ohio River. It was
here that the Ohio Company had selected its site.

Young Washington, looking over the ground, wisely
decided that this site was inferior to one he described as
"extremely well situated for a Fort, as it has the absolute
Command of both Rivers . . . the entire Command of the
Monongahela; which runs up to our Settlements and is
extremely well designed for Water Carriage, as it is of a
deep still Nature. Besides, a fort at the Fork might be
built at much less Expence."

He was already thinking with generalship.

He met here an Indian "King," the Delaware, Shingiss,
who later turned to the French, leading the English to
advertise a reward of $350 for his verminous head.
Shingiss went along with the party to Logstown, where

Washington called on Monakatoocha (or Monacatootha, also known as Scarroyady), and told him the nature of his errand to the French. Monakatoocha sent for the Half-King, Tanacharisson, a Seneca (called half-king because he was a vassal to the Council of the Six Nations, or Iroquois).

"Came to Town four or ten Frenchmen," deserters, who had brought freight up from New Orleans. Failing to meet the escorts supposed to come down from Lake Erie, they decided to decamp. They gave Washington information about the forts on the Mississippi and the "Black Islands" (i.e., the Illinois River) and the Ohio.

"About 3 o'Clock this Evening"—the Southerners still call afternoon "evening"—the Half-King arrived and Washington questioned him concerning the French and the roads. The Indian said the roads were bad and the French worse. The Half-King repeated the magnificent eloquence he had wasted in protesting against French invasion and praising the English good intentions. The French general had answered by declaring that the Indians did not own even so much as the dirt under his fingernails. As the Half-King quoted him, he said:

"Child, you talk foolish, you say this Land belongs to you, but there is not the Black of my Nail yours. I saw that Land sooner than you did. . . . It is my Land and I will have it, let who will stand-up for or say-against it."

The Half-King called a council and Washington made an address, beginning:

"Brothers, I have called you together in Council by order of your Brother, the Governor of Virginia." But it took him several days to persuade them even to grant him aid and protection in reaching the French.

At last he got away with the Half-King and two other Indians and proceeded "without any Thing remarkable happening but a continued Series of bad Weather."

This is making light of his hardships, for even Gist, who also kept a diary,[12] was impressed by the toil and danger they incurred. Everywhere were swollen creeks, where, says Gist, "we were obliged to carry all our baggage over on trees and swim our horses. The Major and I went first over with our boots on. . . . Our Indians killed a bear . . . we had a creek to cross, very deep; we got over on a tree and got our goods over."

At Venango (where Franklin, Pennsylvania, now is, about thirty miles due South of the present city of Erie, Pennsylvania) they "found the French Colours hoisted at a House from which they had driven Mr. John Frazier, an English Subject." In charge was Captain Joincare, half-breed son of a French officer and a Seneca squaw. He invited the party, says Washington, "to sup with them; and treated us with the greatest Complaisance.

"The Wine, as they dosed themselves pretty plentifully with it, soon banished the Restraint. . . . They told me, That it was their absolute Design to take Possession of the Ohio, and by G— they would do it; For that altho' they were sensible the English could raise two Men for their one; yet they know their Motions were too slow and dilatory to prevent any undertaking of theirs. They pretend to have an undoubted Right to the River, from a Discovery made by one La Salle 60 Years ago."

From the wine-loosened tongues of his hosts, Washington cleverly elicited much information as to the forts and numbers of soldiers, while he tried to keep the French from talking to his Indians; but rain detained him and Joincare learned of the Half-King's presence. Washington still strove to prevent Joincare from meeting the chief. But he was not an adept at lies and of all lame excuses, he chose to say that he had not mentioned the Half-King because he thought Joincare did not like Indians!

This was sublime, for Joincare was half-Indian and was famous for his kindliness and skill in Indian dealings.

Joincare greeted the Half-King and the others effusively and talked their own language, dry and wet; gave them presents and got them all drunk.

They sobered up while the frantic young Washington waited. Then they held another long powwow and quarreled among themselves. The wiser ones suspected both English and French of intending to take their lands from them. A few believed that the English intended only to stimulate trade. But even these were afraid of the French, and hesitated to insult them by following Washington's advice that they break off all peaceful relations.

Against Joincare's hospitality Washington could not prevail until he appealed to Gist "to fetch them; which he did with great Persuasion."

Joincare kindly sent a French commissary, La Force, and three soldiers to escort him on the rest of his journey. Four days of hard travel over rain, snow, mire and swamp brought the company to the destination, Fort Le Boeuf (now Waterford, Pennsylvania, about twenty miles south of Erie). They had traversed a total of more than five hundred miles in forty-one days in the worst of weather.

The new commander, replacing the dead General Marin, had arrived only the week before from an exploring expedition in search of the Rocky Mountains! He was an elderly man with one eye, his name Legardeur de St. Pierre. He was courteous to Washington, and not understanding any English, sent for his relative, Captain de Repentigny (of which Washington made "Riparti") to translate the letter from Governor Dinwiddie. Repentigny had about as much English as Van Braam had French, and while he was worrying out a meaning, and the officers were in council over the reply, Washington took advantage of "the Opportunity of taking the Dimensions of the Fort and making Observations." He instructed his people "to take an exact Account of the Canoes" drawn up on shore for the next invasion, thus combining the duties of a spy with those of a man under a technical flag of truce.

The horses he brought along had been so weakened by the journey that he started them back to Venango, while he waited to get his answer. The French tried again to detach the Indians from Washington; and he did his best to get them to make an open breach with the French.

Good sportsmanship is rare in war, and it was perhaps only natural that Washington looked upon his own diplomacy as honorable, while he called St. Pierre's equally honorable devices plots—"Plots concerted to retard the Indians' Business and prevent them returning with me; I endeavor'd all that lay in my Power to frustrate their Schemes."

He finally persuaded the Half-King to return to the French their wampum of friendship, but St. Pierre refused to take it and "made many fair Promises of Love and Friendship" to the Half-King.

Washington asked St. Pierre why the French had made prisoners of English subjects, and was told that "the Country belong'd to them; that no Englishman had a Right to trade upon those Waters; and that he had Orders to make every Person Prisoner who attempted it upon the Ohio, or the Waters of it."

St. Pierre urged Washington to carry Dinwiddie's letter on up to the Canadian governor for answer, but Washington was eager to get back and give Dinwiddie the promptest possible notice of the French intentions. He insisted on St. Pierre answering Dinwiddie's letter, in which Dinwiddie expressed the same sort of polite "surprise" that had come to Céloron. Dinwiddie had written:

"The Lands upon the River Ohio in the Western Parts of the Colony of Virginia are so notoriously known to be the Property of the Crown of Great Britain; that it is a Matter of equal Concern and Surprize to me, to hear that a Body of French Forces are erecting Fortresses, and making Settlements upon that River, within his Majesty's Dominions. . . .

It becomes my Duty to require your peaceable Departure; and that you would forbear prosecuting a Purpose so interruptive of the Harmony and good Understanding, which his Majesty is desirous to continue and cultivate with the most Christian King. I persuade myself you will receive and entertain Major Washington with the candour and Politeness natural to your Nation . . . your most obedient Humble Servant, Robert Dinwiddie." [13]

St. Pierre replied that he would have been glad if Washington

"had been inclined to proceed to Canada to see our General: to whom it better belongs than to me to set forth the Evidence and Reality of the Rights of the King, my Master . . . and to contest the Pretensions of the King of Great Britain thereto.

"I shall transmit your Letter to the Marquis Duguisne. His Answer will be a Law to me. . . . As to the Summons you send me to retire, I do not think myself obliged to obey it. What-ever may be your Instructions, I am here by Virtue of the Orders of my General; and I intreat you, Sir, not to doubt one Moment, but that I am determined to conform myself to them with all the Exactness and Resolution which can be expected from the best Officer. . . .

"I made it my particular Care to receive Mr. Washington, with a Distinction suitable to your Dignity, as well as to his own Quality and great Merit. I flatter myself that he will do me this Justice before you, Sir; and that he will signify to you in the Manner I do myself, the profound Respect with which I am, Sir, your most humble, and most obedient Servant, Legardeur de St. Pierre." [14]

So much bowing and scraping, so much protestation of humility and obedient servitude, was, of course, only the grand way of any two fighters daring each other to strike the first blow.

But St. Pierre's courtesy to Washington was perfection,

and he "ordered a plentiful Store of Liquor, Provision, &c., to be put on Board our Canoe; and appeared to be extremely complaisant, though he was exerting every Artifice which he could invent to set our own Indians at Variance with us, to prevent their going 'till after our Departure. Presents, Rewards and every Thing which could be suggested by him or his Officers—I can't say that ever in my Life I suffered so much Anxiety as I did in this Affair. I saw that every Stratagem which the most fruitful Brain could invent was practiced to win the Half-King to their Interest."

This horror at French perfidy was sincere, but the French were equally sincere in regarding Washington with horror; he was equally bent on seducing the Indians from the French friendship, and was all the while taking notes of the French military situation.

Washington so strongly urged the Half-King to keep his promise to return that he finally pried the thirsty chieftain loose, and they set out for home, pushing their canoes into French Creek, which was "extremely crooked . . . can't be less than 130 miles to follow the Meanders." The water froze to their clothes, and Gist, speaking of the French escort, says, "We had the pleasure of seeing the French overset, and the brandy and wine floating in the creek, and run by them, and left them to shift for themselves." If the French had treated Washington as he treated them more would have been heard of this bit of forest humor.

At Venango there were more delays, and the Half-King was inclined to linger in spite of Washington's warning against Joincare's "Flattery" and "fine speeches." The warning worked both ways. The Half-King would not listen to Washington's speeches either.

Unable to budge him and despairing of making fast travel with the horses "now so weak and feeble and the Baggage so heavy," Washington made an audacious resolve to hasten home on foot. He left Van Braam in charge of the baggage, with money and directions, took his necessary papers, "pulled of my Cloaths; and tied myself up in a Match Coat"—so called because made of matched skins sewed together. "Then with Gun in Hand and Pack at my Back, I set-out with Mr. Gist fitted in the same Manner."

Gist gives Washington credit for more daring than discretion, for he says in his Diary: "I was unwilling he should undertake such a travel, who had never been used to walking before this time. But as he insisted on it, I set out with our packs, like Indians, and travelled eighteen miles. That night . . . the Major was much fatigued."

Gist, the forest-rover, is rather patronizing toward the young and very tenderfoot Washington.

The following day at a place "called the Murdering-Town," [16] says Washington, "we fell in with a Party of French Indians, who had lain in Wait for us. One of them fired at Mr. Gist or me, not 15 steps off, but fortunately missed. We took this fellow into Custody, and kept him till about 9 o'clock at Night; Then let him go, and walked all the remaining Part of the Night . . . to be out of the Reach of their Pursuit."

Suspicion has ever since been cast on Joincare for this attempted assassination, but Gist's Diary conflicts with Washington's, and gives the story in far greater detail, making it plain that the incident was the commonplace effort of an Indian to get two white scalps and a pair of guns. The wonder was that Washington was attacked only once in the whole thousand-mile journey.

Instead of a party, Gist says, "Here we met with an Indian, whom I thought I had seen at Joincare's." He called Gist by his Indian name, pretended to be glad to see him, asked many questions, and consented to show them a short cut. He even relieved the weary Washington of his pack, and they "travelled very brisk for eight or ten miles when the Major's feet grew very sore and he very weary."

The splendid horseman was not so splendid afoot and would have been pleased to drop down and sleep right where he was; but the Indian, seeing him exhausted, kindly offered to carry his gun as well as his pack. When Washington refused this dubious courtesy, Gist says, "the Indian grew churlish and pressed us to keep on, telling us that there were Ottawa Indians in these woods, and they would scalp us if we lay out; but go to his cabin and we should be safe. I thought very ill of the fellow but did not care to let the Major know I mistrusted him. But he soon mistrusted him as much as I."

The Indian said the cabin was within hearing of a gunshot, and later only "two whoops" distant. After he had decoyed them a long way, "the Indian made a stop, turned about; the Major saw him point his gun toward us and fire.

"Said the Major, 'are you shot?' 'No,' said I."

The Indian ran, but they caught him with the gun reloaded. Gist says, "I would have killed him but the Major would not suffer me to kill him."

They pretended to believe that the Indian was lost and had shot merely to attract the attention of someone at his cabin. They let him build a fire for them, as if they intended to sleep there, and bade him go on to his cabin to sleep. Indeed, Gist gave him "a cake of bread" and asked him to bring meat in the morning.

Making sure that he had really gone, Gist and Washington hastened on, travelled all night and all the next day, when they came to the Allegheny River, which was not frozen as they expected, but full of ice "driving in vast Quantities." Says Washington, "There was no Way for getting over but on a Raft; Which we set about with one poor Hatchet, and finished just after Sun-setting. . . .

"But before we were Half Way over, we were jammed in the Ice, in such a Manner that we expected every Moment

our Raft to sink, and ourselves to Perish. I put-out my
setting Pole to try to stop the Raft, that the Ice might pass
by; when the Rapidity of the Stream threw it with so much
Violence against the Pole, that it jerked me out into ten
Feet Water: but I fortunately saved myself by catching
hold of one of the Raft Logs. Notwithstanding all our
Efforts we could not get the Raft to either Shore; but were
obliged, as we were near an Island, to quit our Raft and
make to it.

"The Cold was so extremely severe, that Mr. Gist had
all his Fingers, and some of his Toes frozen; but the water
was shut up so hard, that we found no Difficulty in getting-
off the Island, on the Ice, in the Morning, and went to Mr.
Frazier's. We met here with 20 Warriors who were going
to the Southward to War, but coming to a Place upon the
Head of the great Kunnaway, where they found seven
People killed and scalped (all but one Woman with very
light Hair) they turned about and ran back for fear the
Inhabitants should rise and take them as the Authors of
the Murder. They report that the Bodies were lying about
the House, and some of them much torn and eaten by
Hogs. By the marks which were left, they say they were
French Indians of the Ottaway Nation, &c., who did it.

"As we intended to take Horses here, and it required
some Time to find them, I went-up about three Miles to
the Mouth of Yaughyaughane to visit Queen Aliquippa,
who had expressed great Concern that we passed her in
going to the Fort. I made her a Present of a Matchcoat
and a Bottle of Rum; which latter was thought much the
best Present of the Two."

This bibulous forest-monarch held her state at a point
where McKeesport, Pennsylvania, now stands. Washington does not explain where he got the bottle of rum as a
proof of English friendship, but in those days they seem

never to have travelled so light as to be without liquid passports.[16]

Pressing on, he bought a horse and saddle, and four days later "met 17 Horses loaded with Materials and Stores for a Fort at the Forks of Ohio, and the Day after some Families going out to settle."

This was the party of William Trent, whom Dinwiddie had ordered forward with soldiers and carpenters to start the building of the fort. He had not felt it necessary to delay construction while awaiting the result of Washington's exhausting, futile, and almost fatal errand.

On the eleventh of January, Washington reached Belvoir, where he "stopped one Day to take necessary Rest."

The Fairfaxes must have slain the fatted calf for him, and Mrs. Sally probably looked with new eyes upon the unlettered cub, who was now a man of note, about to be an author published in two worlds.

Washington reached Williamsburg on the 16th, and turned in his "Account of the Success of my Proceedings . . ." with a hope that "what has been said will be sufficient to make your Honour satisfied with my Conduct: for that was my Aim in undertaking the Journey, and chief Study through the Prosecution of it."

Dinwiddie was so delighted at this confirmation of his profound conviction of the French intention to occupy English territory that he asked Washington to write his hasty notes into a connected story for his council to read. Dinwiddie gave him a whole day for this task.

The next thing Washington knew, his manuscript was in the printer's hands and so close to publication that he had barely time to write an apologetic introduction. This shows both modesty and a fine historic conscience, for he says:

"Those Things which came under the Notice of my own

Observation, I have been explicit and just in a Recital of:—Those which I have gathered from Report, I have been particularly cautious not to augment."

He was surely the most reluctant author that was ever shanghaied into print. His first publication "drew on him some ridicule," says Jonathan Boucher.[17] But he never escaped that in his own day.

Too much credit cannot be given to Washington for this feat, though credit belongs also to other brave men who did the same feat before him. This fact diminishes the necessity for exclaiming, with some historians, that Providence selected him for the sublime deed as the one man created for the purpose. He risked grave dangers and "got the message to Garcia." He handled the negotiations, too, with an aristocratic grace impossible to George Croghan, who would readily have gone, as he had gone before, to Thomas Cresap, who was familiar with the region, to Montour or William Trent, or Christopher Gist, who guided Washington, shared his hardships and suffered more from them, though at first he had rather mocked the young man's inexperience. Five years before Washington's expedition Conrad Weiser had also been all over the same territory; but he was a German working for Pennsylvania.[18]

It is interesting to note that Weiser had taken along with him the brilliant bastard of Benjamin Franklin.[19] Nineteen-year-old William Franklin had kept a journal, too, and his father was so much impressed by it that he had sent it to England. William Franklin also fought the French on the Canadian border while Washington fought them on the Virginia frontier.

It is hard now to realize that this great commercial and manufacturing region of Western Pennsylvania was once beyond the frontier, and such a wilderness that it was counted miraculous that the twenty-one-year-old Wash-

ington should penetrate it in 1753, or the nineteen-year-old
Franklin in 1748.

Having had Washington's Journal printed for distribution, without warning to the embarrassed author, Dinwiddie
sent it among the colonies, and even to England to convince
the ministry of his contention that war was inevitable, describing his dispatch of "a Gent." to the French, and what
"the Gent. I sent" had found out.[20] It was reprinted in
London, and thus a young American of twenty-one, innocent
of grammar and spelling, had the distinction of being published at home and abroad. Even more literary distinction
was just around the next corner.

The frenetic Dinwiddie peppered the governors of the
other colonies with letters to convince them of the truth
contained in Washington's quotation of Joincare's words:

"They told me, That it was their absolute Design to take
Possession of the Ohio, and by G— they would do it."

But Dinwiddie was to learn the ghastly indifference of
the colonies to each other's interests, their selfish indifference to each other's alarms.

The Assembly of New York pooh-poohed Dinwiddie's
contention and coldly said that the French were not en-
croaching on any of his Majesty's territory. Pennsylvania
said that the French were in their rights and in their own
dominions on the Forks of the Ohio. The Quakers were
so indifferent that they "seemed to espouse the French
claims."[21]

Even the Virginians, when Dinwiddie got the assembly
together, were not much stirred, and many of them denied
the English claim to the Forks of the Ohio. He wasted on
them all his eloquence:

"Think, You see the Infant torn from the unavailing
Struggles of the distracted Mother, the Daughters ravish'd
before the Eyes of their wretched Parents, and then, with

Cruelty and Insult, butchered and scalp'd. Suppose the horrid Scene compleated, and the whole Family, Man, Wife and Children murder'd and Scalp'd . . . and then torn in Pieces, and in Part devour'd by wild Beasts for whom they were left a Prey by their more brutal Enemies. . . . Such are the People whose Neighbourhood You must now prevent, or with the most probable Expectation, think to see in the Bosom of Your Country these Evils that you as yet have only the melancholy Tidings of from Your Frontiers." [22]

This was not extravagance, either as description or as foreboding, for it all came to pass.

Yet after nine days haranguing, the Assembly voted him only £10,000 and authority to raise six companies "for the encouragement and protection of the settlers upon the Waters of the Mississippi!"

Having done thus much, they absolutely refused to vote the money to send a delegate to the Albany Convention, as urged by the Lords of Trade.[23] Hence Virginia was not represented at that effort to form a union of the colonies, under the preliminary purpose of making a treaty with the Six Nations of Indians to take up the hatchet against the French.

As early at 1751, Archibald Kennedy, of New York, had proposed a confederation of colonies and Ben Franklin had marvelled, as already stated, how strange it was that Six Nations of ignorant savages could form a union while ten or a dozen English colonies could not. But, though he drew up his famous Plan of Union calling for a President and a legislature of representatives from the colonies, and though the delegates at Albany unanimously agreed to it, none of the colonies would approve it and England was ready to refuse to approve it. England thought it too "republican" and a weakening of the power of the Crown. The colonies thought it made the Crown too strong and were afraid to unite under one head lest the King find it too easy to throttle the one neck! [24]

Dinwiddie wrote the Lords of Trade that he thought the Southern Indians, whom he was going to meet at Winchester, "more to be courted than the five (*sic*) Nations, being ten Times their Number." [25] Both conventions accomplished next to nothing. The Indians did not even come to meet Dinwiddie. He waited sixteen days for them, but they were afraid of the French, and sent him three strings of wampum, with a request for presents! [26]

Dinwiddie would not be dismayed. He drove ahead into what Dr. Koontz calls "Dinwiddie's war," adding, "for it was begun in his attempt to protect Virginia territory. The first hostile forces sent out were Virginians; the first blood was shed by Virginians. . . . Washington . . . became so identified with the struggle against the French that he was the sword of this war almost as he was later of the one with the Mother Country." [27]

But if he was the sword of this war, he showed dire need of further fencing lessons, for he cut himself down with his own blade.

VII

HE GOES TO HIS FIRST WAR

AS a reward for his courage and address, Washington was immediately ordered to active duty.

His mother "almost succumbed. 'Oh, this fighting and killing!' she exclaimed, as she entreated him not to go. When convinced that she must sacrifice herself to his duty to his country, she became calm. Laying her hand upon his shoulder, she said solemnly: 'God is our sure trust. To him I commend you.' "[1]

Or so the tale is told; and perhaps she did; but the dialogue has a false ring and her resignation is uncharacteristic.

Dinwiddie summoned the Assembly to convene in February, but did not wait for it to meet and wrangle. He forwarded to William Trent, who was out on the Forks of the Ohio, a commission as captain and ordered him to enlist a hundred men. He ordered Washington to enlist two hundred men, train them, equip them, and then go out and "finish and compleat in the best Manner and as soon as You possibly can, the Fort w'ch I expect is there already begun by the Ohio Comp'a. You are to act on the Defensive, but in Case any Attempts are made to obstruct the Works or interrupt our Settlem'ts by any Persons whatsoever You are to . . . make Prisoners of or kill and destroy them."[2]

All this was easier ordered than done. In the first place, Washington had never drilled a soldier or been drilled in a company. He had merely studied under private tutors,

and he must have endured the agonies of embarrassment that befall every officer who faces for the first time
a body of troops looking to him for instruction and
management.[3]

Nothing but Dinwiddie's frenzy could have led him to
entrust such a task to such a greenhorn. He took a raw
youth and sent him out to meet the trained soldiery of
France, which had the best army in Europe at that time.
The result was inevitable: confusion, disaster, disgrace.

Washington was just beginning that life of troubles, in
whose accumulation and their endurance he was to surpass
almost all other heroes.

In the myth-making process he acquired fame for being
a silent man who bore all bravely. But his pen was never
silent, and he spared nobody in the fierceness of his tremendous temper or the vigor of his self-defence.

His first response to Dinwiddie's orders to enlist and
equip his men was a letter complaining of the difficulties
of getting recruits when the only recruits available were
riffraff, and he could not even pay them:

"I have increas'd my number of Men to ab't 25 . . .
loose, Idle Persons that are quite destitute of House and
Home; and I may truely say, many of them of Cloaths.
. . . There is many of them without Shoes, other's want
Stockings, some are without Shirts, and not a few that have
Scarce a Coat, or Waistcoat, to their Backs . . . but I really
believe every Man of them for their own Credits sake, is
willing to be Cloath'd at their own Expence; they are per-
petually teazing me to have it done, but I am not able to
advance the money, provided there was no risque in it,
which there certainly is, and too great for me to run." [4]

All his life as a soldier he was repeating that pitiful cry
which he first uttered March 7th, 1754: My men are naked,
hungry, disheartened!

He "put a kirb" to his requests lest he be as troublesome to Dinwiddie as his soldiers were to him.

If Washington ever told his father that he could not tell a lie, he found the acquired ability useful in his new life. He had already vied with the French in deception and now he used his skill to keep his own men quiet. Having no knowledge of where money, food, or clothing could come from, he says:

"I have sooth'd and quieted them as much as possible, under pretence of receiving your Honour's Instructions in this particular."

Dinwiddie in the meanwhile was fighting for money with the Assembly, which, when it granted him the £10,000 for the "settlers on the Mississippi," had added the insult of a committee to watch the spending of it. Dinwiddie found this "a republican way of thinking," an "incroachment on the prerogatives of the Crown," and "monstrously unconstitutional." But he received authority to increase the number of troops to six companies and appoint a colonel.

Immediately the ambitious young Major Washington, who was having troubles enough gathering fifty tatterdemalions together to practice on, applied for promotion to a lieutenant-colonelcy.

He rather plumed himself on his modesty in not asking to be commander-in-chief.

Now that Lawrence was dead, he wrote to Richard Corbin, of the Governor's Council, and asked if he could not hope for "a commission above that of major, and to be ranked among the chief officers of this expedition. The command of the whole forces is what I neither look for, expect, nor desire; for I must be impartial enough to confess, it is a charge too great for my youth and inexperience to be entrusted with. Knowing this, I have too sincere a love for my country to undertake that which may tend to the prejudice of it."

He thought that if he were made lieutenant-colonel he could prove himself worthy of the gift after he got it. Colonel Corbin's answer was brief but satisfying:

"Dear George: I enclose you your commission. God prosper you with it. Your friend, Richard Corbin." [5]

Never did a prayer miss fire more completely.

With Corbin's letter came one from Dinwiddie, dated March 15th, 1754, and saying, "Enclos'd You have Com'o. Lieut.-Colo. pay, 12s. 6d. per day Without Any Trouble of Comanding a Comp'a."

Dinwiddie wrote this from Winchester, where he had gone for the futile conference with the Indians.

With this double announcement of his promotion to a lieutenant-colonelcy, Washington learned that he would receive no more than $3.50 a day. He was so indignant at this small money, which was only about half the 22 shillings a day paid to officers with a royal commission, that he planned to throw up the honor. But Colonel Fairfax persuaded him to accept it and promised to get him higher wages. Which he never did.

Dinwiddie answered a letter from Washington, now lost, showing that he was already eager to give his men the invaluable aid of a uniform—coat and breeches of red cloth.

He urged Washington to "march what Soldiers You have enlisted, imediately to the Ohio, and escort some Waggons, with the necessary Provisions." He promised to send three sloops with recruits from other centers, also "24 more Tents, w'ch is all that's to be had here. Picks, Cutlasses, or Halberts, none in the Magazine: so the Officers must head their Comp's with small Arms." [6]

Washington, therefore, appears in his early portrait with a musket slung across his back.

If Washington was having trouble at Alexandria recruiting and clothing and feeding men with all the help of Lord Fairfax, it is easy to imagine the plight of poor William Trent, in the deeps of Old Wilderness, trying to persuade the back settlers to join his little band of men and hold off all France.

When the forty-one men he had gathered were reduced to corn for their sole food, Trent decided to go in person for supplies. He left his lieutenant, Edward Ward, Croghan's half-brother, to command the carpenters, and had gone as far as Will's Creek when a French officer named Contrecoeur floated down the river with a large body of troops and captured the half-finished fort and the half-starved forty-one men.

On the theory that no war had been declared between England and France, Contrecoeur invited Ward to supper, treated him amiably and allowed the men to march out with all the honors of carpentry, taking their tools with them. Then he proceeded to finish the fort and named it Du Quesne, in honor of the Canadian governor.

Poor Trent, lucky enough not to be captured, was unlucky enough to get the blame for Dinwiddie's precipitance in sending him out. Dinwiddie charged him with cowardice and ordered a court-martial. Even Washington accused him of timidity. Washington was soon in a worse plight, and when Trent sued Dinwiddie some years later for malicious slander, the jury awarded him £800 and costs.[7]

Croghan, whom Dinwiddie had put under contract with the Ohio Company, had set out with a pack-train of supplies, but learned of Ward's surrender in time to keep from being included in it.

He immediately devoted himself to stemming the tide of the Indian rush to join the successful French. He wandered in on the orgy of one tribe and had to wait ten

days for the members to sober up. Then they told him
that he was a prisoner. When he reproached them with
breaking certain conditions in the treaties with the traders,
the Indians calmly answered that the traders had probably
written the conditions in after the Indians signed.[8]

For some strange reason, the Indians have never been
willing to trust the white man's honesty or mercy.

Croghan owed his life to the protection of the courteous
French officers, who secured his release. When he reached
Pennsylvania and pleaded for action, the assembly said that
the Forks of the Ohio were not in their jurisdiction. They
also refused him the moneys due him, so he went back to
the Virginians, and with Trent's aid, secured for Washington's men some powder and lead and a little flour, but so
slowly that Washington's men almost starved.

Washington accused Croghan of being "a most flagrant
instance" of the unreliability of the traders, and said he
"had the assurance, during our sufferings to tantalize us."
In return, Washington seized all of Croghan's pack horses
and left Croghan's furs and merchandise for the French to
pick up.

To confound confusion, the colonel whom Dinwiddie
appointed—Joshua Fry, an Englishman, Oxford-bred, professor of mathematics in William and Mary College—
never did reach the troops he was to command.

Thus the young student of war under a tutor, the lad
who had never seen so much as a skirmish, found himself
actually exercising the command he had not ventured to
ask for. He was at the head of all the troops in Virginia,
confronting not only the French, who outnumbered him
overwhelmingly, but all the difficulties of wilderness transportation, supply and maneuver.

His courage equalled his inexperience—a bad combination.
Again we have his own journal to guide us; but we must

take it now in a series of triturations, not merely through a Jared Sparks or a proofreader, but through a French translation of his manuscript and an English translation of the French translation.[9]

While Washington's original notes were captured by the enemy, we have a number of his letters to Dinwiddie to guide in judging the French version, which Washington denounced as deliberately falsified, though it is hard to see any important conflict with his own account.

On his mission to help Trent build forts, he marched away from Alexandria April 2, 1754, with two companies of foot, commanded by Captain Peter Hog and Lieutenant Jacob van Braam. He had about a hundred and fifty men altogether.

On the 19th a messenger brought him an appeal for help from Captain Trent. The next day he received a reinforcement of three companies, but also learned that the fort he was hurrying out to finish and defend had already been captured by the French.

Two days later Ensign Ward arrived with a wildly exaggerated but dismaying enough account of the tremendous force that had gobbled him up. He brought, also, two Indians, one of whom recited a speech from the Half-King telling of the danger that the friendly Indians would be destroyed by the French unless the English came to their aid, in which case the Indians would gladly fight the French.

Having reached Will's Creek, Washington held a council of war, which decided that though he was vastly outnumbered, he should take a chance, dash boldly on to the Monongahela and erect a fort at Red-Stone Creek (now Brownsville, Pennsylvania), where there were storerooms for ammunition, and artillery might be sent by water. It was a brave, rash thing to do, and taught him caution by cruel experience.

He sent Ward back to Dinwiddie with one Indian; he sent two other messengers to the governors of Maryland and Pennsylvania, and sent the second Indian to the Half-King with a speech and a belt of wampum.

In the course of the speech he declared: "Our hearts burn with love and affection towards you in gratitude for your steadfast attachment to us, as also your friendly speech and wise counsels." He explained that his small force was clearing the roads for "a great number of our warriors . . . with our great guns. We know the character of the treacherous French. . . . I desire with greatest earnestness that you . . . should come as soon as possible to meet us on the road, and to assist us in council.

"Your Friend and Brother,
"Go Washington Conotocarious." [10]

This was the name the Indians had given his great-grand-father John, who had earned its meaning, "Destroyer (or Devourer) of Villages." Perhaps George hoped to remind them of his ferocious ancestry, for he had certainly never destroyed so much as a wigwam.[11]

He ordered sixty of his men to "amend the Road," and a little later put his whole force to work; but the jungle was all but impenetrable, and he had to write Dinwiddie that in fifteen days he had progressed only twenty miles.[12] He had worse and worse news from the Ohio: that the English traders were retreating, the French receiving reinforcements; and that Monsieur La Force, who had escorted him on his trip to Fort Le Boeuf, was scouring the country with four men, "under the Specious pretence of hunting Deserters." Washington had only 160 effective soldiers, and had had so much trouble with Captain Trent's men that he was forced to send them out of his camp to "seperate them from the other Soldiers." [13]

He also begged Dinwiddie for some rum for his troops

and his red allies:—"we ought to have Spirit, and many other things of this sort, which is always expected by every Indian that brings a Message or good report: Also the Chiefs who visit and converse in Council look for it."

Croghan, on the other hand, succeeded better with the Indians by trying to prevent the distribution of liquor, for which the savages would trade the very clothes off their backs. He confessed, however, that he occasionally had to yield to pressure: "I am oblig'd to give them a Cag Now and then myself for a frolick, but that is Attended with no Expense to the Government nor no bad Consequence to the Indians as I Do itt butt onst a Month." [14]

Dinwiddie had tried to provide the regular issue of a quart of rum a day to every four men; [15] but supplies were hard to get forward.

The soldiers needed the stimulant, for they were struggling through water up to the armpits of the shortest men. They passed a place called Little Meadows, and another called Great Meadows, and came to the river rejoicing still in the difficult name, Youghiogheny, at whose Great Crossing they were checked. Washington made vain explorations in a canoe among its brawling waters to find a possible passage for his men, and risked his life freely, but had to give up in despair.

There were other reasons for despondency. His officers, wet, weary, and lost in morasses and swamps, were receiving neither rum nor money. He protested to Dinwiddie, who was equally unable to wring funds out of the assembly. Washington's letters reveal a strange and persistent quality in his character; an odd mingling of high personal pride and meek devotion to duty; as to money, a determination to work for nothing, rather than take poor wages or take less than the King's officers received.

His officers had grown mutinous and refused to accept the

pay they did not receive, especially as the usual liquor and table allowances were denied them. They demanded that other officers be sent to replace them, and declared that nothing kept them at their posts but the danger ahead of them. They were grateful to Dinwiddie for their commissions, but disgusted with the Committee.

Washington wrote that he was in sympathy with his officers, and yet, though he found "so many clogs upon the expedition" that he quite despaired of success, he humbly begged to be continued in his post, "but by no means on my present pay.

"Let me serve voluntarily; then I will, with the greatest pleasure in life, devote my services to the expedition without any other reward than the satisfaction of serving my country; but to be slaving dangerously for the shadow of pay, through woods, rocks, mountains—I would rather prefer the great toil of a daily laborer, and dig for a maintenance, . . . than serve upon such ignoble terms; for I really do not see why the lives of his Majesty's subjects in Virginia should be of less value, than those in other parts of his American dominions; especially when it is well known, that we must undergo double their hardships." [16]

Dinwiddie answered that his "ill-timed complaints" were unreasonable; protested that wine and beer were not included in the pay; explained that English officers were "obliged to many more Expences than You are," and that the hardships encountered were usual to a military life, "and are consider'd by Soldiers rather as Opp'ties of Glory than objects of Discouragement." He also promised that when Colonel Fry should reach them they could eat at his table, for which £100 a year was provided.

To this long scolding, spanking letter, Washington retorted: "Nothing is a greater Stranger to my Breast, or a Sin that my Soul more abhors, than that black and detestable one, Ingratitude. I retain a true sence of your Kindnesses and want nothing but opportunity. . . .

"I cou'd not object to the Pay before I knew it; I dare say your Honour remembers the first Estimation allow'd a Lieut. Colo. 15s., and Maj'r 12s. 6d., which I then complain'd very much off; till your Honour assur'd me that we were to be furnish'd with proper necessary, and offer'd that as a reason why the pay was Less than British; after this, when you were so kind to preferr me to the Com'd I now have, and at the same time acquainted me that I was to have but 12s. 6d. This, with some other Reasons, indused me to acquaint Colo. Fairfax with my intention of Resigning, which he must well remember, as it happ'd at Belhaven, and was there that he disswaded me from it and promised to represent the trifling pay to your Honour, who would endeavour (as I at the same time told him that the Speaker thought the Officer's pay too small) to have it enlarg'd.

"As to the Numbers that applied for Commissions, and to whom we were preferr'd, I believe, had those Gentlemen been as knowing of this Country, and as Sensible of the difficulties that would attend a Campaign here, as I then was, I conceive your Honour w'd not have been so troublesomely sollicited as you were; yet I do not offer this as a reason for quitting the Service, for my own part I can answer, I have a Constitution hardy enough to encounter and undergo the most severe tryals, and I flatter myself, resolution to Face what any Man durst, as shall be prov'd when it comes to the Test, which I believe we are on the Borders off.

"There is nothing, Sir, (I believe) more certain than that the Officers on the Canada Expedition had British pay allowed, whilst they were in the Service . . . as this can't be allow'd, suffer me to serve Volunteer, which I assure you will be the next reward to British pay, for as my Services so far as I have knowledge, will equal those of the best Officer, I make it a point of Hon'r [not?] to serve for less and accept a medium.

"Nevertheless, I have communicated your Honour's Sentiments to them; and as far as I could put on the Hipocrite, set forth the advantages that may accrue, and advised them to accept the Terms, as a refusal might reflect dishonour on their character, leaving it to the world to assign what reasons they please for quitting the Service. . . . They have promised to consider of it, and give your Honour an answer.

"I was not ignorant of the allow'e which Colo. Fry has for his Table, but being a depend't there myself, deprives me of the pleasure of inviting an Officer or Friend, which to me w'ld be more agreeable than the Nick Nacks I shall meet with there.

"And here I cannot forbear answering one thing more in your Honour's Letter on this head, which (too) is more fully express'd in a paragraph of Colo. Fairfax's to me, as follows: 'If on the British Establishment Officers are allow'd more Pay, the Regimentals they are oblig'd annually to furnish, their necessary Table and other Incidents being consider'd, little or no savings will be their Portion. . . .

"If they don't save much, they have the enjoyment of their Pay, which we neither have in one sense nor the other. We are debarr'd the pleasure of good Living, which, Sir, (I dare say, with me you will concur) to one who has always been used to it, must go somewhat hard to be confin'd to a little salt provision and water, and do duty, hard, laborious duty, that is almost inconsistent with that of a Soldier, and yet, the same Reductions as if we were allow'd luxuriously.

"My Pay, according to the British Establish't and common exchange, is near 22s. p'r Day, in the R'm of that, ye

Committee (for I can't, in ye least, imagine y'r H'r had any h'd in it) has provided (12s. 6d.) so long as ye Service requires me; whereas one-half of ye other is ascertain'd to British Officers forever. Now, if we sh'd be fortunate enough to drive the French from Ohio—as far as your Honour w'd please have them sent to—in any short time, our Pay will not be sufficient to discharge our first expences. . . .

"The motives that lead me here were pure and noble. I had no view of acquisition but that of Honour, by serving faithfully my King and Country." [17]

This is not the Washington that is usually pictured. But there he had to sit in his tent, and spend his precious hours writing about his own and his officers' money, while the French closed in upon him.

In a letter of his that crossed Dinwiddie's rebuke about the pay-problem, Washington had enclosed a letter from the Half-King, written for him by a Trader. It is so beautiful a piece of backwoods literature as to constitute almost a puzzle. This is the Half-King's warning to "the first of His Majesty's Commanding Officers":

"To the forist, his Majestie's Commander Offwerses—to hom this may concern:
"On acc't of a freench armey to meat Miger Georg Wassionton "therfor my Brotheres I deisir you to beawar of them for deisin'd to "strik ye forist Englsh they see ten deays since they marchd I cannot "tell what nomber the half King and the rest of the Chiefs will be "with you in five dayes to consel, no more at present but give my "serves to my Brothers the English.

"THE HALF-KING,"
"JOHN DAVISON." [18]

Enclosing this with a smile at its bad spelling, Washington went on to say that he had already retreated to Great Meadows as "a convenient spott" and "made a good Intrenchment, and by clearing ye Bushes out of these Meadows, prepar'd a charming field for an Encounter."

He was sending out scouts on wagon horses and was alarmed one night by noises that kept them under arms from two A. M. to near sunrise: "We conceive it was our own Men, as 6 of them Deserted, but cant be certain whether it was them, or other Enemys; be it as it will, they were fired at by the Centrys."

Gist arrived the next morning with news of a detachment of French that he estimated at fifty men, under the command of Monsieur La Force. Gist had seen them within five miles of Washington's camp. Washington promptly sent seventy-five of his men in pursuit, but they were not overtaken.

He sent his report to Dinwiddie by the hand of Gist, and repeated his prayer for goods to give the Indians to offset the generosity of the French, "I really think, was 5 or 600 Pounds worth of proper Goods sent, it w'd tend more to our Interest than so many thousands given in a Lump at a Treaty." [19]

He had been obliged to pay for what rum he had given them, but could not afford it any more. Again he is seen taking from his own slender purse money that should have been furnished him by the state.

Two days later he wrote the long outpouring about pay already quoted, and added to it a slightly longer account of his first skirmish.

And it was a victory!

Little did he dream that it was to earn him ridicule and infamy abroad, and bring about a war in Europe that should last for seven years.

VIII

HE WINS HIS FIRST VICTORY

NOTHING could be finer than the resolution and courage with which Washington awaited his doom, and nothing could have been worse than the spot he selected for his sacrifice.

In the War of 1812 an American general surrendered a fine fortress to an inferior number of the enemy. But he was sick and old. Washington, young and ignorant of military engineering, might far better have trusted to bush-fighting methods with trees for individual fortresses, than have huddled his flock into the little trap where his Virginians and North Carolinians could not stand off twice their number of French and Indians for more than one long rainy afternoon.

Following many harsh critics of Washington's own day, Professor Reuben Gold Thwaites [1] says of "'the buckskin-general'—as the French sneeringly called him," and the spot he chose for a fort: "The place was unfit for defence, for on three sides higher ground, heavily forested, approached closely to the stockade." General Bradley T. Johnson [2] says: "The locality was bad: it was too far out from his supports. The topography was worse. General Sharpe, of Maryland, a soldier of experience, of courage, and sense, criticised the whole performance with remorseless severity."

Still, every one must learn, and it was Washington's sad lot to be educated in the rough school of reality.

Gist had hardly left Washington on his way to the Governor, when there came at about nine o'clock at night an

113

"express" from the Half-King, who was encamped with a few Indians about six miles away.

The Half-King announced, as Washington reports, that he "had seen the Tract of two French Men X'ing the Road, and beliv'd ye whole body were lying not far off, as he had an acc't of that Number passing Mr. Gist." [3]

This dreary forested hillside fastness drenched with a night rain was to become the scene of much tragic history. The Great Meadows lie just over the border of Pennsyl-vania close to the Maryland line, near the town now called Confluence.

They are described by Hulbert [4] as "two large basins, the smaller lying directly westward of the larger and connected with it by a narrow neck of swampy ground. . . . The natural intrenchments or depressions behind which Wash-ington huddled his army . . . were at the eastern edge of the western basin."

The Indians had traced the French to a "low obscure place" where they had built a little hut for shelter from the rain in the lee of a precipice on the other side of Laurel Hill. The seventy-five men that Washington sent out to thresh the woods for them had not yet returned, nor had they seen the French or been seen by them. But the Half-King's Indians had followed their "tracts" and Washington resolved to jump them at dawn. He decided to lead the night-foray in person and strengthen his troops with the Half-King's men. But let him write his own history of this morning of May 28, 1754, as he wrote it to Dinwiddie: [5]

"I set out with 40 Men before 10, and was from that time till near Sun rise before we reach'd the Indian's Camp, hav'g March'd in small Path, a heavy Rain, and Night as Dark as it is possible to conceive; we were frequently tumbling one over another, and often so lost that 15 or 20 minutes search would not find the path again.

"When we came to the Half-King, I council'd with him, and got his assent to go hand in hand and strike the French. Accordingly, himself, Monacatoocha and a few other Indians set out with us, and when we came to the place where the Tracts were, the Half-King sent two Indians to follow their Tract and discover their lodgment, which they did ab't half a mile from the Road, in a very obscure place surrounded with Rocks. I thereupon, in conjunction with the Half-King and Monacatoocha, form'd a disposion to attack y'm on all sides, which we accordingly did, and after an Engagement of ab't 15 Minutes, we killed 10, wounded one and took 21 Prisoners, amongst those that were killed, was Monsieur De Jumonville, the Commander; Princip'l Officers taken is Monsieur Druillorn and Mons'r Laforce, who your Honour has often heard me speak of as a bold Enterprising Man, and a person of great subtilty and cunning; with these are two Cadets.

"These officers pretend they were coming on an Embassy, but the absurdity of this pretext is too glaring as your Honour will see by the Instructions and Summons inclos'd. These Instructions were to reconnoitre the country, Roads, Creeks, &c., to Potomack, which they were ab't to do. These Enterprising Men were purposely choose out to get intelligence, which they were to send Back by some brisk dispatches with mention of the Day that they were to serve the Summons, which could be through no other view than to get sufficient Re-inforcements to fall upon us imediately after; this, with several other Reasons, induc'd all the Officers to believe firmly that they were sent as spys rather than any thing else, and has occasion'd my sending them as prisoners, tho' they expected or at least had some hope of being continued as ambassadors.

"They finding where we were Incamp'd, instead of coming up in a Publick manner, sought out one of the most secret Retirements, fitter for a Deserter than an Imbassador to incamp in, stay'd there two or 3 Days, sent Spies to Reconnoitre our Camp, as we are told, tho' they deny it.

"Now, 36 Men w'd almost have been a Retinue for a Princely Ambassador instead of Petit, why did they, if their designs were open, stay so long within 5 Miles of us with't delivering his Ambassy or acquainting me with it. . . . The name of Ambassador is Sacred among all Nations, but it was by the Tract of these Spy's they were discover'd."

Referring to a Summons carried by the dead Jumonville from the French commander Contrecoeur, ordering the British out of the French possessions, Washington goes on to say:

"The Summons is so insolent and savours so much of Gascoigny that if two Men only had come openly to deliver it, It was too great Indulgence to have sent them back.

"The Sense of the Half-King on this Subject is, that they have bad Hearts, and that this is a mere pretence, they never design'd to have come to us but in a hostile manner, and if we were so foolish as to let them go again, he never would assist us in taking another of them. . . . The Half-King receiv'd your Honour's speech very kind. . . . He has declar'd to send these French Men's Scalps, with a Hatchet, to all the Nations of Indians in union with them. . . .

"I shall expect every hour to be attack'd and by unequal numbers, which I must withstand, if there is 5 to 1, or else I fear the Consequence will be we shall loose the Indians if we suffer ourselves to be drove Back. . . .

"Your Honour may depend I will not be surpriz'd, let them come what hour they will. . . . I doubt not but if you hear I am beaten, but you will at the same hear that we have done our duty in fighting as long there was a possibility of hope. . . .

"I have sent Lieut. West, accompanied with Mr. Sprilldorph [6] and a Guard of 20 Men, to conduct the Prisoners
in. I have shewed all the respect I cou'd to them here, and
have given some necessary cloathing by which I have dis-
furnish'd myself, for having brought no more than two or
three shirts from Wils's C'k, that we might be light, I was
ill provided to furnish them. . . . We have already begun
a Palisado'd Fort; and hope to have it up tomorrow. I
must beg leave to acquaint your honor yt Captn Vanbraam
and Monsr. Peyronney [7] has behaved extremely well."

This destruction of a petty band of Frenchmen, who
claimed to be envoys and denounced the sudden surprise
attack upon them as an outrage amounting to assassination,
created an international wrangle and has been a subject
of fierce debate ever since.

The French published their own account and translated
Washington's Journal in proof of it. It verifies Washington's statement that Jumonville, on finding where the
Virginians were and how many, was to send word at once
to Contrecoeur. This Jumonville did and then seems to
have planned to wait in hiding till Contrecoeur could bring
down enough men to capture the Virginians. If this were
the plan, as Washington afterward suspected, he was right
to act at once. He could not be aware of the fact that
Jumonville had also a summons to deliver if he encountered the Virginians.

Washington gave his own account to Dinwiddie. But
even among his own men there was flat contradiction of
his story. The Indian chief, Monacatoocha (or Monacatootha, or Scarroyady), told the Pennsylvania agent, Conrad
Weiser, his version in December, 1754. According to this,
he encountered the French and was urged to join them.
They pulled him by the arm, but he refused to be persuaded,
fought with the French, killed many of them and took his

bloody hatchet to Washington in proof of his deed, along with the prisoners.

This is, manifestly, false, but Davison, an Indian trader, told Weiser that the Indians did most of the execution:

"Col. Washington and the Half-King differed much in judgment, and on the Colonel's refusing to take his advice, the English and Indians separated. After which the Indians discovered the French in an hollow and hid themselves, lying on their bellies behind a hill; afterwards they discovered Col. Washington on the opposite side of the hollow in the gray of the morning, and when the English fired, which they did in great confusion, the Indians came out of their cover and closed with the French and killed them with their tomahawks, on which the French surrendered." [8]

Knowing that he would soon be attacked by a large force, Washington begged for reinforcements, which Dinwiddie ordered up, scolding the dilatory Colonel Fry, Major Muse, and Captain McKay of the independent company of regulars from South Carolina. He sent Washington a letter acknowledging "the very agreeable Acco't of Y'r Killing and taking Mons'r Le Force and his whole Party, on which Success I heartily congratulate you, as it may give a Testimony to the Ind's that the French are not invincible w'n fairly engag'd with the English, but hope the good Spirits of Y'r Soldiers will not tempt You to make any hazardous Attempts agst a too numerous Enemy. . . . I have also sent out of my private Store some Rum. . . . Pray God preserve You in all Y'r proceedings." [9]

Colonel Fry, smarting under Dinwiddie's rebuke, tried to reach the front but was thrown from a horse at Will's Creek and died from his injuries. So Dinwiddie promptly sent Washington a commission as full colonel. He appointed Washington's military tutor, Major Muse, Lieutenant-Colonel.   He sent along a number of medals for Washington and the Indians, also three barrels of rum.

This promotion crossed another report from Washington, describing his dealings with the Indians.   His friend Monacatoocha had come in "with 4 French scalps, two of which was to be sent to the Wyandotts &c. and the other two to the 6 Nations, telling them that the French had tricked them out of their lands, for which, with their Brothers, the English, who joyn'd hand in hand, they had let them feel the wait of their Hatchet, which was but trifling, yet, as it only lay'd on 30, for that they int'd with their Brothers to drive the French beyond the Lakes. . . .

"If the whole Detach't of the French behave with no more Resolution than this chosen Party, I flatter myself we shall have no g't trouble in driving them to the d— Montreal. . . .

"There was also but 7 Indians with arms, two of which were Boys—one Dinwiddie, Yr Hon'rs God Son [i.e., the Half-King], who behav'd well in action.   There were 5 or 6 other Indians, who served to knock the poor, unhappy wounded in the head, and bereiv'd them of their scalps.   So that we had but 40 men with which we tried and took 32 or 3 men, besides others, who may have escaped.   One, we have certain acc't did."

This one who escaped told a story that shook the world and brought France and England to open war.   Incidentally, he brought down upon the victorious young Washington an overwhelming French force under Jumonville's brother.

In the exultance of his first battle, and in ignorance of its grim sequences, Washington wrote a letter to his own brother from the Camp at Great Meadows, 31 May, 1754:

"Since my last we arrived at this place, where three days ago we had an engagement with the French. . . . Most of our men were out upon other detachments, so that I had scarcely 40 men remaining under my command, and about 10 or 12 Indians; nevertheless we obtained a most signal victory. . . . We expect every hour to be attacked by a superior force, but, if they forbear one day longer, we shall be prepared for them. . . .

"P. S.   I fortunately escaped without any wound, for the right wing, where I stood, was exposed to and received all the enemy's fire, and it was the part where the man was killed, and the rest wounded.   I heard the bullets whistle, and, believe me, there is something charming in the sound." [10]

Unfortunately for him, this letter was doubtless shown about by his proud brother, and a copy of it got over to England, where it was published in the *London Magazine* and caught the eye of the King.

George II had been in the field, and had gone through the great battle of Dettingen, and he sniffed at the enthusiasm of the twenty-two-year-old who would, just twenty-two years later, be maddening his mad grandson, George III.

Horace Walpole, then in the royal exchequer, tells the story:

"In the express, which Major Washington despatched on his preceding little victory (the skirmish with Jumonville), he concluded with these words,—'I heard the bullets whistle, and, believe me, there is something charming in the sound.'   On hearing of this the King said sensibly,— 'He would not say so, if he had been used to hear many.' However, this brave braggart learned to blush for his rhodomontade, and, desiring to serve General Braddock as aid-de-camp, acquitted himself nobly." [11]

Already, at twenty-two, George Washington's name was on the lips of his most sacred majesty, the King.   But, alas, the King was speaking of him with patronizing amusement. Soon, George II would be speaking of him with dismay as he found himself involved in one of the most enormous wars in human history, thanks to the activity of the same young man. The King might have exclaimed with Pyrrhus, "If we have such another victory, we are undone!"

IX

HE MEETS HIS FIRST DEFEAT

THE entire defense of the border against the enfuriated French was now left to the young colonel, whose military history consisted of surprising a handful of scouts. He found to his chagrin that the colonelcy he had received from Dinwiddie did not give him the authority held by the late "Joshua Fry, Esquire," but only the colonelcy of the Virginia regiment. Dinwiddie later appointed to the command of the expedition, Colonel James Innes, a fellow-Scotsman from North Carolina.

This importation aggravated Dinwiddie's unpopularity with the Virginians. Extra pay was offered to induce recruits, but the other colonies were derelict in help, though Captain McKay arrived with an independent company of a hundred regulars from South Carolina. Still, since he held a royal commission, there was doubt of his accepting orders from a colonel with only a governor's commission. The doubt was well-founded.

Two companies from New York finally landed at Alexandria, but ill-equipped and not in time to reach the battlefield, which Colonel Innes, like Colonel Fry, failed to reach.

There was never a thought of fear or self-preservation in Washington's soul. He realized only that if he retreated the Indians would desert bodily to the French, and prepared himself for the sacrifice. There was less and less hope of sufficient reinforcement or sufficient supplies reaching his paltry command.

This was not Dinwiddie's fault. He dismally wrote to

the Governor of Pennsylvania: "I am sorry Y'r Assembly is so obstinate and disobedient to the royal Comands as I had a thorow dependence on You for a Supply of Bread, the want of w'ch puts me to great difficulties." [1]

He wrote to the Governor of New York that, after ten weeks of daily expectation, two companies from that colony had arrived in a sad state. They were "not agreeable to the Order from Home . . . they are not Compleat in Numbers; many of them old that cannot undergo a March of 200 Miles from Alexa, and burthen'd with thirty Women and Children; and to compleat the Whole, no Provisions . . . no Tents, w'ch obliges me to make new Tents; or any Blankets &c. . . . This Conduct, I acknowledge I am surpriz'd at. . . . As in Duty bound by my Orders, I am determin'd, with the few Men I have, and the little Money, to carry on the Expedition with all the Vigour our small Forces will admit of." [2]

It is not generally remembered that great numbers of women usually trailed along with the soldiers, even in the direst campaigning. Six to a company was the usual allotment. They added to the ease and panic of defeat.

With fine spirit, Washington accepted his position of subordination and wrote to Dinwiddie, saying that he rejoiced at the prospect of being under the command of an experienced officer like Colonel Innes (who had served at Cartagena with Lawrence Washington). And undoubtedly this joy was sincere, for he had a hard job ahead of him. He knew that his little skirmish would bring on a battle with a far greater force than his own. Yet he felt obliged to hold the front to the last drop of blood, "without risquing the imputation of rashness or hazarding what a prudent conduct wou'd forbid."

There was still room for jealousy in the contention for laurels that were to be turned to rue. Washington was

uneasy about this Captain McKay, who had promptly displayed a spirit of insubordination and snobbery to the young
colonial. Washington appealed to Dinwiddie, and said he
hoped that McKay would "have more sense than to insist
upon any unreasonable distinction, tho' he and His have
Com'ns from his Majesty; let him consider tho' we are
greatly inferior in respect to profitable advantages, yet we
have the same Spirit to serve our Gracious King as they have,
and are as ready and willing to sacrifice our lives for our
Country's as them; and here once more and for the last
time, I must say this Will be a cancer that will grate some
Officers of this Regiment beyond all measure, to serve upon
such different terms, when their Lives, their Fortunes, and
their Characters are equally, and I dare say as effectually,
expos'd as those who are happy enough to have King's Commissions."

Washington had carefully refrained from any "foolish
desire" of commanding McKay and had not "intermedled"
in his company. But it was absurd to have Captain McKay
direct a colonel; "it would certainly be the hardest thing
in Life if we are to do double and trible duty, and neither
be entitled to the Pay or Rank of Soldiers."

Captain McKay had complimented Washington on the
road-building of the Virginians, but he could not persuade
his own men to chop trees save for double pay. Seeing them
march at ease or loll about and joke while the Virginians
toiled, had caused Washington's "poor fellows" to grumble.
Nothing incenses soldiers like an unequal distribution of
hardships. Washington begged Dinwiddie to put Captain
McKay in his place, since the rank was to him "much dearer
than the pay."

Having "spun a Letter to this enormous size," he added
that he was sorry that his supplies were so slow coming up.
"God knows when we shall [be] able to do anything for to

deserve better of our Country. . . . The Contents of this
Letter is a profound Secret." [3]

Two weeks later, Dinwiddie wrote a letter which, he
expected, would be delivered by Colonel Innes with the
main body, on whose arrival he hoped that they would be
able to "drive the French from the fort and take full possession of the Ohio river." He reminded Washington that
he was second in command, brevet-lieut.-colonel Clark (of
New York) third, and Captain McKay fourth.

The royal lieutenants were to rank with the Virginia captains, but "this is only Feathers in their Caps to prevent any
ill Blood in regard to rank." [4]

He wrote Major Carlyle quoting Colonel Washington's
letter "full of Complaints of ill Usage. . . . They have
been six days Without Flower . . . he also complains for
want of Ammunition. . . . Send out two Hhds of rum, to
give the People w'n on Extraordinary Duty." [5]

Multiplying himself with his zeal, he wrote to nearly
everybody, not neglecting to flatter Captain McKay, with
the hope that he and the other officers would "lay aside any
little Punctilios in rank." [6]

Next, the poor man was writing of bad news. Everything had gone wrong. Colonel Washington had been
instructed to avoid rashness and not let himself be surprised.
While waiting for Colonel Innes, the New York, and other
troops, he had gone on cutting a road through the forest
toward Red Stone. News of the approach of a large body
of French and Indians led to a hasty council of war. Retreat was decided upon to Will's Creek.

Contrecoeur, having received reinforcements at Fort
Du Quesne, was able to give Jumonville's brother, Villiers,
five hundred men. Later they were joined by newly arrived Indians and probably seven hundred marched against
Washington's three hundred plus.

A chaplain started out with the French and Indians to sanctify the proceedings. But the flesh was weak and he turned back at the first halt after giving both French and Indians absolution in a body. For this or other reasons they behaved extraordinarily well and had no unusual military sins to atone for.

Washington's men fell back in such haste that by the time they reached Great Meadows on July 1st, the troops were too spent to go farther. The fort that should have been completed long before (in the opinion of the Half-King) was feverishly improvised and strengthened and eloquently named Fort Necessity.

On the morning of July 3, 1754, twice their number of French and Indians swarmed down upon them, drove them into the fort, and kept them there under heavy and fatal fire. The French were none too comfortable. Villiers in his report home wrote: "As we had been wet all day by the rain, as the soldiers were very tired, as the savages said that they would leave us the next morning, and as there was a report that drums and the firing of cannon had been heard in the distance, I proposed to M. Le Mercier to offer the English a conference."

The horses and cattle were stampeded in the din and killed by the French and Indians. The rain put many of the muskets out of order. There were finally only two ramrods left to clean them as they fouled. The swivel guns probably hit nobody and were silenced by being exposed to French fire. The stockade was thronged with dead and with wounded men wallowing in the rain. McKay's men in the outworks were knee deep in mud. Food was lacking, but rum was plentiful. All about the fort drunken soldiers reeled and fell till half of those alive were only half alive with liquor.

Still, Washington held out until the third effort of the

French to persuade him to surrender was put in writing and read to him in the light of a candle blown out again and again by the rainy gale. Captain Adam Stephen testified that the capitulation was "written in a bad hand on wet and blotted paper."

If only it had not been put in writing!

Dinwiddie made what he called "the following melancholy account" in his report to the Lords of Trade, July 24th, 1754:

"On the 3d of this Mo. they had Intelligence y't the French were re-inforc'd (at the Fort they took from Us, in May last, near the Ohio,) with 700 Men, and y't they were in full March with 900 Men to attack our small Camp, w'ch consisted of few more than 300 Men besides Officers. They imediately connected and prepared to make the best Defence their small Numbers w'd admit of, by throw'g up a small Intrenchm't, which they had not Time to compleat, before their out Centry gave the Alarm, by firing his Gun, of the approach of the Enemy.

"Imediately they appear'd in Sight of our Camp, and fir'd at our People at a great Distance, w'ch did no harm. Our small Forces were drawn up in good Order to receive them before their Intrenchm'ts, but did not return their First Fire, reserving it till they came nigher. The enemy advanc'd irregularly within 60 Yards of our Forces, and y'n made a second Discharge, and observing they did not intend to attack them in open Field, they retir'd within their Trenches, and reserv'd their Fire, thinking, from their Numbers, they w'd force their Trenches, but finding they made no Attempt of this kind, the Colo. gave Orders to our People to fire on the Enemy, w'ch they did with great Briskness, and the officers declare y's Engagem't continue[d] from 11 o'clock till 8 O'Clock at Night, they being without Shelter, rainy weather, and their Trenches to the knee in

Water, whereas the French were shelter'd all around our Camp by Trees; from thence they gall'd our People all the Time as above.

"About 8 O'Clock at Night the French call'd out to Parley; our People mistrusting their Sincerity, from their Numbers, and other Advantages, refused it. At last they desir'd [us] to send an Officer y't c'd speak French, and they gave their Parole for his safe ret'n to them, on w'ch the Comd'r sent two Officers, to whom they gave their Proposals, copy of w'ch I send You here enclos'd. From our few Numbers, and our bad Situation, they (our forces) were glad to accept of them; otherways, were determin'd to loose their Lives rather than be taken prisoners.

"The next morning a Party from the French came and took Possession of our Encampm't, and our People march'd off with Colours flying and beat of Drum, but there appear'd a fresh Party of 100 Ind's to join the French, who gall'd our People much, and with difficulty were restrained from attacking them; however, they pilf'r'd our People's Baggage, and at the Beginn'g of the Engagem't the French killed all the Horses, Cattle and live Creatures they saw, so y't our Forces were oblig'd to carry off the wounded Men on their Backs to some Distance from the Place of the Engagem't, where they left them with a Guard; the Scarcity of Provisions made them make quick Marches to get among the Inhabit's, w'ch was about 60 Miles of bad road. The Surgeon's Chest was destroy'd, w'ch was a great Loss to the Wounded.

"The Number of the Enemy killed in this Action is uncertain, but by Acc't from some Dutch in their Service, they say were 300, and many wounded. From their great Superiority of Numbers at the Beginning of the Engagem't, it may be presum'd they lost many Men, or some other Disaster y't they desired to parley, so much contrary to the

Expectat's of our Forces, who were determin'd to sell their Lives dear rather than be taken Prisoners. The Number of our People kill'd in the Action were 30, and 70 wounded. Our few Forces have behav'd with great Intrepidity and resolution in this Action. . . .

"I forgot to mention some of the Ind's rem'n with our People, but generally speaking these People side with the Conquerors. The French had pretty many Ind's they bro't from Canada, and high up the river Ohio, who were in the Engagem't and I suspect many of our friendly Ind's on the Ohio, &c., will join them out of fear, and if the French are allow'd a quiet Settlem't on y't river, its more than probable they will ext'd their Incursions into our pres't Settlem'ts; indeed we had several Families settled within a few miles of the Fort they took from Us. I shall comply with the Articles agreed on, by returning the Prisoners, in order to recover our two Capt's who are Hostages for the Performance thereof. . . .

"For the forementioned reasons I fear we shall not be able to dislodge the French from the Fort without Assistance from B[ritain]. This Dom'n has always been in Peace and not accustom'd to War, therefore, their Magazines are quite empty, no Bombs, Coehorns, or Granade Shells, without them cannot carry on a Siege against a Fort; no Ingineer in this Co't'y, w'ch is much wanted, and in my private Opinion, with't a regim't or two from Home, and proper Supplies of the above Articles, we shall not be able to force them from His M'y's Fort and Lands." [7]

Hot on the heels of Washington's first sweet little triumph had come a greater defeat and surrender.

And on the Fourth of July!

But this was not the worst of it.

He had been captured and released by the brother of the man he had killed. The French heaped coals of fire on his head. They were as courteous to him in the battlefield as in the wilderness when they had him at their mercy. They protected him from their Indians, though he had not protected the French wounded from his Indians.

On his way home from his journey to Fort le Boeuf, he had suspected the French of trying to assassinate him, because a lone Indian fired one wild shot in his direction. Now the French not only charged him with the assassination of an envoy, but secured his signature to the confession of it.

In the capitulation it was twice stated that the French were not attacking the English, with whom they were at peace, but punishing the "assassination" of M. de Jumonville. And Washington signed it.

Afterwards he said that he did not understand French, and that the Dutchman, Van Braam, had translated the word simply as "loss" or "death."

This might well be true, seeing that Van Braam had translated "Illinois," "Isle Noire." There was a Frenchman in camp, Peyronie, but he was too badly wounded in the siege to be consulted. McKay, by virtue of his royal commission, signed the capitulation ahead of Washington. He and another officer testified that they never heard the word "assassination" mentioned.

Van Braam was later accused of being an intentional traitor, but at the time he was turned over to the French as a hostage along with Robert Stobo, and he gave proof enough afterward that the French had not bought him, for even as a hostage he was plotting their destruction.

The two hostages were taken back to Fort Du Quesne by the French as a security for Washington's pledge, in the capitulation, that the prisoners Washington had made in the battle with Jumonville should be promptly returned to the French.

But Dinwiddie, after some hesitation, refused to be bound

by Washington's pledge.   He refused to return the French prisoners and the hostages were left to shift for themselves.

In the capitulation there was further a "parole of honor not to work at any construction hereabouts nor beyond the highlands."

Since Dinwiddie had repeatedly ordered Washington and the other officers to go out and build forts, this plainly meant that they would all be kept out altogether.   Some copies had the words "for a year from this day."

But Dinwiddie shiftily took this parole to refer only to the soldiers left to guard the baggage! [8]   In any case, Washington and many of the other officers paid no attention to this pledge; they were back in that region well within the year, building roads and marching to war under Braddock.

If this was not breaking a *parole d'honneur*, what would be?

It is unfortunate that the French should be able to point to so many such instances as justifications for their by-word, "perfidious Albion."

X

HE IS CHARGED WITH ASSASSINATION

PEOPLES that are at war, or have been at war, feel it their sacred patriotic duty to ignore or misrepresent the ideals and injuries of the other side, and to denounce them without knowing what they are.

Since the best friends misunderstand one another's motives, deeds and statements, it is to be expected that nations in competition for trade, glory, or expansion should give conflicting accounts.

Truth never had less chance to prevail than in this Jumonville matter. The English and the colonies were at odds; the colonies were at odds among themselves; the French were the ancient enemy of all of them. They could not even understand each other's languages, to say nothing of their conflicting patriotisms.

They met in a wilderness and strove by hook and by crook to win as allies or destroy as vermin the Indians, who could understand the language of neither and whom neither could understand.

The most vital and subtle matters of life, death, honor, mercy, war and trade had to be discussed with gibberish and gestures—a form of retroversion to the beast.

There is no reason to suggest that George Washington could have intentionally murdered anybody, but it was cruel that he of all men, who had just returned from an experience of the finest courtesy in the French domain, should have shot down a young Frenchman bearing a message exactly like his own. The fact that the Frenchman bore another message of different purport could be too easily justified. It was unfortunate that he should have permitted his savages to scalp the wounded and dead. It was unfortunate that he should not have believed the protestations of the survivors and released them, even if he suspected them of spying, as he knew well that he himself had gone inside the French lines with instructions to spy.

It was not to be expected that the French should take his version of the affair any more than he took theirs.

To a certain type of mind it is sufficient to dismiss with scorn any foreign opinion of any native deed. Another type of mind is eager to know the look of his country's, or his own, actions in the eye of his adversary.

Those who have no desire to know how the French regarded Washington can easily skip this chapter.

Just because Washington is so big a man, it is fascinating to see him through alien eyes. The French certainly did enough for him and his people later to win them a day in court.

What little Americans know of French history is taken from the histories written by their hereditary enemies, the British. This throws everything out of balance, and great events take on an astonishingly different aspect when French historians are studied. They have their prejudices, of course, but they help as a counterweight to American and British prejudices.

First, it is interesting to read the comments of one of Jumonville's companions, one of the prisoners who were not released in compliance with Washington's pledge. After agreeing to release the prisoners, Dinwiddie disdained to keep the promise of his subordinate, because, in the first place, they were in his possession before Washington surrendered and pledged them, and in the second place, "Mr.

Washington had no Power to capitulate for the Prisoners in my Possession." [1]

It was the prisoner Druillon who made the following appeal. If we can forget that it is Washington whom he accuses, his letter has a distinct plausibility:

"I beg Y'r Hon'r's Permiss'n to repeat my representat'n of the Hardship it appear'd to me, to be attack'd by those to whom Mr. Jumonville and I went on an Embassy. The Sieur Jumonville, who was killed, being an older Officer than me, had the written Order w'ch Mr. Washington ought to have sent You.

"Mr. Washington said that he w'd have treated Us in the same manner that he was treated w'n You were pleas'd to send him on an Embassy to Us, if, like him, we had come in a smaller Number. The Kind treatment of the Ind's to all the English on the Belle reviere (Ohio) was an assurance to him of the same kindness from them, and from Us he c'd not apprehend any danger in coming without Forces to a French Fort.

"On the contrary, our Situation was quite different; the Ind's had assured Us that the English Troops were on their March to attack Us; whereupon our Command'r did all in his Power to engage them to conduct Us to their Camp, that we might inform ourselves of your Intent's, and those of Y'r King; but none of them c'd be prevailed on to be our Guides.

"Last Year two of our Couriers were killed by these same Ind's, and the Letters lost; and lest we might meet with the same Fate, he thought proper to give Us the small Compa. y't we had, as You know Sir.

"Mr. Washington might have taken Notice w'n he attacked Us at about 7 or 8 o'clock in the Morning, y't neither we nor our own Men took to our arms: he might have heard our Interpreter, who desir'd him to come to our

Cabbin, y't we might confer together, instead of taking that Opp'ty to fire upon Us.

"Had he come and given Us the reason on w'ch the King of Eng'd founds his Pretent's to the Belle reviere (Ohio), we sh'd have immediately born his Answer to our Com'd'r, who then might have withdrawn his Troops.

"We were encamp'd within one or two Miles of the Road. This Officer w'd not have reproach'd Us with this, if he had observ'd, that being compelled by the Rain to encamp in an extremely mountainous Country, we were obliged to fix on the rivulet where he found Us, for the Conveniency of Water.

"He adds that he c'd not refuse the Solicitations of the Ind's to attack Us. If this reason were sufficient to author-ize his violating the Law of Nat's, yet after the Action was over, and he came to read the Order and Instruct's we were charged with, I sh'd have flatter'd myself, Sir, y't instead of sending Us to You, he w'd have sent Us back to our Camp. . . .

"We had continued a day in the Place where we were attack'd . . . and we were not above 7 miles from the Eng. Camp. We were so far from Knowing this, y't we had only the most uncertain Acc'ts that the Eng. were at all in those Parts. . . .

"Be pleas'd I intreat You to give a favorable reception to the request that accompanies this, [in] w'ch I refute all the Pretences that Mr. Washington has used to induce Y'r Hon'r's Approbat'n of His Conduct in siezing Us and send'g us Prisoners to You. If he has added any y't I am not acquainted with, I beg the Favo. of you Sir to impart them to me, and I do assure You y't I can without any Diffi-culty confute them. . . ." [2]

To this polite and very well-reasoned explanation, Din-widdie wrote with unmerited insolence: "I give You the

Civility of an Answer, tho' I am perswaded You cannot, Y'r Self, think it deserves one. The Protect'n due to Messengers of Peace is so universally acknowledged, and the Sacredness of their Characters is so inviolably preserved y't even amongst the most barbarous Nat's their Persons are always safe and unhurt. You cannot be ignorant how much all the various Tribes of Ind's revere the Calumet, and You must know y't a Flag of Truce w'd have sooner induced our Protect'n and Regard, than a Body of Men arm'd with the Instruments of destruction.

"Thus, I think the Inconsistency of Your Appearance with Y'r Pretent's, obliges me to consider You in no other Light than y't in w'ch You presented Yourselves. You rem'd several days ab't our Camp with't telling Y'r Message, nor w'd not, till You were prepared for our destruct'n. You had neither a right to dem'd, nor Colo. Washington to discuss, the King my Master's Title to the Lands on the Ohio river. . . ." [3]

Dinwiddie wrote to the Lords of Trade and his other correspondents, describing the disaster and laying the blame on the indifference of the other colonies, "their infatuation," their "Lethargic Stupidity." He regretted that the friendship of the Indian allies had been forfeited, but he spoke well of Washington and his men.

He was in dismay and protested that he had "gone thorow monstrious fatigues, but such wrong headed People (I thank God) I never had to do with before." [4]

The French account of the Jumonville affair was as different as possible from that of George Washington. Only one of the Jumonville party escaped back to the French with news of what had happened. He told a story that was doubtless false in many particulars, not only because it contradicted Washington's story, but because it contradicted his lifelong character and all human probabilities.

MÉMOIRE

CONTENANT LE

PRÉCIS DES FAITS,

AVEC LEURS

PIECES JUSTIFICATIVES,

Pour ſervir de Réponſe aux *Obſervations*
envoyées par les Miniſtres d'Angleterre,
dans les Cours de l'Europe.

A PARIS,

DE L'IMPRIMERIE ROYALE.

M. DCCLVI.

TITLE PAGE OF THE FRENCH MÉMOIRE CONTAINING
WASHINGTON'S CAPTURED JOURNAL.

Yet it is not easy to read the French version without being convinced of a certain sincerity and a large element of truth.

In the confusion of Braddock's defeat, Washington left behind his Journal containing an account of the Jumonville affair and all that preceded and followed it. It was sent to France, where it was published in a French translation, which Washington afterward denounced as false in many particulars.

And yet, in reading it with care, it is manifestly in Washington's manner, and no one has pointed out any single detail in which it contradicts Washington's own letters to Dinwiddie, except the matter of Jumonville's posture at the first attack. A copy of the French report was later found on board a French ship captured by the British, who brought it into New York, where it was promptly translated into English and published in New York a year after it appeared in France.

Washington then had the privilege of reading his work in an English translation of a French translation of the original. Mark Twain has described seeing such a double distilled version of his "Jumping Frog" story, and its strange metamorphoses. And Washington must have had an odd sensation as he came upon his own thoughts twice translated.

Washington's comments have disappeared, but Sparks evidently had before him a letter Washington wrote "to a gentleman," in which he says:

"In regard to the journal, I can only observe in general, that I kept no regular one during that expedition; rough minutes of occurrences I certainly took, and find them as certainly and strangely metamorphosed; some parts left out, which I remember were entered, and many things added that never were thought of; the names of men and things egregiously miscalled; and the whole of what I saw Eng-

aucune infulte par nos François, & de maintenir, autant qu'il fera en notre pouvoir, tous les Sauvages qui font avec nous.

I I.

IL lui fera permis de fortir & d'emporter tout ce qui leur appartiendra, à l'exception de l'artillerie que nous nous réfervons.

I I I.

QUE nous leur accordons les honneurs de la guerre; qu'ils fortiront tambour battans avec une petite pièce de canon, voulant bien par-là leur prouver que nous les traitons en amis.

I V.

QUE fi-tôt les articles fignés de part & d'autre, ils améneront le pavillon Anglois.

V.

QUE demain à la pointe du jour, un détachement François ira faire défiler la garnifon & prendre poffeffion dudit fort.

V I.

QUE comme les Anglois n'ont prefque plus de chevaux ni bœufs, ils feront libres de mettre leurs effets en cache, pour les venir chercher lorfqu'ils auront rejoint des chevaux ils pourront a cette fin laiffer des gardiens, en tel nombre qu'ils voudront, aux conditions qu'ils donneront parole d'honneur de ne plus travailler à aucun établiffement dans ce lieu-ci, ni en deçà de la hauteur des terres.

V I I.

QUE comme les Anglois ont en leur pouvoir un Officier, deux cadets, & généralement les prifonniers qu'ils nous ont faits dans l'affaffinat du fieur de Jumonville, & qu'ils promettent de les envoyer avec fauvegarde jufqu'au fort du Quefne, fitué fur la Belle-rivière: & que pour fûreté de cet article, ainfi que de ce traité, M. Jacob Vambrane & Robert Stobo, tous deux Capitaines, nous feront remis en otage jufqu'à l'arrivée de nos François & Canadiens ci-deffus mentionnes.

Nous nous obligeons de notre côté à donner efcorte pour ramener en fûreté les deux Officiers qui nous promettent nos François dans deux mois & demi pour le plus tard.

Fait double fur un des poftes de notre blocus, les jour & an que deffus.

Ont figné M.. { JAMES MACKAYE, G WASINCHTON, COULON, VILLIERS.

P iij

THE CAPITULATION MENTIONING THE "ASSASSINATION"
OF JUMONVILLE.

(From Washington's Captured Journal.)

lished is very incorrect and nonsensical; yet, I will not pretend to say that the little body, who brought it to me, has not made a literal translation, and a good one.

"Short as my time is, I cannot help remarking on Villiers' account of the battle of, and transactions at, the Meadows, as it is very extraordinary, and not less erroneous than inconsistent. . . . That we were wilfully, or ignorantly, deceived by our interpreter in regard to the word *assassination*, I do aver, and will to my dying moment; so will every officer that was present. The interpreter was a Dutchman, little acquainted with the English tongue, therefore might not advert to the tone and meaning of the word in English; but, whatever his motives were for so doing, certain it is, he called it the *death*, or the *loss*, of the Sieur Jumonville. So we received and so we understood it, until, to our great surprise and mortification, we found it otherwise in a literal translation."

A thorough search has been made in France for Washington's manuscript, but it has never turned up. The Library of Congress and the Huntington Library have copies of the original French report as issued in Paris in 1756 (*Mémoire Contenant le Précis des Faits, avec leurs Pièces justificatives, etc.*). The New York translation as published in 1757 was reproduced in the March, 1847, issue of a magazine called *The Olden Time* and devoted to the preservation of documents.

A rather careful comparison proves the English translation faithful enough to the letter and the spirit of the French, though Sparks says that it is "uncouth in its style and faulty in its attempts to convey the sense of the original."

The object of the French in publishing the *Mémoire* was to prove that the English were the first to fire on the

French, and were guilty of wrecking the peace and bringing on the terrible war that followed.

The object of the English translator was "to discover the vile misrepresentations of facts, of which the French have been guilty." He does not succeed.

The French story begins with the arrival of the Marquis Du Quesne in Canada as governor, and quotes the letter sent to him by Dinwiddie, ordering him to withdraw from English territory. The Marquis answered that he was on French ground, and charged the Governors of New England and Virginia with laboring "to engage the Indians to a war with the French."

A French detachment under M. de Contrecoeur advanced in 1754 with five or six hundred men, and found on the banks of the Ohio a fort which the English had begun to build. He took it over and named it Du Quesne.

Then Contrecoeur learned that English troops (under Washington) were marching toward him, and he wrote a summons, advising them to keep out of French territory. He entrusted this summons to M. de Jumonville, and charged him to deliver it to the English commander and return with his answer. This story is given as follows in the New York translation:

"That deputy set out with an escort of thirty men, and the next morning found himself surrounded by a number of English and Indians: The English quickly fired two vollies which killed some soldiers. M. de Jumonville made a sign that he had a letter from his commander; hereupon the fire ceased, and they surrounded the French officer, in order to hear it. He immediately ordered the summons to be read, and as it was reading the second time, the English assassinated him. The rest of the French that escorted him, were, upon the spot made prisoners of war.

"The only one who escaped, and who gave M. de Contrecoeur a circumstantial account of that affair, assured him, that the Indians who were with the English, had not fired a gun; and that at the instant M. de Jumonville was assassinated, they threw themselves in between the French and their enemies.

"That murder produced an effect in the minds of the Indians which Major Washington [in the French version, his name is consistently misspelled Wasinghton], who was at the head of that detachment, did not, in the least expect. Even those, who, by the suggestions of the English, had been most animated against the French, came and offered to go themselves and revenge that crime.

"The Marquis du Quesne would not accept the offer of a nation always cruel in their vengeance. He imagined at first, that the English would disavow the fact and throw it upon the fierceness of some traders; but it has been since proved that nothing was done but by the orders of the Governors of the English Colonies. We have the original journal of Major Washington, from which it is apparent that what he did was by virtue of express orders which he had received. It was a thing before agreed upon, to attack the French wherever they could be met with.

"As the English made no satisfactive to M. Contrecoeur, he, upon receiving instruction from the Marquis du Quesne, endeavored to discover the place where the murderers had retired to. He was informed that Major Washington was in a little fort which the English had built, and called Fort Necessity, where he awaited the arrival of some new troops that were destined to come and attack Fort du Quesne. He thereupon sent out a detachment to recover, if possible, the French prisoners, or at least to oblige the English to withdraw from the lands belonging to the French. M. de Villiers, the brother of M. de Jumonville, was charged with that commission, and the instructions given him were entirely confined to that. He was also expressly commanded not to use any violence if the English would withdraw.

"He left Fort du Quesne the 28th of June, and, having passed the place where the murder was committed, and where the bodies of the French still lay, he arrived the 3d of July, in sight of Fort Necessity. The English who were without the fort, fired a volley and retired into it. The fort was immediately invested, and attacked: The fire was very hot, but M. Villiers put a stop to it about eight o'clock at night, in order to propose to the English a surrender, to avoid an assault, which would have exposed them to all the cruelties of the Indians, even in spite of the French.

"The proposal was accepted, and the capitulation drawn up. The French would not make them prisoners, because they did not look upon themselves as at war. They only demanded that those who escorted M. de Jumonville should be returned. Major Washington engaged to send them to Fort du Quesne, and gave hostages for the performance of his promise. In force, the English were suffered to depart with one piece of cannon, and all their effects. They themselves acknowledged, in the first article of the capitulation, that the design of the French was only to revenge the assassination of a French officer, the carrier of a summons [This is in italics in the French version]. The capitulation being signed, and the fort evacuated, the French destroyed it and returned to Fort du Quesne with the two hostages.

"But that agreement, to which seven or eight hundred Englishmen owed their lives, was by no means executed on their part. The prisoners were never sent back to Fort du Quesne: Out of twenty that were taken, seven have been sent to England where they arrived separately after having suffered the most unworthy treatment. . . .

"Perhaps the motive which induced the English to de-

tain the prisoners, was a piece of cunning. The French
would have made no hesitation in sending back the hostages
immediately; but these had their orders, and their stay at
Fort du Quesne was too advantageous for the English to
think of having them removed. These hostages, named
the one Jacob Ambrane, and the other Robert Stobo, were
two very crafty spies, and found means to carry on a correspondence with the English Generals. These were found
among the papers which fell into the hands of the French
after the battle of the 9th of July, 1755, the letters which
Robert Stobo, one of the hostages, had written to Major
Washington. . . ."

Van Braam's letter is then quoted, begging Washington
to attack the fort, enclosing a plan and saying that a hundred Indians could do it with their Tamkanko (Captain
Stobo wrote *tomahawks!*), and begging Washington, "for
God's sake, speak not of this to many people." He also
says, "The French are so vain of their success that I'd rather
die than hear them speak of it." [5] The story goes on:

"The English were quite of a different temper: Major
Washington did not dare to attempt anything, because he
had not forces enough; but from that time all the English
colonies were in motion to execute the plan of a general
invasion."

In proof of this incontrovertible fact, there follows an
account of General Braddock's famous and fatal expedition,
with quotations from Braddock's papers, which were also
captured when he encountered an even worse defeat than
Washington's.

Other documents reproduced include the orders that M.
de Contrecoeur gave M. de Jumonville. They state that
"the Indians give out that the English are on their march to
attack us (which we cannot believe since we are at peace)."

The summons to the English to withdraw is quoted as it

was given to Jumonville to deliver, as well as Contrecoeur's letter to the Marquis Du Quesne, describing the approach of Jumonville as reported by the one Canadian, Monceau by name, who escaped. The story is completed:

"The Indians who were present when the thing was done, say, that M. de Jumonville was killed by a musket shot in the head, whilst they were reading the summons, and that the English would have afterwards killed all our men had not the Indians, who were present, by rushing in between them and the English, prevented their design. . . ."

Contrecoeur wrote to Du Quesne:

"I believe, sir, it will surprise you to hear how basely the English have acted: it is what was never seen, even amongst nations who are the least civilized, to fall thus upon ambassadors and murder them. The Indians are so enraged thereat, that they have applied to me for liberty to fall upon the English."

There follows as Document VIII what the French version calls the "Journal de Major Wasinghton." A footnote to the first page explains that the "Gouverneur de Virginie" was "M. d'Inwiddie."

And now comes an astounding thing. In a preceding chapter there is liberal quotation from Washington's report to Dinwiddie. Let the reader compare it with what is to follow from the French version of his journal (which Washington denounced as so false), and he will find it almost word for word what Washington wrote to Dinwiddie! In his voyage to the Ohio, Washington had kept rough notes, of which he made a fair copy for the Governor's eyes. All the slight differences between this French Journal and the Dinwiddie report may be similarly explained.

Wherein then lay the outrageous interpolations and omissions of which Washington complained? The French give exactly his explanations, and though the editor makes occasional comments in footnotes, calling attention to Washington's frank admissions of falsehood, and interprets his elaborate excuses as the effects of remorse, one who reads the Dinwiddie report must get the same impression that Washington felt himself in a bad situation and tried to argue himself out of it.

Since the translation is reproduced both in Fitzpatrick's edition of Washington's *Diaries* and in Ford's edition of his *Writings* (Vol. I, 66 *et seqq.*) it can be skimmed rapidly, reproducing some of the French comments.

While the French version omits some of the descriptions of the country passed through, all the omissions are noted. The proper names are spelled wrong, as almost always with the French, but *Joshus Fry, Ecuyer* is easily recognized as "Joshua Fry, Esquire," *Wart* as Ward, though the word "wampum" is well disguised by the French term, which is, *"une branche de porcelaine."*

The captured Journal begins with Washington's receipt of a commission as lieutenant-colonel of the Virginia regiment, whereof Joshua Fry, Esquire, was colonel, and the march from Alexandria into the wilderness. The news comes of the capture by the French of the fort Captain Trent was building; a message of friendship arrives from the Half-King, sent with a belt of wampum.

Washington's letters to the Governors of Virginia and Maryland are given from the copies he must have kept, as well as the very same speech he sent to the Half-King, signed "Washington Conotocarious," which the French editor cannily guesses to be "an Indian name that Major Washington had taken to please those Indians whom he wanted to seduce."

Washington writes: "I gave the Young Indians to understand that the French wanted to kill the Half-King, and they at once offered to go with our people against the French."

The French editor comments: "It would appear that imposture costs M. Washington nothing: here he takes pride in it (*il s'en fait honneur*)."

Compare what follows with the exactly parallel account transmitted to Dinwiddie:

"On the 27th, about eight at night, received an express from the Half-King, which informed me, that, as he was coming to join us, he had seen along the road, the tracts of two men, which he had followed, till he was brought thereby to a low obscure place, that he was of opinion the whole party of the French was hidden there: that very moment I sent out forty men, and ordered my ammunition to be put in a place of safety, under a strong guard to defend it; fearing it to be a stratagem of the French to attack our camp, and with the rest of my men, set out in a heavy rain, and in a night as dark as pitch, along a path scarce broad enough for one man; we were sometimes fifteen or twenty minutes out of the path before we could come to it again; and so dark that we would often strike one against the other. All night long we continued our route, and the 28th, about sunrise, we arrived at the Indian camp, where, after having held a council with the Half-King, it was concluded we should fall on them together; so we sent out two men to discover where they were, as also their posture, and what sort of ground was thereabout; after which, we formed ourselves for an engagement,[1] marching one after the other in the Indian manner. We were advanced pretty near to them, as we thought, when they discovered us; whereupon, I ordered my company to fire, mine was supported by that

---

[1] The French version says: "Après quoi nous formâmes notre disposition pour les envelopper," and there is a footnote saying: "Il est donc certain que les Anglois avoient ordre d'attaquer." This is the vital thing to the French: The English attacked in a time of peace.

of Mr. Wager's, and my company, and his, received the whole fire of the French, during the greatest part of the action, which only lasted a quarter of an hour, before the enemy was routed.

"We killed M. de Jumonville,[1] the commander of that party, as also nine others: we wounded one, and made twenty-one prisoners. The Indians scalped the dead, and took away the most part of their arms after which we marched on with the prisoners and the guard to the Indian camp, where again I held a council with the Half-King. . . .

"After this I marched on with the prisoners; They informed me that they had been sent with a summons to order me to depart. A plausible pretence to discover our camp and to obtain the knowledge of our forces and our situation! It was so clear that they were come to reconnoitre what we were, that I admired at their assurance, when they told me they were come as an embassy; for their instructions mentioned that they should get what knowledge they could of the roads, rivers, and of all the country as far as Potomac: and instead of coming as an Embassador, publicly, and in an open manner, they came secretly, and sought after the most hidden retreats[2] more like deserters than ambassadors; in such retreats they encamped, and remained hid for whole days together, and that no more than five miles from us; from thence they sent spies to reconnoitre our camp; after this was done, they went back two miles, from

---

[1] The French editor gives Washington credit for sincerity, but notes that later he strives to justify himself in response to the remorse that afflicted him: "Le Major Washington n'a gardé de faire ici une relation sincere, mais on va voir plus bas les efforts qu' il fait pour se justifier, & pour répondre sans doute aux remords qui l'accusoient."

[2] The French editor demands, "Why this apology in a simple diary if he did not foresee the reproaches that would be rightfully made:" "Pourquoi dans un simple journal cette apologie! M. Wasinghton ne previent ici ces reproches, parce qu'il fait qu' on est en droit de les lui faire."

whence they sent the two messengers spoken of in the instructions to acquaint M. de Contrecoeur of the place we were at and of our disposition, that he might send his detachments to enforce the summons as soon as it should be given.

"Besides, an ambassador has princely attendants; whereas this was only a simple petty French officer; an embassador has no need of spies, his character being always sacred; and seeing their intention was so good, why did they tarry two days at five miles distance from us? [1] without acquainting me with the summons, or, at least with something that related to the embassy? That alone would be sufficient to raise the greatest suspicion, and we ought to do them the justice to say, that, as they wanted to hide themselves, they could not pick out better places than they had done.

"The summons was so insolent, and favored the gasconade so much [2] that if it had been brought openly by two men it would have been an immediate indulgence [*French: une excessive indulgence*] to have suffered them to return.[3] It was the opinion of the Half-King in this case that their intentions were evil, and that it was a pure pretence; that they were intended to come to us but as enemies; and if we had been such fools as to let them go, they (i.e., the Indians) would never help us any more to take other Frenchmen.

"They say they called to us as soon as they had discovered us, which is an absolute falsehood, for I was there marching at the head of the company going toward them, and can positively affirm, that when they first saw us they

---

[1] The French editor not unreasonably suggests that Jumonville did not know the English were so near: "M. de Jumonville ignoroit parfaitement que les Anglois fussent à cinq milles de lui."

[2] The French words are "sent si fort la gasconnade." In the Dinwiddie report Washington wrote, "Savours so much of Gascoigny!"

[3] Again the editor finds a proof of remorse: "Autre genre d'apologie qui ne prouve que des remords."

ran to their arms, without calling; as I must have heard them had they so done.

"After this the French prisoners desired to speak with me, and asked in what manner I looked upon them, whether as the attendants of an Embassador, or as prisoners of war: I answered them that it was in quality of the latter, and gave them my reasons for it, as above.

"The 30th—I detached M. Wart and M. Spindorph to conduct the prisoners to Winchester with a guard of twenty men. Began to raise a fort with small pallisadoes, fearing that when the French should hear the news of that defeat, we might be attacked by considerable forces.

"June the 1st—Arrived here a trader with the Half-King; they said that when M. de Jumonville was sent here, another party had been detached towards the lower part of the river in order to take and kill all the English they should meet.[1]

"The 13th—I persuaded the deserters to write the following letter to those of their companions who had an inclination to desert."[2]

The Journal ends in a council with the Indians and exchange of speeches.

The ninth document in the Précis gives the story of the capitulation in the words of de Villiers, to whom Washington surrendered:

"As I was the oldest officer and commanded the Indian nations, and as my brother had been assassinated, M. de Contrecoeur honored me with that command, and M. le Mercier, though deprived of the command, seemed very well pleased to make the campaign under my orders. . . .

"The 29th—Mass was said in the camp.

---

[1] The French editor calls this a shameless lie: "Indigne fausseté."

[2] This letter is not given in the Journal, but the editor exclaims: "How can such proceedings be justified?"

"July the 2nd—We had rain all night. . . . We marched the whole day in the rain. . . . I stopped at the place where my brother had been assassinated, and saw there yet some dead bodies."

He marched on to the English fort and describes the fight and the offer of capitulation. He said to the captain who came out, that they were here only to revenge his brother's assassination. The English signed and gave hostages.

There is no little pathos in the story of the dead youth, Jumonville, his brother who so gently avenged him, and indeed the whole luckless family of ardent patriots. According to J. W. Cruzat:

"Coulon de Villiers was the name of a family of seven brothers, six of whom, together with their father, died in the service of France, in Canada. The last surviving brother, the Chevalier François Coulon de Villiers, was made prisoner by the English, together with Aubry, at the siege of Niagara; he was sent to Europe, where he received the cross and was made Chevalier de l'ordre 'Royal et Militaire de St. Louis,' with his superior officer, Aubry, in 1761. The Chevalier was thrice married, 1st to Miss St. Ange, sister of the last French Governor of Illinois, 2dly to Miss Marin, and the third time in New Orleans, to Miss Beaumont de Livandais. Numerous descendants, offspring of his two last marriages, still exist in Louisiana. The Chevalier died in New Orleans in 1794." [6]

The French historian, Thomas Chapais,[7] gives the dead envoy's name as Coulon de Jumonville, and his brother as Coulon de Villiers. Chapais defends Washington from the charge of having known the *qualité de parlementaire* of Jumonville, accepts his misunderstanding of the interpreter who mistranslated the French terms, and says that Contrecoeur "resolved to chastise that which he *proclaimed* as an assassination and a violation of the law of nations."

But almost all other French historians (from whom Sparks [8] quotes excerpts), accept the story of the butchery of the envoy, and Washington is to this day linked in the French mind with Jumonville and his dastardly assassination.

Because the name and story of Jumonville are absolutely unknown to the average American, and because of the importance of the tragedy in Washington's life and fame, it has seemed fit to give it so much space.

Though the English and Americans have largely ignored Washington's alleged guilt, the French were wrought to a fury by it. To them there was no question that the English were lying when they pretended to desire peace with France; while disguising their perfidy they were gathering troops for open invasion.

The infamous massacre of a peaceful band carrying a message, and the refusal to surrender the prisoners, as solemnly promised, were typical of English insolence. And soon General Braddock was in the field.

He, too, ended his campaign in death and disgrace, and his journals were also captured by the French. They almost recaptured the murderous "Wasinghton," *le cruel Wasinghton*, who had added another defeat to the poor promise of his life thus far.

Washington brought away from the too-well-named Fort Necessity a copy of the capitulation, and admitted that it contained the odious word assassination twice. The French *Mémoire* gives it in full. A part of the translation follows:

Capitulation granted by M. de Villiers, Captain and commander of His Majesty's troops, to those English troops in the fort of Necessity.

July 3, 1754, at 8 o'clock at night.

As our intentions have never been to trouble the peace and good harmony subsisting between the two Princes in amity, but only to revenge the assassination committed on one of our officers, bearer of a summons, as also his escort, and to hinder any establishment on the lands of the dominions of the King my master; upon these considerations, we are willing to show favor to all the English who are in the said fort, on the following conditions:

ARTICLE I

We grant leave to the English commander to retire with all his garrison. . . .

ARTICLE VII

As the English have in their power, one officer, two cadets and most of the prisoners made at the assassination of M. de Jumonville, and promise to send them back with a safe guard to Fort du Quesne; for surety of their performing this article as well as this treaty, M. Jacob Van Brame and Robert Stobo, both Captains, shall be delivered to us as hostages, till the arrival of our French and Canadians above mentioned. We oblige ourselves on our side, to give an escort to return these two officers in safety, and expect to have our French back in two months and a half at farthest. A duplicate of this being fixed upon one of the posts of our blockade, the day and year above mentioned.

Signed

Ont signé Mrs.
$\left\{ \begin{array}{l} \text{JAMES MACKAYE} \\ \text{G. WASINGHTON} \\ \text{COULON} \\ \text{VILLIERS.} \end{array} \right.$

In Stobo's [9] memoirs, the appendix, it is stated that "Washington kept a copy of this capitulation, but the publication in this country omitted the preamble, article first being the beginning and Article VI had at the end, 'pendant une année à compter de ce jour': How these discrepancies arose it would be useless now to enquire."

Still more strange is the statement of Paul Leicester Ford

and Thomas E. Watson: [10] "One of the Virginia officers had refused to sign because of this confession of assassination." This throws the whole question up in the air, but neither Mr. Ford nor Mr. Watson gives his authority, and both are now dead.

A picturesque and amusing example of the bitterness of the French against Washington at this time was a French poem inspired by the event. It is discussed at length in Appendix III.

XI

HE RESIGNS FOR THE FIRST TIME

THAT word "assassination" rankled in the English soul. It not only brought on the long-deferred war, but it threw an ugly glare on the English cause.[1]
It was like the blowing up of the *Maine* in Havana harbor, which thrilled a nation to fury, and doubtless with as little guilt on the part of the Spanish government as there was in the act of George Washington.

It was like the assassination of the Archduke at Serajevo, which brought on the World War.

Nine months after Washington gave the order to fire on the Frenchmen huddling in their little cranny, Dinwiddie was still trying to explain away the scandal in a letter to Lord Albemarle:

"The Skermish between the English Forces and those of Fr. is very unjustly reported with You. . . . It is true the prisoners s'd they were come on an Embassy . . . but Yr L'ds. Knows y't Ambassadors do not come with such an arm'd Force, with't a Trumpet or any other sign of Friendship. . . . We are in daily Expectat'n of a Reinforcem't from B., w'n I hope our Affairs will be conducted with more Military Knowledge than hitherto."[2]

Like Napoleon's, Washington's career began with defeat. He was not put under arrest as Napoleon was, but he suffered shame and ridicule at home, infamy and contempt abroad.

A more pitiable figure could not be seen. Leaving his

155

men to straggle back in pitiable condition, the medicine chest destroyed by the Indians, and wounds, exposure, hunger and lack of horses making their road a *via dolorosa,* he rode to Williamsburg with Captain McKay to make his report. He had need of all his bravery, and Captain McKay said he was very sad company.

Dinwiddie stood by him with a loyalty partly spurred by the fact that his own prestige was involved with Washington's, but he wrote letters of highest praise to the powers in England and to the governors.

There was no questioning the fact that Washington had behaved with faultless valor, and had been overcome by double his numbers. His "assassination" was the prompt destruction of a force carrying two messages, one claiming ambassadorial courtesies, if caught; one, orders to reconnoiter and report.

The House of Burgesses, on August 30th, voted its thanks to Washington and his officers, with the exception of Major Muse, who was charged with cowardice (though he had taught Washington war) and poor Van Braam, whom they blamed for duping Washington into signing the assassination document. Van Braam was left as a hostage for six years, but the charges against him were eventually recognized as ridiculous, and he was rewarded with a gift of 9000 acres of land.

The Burgesses voted, also, a pistole from the public treasury to each of the soldiers.

But nothing could disguise the fact that Washington had brought home defeat, left the frontier defenceless, and convinced the Indians that the English could not protect them or their lands from the French.

Governor Sharpe of Maryland had sent no reinforcements, but he wrote that "everybody was talking of the unmilitary conduct of Colonel Washington," and ridiculed

Fort Necessity as "a little useless intrenchment between two eminences."

The hot-headed young colonel evidently wrote to Governor Sharpe, indignantly rebuking him for his criticism. Washington's letter does not appear, but Sharpe's letter exists, full of hemming and hawing evasion, showing that even in defeat Washington could demand and receive respect from superiors as well as subordinates. For the Governor wrote him from Annapolis, October 1, 1754, rather tactlessly alluding to newspaper abuse and general disapproval of Washington's collapse:

"I am sorry to learn that any Person has represented any Expressions or Observations of mine concerning the late Engagement to You in such a light as may give You cause for the least uneasiness. indeed at seeing some things inserted in the Public papers soon after the Action & at hearing other Stories that were propagated, & which for want of a more timely Confutation, made an impression on many Minds; I might perhaps have observed that if the measures taken before & the Terms accepted upon the Engagement were really as we had them represented to us, I was apprehensive the Action might be attended with evil Consequences, & would but little encrease the Reputation of the Gentlemen who had been principally concerned therein.

"That such Conclusions were by many People drawn, I believe You cannot be much surprised if You are not an entire Stranger to the Stories & Representations that were at that time received; but after some of the Gentlemen who had been Witnesses of the Affair had honourable submitted an Account thereof to the Publick, & Circumstances were made known, & the Actor's Conduct scrutinized, it appear[d] in a more Advantageous View & many found themselves disposed to exculpate who had been forward to condemn Your Behaviour, & I believe there were few Readers in whom a Different Description of the same Action did not raise different Sensations, & induce them to entertain very dissimilar Sentiments of the Agents; the Prejudices they had before contracted I make no doubt but they again divested themselves of, & Your Reputation again revived.

"for my own part I assure You I am not insensible of the Difficulties You had to encounter & I do not by the Issue of that Enterprise in the lease measure the Merit of the Gentlemen concerned therein, that the Blame with respect to the Terms of Capitulation does not lye at your Door concurrent Circumstances would have inclined me to think, had You not made such Professions as confirm me in my opinion. Your writing to me with so much freedom & such ingenuity is highly agreeable, & I make no doubt but Your future Behaviour will convince the World of the Injustice done You by the Suspicions they have entertained." [3]

The worst of it was that Washington disgusted the Indians, who turned to the French in spite of all the fine speeches, the wampum, the medals, the rum and the dry goods squandered on them.

Dinwiddie had paid the most grovelling court to them, and Monacatoocha must have felt sick as he recalled the letter Dinwiddie had sent to him:

"*Good and faithful Friend Monacatoocha:* . . . I send this as Y'r best Friend, to warn You to beware of the cunning Devices of those who under the Pretence of embracing You do but mean to squeeze You to Death; Such Treachery deserves to be chastised, and I therefore advise You to loose no Time, but directly to stretch out the rod that Onontia put in Y'r Hand to Chastise him with w'n he sh'd grow Foolish, as now he has done." [4]

Far up north, the Six Nations were "dejected on the defeat of Colo. Washington," as Dinwiddie learned from the Governor of New York. [5]

The Half-King had to hide his wife and children from the French, and falling sick, died soon after under the spell of the superstition that the French had bewitched him for slaying Jumonville.[6]

The Indians had not liked Washington from the first any more than he liked them. They accused him of regarding them as slaves to be sent out alone every day scouting and attacking the enemy. In spite of great efforts on the part of the trader Croghan, with whom Washington quarreled and whose horses he took by force, "but thirty warriors joined Washington and of these not more than half were in service at any one time. . . . After Washington's retreat, not an English flag waved beyond the Alleghenies and soon nearly all the Ohio tribes drew their scalping knives to aid the French." [7]

Governor Hamilton of Pennsylvania sent his agent, Conrad Weiser, a German settler whom he later made Colonel, to find out what had happened. In his report, Weiser said:

"It was very unfortunate for the English Interest, that, at the same Time the Affections of the Indians were alienated from us by the Abuses committed in Trade, and by our dispossessing them of their Lands, their Opinion of our Military Abilities was very much lessened. But a few months before this Treaty at Aughwick, Colonel Washington was defeated, whose conduct and Behavior gave so much Offence to the Indians that Thanachrishon, a Seneca Chief, commonly known by the Title of the Half-King, as being at the Head of the Western Indians, who were dependent on the Six Nations, could not help complaining of it, tho' in a very modest Manner.

"The Colonel, he said, was a good natured Man, but had no Experience: he took upon him to command the Indians as his Slaves, and would have them every Day upon the

Scout, and to attack the Enemy by themselves, but would by no Means take advice from the Indians.

"He lay in one Place from one Full-Moon to the other, without making any Fortifications, except that little Thing on the Meadow; whereas, had he taken Advice, and built such Fortifications as he (the Half-King) advised him, he might easily have beat off the French. But the French in the Engagement acted like Cowards and the English like Fools." [8]

The contemptuous Indian ally of Washington's claimed to have killed Jumonville with his hatchet to avenge himself on the French, who, he declared, had killed, boiled and eaten his father. According to Weiser's report, the Half-King and his seven Indians did most of the execution, and having discovered the Frenchmen in a hollow and Washington on the opposite side, closed with the French and forced their surrender.

Many of Washington's friends stood by him loyally, however, none more devotedly than William Fairfax, who wrote to him July 10th, 1754:

"What a Tedious Suspense to You that Languish for Strength eno to undertake Some notable Action against an Enemy that now Seems to dare Your Meeting in the Field.

"In the D. of Marlbro's Campaigns You'l observe many wise Retreats performd that were not called Flights; perhaps when all the brave Officers and Soldiers are Joined by King Dinwiddie, Prince Washington, Col F—x, Maj.ʳ Montour and their gallant Warriors, Y.ᵉ Councils may even then advise and execute such Stratagems of War as to ambuscade decoy and circumvent the subtil French."

He included a statement of which much has been made as a proof of Washington's piety:

"I will not doubt your having public Prayers in the Camp especially when the Indian Familys were your Guests, that They

seeing your plain Manner of Worship may excite Their Curiosity
to be inform'd Why We dont use the idolatrous and Superstitious
Ceremonys of the French which being wel explaind to their Understandings will more and more dispose Them to receive our Baptism
and unite in strictest Bond of cordial Friendship." [9]

It has been stated that Washington tried public prayers
just once and gave it up promptly as it merely convinced the
Indians that he was performing some kind of incantation.
It was the custom, however, to have some kind of service on
Sunday, and a letter exists from one of Washington's officers asking him to send along any old volumes of sermons
he can find.

The harshness of camp life was softened by letters from
home such as he received from his friends, Colonel and Mrs.
Carlyle. John Carlyle, a merchant, had married William
Fairfax's daughter Sally—who is not the Sally Fairfax who
played so large a part in Washington's romantic experience.
The Carlyles were well matched as spellers. This is part
of the Colonel's letter:

"I received your favor of the 6th by Mr Gist & am Very Sorry
that its not In our power to Supply you faster & better than We doe;
its not for want of Will, but for two reasons first a Scarcity of
Cash & Secondly We are Deceived by Those that we depend
opon . . . you cannot Immadgeon, but that we do all We can,
& as soon as the New Crops Come In, you Shall have plenty.

"Your people you may Ashure them from Me, Shall be paid
to the last Farthing, in A few days. I have a Messinger at
Williamsburg for Money. . . . What shirts we have ready, &
Shous & are Getting Red Coats made for All that has not got for
the 25c/ Given by the Country By the order of the Governour, as
the Intention of the Gift, to put them all In one Dress if possible.

"Mr Gist brings you Cloath for Britches & by the first Shipe
Expect you May have Ye things from London that Ye Sent for.

"The Two Cols Fairfax's are not Very well the Old Gentleman
with Sumthing of the flux the Young Gentleman the fever & ague
I am In hopes they are both on the Recovery.

"Mrs Fairfax is still below.   My Sally promises to write to you but know not whether She'd be so Good as her Word.

"p. S.

I have got 2 hh^d of your Tobacco down & have pd of yr Carpinters y^r order.   the Tobacco is but Indiferent & with Sum trouble passed Inspection."

Mrs. Sarah Carlyle wrote by the same messenger:

"Dr Sir

"I Received your Letter dated the 15 May, Which gave me both pleasure and pain, the first to heare of your health, the latter to be Informed of the many Risques you run, but am hopeful your good Constitution and a kind protecter will bring you out of them all as it has In the last Ingagement preserved you from harm.   If I thought my Letters were Agreeabel to you, I wou'd Continers a Correspondence that I must own Agreeabel to me, but must not Expect it to be Carred on (on my Side) with the Spirret it ought to Inliven you Which wou'd be my desire If I cou'd—

"those pleasing reflections on the hours past ought to be banished out of your thoughts, you have now A Noblier prospect that of preserveing your Country from the Insults of an Enimy.   and as god has blessed your first Attempt, hope he may Continers his blessing, and on your return, Who knows but fortune may have, reserved you for Sum unknown She, that may recompence you for all the Tryals past, however you have my Warmest Wishes and may be assur'd that I ever am

"Your Sincear Wellwisher and

Your Humbel Servent

SARAH CARLYLE."

His friend and fellow-Mason, Daniel Campbell, sent some lodge-news and adds the interesting gossip that his mother was still dancing, though then forty-six:

"Your Mother &c. whom I frequently see are well, very lately I had the honour to dance with her, when your health was not forgot.   Mr Splittdorff waits on her this Evening for her commands to you. . . . I sincerely thank you for the countenance you

shew'd Angus Mᶜ Donald on my Account, I have been lately surpris'd with a story that he was Shot for stricking one of his Officers,
which I hope is false, if not I pity his fate, & rather wish he had
dyed as a Soldier in the field of Battle, If he is alive please desire
him to write me under your Cover."

But the news that Washington sent home was of the
dourest.

It was not only the Indians that abandoned Washington.
His own men grew uncontrollable and deserted in squads.
They had trudged back to their original starting point in
Alexandria, and he had rejoined them, while Dinwiddie set
Colonel Innes to building Fort Cumberland at Will's
Creek.

Dinwiddie ordered Washington to enlist more men and
try to set fire to the corn the French had planted. Washington answered with one of those appeals of which so many
were to be wrung from his aching pen. His recruiting was
going on backward:

"I again take the Liberty of recommending to your Honour the great necessity there is of a regulation in the Soldier's pay. . . . They are now Naked and can't get credit
even for a Hatt, and are teazing the Officers every Day.
. . . The Soldiers are deserting constantly, and yesterday,
while we were at Church, 25 of them collected and were
going off in Face of their Officers, but were stop'd and
Imprison'd before the Plot came to its full height.

"We have catch'd two Deserters, which I keep imprison'd
till I receive your Honour's answer how far the Martial
Law may be extended, and it is absolutely necessary that an
Example be made of some for warning to others; for there
is scarce a Night, or opportunity but what some or other are
deserting, often two or three or 4 at a time." [10]

Mutinies were going on in all the commands. Dinwiddie
had to get a friend to advance forty pounds to persuade a

North Carolina regiment to march at all.   Finally the North
Carolina troops "disbanded Themselves."

He wrote to Colonel Innes, "I find Mutiny is general in
Y'r regim't." [11]

Washington was crushed into such meekness at this time
that he permitted a little man to knock him down in a quarrel.   Then, instead of retaliating or challenging the fellow
to a duel, he apologized.

Washington was twenty-two, the scene was an election
hustings in the summer of 1754.   Elections were drunken
and riotous affairs then.   A quarrel arose between George
William Fairfax and the small but pugnacious William
Payne, who was afterwards an officer in the Revolutionary
Army, a fellow-vestryman in Washington's church and
eventually one of his pall-bearers.   A street in Alexandria
is named after him.

In spite of the fact that Parson Weems publishes the
story, it is well authenticated from other sources, and since
nobody quite rivals Weems in making priggishness delicious, let him tell it in his own way, and point the necessary
moral lesson:

"Washington, a thing very uncommon with him, became
warm; and, which was still more uncommon, said something that offended Payne; whereupon the little gentleman,
who, though but a cub in *size*, was the old lion in heart,
raised his sturdy hickory, and, at a single blow, brought our
hero to the ground.   Several of Washington's officers being
present, whipped out their cold irons in an instant: and it
was believed that there would have been murder off-hand.

"To make bad worse, his regiment, hearing how he had
been treated, bolted out from their barracks, with every
man his weapon in his hand, threatening dreadful vengeance on those who had dared to knock down their beloved
colonel.

"Happily for Mr. Payne and his party, Washington recovered, time enough to go out and meet his enraged soldiers: and, after thanking them for this expression of their love, and assuring them that he was not hurt in the least, he begged them, as they loved him or their duty, to return peaceably to their barracks.

"As for himself, he went to his room, generously chastising his imprudence, which had thus struck up a spark that had like to have thrown the whole town into a flame. Finding on mature reflection, that he had been the aggressor, he resolved to make Mr. Payne honourable reparation, by asking his *pardon* on the morrow!

"No sooner had he made this noble resolution, than, recovering that delicious gaiety which accompanies good purposes in a virtuous mind, he went to a ball that night, and behaved as pleasantly as though nothing had happened! Glorious proof, that great souls, like great ships, are not affected by those little puffs which would overset feeble minds with passion, or sink them with spleen!

"The next day he went to a tavern, and wrote a polite note to Mr. Payne, whom he requested to meet him. Mr. Payne took it for a challenge, and repaired to the tavern, not without expecting to see a pair of pistols produced. But what was his surprise on entering the chamber, to see a decanter of wine and glasses on the table! Washington arose, and in a very friendly manner met him; and gave him his hand. 'Mr. Payne,' said he, 'to err is nature: to rectify error is glory. I find I was wrong yesterday: but I wish to be right today. You have had some satisfaction: and if you think that sufficient, here's my hand; let us be friends.'

"ADMIRABLE youth! Noble speech! No wonder, since it charms us so, that it had such an effect on Mr. Payne, who from that moment became the most ardent admirer and friend of Washington, and ready at any time, for his sake, to charge up to a battery of two and forty pounders.

"WHAT a lesson for our young countrymen! Had Washington been one of the race of *little men*, how sadly different would have been his conduct on this occasion! Instead of going that night to the ball, and acting the lively and agreeable friend, he would, like an angry viper that had been trod on, have retired to his chamber. There he would have found no such entertainment as Washington had at this ball; no sprightly music, no delicious wines, no sweetly smiling friends. . . . The next morning would have seen him on the field, and in language lately heard in this state, calling out to his hated antagonist, *You have injured me, sir, beyond reconciliation: and by —— I'll kill you if I can.* While his antagonist, in a style equally musical and christian, would have rejoined, *Kill, and be ——!* Pop go the pistols—down tumbles one of the combatants; while the murderer, with knocking knees and looks of Cain, flies from the avenger of blood! The murdered man is carried to his house, a ghastly, bloody corpse. Merciful God! what a scene ensues! some are stupefied with horror! others sink lifeless to the floor! His tender sisters, wild-shrieking with despair, throw themselves on their dead brother and kiss his ice-cold lips; while his aged parents, crushed under unutterable woe, go down in their snowy locks broken-hearted to the grave.

"Thus bloody and miserable might have been the end of Washington or of Payne, had Washington been one of those poor deluded young men, who are determined to be *great;* and to be brought forward in *newspapers,* in spite of God or devil. But Washington was not born to exemplify those horrid tragedies, which *cowards* create in society by *pusillanimously* giving way to their bad *passions.*

No—he was born to teach his countrymen what sweet peace and harmony might for ever smile in the habitations of men, if all had but the *courage*, like himself, to obey the sacred voice of JUSTICE and HUMANITY. By firmly obeying these, he preserved his hands unstained by the blood of a fellow man; and his soul unharrowed by the cruel tooth of never-dying remorse. By firmly obeying these, he preserved a life, which, crowned with deeds of justice and benevolence, has brought more glory to God, more good to man, and more honor to himself, than any life ever spent since the race of man began."

Years afterward, George introduced Payne to his wife as "the little man . . . who had the resolution, to knock me down, big as I am." [12]

The Payne family long cherished the anecdote among its heirlooms and Bishop Meade encountered it eighty years later when Bishop Payne of Africa told him of finding a descendant of William Payne in Lexington, Kentucky, who was still repeating it. [13]

Bishop Meade waxes as eloquent over the anecdote as Weems, though in less eccentric style.

Following the complete collapse of Washington's military hopes, the resilient Dinwiddie was suddenly inspired to suggest that if Washington should quietly fill his vacant ranks and make a sudden dash on Fort Du Quesne, he might catch the French napping and retrieve his fame!

That would have been a consummation devoutly to be wished, but the despondent Washington had learned the danger of rash dashes, and in a long letter to William Fairfax he protested against Dinwiddie's impossible project and the paralyzing cold that would be encountered. He had had a taste of winter on his trip to the Ohio.

As for raising more men, he could not keep what he had. The mere rumor of the expedition "immediately occasioned a general clamour, and caused six men to desert last night." The same would happen every night. His almost naked men had no shoes, stockings or hats, and no credit.

"There is not a man that has a blanket to secure him from cold or wet." [14]

How like that sounds to the voice of Valley Forge years later!

August 20th, 1754, he writes to Dinwiddie, recommending "for one of the Vacancy's in the Virginia regiment" a Mr. Wright, whom he credits with "discovering an Inclination to the Art Military." He adds a kind word for the promotion of the poor wounded Frenchman, Mr. Peyronney, whose "behaviour has merited a reward from his Country (such he looks upon this to be)."

His request was granted and he received from the brave expatriate who was for some reason zealously fighting his own countrymen, a letter worth quoting for its devotion to Washington, and its picturesque English—though nobody seems to know who the woman may be that he refers to as one of Washington's flames. His allusion to Muse concerns Washington's military tutor, who seems to have been caught in a blue funk during the battle at Fort Necessity:

"As I imagine you By this time, plung'd in the midst of Dellight heaven can aford: & enchanted By Charms even Stranger to the Ciprian Dame. (+ M's Nel) I thought it would Contribue a litle to the variety of yours amusemens to send you a few lines to peruse.

"I Shan't make Bold to Describe the procedings of the house, which no doute you have had already Some hint of. I only will make use of these three expressions related to those of the oracle: furtim venerunt } invane Sederunt } & perturbate Redierunt }

"But all that is matere of indifference to the wirginia Regiment Collo. Washington will still Remain att the head of it, and I spect with more esplendor than ever: for (as I hope) notwithanding we will Be on the British stabichment, we shall be augmented to Six houndred & by those means entitle you to the Name not only of protector of your Contry But to that of the flower of the wirginians, By the powers you'll have in your hands to prove it So.——

"Many enquired to me about Muses Braveries; poor Body I had pity him ha'nt he had the weakness to Confes his coardise him self, & the impudence to taxe all the reste of the oficiers withoud exeption of the same imperfection.   for he said to many of the Consulars and Burgeses that he was Bad But th' the reste was as Bad as he:——

"To speak francly had I been in town at that time I cou'nt help'd to make use of my horse's wheap for to vindicate the injury of that vilain.

"he Contrived his Business so that several ask me if it was true that he had challeng'd you to fight: my answer was no other But that he should rather chuse to go to hell thand doing of it.   for had he had such thing declar'd: that was his Sure Road——

"I have made my particular Business to tray if any had some Bad intention against you here Below: But thank God I meet allowais with a goad wish for you from evry mouth each one enterting such Caracter of you as I have the honnour to do my Self who am the Most humble

"And Obediant of your Servants
"LE CHEVALIER DE PEYRONEY

"September 5, 1754

"his honour the Governor did Grand me the Capt. Comission after having been recomand to him from the house of Burgess and parlament and you Sir to whom I am infinitly oblig'd. . . ."

Poor Peyroney received his commission in good time to be killed on Braddock's field.

Washington has another complaint to make, and a bitter one.   Dinwiddie had sent to him a Mr. Campbell to help him out as his deputy in his grievous task of enlisting recruits for a naturally unpopular service; the soldiers when privately recruited were paid only once a year.   Their only pay thus far had been nakedness, hunger, defeat and distress.

To Washington's horror, and after all the noise he had made about receiving hardly more than half the pay of a royal officer of his rank, when he met Mr. Campbell, "I was not a little surpris'd to hear him say he was to have the Half of my Salary."

This was the climax of his grievances. He points out to Dinwiddie that Mr. Campbell is demanding far more than other officers pay for their deputies; furthermore, that his duty is much easier; furthermore, that he knows nothing of the duty he has undertaken; furthermore, that Washington can get much cheaper a man that he has taken great pains to teach himself. He signed himself "with all due regard, and imaginable respect." [15]

Dinwiddie's icy answer was to detach forty or fifty of Washington's hard-earned men and send them to Captain Lewis, who would use them to protect the frontier, taking along William Wright, whom he commissioned as ensign. He ordered Washington to march the few remaining of his men to Will's Creek "to join the other Forces in executing such Orders as I may see proper to direct." [16] This work was the filling up of the warehouse of the Ohio Company there and the erection of works "to secure the same." [17]

He confirmed Mr. Campbell's claim of £50, or half of Washington's pay as Adjutant-General. He scolded Washington for not sending in his pay-rolls, and with Scottish canniness, assumed that "there must be a great Saving from the Dead and Deserters."

But he had not been able to procure a proper allowance "for the poor Sick and Wounded." [18]

Thus Washington's handful of ragamuffins was absorbed in Colonel Innes's command at Fort Cumberland, and half of his uncollectable pay was given to a stranger.

And now the erstwhile commander of all the troops, the poor hero left out alone in the wilderness to break the advancing wave of the French, was the mere boss of a score of workmen under a superior officer, with winter coming on, the French closing in, and nothing but his own galled heart to eat.

Yet the doleful Dinwiddie was suffering worse handling from the House of Burgesses. He wrote to his fellow governor of Pennsylvania, "A Gov'r is really to be pitied in the discharge of his Duty to his King and Co't'y, in having to do with such obstinate, self-conceited People." [19]

Then suddenly he came into money. The Assembly voted him £20,000, "a handsome Supply." His joy lasted just long enough to make his chagrin comic: "On the 3d reading of the Bill they tac'd a ryder to it, viz: To pay 2,500£ to Payton Randolph Esq'r, their Agent, sent Home with a Complaint against me." [20]

This was a sardonic joke, indeed: to vote him a decent bit of money, then take a tenth of it to pay the expenses of a man whose mission was to unseat him. In his anger he prorogued them and sent them home to think it over.

Appealing from his unruly sheep to his transatlantic employers, Dinwiddie continued to urge the home government to believe that no dependence was to be placed on the colonies.

"I observe a general Infatuation in all the Assemblies on this Cont't; they are seiz'd with a lethargick Supineness, not regarding their own Safety or the Encroachm'ts of the French, they are now left to perpetuate their malicious Designs, and I dread our poor frontier Settlers this Winter." [21]

The President of North Carolina had raised twelve thousand pounds, and paid his private soldiers the monstrous sum of three shillings a day against the eightpence of the other colonial troops. The result was the expenditure of almost all the money, and the mutinous disbandment of the companies before they reached the front.

With such people to protect the realm, it was small wonder that Dinwiddie suspected the French of planning "a Gen'l Conquest of the B. Empire on this Con't," especially as the French naval plans were most ambitious.

He and the governors of North Carolina, and Maryland met and drew up a plan of military operations,[22] which included the appointment of Governor Sharpe of Maryland to the command in chief. This was agreed to by the King.

The General Assembly and the House of Burgesses convened again and exchanged compliments with the governor they distrusted as much as he distrusted them. The Burgesses reminded him that they were thinking of posterity, and "sh'd they ever be so unhappy as to groan under the galling Yoke of civil and religious oppression, it could not be the effect of Inactivity, Supineness, or Neglect in us, the faithful Guardians of their Liberty." [23]

Still, it was agreed that something must be done, the money was freed for Dinwiddie's use and the home government sent him ten thousand pounds in specie with the promise of ten thousand more. He even received from home the godsend of two thousand firearms.

The new-rich resolved to enlarge the army to ten companies and invented a neat way to prevent jealousies between the officers holding royal commissions and the colonials: he would simply give no colonial a higher rank than captain!

This ingenious device for reducing all the native officers beneath all the foreign officers roused Washington to a fury. His ferocity was not personal altogether, but resentment against the contempt for his native land as well. It involved, as Henry Cabot Lodge says, "the degradation of being ranked by every whipper-snapper who might hold a royal commission by virtue, perhaps, of being the bastard son of some nobleman's cast-off mistress." [24] Or, as Weems put it in his own way: "Hence the poorest shoat, if wearing the proud epaulette of a Briton, might command a Wolfe, if so unlucky as to be an American!!!"

In October, Washington resigned his commission, and would listen to no more of Dinwiddie's wheedlings, though all the other officers were persuaded to remain in the service until Dinwiddie should "hear from Home." He wrote to England beseeching the Ministry to send him blank commissions which should place the colonials on an equality with the royal commissions such as had been issued years before when Lawrence Washington had gone with the Virginia troops to Cartagena.[25]

Doubtless the knowledge of his brother Lawrence's royal commission stiffened Washington's wrath at the discrimination against him.

A few of the colonials had received both royal and colonial commissions, among them Governor Sharpe, now the commander-in-chief of all the American forces. In spite of his previous criticisms, Sharpe decided that he could use the "unmilitary" Washington. His second in command, Colonel Fitzhugh, offered Washington a company, and proposed that he keep his former commission as a colonel, though he would do only a captain's work.

This brought Washington up standing. He answered with thinly veiled courtesy:

"I think the disparity between the present offer of a company and my former rank too great to expect any real satisfaction or enjoyment in a corps, where I once did, or thought I had a right to, command. . . . If you think me capable of holding a commission that has neither rank nor emolument annexed to it, you must entertain a very contemptible opinion of my weakness, and believe me to be more empty than the commission itself. . . .

"I shall have the consolation of knowing, that I have

opened the way, when the smallness of our numbers exposed us to the attacks of a superior enemy; that I have hitherto stood the heat and brunt of the day, and escaped untouched in time of extreme danger; and that I have the thanks of my country, for the services I have rendered it. . . .

"I herewith enclose Governor Sharpe's letter, which I beg you to return to him, with acknowledgments for the favour he intended me. Assure him, Sir, of my reluctance to quit the service. . . . My inclinations are strongly bent to arms." [26]

He would not be tempted back into the army, but retired to Mount Vernon to brood over the crowded shames that had fallen upon him. As a reward for his hardships he had been invited to step down from colonel to captain!

He was already the George Washington who would not brook the thought of condescension from his fellow-Englishmen who lorded it overseas.

He tried to interest himself in dancing, flirting, hunting foxes, and fishing, but as the winter turned toward spring his heart hungered for war, he yearned to be in the uniform again. And he was embittered by the thought of the wrecked Ohio Company and all those beautiful acres in the possession of the cursed French.

As late as December twentieth of that year, he had still not collected the money due him. Dinwiddie wrote him curtly, with a hint of suspicion:

"Sir: I rec'd Y'r Letter, but at Pres't cannot order You the Money You say due you as Adjut't. W'n the Council meets, I shall let them know Y'r Dem'd, and if they agree with me, it will be p'd. I am, Sir, Y'r h'ble Serv't." [27]

On February 12th, 1755, Dinwiddie wrote to Lord Albemarle: "It 's true in the Capitulat'n after they make use of the Assassina'n, but Washington not know'g Fr. was deceived by the Interpreter. If he had not, he declares y't he w'd not have agreed to it, tho' then in great Straits.   The Interpreter was a Poltroon." [28]

He was no longer "Colo. Washington," plain "Washington."

By the tenth of March, Dinwiddie has abandoned him entirely and thrust all the blame on him.

"You know Washington's Conduct was in many Steps wrong, and did not conform to his Orders from me, or he had not engaged till the other Forces had joined him. However, now, I am in great Hopes something essential may be done if the Colonies join with Spirit in strengthening the Gen'l's Hands, and not be parcimonious." [29]

The General was Edward Braddock, who reached Virginia February 19th, 1755.

Great things had been going on since Washington resigned, and he had no part in them.   All the colonies were astir with promises to co-operate with the King, who had been gathering regiments in Ireland, and a real soldier to command them.

A real British army was to rescue the poor colonies from the greedy French.[30]   And Washington, the youth who had braved such perils with such young ardor, was only a farmer, seeking consolation for his military despair in his sole available diversion, the company of women.

XII

THE MYSTERY OF SALLY FAIRFAX

IF ever a man had need of woman's kindness, Washington needed it now. He was disgusted with the world of men. He had finished with "the Art Military." Being only twenty-two, it was perhaps natural that he should turn for comfort to an older woman. He had had enough of proposing to fourteen-year-old chits.

It is no longer questionable that at this time Washington began to yield his heart to the love of his life, who was the wife of his best friend—unless she herself had been his best friend.

The authority is Washington himself, who heaps up the evidence in many documents.

When the infatuation overcame him, how far it carried him, there is no knowing. There is no proof, and no reason to assume, that it went beyond wretched courtship on his part, and teasing yet tyrannical evasion on hers. But that it went that far it is mere obstinacy to deny.

To establish Washington's immunity to human emotions by calling him a liar or suppressing his own fervent protestations, would be twisting both ethics and admiration till they crack.

A Virginia woman, Mrs. Sally Nelson Robins (recently dead), compiled, as the National Historian of the Colonial Dames of America and the second vice-president of the Society in Virginia, a volume called *Love Stories of Famous Virginians*, and it was published under the auspices of that

176

society.   After devoting years of research, Mrs. Robins summed up the affair with Mrs. Fairfax as follows:

"The flame smouldered on and on, and perhaps was never extinguished even to the day of Washington's death.   After Sally married Fairfax, Washington was frequently at Belvoir and Mrs. Fairfax became his patron and instructress in the fine arts of courtesy and good breeding, while her brain, in its strength and flowering, matched his.   She rounded the angles of this sturdy, remarkable young man, and gave him the rare opportunity of mingling with the essence of refinement and culture.

"She enmeshed him with her charm and beauty, and while his affection for her, as he has it, was chaste, it was, probably, no less troublesome.   Again his congenital and marvelous restraint kept him absolutely from the semblance of mischief.   I consider his early romances but zephyrs to this one crimson whirlwind passion of his life." [1]

It has already been mentioned that Sarah Cary, in December, 1748,[2] married George William Fairfax, to whom Washington owed much of his tuition and opportunity as a surveyor, and at whose father's house, "Belvoir," Washington made a long visit during his recovery from his rejection by the Lowland Beauty.   Sally Cary was born in 1730, two years before George.   She was five years younger than her husband.

For a time, according to a disputed story, Sally's younger sister, Mary, consoled Washington so well that he tried to marry her, but lost her to Edward Ambler, as he lost his other loves to other men.   He lost Sally in advance of his love.

His endeavors in the field of war were no luckier.   He was not even lucky at cards.   His military reverses and disappointments kept him in such a frenzy as only those can realize who read his letters and his incessant threats to resign. It was inevitable that an old friend like Sally Fairfax should try to cheer him and persuade him that he was not the hopeless failure that he must have begun to think himself. But the consolation of jilted bachelors and heartbroken heroes is a most perilous charity for married women.

The name of Sally Fairfax did not really enter into Washington's history until 1886, when letters addressed to her by him were discovered and published, exciting much controversy, some horror, and flat denial that they were really to be attributed to her.

This last doubt has no longer any justification.

Sally Fairfax can not be ignored in Washington's life-story. She ought not to be. She deserves the honor of having a profound influence on the formation of his character. She stirred his heart more deeply than any other woman ever did. It was the tragedy of all his tragedies that in a youth, crowded with brave deeds that came to naught, and desperate endeavors that brought only defeat, his wandering heart should finally have settled upon the woman who had been his familiar counsellor for years, and whom he could not make his own because she belonged to his best friend, and would not, or could not, give her life to him.

It must have come upon them both with a devastating amazement, when he said or she read in his eyes:

"It is you I love! After all, I love you!"

For a man of his deep earnestness and high integrity this discovery could only have been terrifying and bewildering. Whatever her heart may have felt for him, there was no temptation to a breach with her husband and a union with Washington. Divorce was almost undreamed-of then, more unimaginable a solution than an airship as an escape from a trap. Sally doubtless tried to prevent her tremendous lover from making a knave of himself or an outcast of her.

There is no knowledge of just what Sally said or did or thought or wrote. But we know that Washington was in an alternation of joy and torment. His letters reveal the torment, and in the last years of his existence he wrote to her that the happiest moments of his life had been spent with her. And he underscored it heavily with an ancient fervor.

Sally Fairfax was a woman of education at a time when learning was available in a high degree to women. Few made the best of their opportunity, but those few shone.

The conditions of early Virginia were such that the men, unless they were educated abroad, had little inclination for reading, because of their outdoor activities in farming, hunting, and Indian-fighting. Their spare time was apt to be devoted to horse-racing, cock-fighting, dancing and drinking-bouts.

The women of the upper classes had slaves to wait upon them and were under no necessity to do the more brutal tasks of housekeeping. They were brought up gently and found both time and encouragement to keep abreast of the books, plays and periodicals that were fashionable abroad. None had better opportunity than Sally Fairfax.

She came of one of the best families of Virginia. Her great grandfather, Colonel Miles Cary of Warwick, the first to settle in America, was a member of the Long Parliament that elected Governor Berkeley in 1660. He was later a member of the King's Council; he built a fort where Fortress Monroe now is, and was killed in its defence from the attack of a Dutch fleet in 1667.

His son, of the same name, was educated abroad and became Surveyor-General of Virginia and collector of the Customs for York River—both positions bringing in a great revenue.

He sent his son to William and Mary College as soon as it was chartered, which was in 1693. Two years before, the

Burgesses had sent Commissary Blair to England to secure the charter, but he had a hard struggle with the Attorney-General, who did not want any waste of money on colleges when a war was going on. Mr. Blair pleaded:

"The people of Virginia have souls to be saved as well as the people of England."

"Souls!" cried the Attorney-General. "Damn your souls! Make tobacco!"

But King William and Queen Mary were more amenable, and the college was opened in their name. Since its foundation, five generations of Miles Carys have been on its rolls, including the Captain Wilson Miles Cary who took his Phi Beta Kappa Key there, and met an untimely death in 1916, after a life devoted largely to genealogical researches.

He left an unfinished monograph on the life of Sally Cary Fairfax, which was privately printed in 1916—with "some affectionate editing to piece it out from his notes and other family MSS." [3]

The frontispiece is a reproduction of Sally's portrait as it hangs at the present-day Belvoir. From the similarity of its pose, it might have been done by the same painter who stood Betsy Fauntleroy up so woodenly before him. But where Betsy is plump and stolid, Sally is singularly alert and lithe.

Her descendants still cherish a rich brocade dress of hers that can only be worn by one of slender figure.

In the portrait she stands in an orchard. Her pose is awkward and the drawing uncertain, her neck not fitting her shoulders. Perhaps she was too restless to hold one posture long enough for her joints to be fitted. Her attitude is constrained, her right hand across her waist. Her left hand, with the little finger stuck far out, holds a rose mincingly. Her gown is cut very low, her sleeves fall about her elbow. Her hair is parted a little to the left, and one tiny ringlet escapes at the right of the very high forehead of a very long face. She turns her head to the right and her eyes to the left, which gives her a quizzical look. Her upper lip is thin, her lower lip full. In spite of the artist's failure to realize her well, she looks intelligent, riantly cynical. On her face is the very expression of kindly amusement with which she must have teased the solemn young Washington to the frenzies he betrays in his letter.

Her father, the eldest son of the second Miles Cary, inherited one of the greatest estates of the time, his mother, Mary Wilson, being also wealthy. Her name was added to his own, so that he became Colonel Wilson Miles Cary— "colonel" being a civilian as well as a military title in that day. He studied at William and Mary College and then at Trinity College, Cambridge. Among his many estates he preferred "Ceelys" on the James River near Hampton and not far from Newport News.

Being on the river, his majestic and hospitable home was constantly visited by travelers whose ships came under his inspection as collector of the port.[4]

Colonel Cary had one son and four daughters and gave them every available advantage, including the season at the capital, gay little Williamsburg; for he was a burgess as well as nearly everything else in Virginia.

His wife was Sarah Pate, daughter of Colonel John Pate of Poropotank in Gloucester. Little is known of either. He is merely mentioned by Bishop Meade (I, 324) as a vestryman of Petsworth Parish, but the church is said to have been "perhaps too gorgeous for our republican simplicity." The altar cloth was imported at a cost of more than £150 and "much refinement and wealth were found in the numerous families who worshipped within the venerable church." One of the ministers was, not uncharacteristically, so unsatisfactory that he was suspended "until the next

shipping" of ministers, "in hopes of his future amendment."
He amended and remained for some years.

Of the four daughters of Colonel Cary, Sally, the eldest,
also "the cleverest and far the most fascinating," married
George William Fairfax; Mary married Edward Ambler;
Anne married Robert Carter Nicholas (the man that wrote
Washington about the mysterious girl and the snuff-box and
moved him to an "extatick paragraph"); Elizabeth married
Bryan Fairfax, half-brother to George William. Bryan was
a clergyman for a while, tried to keep Washington from
fighting the King, and finally succeeded to the title of Lord
Fairfax, so that Elizabeth became the Lady Fairfax that
Sally had expected to be.

In the home of the Carys was a library of remarkable
size and quality for a community so far from London.
Colonel Cary subscribed to the *Gentleman's Magazine*
among others, and imported the books that were praised in
its pages. Even after a fire had destroyed most of the
library, enough remained to show the intelligence in the atmosphere of the home. Sally must have taken full advantage of it, for her letters show that she could even write
French with skill.

She was a woman of wit and of pride, and of such an
honesty that when, in her old age in her long exile as an
aged widow, she was gradually deprived of both British
and American possessions by war and litigation, she could
still write concerning the desperate activities of a relative
to prevent the loss of wealth: "I never can think that any
kind of injustice can prosper, nor could I wish that anyone
that is dear to me should be stigmatized with any kind of
fraud, if by putting it in practice he could possess all the
land in England."

She was sought in marriage at the age of eighteen and

won by George William Fairfax, who was in the line for the title of Lord Fairfax, as the son of William Fairfax.

William Fairfax came of an ancient family that had led the Parliamentary troops against Charles I. William himself had entered the British navy as a boy. Later he was a judge of the admiralty courts, before whom the pirates of the Bahamas were brought. While in the West Indies he married for his second wife Sarah Walker, daughter of a major in the Royal Artillery. George William Fairfax was born of this union at Providence, Bahama Islands. Later there arose a ridiculous story that his mother was a negress, and in one of her letters Sally tells how serious the consequences of this gossip might have been, for a relative was about to bequeath a large property away from the rightful heir, and would have done so, as she writes, "from an impression that my husband's mother was a black woman, if my Fairfax had not come over to see his uncle and convinced him that he was not a negroe's son."

In view of his distinguished ancestry, this scandal was particularly annoying. It did not avail to prevent George William from becoming one of the most influential citizens of Virginia. He was a burgess and colonel of militia, and dwelt at Belvoir with his father, who was the agent for Lord Fairfax's six million acres.

It was George William Fairfax who gave Washington his first opportunity as a surveyor, and they went together into the unknown lands of the Shenandoah Valley. After that, when George visited Belvoir, he found Sally Fairfax installed there.

At that time she was the great personage and he the unlicked cub. He came of a good line, but he was little schooled except in roughing it, and he was earning his own living by running off boundary lines in all weathers in wild lands.

Evidently she saw in him something magnificent that could be marred or made. Perhaps she tried to save him from being a drunken roisterer and blustering soldier such as too many men were in that astonishing mixture of savagery and baronial luxury.

He must have seen in her the value of acquaintance with the fashions not only in clothes but in thought and speech as well. She may have read to him from books. In one of his letters he speaks of his longing to play *Juba* to her *Marcia*. *Juba* was the hero and *Marcia* the heroine of Addison's *Cato*, the tragedy that had such success, following its production in London in 1713, that it was considered better than any of Shakespeare's. It was performed at William and Mary in 1736 "by the Young Gentlemen of the College." After 1750 there were regular engagements of professional actors at Williamsburg.[5]

Washington may have seen a performance of *Cato* there; for he never missed going to the theatre when he had the chance.

It was the custom also in the country houses to read the published plays aloud, sometimes to act them. In any case, Washington must have been impressed by the character of *Juba*, a passionate soldier, like himself, who loved the beautiful *Marcia* in vain.

But Sally Fairfax was no blue-stockinged bookworm with a morbid prediliction for tragedies. She was a wife of such independence that when General Braddock came to America, she was one of the most active contestants for the privilege of his favor. The round-robin she wrote to Washington later shows her high and reckless spirit.

Those audacious women with the free tongues are often misinterpreted. Their mischief is apt to be all on the surface and beneath it may lie a heart of steely integrity.

She probably made fun of George Washington's ludicrous inability to keep a sweetheart from marrying another man. She may have flirted him out of the doldrums now and then.   What is more appealing to a woman than a broken-spirited, abused, misjudged and defeated male?   With a good and tender-hearted woman, a man is at his best when he is at his worst.

Eventually, Sally must have fallen pretty deeply into the romance, unless his letters are not to be believed.   She may have come to be afraid of him.   He could fly into appalling rages and sweep all before him.   She may have taught him some of that discretion and self-control that afterwards rarely failed to hold his passions in leash.

In any case, they dwelt together, in close communion. They were related vaguely by marriage.   Her husband's sister had married his brother Lawrence.   The Fairfaxes and Washingtons had been marrying into each other's families before they ever came to America.

So Sally and George were on terms of intimacy.   And what intimacy meant in some of those country houses on festive occasions can hardly be imagined now.

There is a description of such life in which the name of Washington frequently occurs.   The time is of a later date, the 1780's instead of the 1750's, but the informality was surely rather lessened than increased by the passage of time. Furthermore, it agrees so fully with the descriptions Colonel Byrd [6] gave of Virginia life in 1732 that it cannot be very different from the conditions in Washington's day.

For lack of an actual picture of his amusements in the eighteenth-century homes that young Washington knew, there is an undoubted replica of it in the life that his grandson, Corbin Washington, knew.

Corbin was the son of Washington's brother Jack, and he

married Richard Henry Lee's daughter Hannah. And Hannah was the granddaughter of Washington's early flame, Lucy Grymes.

Another son of Lucy Grymes was Thomas Ludwell Lee, and his daughter Lucinda kept a Diary [7] of her visit among the Washingtons and Lees. It is an astounding book and one of the most vivaciously accurate of social documents. Just such scenes have taken place since the world's beginning and surely young George Washington was no stranger to them. Certainly the atmosphere of kindliness, gaiety, hard drinking, hard dancing and the unflagging pursuit of happiness was no more absent from the air he breathed or the homes he visited than from those that Lucinda describes in the journal she kept for her friend Polly:

"I don't think I ever met with kinder, better People in my life; they do everything in their Power to make you happy. I have almost determined not to go to the races this Fall: every one appears to be astonished at [me], but I am sure there is no sollid happiness to be found in such amusements. . . . They laugh, and tell me, while I am mopeing at home, other girls will be enjoying themselves at races and balls.

(20th) "I have spent this morning in reading *Lady Julia Mandeville*, and was much affected. Indeed, I think I never cried more in my life reading a Novel: the stile is beautiful, but the tale is horrid. I reckon you have read it.

(22nd) "We have supped, and the gentlemen are not returned yet. Lucy and myself are in a peck of troubles for fear they should return drunk. Sister has had our bed moved in her room. Just as we were undress'd and going to bed, the Gentlemen arrived, and we had to scamper. Both tipsy!

(23rd) "To-day is Sunday. Brother was so worsted by the frolick yesterday, we did not set off to-day.

(October 3rd) "Cousin Nancy and myself have just returned from taking an airing in the Chariot. We went to Stratford: walked in the Garden, sat about two hours under a butifull shade tree, and eat as many figs as we could.

(9th) "I was in danger last night of commiting a great piece of rudeness; the Play Mr. Pinkard read us was the *Bell Strattagem.* Mr. Newton was by when it was read. Some one ask't him sometime afterwards what the Play was. He said the *Country Cousin.* I thought I should have burst with laughter!

(10th) "Mr. C. Washington returned to-day from Fredericksburg. You can't think how rejoiced Hannah was, and how dejected in his absence she always is. You may depend upon it, Polly, this said Matrimony alters us mightely. I am afraid it alienates us from every one else. It is, I fear, the bane of Female Friendship. Let it not be with ours, my Polly, if we should ever Marry. Adieu. Harriet calls me to supper. Once more good-by.

(11th) "Hannah and myself were going to take a long walk this evening but were prevented by the two horred Mortals, Mr. Pinkard and Mr. Washington, who seized me and kissed me a dozen times in spite of all the resistance I could make. They really think, now they are married, they are prevaliged to do any thing.

(13th) "How often do I think with rapture on the happy hours we spent sitting on the fence, singing and looking at the river with the Moon shining on it. Oh, how beautiful it look't! Adieu. . . .

(27th) "When we got here we found the House pretty full. Nancy was here. I had to dress in a great hurry for dinner. We spent the evening very agreeably in chatting. Milly Washington is a thousand times prettyer than I thought her at first, and very agreeable. About sunset, Nancy, Milly, and myself took a walk in the Garden (it is a most butifull place). We were mighty busy cutting thistles to try our sweethearts, when Mr. Washington caught us; and you can't conceive how he plagued us—chased us all over the Garden, and was quite impertinent.

"I must tell you of our frolic after we went in our room. We took it into our heads to want to eat; well, we had a large dish of bacon and beaf; after that, a bowl of Sago cream; and after that, an apple pye. While we were eating the apple pye in bed—God bless you! making a great noise —in came Mr. Washington, dressed in Hannah's short gown and peticoat, and seazed me and kissed me twenty times, in spite of all the resistance I could make; and then Cousin Molly. Hannah soon followed, dress'd in his Coat. They joined us in eating the apple pye, and then went out. After this we took it in our heads to want to eat oysters. We got up, put on our rappers, and went down in the Seller to get them: do you think Mr. Washington did not follow us and scear us just to death? We went up tho, and eat our oysters. We slept in the old Lady's room too, and she sat laughing fit to kill herself at us. She is a charming old lady—you would be delighted with her. I forgot to tell, Mr. Beal attended us here. I have been makeing Milly play on the forti-pianer for me; she plays very well. I am more and more delighted with her. She has just returned from the Fredericksburg races, and has given me a full account of them. . . .

(31st) "I have seated myself at Nancy's desk to scribble a little—interrupted already. It is Cousin Molly. She is come to propose dressing Mr. Pinkard in Woman's cloaths. I assent, so away goes the pen.

"Just as we had got Mr. Pinkard dress't, came Corbin, Hannah, and Nancy.

(November 1st) "Mr. Pinkard came in just now, and

like to have taken this from me, tho I luckily got it in my pocket before he could get it. . . .

(12th) "Well, my dear, they are come, and, as I expected, brought Flora with them. She is very genteal, and wears monstrous Bustles. Her face is just as it always was." [7]

An anonymous historian of the Cary family, discussing the incredibly rough manners of that period, says:

"Col. Byrd, the greatest fortune in Virginia, perpetrated jokes which were too coarse even to be hinted in one's secret chamber; especially one is related for which in that duelling age he deserved to be shot, but which was thought by his companions (they were not *our* kin) an admirable piece of practical humor and excited roars of laughter."

All over the nation and at home in England there was quite as much vice as in Virginia, perhaps more, because the hilarity, freedom and extravagance of the Virginia life gave a vent to emotions that in more Puritanical communities had no recourse but to sordid and vicious depravity. The Virginians knew how to play. And played!

In the Virginia *Gazette* for October 1737, is a prospectus of the festivities at a horse race where a pair of handsome shoes was to be a prize for dancing, and a pair of "handsome Silk Stockings of one Pistole value to be given to the handsomest young country maid that appears in the field." It was felt necessary to ask the visitors to be decent and sober and to warn them that the subscribers were "resolved to discountenance all immorality with the utmost rigor."

Washington must have gone innumerable times to just such affairs as the Government Ball at Annapolis in 1744, of which William Black, a Virginian, wrote:

"The Ladies of Note made a Splendant Appearance. In a Room Back from where they Danc'd was Several Sorts of Wines, Punch and Sweetmeats. In this Room those that was not engaged in any Dancing Match might better employ themselves at Cards, Dice, Backgammon, or with a cheerful Glass. The Ladies were so very agreeable and seem'd so intent on Dancing that one might have Imagin'd they had some Design on the Virginians, either Designing to make Tryal of their Strength and Vigour, or to convince them of their Activity and Sprightliness. After several smart engagements in which no advantage on either side was Observable, with a mutual Consent about 1 of the Clock in the Morning it was agreed to break up, every Gentleman waiting on his Partner home." [8]

That was part of the life that Washington led, and loved not least. He was particularly fond of horse-races, a better, a judge, eventually the steward of a jockey club, and a breeder of his own race-horses. Since there was always dancing going on, George and Sally must have danced together often and long; and for grace and insatiable ardor in the dance, Washington was famous. His idea of dancing is seen in his comparison of it to war as the "gentler conflict."

Those who are forced to admit that Washington loved to dance, often blandly assume that he never indulged in anything less stately than the minuet, or held a lady closer than her uplifted finger-tips. But the Virginians had their country dances, too, and jigs and kissing-dances, and as much hugging went on then as now. The prudes were as shocked and as denunciatory of the flying skirts and the wanton behavior as the critics of jazz are now. Horror was expressed even then, as of late, at the custom of leaving off corsets for the dance.

Most perilous of all were those Virginia moonlights, silvering the Potomac and giving the honeysuckle and the jasmine the mystic power of love-philters, not to mention the deep draughts of heady madeira in which the guests pledged the ladies, and the ladies drank to the pledge.

Since George Washington himself wrote himself down a tormented devotee of Mrs. Fairfax, let a better man than Washington destroy his confessions.   The rhapsody of the dance till dawn never wearied him.   The exultant frenzies of the fox-hunt and the horse-race kept him alert to his last years.

Washington did an amazing number of things amazingly well, but he never even tried to be a Puritan.   There was probably no name he would have resented more.

Just when George fell in love with Mrs. Fairfax there is no telling.   He had known her for nearly seven years now, and she was already having his shirts made for him, for about this time he wrote her the following letter:

"DEAR MADAM:

"John informs me that you told him Miss Nancy West was to be at your House in a day or two: and that you would, if I sent my Linnen over, give it to Miss Nancy to make:—I shall readily embrace the opportunity of doing this, tho' I am at the same time, sorry to give you the trouble about the directing of the making.

"I have sent a piece of Irish Linnen, a piece of Cambrick and a shirt to measure by.   The Shirt Fits tolerably well, yet, I would have the others made with somewhat narrower Wrist bands: Ruffles deeper by half an Inch: and the Collars by three quarters of an Inch, which is in other respects of proper bigness.   If Miss Nancy will do me the favour to get thread and buttons suitable it will oblige me much I have really forget to procure them myself. Please to make my Compts. to Miss Fairfax and Miss West when you see her.

"I am Dr. Madam

"Yr. most Obedt. Hble Servt

"G. WASHINGTON." [9]

Who Nancy West was, is a problem.   She might have been the sister of the Lieutenant John West, Junior, of the Virginia Regiment, to whom Washington entrusted the delivery to Dinwiddie of the prisoners taken in the Jumonville affair.

In those days, when there were no haberdashers, the girls and women of the best families took a pride in the making of the shirts for the men. The word "shirts" could be used in conversation or in a letter without thought of offence. Seventy-five or eighty years later, a pretended gentleman who wrote to a lady and included the word would have been regarded with horror as a foul-mouthed boor. It would have been as arrant an outrage as to refer to a woman as having legs.

Shirts still had to be made as legs had to be grown, but the sewing of shirts came to be considered as much a thing to be concealed as the nether limbs. Miss Martineau, visiting New York in 1835, includes in her *Society in America* a vivid dialogue showing the ardent efforts of a blushing, snickering girl caught making a shirt for her father, to disguise the nature of the work from a naughty young man who teased her with impertinent questions. The only effect of prudery, of course, is to extend the number of subjects out of which one can get the thrill of indecency, and the coquettes of the early nineteenth century could blush over shirts more easily than the sadly circumscribed girl of the Twentieth Century over such themes as birth-control and the complexes of repression.

But in Washington's times, early and late, there was nowhere in America the pitiful prudery that made the early Victorian fashions of dress and conversation so indecently "decent."

As a later letter signed by Sally Fairfax lightly proves, she was emancipated enough not only to superintend, and perhaps help make, Washington's shirts, but to allude carelessly to her own legs.

Life was frankly devoted to happiness in Virginia, and the literature and pastimes of the English cavalier court were the models followed as closely as possible by the upper classes, of whose females the London *Universal Spectator* had said in 1732, that they were "women at twelve, men at eighteen, and girls at fifty or sixty." [10]

The women rode to hounds, often in men's breeches. They dined and danced, and in the lightest of costumes, and gracious gallantry was the ideal of as many women as men.

The Virginia *Monitor* of October 15, 1736, includes a letter from one "Arabella Sly," who had witnessed at Williamsburg a performance of Farquhar's risky play, *The Beaux' Stratagem,* and having giggled at one scene received from a companion "a most terrible Hunch with her Elbow" and a warning to cover her face with a fan. This was followed by an essay on the folly of Prudishness.

Sally Fairfax's loyalty to her husband and her interest in George Washington, did not prevent her from competing with other married ladies for the attention of the notorious rake, General Braddock, who held a very gay court in Alexandria, a few miles from Belvoir and Mount Vernon, during the General's stay in that town.

And if George loved Sally Fairfax, his love was of the sort that resented another woman's victory over her, for a little later he sketched out a letter to her, in which he said:

"DEAR MADAM:
I have at last with great pains and difficulty discovered the reason why Mrs. Wardrope is a greater favorite of Genl. Braddock than Mrs. F——x, and met with more respect at the review in Alexandria. The cause I shall communicate, after having rallied you upon neglecting the means which produced the effect. And what do you think they were? Why, nothing less, I assure you, than a present of delicious cake and potted wood-cocks! which so affected the palate as to leave a deep impression upon the hearts of *all* who tasted of them. How, then, could the General do otherwise than admire, not only the *charms,* but the politeness, of this lady!" [11]

For some reason, he decided that he would not forward

this explanation, for he wrote against it in the letter book in which he kept the first draughts of most of his correspondence, "This letter was never sent."

Perhaps he had come to the wise conclusion that referring to a lady's social failure under any circumstances wants exquisiteness of tact. He was learning not to blunder so much among women's hearts. He was also getting back to his first love, soldiering.

For a time he must have endured anguishes of embarrassment in attending the dances and watching as a bystander the drills and reviews of the British soldiery arriving on the shores of Virginia to do with pomp and precision what he had so lamentably failed to do.

He was a nobody there, a man whose horrible non-success and whose undiplomatic "murder" had cast upon the British escutcheon the blot of assassinating the envoy of a nation with which it was at peace.

The French protestations of amazement had filled the English government with the double disgust of fiasco and savagery. War had not yet been declared, but the French alone seemed to think it necessary to pay even formal respect to the alleged truce, which both nations were making feverish preparations to violate at the exact moment.

The British, weary of the inability of the colonies either to agree among themselves or to maintain the narrowing frontiers of the Empire in America, resolved to end the farce once for all with a smashing blow.

The Duke of Cumberland, who had won fame on the battlefield of Culloden, replaced as Secretary of the Board of Trade the Duke of Newcastle, whom Hulbert flatters a little perhaps in calling him "as perfect an ass as ever held high office." [12]

In November, 1754, King George II persuaded Parliament to vote him four million pounds "to secure the duration of a general peace" by the practical device of increasing England's naval and land establishments.

This was merely the tricky disguising of a plan to send a crushing force to drive the French off the vague and contradictory map. For commander-in-chief, Cumberland selected Lieutenant-Colonel Braddock of the Foot Guards, the flower of the army. The commission, in that day when commissions were bought and sold, was rated at eighteen thousand dollars.

Braddock, like so many of England's generals, was of Irish birth, but not, of course, a Catholic. He was the son of Major-General Edward Braddock, and began his career as an ensign in the Coldstream Guards. He served in Flanders and shared the defeat of the British by the French and Irish at Fontenoy. His reputation was that of an incorrigible libertine, but, as a soldier, he was famous for being "greedy to lead" the way into danger, "a very Iroquois" of a fighter, what would be called today "hard-boiled" and a "roughneck."

Still, his character had its good points, and he paid himself one of the finest compliments an officer ever had, and did not boast when he paid it. He had appealed to an officer named Dury to spare a soldier sentenced to a flogging, and Dury had mocked him by asking him how long since he had laid aside his well-known brutality and insolence. Braddock answered:

"You never knew me insolent to my inferiors. It is only to such rude men as yourself that I behave with the spirit they deserve."

What better thing could a brave soldier, or any man in power, have said of him than that he was "never insolent to his inferiors"? And this was true of Braddock in America, though his name is a household word for faults he never revealed, and for things that never happened.

He was sent overseas with two regiments of British regulars, recalled from Ireland, where they had been mutinous. Their depleted ranks were to be filled with colonial volunteers. He landed in Virginia in February, 1755, "all in Health, not one Sick, w'ch is wonderful," said Dinwiddie, who rejoiced: "Gen'l Braddock came to my House last night, and I am mighty glad . . . for these 12 mo's past I have been a perfect Slave, and nothing but his M'y's Com'ds, National Service and the Good of these Colonies c'd have prevailed on me to undergo such Fatigue." [13] "The Fr [ench] are collecting all the Ind's they can, even to the West of the Mississippi, but if our Forces get over the Mount's and shew them some of our Coehorns, I doubt not but many of them will desert. . . . I have sanguine Hopes of Success after our Forces are marched, but Pensylva'a has behaved monstrously bad: the Assembly broke up with't grant'g us any aid." [14]

The great difficulty was to get Braddock and his big coehorns across the Alleghenies to show the Indians, even though the coehorn, named after its Dutch inventor, was only a light grenade-throwing mortar that four men could carry forward on the battlefield. But they could not carry such things all the way to the battlefield. Wagons and horses must be furnished by the colonies. They were promised with warmth, especially as they were to be well paid for. Immediately, the horse traders began to gather their sickliest nags and send them in to the army instead of the glue-works.

While Braddock was heartening Virginia, the French were sending the Marquis de Vaudreuil to Canada as governor to replace Du Quesne, with an army under the Baron Dieskau to offset Braddock's. The two hosts were not to meet, however, for Braddock was to move by way of the Monongahela to the Valley of the Ohio, and Dieskau by the valley of the St. Lawrence to Lake George.

The friendly British fleet tried to cut off the friendly French fleet, but did not quite succeed. While Braddock was recapturing Fort Du Quesne, Governor Shirley of Massachusetts was to capture Niagara, and Sir William Johnson to take Crown Point. All of them failed,—though Dieskau was captured. The only success was the seizure of Acadia by a force from New England.

Braddock, on his arrival, ran immediately into the pleasant refusal of the colonies to agree on anything. His best route would have been by way of Pennsylvania, but the London Quaker, Hanbury, who was a stockholder in the Ohio Company, used his pull at Court to have him ordered up the Potomac, so that the Ohio Company could profit by the business involved. Governor Dinwiddie, another stockholder, seconded this heartily. It was a fatal mistake, though Washington preferred the Virginia route, being also interested in the Ohio Company.

Pennsylvania, having lost the trade to Virginia, lost interest and would not help. The northern colonies had expeditions of their own to supply.[15]

Virginia was doing its best, and the Council addressed the Governor in terms of unwonted cordiality:

"The Forces w'ch H. M'y has been graciously pleased to send over to our Assistance, is a fresh Instance of His royal Care . . . we may reasonably hope to see the Peace of America settled upon Foundat'n y't will not be shaken for ages yet to come. To drive the Fr. from our Borders, to maintain the just rights of the Crown, and to re-establish the Tranquility of the British Empire in No. America, are Views y't must warm the Patriot's Breast. . . . The Great and important Business of the Ohio, we have always considered in a national Light, not as Virginians, but as Britons; and w't will not a Briton surmount, w't Dangers will he not encounter when he is engaged in the Glorious Cause of His King and Country?" [16]

The words have a strange sound now, and they took on a strange sound shortly after they were written.

While all this springtime fervor was in the air with its promise of glorious Summer, George Washington had nothing better to do than to tag after Sally Fairfax, watch the fine straight lines of the British regulars swing past, and hear other voices than his own sing out commands and set the bugles to chanting.

That is torture to any soldier, and it must have been visible in his sad blue-gray eyes. He had written a letter of congratulation to Braddock on his arrival, and he could have gone along as a captain, but he had been a colonel and he would rather die and let the country die than swallow his pride another time.

His yearning must have been brought to the notice of General Braddock. Perhaps Sally Fairfax murmured to him that the finest young officer in Virginia was wasting himself in idleness, the very man who had gone out to the very fort which Braddock was to take, had held his post at Fort Necessity in the face of swarming French and Indians until he had been outnumbered two to one, and even then had compelled them to let him march out with drums beating; the brilliant surveyor who knew the unknown country and made maps that were perfection.

She may have warned the General that the ex-colonel would accept no further humiliation. He had drunk his fill of that.

At any rate, one golden day, Washington was lifted to heaven by the receipt of this letter from the charming Captain Robert Orme, one of Braddock's two personal aides (the other being the charming Captain Roger Morris):

"The General, having been inform'd that you exprest some desire to make the Campaigne, but that you declin'd it upon the disagreeableness that you thought might arise from the Regulation of Command, has order'd me to acquaint you that he will be very glad of your Company in his Family, by which all Inconveniencies of that kind will be obviated.

"I shall think myself very happy to form an acquaintance with a person so universally esteem'd, and shall use every opportunity of assuring you how much I am, Sir, your most obedient servant.
                    "ROBERT ORME, aid de Camp.[17]
"Williamsberg, Mch. 2d, 1755."

To this the hungry Washington, restraining his delight, replied with dignity, honesty and grace two weeks later:

                    "Mount Vernon, 15 March, 1755
"Sir, I was not favored with your polite letter of the 2d inst., until yesterday; acquainting me with the notice his Excellency, General Braddock, is pleased to honour me with, by kindly inviting me to become one of his family the ensuing campaign. It is true, Sir, that I have, ever since I declined my late command, expressed an inclination to serve the ensuing campaign as a volunteer; and this inclination is not a little increased, since it is likely to be conducted by a gentleman of the General's experience.

"But besides this, and the laudable desire I may have to serve, with my best abilities, my King and country, I must be ingenuous enough to confess, that I am a little biassed by selfish considerations. To explain, Sir, I wish to attain some knowledge in the military profession. . . . I shall beg your indulgence while I add, that the only bar . . . is some proceedings which happened a little before the General's arrival, and which, in some measure, had abated the ardor of my desires, and determined me to lead a life of retirement, into which I was just entering at no small expense when your favour was presented to me.

"But, as I shall do myself the honor of waiting upon his Excellency . . . I shall decline saying anything further on this head till then.

"You do me a singular favour, in proposing an acquaintance. It cannot but be attended with the most flattering prospects of intimacy

on my part. . . . I shall endeavour to approve myself worthy of
your friendship. . . ." [18]

On learning that Washington was tampering with fate
again, his distracted mother, who always abhorred war as
much as her son loved it, dashed over to Mount Vernon to
plead against his infatuation. She pleaded in vain.

To match the earlier anecdote of her pious words when
he first went out to fight, the story is told that he answered
her now:

"The God to whom you commended me, Madam, when
I set out on a more perilous errand, defended me from all
harm, and I trust he will do so now; do you not?" [19]

It may be believed that if she ever made the first remark,
he made the pious retort. But both have the smell of the
myth-mint.

The Washington who could have rebuked his tormented
mother with such priggishness does not sound like the gay
young man who wrote at once to Captain Orme:

"The arrival of a good deal of company (among whom is
my mother, alarmed at the report of my intentions to attend
your fortunes) prevents me the pleasure of waiting upon
you today. . . .

"I find myself much embarrassed with my affairs, having
no person in whom I can confide, to entrust the management
of them with. Notwithstanding, I am determined to do myself the honor of accompanying you, upon this proviso, that
the General will be kind enough to permit my return, as soon
as the active part of the campaign is at an end. Colonel
Fairfax . . . sends his blessings to you and desires that by
being a good boy you may merit more of them. . . . I herewith send you a small map of the back country, which,
though imperfect and roughly drawn, for want of proper instruments, may give you a better knowledge of the parts

designated than you have hitherto had an opportunity of acquiring." [20]

The sight of one of Washington's beautiful maps must have clinched the matter.

General Braddock was gracious enough to accede to all Washington's conveniences. Captain Orme wrote that the General's "wishes are to make it agreeable to yourself . . . whenever you find it necessary to return, he begs you will look upon yourself as entire master." [21]

So Washington accepted service without any commission at all. Writing to his friend John Robinson, the Treasurer of the colony, he said:

"I may be allowed to claim some merit if it is considered that the sole motive, which invites me to the field is the laudable desire of serving my country, and not the gratification of any ambitious or lucrative plans. This, I flatter myself, will manifestly appear by my going a volunteer. . . . I expect to be a considerable loser in my private affairs by going." [22]

He explained that he had previously lost "50 odd pounds" as paymaster, as well as valuable papers, clothing, horses and other things he had forborne to mention, "as I knew you were greatly pestered with complaints of this sort from officers that were less able to bear them."

Before Washington was ready, Braddock, helplessly following the bad advice of others, had marched on to Frederscktown "by way of Winchester . . . which gave him a good opportunity to see the absurdity of the route, and of damning it very heartily . . . the absurdity of it was laughable enough," wrote Washington. [23]

General Braddock had bought a chariot and six from Governor Sharpe, and he made the journey in state, riding in a carriage while he could. He even took one review in his carriage, inspecting the troops to the crack of the whips of his outriders. He would get enough of the saddle later.

In the meanwhile, Washington was closing up his affairs and giving farewell orders to his overseers and the black and white servants. He had left Mount Vernon April 23rd.

On the previous December 17th he and Lawrence's widow, now Mrs. Lee, and her husband, had given him a deed of life interest in Mount Vernon, for which he was to pay Anne Lee fifteen thousand pounds of tobacco a year or its equivalent in cash. It meant £93:15 in 1755, and a little less thereafter till her death in 1761 released him from the tax.

On his way to Fredericktown, Washington, in his final survey of his business interests, paused at one of his plantations called "Bullskin." He had patented it in 1748, paying for it by surveying its five hundred acres of unimproved land. In 1750 he had bought 456 acres for 112 pounds. In 1752 he had added to his Bullskin property 552 acres, for 115 pounds, and five years later, he bought "Dogue Run," 500 acres for 350 pounds.[24] With Mount Vernon he thus had over four thousand acres to care for with white and slave labor, and there was reason for his plea that he be allowed a little time before his departure, perhaps to death.

But he was not afraid of death. Love was his chief perplexity, and while at Bullskin he toiled over a letter to Sally Fairfax.

Nothing but a photograph could do justice to his mental chaos as he tried to indite a discreet yet devoted expression.[25] Yet the mere transcription of his words as they appear in his copy book is more eloquent than he was. As a portrait, or at least a sketch, of his soul in action, it may be amusing to try to reproduce this letter as it appears in his original draught with all its scratchings-out and its indecipherable words marked by x's:

WASHINGTON'S FIRST DRAFT OF A LETTER TO SALLY
FAIRFAX.

"To Mrs. Fairfax—Belvoir
"DEAR MADAM

In order to engage your corrispondance I think it ~~expedient~~ is incumbent on me to xxxxx to deserve it, which I shall ~~endeavour~~ to do, by embracing the earliest, and every opportunity of writing to you.

"It will be needless to ~~expatiate~~ dilate [?] on the pleasures that a ~~communication~~ corrispondance of this kind ~~will~~ would afford me ~~as it should~~ let it suffice to say—a corrispondance with my Friends is the greatest satisfaction I expect to enjoy in the course of this Campaigne, and that ~~none of my Friends could afford~~ xxxxx from none shall I derive such satisfaction as from you—for to you I stand indebted for ~~so many~~ many Obligations.

"If an old Proverb xxxxx will apply to my case I shall certainly close with xxxxx success—for ~~surely~~ no Man xxxxx could have made a worse beginning than I have done: out of 4 Horses which xxxxx I brought from home, one ~~was~~ I have kill'd outright, and the other 3 are renderd unfit for use; so that I have been detaind here three days already, and how much longer I may continue to be so—~~the~~ xxxxx ~~of~~ time ~~must~~ only can discover.

"I must beg my Compliments to Miss ~~Hannah~~ Fairfax, Miss Dent, and ~~any~~ other's that think me worthy of their enquirys.

"I am Madam
                    "Yr. most Obedt Servt,
                              "GO. WASHINGTON.
"Bullskin, Apl)
the 30th 1755)"

Washington had asked that the loneliness of camp-life might be mitigated by letters from women. Two agreed to write to him. Sally Fairfax is known to have been one of them.

Sally Fairfax later asked him to send his letters to her through another person. And that was odd. The person was his younger brother.

In a little book of Washington's, in which he kept copies of what he called "Epistles to Ladies," some of his letters to her were found. Others have turned up at long intervals in strange places and caused much debate.

Finally, George Washington, "after a very fatiguing ride and long roundabout," reached Braddock's army and was received cordially. As he wrote to his beloved younger brother "Jack," or John Augustine, "I am treated with freedom not inconsistent with respect, by the General and his family; I have no doubt, therefore, but I shall spend my time more agreeably than profitably, during the campaign, as I conceive a little experience will be my chief reward." He also announced that he hoped to "please without ceremonious attentions or difficulty." [26]

His new position was formally announced in a general order of May 10th, 1755: "Mr. Washington is appointed Aid-de-Camp to His Excellency General Braddock."

XIII

HE GOES TO WAR AGAIN

MR. WASHINGTON was, if not the only gay person about the camp, certainly the gayest. All the surprises and hardships that were maddening the British were old stories to him.

Hardly more than a third of Braddock's age, and with one year of war to the old general's forty odd, Washington was the veteran in these woods and Braddock the raw recruit. The young man did not hesitate to give advice amounting almost to orders, and the old general had to admire his information, though he cursed his impudence.

Their very moods were opposite. Braddock was as morose as King Saul and Washington as lyrical as David. King Saul threw a javelin twice at David, but Braddock never cast anything sharper than a little profanity at Washington.

Braddock was the better prophet of the two, and felt himself under a curse, but Washington had entered the campaign in high spirits, regretting only that there was no prospect of fighting!

He insisted that the French would be kept too busy in the north by General Shirley to cause Braddock any trouble: "As to any danger from the enemy, I look upon it as trifling," he wrote his brother Jack, and rejoiced in being a member of Braddock's staff instead of a line or field officer, since he was "thereby freed from all commands but his, and give his orders to all, which must be implicitly obeyed."

He was so exalted that he took thought of his costume, which must be of the latest: "As wearing boots is quite the mode, and mine are in a declining state, I must beg the favor of you to procure me a pair that is good and neat." He adds the highly significant paragraph, "I have wrote to my two female correspondents by this opportunity, one of which letters I have enclosed to you, and beg your deliverance of it." [1]

He referred doubtless to Sally Fairfax and probably to a Mrs. Spearing. The letter to Sally Fairfax has been already quoted, concerning Mrs. Wardrope's victory over her. Now Washington's notebook says that neither the letter to Mrs. Fairfax nor the one to Jack was ever sent. And this creates a wisp of mystery.

He had evidently an understanding with Jack, who was now nineteen, and living at Mount Vernon.

In the undelivered letter to Sally, Washington had said that he had "at last with great pains and difficulty discovered the reason why Mrs. Wardrope is a greater favorite of Genl. Braddock than Mrs. F——x."

Many things must, therefore, have been talked about in the camp besides strategy. He added with light sarcasm:

"We have a *favourable* prospect of halting here three weeks or a month longer, for waggons, horses and forage; it is easy to conceive, therefore, that my situation will not be very *pleasant* and *agreeable*, when I dreaded this (before I came out) more than all the other incidents which might happen during the campaign." [2]

This delay was driving Braddock into inevitable, ungovernable and excusable rages against the colonies for their failure to regard their pledges.

The forty-nine-year-old Benjamin Franklin, then postmaster-general of Pennsylvania—what was he not?—added to his incredible versatility and efficiency by hastening to Braddock's presence and promising to find him a hundred and fifty wagons and enough horses to pull them. Franklin used, not only his influence, but his personal credit in keeping his promise, and Braddock wrote of his splendid achievement as unique among Americans. The Pennslyvania Assembly voted him thanks, but that was all, and a few months later the owners of the wagons and horses made a demand upon Franklin for almost twenty thousand pounds. His extreme embarrassment was finally relieved by Governor Shirley.

Americans think of Franklin as a lad who entered Philadelphia and was laughed at, as a man who flew a kite and edited an almanac. There is almost universal ignorance concerning his immense and vital influence in the cause of union and independence while Washington was young, ignorant, and a mere sophomore in life, war and politics.

One reason for Franklin's failure to be revered as one of the major gods of America (though the French put him among the four or five greatest men of all time) was that Franklin had to do almost everything with a joke. Washington's jokes are as rare and as rarely amusing as scriptural humor; hence people who consider wit incompatible with wisdom or heroism, deify him and suspect such noble and benevolent figures as Voltaire and Franklin.

Even the matter of getting Braddock his horses had to be done farcically by the irrepressible Franklin. Knowing how the Pennsylvania German immigrants had been panic-stricken at the thought of the Hussars at home, he led them to believe that Braddock's quartermaster-general, Sir John St. Clair, was a Hussar. To his own promises of personal liability for the money he added the hint that "he supposed that Sir John St. Clair, the Hussar, with a body of Soldiers," would come and confiscate what he wanted if he were kept waiting. The horses and wagons were delivered at as near breakneck speed as the necessity for cutting roads would permit.[3]

While Franklin was humorously risking bankruptcy, and the jocund Washington was going out for what he supposed would be a mere parade, and the governors were doing little but rub their hands in anticipation of the surprise-party preparing for the French, the only man in America who seemed to take the situation as seriously as it deserved was Braddock.

It enraged him to foresee disaster and to find himself tied hand and foot and blindfolded by the lying, cheating, greedy, jealous and phlegmatic colonials. When Washington later found himself in Braddock's plight, he became no less frantic.

As Braddock floundered helplessly in the wilderness, he learned what Dinwiddie had been taught again and again: the colonies preferred destruction to co-operation.

It is a disgrace that the schoolbooks and other popular histories should give American posterity the idea that Braddock was a blundering fool among a company of saints. He was a brave and brilliant soldier in a new world whose hardships compelled selfish jealousy, and corruption; and incapacity and inexperience were common even among the honest. Braddock was whipped before he landed.

Washington himself had written: "You may with (almost) equal success attempt to raise the dead as the force of this country." [4] He knew the conditions from having been already defeated by them, and had inveighed against them as strongly as Braddock ever did. But it is one thing for a native to denounce his country, and quite another to hear a foreign visitor denounce it. Nothing inflames patriotism like alien statement of indisputable facts. Patriotism is then the only refuge of either scoundrel or honest partisan. So Washington felt called upon to defend the colonials from the General's wholesale denunciations, even at the cost of insubordination. He must have held up his end, for as he wrote to William Fairfax:

"The General, by frequent breaches of contract, has lost all patience; and, for want of that temper and moderation, which should be used by a man of *sense* upon these occasions, will, I fear, represent us in a light we little deserve; for, instead of blaming the individuals, as he ought, he charges all his disappointments to publick supineness, and looks upon the country, I believe, as void of honour and honesty.

"We have frequent disputes on this head, which are maintained with warmth on both sides, especially on his, who is incapable of arguing without, or giving up any point he asserts, let it be ever so incompatible with reason or common sense." [5]

The fact that Braddock would permit his young aide to wrangle with him at all, is proof less of his bullying contentious nature than of the democracy of his rule. He always treated Washington with respect and with deepening affection. His informality was amazing. "He uses and requires less ceremony than you can easily conceive," Washington wrote his brother Jack. [6]

An old, old man who went along with Braddock's expedition, and remembered the roads they cut through the forests and paved with logs, the howling of the wolves, the flare of the campfires of the watchful Indians, remembered, above all, Washington's arguments with Braddock to the very last. He described how Washington, in his blue uniform and cocked hat, "put his two thumbs up into the armpits of his vest," bluntly contradicted and brutally instructed his general. And all Braddock did was to growl: "What think you of this, from a young hand—from a beardless boy!" [7]

He was sixty and Washington twenty-three, and the old man doubtless had a twinkle in his eye as he made his pathetic complaint of being browbeaten. Rather than be insolent to his inferior, he permitted his inferior to be insolent to him, and did not cashier the youth.

Washington really loved Braddock and there is reason to believe what one William Findley said that Washington said to him long after:

"Braddock was unfortunate, but his character was much too severely treated. He was one of the honestest and best men of the British officers with whom I was acquainted; even in the manner of fighting he was not more to blame than others." [8]

Washington, it is known, was so indignant at the Pennsylvanian desertion of Braddock at the time as to declare that they ought to be chastised for their insensibility to danger and disregard of their sovereign's expectation. [9]

The Virginians did not love the Pennsylvanians, nor the Marylanders, who did not love them.

The desponding Braddock wrote home:

"The £20,000 voted in Virginia has been expended tho not yet collected; Pennsylvania and Maryland still refuse to contribute anything." He wrote again that his total force amounted to "about two thousand effective Men, eleven hundred of which Number are Americans of the southern provinces, whose slothful and languid Disposition renders them very unfit for Military service. . . . Mr. Franklin has executed [his task] with great punctuality and Integrity, and is almost the only Instance of Ability and Honesty I have known in these provinces. . . . It would be endless, Sir, to particularize the numberless Instances of the Want of public and private Faith, and of the most absolute Disregard of all Truth."

He tells how the Governor of Virginia gave him a contract to deliver 1100 Beeves for his troops and charged it against his credit. Then the contractors informed Braddock that the Assembly "had refus'd to fulfill the Governors Engagements, and the Contract was consequently void."

Braddock offered to advance the money himself, but the

contractors said the beef would now cost him one-third more and would take two months longer—by which time it would not be needed.

The agent for Maryland delivered her provisions in such shape that they had to be condemned altogether and Braddock had to send a hundred miles to get more.

The English found Alexandria a bad place for troops, according to Captain Orme, who wrote in his Journal, "The General was very impatient to remove the troops from Alexandria, as the greatest care and severest punishments could not prevent the immediate [immoderate?] use of spirituous liquors. . . . It was ordered that no suttler should dare to sell any more spirits than one gill a day to each. . . ."

An order was issued: "If any Soldier is seen drunk in Camp, he is to be sent immediately to the Quarter Guard, and to receive two hundred lashes the next morning."

But as Washington found out all his life long, the American soldiers could not be kept sober by any amount of whipping.

Of the Virginian recruits Orme says that "they had been well drilled, but their languid, spiritless and unsoldierlike appearance considered with the lowness and ignorance of most of their officers gave little hopes of their good behaviour."

For this bad opinion the Americans took full revenge later.

Braddock had been promised great numbers of Indian allies. He lost them all "through the Misconduct of the Government of Virginia: And indeed the whole Indian Affairs have been so imprudently and dishonestly conducted, that it was with the greatest difficulty I could gain a proper Confidence with those I have engag'd. . . .

"The Difficulties we have to meet with by the best Accounts are very great: the Distance from hence to the Forts

[on the Ohio] is an hundred and ten miles, a Road to be
cut and made the whole way with infinite Toil and Labor,
over rocky Mountains of an excessive Height and Steepness,
and many Stoney Creeks and Rivers to cross." [10]

It is quite too outrageous that posterity should continue
to be as unjust to Braddock as his contemporaries were.

If Braddock was dispirited, so were his officers and his
men. They did not find Virginia a paradise, or the people
angels. It was from the report of one of the officers on this
expedition that the quotation was made in the first chapter,
beginning, "I reckon the Day I bought my Commission the
most unhappy in my Life, excepting that in which I landed
in this Country." [11]

This writer was revolted by the climate, the whites, the
blacks, the food, the drink, the city folk and the settlers in
the cow-pens.

He describes the British soldiers as more mutinous than
they had been even in Ireland, where they had been tainted
by "Pamphlets and Conversation" into believing that they
had the right to criticize both the ministry and their officers.
They even went so far as to "say they are free Englishmen
and Protestants, and are not obliged to obey Orders if they
are not fed with Bread, and paid with Money: now there
is often only Bills to pay them with, and no Bread but Indian Corn. . . .

"The General himself, who understands good eating as
well as any Man, cannot find wherewithal to make a tolerable Dinner of, tho' he hath two good Cooks who
could make an excellent Ragout out of a Pair of Boots, had
they but Materials to toss them up with; the Provision in
the Settlements was bad, but here we can get nothing but
Indian Corn, or mouldy Bisket. . . . We are happy if we
can get some rusty salt Pork. . . .

"We have not as yet had one Man killed by Lightening,

but we have had several died by the Bite of Snakes, which are mortal, and abound prodigiously in the Swamps, through which we are often forced to march."

Almost worse was the tick, or forest bug, that set up such an itch as "makes one ready to tear off the Flesh."

The General tried to allay the dread of the Indians by saying that "where the Woods are too thick so as to hinder our coming at them, they will hinder their coming at us."

In the camps of that time, whether under Washington or Braddock, the sound of the lash was almost more characteristic than the sound of the drum, and this officer speaks vividly when he says:

"The mutinous Spirit of the Men encreases, but we will get the better of that, we will see which will be tired first, they of deserving Punishments, or we of inflicting them."

Two men received a thousand lashes each for theft.

At last Braddock announced to the Virginians that if wagons and provisions did not arrive in two days, he would turn back. He had given the order when "there arrived five Quakers decently dressed, they were pure plump Men, on brave fat Horses, which, by the way, were the first plump Creatures I had seen in this country."

They announced that they had been cutting roads to let the wagons through with their burden of flour, cheese, bacon and the like.

"It was ominous, your Cheese and your Bacon being the Baits that draw Rats to Destruction, and it proved but too true; this Bait drew us into a Trap where happy was he that came off with the Loss of his Tail only."

One Quaker, however, being a man of peace, tried to scare Braddock out of the war by telling him not only of the perils, but "that the Country was not worth keeping, much less conquering. . . .

"Some of the Braggadocio Virginians, who last Year ran

away so stoutly, began to clamor against the Quakers and the General, so we marched."

But they marched without the Indians, and the first disaster was the loss of these allies, on whom Braddock had depended for all his scouting and the protection of his advance.

Dinwiddie and Gist had promised Braddock four hundred Cherokee and Catawbas, but not one came. The Six Nations were aiding Governor Shirley in the North and the Ohio Indians were cowed by the French, who stood between them and Virginia. Croghan delivered to Braddock a hundred Indians, and Braddock gave him a commission.

But many of the Indians insisted on bringing their women and children to the war with them. There the trouble began. The Indians were disgusted because the British did not consult the chiefs but did consult the squaws;—"their Squas bringing them money in Plenty which they got from the Officers, who were scandalously fond of them." [12]

The Indians were at first overwhelmed by the gorgeousness of the British uniforms and the irresistible scarlet. The discipline of the troops, who were drilled with care, impressed the savages. During idle afternoons the officers had horse races.

Then the Indians took their turn at entertainment. The bucks terrified the British troops by their fierce dances, their demoniac yells, their painted bodies and the all-too-vivid pantomime of the tomahawk and the scalping knife.

Braddock, in his instructions, had been ordered by the Duke of Cumberland to be "particularly careful that the troops be not thrown into a panic by the Indians, with whom they are yet unacquainted." [13] But familiarizing the soldiers with the savages rather tightened than quieted their nerves.

Among the Indians were some of Washington's acquaintance. The Half-King was dead and Braddock expressed his grief for the loss, not forgetting to pass round the rum. Monacatoocha (or Scarroyady) was there, also White Thunder, whose daughter, called Bright Lightning, led a dance of the women after which they threw themselves into the arms of the red uniforms.

Thirty sailors had been detailed to the troops to act as pioneers and engineers and to work four cannon sent by Admiral Keppel. In a Journal [14] supposed to have been kept by one of them, but probably written by Engineer Gordon, there are quaint impressions of the effect upon the English of the Indian orgies:

"May 14th: Inactive in our Camp. I went to the Indian to see them Dance which they do once or twice a Year round a Fire, first the Women dance, whilst the Men are Sitting, and then every Woman takes out her Man; dances with him; lays with him for a Week, and then Returns to her proper Husband, & lives with him. . . . The General Assured them of his Friendship and gave his Honour, that he never would deceive them, after which they sung their Song of War, put themselves into odd postures, wth Shouting and making an uncommon Noise, declaring the French to be their perpetual Enemies, which they never had done before, then the General took the Indians to the Park of Artillery, Ordered 3 Howtz^{rs}. 3:12 pounders to be Fired, the Drums beating & Fifes playing the point of War, which astonish^t but pleased the Indians greatly. they afterwards Retired to their own Camp to eat a Bullock and Dance in their usual manner, with shewing how they fight and Scalp, and expressing in their Dance, the exploits & Warlike Actions of their Ancestors and themselves—Arrived 80 Waggons from Pensylvania with Stores; and 11 likewise from Philidelpha with Liquors, Tea, Sugar, Coffe &c. to the Amount of 400£ With 20 Horses, as presents to the Officers of the 2 Regiments—An Indian came in 6 days from the French Fort, and assured us they have only 50 Men in the Fort, however they expected 900 more soon, yet they purpose blowing it up whenever the Army Appears—as this Indian was one of the Delawars, who never were our Friends he was suspected to be a Rogue. . . ."

An even more dramatic account is given by the anonymous officer previously quoted.[15]

"This as every Thing in this Country is, was in the Stile of the Horrible; the Sal de Ball was covered with the Canopy of Heaven, and adorned with the twinkling Stars, a large Space of Grass was mark'd out for the Dancing-Place, round which we the Spectators stood, as at a Cricket-match in *England,* in the Centre of it was two Fires, at a small Distance from each other, which were designed as an Illumination to make the Dancers visible; near the Fires was seated the Musick, which were a number of Men and Women, with a Kind of Timbrels or small Kettle-Drums, made of real brass Kettles, covered with Deer Skins made like Parchment by the Indians, and these they beat, and keep good Time, although their Tunes are terrible and savage; they also sing much in the same Stile, creating Terror, Fear, and all dreadful Passions, but no pleasing ones. After this Noise had gone on for some Time, at once we heard a most dreadful Shout, and a Band of horrid Figures rushed into the Ring, with a Nimbleness hardly conceivable; they struck the Ground in exact Measure, answering the rough Musick; at once all the Descriptions of the Fawns and Satyrs of the *Latin* Poets came into my Mind, and indeed the *Indians* seemed to be the same Kind of brown dancing People, as lived under King *Faunus,* some 3000 Years ago in *Italy;* they are most chearful and loving to their Friends, but implacable and cruel to their Enemies."

All of this uncanny, chilling and nerve-wracking business in the jungle was, of course, an old story to Washington. As a young surveyor he had given enough of his rum to make the Indians dance for him and the young Fairfax.

But there was so much quarreling over the love-making between squaws and soldiers that Braddock was advised to send the women and children out of the camp before the Indian braves grew too ugly.

He made the suggestion as politely as he could and the Indians accepted it with the same courtesy. They asked only to be allowed to accompany their dusky ladies home.

They did.

They never came back.

Braddock's ideas of discipline offended the mighty Indian-fighter, "Jack the Black Hunter," and he and his gang refused to go along. But then he had previously refused to go with Washington.

Only eight Indians stuck to Braddock and they were really swayed by Croghan. They did good service, but in spite of all that Croghan and his lessening squad of redskins could do, many of Braddock's stragglers were killed and scalped by the French Indians.

With food bad and his men increasingly surly for lack of pay or hope of it, Braddock grew so desperately hard up for cash that he sent Washington, on May 30th, to fetch some by hook or by crook. Washington set out on one of those amazing rides of his. He travelled from Fort Cumberland, at Wills' Creek, to Winchester in a day. Thence he sent a messenger to Colonel Hunter, saying that he would be waiting for the four thousand pounds in Williamsburg.

This gave him an opportunity for a dash to Mount Vernon. There he was "detained a day in getting horses." Since he carried away one of Sally Fairfax's horses, he must have seen her, and that was probably his reason for the side-ride.

As he hurried on South, he met a messenger with a word from Governor Dinwiddie that there was no chance of his getting the money.   He rode on anyway and met a partner of Hunter's, who happened to be in funds, and next day borrowed enough to make up four thousand pounds.

So much treasure must have a convoy, and failing to find the light-horse he expected, Washington rounded up some militia men, of whom he wrote that the "8 men were two days assembling; but I believe they would not have been more than as many seconds dispersing, if I had been attacked." [16]

While he was detained at Winchester, he wrote to his brother Jack, expressing the hope "that you live in perfect harmony and good fellowship with the family at Belvoir, as it is in their power to be very serviceable upon many occasions to us, as young beginners . . . to that family I am under many obligations, particularly to the old gentleman [William Fairfax].

"Mrs Fairfax and Mrs Spearing having expressed a wish to be informed of the time and manner of my reaching this place (with my charge), you may acquaint them that I met with no other interruption than what proceeded from the difficulty of getting horses.   After Mrs. F——x's grew lame, I was obliged to get a fresh one every 15 or 20 miles, which rendered the journey tedious.   I should have been more refreshed from the fatigues of my journey, and my time would have been spent much more agreeably, had I halted below, instead of being delayed in this place; but I little imagined I should have had occasion to wait for a guard, which ought to have waited for me—if either must have waited at all."

This refers, of course, to his wish that he had spent the time at Belvoir.   He knew that Jack would show the letter to Sally.

LIEUTENANT-GOVERNOR ROBERT DINWIDDIE.

(From the Dinwiddie Papers.)

He added a long and amazing postscript,[17] revealing a sudden desire to get into politics, and asked Jack to find out secretly if Colonel Fairfax intended to offer himself as a candidate. "If he does not, I should be glad to take a poll, if I thought my chance tolerably good. Majr. Carlyle mentioned it to me in Williamsburgh in a bantering way . . . I should be glad if you could discover Maj. Carlyle's real sentiments on this head; also those of Mr. Dalton, Ramsay, Mason &c., which I hope and think you may do without disclosing much of *mine*, as I know your own good sense can furnish you with contrivances. . . .

"The Revd. Mr. Green's and Capt. McCarty's interests in this matter would be of consequence, and I should be glad if you could *sound* their pulse upon that occasion. Conduct the whole 'till you are satisfied of the sentiments of those I have mentioned, with an air of indifference and unconcern. . . . Capt. West, the present Burgess, and our friend Jack West, could also be serviceable, if they had a mind to assist the interest of, Dear Jack, Your loving brother."

Can this be George Washington counselling a younger brother?

He was disgusted with the slothfulness of his military excursion for experience; otherwise full of hope. But poor Braddock was going out to make good the prophecy he uttered on his last night in London, according to a friend who wrote: "Before we parted, the General told me that he should never see me more; for he was going with a handful of men to conquer whole nations; and to do this they must cut their way through unknown woods. He produced a map of the country, saying, at the same time, 'Dear Pop, we are sent like sacrifices to the altar.'" [18]

This sombre document should end once for all the eternally reiterated slander that Braddock was full of self-confidence and indifferent to advice.[19]

The United States should rather enshrine his memory, for, while Dinwiddie discovered Washington and gave him his first opportunities, he dropped him after the woeful first failures, and it was left to Braddock to coax the young Achilles out of the tent where he sulked, give him affection and the chance, not only to air his views and prove them right, but to be present at the fearful calamity where Washington for the first time revealed the sublimity of his valor and his godlike calm in general panic.

It was Braddock who recognized Washington as worthy of his intimate friendship and soldierly counsel, and lured him to that great hour whence he emerged as the one perfect hero in the eyes of the whole world, the very redeemer of colonial honor.

XIV

BRADDOCK TAKES HIS ADVICE

WASHINGTON always made war at his own expense. Close as he had to be in financial matters, he was generous to those in real need, and never so generous as when his country was in need. He loved fighting so well that he was ready to fight for nothing—or even less.

And now, foreseeing neither the tempest nor the after splendor, nor any of the following storms and calms, the commissionless and wageless young Mr. Washington was proud enough of the fact that he was convoying four thousand pounds of cash across the country with an army of eight comic and dubious militiamen as his entire command. He had to threaten to have them flogged to keep them sober enough to stay on their horses.

When he galloped into camp, he learned that a miracle had happened: the army had already begun to move—though "already" is flattery, seeing that Braddock had arrived in February, and on May 29th was able to push out only five or six hundred men under Major Chapman, with two field pieces and fifty wagons.

The engineers, under Quartermaster-General Sir John St. Clair, were still chopping down the trees and grubbing the stumps to open a swathe wide enough for the wagons. The road they cut still lives in places as a long "unhealed wound" across the landscape.[1]

The vanguard trickled away so slowly into the jungle that it was not until June eighth [2] that Sir Peter Halkett could get away with the first brigade of 984 men, including 700 Grenadier Guards of the 44th Regiment, two independent companies from New York, commanded by Captains Rutherford and Gates—this latter the Gates to whom Burgoyne would surrender in an unimaginable war, and who came within an ace of replacing as Commander-in-Chief the same George Washington who was Braddock's aide. There were also in this brigade Captain Polson's carpenters and two companies of Virginia Rangers, as well as forty-nine Maryland Rangers under Captain Dagworthy, with whom Washington would soon be having a quarrel that drove him north into another love affair.

Sir Peter Halkett was an old soldier who had been captured by Charles Edward the Pretender in 1745, and released on parole. When he was ordered by the Duke of Cumberland to return to the war against the Pretender, he had the strength to refuse, saying "His Royal Highness is master of my commission but not of my honor."

Which makes some contrast with Washington's appearance here, though he and many others with him at Fort Necessity had been released by the French on their word of honor not to come back.

The King had defended Halkett from Cumberland and he was sent out with Braddock. In his command was his son James, who shared his fate with devoted heroism. In this army went also to his death the young son of Governor Shirley.

On June ninth the Second Brigade of 993 men set out, its commander, Colonel Dunbar, being detached for rearguard duty and Lieutenant-Colonel Gage of the Forty-eighth regulars taking his place. This was the very Gage who caused so much trouble later in Boston, where he was besieged by Braddock's aid-de-camp, Mr. Washington.

In Gage's brigade were rangers from North and South

Carolina, three companies of Virginia rangers and a company of carpenters.

On the 10th, Braddock moved off with the rest of the army, taking with him the unsuspected grandeur of Washington.

The seventh of June had been a busy day for the youth. Though he must have had much to do in carrying messages to put the first brigade under way in the morning, and the camp must have been clamorous with bugles, drums and all the last moment panic of getting an army started, he found time to write four letters, one to his mother, one to his brother, one to William Fairfax, and one to Sally.

By some irony of mismanagement, he received in this remote and turbulent camp a letter from his mother asking him to get her a Dutch servant and some butter!

He answered with the greatest respect and patience:

"Hon'd Madam, I was favored with your letter, by Mr. Dick, and am sorry it is not in my power to provide you with a Dutch servant, or the butter, agreeably to your desire. We are quite out of the part of the country where either is to be had, there being few or no inhabitants where we now lie encamped, and butter cannot be had here to supply the wants of the army. . . . I hope you will spend the chief part of your time at Mount Vernon, as you have proposed to do, where I am certain every thing will be ordered as much to your satisfaction as possible, in the situation we are in there." [3]

In the gossipy letter to old Fairfax he described his safe arrival with the money, commented on Braddock's inability to argue reasonably with him, as already quoted, spoke angrily of the Pennsylvanians as deserving a flogging; told how the bloody flux had filled one hospital and was growing worse, though it had "not yet proved mortal to many."

He paid his old chief, Colonel Innes, a left-handed compliment, saying that he had "accepted of a Commission to be Governor of Fort Cumberland, where he is to reside: and will shortly receive another to be hangman, or something of that kind, and for which he is equally qualified."

He mentioned the news that three hundred Frenchmen had been seen on their way to Fort Du Quesne, and more were expected, and nine hundred had certainly gone thither already: "So that from these accounts we have reason to believe, that we shall have more to do than to go up the hills and come down."

He ended with, "We are impatient to hear what the powers at home are doing; whether peace, or war is like to be the issue of all these preparations." [4]

An odd query! He was with an army en route to battle and everybody wondered if war would be declared?

Governor Dinwiddie, nine days later, was writing to Braddock that his letters from England "say y't War is unavoidable, and I am apt to think before y's it is declar'd." But it was not.

Washington's letter to Sally Fairfax showed a more serious concern as to whether or not she had declared war against him.

His letter to her was prepared for delivery under cover to some common friend of theirs, who must have been in the secret, and whose memoirs would be interesting, indeed. It was probably his brother Jack, to whom he had entrusted other secrets.

Washington refers to his safe arrival with the treasure chest as something that, he imagined, must have delighted her as much as it did him. But he is deeply alarmed by the fear that, in asking him not to address his letters to her openly, she might be hinting that she would have preferred that he did not address her at all.

Sally was plainly a woman who kept him guessing. She

keeps us guessing also, for in the very letter that describes her insistence that the correspondence shall be clandestine, Washington asks her to make his compliments to "Miss Hannah and Mr. Bryan."

Now Hannah was the daughter of William Fairfax and the youngest sister of Sally's husband, George William; while Bryan Fairfax was George William's half-brother (nine years younger and the son of the third of William Fairfax's three wives,[5] George William being the son of the second).

Washington's hidden correspondence with Sally was a strange secret to be kept by so many close relatives. How the husband was kept out of it, it is difficult to understand, but he was at this time a colonel in the militia of Frederick County; and he was doubtless absent from home recruiting men, since Dinwiddie more than once refers to money sent to him to pay off troops.

Fredcrick was one of the western frontier colonies, and along with Hampshire and Augusta (which stretched into the Shenandoah Valley) would receive the first attentions of any Indian marauders.

Lord Fairfax must have been with George William, for on July fourth, Governor Dinwiddie wrote urging him to call out the Frederick and Hampshire militia and organize rangers to protect the frontiers where Indians in a sudden descent had butchered nine families.

Lord Fairfax and Colonel George William, or their troops, evidently had scruples against marching beyond the county boundaries, for Dinwiddie, after writing, "I entreat Y'r L'ds will imediately put the foremention'd Orders in execu'n," wrote to another officer, Colonel Martin, that he was "surpriz'd Lord Fairfax sh'd scruple in march'g the Militia out of Frederick C'ty."

He learned that the people were in too great a "pannick"

to let their troops go out, and on July 9th he wrote Colonel
George William Fairfax, pleading with him to bestir himself, recruit rangers, and advance the necessary money. He
added, "Excuse y's Freedom, and be assur'd I am with very
great Respect, Worthy Sir, Y'r most ob'd't h'ble servt." [6]

A little later he was writing abroad, "I found the Militia
were a cowardly People or seiz'd with such Pannick as not to
resist the Insults of the Enemy," again, "A dastardly cowardly People y't w'd not stand to the Defence of their Lives
and Fortunes." [7]

There seems to have been something lacking therefore in
the martial ardor of Colonel George William Fairfax, and
his wife must have noted the contrast with Washington, who
was now appealing to her so pitifully.

There are two versions of this letter, as of many of Washington's, since some of them are extant as sent, while others
exist only in his copy-book, and it was his custom to make
slight changes from his first draught.

But this is the letter, as Washington wrote it, save for the
italicizing of certain significant phrases:

"DEAR MADAM:
"When I had the happiness to see you last you expressed an inclination to be informed of my safe arrival in camp with the
Charge that was intrusted to my care, but at the same time desired
it might be communicated in a letter to somebody of your acquaintance.

"This I took as a *gentle rebuke* and a polite manner of forbidding my corresponding with you; and conceive this opinion is not
illy founded when I reflect that *I have hitherto found it impracticable to engage one moment of your attention.* If I am right in
this, I hope you will excuse the present presumption and lay the
imputation to elateness at my successful arrival.

"If, on the contrary, these are fearful apprehensions only, how
easy it is to remove my suspicions, enliven my spirits, and *make me
happier than the day is long by honouring me with a correspondence
which you did once partly promise to do.*

"Please make my compliments to Miss Hannah and to Mr. Bryan, to whom I shall do myself the pleasure of writing so soon as I hear he is returned from Westmoreland.

"I am, Madam, Y'r most obedt & Hble Servt

G. WASHINGTON." [8]

Why did Mrs. Fairfax ask George to keep her informed of his welfare, but not to write to her about it? Was her husband jealous? Why did George speak of his own suspicions? Was he jealous?

But his riddle went unanswered while he turned his face toward the wilderness and rode alongside Braddock, whose army was as cumbersome and as slow as a huge red caterpillar crawling through a thicket infested by red ants.

Franklin had warned Braddock that his slender line was in danger of ambuscades, and might be "cut like a thread, into several pieces, which, from their distance, cannot come up in time to support each other."

It is often reported that Braddock "smiled" or even "laughed at the prophecy," and that is given as a proof of his stubborn imbecility.

But in the first place, there was no other way for an army to move through such a forest except in a long thin line without taking so much time that it might as well stay at home. In the second place, as Braddock shrewdly said, the woods that were so thick as to hide the Indians were thick enough to protect him from them.

And in the third place, he never was ambuscaded, nor his line broken.

As a further disproof of the charge that Braddock took no advice, Washington himself, in a letter to Jack, speaking of the dangers of a too slow advance, and the importance of beating the French reinforcements to the fort, says:

"The General (before they met in council) asked my

private opinion concerning the expedition. I urged it, in the warmest terms I was able, to push forward, if we even did it with a small but chosen band, with such artillery and light stores as were absolutely necessary; leaving the heavy artillery, baggage &c with the rear division to follow by slow and easy marches.

"This advice prevailed . . .

"We set out with less than thirty carriages (including those that transported the ammunition for the howitzers, twelve-pounders, and six-pounders, etc.), and all of them strongly horsed; which was a prospect that conveyed infinite delight to my mind, though I was excessively ill at the time. But this prospect was soon clouded, and my hopes brought very low indeed, when I found that instead of pushing on with vigor, without regarding a little rough road, they were halting to level every molehill, and to erect bridges over every brook, by which means we were four days getting twelve miles.

"At this camp I was left by the Doctor's advice, and the General's absolute orders, as I have already mentioned, without which I should not have been prevailed upon to remain behind; as I then imagined, and now believe, I shall find it no easy matter to join my own corps again, which is twenty-five miles advanced before us. Notwithstanding, I had the General's word of honor, pledged in the most solemn manner, that I should be brought up before he arrived at Fort Duquesne." [9]

Braddock was not to blame for the engineering. That was in charge of General St. Clair, who had been in the country long before Braddock arrived, and had laid out the route with Governor Sharpe, who later criticized Braddock severely, but not so severely as Forbes criticized St. Clair, accusing him not only of ignorance but of actual treachery.[10]

The Hon. J. W. Fortescue, the historian of the British

army, asserts that the first grand error was in dividing the British attack into two armies.   Both should have been combined against Fort Niagara.   Once that fell, Du Quesne would collapse for lack of supplies, as was later proved. Prof. Thwaites says, "Braddock committed a fatal blunder in following Washington's wilderness road to the Ohio, and making Fort Cumberland his principal base . . . had he proceeded westward from Philadelphia he would have had the advantage, much of the way, of a settled country abounding in supplies and the means of transport."   This also was later demonstrated by General Forbes.

Washington's impatience at the delay was aggravated by grave illness.   Four days after he set out on the march he was "seized with violent fevers and pains in my head which continued for nine days without intermission 'till the 23d following, when I was relieved, by the General's absolutely ordering the physicians to give me Dr. James's powders (one of the most excellent medicines in the world), for it gave me immediate ease, and removed my fevers and other complaints in four days' time.   My illness was too violent to suffer me to ride; therefore I was indebted to a covered wagon for some part of my transportation; but even in this, I could not continue far, for the jolting was so great, that I was left upon the road with a guard, and necessaries, to wait the arrival of Colonel Dunbar's detachment, which was two days' march behind us, the General giving me his word of honor, that I should be brought up, before he reached the French fort.   This *promise,* and the doctor's *threats,* that, if I persevered in my attempts to get on, in the condition I was, my life would be endangered, determined me to halt for the above detachment."

His servant, "poor John Alton," fell ill at the same time and got well at the same time.

Twice in this letter to his brother, he refers to Braddock's solemn promise to let him share the fight for the fort.

Braddock shines here as tender-hearted and considerate, pleading with an unruly youngster as long as possible, prescribing for him, and finally ordering him to bed, but consoling him with absolute promises that he should not miss the great day.

Washington shines as a sick warrior, surrendering his best horse to help out the dreadful need of horses, but forcing his brain to the point of giving fine strategic advice to the veteran. Finally he collapsed, and was left by the roadside for two days until the rear-guard came up and shoved him into a covered wagon that jolted him along at worse speed than ever, because of the wretchedness of the few horses:

"I have been now six days with Colonel Dunbar's corps, who are in a miserable condition for want of horses, not having enough for their wagons; so that the only method he has of proceeding, is to march with as many wagons as those will draw, and then halt till the remainder are brought up with the same horses, which requires two days more; and shortly, I believe, he will not be able to stir at all. But there has been vile management in regard to horses. . . ."

In his distress, he worries over the loss of his own best mount and the disappearance of several horses sent on by Colonel Fairfax. He is peevish because nobody has written the sick man. One can imagine whom he is thinking of from the words he underlines:

"You may thank my friends for the letters I have received from them, which, tell them, has not been *one* from *any mortal* since I left Fairfax, except yourself and Mr. Dalton. It is a specimen of their regard and kindness which I should endeavor to acknowledge and thank them for, was I able and *suffered* to *write*. . . . Make my compliments to *all* who think me worthy of their enquiries."

His friends may have neglected him, but Braddock did not forget him. He sent word by his aide, Captain Roger Morris:

"DEAR WASHINGTON,

"I am desired by the General to let you know that he marches tomorrow & next day but that he shall halt at the meadows two or three days, It is the desire of every particular in this family and the general's positive Commands to you not to stir but by the advice of the person under whose care you are till you are better which in all hope will be very soon. &c." [11]

Washington writes to his friend, "Dear Orme" [12] for news, saying that his fevers are moderate and nearly well. His one trouble is "weakness, which is excessive, and the difficulty of getting to you, arising therefrom; but this I would not miss doing, before you reach Duquesne, for five hundred pounds. However, I have no doubt now of doing this, as I am moving on slowly, and the General has given me his word of honor, in the most solemn manner, that it shall be effected. . . .

"I am too weak to add more than my compliments to the General, the family, &c. and again to desire, that you will oblige me in the above request, and devise the most effectual means for me to join you. I am, dear Orme, your most obedient servant." [12]

Soon it was Orme who was in the covered wagon.

XV

HE SHARES IN BRADDOCK'S DEFEAT

WHEN Washington complained that Braddock's roadmakers were determined to level every molehill and were so slow that he despaired, he forgot his own experience in the same country a year earlier.

It took Braddock seven days to carry two thousand men and some heavy artillery from Fort Cumberland at Will's Creek to Little Meadows; but it had taken Washington with only a hundred and fifty men fourteen days to cover the same twenty odd miles.[1]

Both officers followed and enlarged what was originally called Nemacolin's Path, after the Indian who guided Christopher Gist to the Forks of the Ohio, as Gist later guided Washington, and again Braddock.

Thus the weaving Indian trail became in time a great highway into the unknown West.

Braddock has been abused for carrying useless baggage[2] and taking too great care with his road; but he was not trying to pull off a flying raid; he was aiming at permanent conquest and the establishment of a channel for settlers.

He had his one bit of luck at the Great Crossing of the Youghiogeny since he arrived at a time of low water. Washington the previous year had been unable to get his men over at all.

While Washington lay raging with fever and inactivity and watched Colonel Dunbar's dreary progress, Braddock's men found that everything forbade the speed they had hoped to attain. The horses were so few and of such poor quality that though the officers had surrendered their extra mounts and given up all but their necessary baggage, it took the army fifteen days to make the thirty-seven miles from Fort Cumberland to the Great Crossing of the Youghiogeny.

In the van, from three to six hundred axes kept up a savage music as they gnawed what was rather a tunnel than a road through the dense and lofty growth. The fallen trees with their interlocking branches must be dragged out of the path, but removing all the stumps was impossible and the wagon train had an infernal task.

Bogs, gullies, rocks and creeks presented varied obstacles. Rattlesnakes whirred and struck; wood-ticks silently invaded the skin and caused an itching that was mania. The screaming victims, scratching at their tingling flesh, made wounds that festered and crippled. More than one soldier had his legs amputated as a result of ticks instead of bullets.

The horses wrecked themselves and the rickety wagons as they plunged and tugged under the merciless whips. The spokes splintered on the craggy boulders or the stumps and writhing roots left by the pioneers; or the wheels sank over their axles in the marshes.

The poor wind-broken beasts foisted upon the soldiers by the traitorous jobbers in horseflesh foundered and perished at the side of their ruined wagons and their stalled cannon and coehorns.

The stronger horses were the unluckier, for after they had wrestled their burdens to the evening camp they were whipped back along the road to bring up the wagons of their martyred fellows. Nothing in all the pities of war is more pitiable than the fate of horses.

The failure of the wagon-train meant that the soldiers must fast as well as labor. They had grown mutinous enough at Fort Cumberland for lack of human food and

over-abundance of Indian corn.   Now they lacked the corn.
The woods were full of everything green but vegetables.
The salt pork, salt beef, salt horse, brought a plague of
bloody flux upon the men.   This tortured many of them to
death and saved them from the less cruel Indians.

The worst of the march was the absence of liquor which
was vital to the morale of the soldiers, who had little else
to cheer them.   They complained afterwards that they were
overworked, short of numbers, starved, compelled to drink
only water (and that both scarce and bad), and "that the
provincials had disheartened them by repeated suggestions
of their fears of a defeat should they be attacked by Indians,
in which case the European method of fighting would be
entirely unavailing." [3]

Their despondency was natural.   They had been drilled
and flogged all their lives to make them automatons on the
battlefield.   Now they were told that their mechanism
would not work against the enemy they were approaching.

The little grog "for the stomach's sake" was missing and
their bellies were cold and rumbling with swamp water.

The road that Braddock's men carved and agonized upon
is not yet effaced and Archer Butler Hulbert, who has traced
its scars, describes vividly how the memory of its builders
still haunts the region:

"In the forests it is easy to conjure up the scene when this
old track was opened—for it was cut through a 'wooden
country,' to use an expression common among the pioneers.
Here you can see the long line of sorry wagons standing
in the road when the army is encamped; and though many
of them seem unable to carry their loads one foot further—
yet there is ever the ringing chorus of the axes of six hundred choppers sounding through the twilight of the hot May
evening.   It is almost suffocating in the forests when the
wind does not blow, and the army is unused to the scorch-

ing American summer which has come early this year. The
wagon train is very long, and though the van may have
halted on level ground, the line behind stretches down and
up the shadowy ravines. The wagons are blocked in all
conceivable positions on the hillsides. The condition of the
horses is pitiful beyond description. If some are near to the
brook or spring, others are far away. Some horses will
never find water tonight. To the right and left the senti-
nels are lost in the surrounding gloom.

"And then with those singing axes for the perpetual re-
frain, consider the mighty epic poem to be woven out of the
days that have succeeded Braddock here. Though lost in
the Alleghenies, this road and all its busy days mirror perfectly the social advance of the western empire to which it
led. Its first mission was to bind, as with a strange, rough,
straggling cincture the East and the West." [4]

But the sad men who opened the way had no comfort from
visions of the magnificent future of these realms. They
foresaw neither the glory that would be McKeesport nor the
grandeur of a Pittsburgh-to-come.

They wondered why they were there; why they had not
preferred any poverty or toil in the slums of London or
the factories or farms of England to going for a soldier.
The gaps in their ranks when they left Ireland had been
partly filled with raw recruits from Virginia, most of them
young immigrants or the children of poor indentured
servants. Of Braddock's total of two thousand men, eleven
hundred were colonials. He had drilled them bitterly before they marched, to try to whip them into shape for obeying commands in the stress of battle.

The regulars made fun of them and they took refuge
in having fun with the regulars. When they halted, they
ridiculed the British tactics and spun yarns of Indian
horrors.

There still exists a silly fancy that all frontier-folk are brave and hardy and exceedingly courageous in fighting Indians. The Virginia lads may have given the regulars that impression of themselves. But it was not true. Most of them had no experience whatever. Already in that young country there were countless instances of colonial cowardice that could not be surpassed. At this very moment Dinwiddie was shrieking in vain at the timorous home-guarding militia, who were afraid to defend their borders from such Indians as had slunk along the flanks of the column to break its communications and perhaps divert it from its purpose by massacres in the rear.

The Virginia soldiers with Braddock, like children who tell ghost stories to children, frightened themselves as well as their audience. The worst of the Indians was that while they were ghostly in their mystic appearances and disappearances, they were not ghosts, but painted, naked demons with hatchets that split the skull and knives that stripped it of its hair and flesh.

The soldier who fell behind because of a bruise, or a throe of dysentery, or a leg disabled by the chigger-frenzy, had not only the wolves and the mosquitoes and the rattle-snakes to fear, but the velvet-footed approach of the Indians or their Indianized French companions who loved to carve scurrilities on the trees for the British eyes. The scouts, who must push ahead and the flankers who must steal through the thickets far from the road, were always encountering the Indians. The report of a musket that fired and could not be reloaded for an age, a yell of fear, a cry of pain, and groans of woe would check the symphony of the axes or the dreary flutter of the drums, and the rescuers would come in with a dripping corpse or some living wretch hideous with his red skull bare and his brains oozing.

The roots of the hair are the very seat of the thrill of

fear, and scalping has a horror of irresistible grisliness. The ferocity of the warfare had made the white men vie with the Indians in the art of slicing away the hair of one another. Whether the Indians had invented their other methods of torture or had learned them from Christian Europe, they did exceedingly well without the machineries and ingenuities of civilization.

The soldiers, both British and Colonial, were frightened through and through, and with good reason. They were preparing themselves for one of the most famous panics in history.

Fate, like a grim dramatist, a Sophokles or a Shakespeare, built toward the gory climax with many a little touch of ghastliness. The engineer Gordon, whose Journal has been already quoted, tells of two by-incidents that befell the army a fortnight deep in the June woods:

"25th: it was reported that a party of Indians had Surprized Kill'd, and Scalp'd 2 families to the Number of 12 within 4 miles of ye Fort

"June 26th: Accounts of another family's Scalp'd within 3 Miles of us. The Governor detach'd a party to bury the Dead, and to look for the Indians, they found a Child standing in the Water scalp'd, which had 2 holes in its Skull, they brought it to the Doctor, who dressed it but Died in a Week." [5]

The only Indians that Braddock possessed to fend off the swarms of the French allies, were Croghan's handful. On the 19th of June, Monacatoocha and his son went out for information and were captured by the French, and 'would have been killed but for their release by some of the French Indians, who must have had a momentary glimpse of the folly of helping either of the white invaders to destroy their own race.

On July sixth British soldiers, coming upon a party of

Indians and not recognizing them as friendly, fired into them and killed this same son of Monacatoocha.[6]

Towards the last, Croghan's Indians grew too cautious to bring in any information, feeling that they were hopelessly outnumbered. But, as the army drew toward the end of its forest-imprisonment, two Indians stole away and crept up to within half a mile of Fort Du Quesne where they chopped down a French officer. They brought in his scalp to add to the paltry eight or nine they had taken on the march "a Number much inferior to the Expectations." [7] The trophy was none too cheering for Braddock's regulars, some of whom were Cockney convicts who felt the hair rising on their own scalps for the last time that night.

Braddock, realizing that his goal was at hand, sent out a reconnoitering party including Croghan and his Indians. Then he held a final council of war, and a plan was unanimously agreed upon.

Since Virginian carpenters under Trent had originally started to build the fort, which its French commander Contrecoeur had taken away from them; and since Gist and Washington had been over all this ground and made a map of it, Braddock's officers were in no doubt as to the lay of the land, though Washington, who came up that evening in a covered wagon, was too late and too ill to attend the council.

The Ohio River is the joint name of the Allegheny and the Monongahela rivers, which meet and form in a crooked letter Y fallen over on its side. The Allegheny comes down from the northeast; the Monongahela up from the southeast. They unite at an almost perfect right angle and the stem of the Y follows the northwestern course of the Monongahela for about thirty miles before it turns south and west and begins its drift toward the Mississippi.

The meeting place of the Monogahela and the Allegheny

was called at that time the Forks of the Ohio. Fort Du
Quesne nestled in the crotch of the Y on the north bank of
the Monongahela, and the eastern bank of the Allegheny.

Washington and Christopher Gist had studied the ground
carefully as they had passed on north to deliver to the
French Dinwiddie's invitation to get out. The French had
not obeyed, and now Washington and Gist were back again
with a gorgeous British army to enforce the request; for it
was only a request since war had not yet been declared.

It is odd that two of England's greatest defeats were
suffered during a truce: Braddock was whipped and killed
before war was declared: Pakenham was whipped and killed
at New Orleans two weeks after a treaty had been signed.
"Peace hath her victories no less renowned than war."

Braddock's army came up along the northern bank of the
Monongahela, on the same side as the fort, but encountered
high and ragged bluffs crowding almost to the water's edge.
On the south side of the river there was a level open space
free of those accursed trees that had mourned over them
all the way.

So it was decided to cross the river about fifteen miles from
the fort, march up the south bank about six miles, beyond
the mouth of Turtle Creek which came in from the north,
then cross the river again. Here they would emerge on a
slightly elevated plain, which after half a mile or so would
rise into hillocks and rolling country once more covered with
forest.

The army would come out of the dark, march a few miles
in the blessed sunlight and then return into the gloom of
the woods, beyond which Fort Du Quesne awaited them
in terror.

Braddock believed, and had good reason to believe, that
he had only to parade his army in front of Fort Du Quesne
in full panoply to scare its commander into surrender. The

French commander was, indeed, already defeated, ready to burn the fort and take his men back to Canada where they would be needed to help resist the other attacks of the divided British power.

It is a kind of cowardice to award blame after the event, and deny intelligence to one whom blind luck has overthrown. Many a fool has stumbled into a victory and been hailed a genius and many a genius has been tripped and thrown by a fool or a pack of fools, and lain in the unmerited dust for other fools to mock.

In the American Civil War there was just such another case. General MacDowell's plans for the battle of Bull Run, or Manassas, were so finely conceived that they were long afterward offered to students of strategy as a model, for the military scholars were not duped by the mere fact that, owing to the unforeseen and illegal brilliance of Stonewall Jackson and the unwillingness of the Northern soldiers to pay any heed to their officers, the Federal troops were thrown into a panic that ranks next to that of Braddock's men and makes Bull Run another by-word of disgraceful rout.

As MacDowell, fighting J. E. Johnston, smashed his army against Stonewall Jackson, so Braddock, fighting Contrecoeur, ran into Dumas. Stonewall Jackson is revered in the memory even of his enemies; but the name of the superb Dumas is known to few Americans.

Braddock's council of war acted with faultless energy. Sleep was forgotten. An advance party of three hundred under Lieutenant-Colonel Gage marched out of the woods an hour or two after midnight and secured the ford. An hour later, General St. Clair with his pioneers went forward to level the banks of the stream for the wagons and cannon and prepare the road.

At six o'clock in the morning General Braddock and the main body, with bayonets fixed and gleaming, splashed across the Monongahela. Washington afterwards called it "the most beautiful spectacle I ever beheld."

The advance party scared some Indians out of the bushes but was not interrupted in its march to the second ford where the army was to regain the north bank of the river.

The French knew, of course, just where Braddock was and how strong, and he knew they knew. The first surprise he had that day was in being allowed to straddle the Monongahela twice without even a detaining attack. The failure to surprise him was due to a failure in the French plans.

While he was on the open plain south of the Monongahela and only a few rugged miles stood between him and the fort, he felt that there was plenty of time for the conquest and thought it well to steady his men with a drill and a bit of food.

They had need of sunshine after their long crawl through the cavernous forest. They had need of exercise in deployment and battle maneuver. They had here a parade-ground such as he and his officers and the regulars were used to.

It was a wise and cautious idea and not at all the mere display of pomp and circumstance that he has been accused of intending.[8] MacDowell's troops that lost at Bull Run had never once been drilled in deployment or shift of position. If they had been they might have won. If Braddock's men had met the enemy on a decent field of honor, this drill would have been hailed as a proof of generalship. If!

If they had had more such drills they would not have lost the habit of obedience and would automatically have obeyed their officers. Braddock had already beaten the French to the logical and dangerous place for an ambush.

He had a right to expect to win. After all his miserable disappointments the sun had come out of the clouds and was bright upon his bayonets.

Busy as he was and triumphant, he was not too grand to be solicitous for that inescapable leech of a Washington, who had arrived the night before. Dunbar had sent forward a wagon train of provisions with an escort of a hundred, and Washington had come up flat on his back in one of the provision carts. He would not be kept from his day. He appeared in a fringed buckskin shirt instead of the uniform he had been wearing, in common with the other officers.[9] Here the cub was, gaunt with past fevers, in the saddle for the first time since he was stricken, so lean that he had to have a ridiculous pillow under his bony frame, and swaying like a novice. Faithful Doctor Craik had given him medicine, and rum for breakfast to hold him up. Yet his incomparable soul had more advice to give, and he was grasping after glory.

All he wanted to do was to be permitted to lead the way through the woods with his Virginians and Croghan's Indians. He promised to clear the path to Fort Du Quesne, all by himself.

He had no commission and had no right to command troops; his own colony had reduced him from his colonelcy; he had come along as a personal messenger; the poor young man was fitter for the hospital than the drillground. And he wanted to do all the fighting and lead the army to victory with his green provincials!

Instead of ordering him out of his sight, Braddock's answer was to call up the old British regular who had been his bodyservant for years and say to him:

"Bishop, this young man is determined to go into action, although he is really too sick and weak. Keep an eye on him!"[10]

Braddock rebuked his indomitable grit and his incorrigible audacity by giving him his own bodyservant! And thus he saved Washington's life.

On the other side of that forested ridge another young man of wonderful heroism had similarly fought his superior officer into submission. Contrecoeur was too wise a man to believe that his inferior force could whip Braddock's army either in the open or behind his stockade, in case Braddock ever got his troops and his big artillery through the wilderness. That seemed the impossible thing. But Braddock accomplished it. He had built a road and brought an army across the jungled mountains. He was knocking at the outer gate.

Captain Contrecoeur did not dream of going into the woods to grapple with Braddock, much less to meet him on the plain. But he had three subordinates, Captains de Beaujeu, Dumas and Ligneris. Dumas had an idea which he passed on to Beaujeu, who made the same plea to Contrecoeur that Washington made to Braddock: "Give me my own men and some Indians and let me lead the attack." [11] Since Beaujeu had been sent to relieve Contrecoeur of the command, Contrecoeur yielded, and according to his own report, "formed a party of all I could spare . . . 250 French and 600 savages, a total of 900 men." Beaujeu ran to the Indians whose tents made a suburb to the fort. He summoned a council of chiefs, threw a tomahawk at their feet and asked them to come out with him and fight.

The Indians shook their heads. Braddock's power had already impressed them, as he hoped. Emotions which we call patriotism and sacred ardor in our own heroes, but ambition and obstinacy in foreigners, led Beaujeu to return to the Indians and plead:

"I am going anyway. Will you let your father go alone?" They pledged him their aid and on the morning while

Braddock's army was debouching from the forest, Beaujeu was summoning his red warriors to keep their pledge. They kept it, but it was hard to get them started and some of them refused to go at all though they joined in the carnage later. Those who went had to put on their war-time make-up, their grease-paint and feathers. They had to hear a certain number of speeches, and drill their voices for the war-cry, and their hands with the war-hatchet.

Beaujeu was frantic with the delay, but his French and Canadians were kept waiting till the Indians had howled and hopped themselves to the high pitch of slaughter.

Kegs of powder and bullets stood near the gate of the fort and the Indians helped themselves. Among them was the Huron chief called Athanase, a great warrior; the Ottawas were probably led by Pontiac, an unknown chief of future fame, and the Ojibways were commanded by a brilliant Frenchman, Charles de Langlade.

It was eight o'clock before the force could start and it did not come in touch with Braddock's army until after noon. It had no artillery. It consisted of thirty-six French officers and cadets, seventy-two regulars and a hundred and forty-six Canadians, who must have been mere lads, since Contrecoeur says that *"une grande partie des Canadiens qui n'estoient malheureusement que des enfants s'estoient retirés à la première décharge."*

What would have happened if Braddock had taken the advice of the ague-ridden young Washington and let him lead the Virginians and eight Indians into that divinely arranged death-trap where Beaujeu was compelled to fight instead of following the standardized program of attacking at a ford?

A year before, Jumonville's brother, Villiers, had with about the same number of French and Indians driven Wash-

ington's three hundred men into Fort Necessity and captured them after inflicting heavy casualties.

In view of what Beaujeu and his men did on that ninth
of July to so many experienced officers, British and American, and so many soldiers as Braddock had with him, it is per-
missible to believe that Washington's party would have
been promptly and utterly destroyed.   When Braddock
refused to heed Washington's prayer, he earned the gratitude of posterity.

It is generally forgotten that Braddock's regular regiments were partly made up of Virginian recruits, and that
Braddock sent out as his advance party such unsurpassed
woodsmen as Croghan with his eight Indians and Christopher Gist with mounted Virginians.

Three things every school child and grown-up American
knows of Braddock's Defeat: that he was surprised, that he
was ambushed, and that if he had allowed his men to hide
behind trees, as Washington begged him to, he would have
won the battle.

All three beliefs are absolutely false, even though George
Macaulay Trevelyan,[12] as late as 1926, says that Braddock's
expedition was "cut to pieces in an ambush of French and
Red Indians."

Braddock was not surprised, but the French were, and
Braddock's men fired first.   According to the testimony of
the French officers present, the first British volley put to
flight the entire force of Canadians, who returned to the fort
and stayed there.   It also threw the Indians into a panic hard
to overcome, especially as Beaujeu fell dead at the third
British volley, leaving Dumas in command unexpectedly.

Braddock was not ambushed; for the French were not
yet ready to attack when his advance party marched across
the sunken gullies,[13] which did not run parallel with Brad-

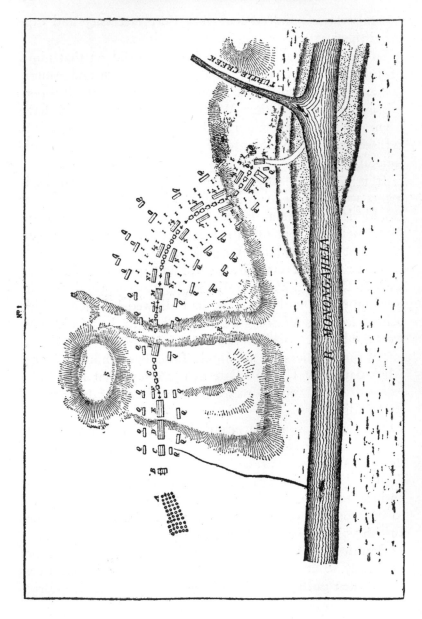

No. 1.

A Sketch of the Field of Battle of the 9th of July, upon the Monongahela, seven miles from Fort du Quesne, shewing the Disposition of the Troops when the Action began.

EXPLANATION.

▯ British Troops; the long lines express the number of Files. O French and Indians. + Cannon and Howitzers. ⊡ Waggons, Carts, and Tumbrils. I Cattle and Packhorses.

A, French and Indians when first discovered by the Guides.

B, Guides and six light Horse.

C, Vanguard of the advanced Party.

D, Advanced Party, commanded by Lt. Col. Gage.

E, Working Party, commanded by Sir Jn. St. Clair, D.Q.M.G.

F, Two Field Pieces.

G, Waggons with Powder and Tools.

H, Rear Guard of the advanced Party. I, Light Horse leading the Convoy. K, Sailors and Pioneers, with a Tumbril of Tools, etc. L, Three Field Pieces. M, General's Guard. N, Main Body upon the Flanks of the Convoy, with the Cattle and Packhorses between them and the Flank Guards. O, Field Piece in ye rear of ye Convoy. P, Rear Guards. Q, Flank Guards. R, A Hollow Way. S, a Hill which the Indians did most of the Execution from. T, Frazer's House.

(Signed)   Pat. Mackellar, Engr.

Proof that Braddock Was Not Ambushed.

(From Parkman's "Montcalm and Wolfe," by Permission of the Publishers, Little, Brown & Co., and of the Parkman Estate.)

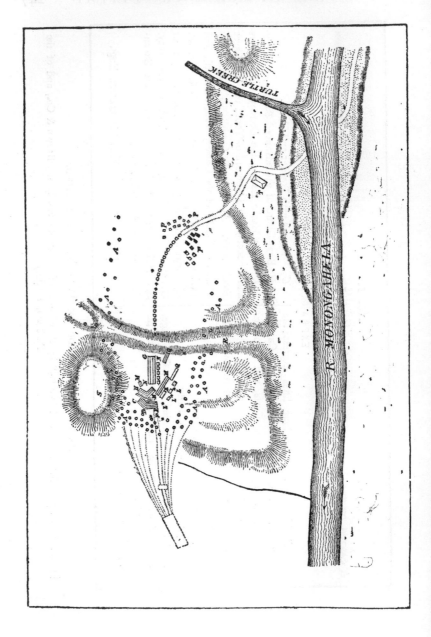

No. 2.

A SKETCH OF THE FIELD OF BATTLE, SHEWING THE DISPOSITION OF THE TROOPS ABOUT 2 O'CLOCK, WHEN THE WHOLE OF THE MAIN BODY HAD JOINED THE ADVANCED AND WORKING PARTYS, THEN BEAT BACK FROM THE GROUND THEY OCCUPIED AS IN PLAN No. I.

EXPLANATION.

A, The French and Indians skulking behind Trees, round the British.

F, The two Field Pieces of the advanced Party abandoned.

C, D, E, H, K, M, N, Q, The whole Body of the British joined with little or no Order, but endeavouring to make Fronts towards ye Enemies Fire. *L*, The three Field Pieces of the main Body. *P*, The rear Guard divided (round the rear of the Convoy now closed up) behind Trees having been attack'd by a few Indians.

N.B. The Disposition on both Sides continued about two hours nearly as here represented, the British endeavouring to recover the Guns (*F*) and to gain the Hill (*S*) to no purpose. The British were at length beat from the Guns (*L*). The General was wounded soon after. They were at last beat across the Hollow Way (*R*) and made no further Stand. The Retreat was full of Confusion and Hurry, but after a few Miles there was a Body got to rally.

(Signed) PAT. MACKELLAR, Eng^r.

PROOF THAT BRADDOCK WAS NOT AMBUSHED.

(From Parkman's "Montcalm and Wolfe," by Permission of the Publishers, Little, Brown & Co., and of the Parkman Estate.)

dock's march, as so often stated, but across it.   He did not
enter a ravine, but was caught in the narrow space of the new
road his men chopped through the dense growth of trees.

Since the French and Indians with amazing speed, courage
and good fortune divided, covered both flanks, and fired
from both sides, from all sides, on Braddock's men, a man
behind a tree was no safer than one in the open, as was well
proved by the appalling losses of the Virginian troops.   The
traditional view, supported by all too many historians, is
completely and demonstrably wrong.

But this is anticipating the battle itself.

While the rest of the British army fed, the scouts and the
advanced and working parties were ordered to march.
Croghan with his eight Indians, Gist with six mounted Virginians, Gordon with his engineers and three hundred men,
led out the British advance party in charge of Lieutenant-
Colonel Thomas Gage.   They crossed the river the second
time, then a slightly elevated plain, where the bulk of the
army waited while the pioneers mounted a rolling forested
hill and began to clear a path through it.

The whole army was now stretched out in a long series of
groups at intervals: Sir John St. Clair, Quartermaster-
General, with two six-pounders and the wagons of the
working party; next, General Braddock, Sir Peter Halkett,
Orme, Morris, Washington and the main body; the artillery
and the baggage-train; finally, a rearguard of colonials.   In
all about 1300 men, though some accounts say that Colonel
Dunbar had sent up enough men from the reserves to make
a total of 1486.   This would be the convoy that brought
Washington to the battle in the covered wagon.

They were actually now within the present city limits of
Pittsburgh, what is known as the borough of Braddock, and
a recent photograph shows the battleground covered with
the tall chimneys of blast furnaces.

As the vanguard climbed a hill through thick woods and tall grass, it crossed the first leg of a horseshoe-shaped ravine lying across their route, with a high hill on their right flank.

Suddenly Gordon caught sight of a pack of French in hunting shirts, and naked Indians, led by three French officers with their hats in their hands. The British fired promptly. A hundred young Canadians started to run and did not stop till they reached Fort Pitt. Beaujeu waved his hat and his men spread out in a crescent-shaped skirmish line, then charged. The British seeing them vanish, joyously shouted, "God save the King!" as they fired again, and the two cannon mouths belched grape. The Indians fell back in terror.

Only a hundred French regulars confronted them and the British advanced firing. At the third cannon discharge the French leader Beaujeu fell dead.

Despairing but determined to perish rather than flee, Captain Dumas brilliantly rallied the French and advanced. His platoon fired so well that the British stopped short and fell back. The Indians paused and returned, interested. They always want to be the first to scatter from defeat and to crowd in on victory.

Dumas, with fine control, split his line and shoved it down both sides of the British column like a two-tined fork. Other Indians seized the high hill at the British right and fired as from a citadel. The British were jammed in a narrow twelve-foot channel where they could not deploy. They could not decide which way to fire, for the Indians were on both sides of them, drowning their shouts with demoniac yells, hidden from sight and pumping lead into the huddled, bewildered soldiers.

At the sound of cannon, General Braddock with his staff, including George Washington, sprang up from dinner and hurried up with supporting troops. Some of the officers forgot to unpin their napkins from under their chins, where polite persons wore them at that time. And they died so, for their arrival only added more victims. They merely jumped into the quicksands to confound the men they wanted to rescue.

The Indians filled the woods alongside the column and attacked it as ants attack a caterpillar—from the side as well as at the head. And a column marching forward is a difficult thing to swing to the flank, impossible in a narrow road twelve feet wide and under fire from invisible assailants. That is why it is considered the most criminal thing an officer can do, to let the enemy catch him in column. The French and British columns had met head on, but the French had divided and straddled the British at once.

The British were plucky but unwieldy and they could not undo in a moment what had been drilled into them for years. Bunker Hill would still find them fighting in close order, to the great comfort of the enemy. Majuba Hill would still find them unable to prevent the Boers from climbing a hill as individuals and destroying the massed British.[14]

The Indians believe in discretion as valor's better part, until they begin to win; then they are prodigiously brave. These naked savages not only met British volleys now with individual fire from behind logs and trees and bushes, but charged and charged the red line, spreading havoc with their war-hatchets and stealing back again into the thicket. The British could not find them to aim at. One officer said he did not see above five Indians during the whole battle. Modern warfare was revolutionized by the Indians, who taught us the great art of taking cover.

The British and the colonials among them tried to imitate their masters and dispersed behind the trees, but "Bull-dog Braddock" rode about driving them back into the line with the flat of his sword.   He kept trying to form them into platoons.

His men shouted at him: "We can't fight bushes!" but he flogged them with his blade as he God-damned them for cowards.   His horse went down in a heap.   He picked himself out of the grass, ordered another officer out of his saddle, climbed into his place and resumed the belaboring of his own soldiers and the business of chasing them into line. His red coat, gorgeous sash and the fine mark he made on his plunging, rearing horse offered him as a perfect target for the Indians.   But it was always his horse that died.   He is said to have had his hat bound down on his head with a white handkerchief—perhaps it was really his dinner-napkin. A black servant, Billy Brown, who kept close to him, said that some suspected this white handkerchief was a signal for the French not to shoot him, as he had an understanding with them!

The stories told of that battle are as confused as the battle was itself.   Braddock was so hated, before and after, that no shame was spared him.   He was said to have worn a breastplate from which the bullets glanced.

Though no historian has apparently found a good word to say for Braddock's effort to get his men from behind the trees, it would seem on sober consideration that he was attempting the only wise thing in the circumstances.

By one of those bits of bad luck that generals dread, his men had been pinched in a tight place by the accidental arrival and dispersal of a luckier army.   By one of those mysteries that cause cattle, human and quadruped, to stampede with no excuse, his men had been taken in an off-hour. They broke, but were unable to get to the rear (as American and other soldiers have done innumerable times), because they were blockaded by the main body hurrying up to their rescue.

They were like men or rats caught swarming in an alley or a trench. They could not spread out into the woods for the Indians and French were there coiled under every bush, deadlier than rattlesnakes.

Braddock, taking in the situation at a glance, saw that the only wise thing, the only possible thing to do, was to accept his losses, form in column and march either forward or to the rear, anywhere to get out of the vise.

But first he must drive his men back into the ranks. He could not save them or move them otherwise. As a man rescuing a drowning person is permitted to knock him senseless, so he used the flat of his sword to whip his men away from the trees where they were sure to die since the Indians were firing from every direction. Once in the column they would have a chance not only of safety but of victory.

He ordered the standards planted for them to rally on. With sublime self-sacrifice and valorous intelligence he rode about from tree to tree taking all the risks upon himself, trying with voice and sword to snatch his men from the false security they hugged.

If he had been able to get them into column and retreat to the plain, the French and Indians would never have followed him. They did not even follow his men beyond the first ford when at last they broke and ran.

Once on the plain, Braddock could have re-formed his lines, shelled the enemy out of the woods and pushed through to the fort where the commander was waiting to surrender or retire.

Or, if Braddock could have thrust his men back into column and charged on ahead, he could still have won, for he would have removed his men from the range of that fatal hill; the French and Indians would have found themselves cut off from their base and caught between Braddock's advance and the body still left on the plain below. They would probably have dispersed in panic as they had already done at the first fire of the advance party.   Then Braddock would have found the fort an easy prey, with Contrecoeur already despondent and now almost destitute of troops.

That sort of triumph wrested from preliminary disorder has been won innumerable times by other generals.   If Braddock had only succeeded in quelling the first dismay of his men and if the custom of obedience had not been lost in the long lawless struggle through the wooded mountains and swamps, he might well have gained a victory that would have immortalized him as a genius of the first order.

This defense of Braddock from almost unmitigated abuse is verified by the account of his aide, Captain Orme, who vainly dedicated his life to redeeming Braddock's good name.   He says in his Journal:

"The general ordered the officers to endeavour to form the men, and to tell them off into small divisions and to advance with them; but neither entreaties nor threats could prevail.   The advanced flank parties, which were left for the security of the baggage, all but one ran in.

"When the General found it impossible to persuade them to advance, and no enemy appeared in view; and nevertheless a vast number of officers were killed, by exposing themselves before the men; he endeavored to retreat them in good order; but the panick was so great that he could not succeed.   During this time they were loading as fast as possible and firing in the air.   At last Lieutenant Colonel Burton got together about one hundred of the 48th regiment and prevailed upon them by the General's order to follow him towards the rising ground on the right, but he being disabled by his wounds, they faced about to the right and returned.

"When the men had fired away all their ammunition and the General and most of the officers were wounded, they by one common consent left the field, running off with the greatest precipitation." [15]

It is bad historical ethics to deny a man the merit of his intention and his intelligence because the cards fell out of the dealer's hand.

As for his temper, Washington himself would soon be displaying just as wild a frenzy again and again, demanding and inflicting the penalty of death for the cowardice and disobedience that he abhorred beyond all crimes.

Later in life he would be crying to heaven with horror at the perfect cowardice shown by Americans fighting Indians when Harmar and St. Clair could control their panics no better than Braddock his.

It amounts to an odious caddishness for Americans to explain Braddock's defeat on the silly assumption that if he had had only the fearless Americans there or listened to American wisdom, he would have won. Americans were there, outnumbering the British. He listened to American wisdom. He had American Indians and Virginians out in front. The Americans proved themselves no braver than the British.

With such facts in mind, the mere "intrepidity" so freely conceded to Braddock, along with contemptuous allusions to his being a brutal fool, should be changed to tributes to his magnificent and fearless wisdom.

Down went his second horse in the dust, and collapsed with a snort and a gush of blood.

Up he climbed on another. As fast as he flailed the men from behind the trees, they went back to them, trusting more in the thick trunks of the trees than in the unappreciated generalship of the maniac bawling and wasting his useless steel on his own men.

George Washington, who ought to have been in the

hospital, was wavering in the saddle, sick with fever and disgust, but never with fear.   Discipline withheld him for a while, as he recalled the hot arguments he had waged with that old man who always outbawled him.

He followed like a faithful aide till his own horse was killed between his legs and the bullets began to cut up his own clothes.   His experience in fox-hunting is said to have taught him to fall clear when his horse went down.   But in fact he was so entangled and so weak that Braddock's man Bishop had to extricate him, find him another horse and help him to mount.   Then he went to Braddock and begged to be allowed to ride back, bring up the Virginians, and flank the enemy.   Billy Brown testified afterward that Washington went on his knees before Braddock consented with an oath and a cry of "I've a mind to run you through the body." [16]   This is an example of the after-myths of battle.

In any case, Braddock gave his consent and Washington made his difficult way through that hurly-burly of insane men, insane horses, wounded, dead, wagons, cannons, shovels, pick-axes, muskets, knapsacks.

Many must have taken him for a coward in flight.   Many joined him, clinging to his stirrups and even to the mane of his plunging horse.   He got through to the Virginians with the orders and watched them formed up by their own officers, while Braddock raved on.   The lieutenants, with their napkins still pinned to their breasts, finding themselves unable to wheedle the soldiers into action, formed squads of officers and charged into the bushes.   They never returned.

Braddock was down again.   He swung into the fourth saddle, thinking what they would say of him and his men in England if he lost the battle to the scurvy French and the lousy Indians. That was all he was afraid of—the scandal of retreating before frog-eaters and dog-eaters—he and his roastbeef-eaters!

Colonel Gage had jabbed the standards of the two British regiments into the ground to mark their forming-point. But they would not fall in. Driven up, they fell out or down.

Milling miserably together, they fired every which way, because there was no visible target to fire at and because of the strange soldierly instinct in battle to be rid of ammunition noisily.

There were two instances, however, of a carefully placed volley. They made out a body of men going through the woods along the flank at a distance. They must be Frenchmen because of their fringed hunting shirts. Let 'em have it!

It was a well-aimed volley, and brought down two-thirds of its recipients. Unfortunately, it was Colonel Washington's Virginians who fell. According to one account, he had rushed them up, but not into the choked ravine. He guided them into the woods back of the Indians, faced them to the left and charged into the Indians, who were too much absorbed in butchering Englishmen to notice what Washington was up to until he was upon them. He drove them away from that flank for the time, and added his woodsmen to the British regulars.

This is probably a duplication of the true account of Captain Waggener, who led eighty men to the brow of the hill where they fell prone behind logs and opened a hot fire on the enemy. At the first flash of their first volley, the English, supposing them to be French and Indians, poured into them a fire, so accurate for once, that fifty of Waggener's men were killed and the rest driven to flight.

If Braddock's men had not killed so many of the

Virginians, the reserves might have saved the day. Washington's second horse fell dead, and he fought on foot, moving about among his woodsmen and warning them to shoot straight: "Draw your sights for the honour of old Virginia!"

By and by it was too late to retreat. The Indians were attacking from the rear, from the head, and from both sides. Braddock was down again on a dead horse. On his fifth steed, the bleeding, sweating old hero tried to compel success. He was so enraged that he began to kill his own men instead of merely smacking them with his sword.

He hated the Pennsylvanians who had not kept their promises to him—the canting Quakers!—and they hated him for what he said of them in his famous manner. It was told that he cut down one Pennsylvanian, named Fawcett, because he skulked behind a tree. And the dead man's brother, Tom Fawcett, revenged the deed. From behind another tree he fired at close range, the bullet cutting back of the breastplate through the General's right arm into his lungs.

This brought old Braddock off his fifth high horse. He fell into the arms of Captain Stewart. He did not rise again.[17]

With nearly all their officers slaughtered, the surviving soldiers were running about like beasts encircled by a forest fire. When they saw big Braddock lurch along the neck of his horse and vanish, and the charger buck and bolt with an empty saddle, all pretence of discipline ended.

Braddock's secretary, the son of General Shirley, had been killed; Colonel Sir Peter Halkett was shot dead and his son, bending to lift his father's corpse, was shot dead across it. Their two skeletons were found interlocked long afterward.

Sir John St. Clair was wounded, also Colonel Burton.

Captain Orme and Captain Morris were both desperately shattered; Gates and Gage and Gladwin were wounded. Of Washington's comrades at Fort Necessity, Splitdorph was killed, and the Frenchman, Peyronie, and Waggener, and Polson, of whose company of 48 "carpenters" or as we should say, pioneers, only one man escaped. Even William Wright, for whom Washington had asked a commission as showing "an inclination to the Art Military," had won his commission just in time to die in Braddock's gory slaughterpen.

Of eighty-six commissioned officers, sixty-three were killed or disabled, four hundred and thirty-seven men were killed, and almost as many wounded.

Of the French, three officers were killed, four wounded; four regular soldiers were wounded and five Canadians. The Indians lost twenty-seven known dead; perhaps others not reported.

Rarely in history has an army suffered such destruction; never perhaps from an enemy of only half its numbers. It was not bravery alone that kept the British there for three hours. There was no way out; nobody to say retreat. When at last the order came, from the fallen Braddock, the men charged pell mell like a mob in a theater fire. Washington said they could no more be stopped than "a gang of wild bears from the mountains."

Standing over the shattered hulk of Braddock to keep him from being trampled to death, Captain Orme, bleeding from his own wounds, tried to check a few of the soldiers long enough to carry off their prostrate general. They would not stop at his request, or at his command. When he seized them they wrenched free. He tried to bribe them. He shouted at the wretches who were paid eightpence a day, offers of guineas for a little charity: "Ten guineas! Twenty guineas! Forty! Fifty! Sixty guineas!"

That was more than five years' pay for a half hour's work.[18] But what good would it do a dead man? And what chance had the officer who promised it of living to pay it?

They ran on, casting aside weapons, knapsacks, caps, coats, fighting one another, treading on wounded, dead, or the unlucky living who stumbled.

To the weeping Captain Orme came his friend and fellow aide-de-camp, George Washington, and the woodsman, George Croghan.

Bishop was kneeling and upholding the reeking body of his general, and he afterwards told the improbable story that Braddock seized the hand of Washington and groaned:

"Oh, my dear colonel, had I been governed by your advice, we should never have come to this!"

In the effort to save the mortally wounded hero from adding his scalp to the dripping multitude the Indians were harvesting as they crept closer and closer to the almost undefended road, Washington and Croghan, for lack of a better litter, unwound Braddock's wide silk sash and lifted him into it.

He begged to be left to die on the field of his shame. He commanded them to leave him, and when they disobeyed, he tried to jerk Croghan's pistols from his belt and kill himself.

But Washington and Croghan overpowered him. He was too weak to resist. They toted him to a horse and with great difficulty hoisted him into the saddle. Bishop supported him back to a wagon, in which he was carried over "the worst road in the world," jolting his life away.

It was hard to find a wagon to put him in, for most of the drivers had cut the traces and lashed their horses all the way back to Colonel Dunbar, who was bringing up the reserves forty miles in the rear. Shouting "All is lost!" the relics of the army gradually staggered in with such tales that Colonel Dunbar had difficulty in keeping his big force from fleeing in disorder at once. Among the wagoners were Daniel Morgan and Daniel Boone.

Washington, with a coolness, a dauntlessness, and a military genius that sent his name across Europe again, but now with glory, mounted his horse and joined the British officers in organizing a dogged rearguard action with the steady soldiers fighting from tree to tree till they were clear of the woods. He said afterwards that the rangers "fought like soldiers and died like men."

The histories give the impression that Washington single-handed wielded the dauntless Virginians into a rearguard that saved the remnants of the British. As a matter of fact, he was an aide-de-camp, a messenger with no authority or commission to command anybody. His business took him to and from his wounded chief, who was still giving orders. The British and Virginian officers took charge of their own men. As he said himself, his work was greatly increased by the wounding of the other two aides.

Beyond the first ford Braddock's officers rallied a hundred soldiers, but they abandoned him in a sudden break. Colonel Gage then collected eighty men and held the ford.

If Dunbar had come up, he could probably have captured the fort, as the French themselves admitted. But the look of the panic-stricken fugitives inspired neither him nor the reserves.

The Indians did not follow far. At the river they found resistance, and they turned back to that incredible feast of spoils in the woods: dead and wounded by the hundred to be scalped, weapons, cannon, ammunition, uniforms, swords, jewels to be gathered. Never had the god of the French sent such a reward to his faithful followers or dealt such a blow to the heathen English.

A young prisoner, James Smith, who had been previously captured by the Indians, made to run the gauntlet, rescued by the French and taken into Fort Du Quesne to recover, used to describe the return of the Indians and the French with the caps, canteens, bayonets, bloody scalps, wagon horses.   Finally came a dozen prisoners, stripped naked. The Indians burned them to death jubilantly on the river bank opposite the fort.[19]   Three women captives were spared.

The next day all of the Western Indians left for home with their booty, and Contrecoeur shivered in his fort, wondering if the British would not still return.   He could not imagine the destruction that had been wreaked on that majestic host, by his few men under Captain Dumas and the great Indian chief Athanase and Langlade, the trader, who had handled their savages with tactical genius.

Washington stayed with General Braddock until midnight, when the dying veteran asked him to hurry to Colonel Dunbar and demand wagons for the wounded and provisions for the starving.   Washington and Croghan and six lighthorse pushed through a darkness so thick that at times they had to lead their horses and kneel to feel their way along the road.

They made Dunbar's camp at Gist's plantation by sunrise and returned at once with a few supplies to the still fleeing rabble that had been the finest army the New World had ever seen.

Captain Orme bribed, with money and rum, litter-bearers to carry Braddock along with the unceasing panic.

When they had all retreated to Dunbar's camp, Dunbar showed no disposition to fight, but fell back on Fort Cumberland in disorderly panic, after destroying everything that might delay the flight.   A hundred wagons were burned, vast amounts of gunpowder thrown into a brook, big guns wrecked, shells exploded or buried. Some of these were found long after.

If Dunbar had advanced, he might have retrieved the disgrace, for the French, instead of pursuing, were despondent over the inevitable return.

Braddock died on July 13th, 1755, at Great Meadows, muttering in his infinite bewilderment: "Is it possible? Is it possible?" "Who would have thought it?" "What will the Duke say?" "We shall know better another time."

Washington was with Braddock when he went out at midnight, and it must have been a somber hour for him, for he was in the Great Meadows, near the ruins of Fort Necessity where he had failed so wretchedly. And it was to redeem that failure that Braddock had crossed the seas, to fail more direly and die in the black woods.

Among the last words of the old martyr to bad luck were a good counsel to his war-wrung body-servant:

"Bishop, you are getting too old for war; I advise you to remain in America and go into the service of Colonel Washington. Be but as faithful to him as you have been to me, and, rely upon it, the remainder of your days will be prosperous and happy."

Bishop took this advice, and Washington kept Braddock's promise for him.

They buried him in the center of the road he had made, some say, at midnight: some, at dawn. The chaplain, Mr. Hamilton, who had behaved bravely in action, was badly wounded, and Washington is said to have read the funeral service of the Anglican church over the grave in the wilderness. Then such wagons as had not been lost or burned were driven over the grave to hide it from the Indians.

Many years later Washington revisited the field and sought for the grave in vain. But in 1823, in repairing the old road, Braddock's bones were found, with insignia of rank; and old Tom Fawcett, still boasting of his assassination, identified the spot. The remains were committed to the earth again at a little distance. Seventy years later, four hemlock trees were planted around the neglected grave, and in 1913 a monument of granite and bronze was set up by the citizens of Fayette County.[20]

How different was the fate of Baron Dieskau, who had come over to head the northern French army. Leading his Indians against Colonel William Johnson, he fell into the hands of the English and was saved with difficulty from being boiled and eaten by the English Indians, whose chiefs he had killed. But Johnson's victory came to naught. Shirley had a cabal formed against him, and the Quakers said that Braddock's defeat was a judgment of God against wars on the Indians.

Thousands of pounds in money fell into the hands of the French, also Braddock's and Washington's papers. These were the papers already discussed following the surrender at Fort Necessity, which the French published. They included Washington's Journal and the assassination capitulation as convincing evidence that the British had been preparing for war month after month while they protested the most peaceful intentions.[21]

Perfidious Albion was well punished for making war in time of peace—456 killed and 421 wounded out of a total of 1,300 or 1,400 men. The French claimed to have counted 1,300 dead. Captain Stewart's light-horse had twenty-five of the twenty-nine killed. The Virginia troops were all but wiped out. The French and Indians lost only Beaujeu and about thirty others!

Among the stories told of Washington was that of Dr. Craik, who said that in later years he and Washington were visited by an old Indian chief, who had fired at Washington again and again in vain. At last he concluded that the Great

Spirit shielded him, and ceased to fire. But the Great Spirit must have been reckless, for Washington had four bullets through his clothes, and two horses killed under him. His hat with the two holes in it was long a relic at Mount Vernon. Providence was doubtless aided in his rescue by the fact that he had changed his brilliant coat for a neutral-toned hunting shirt.

There is one popular belief about this battle that is true. George Washington performed prodigies of valor. He did not, however, say or pretend that he took command in the retreat, nor did anybody else say so at the time. He did not deny that the regulars, who behaved so badly, contained many Virginians. He referred to them as "the regulars (so-called)" and spoke of "the incomparable bravery" of the officers, who were largely British.[22] His devoted friend Orme praised his bravery but did not mention him in his battle account.

But at the time he felt only dismay at the appalling failure that had rendered his previous defeat petty by comparison. His men, at least, had been outnumbered at Fort Necessity, had fought long and hard in rain and fog, and had accepted only a deliberate capitulation allowing them to march out with the honors of war. But now he must write:

"We have been beaten, shamefully beaten by a handful of men, who only intended to molest and disturb our march. . . . But see the wondrous works of Providence! . . . We, but a few moments before, believed our numbers almost equal to the Canadian force; they only expected to annoy us. . . . Yet . . . we were totally defeated, and sustained the loss of everything . . . had I not been witness to the fact on that fatal day, I should scarcely have given credit to it even now!"[23]

The most important and best-earned tribute paid to the

Washington of this period is that of General B. T. Johnson, who says, with some preliminary exaggeration:

"Beyond a peradventure, his coolness, his self-control, his will, saved all that was saved. If it had not been for him, every British soldier would have been scalped. Twelve of them, taken prisoners, were burned alive at Fort Du Quesne the next evening.

"And the endurance of the Virginian captain is wonderful. After the entire day, from four o'clock in the morning of the 9th until dark of the 10th, in the saddle, four hours of it under the fiercest fire, which is the most exhausting excitement known to man, he rode and walked all night back to Dunbar's camp and returned at once to his wounded chief, and from the 9th until the 16th never took his clothes off. . . . The iron will was equaled by the iron frame and the iron constitution, and this prodigious effort was made by a man who had been left behind at Dunbar's camp, too ill to accompany the command, and had only reached the army the evening before the battle, hauled in a wagon because he was too weak to ride. The exhibition of endurance by Captain Washington for seven days after the battle exceeded that of courage, coolness, and self-control by him on the disastrous field." [24]

Washington was moved to one flash of bitter wit, in which he partly anticipated Mark Twain's "exaggerated death-reports" by writing to his brother Jack:

"As I have heard . . . a circumstantial account of my death and dying speech, I take this early opportunity of contradicting the first, and of assuring you that I have not as yet composed the latter. . . . You may expect to see me there on Saturday or Sunday se'night. . . . I shall take my Bullskin Plantations in my way. Pray give my compliments to all of my friends." [25]

For a brief, vivid and accurate account of the battle with none of the embroideries of after-history, one might search far for a better than the one Washington wrote to his mother on July 18, 1755, from Fort Cumberland:

"HONORED MADAM,

"As I doubt not but you have heard of our defeat, and, perhaps, had it represented in a worse light, if possible, than it deserves, I have taken this earliest opportunity to give you some account of the engagement as it happened, within ten miles of the French fort, on Wednesday the 9th instant.

"We marched to that place, without any considerable loss, having only now and then a straggler picked up by the French and scouting Indians. When we came there, we were attacked by a party of French and Indians, whose number, I am persuaded, did not exceed three hundred men; while ours consisted of about one thousand three hundred well-armed troops, chiefly regular soldiers, who were struck with such a panic, that they behaved with more cowardice than it is possible to conceive. The officers behaved gallantly, in order to encourage their men, for which they suffered greatly, there being near sixty killed and wounded; a large proportion of the number we had.

"The Virginia troops showed a good deal of bravery, and were nearly all killed; for I believe, out of three companies that were there, scarcely thirty men are left alive. Captain Peyrouny, and all his officers down to a corporal, were killed. Captain Polson had nearly as hard a fate, for only one of his was left. In short, the dastardly behaviour of those they call regulars exposed all others, that were inclined to do their duty, to almost certain death; and, at last, in despite of all the efforts of the officers to the contrary, they ran, as sheep pursued by dogs, and it was impossible to rally them.

"The General was wounded, of which he died three days after. Sir Peter Halket was killed in the field, where died many other brave officers. I luckily escaped without a wound, though I had four bullets through my coat, and two horses shot under me. Captain Orme and Morris, two of the aids-de-camp, were wounded early in the engagement, which rendered the duty harder upon me, as I was the only person then left to distribute the General's orders, which I was scarcely able to do, as I was not half recovered from a violent illness, that had confined me to my bed and a wagon for above ten days. I am still in a weak and feeble condition, which induces me to halt here two or three days in the hope of recovering a little strength, to enable me to proceed homewards; from whence, I fear, I shall not be able to stir till towards September; so that I shall not have the pleasure of seeing you till then, unless it be in Fairfax. Please to give my love to Mr. Lewis and my sister; and compliments to Mr. Jackson, and all other friends that inquire after me. I am, honored Madam, your most dutiful son." [26]

He claims nothing and reveals no errors except the astounding and exceedingly rare mistake of estimating the enemy at less than half their number.

XVI

CHAOS AND TERROR

BONFIRES were waiting to be lighted as soon as the good word came from Braddock that the fort at the Forks of the Ohio was taken back from the French papists, whose designs on America all truly good religious people had dreaded since Roger Williams in 1670 had cried:

"The French and Roman Jesuits, the firebrands of the world, for their godbelly sake, are kindling at our back in this country their hellish fires with all the natives of this country." [1]

The fear of Catholicism was what most of the people of that time, Puritan, Anglican and other Protestants, meant by maintaining their "civil and religious liberties." It was the only thing that could force the colonies to the semblance of concerted action. But since bringing them together always brought their prejudices into the contiguity that always favors a fight, they were as apt as the pithballs in the electric experiment to fly apart as soon as they were brought together.

But now England had sent an army and the colonies were on the march in all directions. Braddock was to explode the first bomb under the French foundations.

Fussy old Dinwiddie could hardly wait. Ben Franklin had to quench the enthusiasm in Philadelphia by refusing to subscribe for fireworks before the victory was won. But Dinwiddie was genuinely happy for the first time—aside, that is, from such minor disturbances as the French and Indian raids on the frontiers, the destruction of a few poor families and the dastardly inactivity of the two Fairfaxes and their militia.

His letters and speeches are dramatic as they mirror the public feelings when the news began to trickle back over the dark long-trail to Fort Du Quesne.

The very day when Braddock reached the Monongahela and came out of the woods, Dinwiddie prorogued the Assembly to the following Tuesday with a pleasant farewell message of good news to come:

"Gen'n, I am in great Hopes before y's y't Gen'l Braddock is in Possess'n of the Fort on the Ohio the French took from us last year." [2]

On July 14th, five days after the calamity, he writes to Sir Thomas Robinson in England: "I y's Morn'g rec'd a Let'r from Colo. Innes . . . and another from L'd Fairfax, Copies thereof I enclose You. These Let's gave me a sensible Concern for the melancholy disaster attend'g Gen'l Braddock and his Forces. . . . I daily expected an Acc't of his hav'g taken the Fort on the Ohio."

On July 18th he writes to Colonel Carter: "The News from Colo. Innes surpriz'd me at first, but on reading the Let'r over some Times I concluded it was wrote imediately on the Acc't given him, which Acc't I was willing to think was from a Deserter who, in a great Pannick, represented w't his Fears suggested . . . the length of Time gives me still greater hopes the first News is false, or at least not so bad."

On July 21st he writes to Colonel Innes: "This Day Week I dispatch'd an Express to You, and it gives me the greatest Uneasiness not to hear from You. As Your Let'r of the 11th was wrote in a great Hurry . . . I am in hopes Things are not so bad as You then wrote."

Not until July 25th could he write Sir Thomas Robinson: "I was in Hopes y't the News was false. . . . But, alas! last night I rec'd an Acc't of our Defeat and the Enemy's being in Possess'n of our Train of artillery. The Gen'l died like himself, hav'g had five Horses shot under him before he dropt. All the officers and Men rais'd here behav'd well, but am sorry to hear the private Men of the Regulars were seiz'd with a Panick, run away like Sheep. But I refer You to the enclosed Copy of a Let'r from Colo. Washington."

He describes the fear of French invasion with the captured artillery. He writes to Colonel Dunbar, who succeeded Braddock in command:

"I was the more astonish'd w'n I am inform'd y't 300 Fr'h and Ind's have defeated 1300 British Forces. . . . Such advantages by so few Men is not to be met with in History, and surely must raise a just resentm't in the Heart of every British Subject. . . . W't a fine Field for Hon'r will Colonel Dunbar have to confirm and establish his Character as a brave Officer, and w't will he have in View to retrieve the Loss . . . ! Recover the Train of Artillery and the Hon'r of the British Forces."

He writes to Captain Robert Orme, who was badly wounded, that he read his letter "with Tears in my Eyes. . . . The dastardly Conduct of the Private Men is with't Precedent; or can History produce when so many British Forces were defeated by so few of the Enemy." He advises Orme to ride back in General Braddock's chariot and invites him to his house. Later, Dinwiddie was called on to apologize to Orme for slandering the British regulars, and he explained that he was only trying to get Virginians to enlist, but he snapped: "There were no Fellons among the Draughts from our Men." And he wrote to the Cherokee chief, Old Hop's Son: "I am sensible Y'r Nat'n can fight the Enemy Ind's better than Y'r Broth's, the English."

By his bravery Washington had won back all of Dinwiddie's old esteem. He, who had been the blameworthy "Washington," reappears as "Colo. Washington," and in a letter of July 26th Dinwiddie was so moved by his heroism as to begin his letter for the first and last time, "Dear Washington," and to exclaim upon his delight that "You came safe off with't any Wound, after Y'r gallant Behav'r, on which I congratulate You. . . . But pray, S'r, w'th the Numb'r of Men remain'g is there no Possibility of doing someth'g the other Side of the Mount's before the Winter Mo's?" [3]

On August 5th Dinwiddie addresses the dismal General Assembly, describing how open the colony lies to French and Indian invasion, and comments on the "Virginia Forces who purchas'd with their Lives immortal Glory to their Country and themselves on the Banks of Monongahela." He reminds them that they still have one first duty: "to preserve to us and our Posterity the most dear and desirable of all human Treasures—Religious and Civil Liberty." [4]

The next day he writes in horror to the Earl of Halifax that Colonel Dunbar, instead of recapturing the field, has marched off "to Winter Quarters" in Pennsylvania—winter quarters in August! "There appears to be an infatuat'n attending the whole of ys Evpedit'n."

In his despair he tries to wheedle some help from the Catawba and Cherokee allies. It was alleged that Braddock's contempt had driven them from his side; and his defeat had certainly not endeared the English to them. Dinwiddie pleaded:

"If we had had some of Y'r Warriors to fight the Ind's in their own Manner we sh'd have demolish'd them. . . . The Love and F'dship y't has always subsisted between Y'r Nat'ns and Y'r Bro's, the English, I hope will continue as long as the Sun and Moon gives Light."

On the same day he writes to the Captains of the Virginia Forces, scolding them for complaining of not being paid, and offering a bounty of ten pounds "for every French or French Indian Scalp y't may be bro't in by You. . . . It gives me Concern to hear of the great Desertions from Y'r Companies."

With a few brilliant exceptions, the British and their colonists were unable to manage the Indians except by annihilation. Braddock's disaster was a result of this. He was destroyed by an inferior number of French and Indians largely because he could not attach friendly Indians to him. He blamed the colonists for having alienated them before his arrival. Only a hundred ever visited him. The colonial troops warned the regulars of what would happen and were later accused of undermining their morale!

Now their own morale was gone. Too many of their comrades had been left dead and dying on Braddock's field for the Indians to scalp and leave to the wolves that were stripping their bones for the ants to cleanse of mortal flesh and bury under the soil.

George Washington's tremendous energy had thrown off the fever that should have kept him from the battle; he had endured sorrows and anguishes of heart and hardships unspeakable on that frightful road home from the Monongahela; he had upheld his dying general and hidden his corpse under the wagon tracks for fear of Indians and wolves; he had found Colonel Dunbar in panic and Colonel Innes no better than he had expected.

He had done all he could, and now he had time to be ill again.

He came back from Braddock's defeat, lucky to be alive, but such a physical wreck that he thought himself doomed to die. He found no end of pretty nurses, and had made

himself so indispensable to the women that old William
Fairfax (never dreaming, surely, that his daughter-in-law,
Sally Fairfax, had indulged in a clandestine correspondence)
wrote to him July 26th, 1755:

"We have been in torturing suspence. Each one for their best
beloved. Now You are by a kind Providence preserved and returned to us, we can say the Catastrophy might have been
worse. . . .

"If a Satturday Nights Rest canot be sufficient to enable your
coming hither to Morrow, the Lady's will try to get Horses to equip
our Chair or attempt their strength on Foot to Salute You, so desirous are they with loving Speed to have an ocular Demonstration
of your being the same Identical Gent'n—that lately departed to defend his Country's Cause."

To this letter was appended the following postscript [5]
from "the Lady's" themselves:

Dear Sir
After thanking Heaven for Your safe return
I must accuse you of great unkindness in refusing us the
pleasure of seeing you this night I do assure You nothing
but our being satisfied that our company would be
disagreable should prevent us from trying if our Legs
would not carry us to Mount Virnon this night, but if
you will not come to us to morrow Morning very early
we shall be at Mont Virnon

S Fairfax.
Ann Spearing
Eliz[th] Dent

A LETTER FROM SALLY FAIRFAX TO WASHINGTON.

"DEAR SIR,—After thanking Heaven for your safe return I
must accuse you of great unkindness in refusing us the pleasure of

seeing you this night. I do assure you nothing but our being satisfied that our company would be disagreable should prevent us from trying if our Legs would not carry us to Mount Virnon this Night, but if you will not come to us tomorrow Morning very early we shall be at Mont Virnon.

"S. Fairfax,
"Ann Spearing,
"Eliz'th Dent." [5]

The manuscript is in the hand of Sally Fairfax. Though it is written in the first person, with her usual caution, she had two other women sign it with her.

Mrs. Robins says of "this famous round-robin," as she calls it: "With all of her culture and social powers, Sally did not know how to spell Mount Vernon, and she did have legs, destroying the myth of years, that young ladies of the day before ours neither had legs, mentioned legs, nor showed legs." [6]

This letter in itself means no more, of course, than that Washington was a favorite with these women. And why not?

He was not yet twenty-four, and a man of peculiar history. He had been a pathfinder in the wilderness, he had proved himself fearless of any danger, ready to sacrifice himself to any public duty, he had been defeated twice by the French and Indians, he had been accused of being an assassin, he had surrendered a fort to the French; yet always he came out a hero. No wonder the women admired him. No wonder they feared to marry so restless an adventurer. As Archibald Cary wrote him: "Miss Cary and Miss Randolph joyn in wishing you that sort of Glory which will most Indear you to the Fair Sex." But to be endeared to a sex was coldly far from being dear to one woman.

In Braddock's downfall, the colonies had lost all their reverence for the British troops. Virginia woodsmen had witnessed their "dastardly cowardice," had saved them from utter destruction, and seen the wretched survivors retire to winter quarters near Philadelphia in August, where their officers flogged them almost daily for their disobedience.

"From a military point of view," says James Truslow Adams,[7] "whenever the colonists had come into close co-operation with the British troops and navy, as in the Canadian and Jamaican expeditions of the first decade of the century, the Cartagena expedition of 1740, and the joint operations of the Seven Years' War, England had been too apt to show herself at her lowest point of efficiency and military ability, and this led many to underrate her strength."

Braddock's army had gone like the Spanish Armada, leaving Western Pennsylvania and Virginia to take the consequences. The consequences were dire.

The magnificent Dumas who had gained with inferior forces one of the greatest victories in human chronicle and one of the most influential, took the place the dead Beaujeu had been sent to fill as the successor of Contrecoeur, who went home and received his well-earned pension and the cross of Saint Louis.

Dumas had now extraordinary success in gathering the Indians to his side. The news of the spoils of Braddock's defeat had made him a god for dispensing treasures. The Delawares and Shawanese, sulking at British tactlessness, and worse, went over to the French. The Mingoes and other tribes beyond the Ohio remembered ancient grudges. "The West rose like a nest of hornets, and swarmed in fury against the English frontier."[8]

Soon Dumas was able to write home:

"It is by means varied in every form to suit the occasion, that I have succeeded in ruining the three adjacent provinces, Pennsylvania, Maryland, and Virginia, driving off the inhabitants, and totally destroying the settlements over a tract of country thirty leagues wide, reckoning from the line of Fort Cumberland. M. de Contrecoeur had not been gone a week before I had six or seven different war-parties in the field at once, always accompanied by Frenchmen. Thus far, we have lost only two officers and a few soldiers; but the Indian villages are full of prisoners of every age and sex. The enemy has lost far more since the battle than on the day of his defeat."

Dumas and all the French officers were revolted by the ferocity of the Indians; but, since the English used them, they had to, and the French officers were a trifle more merciful than the colonial. Both were afraid to quarrel with the methods of their allies lest they feel them. "They kill all they meet," writes a French priest; "and after having abused the women and maidens, they slaughter or burn them."

The frontiers were ghastly with unheard-of horrors. Even the brave Moravian missionaries in Pennsylvania and New York lost their welcome among the Indians and had to abandon their work.[9] No wonder, since many of the Indians had been taught that Christ was a Frenchman crucified by the English. They but carried out the work of the Inquisition among heretics.

As Croghan's friend, Adam Hoops, wrote to the Governor of Pennsylvania:

"We, to be sure, are in as bad Circumstances as ever any poor Christians were ever in, For the Cries of Widowers, Widows, fatherless and Motherless Children, with many others for their Relations, are enough to Pierce the most hardest of hearts; Likewise it's a very Sorrowful specticle to see those that Escaped with their lives not a Mouthful to Eat, or Bed to lie on, or Cloths to Cover their Nakedness, or keep them warm, but all they had consumed into Ashes."

The horrors were such that the non-resisting Quakers

were ousted from their hold on the colony and 60,000 pounds was appropriated for defence, with land bounties for soldiers, as well as a bounty of $150 for the scalp of every male Indian over ten years old and $50 for every Indian woman's hair.[10]

But the Indians were willing to collect scalps for nothing. There is no telling all the ghastly border scenes. Jumonville's brother, Coulon de Villiers, revenged him handsomely by his forays, until he and Ligneris were captured by Amherst in 1759.

The ignored lives and trials of such men as Croghan must be studied for those phases. Croghan raised a volunteer company, built a fort, and when commissioned a captain by Pennsylvania, did splendid work, though always at war with the Quakers as was his new chief, Col. William Johnson, who drew his sword against one of them at a conference with the Indians.[11]

Virginia had her own hands full. Women were being cut to pieces in their beds, their babes and clinging children tomahawked in their arms.

While the scalps of Indian boys were selling at $150 apiece, American boys were losing theirs. In the Shenandoah Valley, a Mrs. Painter saw her husband consumed in their blazing house; saw four of her children hung to trees and shot to death. A neighbor's child of twelve, little Jacob Fisher, was carried away to a distance where he was ordered to collect a pile of dry wood for his own funeral pile, as little Isaac was. This was heaped around a tree to which he was tied by a rope. The humorous Indians then made the lad run in a circle "until his rope wound him up to the sapling, and then back until he came in contact with the flame, whilst his infernal tormentors were drinking, singing, and dancing around him. . . . This was continued for several hours, until the poor and helpless boy fell and expired with the most excruciating torments." [12]

Mrs. Painter, five of her daughters and one of her sons were dragged into the wilderness and only released after an absence of three years: three of the daughters remained with the Indians by choice, refusing to return. From this same community a Mrs. Smith was carried away, and afterward "had the honor, if it could be so deemed, of presenting her husband with an Indian son, by a distinguished war chief," wrote Samuel Kercheval, who added that Mr. Smith took back his wife "and never maltreated her on this account, but had a most bitter aversion to the young chief." The boy grew up, revealing Indian traits, and scorning education. He enlisted as a soldier in the Revolution and never returned.

Some of the worst atrocities were committed by white renegades disguised as Indians, who sought plunder at any cost.

One does not think nowadays of Virginia as a scene of such horrors as we associate with later frontiers. As the whites flowed out across the West in a creeping tide, the frontier moved forward like a troubled surf, always in torment and always crimson.

The roadways that had been built at such effort and drenched with so much blood "to reach the foe were now the ways which the foe was using to reach the hearts of the colonies," says Dr. Koontz.[13] "The situation was almost as though the dykes of Holland had been cut and the ocean had begun its inundation. Through every gap and mountain pass . . . the gleeful, triumphant savages now rushed in. . . . For a time it looked as if the British would be swept from the American continent."

To put an end to such grisly revelry as this, Virginia looked to Washington. He was still so weak with fever that he could hardly move about his beloved glebe. He was sick, too, of war as a business. He wrote bitterly to his half-brother Augustine, August 2, 1755:

"I am always ready and always willing, to render my country any services that I am capable of, but *never* upon the *terms* I have done; having suffered much in my private fortune, besides impairing one of the best constitutions.

"I was employed to go a journey in the winter (when, I believe, few or none would have undertaken it), and what did I get by it? My expenses borne! I then was appointed, with trifling pay, to conduct a handful of men to the Ohio. What did I get by *this?* Why, after putting myself to a considerable expense, in equipping and providing necessaries for the campaign, I went out, was soundly beaten, lost them all!—came in and had my commission taken from me, or, in other words, my *command* reduced, under *pretence* of an order from *home!* I then went out a volunteer with General Braddock, and lost all my horses and many other things; but this being a *voluntary* act, I ought not to have mentioned *this;* nor should I have done it, was it not to show that I have been upon the losing order ever since I entered the service, which is now near two years. So that I think I cannot be blamed, should I, if I leave my family again, endeavour to do it upon such terms as to prevent my suffering; (to *gain* by it being the least of my expectation)." [14]

A fortnight later he was scolding his mother for advising him not to accept further hardship in the service.

The distracted soul, having imagined him dead and scalped as the rumor came, had received him back under the mercy of providence, and had seen how heartbroken he was and broken of body and creeping about like a sick cat.

The thought of his taking another chance with the fate

that had spared him thrice was too much. To her frantic plea he wrote with a calm that is less lovely than some of his others:

"Honored Madam,

If it is in my power to avoid going to the Ohio again, I shall; but if the command is pressed upon me, by the general *voice* of the country, and offered upon such terms as cannot be objected against, it would reflect dishonor upon me to refuse; and *that*, I am sure, must or *ought* to give you the greater uneasiness, than my going in an honorable command, for upon no other terms I will accept of it. At present I have no proposals made to me, nor have I any advice of such an intention, except from private hands. I am, etc." [15]

The stilted tone must be discounted, for children were taught to address their parents in a tone of awe next to that reserved to the deity. But that word "ought" (and underlined) is shocking.

On the same day he wrote Warner Lewis, brother to the husband of his sister Betty, that he was well of his disorder, but not of his discontent:

"The chief reason (next to indisposition), that prevented me from coming down to this Assembly, was a determination not to offer my services; and that determination proceeded from the following reasons. First, a belief that I could not get a command upon such terms as I should incline to accept; for I must confess to you, that I never will quit my family, injure my fortune, and, (above all,) impair my health to run the risk of such changes and vicissitudes, as I have met with, but shall expect, if I am employed again, to have something *certain*. Again, was I to accept the command, I should insist upon some things, which ignorance and inexperience made me overlook before, particularly that of having the officers appointed, in some measure, *with* my advice and with my concurrence, for I must add I think a commanding officer, not having this liberty, appears to me to be a strange thing, when it is considered how much a commanding officer is answerable for the behaviour of the inferior officers, and how much his good or ill success, in time of action, depends upon the conduct of each particular one, especially too, in this kind of fighting, where, being dispersed, each and every of them at that time has a greater liberty to misbehave, than if he were regularly and compactly drawn up under the eyes of his superior officer.

"On the other hand, how little credit is given to a commander, who, after a defeat, in relating the cause of it, justly lays the blame on some individual, whose cowardly behaviour betrayed the whole to ruin! How little does the world consider the circumstances, and how apt are mankind to level their vindictive censures against the unfortunate chief, who perhaps merited least of the blame!"

This surely is a warm defense of his late chief, Braddock, to whom he wanted to raise a monument. He goes on:

"I believe our circumstances are brought to that unhappy dilemma, that no man can gain any honor by conducting our forces at this time, but will rather lose in his reputation if he attempts it.

"But if the command should be offered, the case is then altered, as I should be at liberty to make such objections, as reason and my small experience had pointed out. . . . I am, dear Warner, your most affectionate friend, and obedient servant." [16]

The Assembly, however, frightened by the hideous tales of Indian havoc among the unprotected back settlements, had already voted £35,000 for the public service. Dinwiddie wrote, "I believe they w'd have given 100,000." [17] They also ordered the Virginia regiment increased to sixteen companies, and granted cash rewards of five pounds to every soldier, seventy-five pounds to the captains, and three hundred pounds to George Washington, as "a reward and compensation for their gallant behaviour and losses."

On August 14th, Governor Dinwiddie sent to the commissionless hero of the battle, a commission as "Colonel of the Virg'a Regim't and Com'd'r-in-Chief of all the Forces now rais'd and to be rais'd for the Defence of y's H. M'y's Colony. . . . And You are hereby charg'd with full Power and Authority to act defensively or Offensively, as You shall think for the good and Wellfare of the Service."

But, alas, it was not a royal commission—only another one of Dinwiddie's!

On September 17th, Dinwiddie wrote and modestly suggested to the new Commander-in-Chief that he teach his recruits "as much as possible Bush fighting."

This was a tribute to the young Virginian of twenty-four, and another tribute to the Indians who had taught the world a new tactics and revolutionized the Art Military.

He accepted, selected his officers, enlisted soldiers, made a tour of inspection around the blockhouses from Fort Cumberland to Fort Dinwiddie and found everywhere the same old inefficiency, dearth of equipment, selfishness, drunkenness, insubordination and general unfitness that he was doomed to find about him all his life—the very thing that the foreigner Braddock was loathed for remarking upon in his blunt manner.

There is nothing that Washington inveighed against all his life so much as American military methods; and in nothing has his most earnest advice been more persistently ignored. Nothing in American history—to one who reads beyond the schoolbooks and sermons—is more misleading than the eternal reliance on an unprepared militia, in spite of the almost unrelieved chronicle of its odious and costly failures. This history has been so well suppressed, smothered or disguised in hymns to the ultimate victories secured by ultimately trained troops, that the average American has actually always taken pride in the militia.

Washington kept up an unrelenting clamor against reliance on untrained citizen soldiery. He suffered disaster after disaster from the "sheep" he had to try to lead. In every American war the patriotic laity has revealed a cowardice and panic that are inevitable when rabbles of well-meaning souls find themselves in the presence of an organized enemy.

The nation has lost tens of thousands of lives and risked its very existence again and again from its addiction to militia. And yet so shameless has been the concealment of these collapses, or so short the memory of them that this silliest of superstitions still controls all national plans.

If children were taught a little more of the truth and a little less of the flapdoodle, they would not be so easily victimized by the claptrap of politicians and the pious hosannas of the professional lovers of "peace," which nobody loves better than men of Washington's mind, though they realize that it needs strength to maintain it.

So now, with the Indians torturing and burning, and Dinwiddie railing against the "dastardly cowardly" militia and sending Rangers out to replace them, Washington wrote to him from Winchester, "Oct'r ye 11th, 1755," confessing that his men deserted at will and were protected when caught by the judges before whom they had to be tried.

Washington denounced the judges as "absurd, irregular and illegal."

The soldiers were so mutinous that he had to draw his sword on his own soldiers and was threatened with having his brains blown out by his own men:

"I was desirous of proceeding immediately at the head of some Militia to put a stop to the Ravages of the Enemy . . . but was told by Colo. Martin, that it was impossible to get above 20 or 25 Men, they having absolutely refus'd to stir, choosing, as they say, to die with their Wives and Family's.

. . . I sent off expresses to hurry the Recruits from below
. . . and also hired Spies to go out and see . . . and to
encourage the Rangers, who, we are told, are block'd up by
the Indians in small Fortresses; but . . . I believe they are
more encompass'd by fear than by the Enemy. . . .

"In all things I meet with the greatest opposition.　No
orders are obey'd but what a party of Soldiers, or my own
drawn Sword Enforces . . . to such a pitch has the insolence of these People arriv'd, By having every point hitherto
submitted to them, however I have given up none . . .
nor will it, unless they execute what they threaten—i.e. 'to
blow out my brains. . . .'

"Unless the Assembly will enact a Law to enforce the
Military Law in all its Parts, I must, with great regret,
decline the Honour that has been so generously intended
me, and for this only reason I do it—The foreknowledge
I have of failing in every point . . . under our present
Establishment we shall become a Nuisance. . . . If these
Practices are allow'd off, we may as well quit altogether,
for no duty can ever be carried on if there is not ye greatest
punctuality observ'd, one thing always depending so immediately upon another." [18]

The reluctance of the militia to march was not altogether
fear of the Indians, nor their devotion to their families a
mere pretence.　What the Virginians feared most of all was
an uprising of the slaves.

In a report of the population made by Dinwiddie a little
later, he says: "The No. of our People, Whites and Blacks,
are as follows: White Men, Women and Children are
173,316 . . . the Militia may be reckon'd at 35,000 Men
fit to bear Arms, but the greatest Part of 'em are Free-
hold's . . . they plead their Privilege not to be forc'd to
serve but on Invas's and Alarms. . . . The No. of our
Negroes are 120,156. Y's No. of Negroes alarms our

People much and are aff[rai]d of bad Consequences if the Militia are order'd to any great Distance from the pres't Settlements." [19]

The first result of Braddock's defeat was a noticeable restlessness among the negroes. Before the bad news was fully confirmed, Dinwiddie wrote to Colonel Charles Carter (whose daughter was the mother of Robert E. Lee), owner of a thousand slaves, "The Villany of the Negroes on any Emergency of Gov't is w't I always fear'd." A body of them had threatened Colonel Carter's son, and Dinwiddie advised the seizure of "all Horses used by Negroes in the Night time."

He wrote to England that he could not call out all the militia, but must leave a proper number in each county "to protect it from the Combinations of the Negro Slaves, who have been very audacious on the Defeat on the Ohio. These poor creatures imagine the Fr. will give them their Freedom. We have too many here." [20]

With the plantations scattered as they were, the Indians torturing and burning on the whole frontier, so many families in mourning from the massacre of the Monongahela, and the sinister blacks beginning to lift their heads and mutter their blood-chilling threats, what soldier but would feel that home was his first allegiance? Everybody was in a state of nerves, and with all too much reason.

Washington describes two panic-stricken messengers bringing in news of Indian butchery and his hasty dash to the spot "where these horrid Murders were said to be committed. . . . Who shou'd we find . . . but 3 drunken soldiers of the Light Horse, carousing . . . the Party of Indians discovered by Isaac Julian prov'd to be a Mulattoo and negro seen hunting of Cattle."

He tells of one Captain of Militia, who, when called to march, "answer'd that his Wife, Family and Corn was at

Stake, so were those of his Soldiers, therefore it was not possible for him to come; such is the Example of the Officers! Such the behavior of ye Men! and such the unhappy circumstances on which this Country depends!" [21]

He tells of purchasing 650 fine Beeves, and giving his own bond for them; also he tells of sending a letter to Andrew Montour, who had with him 300 friendly Indians to whom Washington wrote a wily letter, which he says "savours a little of flattery &c, but I hope is justifiable on such occasions." [22] That "&c." is eloquent, from the George who could not tell a lie—at least as a little child.

In the following letter he says of the Indians, using his Indian name, Conotocarius:

"I was greatly enraptur'd when I heard you were at the head of 300 Indians, being satisfied that your hearty attachment to our glorious Cause, your Courage, of which I have very great proofs, and your Presence among the Indians, wou'd animate their just Indignation to do something Noble, something worthy themselves, and honourable to You. . . . Assure them that as I have the chief Comand, I am invested with Power to treat them, as Brethren and Allies, which, I am sorry to say, they have not been of late. Recommend me kindly to our good Friend, Monocatootha, and others; tell them how happy it wou'd make Conotocaurious to have an opportunity of taking them by the hand . . . and how glad he wou'd be to treat them as Brothers of our great King beyond the waters." [23]

But the Indians would not be wheedled and the militia would not obey.

Sally Fairfax's husband was still so fond of George Washington and such an admirer of his that he was struck with a sudden desire to go out and fight under his command, perhaps to redeem the loss his prestige endured when his men refused to protect their own frontier.

He wrote to Dinwiddie a letter that is lost to us as to Dinwiddie, who replied, October 18th, 1755, that it was mislaid so that he could not answer it in a particular manner, "but I remember You propos'd an Inclinat'n to go out with Colo. Washington, w'ch if You had mention'd sooner it w'd have been mighty agreeable to me, but as the Assembly is to meet the 27th I hope of seeing You here w'n shall talk y't Affair over."

The governor had evidently seen Sally on her way home to her father's for a visit, since he adds: "Y'r Lady was very well a few Days ago and is gone to Hampton."

By chance, we have a vivid description from one of Washington's officers of the state of affairs within the army and the scenes encountered. Captain Charles Lewis, among the troops of the Major Lewis referred to, kept a Journal,[24] from which a few quotations are made:

"October 10th, 1755. Left Fredericksburg under the command of Major Andrew Lewis with eighty men. . . . The men being most of them drunk. . . . This night two of my company deserted.

"October 11th. (at Martin Hardin's) Here we had good entertainment, a merry landlady and daughter. . . ."

"Took on the march a deserter and a drunken schoolmaster. . . . We joined the Hon'ble George Washington, Commander of the Virginia Regiment . . . a remarkable battle between two of our servants. . . . A remarkable dispute between Lieutenant Steenberger and an Irish woman . . . much shocked at the havoc made by the barbarous, cruel Indians at one Mecraggin's. I found the master of the family . . . half out of the grave and eaten by the wolves. . . . We had this day two women ducked for robbing the deserted houses . . . an Irishman arrived with two scalps . . . to the plantation of one Williams. The body of a woman layed near one of the houses, her head being scalped, and also a small boy and a young man. . . . Five deserters were this day punished, each receiving one thousand lashes. . . .

"December 6th. I saw the most horrid shocking sight I ever beheld . . . the bodies of three different people who were first massacred, then scalped and after thrown into a fire . . . the instruments of their death still bloody and their brains sticking on them. . . .

"December 24th.   Being Christmas, we spent the time in drinking loyal healths and dancing till 11 o'clock.

"December 25th.   After dinner drank the Royal Healths and sung some entertaining songs with 3 Huzzas and Rolls of Drums to every health and song.   Then took partners and spent the evening in dancing, about 12 o'clock broke up."

Two more entries conclude the Journal.

Dinwiddie begged the Burgesses to strengthen Washington's hands, especially against the magistrates who actually protected the deserters.   He said in a letter to the Earl of Halifax:

"The bad Conduct of all the Colonies is very unaccountable. . . . I am really wore out with Concern.   I never heard or saw a People so very defective of their Duties to H. M'y's Com'ds, so absurdly neglectful of their Liberties, Lives, and Estates." [25]

He complained of the cabals and secret factions already ruining the spirit of the Assembly.   It was Congress a little in advance, and refused to enact the military laws that Washington demanded.

In one of his letters, he wrote to his lieutenant-colonel, Andrew Stephen:

"Things not yet being rightly settled for punishing deserters according to their crimes, you must go on in the old way of *whipping stoutly*. . . . The Governor . . . seems uneasy at what I own gives me much concern, i. e. that gaming seems to be introduced into the camp.   I am ordered to discourage it, and must desire that you will intimate the same." [26]

Washington was always a great believer in flogging, and kept it up through the Revolution.   He did not approve of gambling in camp, though he gambled himself, lightly.

To add to his other confusions, Washington had a familiar and sorry wrangle with a Maryland officer, Captain Dagworthy, who had fought at Braddock's field under a royal commission. He would not obey Dinwiddie's Colonel Washington, and was insulting in his manner. Since Fort Cumberland was in Maryland, Washington was in a quandary that Dinwiddie could not solve.

Dagworthy, on the strength of an obsolete commission, though he had only 30 men under him, refused to obey Washington, who commanded 500. Dagworthy refused to accept even a countersign or let Washington touch the provisions at the fort. Dinwiddie wanted Washington to arrest Dagworthy, but Washington declined to risk the decision of the foreign ministry on such a colonial presumption.

He offered to resign, "rather than submit to the Comand of a Person who I think has not such superlative Merit," but that solution was refused. His officers, who shared his indignation, drew up a memorial and asked him to take it to Governor Shirley of Massachusetts, who had been made commander-in-chief of all the British forces in America after Braddock's death. They begged to be put on the same footing with royal officers.

Washington asked Dinwiddie's permission to go and Dinwiddie gladly gave it. He wrote in high praise of Washington, and prepared for him, not only a strong letter to Shirley, but cordial introductions to other governors, with requests for information to be transmitted by the young colonel.[27]

It was a long ride for a colonel to take to discipline a captain, but it gave Washington the first glimpse of the country he was to unite and hold together, and it gave the country the chance to see what a magnificent creature he was before it invited him to make another ride to Boston twenty years later.

Before leaving he wrote to Lieutenant-Colonel Stephen, that he had solicited permission to go to Boston to lay the situation before General Shirley, with whom he had "a personal acquaintance, which I thought might add some weight . . . as I have taken the fatigue &c of this tedious journey upon myself. . . . I hope you will conduct everything in my absence for the interest and honor of the service. . . . You may tell Mr. Livingston for me, that, if the soldiers are not skilled in arms equal to what may reasonably be expected, he most assuredly shall answer it at my return. And I must ingenuously tell you, that I also expect to find them expert at bush-fighting." [28]

He did his utmost to keep officers and men up to the standard, and when an ensign was court-martialled and dismissed for conduct which Washington called infamous, he delivered an address to his officers that shows his own high opinion of the service:

"This timely warning of the effects of misbehaviour will, I hope, be instrumental in animating the younger officers to a laudable emulation in the service of their country. Not that I apprehend any of them can be guilty of offences of this nature: but there are many other misdemeanors, that will, without due circumspection, gain upon inactive minds, and produce consequences equally disgraceful.

"I would, therefore, earnestly recommend, in every point of duty, willingness to undertake, and intrepid resolution to execute. Remember, that it is the *actions*, and not the commission, that make the officer, and that there is more expected from him, than the *title*. Do not forget, that there ought to be a time appropriated to attain this knowledge, as well as to indulge pleasure. And as we now have no opportunities to improve from example, let us read for this desirable end. There is Bland's and other treatises which will give the wished-for information.

"I think it my duty, gentlemen, as I have the honour to preside over you, to give this friendly admonition; especially as I am determined, as far as my small experience in service, my abilities, and interest of the service may dictate, to observe the strictest discipline through the whole economy of my behaviour. On the other hand, you may as certainly depend upon having the strictest justice administered to all, and that I shall make it the most agreeable part of my duty to study merit, and reward the brave and deserving. I assure you, gentlemen, that partiality shall never bias my conduct, nor shall prejudice injure any; but, throughout the whole tenor of my proceedings, I shall endeavour, as far as I am able, to reward and punish, without the least diminution." [29]

In spite of his bad material and all the wretched handicaps he had to overcome, his own earnestness, his studiousness, his fairness and his tireless energy whipped his raw and unwilling, drinking, gaming, quarrelsome men into the best provincial troops in America by 1760. But 1760 was a long way off.

He set out on February 4th, 1756, on a five-hundred-mile ride in the dead of winter. He made it a tour of state, taking along his aides-de-camp, Captain Mercer and Captain Stewart, also Bishop and another servant. He was received officially as a hero of the late tragedy, and colonial governors greeted him with respect.

He kept his accounts with his usual care, and must have had a good time. He had spoken of "the Fatigue &c of this tedious journey." There was more "&c" than tedium, for it gave his heart, sick of frontier horrors and failures, the respite of northern drawing-rooms and beautiful ladies, who were not Virginian, but very human. It brought him an escape from the teasing of Sally Fairfax and his only recorded love affair with a Northerner—or should one say, a Northerness?

XVII

HE RIDES NORTH TO A NEW LOVE

A MORE gorgeous dandy never rode than the Colonel Washington of 1756. As even Thomas Jefferson called him "the best horseman of his age and the most graceful rider that could be seen on horseback," it can be imagined how the women fell before him.

He was always of a foppish turn and he kept his toilet as minutely as his expense books, which show heavy outlays with the Taylors, the Hatters, the Jewellers and the Sadlers. He spent his twenty-fourth birthday in Philadelphia and reached New York February 15th. He had a cordial welcome. He went to "Mrs. Barons Rout."

He lost 8 shillings at cards one night, also he did a good deal of shopping. He paid twelve pounds ten "for a Hatt," a Taylors Bill of ninety-five pounds seven and three, and for "Silver Lace" almost ninety-five pounds.

Though his business was in Boston, and the Indians were scalping and burning everywhere along the diminishing frontier of Virginia, Washington found reason to tarry in New York.

The reason was Mary Philipse of Yonkers.[1]

He had been persuaded to lodge at the house of a fellow-Virginian who had married North and rich—Beverly Robinson, son of the speaker of the House of Burgesses. Robinson had married Susanna Philipse, an heiress of the founder of Philipse Manor on the Hudson, and appallingly wealthy. Susanna had a younger sister, Mary, called Polly, very pretty, still a spinster at twenty-six, but most attractive.

Washington always had an insatiable love for land, acreage.   And it probably did not hurt Mary Philipse in his eyes, when he learned that, though she was nearly two years older than he, she would bring to her husband her share of the estate, a small matter of 51,102 acres.[2]   That was more than Washington ever accumulated, counting his wild Western lands.

The Beverly Robinson house in New York was one of the most important in town.   Beverly Robinson had recently been a major, and distinguished himself at the storming of Quebec.   In God's good time, he would be one of the leaders of the New York opposition to the stamp tax, but when the test of loyalty came, he would abide by his King, raise a Loyal Regiment, and serve as its colonel.[3]   At the end of the war, all his estates would be confiscated.   But at this time a war of the colonies with England was unimaginable and Washington would probably have knocked down anybody who prophesied that he could ever be disloyal to his King.

Among the brilliant company at Beverly Robinson's, Washington was at first delighted to find a comrade of Braddock's battlefield, one of the three musketeers who had served as aides of the old bulldog—no less a friend than Captain Roger Morris.   Washington alone had not been scratched, though his hat and clothes were bullet-riddled and two horses killed under him.   Captain Morris and Captain Orme had been wounded severely, and shipped back North for repairs.

Captain Morris was an Englishman born, and just now thirty.   After the first cordial greetings of so close a friend in so fierce an experience, Col. Washington was chilled to learn that Captain Morris was making a prior claim on Mary Philipse, who was not indifferent to him.

Washington, riding all the way to Boston to suppress an English captain who showed no deference to a Virginia colonel, found himself in exactly the same predicament in a matter of love. Governor Shirley had no jurisdiction here and Washington was hugely embarrassed.

He lingered for ten days, fascinated by Mary Philipse and life in what he would have called a great "Matrapolis." New York had the immense population of 10,381 by last year's census, and was growing.

It was probably Mary and her sister that Washington took to see the Microcosm, a contraption which the New York *Mercury* in 1756 advertised as "that elaborate and celebrated piece of mechanism called the Microcosm or the World in Minature. Built in the form of a Roman Temple, after twenty-two years close study and application by the late ingenious Mr. Henry Bridges of London. . . . It will be shown every day from six in the morning till six at night, to any select company (not less than six) at six shillings each." [4]

Washington saw it twice and noted in his never-neglected expense book, "for treatg Ladies to ye Mm. one pound eight shillings," and again, "treatg Ladies to ye Microcosm, one pound four shillings."

But duty called him louder and louder and he had to move on. He bought three mares in New York and tipped Mr. Robinson's servants one pound, eight shillings for the ten days.

He paused in Rhode Island long enough to make the puzzling entries, "By cash to Mr. Malbones servants four pounds; to a Bowle broke four pounds." That sounds like a lively party. For one night in Rhode Island he gives the servants four pounds and damages. For ten days in New York, one pound, eight. For his eleven-day stay in Boston he gave the chambermaid a bit over a guinea.

He stopped at the Cromwell's Head Tavern, attending the sessions of the Legislature and accepting the hospitality

of various prominent people.   He is said to have sat for
his portrait to Copley, a native of the town, and a miniature
was declared to be that picture of him at twenty-five but
has since been assigned to a later date.[5]

He had worse luck at cards than in New York, for he says
he lost three pounds on one occasion and one pound, two-
and-six on another.   But no heart entanglements are reported in Boston.   He was, perhaps, still thinking of Mary
Philipse.

With Governor Shirley he had the best of luck.   A few
years before, the old gentleman had dared to bring back
from Paris as his second wife, a Catholic French girl, the
daughter of his landlord.   Having safely established a
pretty young papist in the heart of Puritania, he was not
afraid of anything.   His wife did not frighten him from
the most thorough-going plans to destroy the French power
in America.   His sixty years of life without military training did not prevent him from becoming a general and entering on an active campaign in which his failures were at least
no greater than those of lifelong soldiers.   They could not
have been.

By his first marriage he had had two sons.   William went
as secretary to Braddock and was killed in battle.   His son
John went along with his father on the Niagara expedition
and died of bloody flux.   As Governor Morris of Pennsylvania wrote to Governor Dinwiddie:

"My heart bleeds for Mr. Shirley.   He must be overwhelmed
with Grief when he hears of Capt. John Shirley's Death, of which
I have an Account by the last Post from New York, where he died
of a Flux and Fever that he had contracted at Oswego.   The loss
of Two Sons in one Campaign scarcely admits of Consolation.   I
feel the Anguish of the unhappy Father, and mix my Tears very
heartily with his.   I have had an intimate Acquaintance with Both
of Them for many Years, and know well their inestimable Value."

To Governor Shirley, Morris wrote:

"Permit me, good sir, to offer you my hearty condolence upon the death of my friend Jack, whose worth I admired, and feel for him more than I can express. . . . Few men of his age had so many friends." [6]

A cabal was formed against the poor old man and he could see that he would soon lose his place as commander-in-chief, for the Earl of Loudoun (Loudon or Lowden) was to come over to fill the long-vacant post of Governor of Virginia, which Lieut. Governor Dinwiddie had tried to fill so tirelessly.

We hear so much of the atrocities of British Governors, that it is surprising to find how human and pitiful they really were.

To this despondent humbled governor at Boston came the young Colonel Washington with many a tale to tell of the death of young Will Shirley. He got inside the old man's heart, no doubt. His own fame was so clean and bright and Governor Dinwiddie had written so warmly of him and given him so strong a letter to deliver, that he had no difficulty in persuading the Governor to suppress the pretensions of Captain Dagworthy.

Though he apparently made no answer to the memorial of the officers asking to be put on the royal establishment, Shirley issued an order March 5, 1756, placing Washington and Dagworthy in their proper positions:

". . . I do therefore give it as my opinion, that Captain Dagworthy, who now acts under a commission from the Governor of Maryland, and where there are no regular troops joined, can only take rank as a provincial Captain, and of course is under the command of all provincial field officers; and, in case it should happen, that Colonel Washington and Captain Dagworthy should join at Fort Cumberland, it is my order that Colonel Washington shall take the command." [7]

Furthermore, he wrote a little later to Governor Sharpe of Maryland (whose attitude toward Washington always varied from lukewarm to chilly but who had now recommended him for the post of second in command of the next great Westward push):

"I beg you would be pleas'd to acquaint Col: Washington, that the Appointment of him to the second Command in the propos'd Expedition upon the Ohio, will give me great satisfaction and pleasure; that I know no Provincial Officer upon this Continent to whom I would so readily give it as to himself; that I shall do it, if there is nothing in the King's Orders, which I am in continual Expectation of, that interferes with it; and that I will have the pleasure of answering his Letter immediately after my receiving them." [8]

But Washington did not get the post.

Having conquered Boston, and never dreaming that the next time he saw the city he would visit it at the head of an army trying to drive out of it his old comrade of Braddock's field, Col. Gage, he hurried back to New York to see what his other crony of Braddock's field had done in the siege of Mary Philipse.

He rode through New England in the pleasant weather of March and spent several days at New York, of which there is no record. But Mary Philipse must have kept him hoping; for a year and a half later he was writing to his friend Joseph Chew to find out how the land lay, and was urged to hurry to New York and storm her heart.

Chew rebuked Washington for his timidity with ladies. He did not know how often the poor man had been rejected.

That his heart was not allowed to rust entirely from disuse is evident from a letter written to him by Robert Carter Nicholas January 3rd, 1756, concerning a mysterious flirtation with some unknown girl who stole his snuff-box or whose snuff-box he stole:

"The Snuff Box was properly return'd and I took the Liberty of communicating the extatick Paragraph of your Letter.   What Blushes & Confusion it occasioned I shall leave you to guess." [9]

He leaves us also guessing; but some day the letter may turn up as startlingly as did the letters to Sally Fairfax, and confound a world reluctant to believe that Washington could writhe in extatick misery.

XVIII

SCANDAL, ABUSE, MUTINY, LITIGATION, DESPAIR

IS heart was filled with uncertainty as to Mary
Philipse. His only satisfaction was that he carried
bad news for Captain Dagworthy, whom his protector, Governor Sharpe, thereafter kept under his wing as
Maryland's exclusive property.

But there was worse news for Washington. The moral_
ists were scandalized by the immorality of his soldiers, and
the French and Indians were burning and murdering in the
very outskirts of Winchester. They had cut off Fort
Cumberland.

The Assembly was convening at Williamsburg and there
was great talk of another drive against the French. But as
always, the colonies were still unwilling to get together.

Virginia passed a bill to increase her own army to fifteen
hundred, by drafting enough militia to supply the deficiency
of recruits. But it was stipulated that they must never be
marched out of the province.

Still, the Indians and French were deep inside the province and there was enough to do to throw them back across
the boundaries. Washington was welcomed to Virginia by
the story of attacks in broad daylight on the little forts he
had established wherever he could.[1]

The day after he reached Winchester, on April 7th, 1756,
he wrote Dinwiddie, telling of several murders near there;
the terror of the people was so great that "unless a stop

301

is put to the depredations of the Indians, the Blue Ridge will soon become our frontier."

He strongly urged that the inhabitants be concentrated in defensive positions, working each other's farms by turns. The Burgesses proposed a chain of forts, but he objected that that would require "an inconceivable number of men." His objections were not heeded. He urged the enlisting of friendly Indians. "It is in their power to be of infinite use to us; and without Indians we shall never be able to cope with those cruel foes to our country."

He sent along with this letter the scalp of a French officer, Monsieur Douville, overtaken by some of the soldiers of Washington. He added this comment on the white man's scalp: "I hope, although it is not an Indian's, they will meet with an adequate reward at least, as the monsieur's is of much more consequence. The whole party jointly claim the reward, no person pretending solely to assume the merit.[2]

One may read a vast amount about Washington without finding any reference to this ghastly business of his sending a Frenchman's scalp and asking that the soldiers who took it should receive adequate reward for their "merit." But he was like all the rest, subdued to the conditions of the war about him. Scalps, white or red, meant no more in their day than the motor-massacre of our day.

By this time the colonies were frantic for scalps. The best people wanted them; as in Massachusetts long ago, the good folk had earned good money for the little skulls of Indian children, and had brought them in in meal sacks like cabbages. In August, 1755, Virginia had made the standard offer of £10 for every male Indian scalp over twelve years old. In April, 1757, the price was raised to £15, with a bonus of £1 for every further scalp taken by the same scalper in the next two years. Maryland still kept her price up to £50. Scalps were worth more than any other form of fur—worth more than gold.

The pathetic thing about Douville was that the Virginians who scalped him had found on his person orders from Captain Dumas, the conqueror of Braddock, bidding Douville to harass convoys, burn magazines, and take prisoners, but to "employ all his talents to prevent the savages from committing any cruelties upon those who may fall into their hands. Honor and humanity ought, in this respect, to serve as our guide. Dumas." [3]

It is desolating to find George Washington passing along with approval the scalp of a young French officer ordered to prevent atrocities.

More than a year later, he sent a still more dreadful bundle, mentioned by Dinwiddie in a cheerful postscript:

"This Minute by Express from Colo. Washington, that a Party of our Indians, under comand of Lieut. Baker, with some Cherokee Indians, met with 10 Frenchmen at Turtle Creek, near Ft. Du Quesne and kill'd and scalp'd 5, 2 of which were officers." [4]

But scalping was part of the day's work.

On April 9th, Washington reports the death of Douville to Governor Morris of Pennsylvania, commenting: "The accident that has determined the fate of Monsieur has, I believe, dispersd his party, for I don't hear of any mischief done in this colony since." He warns the Governor that it will be in French power "if the colonys continue in their fatal lethargy, to give a final stab to liberty and property. Nothing I more sincerely wish than a union to the colonys in this time of eminent danger. . . . Virginia will do everything that can be expected to promote the publick good. . . .

"I went to Williamsburg fully resolved to resign my commission, but was diswaded from it at least for a time. If the hurry of business, in which I know your Honor is genly.

engaged, will admit of an opportunity to murder a little time in writing to me, I shoud receive the favour as a mark of that esteem which I coud wish to merit." [5]

Young Washington is now a man of inter-colonial importance, able to ask the Governor of Pennsylvania to "murder a little time" and write to him. Even Governor Sharpe is beginning to appreciate him, and on April 10th writes to Governor Shirley urging what Governor Shirley had already thought of:

"The enclosed letter I am desired to forward to your Excellency from Colo. Washington, and to request you to commissionate and appoint him second in command, in case these colonies shall raise a sufficient number of troops for carrying on an expedition or making a diversion to the westward this summer. As Mr. Washington is much esteemed in Virginia, and really seems a gentleman of merit, I should be exceedingly glad to learn that your Excellency is not averse to favoring his application and request." [6]

In his next letter to the Governor Washington has learned the glorious news that the Assembly is going to increase the establishment still further. It saved him from a certain humiliation, since almost nobody had paid any attention to his call in spite of the utter dismay of the settlers.

"All my Ideal hopes of raising a Number of Men to scour the adjacent Mountains have vanished into Nothing. Yesterday was the appointed Time for a general Rendezvous of all who were willing to accompany Me for that desirable End, and only 15 appeared; So that I find myself reduced to the further Necessity of waiting at this Place a few Days longer till the Arrival of a Party which was ordered from Fort Cumberland to escort Me up, the Roads being so infested that none but Hunters who travel the Woods by Night can pass in Safety.

"I have done every Thing in my Power to quiet the Minds of the Inhabitants, by detaching all the Men that I have any Command over, to the places which are most exposed; there have also been large Detachments from Fort Cumberland in Pursuit of the

Enemy these 10 Days Past, and yet nothing, I fear, will prevent them from abandoning their Dwellings and flying with utmost Precipitation.   There have been no Murders committed since I came up, but the Express I sent to Colo. Stephen (notwithstanding he was an excellent Woodsman and a very active Fellow) was fired upon 5 Times at a place called the Flats, within 6 Miles of Fort Cumberland.   He had several Balls thro' his Coat, and his Horse shot under him, yet made his Escape from them.

"By a Letter from a Gent. in W'msburg, we are informed that the Assembly have generously given the further Sum of £20,000, and voted the augmenting our Forces to 2,000 Men. . . ."

He gives a carefully-thought-out plan for raising these men by drafting; he describes their proper pay, and outlines an organization scheme "established more after the British Manner than We now are . . . and I humbly conceive where we can pattern after our Mother Country upon as easy Terms as pursuing Plans of our own, that we shou'd at least pay that Deference to her Judgment and Experience. . . ."

His prestige was so great that his military enthusiasm for his mother country prepared another sorrow for his pacifistic mother:

"P.S.—I have a brother that has long discovered an Inclination to enter the Service, but has till this been disswaded from it by my Mother, who now, I believe, will give consent.   I must, therefore, beg that if your honour shou'd issue any new Commissions before I come down, that you will think of him and reserve a Lieutenancy.   I flatter myself that he will endeavour to deserve it as well as some that have, and others that may get." [7]

To this last request, Dinwiddie answered April 23rd, "I have not the least Objection to your Broths' being a Lieut." [8]

But which brother it was and what, if anything, was ever done about it, does not appear.

Perhaps the service lost its charm, for troubles thickened

about Washington's head.   Captain John Fenton Mercer
(younger brother of the Colonel Mercer who had ridden
north with Washington) went out with a party of a hundred men and was surprised by the French and Indians.
His sergeant and other men shamefully abandoned him,
leaving him to be scalped and killed.   Washington could
not persuade a small force to go in pursuit of the enemy.
There was a court-martial, the sergeant was sentenced to
death.   Washington approved the sentence, but had no
authority to execute deserters or cowards, much as he wanted
it.   Still, on May 8th, Dinwiddie wrote: "I sent You a death
Warrant for shooting Sergeant Lewis, which, I doubt not,
you will order to have executed by having as many of
the forces present as You can that he may be a publick
Example." [9]

But Washington and his officers and men were subjected
now to a new attack.   The Puritans assailed them.   In spite
of all his strictness of discipline, his good example, and the
unpopularity and difficulty of the service, his troops and
officers were accused of gross immorality, outrageous intoxication and general corruption.

"I hope the Affairs of the Regim't are not in so bad a
condit'n as represented here," Dinwiddie wrote him April
8th, 1756.   "The Assem'y were greatly inflam'd, being told
y't the greatest Immoralities and drunkenness have been
much countenanced and proper Discipline neglected.   I am
will'g to think better of our Officers, and therefore suspend
my Judgm't till I hear from You.   I desire you will keep
them properly employ'd in patroling the Woods, and, if
possible, to Scalp some of our barbarous Enemies to prevent and discourage Y'r inhuman Murders in our back
Settlem'ts." [10]

This cut Washington to the quick and he answered on
the 18th:

"It gave me infinite concern to find in yours by Governor Innes, that any representations should inflame the Assembly against the Virginia regiment, or give cause to suspect the morality and good behaviour of the officers. How far any of the individuals may have deserved such invidious reflections, I will not take upon me to determine, but *this* I am certain of, and can call my conscience, and what, I suppose, will still be a more demonstrable proof in the eyes of the world, my orders, to witness how much I have, both by threats and persuasive means, endeavoured to discountenance gaming, drinking, swearing, and irregularities of every other kind; while I have, on the other hand, practiced every artifice to inspire a laudable emulation in the officers for the service of their country, and to encourage the soldiers in the unerring exercise of their duty. How far I have failed in this desirable end, I cannot pretend to say. But it is nevertheless a point, which does in my opinion merit some scrutiny, before it meets with a final condemnation. Yet I will not undertake to vouch for the conduct of many of the officers, as I know there are some, who have the seeds of idleness very strongly ingrafted in their natures; and I also know, that the unhappy difference about the command, which has kept me from Fort Cumberland, has consequently prevented me from *enforcing* the orders, which I never failed to *send*.

"However, if I continue in the service, I shall take care to act with a little more rigor, than has hitherto been practised, since I find it so necessary." [11]

He was once more ready to resign. Dinwiddie understood and approved him, but there were busybodies elsewhere at work, and there was no cessation of the criticism.

Washington's moral orders included the arrest of any officer who did not endeavor to quell irregularities; for any soldier who should presume to quarrel or fight, five hundred lashes; for any soldier drunk, one hundred lashes, both without benefit of court-martial.

The gloom thickened as more and more people were killed closer and closer to his helpless little force. His heart cried out to Dinwiddie in a letter of unwonted passion:

"I am too little acquainted, Sir, with pathetic language, to attempt a description of the people's distresses, though I have a generous soul, sensible of wrongs and swelling for redress. But what can I do? If bleeding, dying! would glut their insatiate revenge, I would be a willing offering to savage fury, and die by inches to save a people! . . .

"I see inevitable destruction in so clear a light that unless vigorous measures are taken by the Assembly, and speedy assistance sent from below, the poor inhabitants that are now in forts, must unavoidably fall, while the remainder of the country are flying before the barbarous foe.

"In fine, the melancholy situation of the people . . . the gross and scandalous abuses cast upon the officers in general, which is reflecting upon me in particular . . . and the distant prospects, if any, that I can see, of gaining honor and reputation in the service, are motives which cause me to lament the hour that gave me a commission, and would induce me, at any other time than this of imminent danger, to resign without one hesitating moment, a command, which I never expect to reap either honor or benefit from; but on the contrary, have almost an absolute certainty of incurring displeasure below, while the murder of poor innocent babes and helpless families may be laid to my account here!

"The supplicating tears of the women, and moving petitions from the men, melt me into such deadly sorrow that I solemnly declare, if I know my own mind, I could offer myself a willing sacrifice to the butchering enemy, provided that would contribute to the people's ease!" [12]

His next letter begins "Not an hour, nay scarcely a minute

passes, that does not produce fresh alarms and melancholy accounts. So that I am distracted what to do? . . . Three families were murdered the night before last, at the distance of less than twelve miles from this place." Worse yet, there was cabal within the fort to surrender to the French! The inhabitants despairing of protection planned to make peace with the French! And his force was too weak to punish them!

There was a cabal going on against him in the Assembly, too. His advice was disregarded and the plan to build a chain of forts approved on an even greater scale than the plan which he had opposed as requiring an inconceivable number of men.

On April 27th, Washington wrote: "Desolation and murder still increase. . . . The Blue Ridge is now our frontier. . . . There are now no militia in this country . . . when there were they could not be brought to action." [13]

His helplessness was complete. Every time word came of an Indian atrocity, a number of men deserted! He urged that death penalties be dealt more freely. But the Assembly would not authorize him to inflict more than corporal punishment for desertion.

In the draft, six Quakers were caught and they were a problem. They would "neither bear arms, work, receive provisions or pay, or do anything that tends, in any respect, to self-defence." [14] He did not want to whip them, or to let them go unpunished. Dinwiddie answered his appeal by suggesting bread and water. Later, a great body of Quakers waited on Dinwiddie, praying that the drafted Friends be not whipped, so he advised that they be used with lenity.

In August, while trying to carry out the Assembly's plan for a chain of forts, he had to describe another disgrace, with the usual "dastardly behaviour of the militia, who ran off

without one-half of them having discharged their pieces."
It was common for twenty or more to desert of a night.

In his despair Washington thought that a chaplain might
have a good influence on his cowardly brigands. To his
appeals for such help, Dinwiddie answered, September 30th:

"A Chaplain for the Regim't I have recomended to the
Comissary to get one, but he can't prevail with any Per-
son to accept of it. I shall again press it to him." And on
June 24th, 1757, he still had to write:

"There, as yet, has no Clergyman offer'd to be Chaplain;
if not one of good character, better have none." [15]

From Bishop Meade's accounts of the old-style Virginia
clergyman, a chaplain would have been of little help in de-
creasing drunkenness, unless by diminishing the available
supply. As Albert Jay Nock remarks, "The Bishop of London had the spiritual direction of the colony, and he could
not always resist the temptation to unload upon Virginia
such of his clergy as for one reason or another he thought
could be best employed away from home." [16]

A startling picture of the clergy of the day is given by
Dinwiddie himself in a letter of September 12th, 1757, to
the Lord Bishop of London, describing the trial of a clergyman "for monst's Immorality, profane Swear'g, Drunk's and
very imodest Acts." The accused declined a secret trial and
"every Th'g was prov'd in a much more heinous Mann'r
y'n was in the Original Compl't." He was "almost guilty
of every Sin except Murder, and y's last he had very near
perpetrated on his own Wife by ty'g her up by the Leggs to
the Bed Post and cut'g her in a cruel Man'r with Knives,
and guilty of so many Indecencies, y't Modesty forbids my
troub'g Yo. with a detail of. This Tryal and Sentence is
much resented by 2 or 3 hot-headed, inconsiderate Clergy-
Men."

This same letter describes the Immorality and Drunkenness of other clergymen, who were also teachers.[17]

Washington found it simply impossible to comply with the Assembly's demand for the building of a chain of forts.[18] He wanted to give up Fort Cumberland altogether. He had said that its "situation, which is extremely bad, will ever be an eyesore to this colony." A council of war was held in his absence and his subordinates voted to retain it, though he said it was "very useless in itself, expensive to the country, containing over 150 men solely employed in guarding the stores, which could be better defended at any other place."

But he was overruled, as on so many points.

"The Militia now can neither serve nor disserve us, for they are all called in." He cannot get his men to make correct returns of pay. He has only 926 men, yet gets pay returns for 1080. For this, Dinwiddie abuses him: "Great and scandalous desertions continue." Sixteen men got away at once, hoping to enlist with the Pennsylvania troops. Pennsylvania butchers were driving off his cattle. Two deserters reached Fort Du Quesne and rejoiced the French with stories of Virginian weakness. An attack on Fort Cumberland was to be expected.

His dead brother Lawrence's estate is in trouble, and he wants a leave of absence, "as I am very deeply interested, not only as an executor and heir to part of his estate, but also in a very important dispute, subsisting between Colonel Lee, who married the widow, and my brothers and self."

Dinwiddie answers: "I can't refuse Your Liberty of Absence." The dispute, a very painful one, with his brother's widow and her husband over Mount Vernon, did not really end until 1761 with Washington in full possession.

On August 19th, he gets word from Dinwiddie that "Warr against France was proclaim'd here the 7th," and sending instructions how it is to "be done."

"The Method that Yo. are to declare War is at the h'd of Y'r Comp's with three Vollies of Small Arms for his Maj'ty's Health and a successful Warr." [19]

So now, after a year or two of mutual butchery, scalping and arson, and after Braddock's destruction, they were actually going to have a war.

The letters of Washington are still but catalogues of dismay. He makes his usual effort to keep his men from pillaging the few inhabitants. Of two men, Waters and Burrass, whom he accused of having "sold or swapped" a stray mare, he writes: "If I could lay my hands on them, I would try the effect of 1000 lashes on the former, and whether a general court-martial would not condemn the latter to a life eternal!" [20] But neither threats of death nor the clatter of the bloody lash do any good. He instructs his officers (in his general orders in August, 1756) "if they hear any man swear, or make use of an oath or execration, to order the offender twenty-five lashes immediately, without a court-martial. For the second offense, they will be more severely punished."

He berates his officers: "Your suffering such clamors among the men argues great remissness in you . . . you are afraid to do your duty." To a captain he wrote of a lieutenant: "Tell him not to stir from thence at his peril until he has leave; if he does, I will arrest him for disobedience of orders, and try him so soon as he arrives here."

He gives out orders that no man should cut off his hair, and they actually disobeyed even that. He orders the offenders imprisoned. [21]

In spite of the attractiveness of the service and such easy conditions, with the Indians taking the hide off the head of those who were good soldiers, and the officers taking the hide off the back of those who were poor soldiers, recruits will not pour in. At last he is driven to enlisting indentured servants, but their masters must be paid for them. His men are, "so long as their pay holds good, incessantly drunk," though the rates for liquor are immoderately high, and he complains of "the great nuisance the number of tippling-houses are to the soldiers."

To crown his distresses, he learns that there is general dissatisfaction with him. He can please neither his men nor his masters. He is blamed for the gross drunkenness and immorality of his troops. A ferocious attack on his army is published in the *Virginia Gazette*, signed "Centinel No. X."

XIX

"CENTINEL NO. X" CALLS HIS TROOPS DASTARDLY DEBAUCHEES

THIS amazing onslaught gives a startling view of the miserable state of affairs in astonishingly scholastic language. As it is constantly referred to and never quoted, a long extract from the exceedingly rare document may be interesting.[1]

It is headed "The Virginia Centinel No. X," and begins with an excerpt from Virgil, a praise of the profession of arms, and a protest against harsh criticism of soldiers by "Chimney corner Politicians, who lie sneaking at Home." This was a phrase that Washington had used. Still, the author urges, there is a time when protest is compulsory. The assault opens with a reference to the drinkers of "Bombo," a punch made of sweetened rum and nutmeg:

> " 'But Soldiers differ; some will shed their *Blood*.
> And some drink *Bombo*—for their Country's Good,
> Some in the Field will nobly risque their Lives;
> Some Hero like, will *swear*, or play at *Fives*.
> Some shew themselves the genuine Sons of Mars;
> Some brave in *Venus*' or in *Bacchus*' Wars
> Can shew their *lecherous* and *drunken* scars.'

"No Profession in the World can secure from Contempt and Indignation a Character made up of Vice and Debauchery; and no Man is obliged to treat such a Character as sacred.

"When raw Novices and Rakes, Spendthrifts and Bankrupts, who have never been used to command, or who have been found

314

insufficient for the Management of their own private affairs, are honoured with Commissions in the Army; when Men are advanced according to Seniority, the Interests and influence of Friends, &c. and not according to Merit; when the common Soldiers are abused, in a fit of Humour or Passion, or through an Ostentation of Authority; and in the mean Time, perhaps, tolerated or connived at, in practices really worthy of Correction; when the Militia Men are brow-beat and discouraged in every noble atchievement, as claiming a Share with the Soldiery in their Monopoly of Honour; when the Officers give their Men an Example of all Manner of Debauchery, Vice and Idleness; when they lie sculking in Forts, and there dissolving in Pleasure, till alarmed by the Approach of the Enemy, who could expect to find them no where else; when instead of searching out the Enemy, way laying and surprising them, obstructing their Marches, and preventing their Incursions, they tempt them by their Security and Laziness, to come in quest of them and attack them in their Fortifications— When this is the Case, how wretchedly helpless must a Nation be? What useless Lumber, what an Encumbrance, is the Soldiery;

> " '*Conscius ipse de se portat omnia dici.*'

"I would by no Means make the *Event* the Standard by which to judge the Measures taken,[2] though this be undoubtedly the Standard of the Crowd. Successful Rashness will never fail of popular Applause, and unfortunate good Conduct will never escape Censure. But when nothing brave is so much as *attempted*, but very rarely, or by Accident, or for necessary Self defence; when Men whose Profession it is to endure Hardships, and encounter Dangers, cautiously shun them, and suffer their Country to be ravaged in their very Neighbourhood; then, certainly, Censure cannot be silent; nor can the Public receive much Advantage from a Regiment of such dastardly Debauchees.

> " 'Shew me one scar character'd on their skin:
> Men's Flesh preserv'd so whole but seldom win.'
> "SHAKES."

"Men of Virtue and true Courage can have no Heart to enlist, and mingle in such a Crowd. And the few of that Character, that may be among them, are in Danger of catching the general Contagion; or of being damped and mortified at the Sight of such Scenes of Vice, Extravagance and Oppression.

"*Horace,* who knew the Estate of the all-conquering *Roman* Army, in the Period of its highest Glory, and most illustrious Victories, will teach us the Discipline proper for Soldiers.

> " 'Our hardy Youth should learn to bear
> Sharp Want, to win the warlike Steed,
> To hurl the well directed Spear,
> With pointed Force, and bid the *Parthian* bleed.
> In War's illustrious Dangers bold,
> Inur'd to Summer's Heats, and Winter's Cold.'

"But it seems the Delicacy of modern Soldiers cannot bear such hardy Discipline. Their Ease and Pleasure must not be disturbed by the Fatigues and Dangers of the Field or Woods.

> " 'Their Country calls; and see! the Heroes run
> To save her—if the Game or Dance is done.'

"Luxury and Sensuality have unmanned many an Army, and enslaved or ruined many flourishing Cities and Kingdoms. Let me enumerate a few Instances, for the Warning of surviving Nations. —The first great Empire of the World, viz. the Assyrian, owed its Destruction entirely to the Luxury of its Prince, Sardanapalus: an effeminate Creature, that never went out of his Palace; but spent all his Time in the Company of Women. Feasting, rioting, and all manner of sensual Indulgencies were his daily Employ. At Length his Generals cut him off in the Midst of his Debaucheries, and overturned the Empire.—Babylon, the strongest City, perhaps, that ever was built upon Earth, was taken in the Night by Surprise, while the King, his Wives and Concubines, with a Thousand of his Lords, were carousing in a Debauch, unapprehensive of Danger. . . ."

After listing numerous other eminent drinkers and debauchees, the article ends with a warning: "The Application of these pieces of History is easy."

As a piece of writing, this unrivalled onslaught was what used to be called "elegant." It created an earthquake in Virginia.

To its devastating abuse, the officers answered, October 6, 1756, that the attack was "so scandalous and altogether so unjust" that they unanimously agreed to apply to their Lieut-Col. Stephen for Orders. Out of "the great and just Regard we have for Collo. Washington and yourself join'd to the Duty we owe to our King in Defending as much as it is in our Power His Colony of Virginia to which we belong, we do with the greatest exactness obey the Orders of our Superior Officers. But unless we have ample Satisfaction for these so groundless and barb'rous Aspersions, we are one and all (at this Garrison) fully determin'd to present our Commissions to the Governor (as in that Paper it is hinted) given to a Reg't of dastardly Debauchees; and desire that you will inform His Honor we expect that he will provide a Sett of Men for the Service, that will better answer the expectations of Our Countrey and of himself; we say Himself, believing The Printer wou'd never have dar'd to insert such a Paper in His Gazette without His previous knowledge or Consent, in either of which cases He must have believ'd the Censures therein to be just.

"You, Sir, may therefore assure Him, we are resolv'd to obey as Officers no longer than the twentieth day of November next, unless we have as Publick Satisfaction, as the Injury receiv'd."

XX

HE DRAINS THE DREGS OF HUMILIATION

THIS sensation shook all Virginia and drove Washington to another of his determinations to resign. It took all the prayers and persuasions of his friends to keep him in the service. Landon Carter exclaimed: "How are we grieved to hear Colonel George Washington hinting to his country that he is willing to retire! . . . No Sir, rather let Braddock's bed be your aim, than anything that might discolor those laurels, which I promise myself are kept in store for you." [1]

Colonel Fairfax added his protest and praise: "Your good health and fortune are the toast of every table." The Speaker of the House of Burgesses wrote: "Our hopes, dear George, are all fixed on you for bringing our affairs to a happy issue. Consider of what fatal consequences to your country your resigning the command at this time may be: more especially as there is no doubt most of the officers would follow your example."

It had taken the abuse to bring forward the praise. He needed it. It restored him to reason and patriotism, but it left him sick and irascible. He was always enfuriated when the purity of his motives was befouled in the public press, as it was at intervals from then on.

He withdrew his resignation and went back to the treadmill. But the intrigues against him did not cease. Poor Dinwiddie was accused of being interested in replacing him. This charge is what he would have called "monstrous," though it is still repeated by historians.

Dinwiddie had actually written to England begging that Washington should receive a royal commission, and saying that if Braddock had lived, "he would have provided handsomely for him in the Regulars. He is a person much beloved here and has gone through many hardships in the Service, and I really think he has great Merit, and believe he can raise more Men than any one present that I know. If his Lordship will be so kind as to promote him in the British Establishment I think he will answer my recommendation." [2]

But the prayer was never answered. Following the Centinel No. X scandal, Dinwiddie turned peevish with the dangerous illness of "a Paralytick Disorder in my head."

Washington's tone to him grew a trifle impatient and Dinwiddie resented it. On November 16, 1756, he wrote with unusual harshness: "You seem to charge Neglect in me. . . . This Charge is unmannerly. . . . You ment'n hav'g made a Choice of a Person [for Commissary] with't mention'g his name for my Approbat'n; . . . I can't consent to it. . . . the same in reg'd to a Chaplain. . . . I hereby order You im'dtly to march 100 Men to F't. Cumb'l'd. . . . These Orders I expect You will give due Obedience to." [3]

Always the good soldier who finds his highest pride in that subordination to his superiors which he demands and desires from his inferiors, Washington wrote, disclaiming any disrespect:

"I am very sorry any expression in my letter should be deemed unmannerly. I never intended insults to any; on the contrary, have endeavoured to demean myself in that proper respect due to superiors. . . .

"I seem also to be reprimanded for giving a vague account of my tour to the southward. I was rather fearful of blame for prolixity and impertinence in meddling with matters I had no immediate concern with. . . . And am sorry to find, that this, and my best endeavours of late, meet with unfavorable constructions. What it proceeds from, I know not. If my open and disinterested way of writing and speaking has the air of pertness and freedom, I shall correct my error by acting reservedly, and shall take care to obey my orders without offering any thing more. . . .

"When I spoke of a chaplain, it was in answer to yours. I had no person in view, tho' many have offered; and only said, if the country would provide subsistence, we could procure a chaplain, without thinking there was offence in the expression. Because I was told the commissary had endeavored but could get no one to accept of it.

"When I spoke about scalps, I had the Indians chiefly, indeed *solely* in my view, knowing their jealous, suspicious natures are apt to entertain doubts of the least delay and a suspension of rewards causes a dissatisfaction and murmuring among them, which might be productive of bad events at this critical juncture." [4]

Washington's eagerness that there should be no delay in paying the Indians for scalps was opposed by others. Edmund Atkin, the Indian agent for the South, disapproved of offering high rewards to Indians for scalps, as it encouraged "private scalping, whereby the most innocent and helpless persons even women and children" were murdered for their scalps. He instanced also some cases where the Indians picked quarrels among themselves that the scalp of the killed might be sold. Further, the high rewards sharpened the ingenuity of the Indians; "for the Cherokees in particular have got the art of making four scalps out of one man killed." Atkin asserted that he was "well assured Lord Loudoun detests that practice, and that the French general Montcalm in Canadas does the same. Sir Wm. Johnson gives no reward at all for scalps." [5]

Washington, with gruelling meekness, said that he would

obey Dinwiddie's order to march without further question
though it meant the exposure to pillage and destruction of
all the works and stores, and though the "late and unexpected order has caused the utmost terror and consternation
in the people." [6]

The drafted troops were homesick and tired of work.
The friendly Indians had promised to stay "only one moon."
There was a cabal, "a very base and villainous scheme" in
the camp, led by Denis McCarty, to encourage desertion.
McCarty privately resigned before Washington could court-
martial him.   There was the old cry for clothes; the old
watchword: the men are "naked."

He could not keep his men warm even with the whip, nor
could he break them to discipline with any increase of severity. He wrote to Dinwiddie that he had flogged without
legal right and had deceived prisoners into thinking he
would have them killed:

"I had sent Colo. Stephen with a detachment to bring in
the mutineers on the Branch to this place in irons. . . . We
have held a General Court Martial on the Ring-leaders;
flogged several severely; and have some under sentence of
death . . . we have no Law to inflict punishments even of
the smallest kind. I shall keep these criminals in irons, and
if possible, under apprehensions of death, until some
favourable opportunity may countenance a reprieve." [7]

But Dinwiddie, incensed perhaps by Washington's most
irritating obedience, was still sore at his own creature.

To humiliate him further, Dinwiddie sent him a criticism
of his actions from the hand of Lord Loudoun, who had
come over to take charge of American affairs. Washington
could not even understand what he was blamed for. He
wrote to his friend, John Robinson, Speaker of the Colony:

"My strongest representations of matters relative to the
peace of the frontiers are disregarded as idle and frivolous;

my propositions and measures, as partial and selfish; and all my sincerest endeavours for the service of my country perverted to the worst purposes. My orders are dark, doubtful, and uncertain; *to-day approved to-morrow condemned.* Left to act and proceed at hazard, accountable for the consequences, and blamed without the benefit of defence, if you can think my situation capable to excite the smallest degree of envy, or afford the least satisfaction, the truth is yet hid from you, and you entertain notions very different from the *reality* of the case. However, I am determined to bear up under all these embarrassments some time longer, in hope of better regulation on the arrival of Lord Loudoun, to whom I look for the future fate of Virginia. . . .

"The severity of the season, and nakedness of the soldiers, are matters of much compassion, and give rise to infinite complaints." [8]

To Dinwiddie he wrote in abject misery, bewilderment and humility:

"I have read that paragraph in Lord Loudoun's letter, (which your Honor was pleased to send me,) over and over again, but am unable to comprehend the meaning of it. What scheme it is, I was carrying into execution without waiting advice, I am at a loss to know, unless it was building the chain of forts along our frontiers, which I not only undertook conformably to an act of Assembly, and by your own orders, but, with respect to the places, in pursuance of a council of war. If, under these circumstances, my 'conduct is responsible for the fate of Fort Cumberland,' it must be confessed, that I stand upon a tottering foundation indeed. . . .

"I see with much regret, that His Excellency Lord Loudoun seems to have prejudged my proceedings, without being thoroughly informed what were springs and motives, that have actuated my conduct. How far I have mistaken the means to recommend my services, I know not, but I am certain of this, that no man ever intended better, or studied the interest of his country with more affectionate zeal, than I have done; and nothing gives me greater uneasiness and concern, than that his Lordship should have imbibed prejudices so unfavorable to my character, as to excite his belief that I was capable of doing anything, 'that will have a bad effect as to the Dominion, and no good appearance at home.' " [9]

And so Washington wrote to his friend Robinson as "the Speaker of the House of Burgesses" a formal proffer of resignation with a deal of heartbreak in it:

"This I am certain of; and can with the highest safety call my conscience, my God! . . . I can not help observing, that if the country think they have cause to condemn my conduct, and have a person in view that will act; that *he* may do. But who will endeavor to act more for her Interests than I have done? It will give me the greatest pleasure to resign a command which I solemnly declare I accepted against my will.

"I know, Sir, that my inexperience may have led me into innumerable errors. For which reason, I shou'd think myself an unworthy member of the community and greatly deficient in the love I owe my country which has ever been the first principle of my actions, were I to require more than a distant hint of its dissatisfaction to resign a commission which I confess to you I am no ways fond of keeping. . . .

"I have diligently sought the public welfare; and have endeavoured to inculcate the same principles on all that are under me. These reflections will be a cordial to my mind so long as I am able to distinguish between Good & Evil." [10]

At the same time his officers expressed a wish to be relieved of the service that brought them no rewards except such castigations as Centinel No. X had dealt out. [11]

Neither Washington's, nor his officers', prayers for dismissal were accepted. In March, 1757, Washington wrote a long and eloquent letter to Lord Loudoun outlining his difficulties, explaining how his recruits were left without clothes, tents or subsistence and "thought themselves bubbled and that no reward for their service was intended. This caused great desertion."

The deserters showed their rags and poverty to the people and gave a bad impression of the service. He complains of the absurd law, or lack of it, and the "difficulty of keeping soldiers under proper discipline, who know that they are not (legally) punishable for the most atrocious crimes." He recounts his own confusing orders, "I am left like a wanderer in a wilderness, to proceed at hazard." He had foreseen this situation and rejected the commission "until I was ashamed any longer to refuse, not caring to expose my character to public censure." [12]

This report now in the Huntington Library at San Marino, California, is an exquisite masterpiece of penmanship.

Washington's fine loyalty and frankness won over the Earl and though, in Dinwiddie's words, he conducted "his Affairs with great Secrecy, that nothing perspires," [13] Loudoun's aide wrote Washington that "His Lordship seems very much pleased with the accounts you have given him." [14]

Loudoun never did get to Virginia while he was Governor of the colony. Instead, he called a council of Governors to Philadelphia.

Washington decided that he would like to go to Philadelphia. Dinwiddie did not see any reason for him to make the journey with affairs in such a tangle. Washington pleaded. Dinwiddie yielded impatiently:

"I cannot conceive what service you can be of in going there as the plan concerted will in course be communicated

These Things were productive of great murmering and discontent, and render the Service so distasteful to the Men, that not being paid immediately upon coming in, they thought themselves bubbled, and that no reward for their Services ever was intended. This caus'd great Desertion: and the Deserters spreading over the Country recounting their Sufferings and want of Pay, which Rags and Poverty sufficiently testified) fixed in the Populace such horrid Impressions of the hardships they had Encountered, that no Arguments coud remove their prejudices, or Facilitate the Recruiting Service

This put the Asembly upon enacting a Law to Impress Vagrants; which compleated our Misfortunes:

for,

A PAGE FROM WASHINGTON'S REPORT TO THE EARL
OF LOUDOUN, 1757.

(From the Henry E. Huntington Library.)

to you and the other officers.   However, as you seem so earnest to go I now give you leave." [15]

So Washington went and was received with respectful attention by the Earl, who decided that the next attack on the French would be made in the North.   Virginia had had her chance and her great road to the Ohio had led to deathless regret.

Fort Cumberland was turned over to Maryland and Colonel Washington's dear enemy, Captain Dagworthy, put in charge of it as soon as Washington should march out.[16] This must have been an exquisitely nauseating pill for Washington to swallow.   He was now ordered to a smaller parish with nothing much to do but sit and watch for news from the north.

His hopeless prospect led him to review his futile past in a letter to a London merchant, Richard Washington, who dealt in indentured servants and tobacco:

"I have been posted for twenty months past upon our cold and barren frontiers, to perform, I think I may say, impossibilities; that is, to protect from the cruel Incursions of a crafty, savage enemy a line of inhabitants, of more than three hundred and fifty miles in extent, with a force inadequate to the task.   By this means I am become in a manner an exile, and seldom informed of those opportunities, which I might otherwise embrace, of corresponding with my friends."

He thought it would be a good time to attack the French while their attention and forces were distracted to the north by Lord Loudoun's attack, but he had his thoughts for his reward.

"I am so little acquainted with the business relative to my private affairs, that I can scarce give you any information concerning it.   I know that I ought to have some tobacco, and that it ought to be shipped . . . whatever goods you may send me, where the prices are not absolutely limited, you will let them be fashionable, neat, and good in their several kinds." [17]

He sat at his doleful post awaiting the worst. He told one man that his men would be no more "than a breakfast to the French and their Indians." [18]

They were taking even his perquisites away. He was receiving as colonel "30 shillings, per day, pay, and two per cent commissions for examining, settling, and paying off accompts." This was thought to be high and he pleaded that the Governor should not, having promised "to better my command, render it *worse* by taking away the only perquisite I have; and the only thing that enables me to support the expence which unavoidably attends my Table." [19]

The governor took away his two percent and gave him two hundred pounds a year for his table and extras.

He was relieved of the management of Indian affairs. He was also placed in subordination to Colonel Stanwix, whom Loudoun put in command of the Pennsylvania, Maryland and Virginia troops.

An interesting evidence of his tormented frame of mind has recently come to light. In 1920, Mr. Victor Hugo Paltsits, keeper of the manuscripts at the New York Public Library, on looking over a small memorandum book (called "A Roll of the Artificers . . . under the command of Captain William Peachy with an account of their Lost Time") discovered that most of it was filled with memoranda in the handwriting of George Washington—the so-called round hand that he used between 1750 and 1760. Worthington C. Ford verified the documents and they were published in the Bulletin of the Library. [20]

Comparisons with his correspondence showed that this little book contained his reminders of letters to be written and errands to be done; as well as a list of the pedigrees,

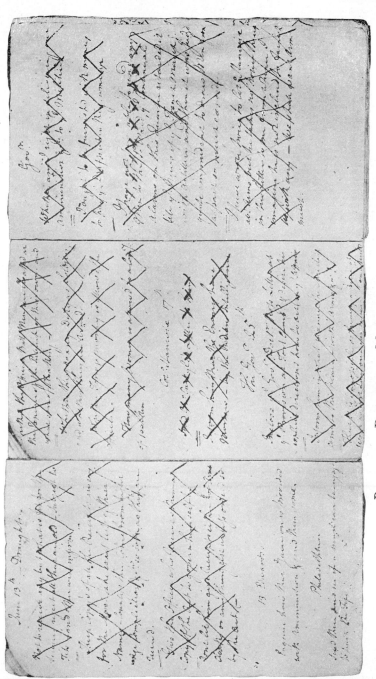

RECENTLY DISCOVERED MEMORANDA OF 1757.
(Found in the New York Public Library by Victor Hugo Paltsits.)

brands and marks of his military wagon horses, Nelly, Bull, Jack, etc.

Some of these picturesque notes run as follows:

"8 June 1757. Get the Priccs of all the Soldiers Clothg from Colo Carlyle—with a reasonable advance: and give it to each Captain with Orders to examine his Company's necessary Roll once a Week (every Saturd'y) with't fail and to make stopages for every thing difficient besides punishing the Soldiers for neglect of Duty. this to be done before they are paid. . . . Write the Governor that Capt'n Paris has got a Commission in the Maryland Force—That Gove'r Denny has sent Invitations to the Cherokees to treat with him at Fort Loudoun in his Govt . . . That I am apprehensive the diff't Colonies striving against each other must be bad.

"Also know how far and in what points I am to pay Obedience to the Orders of Colo Stanwix & if it should happen that I receive Orders from himself & Col Stanwix differing (which is not unlikely) whose Orders I am to Obey . . . Take care also to acquaint the Gov'r ab't the bad Provisions at Fort Cumberland . . . There has been foul play us'd with it.

"June 13th—Draughts. Not to receive any but what is fit for the Service. reject all that are old—Subject to Fits —and otherwise infirm.

"I have wrote twice to Colo. Stanwix ab't Arms, but he takes no notice thereof in his Letters to me from whence I imagine he is not inclin'd to furnish us with any—We shall want Arms much.

"Memorandom of Sundry things to be done in Williamsburg if I go down in November—

"Get my acc'ts with the Governor & Commit settled . . . Get some Tea—Hyson . . . Is all the Parties of Ind'ns to be furnished with Ammunition from ye Publick Stores here . . . Unless Troops March out in ye Spring there wont be one Inhabit. left in this County—the People hav been perswaded to wait ye event of ye Spring.

"If this County brakes ye others will go (being much thinner settled) infinitely faster & then an Army can never be supported."

In this same book is a recipe in his hand for brewing something to quiet his nerves.

Early in 1926, during an agitation concerning the prohibition law, a number of newspapers reprinted this document; and a Southern congressman noted both for his ardent support of the Eighteenth Amendment and of the traditional Washington, advocated the prosecution of the newspapers, who violated the law against the publication of recipes for intoxicating liquors. Since none of the newspapers were haled into court, it may be safe to reproduce it here as an historical evidence of how far the nation has travelled since 1757:

"To make Small Beer

"Take a large Siffer full of Bran Hops to your Taste.— Boil these 3 hours then strain out 30 Gall'ns into a Cooler put in 3 Gall'ns Molasses while the Beer is Scalding hot or rather draw the Mellasses into the Cooler & Stain the Beer on it while boiling Hot. let this stand till it is little more than Blood warm then put in a quart of Yeat if the Weather is very Cold cover it over with a Blank[et] & let it Work in the Cooler 24 hours then put it into the Cask—leave the Bung open till it is almost don Working—Bottle it that day Week it was Brewed."

His business affairs and the threat of litigation over Mount Vernon alarmed him so that he asked leave of absence for a brief trip home.

Both Stanwix and Dinwiddie expressed amazement at his wanting to abandon his post at such a time. He was accused of keeping too large and expensive a retinue—more than Colonel Stanwix had.

He wanted a regular pension allotted to all wounded soldiers to save them from having to come down individually and petition the Assembly for service.[21]   No heed was paid to his plea.

He was still begging for power to punish offenders and deserters. He wanted blank warrants so that he could execute the court-martial sentences. Out of 400 drafted men, 114 had deserted. He wrote to Colonel Stanwix, July 15, 1757:

"I have a Gallows near 40 feet high erected (which has terrified the rest exceedingly) and I am determined if I can be justified in the proceeding, to hang two or three on it, as an example to others." [22]

A fortnight later:

"Two were hanged on Thursday last." [23]

He apologized to Dinwiddie for "hanging instead of shooting them. It conveyed much more terror to others, and it was for example sake that we did it."

He begged again for permission to go to Mount Vernon for twelve or fourteen days "because the first of August is the time appointed for the meeting of the executors (of which I am one) of an estate that I am much interested in a dividend of, and have suffered already by the unsettled state it has remained in."

One thing Washington could never be justly accused of: thinking that a preposition is a bad word to end a phrase with.

They had the poor man so put upon, so denied his liberty, that he was all but insane with frustration, helplessness and disgrace.

XXI

HE LOSES ANOTHER SWEETHEART

AT this time came an accusation of another sort of cowardice. When he had left New York and Mary Philipse, he had evidently confided his love to Joseph Chew, a friend of aforetime, now living in Connecticut; and had asked to be kept in touch with affairs in New York. He had not forgotten Mary Philipse. He still had hopes of her.

Whether he ever told Sally Fairfax about his New York courtship or not, there is no evidence. He was still on excellent terms, as always, with Sally's husband, Colonel George William Fairfax. When he rode up to Philadelphia to meet Lord Loudoun he must have carried with him a letter from Fairfax to Governor Dinwiddie; for March 2, 1757, Dinwiddie wrote to Fairfax about his absence, beginning, "I rec'd Y'r L're by Colo Washington," and ending, "my Comp'ts to all the agreeable Family." [1]

While Washington was in Philadelphia he had learned from Joseph Chew that "Polly" Philipse had not yet been conquered by Capt. Roger Morris, for Chew wrote him:

"I am now at Mr. Robinson's, he Mrs. Robinson and his Dear Little Family are all well they desire their Compliments to you. Pretty Miss Polly is in the same Condition & situation as you saw her. . . ." [2]

Washington must have been kindled by the good word that Polly was still single and must have written to Chew to reconnoiter and spy out how the land lay, for Chew wrote to him on July 13, 1757, in evident response to some anxious letter that has, alas, disappeared:

"As to the Latter part of your Letter what shall I say. I often had the Pleasure of Breakfasting with the Charming Polly, Roger Morris was there (dont be startled) but not always, you know him he is a Ladys man, always something to say, the Town talk't of it as a sure & settled Affair. I can't say I think so and that I much doubt it, but assure you had Little Acquaintance with Mr. Morris and only slightly hinted it to Miss Polly; but how can you be Excused to Continue so long at Phila.

"I think I should have made a kind of Flying march of it if it had been only to have seen whether the Works were sufficient to withstand a Vigorous Attack, you a Soldier and a Lover, mind I have been arguing for my own Interest now for had you taken this method then I should have had the Pleasure of seeing you—my Paper is almost full and I am Convinced you will be heartily tyred in Reading it— however will just add that I intend to set out tomorrow for New York where I will not be wanting to let Miss Polly know the sincere Regard a Friend of mine has for her. and I am sure if she had my Eyes to see thro she would Prefer him to all others . . ."

Everybody was scolding Washington for lack of courage. In August, Chew mentions Polly Philipse again:

" . . . I arrived here a few days agoe Mrs. Robinson & her Dear little Family are well. Miss Polly has had a pain in her Face but is on the mendg hand."

There is uncertainty about the pain in Washington's heart. The English descendants of Mary Philipse claim that Washington did propose eventually. In an article on Mary Philipse, Mrs. Amherst Morris says:

"Mr. Chew's letter had the desired effect, and Washington set out for New York, arriving there one winter's evening; late as the hour was he sought and obtained an interview with Miss Polly." [3]

But whether he made the legendary journey or not, the result was all one. Washington once more lost the battle. On January 28th, 1758—which was Captain Morris' thirty-first birthday—Mary Philipse married the Englishman.

The story was long told by an old colored valet of the Philipse's that at the wedding-feast a lone Indian in a scarlet blanket appeared at the door of the banquet hall and prophesied: "Your possessions shall pass from you when the eagle shall despoil the lion of his name."

This warning referred of course to the confiscation by the Americans of the magnificent domain of the royalist Philipses after the Revolutionary War. It has the characteristics of most prophecies in that it was plainly written after the event and betrays itself by its anachronism. It is doubtful that even a lone Indian could have foreseen in 1758 that America would eventually choose the eagle as the national fowl, in spite of Ben Franklin's preference for the wild turkey. [4]

Captain Morris built for his bride a house in town (probably with her money). It was burned in September, 1776, in the great fire supposed to have been set by the ousted American army under Washington.

A month after his marriage, Captain Morris purchased a major's commission (probably with his wife's money) and fought the Indians in Nova Scotia, while Washington fought them in the south. Captain Morris was with Wolfe at the taking of Quebec (in which battle Mary's brother-in-law, Beverly Robinson, also served as a major), was promoted lieutenant-colonel and took part in the capture of Montreal, sold his commission in 1764, and was appointed to the Executive Council of New York Province.

A year later Morris bought a farm on Harlem Heights,

"the most desirable and commanding site on the island of Manhattan." There Morris built a fine home that still stands and is cherished as the most interesting historical building in New York, partly because it served for a while as Washington's headquarters, but more because it was the home of the famous or infamous Betty Jumel.

Mary Philipse Morris bore her husband two sons and two daughters; one of the sons became a vice-admiral in the British navy.

All the women who jilted Washington seem to have had many children.

XXII

HE LOSES HIS FIRST ELECTION

TO the new wounds of Washington's disprized love was added the hot pepper of a crushing humiliation in politics. Even the voters jilted him.

He had long cherished an ambition to enter the House of Burgesses. He stood well with the church folk, though he was not a vestryman and it was practically necessary to hold that quasi-political office before one could hope to be a Burgess. Furthermore, the less reputable elements had equally to be enticed, and he was in poor standing with the politicians.

His letter to his brother Jack [1] written on his way back to Braddock's army in 1755 showed that he was already feeling out the chances of his election, for he had asked Jack to ferret the opinions of the Reverend Mr. Green, also of Captain West, "the present Burgess and our friend Jack West."

The result of his brother's canvass was the opinion that he had better not try to run in his home county.

This is the account as given in the only available sources, yet there exists a letter to Washington from Colonel Adam Stephen, written at Fort Cumberland December 23rd, 1755, which strongly indicates that Washington did, at the last moment, decide to run and was not only defeated but insulted. What else can be assumed from this letter:

"Dr Sir

"Such a Spirit of Revenge and Indignation prevaild here, upon hearing you were insulted at the Fairfax Election, that we all were ready and violent to run and tear Your Enemies to pieces. As I imagine myself interested in all that Concerns you, I cannot forbear telling you that it would have been far better to have acquainted me with your Intention of Standing Candidate for Frederick, my acquaintance there is very general, and I would touchd on the tender part So gently, that with a Weeks Notice, I am perfectly Sure you would have gone Unanimously, in the mean time I think your Poll was not despicable, as the people were a stranger to your purpose, Untill the Election began." [2]

Three days later he writes again, giving an account of Christmas conditions at Fort Cumberland:

"The State of the Regiment is much the Same as at last Return. Cap.t Peachy is a good deal Better—M.r Lowry pines after the Babby, and has been of no Service here, the gentlemen who are best acquainted with him, tell me they are of Opinion he is tired of ths Service and being a Malingeror here, I gave him Leave to Wait on you to inform how he stood affected.

"I had the honour to dine at the head of 24 fine Gentlemen yesterday—We had an extreamly Good dinner, and after drinking the Royal Healths in a Huff and a Huzza at every Health we pass'd an hour in Singing and taking a Cheerful glass. We then amus'd ourselves with acting part of a Play, and spending the Night in mirth, Jollity and Dancing, we parted very affectionately at 12 O'Clock, remembering all Absent Friends.

"I am with Respect, wishing you a happy Year, and that it may be remarkable for your Victorious Atchievments."

Washington evidently remembered Colonel Stephen's advice, but did not put himself up in Frederick County until 1757. Even this candidacy was forgotten or denied until the records were discovered in 1892. The result by no means confirmed Colonel Stephen's promise that he would have "gone Unanimously."

Captain West had several sons, including John West, Jr., and Hugh West, Jr. Hugh, Jr. was elected a Burgess for Frederick County in 1756, though he was a lawyer in Alexandria.[3]

In the summer of 1757 Washington decided to run against him. Washington was not a resident of Frederick County, but neither was Hugh West, Jr. To represent a county, one had to have a sufficient number of "tithables" there. White tithables, or taxables, were adult males. Black tithables were slaves.

Dinwiddie in a report to the Lords of Trade in 1756 computed that there were then in Virginia, 43,329 White Tithables, and 60,078 Black Tithables, explaining, "the White Tithables are only the Males from 18 years and upw'ds. Women and those under the Age of 18, both Males and Females, are not tithed. . . . The Negroes or Blacks are Tithables from the Years of 16 and up upwards, both Males and Females." [4]

From this he computed the total population of Virginia in 1756 as 173,316 whites, 120,156 slaves. In Frederick County there were 2,173 white tithables and 340 slaves.

Washington owned in 1757 at least thirty-three black tithables. He had inherited ten or twelve slaves from his father. He acquired eighteen more with Mount Vernon. In 1754 he had bought two "fellows" for forty or fifty pounds apiece and a woman named "Clio" (a black muse of history) for fifty pounds. In 1756 he had bought two men and a woman for eighty-six pounds and, from Governor Dinwiddie, a woman and child for sixty pounds. [5]

A voter had to own fifty unimproved acres, or only twenty-five acres if there were a house on them. Bullskin Plantation was in Frederick County, and it had five hundred acres, to which he had added five hundred more in 1752.

In those days white freemen whose religious conformity and tax-paying importance were sufficient, could vote. In fact they must vote or pay a fine of two hundred pounds of tobacco. [6]

Washington not only owned property but, with his soldiers, was protecting the property of everybody else.

He was, however, in the worst possible estate for a candidate. He had disgusted all the good horse-dealers who
flocked to Braddock's army with their equine wreckage, for
he denounced them in unbridled language as corrupt traitors and jobbers in human life. So the rural vote was
against him.[7]

The saloon vote was also enthusiastically against him; for
he had fought the tippling-houses with all his might and had
flayed the drunken soldiers with great vigor and regularity.
He had furthermore tried to close up many drinking resorts,
including that of one Lindsay, a local boss of power.[8]

The moral element was against him, too, and he was
blamed for the state of affairs outlined by Centinel No. X.
He was even accused of being responsible for the massacre
of the inhabitants!

Of what infamy was Washington not falsely accused
during his lifetime?

The election was held in Washington's absence. There
were three candidates, and he made a very poor third. Out
of 581 voters, only 40 voted for him. Hugh West, Jr. was
re-elected by 271 votes, and Thomas Swearingen got in with
270, although (or because) he was "a man of great weight
among the meaner class of people," as Washington wrote.[9]

It was a stinging rebuke to a dry candidate, and Washington resolved that the next election should be as wet as
need be.

In the meanwhile, this chagrin, added to his other cha-
grins, all but broke his spirit. He had been defeated in
everything he had undertaken. Probably nobody ever
lived who accumulated more defeats than Washington. Yet
he was never really defeated.

Grief piled on grief. He had been only eleven when his

father died, leaving the family in straits from which the half-brothers did their best to relieve it.   His half-brother Lawrence, who had tried to take the father's place, fell ill when George was nineteen, and died the next year. Now, in the thick of his perplexities, he lost William Fairfax, who had treated him like a son.   The death of the old man on September 3, 1757, must have wounded him sorely.

There was a great book of pedigrees at Belvoir which came to be used as a kind of autograph album for distinguished visitors.   The last colonial entry in it is in Sally Fairfax's "beautiful tall chirography."

Under the line recording William Fairfax's death, she comments that misfortunes never come singly; one never prizes a thing enough till it is lost.   Only she puts it in almost perfect French:

"Un malheur ne vient jamais seul.   On n'estime jamais une chose assez avant que nous l'avons perdu." [10]

The editor of her biography says: "The curiosity of subsequent generations has always been piqued as to what was the other *'malheur.'* "

XXIII

HE FEELS THAT DEATH IS NEAR

SO many and such intolerable humiliations were heaped upon Washington that he began to reveal what was later to be called an "inferiority complex"—the sort of reaction to life that makes a shy man boastful, keeps a modest man harping on his own virtues.

He almost reached the "mania of persecution."

His physical health began to break under it. He believed that his best friends were traitors to him. He believed any cruel gossip and could even imagine that Colonel Richard Corbin had made "gross and infamous reflections on my conduct last Spring." [1]

This was the very Corbin to whom he had appealed in 1754 for a lieutenant-colonelcy, and who had sent it to him with a note, "Dear George: I enclose you your commission. God prosper you with it. Your friend, Richard Corbin." [2]

One of his Captains, William Peachy, had written to Washington that a Mr. Carter had said that a Mr. Robinson had said that Colonel Richard Corbin had said that Washington had tried to put through "a scheme of yours to cause the Assembly to levy largely both in men and money, and that there was not an Indian in the neighborhood . . . that that piece of deceit, or imposition of yours (as they term it) had lessened the Governor's and some of the leading men's esteem for you." [3]

Peachy added that he himself was accused of padding

his payrolls: "That I generally mustered between 30 or 40 Men & had only 6 or 7."

For such a ridiculously vicious libel, Washington had no laughter to save him. It drove him out of his wits. He wrote to the Governor and demanded to know if the author of that "stupid scandal . . . that malice so absurd, so bare-faced," could possibly be Colonel Corbin. "That I have foibles and perhaps many of them, I shall not deny. I should esteem myself, as the world also would, vain and empty, were I to arrogate perfection . . . but this I know, and it is the highest consolation I am capable of feeling, that no man, that ever was employed in a public capacity, has endeavoured to discharge the trust reposed in him with greater honesty." [4]

To Peachy he wrote with an unamused ferocity of irony that Corbin's "sporting with my character, is a little less than a comic entertainment, discovering at one view his passionate fondness for your friend, his inviolable love of truth, his unfathomable knowledge, and the masterly strokes of his wisdom in displaying it." [5]

And he told Peachy he could show his letters to anybody.

Dinwiddie replied that he had never even heard of the story, and tried to calm him, "I'd advise Yo not to give Credit to ev'ry idle Story Yo hear, for if I was to notice Reports of Diff't kinds, I s'd be constantly perplex'd."

This counsel to calm from the most irascible of men was none the less good advice, but Washington was unable to take it to his dying day. Few men have been purer in intention, more bespattered with abuse and slander, and more incapable of ignoring them.

While he is talking about false friendship, Dinwiddie puts in a dig on his own: "My Conduct to Yo. from the Beginning was always Friendly, but Yo. know I had g't

Reason to suspect Yo. of Ingratitude, w'ch I'm conv'c'd your own Conscience and reflect'n must allow I had Reason to be angry, but this I endeavour to forget; but I can't think Colo. Corbin guilty of w't is reported.

"However, as I've his M'ty's Leave to go for England . . . I wish my Successor may show Yo. as much Friendship as I've done." [6]

Washington replied that he was not aware of any ingratitude, "a crime I detest. . . . If instances of my ungrateful behavior had been particularized, I would have answered to them. But I have long been convinced, that my actions and their motives have been maliciously aggravated." [7]

He asked permission to come down to Williamsburg to settle up his accounts with Dinwiddie and the Council.

Dinwiddie wrote once more refusing Washington's plea for leave of absence even to clear up his accounts, of whose "loose writing" Dinwiddie had complained. He scolds the wretched leader like a schoolboy: "You have been frequently indulg'd with Leave of Absence. Little will be done, and Surely the Commanding Officer should not be Absent when daily Alarm'd with the Enemy's Intent's to invade our frontiers. I think you are in the wrong to ask it. You have no Acco'ts, as I know of, to Settle with me." [8]

Spanked once more, Washington wrote plaintively to John Robinson that Dinwiddie evidently thought "I had some party of pleasure in view." His final letter to Dinwiddie re-tells the old, old story of further troubles with the increasingly bold deserters, the tippling-house keepers, the lack of clothes for his men, and other dismal matters. He mentions incidentally the scalping of another young French officer. He even pleads for better treatment of the friendly Cherokee Indians, and as always, beseeches money.

To this, Dinwiddie sent his last letter, mournfully saying that he had thought no more money was due. In a letter to Captain Stewart, the departing Dinwiddie twice states: "I leave it to Colo. Washington." [9]

But Colonel Washington was in a parlous state, too ill to write, so Captain Stewart wrote for him on November 9, 1757 from Fort Loudoun:

"For upwards of three Months past Colo Washington has labour'd under a Bloody Flux, about a week ago his Disorder greatly increas'd attended with bad Fevers the day before yesterday he was seiz'd with Stitches & violent Pleuretick Pains upon which the Doct'r Bled him and yesterday he twice repeated the same operation. This complication of Disorders greatly perplexes the Doct'r as what is good for him in one respect hurts him in another, the Doct'r has strongly recommended his immediately changing his air and going some place where he can be kept quiet (a thing impossible here) being the best chance that now remains for his Recovery, the Colo. objected to following this Advice before he could procure Y'r Hon's Liberty but the Doc'r gave him such reasons as convinc'd him it might then be too late and he has at length with reluctance agreed to it; therefore has Directed me to acquaint Y'r Hon'r (as he is not in condition to write himself) of his resolution of leaving this immediately."

To this the sick Dinwiddie replied at once:

"The violent Complaint Colo Washington labors under gives me great Concern, it was unknown to me or he shou'd have had Leave of Absence sooner, & I am very glad he did not delay following the Doct'rs Advise, to try a Change of Air, I sincerely wish him a speedy Recovery."

Dinwiddie's final letter in America was addressed to Colonel Richard Corbin, but made no mention of Washington's suspicions. It is taken up with his own complaints of the attacks on his own character, mentions a gift of "a Cheese and some porter," and a "chest of Lemmons, which I begg your acceptance of.   My health continues but very poorly, tho' I have travelled upwards of 1,300 miles this summer. My Paralisise Complaint continues, and effects my spirit a little.   My Wife and two girls Join me in Sincere respects to your Lady and pretty family."

Then Dinwiddie sailed for Europe in January, 1758, relieved of the Lieutenant-Governorship at his own request, and complimented by an address of the corporation of Williamsburg, wishing him "an agreeable Voiage."

The previous October, Dinwiddie had made a Charge to the Grand Jury, in which he gave a startling picture of Virginia as he left it in 1757:

"Wickedness, Immorality and profaneness are become So epidemical, that Nothing but Strict discipline and wholesome rigour, can prove cure for those g't Enormities.

"Your conscientious presentation against Offenders, and due Execution of the Laws is the only probable method, to put a Stop to that torrent of Impiety, w'ch is a Scandal to our Country, and in time, if not prevented, may prove the ruin of our happy Constitution.   It is your duty, Gent'n, to present to the Court, all profane Swearers, drunkards and Common Gamesters, those professing the Establish'd religion, not attending divine Service in their parish Churches, all Cabals, unlawfull or unwarrantable Assemblies, Conventions or meetings, or those that, without Authority, dare to publish by way of Advertisem't in the Gazette   Such irregular meet'gs, contrary to Law and good order, w'ch tend to cause discontent and uneasiness in the minds of the people and Apt to make divisions Amongst us." [10]

But then, he had made a charge six months before to the Grand Jury, in which he had said:

"Wickedness is grown to such a Head, Immorality and Profaneness are become so epidemical that Nothing but strict Discipline and wholesome Rigour . . . can put a stop to that Torrent of Iniquity which is the Scandal of our Country." [11]

Going on backward, in October, 1756, he had been assured that the warfare was a divine protest against the general depravity:

"We have reason to dread y't our manifold Crimes and Iniquities have provok'd the Almighty God to punish us with the impend'g Prospect of Famine and the real Invasion of a barbarous and inhumane Enemy who delight in shed'g of Blood and the most unheard of Cruelties." [12]

It was the doleful custom of those times, and is to some degree of ours, to lay the blame for wars, earthquakes, plagues and volcanic eruptions on the displeasure of the deity. In 1675, during King Philip's War, the Massachusetts General Council had announced that the Indian atrocities were God's way of punishing the immodest girls and boys of the time. It seems to imply a certain clumsiness and lack of discrimination in the deity, but it satisfies a familiar type of mind to impute its own vindictive wrath to its god.

Dinwiddie was a pious Scot, and in his first message to the Burgesses he had stated:

"We have an open and extensive Country, without Fortifications, so that the Protection of our Lives and Estates depend Chiefly (under God) on our Militia, and it's the Maxim of all wise Nations, in Time of Peace to prepare and provide against the Exigencies of War." [13]

If he could believe that that Militia was "under God," his faith was indomitable.

One who reads about Dinwiddie, despises him. But it is not easy to read his voluminous letters without coming to love the man and sympathize with him keenly. He suffered from the same difficulties that maddened Washington. He co-operated with Washington as best he could.

The hostility to Washington, the slanders and conspiracies came from his fellow colonists.

Dinwiddie has not been fairly treated by American historians, Sparks, Washington Irving, Parkman, Lodge and others heaping unmerited abuse upon him.   But then, no foreigner has been treated fairly, nor any native, who happened to clash with the heroes of the struggling republic, since everything is viewed from its aftermath.   It is perhaps inevitable that Americans should see in all who contributed to the final independence a prophetic and patriotic self-sacrificing idealism, and in all who resisted any of the prophets in any of their moods, enemies of good men and opponents of freedom.

But independence was an evolution.   When it came, it surprised nobody more than some of those who are given most credit for it.   Many of the forefathers were as innocent of ideals and as greedy of personal profit as ever men were.   Many of those who resisted freedom were aglow with idealisms that time and confusion frustrated.

Washington, at this period, had certainly never dreamed of a republic.   He was as loyal to his king as any man in England.   He raged more violently and with better cause against the selfish laziness of his fellow-Virginians and the odious indifference of the other colonies, than against any of His Majesty's representatives.

"We seem to act under an evil genii," he wrote to John Robinson.[14]

Dinwiddie may justly be said to have discovered Washington.   At least he gave him all his opportunities, and in only one of his letters [15] to other people is there any criticism of Washington.   To Washington, he was full of encouragement and praise, except when he himself was rendered frantic by the inability to get support either from the Vir-

ginia Assembly or from the other colonies, and was crippled
with the paralysis that forced him to ask to be relieved.

He died in England in 1770, and the best part of his
lengthy epitaph is found in these lines:

"As his happy dispositions for domestic life
were best known to his affectionate wife and daughters,
they have erected this monument
to the memory of his conjugal and paternal love,
which they will ever cherish and revere
with that piety and tenderness he so greatly merited.

Farewell, blest shade! no more with grief opprest,
Propitious angels guide thee to thy rest!"

While the half-paralyzed Dinwiddie was making ready
to sail for home in the expectation of an early death, Washington was in the throes of fever and dysentery, and so ill
that Doctor Craik ordered him home.

He set out for Williamsburg, but as he wrote January
31, 1758, to Dinwiddie's temporary successor, President
Blair: "I was unable to proceed, my fever and pain increasing upon me to a high degree, and the physicians assured
me, that I might endanger my life by prosecuting the
journey." [16]

He reached Mount Vernon where he continued gravely
ill. On March 4th, 1758, he wrote from there to Colonel
Stanwix concerning a wild plan of campaign suggested by a
Major Smith, whose ideas for moving soldiers about the
mountain fastnesses he ridiculed with the comment: "Surely
he intended to provide them with wings."

He railed equally at Major Smith's invitation to ride two
hundred miles to meet him, explaining: "I have never been
able to return to my command. . . . At certain periods I
have been reduced to great extremity, and have now too

[Facsimile of Washington's handwritten letter]

A PAGE FROM WASHINGTON'S LETTER OF MARCH 4, 1758, TO COLONEL STANWIX ANNOUNCING HIS "APPROACHING DECAY."

(By Permission, from the Henry E. Huntington Library.)

much reason to apprehend an approaching decay, being visited with several symptoms of such a disease.

"My constitution is certainly greatly impaired. . . . I have some thoughts of quitting my command, leaving my post to be filled by some other person more capable of the task, and who may, perhaps, have his endeavors crowned with better success than mine have been. But wherever I go, or whatever becomes of me, I shall always possess the sincerest and most affectionate regards for you." [17]

It was odd that this young man just twenty-six, who had surrendered a fort on a Fourth of July, should on a fourth of March decide that his life was not only a failure but drawing to its close.

His historians usually write of him as if he always knew the destiny that Providence selected him for, and for him. They describe him as so silent and strong and serene that he might almost have foreknown that on a March fourth thirty-five years later he would be inaugurated for his second term as the unanimously elected and re-elected president of the divinely constructed United States.

But the pitiful victim of defeat upon defeat, disgrace, abuse, frustration, blazing with fever and sick with dysentery, cowered alone at Mount Vernon and reviewed a life of miseries almost unbroken, and resigned himself to "an approaching decay."

There was not even a woman to love him. He had no hope of that "domestic felicity" which was perhaps the chief of his desires.

The world was such a failure, and he such a failure in it, that he rather hoped, than feared, his release. His one regret was doubtless that he had not indeed shared "Braddock's bed" and died in battle. Did he not write, a little later, to the one woman he truly loved, and all in vain, speaking of some men of his who had been slaughtered in a foolish battle:

"But who is there that does not rather Envy than regret a death that gives birth to honor and glorious memory?"

XXIV

HE WINS A RICH WIDOW

WITH a singular irony, the makers of pretty legends have thrust the prettiest of all into this bleakest and loneliest period of Washington's young life.

Though he was writhing in mental and physical anguish at Mount Vernon on March 4th, 1758, they have him blithely riding on February 25th toward Williamsburg with despatches. He comes to William's Ferry, where he must cross the pretty stream burdened with the name Pamunkey, which it is always hastening to lose with itself in the broad York River.[1]

Here his friend Major Chamberlayne invites him to rest for a day or two. But the eager soldier remembers his despatches and refuses until he catches sight of the beautiful guest, the young widow with two darling children, Martha Dandridge Custis.

As Oliver Herford said: "A little widow is a dangerous thing."

Even Washington forgets in her presence that he has told Bishop, his body-servant, the one that Braddock gave him, to wait outside with his horse, the one that Braddock gave him. Bishop walks the gravelled road for hours, followed by the two wondering steeds. Their footsteps crunch the pebbles in vain until at a late hour they are dismissed till daybreak.

They are forgotten and unheeded as Washington and

DISPUTED PORTRAIT OF MARTHA CUSTIS WASHINGTON.

Martha, infatuated with love at first sight, talk the moon down and the sun up.

And when, at last, Washington comes forth with the dawn, there is a light of heaven in his countenance, for he is in love with one who loves him, and he rides away in the dream of bliss that made them live happily ever after.

One of those painters who have done so much to fasten picturesque falsehoods on the public mind, has shown the wooing, with the widow's pretty children playing on the floor while George and Martha stand by the mantelpiece as still as the statuary they have since become; though the tradition-builders have had the kindness to make Martha of bisque instead of the marble they selected for George. And she is the more lovable of the two; they allow her humanity at least. Even in legend she is such a woman as everybody knows, while nobody ever knew such a man as the George Washington of myth. If such a man ever lived, he himself was not that man, but the opposite.

One thing is certain, that George did not meet Martha on the Pamunkey on February twenty-fifth of that year. And if Bishop were kept waiting, it was because of his poor master's dysentery, not his courtship.

Others place the date of the meeting in May, 1758, and it might well have taken place then, for Washington was in Williamsburg in May, and wrote to the President of the Council, May 28th:

"I came here at this critical juncture, by the express order of Sir John St. Clair, to represent in the fullest manner the posture of our affairs at Winchester." [2]

He explains "how absolutely necessary is despatch." Among other customary woes, he mentions that the soldiers "have had no clothes for near two years." There is trouble over an unfair promotion of a Lieutenant Baker for taking some scalps when others had an equal right to the honor.

"Ensign Chew, for instance, was with him when the scalps were taken." This is the very Chew who had been unable to mate Washington with Mary Philipse.

In May, 1758, Washington would have been in a hurry, for great things were astir, another expedition against Fort Du Quesne was afoot, and he might well have kept Bishop waiting while he tried to tear himself away from Martha.

He might have met her previously in Williamsburg when he rode slowly down in March to see the physicians who finally cured him. It was strange that he had not encountered her on some earlier visit than this, for he was a famous young man, who dined and danced vastly, and she was a pretty young thing who married a Williamsburg man in her youth, a man of wealth who had a place in town so imposing that it was known as the Six Chimney House, also a country place on the York River, called the White House.

Martha was eight months older than George, but Sally was two years older. So was Mary Philipse. Many historians say that Martha was eight months younger.[3] But he was born in February, 1732; and her family Bible stated that she was born June 2, 1731—some say, June 21, 1731.

She was the daughter of Colonel John Dandridge, a planter in New Kent, and his wife, Frances Jones, whose grandfather graduated from Merton, Oxford, and came to Virginia in 1674. This great-grandfather of Martha was a clergyman and the son of a clergyman of the same name, for as his tombstone puts it:

Hic jacet Rolandus Jones, Clericus, filius Rolandi Jones, Clerici.

He was the first minister at old Bruton church in Williamsburg. When he dedicated the church, the vestry proclaimed that the law against staying away from church would be enforced in tobacco-fines. His salary of a hundred

pounds was commuted for sixteen thousand pounds of tobacco a year.[4]

The young Martha was taught little about spelling, but
much about "stitchery." She could play the spinet well
enough to give lessons to her granddaughter when the time
came for her to have one.

She was the eldest daughter of a large family, and learned
housekeeping. But her light-brown hair, hazel eyes, and
tiny stature caught the fancy of Daniel Parke Custis, descendant of a picturesque family including Colonel John
Custis, who suffered so much during his marriage to Frances
Parke as to order it put on his tombstone, that his seven
years of bachelorhood between his majority and his marriage were his only years of real life.

The epitaph may still be read at Arlington:

> "Aged 71 Years and yet lived but seven years
> Which was the space of time he kept
> A Bachelor's house at Arlington
> On the Eastern shore of Virginia.
> This information put on this tomb was by his
> Own positive order." [5]

His wife inherited her temper from her father, who had
a famous one. In one of his rages at a lady who occupied
what he considered his pew in church, he pulled her out of
it with great fury and violence one Sabbath morning. Before this he had been aide-de-camp to the Duke of Marlborough and brought back from the battle of Blenheim to
the Duchess and her friend, Queen Anne, the first news of
that glorious victory. One of his daughters married Colonel William Byrd of Westover; the other married the
hen-pecked Colonel Custis.

The violent tempers skipped the generation of the

son, and Daniel Parke Custis, at the age of thirty, courted and captured Martha Dandridge, who was eighteen when she married him in 1749. They dwelt alternately in the White House on the York River and the Six Chimney House in Williamsburg, and lived happily together for ten years. In 1755 Dinwiddie made him a lieutenant of Kent County and later a colonel of militia. He was about to become a member of the Council when, in 1757, he died of a bilious fever. One of his gifts to Martha was a watch with the twelve letters of her name, "Martha Custis," over the numerals.

Custis' health had been poor and the children were not strong. Two of them died in infancy, and one of the survivors, Martha—called Patsy—was a victim of fits that kept her mother harrowed and anxious until her death in her girlhood. The son, John Parke Custis, had a good heart but lacked initiative and ambition.

There is a tradition in Fredericksburg that Martha first met Washington while her husband was alive, at the beautiful home of Colonel William Fitzhugh, just across the Rappahannock from the town.[6] It is still beautiful, still known as Chatham Manor, for it was named after the Earl of Chatham. But it could not have been called by his name then, since he was only Mr. Pitt, and it was not until 1766 that he was bribed with the title of Earl of Chatham; hence the Fitzhugh manor must have worn only the family name when (and if) Martha and George first saw each other there. Fitzhugh's daughter, Mary, later married Martha Custis' grandson, and their daughter became Mrs. Robert E. Lee.

In her book, *In Tidewater Virginia*, Miss Dora Chinn Jett describes beautifully the beautiful home and its gardens:

"Tradition asserts that those rare old trees at Chatham,

or the lofty panelled walls of the interior were silent witnesses of the plighted troth of George Washington and Martha Dandridge Custis, and of Robert E. Lee and Mary Custis. Of the love affairs of the former in connection with Chatham, one flounders in the dark.

"But it is certain that Washington's frequent visits to Chatham were among his most 'interesting memories,' and that he enjoyed, as nowhere else, Mr. Fitzhugh's 'good dinners, good wine, and good company.' One is satisfied that, at least, a subsequent recital of the old story was whispered here, if not the original." [7]

Furthermore, Washington must have been interested in Fitzhugh, because of their common interest in racehorses. Fitzhugh was one of the first to import thoroughbreds and he had a private track of his own. Miss Jett vividly imagines such a scene as Washington loved:

"Here are representatives from the Fredericksburg Jockey Club, and Carters, Randolphs, Tayloes, Byrds, Wormeleys, Lees, Fairfaxes, and many more are here, and three-cornered hats, silver knee-buckles, and powdered wigs are in evidence. And consorts and daughters are here, too, with panniers, hoop skirts, and hair craped high, and poke bonnets over charming faces, and chivalry and beauty, and gallantry, all are characteristic of the gay assembly.

"Conspicuous on the track, impatient to be off, and held in check by the ebony jockey in gay attire, are Yorick and Traveller, the pride of the Mt. Airy Stables; Kitty Fisher, Regulus, Brilliant, and Volunteer of William Fitzhugh, Thomas Minor's Fearnought, Robert Slaughter's Ariel, Peter Conway's Mary Gray, Alexander Spotswood's Sterling, and other famous horses."

Assuming that Washington met Mrs. Custis at the Chamberlayne home on the Pamunkey in May, 1758, Woodrow Wilson, also a Virginian, said in the life of Washington that he wrote long before he dreamed of joining the line of Virginian presidents:

"This was not his first adventure in love. . . . No young Virginian could live twenty-six years amidst fair women in that hale and sociable colony without being touched again and again by the quick passion; and this man had the blood of a lover beyond his fellows. Despite the shyness of a raw lad who lived much in the open, he had relished the company of lively women from the first, meeting their gay sallies sometimes with a look from his frank blue eyes that revealed more than he knew. Love had first found him out in earnest six years ago, when he was but just turned of twenty; and it had taken all the long while since to forget his repulse at the hands of a fair young beauty in that day of passion. Mary Philipse had but taken his fancy for a moment, because he could not pass such a woman by and deem himself still a true Virginian. It was more serious that he had been much in the company, these last years, of a fair neighbor of the vivacious house of Cary, whose wit and beauty had haunted him in the very thick of campaigns upon the frontier, and who still mastered his heart now and again, with a sort of imperious charm. . . . It may well have made him glad of misadventures in the past to know his heart safe now." [8]

In this guarded allusion to Mrs. Sally Cary Fairfax, the then President of Princeton adroitly evaded direct mention of the most pathetic and baffling incident of Washington's life. Washington himself may have thought that he was "safe now," and had smothered a fire that had long tortured him. But it broke out once more and leaves a haunting memory in the hearts of all who know of it.

In wooing Martha Custis he was certainly doing the wise thing, but he was escaping from romance and compromising with his soul. This he did from no choice of his own, but, perhaps, because of his inability to persuade Sally Fairfax to be as madly rash as he was ready to be.

When Washington first met Martha he must have been startled, for she was the absolute image of Mary Cary, Sally's younger sister, whom he is said to have loved and proposed for long before he loved Sally, whom he could not propose for.[9]

But Mary in her portrait does not resemble her sister at all. She looks plump and sentimental where Sally was thin and intellectual.

The contrast of Martha with Sally was complete. Washington could not have talked long with her before he realized that she was neither well-educated nor eager to be. Her letters must be an index of her mind, and they are spelled almost as badly as the letters of George Washington's mother—worse even than the spelling of George's writings before he met Sally, who may or may not have had some influence on the marked change in the nature of his written thoughts and their expression.

Washington must soon have noted the difference between Martha's letters and Sally's. Their spelling was not their only difference. Sally was wooed in vain for years. Martha was willing at once.

Sally was the great lady, the essential aristocrat. Martha was the pure housewife at her best—and worst. She was prophetically named Martha.

Her interest in Washington may have been one of instant love, for he was a noted soldier, already the commander-in-chief of all the Virginia troops. And Virginia was the world. He was tall and handsome, too. But the canny housewife had her share in her decision, for Mr. Washington was a very able man. He had already acquired a good deal of property for a soldier, and he was on his way to becoming one of the biggest land-speculators in the country. At this time he was land-poor and deeply involved in debt. But she may not have known that. He probably did not emphasize it. She had a natural taste for the easy profits that come from money-lending.[10] He was fond of that business, too.

She was a widow with two ready-made children, but Washington had an extraordinary affection for children, and there was every reason to expect that she would bring him some of his own. She had already had four, though two of them had died. She raised half of them, which was a high percentage at that time.

In any case, the meeting with Martha was a blessing to him. He was none of your intellectuals himself, no bookworm. He had gone through years of loneliness in rain and snow, in horror, bloodshed and defeat. He needed above all things a plump little widow to take him to her soft breast and give him repose and the luxury of a home. If he could not give her the passionate ardor of his first love, neither could she give him hers.

Wherever he first met Martha, and whenever they became engaged, it was a fair exchange, for he was a bachelor in spite of himself, and she was a widow in need of a manager.

There are two anecdotes that may or may not be true, but are, for once, in no conflict with the facts.

When Martha was teased with her engagement, she explained: "I had to have a manager for my estate."

That was not a pretty thing for a fiancée to say, but it was quite as handsome as what he wrote, in a letter said to be still extant, to a friend who had joked with him:

"You need not tease me about the beautiful widow. *You* know very well whom I love." [11]

There were numbers of people that knew he had loved Sally Fairfax for a long time.

She kept that love hopeless, either because she did not love him at all, or because she did not love him well enough to destroy him and herself and the home of her admirable husband.

In spite of his infatuation for her, Washington had made a try for the hand of Mary Philipse, who had fifty-one thousand odd acres coming to her—which (in those days when a woman lost her legal integrity on marriage) meant, coming to her husband.

By a strange coincidence, Martha Custis also had acres; not so many as Miss Philipse, but more than any other eligible woman in Virginia. She had inherited about fifteen thousand acres, much of the land valuable from its vicinity to Williamsburg, a number of town lots, 150 negroes, and about a hundred thousand dollars in cash.

She admitted that she did not have brains enough to take care of all this, and her lawyer had advised her to "employ a trusty steward, and as the estate is large and very extensive . . . you had better not engage any but a very able man."

She had found him. And he had found her. He proposed, it seems, and she asked for time to think it over, and invited him to call upon her at the White House on his way North from Williamsburg.

On his way back he turned aside to the York River and found a slave in a rowboat on the shore. When he asked if Mrs. Custis were at home, the negro is said to have answered:

"Yes, sah. I reckon you'se the man what's 'spected." [12]

Martha's answer was Yes, and they decided to spend their honeymoon at the White House.

Then he rode away to the wars in triumph, for after his long and futile campaigns as a lover, he had at last found a woman who would marry him. [13]

When the news of this arrangement reached Mrs. Fairfax is unknown. But she commented upon it in September in a lost letter that moved him to write the most amazing letter among all his thousands of letters.

XXV

HE WINS AN ELECTION

AFTER giving himself up to a graveyard mood in March, 1758, Washington had been advised to "set out for Williamsburg to receive the advice of the best physicians there." He went down, convinced that his constitution was so impaired that nothing could "retrieve it but the greatest care and the most circumspect conduct." [1]

The doctors at the capital persuaded him that his earthly career had not quite ended, and in three weeks he was on his way back to his command at Fort Loudoun.

He had the pleasure of dissipating another of the rumors that he was already in heaven. He wrote to his friend Robert Carter Nicholas, who answered:

"I have heard of Letters from the dead, but never had the Pleasure of receiving one, till your agreeable Favour came to Hand the other Day. It was reported here that Colo. Washington was dead."

The name, Fort Loudoun, was all that Virginia ever had of that blundering Lord, for he was called home by the new Secretary of State, William Pitt, who boldly declared to England and Englishmen:

"I can save this country and no one else can."

What is more, he proved it.

He was the great Mr. Pitt, the new hope of England and the colonies. He had formed a partnership with the ineffective Duke of Newcastle, then attacked him and been ousted from his office, then joined forces with him again and become Secretary of State. Newcastle was Lord of the

Treasury, but Pitt took up the slack reins of government and put such life into England as lifted the empire out of inanition into one of its golden ages.

As George Macaulay Trevelyan says of him:

"He alone was trusted by the middle and labouring classes as the one disinterested politician. . . . He alone of British statesmen carried the map of Empire in his head and in his heart. He alone understood the free and impatient spirit of the American colonials, and he alone knew how to evoke and use it for the common purpose. . . . As a war minister he surpassed Lincoln." [2]

Unfortunately, poor Washington had little share in the miracles that he worked; for Washington's advice was completely ignored and when he urged it with deep emotion, he was ordered to keep his place.

The historians who make so much of Braddock's failure because he declined Washington's advice—though he failed in spite of accepting it—are strangely mute about the indisputable fact that when the blundering English actually did refuse his advice, they succeeded completely. Yet too much should not be made of that, either.

Still, this final humiliation, in the service of his beloved King and befuddled ministers, was as yet unforeseen, and Washington rejoiced in that most welcome act of Pitt's which removed the offensive distinction between royal and colonial commissions.

Colonel Washington, of Virginia, now ranked any lieutenant-colonel, to say nothing of a mere captain like Dagworthy.

Another thing that medicined the soul of Washington was Pitt's decision to make another grand assault on Fort Du Quesne. This meant, not only the wiping out of an old disgrace, but the redemption of the Ohio Company's property, and all those lands that Dinwiddie had promised to the soldiers who went out to the Ohio, of which many, many acres belonged to Washington, to whom the French paid no rent.

To replace Lieutenant-Governor Dinwiddie, a real governor came out, Francis Fauquier, who made a good start and treated Colonel Washington with the deference he had earned by his hardships.

Mr. Pitt, always the best friend the colonies ever had in England, did not ask too much of them. He offered to provide all munitions and supplies, requesting the colonies merely to pay the wages of their own soldiers and feed them and find them in clothes.

The assembly rose to the occasion and enlarged Colonel Washington's army to two thousand, besides three companies of rangers—on paper. To take them off the paper and put them in the ranks, a bounty of ten pounds was offered to every recruit. That ought to have ended the eternal difficulty of procuring enlistments. But it didn't. Colonel Washington was to command the brigade, and be personal commander of the first regiment, with his old friend Colonel Byrd at the head of the second, and Adam Stephen as Washington's lieutenant-colonel.

The promise Governors Sharpe and Shirley had given Washington that he should be second in command of any expedition—well, it was forgotten in the grandeur of the new plans; besides, the two governors were thrust into the background with him.

Pitt appointed Major General Abercromby to replace the indolent Loudoun, sent General Forbes to command the Fort Du Quesne attack, promoted Washington's friend Colonel Stanwix to Brigadier, and assigned a Swiss officer, Lieutenant-Colonel Henry Bouquet, to do the advance work.

It was spring, indeed, in Virginia! Washington's heart beat high again.

When it came to the actual clothing of his naked soldiers, there was the usual trouble about raising the money; but, instead of making vain complaints as of old, he designed a new uniform, a kind of Indian dress. He fitted out two companies so and sent them on to Col. Bouquet for his inspection. He was so delighted that he wanted to have the whole expedition dressed in the uniform, of which, he said, "we see nothing but shirts and blankets." It was an early form of camouflage or protective coloration.

Washington hoped now to retrieve not only the lost glory of British arms, but to recover as well from the wolves the reliques of the scattered dead. Sir Peter Halkett's son, Major Halkett, had come back overseas to find the bodies of his father and his brother, and Washington welcomed him with a beautiful letter:

"MY DEAR HALKETT: Are we to have you once more among us? And shall we revisit together a hapless spot, that proved so fatal to many of our (former) brave companions? Yes; and I rejoice at it, hoping it will now be in our power to testify a just abhorrence of the cruel butcheries exercised on our friends, in the unfortunate day of General Braddock's defeat; and, moreover, to show our enemies, that we *can* practise all that lenity of which they *only* boast, without affording any adequate proofs at all."

His friend Joseph Chew, having failed as a match-maker, had joined him and in pursuing some supposed enemies had by mistake shot dead two Virginians. It was most unfortunate; but Washington secured his exculpation.

He also persuaded the Assembly to vote him pay for a chaplain. All he needed was "a sober, serious man for this duty. Common decency, Sir, in a camp calls for the services of a divine, and which ought not to be dispensed with, altho' the world should be so uncharitable as to think us void of religion, and incapable of good instructions." [3]

There was good news from Gist (now Lieutenant, soon Captain): he had gone scouting about Fort Du Quesne and had the luck to kill and scalp two Frenchmen. It was not so pleasant when an Indian tried to palm off two white English scalps as French pelts.[4] Sometimes the canny savages sold the same scalp to three or four colonies.

Still, "a pretty good supply of Liquor came up with the last convoy."

Everything was coming Washington's way. He had been "persuaded" to run again for the House of Burgesses. The campaign was hot and his friends urged him to come down and help with his personal appeal. They had even written to Bouquet and asked leave of absence for their peerless standard-bearer. Bouquet graciously granted it, but Washington made up his mind not to do any speaking. He doubted his abilities as a spell-binder, wisely "determining rather to leave the management of that matter to my friends."

He was already speaking the politician's language: "I am in the hands of my friends."

For a time there was grave anxiety and his manager, Gabriel Jones, wrote him on July 5, 1758:

"I am sorry to find that ye people & those whom I took to be y'r friends in a great measure change their sentiments . . . this is ye consequence of ye back being turned—your Potowmack people I am afraid will not be stedfast they talk now of the Old Burgesses." [5]

His other manager, James Wood, wrote to Bouquet of Washington: "If he could come down & show his face success would be certain."

But he did not show his face, and won anyway.

His friends managed so very well that Thomas Swearingen, that favorite of "the meaner class," exchanged places with him on the see-saw of public favor. At the previous election, Swearingen had polled 270 votes and Washington 40. On July 24th, 1758, Washington drew 310 votes and Swearingen 45, out of a total of 794. Hugh West, ousted from his seat, ran third with 199; Col. Thomas Bryan Martin became the other Burgess with 240 votes. He was Washington's friend, the son of Lord Fairfax's sister Frances, and the successor, as his agent, of William Fairfax, whose death the year before had been one more of Washington's woes.[6]

With all deference to Washington's worth and desert, worth and desert have never been enough to win elections. The victory was at least partially due to his clever manager, Colonel James Wood, who must have somehow quieted the hostile horse-traders as well as Lindsay and his tippling-house man.

The method of winning over the saloon-keepers may be judged from Washington's liquor bill. It was one of the most remarkable reversals of policy ever known. Washington, the irreconcilable enemy of the wet interests, became their very patron saint. This was the successful candidate's expense account:

	£	s	d
To 40 gallons of Rum Punch @ 3/6 pr. galn	7	0	0
15 gallons of Wine @ 10/0 pr. galn	7	10	0
Dinner for your Friends	3	0	0
13½ gallons of Wine @ 10/	6	15	0
3½ pts. of Brandy @ 1/3		4	4½
13 Galls. Bear @ 1/3		16	3
8 qts. Cyder Royl. @ 1/6		12	0
Punch		3	9
30 gallns. of strong beer @ 8 d. pr. gall.	1	0	0
1 hhd. & 1 Barrell of Punch, consisting of			
26 gals. best Barbadoes rum, 5/—	6	10	0
12½ lbs. S. Refd. Sugar 1/6		18	9
6 galls. best Madeira Wine 10/—	3	0	0

Facsimiles   Æt. 13.

March 12th 1744/5

Geo Washington

Æt. 17.

Beginning this Eleventh Day of November 1749 —

Washington

Æt. 25.

I am Sir. Yr. Most Obedt. Hbble Serv.

Fort Loudoun
10th Sepr. 1757 — G. Washington

Æt. 44.

Yr. Most affect Brother,

G. Washington

New York 29th of April 1776.

Four days before his Death. Æt. 67.

Mount Vernon
December 10th G. Washington
1799

EXAMPLES OF WASHINGTON'S HANDWRITING AT VARIOUS AGES.
(From Jared Spark's Edition of "The Writings of George Washington.")

	£	s	d
3 galls. and 3 quarts of Beer @ 1/ pr gall.		3	9
10 Bowls of Punch @ 2/6 each	1	5	0
9 half pints of rum @ 7½ each		5	7½
1 pint of wine		1	6

The total bill was £39 6 0, or about $195 for liquor, [7] barring $15 devoted to "dinner for your friends."

This expense for "entertainment" did not shock Washington. He said his only fear was that Colonel Wood "spent with too sparing a hand"; he hoped that "all had enough."

Evidently all had more than enough, for there was a grand rally after the election and the rum punch did its work so well that Colonel Wood, as Washington's proxy, was picked up on the shoulders of his partisans and carried about the town "in the midst of a general applause and huzzaing for Colonel Washington." [8]

The absent soldier wrote to his political manager a tribute of thanks of the sort that elected candidates always write:

"If thanks flowing from a heart replete with joy and Gratitude can in any Measure compensate for the fatigue, anxiety and Pain you had at my Election, be assured you have them; 'tis a poor, but I am convinced, welcome tribute to a generous Mind. Such, I believe yours to be.

"How shall I thank Mrs. Wood for her favorable Wishes, and how acknowledge my sense of obligations to the People in general for their choice of me, I am at a loss to resolve on. But why? Can I do it more effectually than by making their Interest (as it really is) my own, and doing everything that lyes in my little Power for the Honor and welfare of the Country? I think not; and my best endeavors they may always command. I promise this now, when promises may be regarded, before they might pass as words of course.

"I am extremely thankful to you and my other friends

for entertaining the Freeholders in my name. I hope no Exception was taken to any that voted against me, but that all were alike treated, and all had enough. It is what I much desired. My only fear is that you spent with too sparing a hand.

"I don't like to touch upon our Public Affairs. The Prospect is overspread by too many ills to give a favourable account. I will, therefore, say little, but yet say this; that backwardness appears in all things but the approach of winter—That joggs on apace." [9]

Immediately after, if not immediately because of, the drunken hilarity following Washington's election, the House of Burgesses passed a law disqualifying any candidate to hold his seat who should "before his election, either himself or by any other person or persons on his behalf and at his charge, directly or indirectly give, present or allow any person or persons having voice or vote in such election any money, meat, drink, entertainment or provision, or make any present, gift, reward, or entertainment, &c. &c., in order to be elected." [10]

This law Washington seems to have disregarded thereafter with perfect equanimity. The news continued to warm his electors.

What Washington wrote to Martha about his new dignity is unknown, for she burned almost all their correspondence after his death, as ruthlessly as many another widow has destroyed her husband's letters, but with how much more loss to history, and to her husband!

Out of all the mass of them that he must have written, there remains only one relique of their betrothal, a brief note written four days before his election:

July 20, 1758

"We have begun our march for the Ohio. A courier is starting for Williamsburg, and I embrace the opportunity to send a few words to one whose life is now inseparable from mine. Since that happy hour when we made our pledges to each other, my thoughts have been continually going to you as another Self. That an all-powerful Providence may keep us both in safety is the prayer of your ever faithful and affectionate friend." [11]

This celebrated letter is so brief in its fervor that it makes a bewildering contrast with the long, long letters he was soon pouring out to Sally Fairfax.

The election to the Burgesses came to him in a lucky time, for he was worn out with soldiering. New disappointments and humiliations were lurking just around the corner and he would be glad to have something to do for the state besides bribe Indians with sickening eloquence and fire-water, sleep in the dirt that his neat soul abhorred, flog his mutinous soldiers and set them a futile example by his humility before his own superiors.

The House of Burgesses was an academy of politics, a subject of which he was abysmally ignorant at that time. In all America there was probably no other school so good for a future statesman.

Its importance in his career merits a brief description of it from the pages of Dr. James Miller Leake:

"The General Assembly of Virginia was composed of two houses, the Council and the House of Burgesses. The former was appointed by the Crown, usually from a number of persons suggested by the governor, while the latter was composed of representatives elected by the freeholders of the colony. But while the Council had legislative functions as the upper house of the General Assembly, it had in addition executive duties as an advisor to the governor, and judicial functions as the general court of the colony. The House of Burgesses, being only a legislative body and directly responsible to the people who elected it, was looked to by them as the maker of their laws and the guardian of their rights. Any fight made against the encroachments of Parliament would naturally be waged by the House of Burgesses. It was in this body that most of the colonial legislation originated, and as the volume of legislative work increased, its system of legislative committees was developed and perfected. . . .

"No woman, sole or covert, infant, or Popish recusant was allowed to vote. . . .

"The basis of suffrage in Virginia was much wider than it was in England at a corresponding period. It is also evident that, whatever defects the Virginia system of representation may have shown, its basis was more uniform and it was better regulated by law than was the representation in the House of Commons. While Parliament was controlled by corrupt and vicious methods, by flagrant and notorious bribery, the House of Burgesses through its committee of privileges and elections was enforcing strict and uniform election laws. . . .

"Elected by so wide an exercise of the privilege of suffrage, in elections around which the law threw every safeguard, it is not strange that the Virginia House of Burgesses should have been a body very representative of the interests of its constituency. Nor do we wonder that, within its hall, there should have developed some of the most powerful champions of popular sovereignty that the world has known. In this legislative assembly such men as Patrick Henry, Richard Henry Lee, Thomas Jefferson, Richard Bland, George Mason, and George Wythe gained their legislative experience, and formed those ideas of democracy that made them leaders in the advance guard of those who contended for constitutional government and representative institutions. When one looks at the roll of great Americans whose training in politics and government was received in the House of Burgesses, he feels that it was something more

than accident or coincidence which made that body the training school of statesmen. Its representative character, the
high average of its membership, and the system of local
self-government which it had built up, its well-regulated
committee system of legislative procedure,—all of these
help to explain the number of great men who went from
its hall into the larger leadership of State and Nation." [12]

Washington was not able to take his seat for many
months, and when he entered the hall with the meekness
inherent in him wherever he was a novice, his old friend
John Robinson, the Speaker, is said to have announced to
him that a vote of the House had directed him to return its
thanks to Colonel Washington on behalf of the colony, for
the distinguished military services he had rendered the
country.

According to the disputed but none the less plausible
legend, Washington rose to express his thanks for the honor,
but was so embarrassed that he could not utter a syllable.
The speaker relieved the blushing, stammering hero by
exclaiming:

"Sit down, Mr. Washington, your modesty equals your
valor; and that surpasses the power of any language that I
possess." [13]

He needed some such salve for his wounded pride, for he
had gone down into the depths again in his military career.

If the Burgesses ever honored him so, they felt absolved
by the tribute, for his voice was practically unheard and
the first dignity they gave him was appointment on a committee to draught a law forbidding hogs to run at large in
Winchester.[14]   Still, hogs were important members of
society then, and the punishment for stealing one was death.

Washington was representing Frederick County, not his
own home district, where he did not feel called upon to run
for seven years.

XXVI

HE IS IGNORED IN THE NEW WAR

WASHINGTON has been left all this while at Winchester trying to compile two regiments. The newly betrothed of the wealthy Mrs. Custis, the newly elected Burgess, the commander-in-chief of all the Virginia troops, was to learn how small a part he was of England's sudden awakening from years of defeat in every direction.

Americans naturally see America magnified out of all perspective in that gigantic Seven Years' War, which we call the French and Indian War (instead of the English, French, German, Austrian and Russian War). But so we do in the War of 1812 where our army and navy were but a detail in the gigantic death-wrestle with Napoleon.

England, however, was fighting all over the continent of Europe and on all the seas, hiring German troops and devastating the French coasts, burning three ships of the line, twenty-four privateers and sixty merchantmen at St. Servan, burning twenty-seven ships and destroying the forts at Cherbourg, driving the French away from Senegal and the Guinea Coast of Africa.

In America, Pitt's eyes were on Louisbourg and then Quebec, then Ticonderoga, and finally Fort Du Quesne. He made Colonel Amherst a major-general and gave him three brigadiers, including Wolfe. He brought in whole armies of Highlanders and sent two regiments of kilties to America.

At the same time Frederick the Great was matching his five million Prussians against a hundred million enemies.[1] The Seven Years' War that the hitherto-unheard-of Washington had kindled when his men shot down the hitherto-unheard-of Jumonville, was raging to its close.

"Maria Theresa with her two allies, Pompadour and the Empress of Russia," as Parkman puts it, were allied against the woman-ignoring Frederick, but he was winning all the victories, when Pitt took up the idle sword of England and wielded it everywhere about the world.

The campaign against Fort Du Quesne was only one item in a long catalogue, yet he called for two thousand troops from Pennsylvania, two thousand from Virginia and the same from Maryland. Maryland's Assembly voted for one thousand, but a quarrel with the governor over the tax to pay for them ended in her sending only two or three hundred. North Carolina sent that many. Pennsylvania raised nearly three thousand; Virginia only sixteen hundred. But these, with twelve hundred Scots and others, brought the army of General Forbes beyond six thousand, as against Braddock's two. In the North, for the northern expeditions, Massachusetts had promised 7000 men, Connecticut 5000, New Hampshire 3000.

Forbes had nearly as many Highlanders as all the troops that Braddock got to Fort Du Quesne, and many of them met as frightful a conclusion.

Under Dinwiddie's luckless management Washington had tried to defend a frontier of three hundred miles with a single regiment of disgruntled, drafted, all-but-worthless troops. Dinwiddie had urged him to attack Du Quesne when the project was ridiculous. When he pleaded for strength and authority to attack the hated fort, he was denied the chance.

But now it looked as if his day had come. The Scotsman

Forbes reached Philadelphia in April, where he fell ill with the bloody flux; worse yet, he fell into the hands of the Pennsylvanians whom Washington had wanted flogged.

They had tried to persuade Braddock to cut through the Pennsylvania wilderness instead of following the route of the Ohio Company, but the Company's Quaker director in London had exerted his pull and Braddock had landed in Virginia.

Now there seemed to be no way for the Virginians to get at Forbes. He was a sick man entirely surrounded by Pennsylvanians. And they upheld the outrageous pretence that the present site of Pittsburgh belonged to them and not to Virginia. They succeeded in seducing Quartermaster-General Sir John St. Clair (or Sinclair). He had marched in the van of Braddock's army and been wounded at the Monongahela. He had been so fiercely blamed for selecting that road that treason was hinted.

He had had enough of Braddock's Road. The Pennsylvania route was a short-cut with more convenient sources of supply and forage.[2]

Forbes agreed with St. Clair and so did Bouquet. They planned to move up slowly, establishing magazines on the route, instead of taking Washington's advice as Braddock had done and pushing through on one long march.

Forbes believed in fighting Indians the Indian way, but he had more contempt for the colonial soldiers than Braddock ever expressed. The sight of them with their duck-hunting guns and old muskets patched with twine, and some of them with only walking-sticks or clubs, disgusted him. Many of these alleged denizens of the woods had never pulled a trigger in their lives.

Forbes wrote to Pitt, "I vainly at the beginning flattered myself that some very good Service might be drawn from the Virginia, & Pennsylvania Forces, but am sorry to find

that a few of their principal Officers excepted, all the rest
are an extream bad Collection of broken Inn-keepers, Horse
Jockeys, & Indian traders, and that the Men under them,
are a direct copy of their Officers, nor can it well be otherwise, as they are a gathering from the scum of the worst of
people in every Country, who have wrought themselves up,
into a panick at the very name of Indians." A short while
after this Forbes commended the behavior of some of the
provincial troops in resisting an attack of the French. "I
was extremely angry to find our people had not pursued
and attacked their rear in their retreat, from which we might
have made reprizalls, but as our troops were mostly provin-
cialls, I was obliged to attribute it to their ignorance, for to
do justice I must commend the spirit of some of the provin-
cialls particularly the Maryland troops, who I retained in
the Service, after being left to disband by their Province." [3]

The provincials, said Forbes, were generally "a parcel of
scoundrels" and he advised Bouquet to "drop a little of
the gentleman and treat them as they deserve."

When Forbes moved at last he had to be carried in a
litter slung between two horses—which was worse than
Braddock's coach-and-six. He groaned with "excruciating
pain" and was "weak as a new-born infant."

As for the feud between Pennsylvania and Virginia, he
followed his own intuition, and wrote to Bouquet that he
had told the two Virginia colonels, Washington and Byrd,
"that the good of the service was all we had at heart, not
valuing provincial interests, jealousies, or suspicions one
single two pence." [4]

Washington's motives were undoubtedly sincere, though
they excited grave suspicion, but it is not surprising that he
sickened of war when, in his final campaign, his advice was
bluntly refused and his prophecies of disaster were falsified
by the triumphant event.

He had begun by asking Colonel Stanwix to say a good word for him to Forbes:

"I must, nevertheless, beg, that you will add one more kindness to the many I have experienced, and that is, to mention me in favorable terms to General Forbes, (if you are acquainted with that gentleman,) not as a person, who would depend upon him for further recommendation to military preferment, for I have long conquered all such inclinations, (and serve this campaign merely for the purpose of affording my best endeavors to bring matters to a conclusion), but as a person, who would gladly be distinguished in some measure from the *common* run of provincial officers, as I understand there will be a motley herd of us. Nothing can contribute more to his Majesty's interest in this quarter, than an early campaign, or a speedy junction of the troops to be employed in this service. Without this, I fear the Indians will with difficulty be restrained from returning to their nation before we assemble, and, in that event, no words can tell how much they will be missed." [5]

Forbes answered with great courtesy. After all the impertinences Washington had endured from Captain Dagworthy of Maryland with his royal commission, it must have been an irresistible delight to him to have the martinet come meekly to him to take his commands. He was too big a man to gloat, but it could not have given him any pain to write to Colonel Bouquet:

"Captain Dagworthy's party returned hither yesterday in consequence of orders from Sir John St. Clair, forwarded by the commanding officer at Fort Frederick. I have directed him to finish a bridge at this place, which I imagine he will effect by to-morrow night; with his tools I will next day send out a party on General Braddock's road, which I shall be able to reinforce when Colonel Mercer returns." [6]

Triumph was in the sky and the Indians were barometers.

To Braddock only a hundred had come; and only eight remained to the end. Now, Washington could write to General Forbes:

"The Indians seem to anticipate our success, by joining us, thus early, with seven hundred of their warriors." [7]   He did not trust them but he imagined the French were having equal trouble with them and he urged that they be humored. What Indians he could retain, he kept busy at scalping, the work they did best. Like Dumas, he always sent a white man along, as he wrote to Colonel Bouquet:

"I must confess, that I think these scalping parties of Indians we send out will more effectually harass the enemy . . . than any parties of white people can do." [8]

It is noteworthy that Sparks, in his edition of Washington's writings, and Irving in his biography, both quote this letter and omit the word "scalping" from "scalping parties." [9]

The motives are evident, but they do not belong in faithful history. Washington never expressed the least abhorrence of the practice of scalping. He would always rather have a French scalp than a savage warlock.

But the Swiss Bouquet could not learn to love the Indians. They were unreliable thieves and he protested:

"It is a great humiliation for us to be obliged to suffer the repeated insolence of such rascals. I think it would be easier to make Indians of our white men, than to cox [coax] that damned tanny race." [10]

No more would St. Clair be persuaded to provide the band of naked Cherokee Indians with guns and clothes. He vowed he would have nothing to do with the "unreasonable nations of Indians." The good services of the Cherokees were therefore lost and Washington had no confidence in the Catawbas who had "not this year brought in one prisoner or scalp." [11]

Knowing what the Indians had done to Braddock, Washington grew so alarmed at the scornful attitude of these visiting Britishers that he wrote a fervid appeal to Forbes, imploring him to appease the Cherokees and by no means to neglect the other red allies.   He began very humbly:

"Pardon the liberty I am going to use—a liberty that nothing but the most disinterested regard for the safety and welfare of these Colonies would induce me to take.   How far my Ideas on what I am about to observe are compatible with reason, and may correspond with your Sentiments on the matter, I candidly submit to your Excellency's determination.

"The unfortunate arrival of the Cherokees into these Governments so early in the Spring, and the unavoidable accidents that have hitherto prevented a junction of the Troops intended for the Western Expedition, have caused them (as they are naturally of a discontented temper) to be tired of waiting; and *all* except those who came last, with Colo. Byrd, and a few others that have joined since, to return home. . . . We shall be left to perform without them a march of more than 100 miles from our advanced Post, before we shall arrive at Fort du Quesne; a great part of which will be over mountains and Rocks, and thro' such Defiles, as will enable the Enemy, with the assistance of *their* Indians, and Irregulars, and their superior knowledge of the country, to render extremely arduous, unsafe, and at best, tedious, our intended Expedition; unless we also can be assisted by a Body of Indians; who I conceive to be the best if not the *only* Troops fit to cope with Indians in such grounds. . . .

"The Southern Indians, of late, seem to be wavering; and have, on several occasions, discovered an inclination to break with us.   I think it will admit of no doubt, that, if we should be unsuccessful in this Quarter, which Heaven avert! the united force of several powerful nations of them might be employed against us; and that such an acquisition to the Enemy would enable them to desolate our Southern Colonies, and make themselves masters of that part of the continent, is not to be questioned. Wherefore, that nothing should be omitted that might contribute to prevent so dreadful a calamity, I suggest the idea of sending a proper person immediately to the Cherokee nation; who may not only heal the differences which now subsist, but get a Body of them to join the army on their march, and no person, surely, who has the interest of our important cause at heart, woud hesitate a moment to engage in such a Service, on the event of which our all, in a manner, depends. . . .

"It woud be presuming too much after I have endeavored (tho' a little indigestedly) to shew the necessity of Indians, and the advantages and disadvantages of a late campaign to say any thing further, unless it be to apologize once more for the freedom I have taken of mentioning matters, which I suppose you are equally (if not better) acquainted with than I am." [12]

He wrote again:

"The malbehaviour of the Indians gives me great concern. If they were hearty in our interest, their services would be infinitely valuable. As I cannot conceive the best white men to be equal to them in the woods. But I fear they are too sensible of their high importance to us, to render us any very acceptable service." [13]

It was at this anxious moment that the day of election came round. He was too deeply worried to accept the permission to absent himself, and stuck to his post.

And now it dawned upon him that, after all, the expedition was not to go by Braddock's Road but by a new one to be cut through an old trading path running through Raystown or Rea's Town (now Bedford, Bedford County,

Pennsylvania), thirty miles north of Fort Cumberland.

All the toil and money that had been spent on Braddock's route by the Ohio Company, by his own troops when he pushed beyond Fort Necessity, and by General Braddock, who had widened it for artillery—all that was to be rejected and a new path chopped out!   The thought was unbearable.

He pleaded with Bouquet and, to make his points clearer, went to his tent and wrote them out, warning him of "most destructive consequences," and of "the despicable light" in which the Indians looked on the Southern Colonies.

He ridiculed the alleged shortness of the Raystown road:

"I must beg leave to ask if it requires more time, or is it more difficult and expensive, to go 145 miles in a good road already made to our hands, or to cut a road 100 miles in length, great part of which over almost inaccessible mountains?" [14]

He wrote a very long and keenly reasoned letter, taking up every point of economy, speed, forage, strategy.   But he pleaded in vain.

He wrote dismally to Major Halkett:

"I am just returned from a conference held with Colonel Bouquet.   I find him fixed, I think I may say unalterably fixed, to lead you a new way to the Ohio, thro a road, every inch of which is to be cut at this advanced season, when we have scarce time left to tread the beaten track, universally confessed to be the best passage through the mountains.

"If Colonel Bouquet succeeds in this point with the General, all is lost,—all is lost indeed!   Our enterprise will be ruined, and we shall be stopped at the Laurel Hill this winter; but not to gather *laurels*, (except of the kind that covers the mountains.)   The southern Indians will turn against us, and these colonies will be desolated by such an acquisition to the enemy's strength." [15]

He wrote to Governor Fauquier on August 5th, 1758:

"We are still encamped here, and have little prospect of de-camping, unless a fatal resolution takes place, of opening a new road from Rays Town to Fort du Quesne."[16] In a mournful afterword he added:

"P. S. I was this moment presented with a letter from Colo. Bouquet telling me that the General had directed the other road to be opened. I expect therefore to be ordered that way immediately."

In the meanwhile St. Clair, who had insisted on the new road, had changed his mind and come round to the Braddock route as the best. Governor Sharpe had apparently persuaded him to Washington's point of view.[17] But St. Clair's sudden shift only angered Forbes. "This he ought to have said two months ago or hold his peace now." Forbes believed that Braddock's road would "save but little labour, as that road is now a brush wood by the sprouts from the old stumps."

Bouquet was set against Braddock's Road because, as he wrote Forbes, "some foolish people have made partys to drive us into that road," and "I utterly detest all partys and views in military operations."

None the less, he sent orders to have Braddock's Road reconnoitred and cleared. It would at least deceive the enemy.

Forbes, learning from other guides that the Raystown route was feasible, grew angrier and angrier with St. Clair. He wrote to Bouquet: "I conceive what the Virginia folks would be att, for to me it appears to be them, and them only, that want to drive us into the road by Fort Cumberland, no doubt in opposition to the Pennsylvanians, who by Raes town would have a nigher Communication (than them), to the Ohio."

He was still more furious when Washington's Colonel

Byrd wrote that he had sixty Indians ready to go with
Forbes, but only on condition that he went by Fort Cumberland.   At this Forbes fairly roared on paper:

"This is a new system of military Discipline truly; and
shows that my Good friend Byrd is either made the Cats
Foot of himself, or he little knows me, if he imagines that
Sixty scoundrels are to direct me in my measures."

Bouquet, after praising Washington's "sincere zeal," was
so annoyed by his pressure, that he wrote to Forbes (on
July 31st):

"I have had an interview with Colonel Washington, to
ascertain how he conceives the difficulties could be overcome; I got no satisfaction from it; *the majority of these
gentlemen do not know the difference between a party and
an army,* and, overlooking all difficulties, they believe everything to be easy which flatters their ideas.   What I shall
have to tell you on this point cannot be discussed in a
letter. . . ." [18]

This was a slap indeed at Washington, who had never
led more than a party of 300 men to battle, had been unable
to feed them, and had surrendered them promptly at Fort
Necessity.   He had had no practical experience in command
with Braddock, since he did not join till late, was a messenger only and was ill during the greater part of the march.

Forbes was moving six thousand men and moving them
slowly on purpose—on two purposes: one, to keep in touch
with the campaigns to the north, which might need his help;
the other, to allow more time for the Indian traders like
Croghan, and the Moravian missionary, Christian Frederick
Post, to work on the French Indians and decoy them away.
This secret and subtle campaign was succeeding marvellously
and undermining the French control. [19]

Washington would not be rebuffed, and even after he had
received orders that Braddock's Road was to be given up,

he wrote again to Bouquet "to say what I could to divert you" from the resolution.[20]

One of his too ardent letters to somebody was turned over to Forbes, who wrote to Bouquet a fierce denunciation of him:

"By a very unguarded letter of Col. Washington's that accidently fell into my hands, I am now at the bottom of their scheme against this new road, a scheme that I think was a shame for any officer to be concerned in, but more of this at meeting." [21]

Just which unguarded letter of Washington's it was that enraged Forbes, nobody knows. He could hardly have seen the one to Governor Fauquier, though being a British officer, Fauquier might have felt called upon to forward it to Forbes.

Perhaps it was the letter he wrote to an unknown friend, probably Gabriel Jones, who had helped in his election:

"God knows what's intended; for nothing seems ripe for execution; backwardness, and I would if I dare, say more, appears in all things." [22]

That would not have been the most pleasant sort of letter for a General to read in a Colonel's hand, especially the hand of the unrelenting Washington.

A month later Forbes was still fuming: "His Behaviour about the roads, was in no ways like a soldier."

Concerning this losing battle of Washington's, even so ardent an admirer as Prof. Archer Butler Hulbert finds nothing to say in his defence. He finds that the letter to Governor Fauquier "does Washington no credit"; his accusation against his general is "unreasonably bitter," and "Forbes' correspondence with Bouquet is convincing proof of the falseness of Washington's theory that the Pennsylvanians 'had prejudiced the General absolutely against the old road.'"

He quotes Forbes' letter of September 17th to Bouquet, showing that the old Scot hated both colonies alike:

"I believe neither you nor I values one farthing where we get provisions from, provided we are supplyed, or Interest ourselves either with Virginia or Pennsylvania, which last I hope will be damn'd for their treatment of us with the Waggons, and every other thing where they could profit by us from their impositions, altho at the risque of our perdition." [23]

In the ferocity of this intercolonial war over the building of a road, Prof. Hulbert sees the vital importance of a highway to either of the colonies. To Pennsylvania it meant the turning of an Indian trading path into a grand avenue of commerce. But this was just what the Virginians did not want, for they "called the West their own. This rivalry was intense for more than a quarter of a century and came near ending in bloodshed; the quarrel was only forgotten in the tumultuous days of 1775." Was it forgotten then?

There was another great argument between Virginia and Pennsylvania over the opening of a later and farther west. The conference took place for three days at Gettysburg, ending with the Virginians on their way home on the Fourth of July, 1863—to the immense relief of Pennsylvania.

Prof. Hulbert admits that Pennsylvania had not "deserved the opening of the road," since "Virginia men and capital were foremost in the field for securing the Indian trade of the Ohio; they had, nearly ten years before, secured a grant of land between the Monongahela and the Kanawha, and sent explorers and a number of pioneers to occupy the land; their private means had been given to clear the first white man's road thither and erect storehouses at Will's Creek and Redstone; the activity of these ambitious, worthy men had brought on the war now existing. When open strife became the colonies' only hope of holding the West,

Virginia was first and foremost in the field; the same spirit that showed itself in commercial energy was very evident when war broke out, and for four years Virginia had given of her treasure and of her citizens for the cause. During this time Pennsylvania had hardly lifted a finger, steadily pursuing a course which brought down upon her legislators most bitter invectives from every portion of the colonies. And now, in the last year of the war, the conquering army was to pass through Pennsylvania to the Ohio, building a road thither which should for all time give this province an advantage very much greater than that ever enjoyed by any of the others. . . . But Forbes had the present to deal with, not the past, and the shortest route to the Ohio was all too long."

Forbes wanted a short road, but he was not, like Washington, frantic to get to Du Quesne in a short time. As he wrote Bouquet in August:

"Between you and I be it said, as we are now so late we are yet too soon."

That was what Washington could not understand, and with him, as in all such cases, human nature disguised and ennobled its more material motives. He was a Virginian first and a Britisher second, when it came to matters of inter-state rivalry over trade, just as Robert E. Lee was a Virginian first and an American second when the commercial interests of the north tried to cramp the south to the northern policies. Both sides, as the behaviorists say, "rationalized" their selfish impulses.

Washington was unquestionably convinced of the purity of his ideals and the high virtue of his aims. But so everybody is.

Meanwhile the poor Indians, who after all did little to deserve their territory except to be born in it, watched like the wolves and panthers the gradual rising of the white sea about their forests. They were being drowned out or driven into other wildernesses already occupied. They began to weary of the French and for sheer variety to prefer the English, whose traders and soldiers, governors and colonels, plied them with whiskey and rum. Even the Quakers kept the Indian delegates drunk for days at a time when it suited their purposes.[24] Much has always been made of the fact that William Penn acquired his territory by purchase and not by bloodshed; but the Indians of 1758 asked how a few chiefs of an earlier generation could give away so much land for so little recompense. In 1754 at Albany the later Penns had secured from a few Iroquois chiefs a deed for all of southwestern Pennsylvania. They claimed more than they had paid for and the Indians grew ugly as they realized it. Croghan in 1757 drew up a memorandum advising that the Penns in England deed back most of this land, and they consented.

The English were all for sweetness and light now. The brave Moravian missionary Post was sent out to the Ohio tribes by Governor Denny of Pennsylvania in July, 1758, and, as Volwiler says, "with sublime courage went into the heart of the enemy's country and placed himself in the hands of a treacherous and cruel foe."[25] He held conferences west of Fort Du Quesne and the French officers were dismayed to find that the Indians would not let them take him prisoner. This change in Indian sentiment weakened the French morale more than the approach of Forbes' army.

Everywhere in every manner the attack on the French was being pressed, and their power was crumbling. In this attack Washington had no part at all except to wreck his own prestige with counsels that were not heeded.

It would be unjust to him to say that his advice was wrong because Forbes succeeded in spite of refusing it. In other circumstances his advice would have been proved to be perfectly wise. It was luck that won the victory for

Forbes, meaning by "luck" the whole complex of forces that interplay and bring about results in which no one man has a controlling influence.

And yet Forbes must not be robbed of the glory that a man deserves by being lucky, for luck itself must be managed and improved. It must not be forgotten that the brave old man, dying slowly, slowly, kept following the army and directing nearly every step though he was so feeble that he went to bed "at eight at night, if able to sit up so late."

Bouquet was having his troubles, too. The new road was an appalling task. St. Clair wrote him on August 12th:

"Send as many men as you can with digging tools, this is a most diabolical work, and whiskey must be had." [26]

There was the usual complaint of "unaccountable slowness" and Washington's prophecies were beginning to justify themselves a little. And yet the toilers finished the road across the steep Laurel Hill and were forty miles from Fort Du Quesne before the French suspected its existence. They were too busy fortifying and ambushing Braddock's Road.[27]

Washington would not be quieted from muttering. As late as August 28th he was writing to Bouquet with a rash sarcasm; and sarcasm is among the most irritating of insubordinations:

"Since you hope our point may be carried I would fain expect the surmounting these obstacles. 'Tis a melancholy reflection tho' to find there is even a doubt of success, when so much is depending, and when in all Human probability we might have been in full possession of the Ohio by now, if rather than running ourselves into difficulties and expence of cutting an entire new road the distance we have, first and last Braddock's had been adopted.

"Every one knows what could have been done [on] the old road—few can guess what will be the new, their being not only the difficulties of the Road to encounter, but the chance of a French reinforcement also, but it is useless to add on this head. I should rather apologize for what I have said." [28]

He wrote to the Speaker of the House, September 1st, 1758, from Fort Cumberland:

"We are still encamped here, very sickly, and quite dispirited at the prospect before us.

"That appearance of glory, which we had once in view, that hope, that laudable ambition of serving our country, and meriting its applause, are now no more; but dwindled into ease, sloth, and fatal inactivity. In a word, all is lost, if the ways of men in power, like (certain) ways of Providence, are not inscrutable. But why may not? For we, who view the actions of great men at a distance, can only form conjectures agreeably to a limited perception; and, being ignorant of the comprehensive schemes, which may be in contemplation, might mistake egregiously in judging of things from appearances, or by the lump. Yet every fool will have his notions,—will prattle and talk away; and why may not I? We seem then, in my opinion, to act under an evil genii. The conduct of our leaders, (if not actuated by superior orders,) is tempered with something I do not care to give a name to. But I will say they are —— or something worse to P—j—v—n [Pennsylvanian?] artifice, to whose selfish views I ascribe the miscarriage of this expedition; for nothing now but a *miracle* can bring this campaign to a happy issue."

He was almost insane with impatience, for he had sent out his friends Chew and Allen, two officers of the First Virginia, to reconnoitre, and they had lain a day or two in hiding with a full view of Fort Du Quesne and discovered that the whole French garrison was only eight hundred men, half of them Indians:

"See, therefore, how our time has been misspent. Behold how the golden opportunity is lost, perhaps never more to be regained! How is it to be accounted for? Can General Forbes have orders for this? Impossible. Will, then, our injured country pass by such abuses? I hope not. Rather let a full representation of the matter go to his Majesty. Let him know how grossly his glory and interest, and the public money, have been prostituted. I wish I were sent immediately home, as an aid to some other on this errand. I think, without vanity, I could set the conduct of this expedition in its true colors. [By "sent home" he meant "sent to England." He wanted to go to England to fight for Braddock's Road!] . . .

"Adieu, my dear Sir. It hath long been the luckless fate of Virginia to fall a victim to the views of her crafty neighbors, and yield her honest efforts to promote their common interests, at the expense of much blood and treasure! whilst openness and sincerity have governed her measures. We *now* can only bewail our prospects, and wish for happier times, but these seem to be at so remote a distance that they are indeed rather to be wished, than expected."

How he loved those Pennsylvanians!

It seems strange to find George Washington writing with sincere humility of irony: "We who view the acts of great men at a distance can only form conjectures," and "every fool will prattle, and why may not I?" But his eloquence in the last paragraph was not exactly his own. He quoted it almost literally from a letter he must have just received. On August 23rd an admirer of his, John Kirkpatrick, had written to him from Alexandria using these very words:

"It has long been the luckless fate of Virginia, to fall a Victim to the Views of crafty neighbours and yield her honest efforts to promote their common interest—at the expense of much Blood and Treasure—While her Sincerity Justified her measures—We now, can only bewail that Blindness—and wish for happier times—which seem at so remote a distance—that it is rather to be wished than expected." [29]

Washington did not give Mr. Kirkpatrick credit for his phrases, but he did correct the grammar of the last sentence, and give the plural noun a plural verb—which was more than he always did in his own writings.

He wrote in the same strain to Governor Fauquier, castigating the neighboring colony:

"The Pennsylvanians, whose present as well as future interest it was to conduct the Expedition thro' their Government, and along that way, because it secures at present their frontiers and the trade hereafter—a chain of Forts being erected—had prejudiced the General absolutely against this road; made him believe we were the partial people; and determined him at all events to pursue that rout. So that their sentiments are already known on this matter and to them, as instigators, may be attributed the great misfortune of this miscarriage—for I think now nothing but a miracle can procure success. . . .

"I may possibly be blamed for expressing my sentiments so freely—but never can be ashamed of urging the truth; and none but obvious facts are stated here. The General, I dare say from his good character, can account fully, and no doubt satisfactorily, for these delays, that surprize all who judge from appearances only; but I really can not." [30]

As a result of Washington's ferocious criticism of his superiors, when the Virginia Assembly met on the 12th of September, there was a rancorous indignation against Pennsylvania, and general despair that the campaign would ever end. It was, therefore, voted to withdraw the first regiment, Washington's own, from the expeditionary forces after the first of December. Later, when it was learned that unsuspected progress had been made, the Assembly was recalled and the date extended to January first. [31]

Washington was summoned at last to leave Fort Cumberland and march his men up to the abominated new road. It had been chopped, blasted and built through swamps and around the sides of precipices, across the Allegheny Mountains and the long harsh parallel ridge of Laurel Hill, as far as Loyalhannon Creek near Fort Ligonier in Westmoreland County.[32] Here Washington was put in charge of the road construction gang and he did his utmost to push the road through. He had the temporary rank of a brigadier-general of pioneers, and a thousand men under him. Bouquet established a depot of supplies at Loyalhannon Creek as his last base for the advance to Du Quesne.

The French had learned by now all about the new path of the new army and were doing their utmost to reinforce the fort. But they were being pressed at too many points to accomplish much.[33]

They were chiefly afraid of the fidelity and patience of the Indians; and with good reason, for the redskins were listening to the gentle suasions of the English missionaries of trade and religion.

Forbes was inspired to suggest a great powwow of whites and Indians for the purpose of making peace between them. It was announced for October 8th at Easton, Pennsylvania, and invitations were broadcasted to all Indians, especially the tribes most devoted to the French.

Since everybody else was in trade, the Indians were not superior to business motives. The gifts from the French had been notably few of late, thanks partly to the success of the British fleet in capturing French vessels. The English had become lavish in gifts. Where Washington had begged almost in vain for a little goods, dry and wet, Forbes had celebrated his arrival by dealing out presents worth thirty thousand dollars. At the Easton conference the stingy Pennsylvanians decided to distribute a wealth of 3 dozen pairs of women's stockings, 4 dozen ivory combs, trinkets, 9 gross of starred gartering, 50 pairs of shoes,

100 blankets, 160 match-coats of fur, and 433 plain and ruffled shirts.[34]

With such pretty things before them or in the offing, the Indians were hypnotized; and it may well be believed that the immensity of the army approaching the French fort had not been minimized in British propaganda. Even the Delawares were wavering.

In the everlasting auction for Indian favor the British were making all the high bids. The Moravian missionary Post, who spoke Delaware and had married a squaw convert, was spreading the gospel of peace among the Indians. This German did not ask them to butcher other Christians as many missionaries did, particularly the Jesuits; but merely to lay down the war-hatchet and live at peace with the world. His absolute fearlessness and his innocent spirituality melted the hearts of the barbarians. A German was thus the chief influence in the defeat of the French in this wilderness so far from the battles Frederick of Prussia was winning on the continent. In the very presence of the helpless French officers Post won the promise of the chiefs to attend the convention at Easton.

It was well for the English that his gentle might was exerted at that very time, for the French had recently given another bloody demonstration that they could still destroy all English forces that dared approach Du Quesne. They had inflicted another Braddock's Defeat on another mixed army of British and colonials.

Washington was not the only one in the army who was eating his heart out with restlessness to be at the French throats. Major Grant of the Highlanders begged Bouquet to let him take out a strong force for an armed reconnaisance of Fort Du Quesne. He hoped to capture useful prisoners for intelligence purposes and shake up the French and Indians by a quick raid.

Bouquet was so impressed by his enthusiasm that he did not pause to ask permission of General Forbes, but gave Grant his kilties and some of the so-called Royal Americans, and some of Washington's men.

Washington was not permitted to go along since he was a colonel, but his friend Major Lewis took his place, with seven other officers and Captain Bullet and 168 Virginia men.

Grant took out eight hundred altogether and reached the neighborhood of the Fort on the night of September 13th, 1758. At two in the morning he mounted a hill within half a mile of the fortress. Since that day it has been known as Grant's Hill, for the same red reason that gave Braddock's name to Nemacolin's Path.

The forests that had seen Braddock's ruin hid the Scots and the colonials from the unsuspecting French. Grant ordered Major Lewis with half his Virginians to charge the Indian camp outside the fort and then, by a feint of retreat, lure the pursuers up the hill into ambush. While Grant waited in increasing suspense, Lewis and his woodsmen were so completely lost that they returned in the foggy dawn with nothing done.

Grant sent some of his own men to set fire to a log warehouse and decoy the enemy to their ruin. He sent Lewis to the rear with two hundred men as guard of the wagon-train, where he joined Captain Bullet's company of Virginians.

Grant sent a hundred Pennsylvanians off to his right and the Scots Captain Mackenzie off to the left to form the walls of the trap. He sent his Captain Macdonald down into the plain to sketch the fort ostentatiously, while he hid himself in the high forest with his own remaining hundred and a company from Maryland.

He took the perilous step of dividing his forces in the

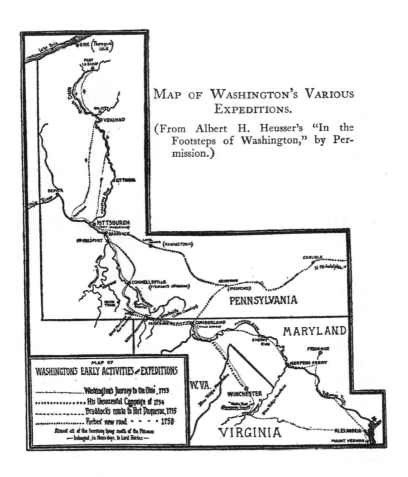

MAP OF WASHINGTON'S VARIOUS
EXPEDITIONS.

(From Albert H. Heusser's "In the
Footsteps of Washington," by Permission.)

presence of the enemy, believing that only a trapful of them would come out.

He waited for his victims, but they did not appear, so Captain Macdonald had the drums beaten here and there and the reveille sounded. It was answered without delay.

The Indians leapt from their grassy beds in their usual costume of next-to-nothing. The French did not stop to put on their breeches but came out in their shirts, true *sans-culottes* and no less bloodthirsty.

If Macdonald had tapped a hornets' nest he could not have met a more speedy response to his summons. He stopped the enemy a moment with a volley, but there were so unexpectedly many of them that they flowed all the way round him and cut him off from Grant.

The Highlanders charged through, but Macdonald was killed in the rush. The French chased them up the hill and broke Mackenzie's left wall of the trap, crushing it in on Grant. For nearly an hour the Scots endured the unwonted terrors of their painted, whooping, dancing enemies.

Then, as it was with Braddock's Englishmen, their spirits caved, and they ran like defenceless sheep. Grant afterwards said, "I trust I shall never again see such a panic among troops." [35]

He fell back toward Major Lewis and the Virginians who formed the rear-guard as in Braddock's battle. Lewis, unfortunately brave, had commanded Captain Bullet to keep his post and had dashed forward with his men at the first sound of firing. He made a bee-line for the front, while Grant retreated on a winding path, and so to his horror found only Bullet.

He cried, "I am a ruined man!" and gathering what few of his scattered men he could, made for the Allegheny. Bullet and his men fought like Virginians at their best, and there is no better.   But dead men cannot fight, and two-thirds of them were swiftly slaughtered.

The French cried for a truce but the living men leapt into the river where some were drowned and the good swimmers made the opposite shore.   Out of 813 men, 540 got back alive.   But Grant was captured and Major Lewis, coming to his rescue, was overwhelmed.   Two hundred and seventy-three men were killed, wounded or captured.

When the news reached Forbes, he wrote mildly enough to Bouquet, that he read his report "with no less surprise than concern, as I could not believe that such an attempt would have been made without my knowledge and con-currence . . . my friend Grant most certainly lost his wits, and by his thirst of fame brought on his own perdition, and ran great risk of ours."

Washington received the news with anger and dismay. He ridiculed the behavior of Major Grant, and regretted it as "a heavy blow to our affairs here and a sad stroke upon my Regiment." . . . "Among the Slain was our dear Major Lewis. . . . Your old acquaintance Capt. Bullet, who is the only officer of mine that came off untouched, has acquired immortal honor by his gallant behavior." [36]

He made this report in a letter written eleven days after the battle, to Sally Fairfax.

XXVII

SALLY FAIRFAX AGAIN

THE part that women played in war in those days is apt to be misunderstood in these days. When troops were in the field at that time, six women were regularly allowed to a company, but this was often exceeded. Dinwiddie had complained a year before of the excessive number carried by Washington's troops.[1] These were washerwomen, the wives and mistresses of common soldiers, good faithful women as well as common trulls who were apt to make trouble, get drunk and shift their partners.

Some of them were indentured servants, and were in a more or less helpless situation, the pathos of which can be seen from a letter written to Washington by Captain Peter Hog concerning Joseph Chew's indentured girl, who seems to have been passed about a bit. In some unpublished or perished letter Washington called Hog to account for not paying her master the money for her services, and Hog answered:

"I am sory that you are either Misinformed or Misapprehend the Case of Chew's Servant, I never spoke to her in my life Untill I was ordered by Gen! Braddock to take the Command of the Detachm.ᵗ for the pensilv.ᵃ Road when she was recommended to my care in her way to Phil.ᵃ by some of the officers who Lodged at her Masters & by M.ʳˢ English who waited on M.ʳ Allen & me, it is here I made her Change her resolution of going to Phil.ᵃ and brought her back to Wills Creek where she was openly Seen in the Camp, I never intended to Conceal her, but on the Contrary tho there was never no Enquiry made after her all the time I had her at Wills Creek, I Emploied M.ʳ Slatker to buy her time and told him he might draw on me for the money. . . .

"I dont See that I have acted either Unlike an officer or a Gent. unless that a Great many would have made the same Use of a Mans Maid without making any Satisfaction to the Master or reckoning themselves under any Obligation to free the Maid from a harsh Servitude, which I all along Intended and declared, tho' I never had any Application made to me by M.ʳ Chew or any other person for him till y.ᵉ note that Came with Yours: and Accordingly have Sent Bills to Cap.ᵗ Stewart for £10—who will deliver them to any Safe hand that you shall order going to Alexandria who may bring up the Indenture & deliver it to him.

"She tells me that was the original price given by Chew to M.ʳ Kirkpatrick & she served him 9 Months however if it is a trifle more Cap.ᵗ Stewart will advance it for me." [2]

This same Captain Stewart, one of Washington's closest friends, wrote from Fort Loudoun to say that "The Girl kept by the Quartermas'r had some difference with Bonnet a Soldier that waited on Hamilton." [3]

There was a camp broil over her.

Many women came over from England with Braddock's army. Three of them were captured, and the French commander is said to have kept one of them for himself at Venango, and sent the other two up to Canada to be sold. [4]

But these poor white trash and the half-slaves were not the only ones who mitigated the harsh life of the soldier. Aristocratic women also visited the camps. At Alexandria Braddock and his officers led so vivacious an existence that a Philadelphia paper spoke with disgust of "his feasts and his women." Mrs. Fairfax was among those who helped amuse the general, as Washington's letter concerning her rivalry with Mrs. Wardrope showed.

Evidently the soldiers talked freely about their love affairs, for it was in camp that Washington had learned how Mrs. Wardrope won the general.

Washington was complete man enough to appreciate both the beauty of women and their amiability, and when they were not present he must have been glad of the pale substitute of conversation about them—and that sort of art criticism that goes on where men of no prudery are gathered.

Else, his aid-de-camp, Captain George Mercer, would never have dreamed of writing, never have dared to write, his commanding officer such a letter as he wrote from Charleston, South Carolina, when he and other officers of Washington's Virginia Regiment were stationed there in August, 1757.

Washington was to the last an aristocrat of the slightest possible interest in the common people, and his lack of democracy caused him his final conflicts and defeats and most of his final deluges of abuse in his final years.

So now Captain Mercer, who was a gentleman, if not a scholar, expatiates on the amazement of the British royal officers when they found that Virginia officers were not all from the low herd of colonials. They could hardly believe their eyes when they saw "Officers whom they found to be Gent. to see a Sash & Gorget with a genteel Uniform, a Sword properly hung, a Hat cocked, Persons capable of holding Conversation when only Common Sense was requisite to continue the Discourse, and a White Shirt, with any other than a black Leather Stock, were Matters of great Surprise and Admiration. . . . We have lost that common Appellation of Provincials & are known here by the Style & Title of the Detachment of the Virg'a Regiment." [5]

In this same letter Captain Mercer, a gallant gentleman in both senses (he had not only ridden North to Boston with Washington and lingered with him in the philanderings at New York, but had been wounded at Braddock's Defeat) wrote what he must have assumed to be interesting reading matter for his Colonel:

"Youl be surprized I have not yet mentioned the fair Ones I wish I could call Them so, I assure you they are very far inferior to the Beauties of our own Country, & as much on the Reserve as in any Place I ever was, occasioned by the Multiplicity of Scandal which prevails here; . . . you hear the Termagant the Inconstant, the Prude & Coquette the fine Gent. & the fine Lady laid off in their most beautiful Colors. . . . A great Imperfection here too is the bad Shape of the Ladies, many of Them are crooked & have a very bad Air & not those enticing heaving throbbing alluring plump Breasts common with our Northern Belles— I am afraid I have tired your Patience & doubt not but you are as much disappointed at reading This, as I was of having an Opportunity of writing it to you."

Accompanying this letter from Washington's aide, was one from his next in command, Lieutenant-Colonel Adam Stephen, who felt called upon to report the results of his reconnaissances:

"I am but little acquainted with the Ladies, but if you will allow me to be a Judge, The Fair in this place must give way in Beauty, Easy Behaviour, & other female Accomplishments to the Daughters of the more northern Climes." [6]

Even in the hardships of the new campaign against Fort Du Quesne, Washington was apparently hungry for talk of love and for gossip of romance, for in the previously quoted letter from John Kirkpatrick these items occur, evidently referring to a lost letter of Washington's:

"To drop the dull topick of politicks—and touch the subject of social entertainment—woud require a readier genius, to dress the insipid occurancies so as to yield you any degree of Satisfaction—but to take them according to your own Arrangem.—Love, reigns with gentle sway—and rarely in this Age warms the heart beyond the common degree of Fondness—hence, this defficiency of Romantick Lovers Knight Errants—&c. in short his influence is seldom seen. However as an exception I hear Charles Eskridge intends to Batter down the Gates of Miss Guby's affections in a little time, The Surrender being suspended till Mons.ʳ Ramsay the commandant consent to the Terms of Capitulation—Charles' Colo. viz.ᵗ, C——le resists the scheme with fruitless arguments. I am almost induced to believe our Friend B. Fairfax has some thoughts of softening his austerity in the arms of some fair Nymph—coud he reconcile the Toying, Triffling, Billing Sports of Love to the Solemnity and Gravity of his Deportment—Amusements and joys unbecoming his Philosophic Temper—tho' I cant think he has any inherent aversion to what some esteem the end of Creation. . . .

"I am extremely Yours in every respect—as in Duty I ought—& always will be dear Sir Your very much oblidged & Obed.ᵗ Hum.ᵉ Serv.ᵗ, Jn.º Kirkpatrick." [7]

There must have been considerable gaiety at Fort Cumberland. One woman may have diverted the officers' minds in their martial doldrums. This was Mrs. Spotswood, a vivacious widow of a year's standing; her husband had been the son of Governor Spotswood, and she did not mourn him long.[8]

Judging from Washington's comments, she was exceedingly popular with the officers and there was keen rivalry for her society and for her hand in marriage. Her wealth would be easily forgiven. She may or may not have been in the camp when he wrote.

During her reign in camp Washington received a note from Sally Fairfax that stirred him to the depths, and led him to write in reply an amazing letter whose very existence was unknown till it came back from England nearly a hundred and twenty years later among the personal papers found in Sally Fairfax's old trunks at Bath, where she died.[9]

Washington's letter involved him so deeply in a carelessly veiled confession of desperate love for his friend's wife (at a time when Washington was already engaged to Martha Custis) that equally desperate efforts have been made to attribute it to some other woman, to Mary Cary, to Martha Custis, to anybody but its manifest recipient.

Those who cannot believe that Washington could have written such a document have all overlooked an absolute proof that he did; for in Washington's own files there is a letter written to accompany Sally Fairfax's note, saying that she was writing to Washington by the same impatient messenger, and giving certain facts that reappear in Washington's crucial letter in reply to Sally Fairfax.

This confirmatory letter was written by young William Fairfax—the "Billy" Fairfax for whom the late venerable William Fairfax had, before his death, requested a commission from Washington.

On September 1st, 1758, this young Billy Fairfax wrote to Washington acknowledging receipt of two letters, "of the 23d and 27th Ultimo." These two letters are either lost or lie hidden among the mass of Washington's letters that have not yet been published.

Fairfax says: "The first [letter] Mrs. Fairfax undertakes to answer, as I dont care to detain the bearer." He speaks of "an impatient Man at my Elbow" as an excuse for his brevity, and adds the statement, "I am really sorry the Ladies wont dispense my going with them to Hampton." [10]

The note of Sally's that Billy refers to must have been brief, for in his famous reply to it Washington expresses regret that his messenger should have been too impatient to wait while she wrote a longer letter. He gives her assurance that his second messenger is entirely at her disposal, as he does not want to miss a line. Furthermore, he begs her to tell him just when she is to set out for Hampton and when to return.

Though he preserved in his files Billy Fairfax's dull letter, Sally's priceless note is lost. Washington did not keep it—perhaps dared not keep it.

Yet his answer to it is so explicit that one may easily reconstruct the essence of Sally's note though the precious phrases are beyond recapture.

She probably said something to this effect, but said it with a taunting irony that stung her supposedly fickle lover to an outcry of frenzy: "Sir, All Virginia is ringing with your impatience at General Forbes' delay in moving the army and your indignation at his taking the time to cut a new road when Braddock's road is waiting. But I imagine there is a lady in the case, for you always profess yourself a votary of love. Your opposition to the management is, then, perhaps due less to your love of country than to the animating prospect of possessing Mrs. Custis. I am very happy in your new happiness, and I am sure that you must be. I hear that Mrs. Spotswood is in your camp and doubtless so charming that I could almost wish myself a fine gentleman for her sake.

"I would write you much more, but your messenger is in such haste that I dare not detain him, except for a last question. Shall I make the exchange of carpets, since I cannot avail myself of your offer of your own?

"Enclosed with this is a letter to Captain Gist, which please forward to him. The family at Belvoir sends compliments to Col. Mercer, as well as to you with all felicitations."

This is dull and heavy where Sally must have been

radiantly sparkling. She may have been biting and taunt-
ingly reproachful. She may have said that he had no heart
in him since he engaged himself to Mrs. Custis so precipi-
tately after avowing undying love to her.

She may have written in the bitterness of jealousy. She
may have let her bright unattainable spirit dance across his
vision like the will-o'-the-wisp she always was to him.

In any case, this is the answer that poured from his heart
with an uncharacteristic fervor that broke through all his
awkward efforts to conceal his meaning—the italics are not
his, but are added to emphasize the things he tried to
disguise:

"Camp at Fort Cumberland, 12th September, 1758.
"DEAR MADAM,

"Yesterday I was honored with your short but very agreeable
favor of the first inst. How joyfully I catch at the happy occasion
of renewing a correspondence which I feared was disrelished on
your part, *I leave to time,* that never failing expositor of all things,
and to a monitor equally faithful in my own breast, to testify. *In
silence I now express my joy; silence, which* in some cases, I wish
the present, *speaks more intelligently than the sweetest eloquence.*

"If you allow that any honor can be derived from my opposition
to our present system of management, you destroy the merit of it
entirely in me by attributing my anxiety to the animating prospect
of possessing Mrs. Custis, *when—I need not tell you, guess yourself.* Should not my own Honor and country's welfare be the excitement? 'Tis true, *I profess myself a votary of love. I acknowledge that a lady is in the case, and further I confess that this lady
is known to you. Yes, Madame, as well as she is to one who is too
sensible of her charms to deny the Power whose influence he feels
and must ever submit to.* I feel the force of her amiable beauties
in *the recollection of a thousand tender passages* that I *could wish to
obliterate, till I am bid to revive them.* But experience, alas! sadly
reminds me *how impossible this is,* and evinces an opinion which I
have long entertained, that there is a Destiny which has the control
of our actions, not to be resisted by the strongest efforts of Human
Nature.

"You have drawn me, dear Madame, or rather I have drawn myself, into *an honest confession of a simple Fact. Misconstrue not my meaning; doubt it not, nor expose it. The world has no business to know the object of my Love,* declared in this manner to you, when I want to conceal it. *One thing above all things in this world I wish to know, and only one person of your acquaintance can* solve me that, or guess my meaning. *But adieu to this till happier times, if I ever shall see them.* The hours at present are melancholy dull. Neither the rugged toils of war, nor *the gentler conflict of* A——B——s [Assembly Balls?], is in my choice. I dare believe you are as happy as you say. *I wish I was happy also.* Mirth, good humor, ease of mind, and—what else?—cannot fail to render you so and consummate your wishes.

"If one agreeable lady could almost wish herself a fine gentleman for the sake of another, I apprehend that many fine gentlemen will wish themselves finer e'er Mrs. Spotswood is possest. She has already become a reigning toast in this camp, and many there are in it who intend (fortune favoring) to make honorable scars speak the fullness of their merit, and be a messenger of their Love to Her.

"*I cannot easily forgive the unseasonable haste of my last express, if he deprived me thereby of a single word you intended to add. The time of the present messenger is,* as the last might have been, *entirely at your disposal.* I can't expect to hear from my friends more than this once before the fate of the expedition will some how or other be determined. I therefore beg to know when you set out for Hampton, and when you expect to return to Belvoir again. And I should be glad also to hear of your speedy departure, as I shall thereby hope for your return before I get down. The disappointment of seeing your family would give me much concern. From any thing I can yet see 'tis hardly possible to say when we shall finish. I don't think there is a probability of it till the middle of November. Your letter to Captain Gist I forwarded by a safe hand the moment it came to me. His answer shall be carefully transmitted.

"Col. Mercer, to whom I delivered your message and compliments, joins me very heartily in wishing you and the Ladies of Belvoir the perfect enjoyment of every happiness this world affords. Be assured that I am, dear Madame, with the most unfeigned regard, your most obedient and most obliged humble servant.

"N.B. Many accidents happening (to use a vulgar saying) between the cup and the lip, I choose to make the exchange of carpets myself, since I find you will not do me the honor to accept mine." [11]

This letter was printed in the New York *Herald* of March 30th, 1877, as having been found among eighty-one letters still in the possession of the Fairfax family, "showing that Washington had never forgotten the influence of his youthful disappointment" over her whom Constance Cary Harrison called "the object of George Washington's early and passionate love."

Certain things are inescapable in this letter. Washington cries, "How joyfully I catch at the happy occasion of renewing a correspondence which I feared was disrelished on your part . . . In silence I now express my joy; silence, which . . . speaks more intelligently than the sweetest eloquence."

Then he protests that he really did oppose the military system. He admits "the animating prospect of possessing Mrs. Custis," but denies that she was the reason of his anxiety.

Then he professes himself "a votary of love." This is George Washington writing! And he professes himself a votary of love!

Then, as lovers have always done, he speaks to his beloved in the you-know-whom-I-mean dialect. "This lady is known to you. Yes, Madame, as well as she is to (me, i.e., to) one who is too sensible of her charm to deny the power he must ever submit to."

He is not writing of his fiancée, Martha, whom he had seen only three or four times, when he fairly reels with the memory of "the force of her amiable beauties in the recollection of a thousand tender passages that I could wish to obliterate, till I am bid to revive them."

Can this mean anything but that he and Sally Fairfax had enjoyed a thousand tender passages? He would ask to renew them, too, but—"experience, alas! sadly reminds me how impossible this is."

He could not have been writing to Martha, for he mentions her as "Mrs. Custis." He could not possibly be referring so intimately to Martha, because he was going to renew what few tender passages he may have had with her. Besides, he says he wishes he could obliterate them; and that the "renewal" of the thousand tender passages is "impossible."

What makes it impossible? Destiny! "not to be resisted by the strongest efforts of Human Nature."

There he sits in his camp at Fort Cumberland, and in the secrecy of his tent pours out his tortured soul. It is a fearful secret and it must be kept.

"You have drawn me, dear Madame, or rather I have drawn myself, into an honest confession of a simple Fact. Misconstrue not . . . nor expose it. The world has no business to know the object of my love, declared in this manner to you, when I want to conceal it."

This is George Washington writing: It's none of the world's business who the object of my love is. It will soon know that Mrs. Custis is to be my wife, and that is all it needs to know.

But there is "one thing above all things in this world" that he wishes to know, and "only one person of your acquaintance can solve me that."

Of course, he wants to cry out the ancient, "Do you love me as I love you?" He breaks off impatiently. "But adieu to this till happier times, if I ever shall see them.

"You say you are happy. I dare believe so. I wish I was happy also." "What else" do you want?

As for me, I am stuck here in this dreary camp. The hours are melancholy dull. I cannot fight. I cannot indulge in "the gentler conflict" of the dance!

You said you would like to be a gentleman for my sake, so that you could go to war as Mrs. Spotswood does, who has many courtiers here.

I cannot forgive the haste of my last messenger if, as you say, you had not time to say all you had in mind.—To think that he deprived me of a single word you intended to add! Don't forget that this messenger can wait as long as you want him to.

Let me know when you go to your father's home for a visit and when you get back to Belvoir. I hope you get away soon so that you can get back before I do. "The disappointment of seeing (he means, of course, not seeing) your—er—family would give me much concern."

"Concern" was a strong word with Washington. When he had to hang so many of his soldiers for deserting, he wrote: "I always hear of capital executions with concern."

The letter ends with a postscript about some mysterious lovers' quarrel over "carpets." She would not accept his and he scolds her tenderly.

There was a great stir at Mount Vernon, which he was having rebuilt and refurnished for the bride he was going to establish there on his return from the war. He had perhaps offered to give Sally one of the carpets in the house, or to exchange one of his for one of hers.

The most important, the most convincing, the most dramatic, thing in the whole letter is his groan of despair, "I dare believe you are as happy as you say, I wish I was also." He could not have written this to Martha, yet he was engaged to her when he wrote it to another woman.

It would be hard to imagine a more distraught lover trying more clumsily to disguise his despair and his adoration in a true-lover's code chosen to blind the eyes of possible strangers. He adds that there are so many accidents happening—if you will pardon the slang, the vulgar saying, "between the cup and the lip," that I will wait to talk this over with you and see if we cannot come to some agreement about my gift of a carpet.

Not the least astounding puzzle in this letter is the motive for writing it at all in the circumstances. Yet the motive is perhaps the finest thing about it, and reveals his fierce humanity, against which he always fought, conquering him at the time of all times when it should have been most repressed.

He loved Sally. He was going to marry Martha. Sally mocked him, perhaps, with a deep hurt beneath her raillery —laughter lest she weep. She may well have implied that he could not really love anybody.

This was the ultimate unbearable accusation. His love asserted itself with volcanic fire. He had to tell her that he loved her. She had the right to know it. She must know it. He was like a mad Samson trying to bind himself in withes of discretion.

It is the suppression, the editing and the destruction of such letters that have led people to describe Washington as a silent man, a cold man, a man under almost perfect self-control.

But he could love. He did love.

His letter, however confusing to his idolaters, redeems him to humanity and, however pitiful as a confession, is magnificent as passion.

A biographer of Sally Cary's, Captain Wilson Miles Cary, has written eloquently of this letter. He justified his little volume as a defence of Sally from the scorn directed against her since the appearance of that "bundle of faded letters, pale skeletons of a buried passion, that have been uncoffined from their long hidden caskets and pitilessly exposed to a mocking age. . . . The microscope of history has been levelled for the past century upon the character and personality of Washington. On the other hand the world knows nothing of the beautiful and talented woman who had no little share in shaping the destiny of one of its foremost men."

Marvelling, as every one must, at Washington's choice of this occasion for his declaration of the doubly vain love of a man betrothed to a woman married, Captain Cary wrote, with a fervor matching Washington's:

"Those who have always been accustomed to regard Washington as a most prudent and unimpassioned man of method and moderation in all things will be amazed and well-nigh confounded at such an exhibition of uncontrollable feeling on his part, evinced at a time when there seemed no special occasion to call it forth, but every prudential reason to conceal a passion which he had entertained hitherto without daring to give it birth in words. Why should he select this juncture, of all others, to make such an avowal? . . .

"Ah, the secret spring of an action so extraordinary cannot be doubted. It is a sudden revolt in the soul of a man intensely wrought who has nerved himself to take a step against which his rebellious heart makes its final emphatic protest, and who, before he crosses the irrevocable Rubicon of matrimony, pauses to falter forth his real, feeling soul in a piteous sort of frenzy to the long unattainable love of his life, to clasp his hopeless attachment in one mad embrace, as it were, ere he parts with his cherished ideal forever." [12]

A woman's point of view in matters of love is always interesting, and not at all apt to be that of a Jared Sparks or a Fourth-of-Julying politician. Mrs. Sally Nelson Robins, a Virginian, wrote of this letter and Sally:

"It was just four months before his marriage to Martha Custis (we can scarcely believe it) that he felt himself powerless to be prudent any longer. The following letter is the incontrovertible witness in the case, and is the one evidence we have of the impassioned recklessness of the austere Washington. It is great to know that he was human enough to love in such a way; that he was strong enough to conceal his true feeling, till it was to him the blessed privilege of her he loved to know it. The greatest tribute he could pay her was to tell her all. Here is the compromising but noble letter:"

She follows the quotation of it with these comments:

"Through all the fervor and surprise of her Washington experience Mrs. Fairfax was discreet; there is no record of the slightest deviation from the most rigid interpretation of her marital code. Certainly so far as anybody can tell at this late day, Washington did all the talking. His former affairs were but flimsy showers, gently falling on a restrained and calculating nature, to the torrential storm which swept prudence away and bared his big heart to the wife of George Fairfax.

"One visualizes her as a prismatic iceberg on which the rays of his passion fell very colorful and beautiful, but by no means capable of melting, in the least degree, the high standard of matrimonial virtue which the proud Sarah had set for herself. . . .

"Love and the ladies were certainly softening the grim aspects of war and making life amorously sweet or amorously bitter for George Washington. This letter, no doubt, rather surprised Sarah Fairfax, who, though secretly enjoying the prudent but perceptible dangling of a crimson cluster of forbidden fruit—enjoying it as the most careful women will invariably do—never expected the forbidden fruit to fall bruised and bleeding into her hands or rather into her heart; for she must have received with a certain amount of feeling, no matter how absolutely chaste it was, this undiluted message from a strong man's heart.

"Where is Sarah's reply? Was it cold and reproachful?

Full of surprise (?) and horror at the rash declarations of him whom she valued highly as a friend and only as a friend? Did its sarcasm sting, its holy indignation make the will-of-steel conscious of his unpardonable weakness? Did he wish the letter were unwritten? Who can tell? But we, ourselves, accord him full forgiveness; this letter to Sarah Fairfax reveals the gorgeous passion-flower in his crown of red immortelles, the white rose in his laurel wreath. We are glad to know that he could love as he loved her, and American emotion would have lost a note but for this letter written by our first American from Fort Cumberland in September, 1758.

"Sarah must have reproved him, and that severely, as her sense of wifely duty and her high ideals would demand. He answers her. But there was only one letter of its kind from Fort Cumberland; it was the great expression—what use for more?" [13]

To this tense letter that special messenger, instructed not to hurry Mrs. Fairfax's pen, brought back some answer that would be worth worlds to the lovers of the real Washington.

We know nothing of it beyond his quotation from it and his allusions to it. She evidently wrote from her father's home at Hampton, whither she made the journey already referred to. She apparently mentioned an amateur performance or a reading from Addison's *Cato*, in which she took, or was to take, the part of Cato's daughter *Marcia*, for Washington expresses a longing to play the part of Marcia's soldier lover *Juba*, who loved the unattainable heroine. The play abounds in Juba's rhapsodies upon the beauty of the adorable queen of his heart.

Sally evidently mentioned her sisters and Nancy Gist and various flirtations in which Washington shows his usual keen interest. She asked him if she had not already wearied him by the length of her letter, and she may have still pretended to doubt his love or warned him to be more discreet in his correspondence.

Some day her letter may turn up, but he probably destroyed it, knowing that he might be killed at any time, knowing that he was about to move from Fort Cumberland into the wilderness where Forbes' army was clearing a pathway to what he was sure would be destruction.

It would have been criminal of Washington in the field to leave Mrs. Fairfax's letters about. But she had old garrets and trunks in which to hide his answer, and perhaps to read it in England stealthily and gloat over what she knew of this Washington whom she had known as a cub, and whom the world even of England came to accept as the greatest, noblest man of his time—or, perhaps, of all time.

Whatever she wrote him then must have been playfully or tormentingly vague, for this is what he answered from his new station at Raystown with the most transparent disguise, —the italics still being interpolated. The detailed account he hastened to give her of Major Grant's disaster proves how close he was to her and what interest she must have taken in his military affairs:

"Camp at Rays Town, 25th Sept'r. 1758.
"DEAR MADAM:

"Do we still misunderstand the true meaning of each other's Letters? I think it must appear so, tho' I would feign hope the contrary as *I cannot speak plainer without.—But I'll say no more and leave you to guess the rest.*

"I am now furnished with news of a very interesting nature. I know it will affect you, but as you must hear it from others I will state it myself. The 12th past, then Major Grant with a chosen detachment of 800 men, march'd from our advanced post at Loyal Hanna against Fort Duquesne.

"On the night of the 13th he arrivd at that place or rather upon a Hill near to it; from whence went a party and viewd the Works, made what observations they could, and burnt a Logg house not far from the Walls. Egg'd on rather than satisfied by this success,

Major Grant must needs insult the Enemy next morning by beating the Reveille in different places in view. This caus'd a great body of men to Sally from the Fort, and an obstinate engagement to ensue, which was maintained on our Side with the utmost efforts that bravery could yield, till being overpowered and quite surrounded they were obliged to retreat with the loss of 22 officers killed, and 278 men besides wounded.

"This is a heavy blow to our affairs here, and a sad stroke upon my Regiment, that has lost out of 8 officers, and 168 that was in the Action, 6 of the former killd, and a 7th wounded. Among the Slain was our dear Major Lewis. This Gentleman as the other officers also did, bravely fought while they had life, tho' wounded in different places. Your old acquaintance Captn. Bullet, who is the only officer of mine that came of untouched, has acquired immortal honor in this engagement by his gallant behavior, and long continuance in the field of Action. It might be thought vanity in me to praise the behavior of my own people were I to deviate from the report of common fame,—but when you consider the loss they have sustained, and learn that every mouth resounds their praises, you will believe me impartial.

"What was the great end proposed by this attempt, or what will be the event of its failure, I can't take upon me to determine; it appears however (from the best accounts) that the enemy lost more men than we did in the engagement. Thus it is the lives of the brave are often disposed of. But who is there that does not rather Envy than regret a death that gives birth to honor and glorious memory.

"I am extremely glad to find that Mr. Fairfax has escap'd the dangers of the Seige at Louisburg. Already have we experienced greater losses than our army sustained at that place, and have gained not one obvious advantage. So miserably has this expedition been managed that I expect after a month's further tryal, and the loss of many more men by the sword, cold and perhaps famine, we shall give the expedition over as perhaps impracticable this season, and retire to the inhabitants, condemned by the world and derided by our friends.

"*I should think our time more agreeably spent believe me, in playing a part in Cato, with the company you mention, and myself doubly happy in being the Juba to such a Marcia, as you must make.*

"Your agreeable Letter contained these words. 'My Sisters and Nancy Gist who neither of them expect to be here soon after our return from Town, desire you to accept their best complimts. &c.'

"Pray are these ladies upon a Matrimonial Scheme? Is Miss Fairfax to be transformed into that charming domestick—a Martin, and Miss Cary to a Fa——? What does Miss Gist turn to—a Cocke? That can't be, we have him here.

"One thing more and then have done. *You ask if I am not tired at the length of your letter? No madam, I am not, nor never can be while the lines are an Inch asunder to bring you in haste to the end of the paper.* You may be tird of mine by this. Adieu dear Madam, you will possibly hear something of me, or from me before we shall meet. I must beg the favor of you to make my compliments to Colo. Cary and the Ladies with you, and believe me that I am most unalterably." [14]

Some historians express a doubt that either of these letters was written to Mrs. Fairfax. Mr. Everett first made the ascription to Martha, which is manifestly inconceivable. Washington speaks of Belvoir and Hampton in the first letter and Colonel Cary in the second. Dr. Neill, in his *Fairfaxes of England and America*, assigned it to Mary Cary. But they had evidently never noted the letter of William Fairfax previously quoted. The reference to Mr. Fairfax escaping the dangers of Louisburg is further proof, especially as there exists a letter to Washington from Sally's husband written in New York City and referring to Louisburg.

All caution is necessary in such matters, and the dubious should be left in doubt. Yet it is impossible not to link this second letter with the first. In the first, dated September 12th, he sends a messenger to wait for an answer.

It took time for a horseman to ride from Fort Cumberland to Mount Vernon, and back.

The second letter, dated a fortnight later, refers to another letter, a veiled correspondence which he dares not discuss too plainly: "Do we still misunderstand the true meaning of each other's letters?" "I cannot speak plainer without—but I must be careful and you must guess."

He quotes her reference to her "return from Town," and the previous letter spoke of her prospective journey to Hampton. He quotes her words, "my sisters," and makes his compliments to Col. Cary. Mrs. Fairfax had sisters, and her father was Colonel Cary. He asks if Miss Cary is to be transformed "to a Fa——?" Sally's sister, Elizabeth Cary, married Bryan Fairfax the following year.

And he signs himself "most unalterably," which is a good phrase, since lovers have degrees of unalterableness, plain unalterably, more unalterably and most unalterably.

Written to Sally Fairfax, that "unalterably" meant something; for twenty-five years later Washington wrote to Sally Fairfax that he had spent with her the happiest moments of his life, and gently hinted that she ought to return from England.

Those who think to escape the horror of Washington's love for Mrs. Fairfax by assigning the letter to her sister Mary Cary, fall into another pitfall, since Mary Cary had been Mrs. Edward Ambler for six years, and he would still be writing to the wife of somebody else.

There is simply no escaping the facts that while engaged to Mrs. Custis, Washington was trying to appease some angry woman to whom he was unalterably devoted, and that Mrs. Sally Fairfax was the pathetic impossible love of Washington's life.

The editor of Wilson Miles Cary's study of Sally Fairfax makes this striking statement after an examination of documents not open to the public:

"It appears from the family correspondence of the time that Sally Cary entertained some personal feeling against her brother-in-law Bryan Fairfax, which estranged him and his brother for years. It has remained for the feminine intuition of a later generation to conjecture that Bryan had rebuked Sally for her flirtation with Washington." [15]

Many worshippers of Washington find it impossible to imagine that he could have loved his friend's wife. But it is still more impossible (if possible) to doubt Washington's own frantic protestations.

There is nothing to do but marvel at the contrast between the strangled agonies of Washington's letters to Sally Fairfax and the letter he wrote to his betrothed, Martha Custis, during this same absence at the wars.

This letter has been infinitely quoted with all the praise due its brief beauty, but with a perplexing assumption that it proved the perfect devotion of its author to its recipient.

Washington must have written many other letters to Martha, and they may well have been longer and more passionate, but they were doubtless consumed in the flames to which Martha meant to consign all of Washington's writings to her. This brief note escaped oblivion, and it makes such a pitiful appearance alongside the long tumultuous letters to Mrs. Fairfax that it will bear repeating.

It was on July 20th at Fort Cumberland that he indited this classic fragment to Martha:

"We have begun our march for the Ohio. A courier is starting for Williamsburg, and I embrace the opportunity to send a few words to one whose life is now inseparable from mine. Since that happy hour when we made our pledges to each other, my thoughts have been continually going to you as another Self. That an all-powerful Providence may keep us both in safety is the prayer of your ever faithful and affectionate friend." [16]

This is perfect enough, if only he had not been goaded two months later into the helpless treason of the far more passionate letters to Sally Fairfax.

There is no reason on earth to regard Sally Fairfax with anything but homage. She was the last of the women who refused George Washington's heart.

Seeing that he was denied the tall, the keen, vivacious, fascinating, elusive Sally, it would have been a pity if he had taken a feeble imitation of her.

Martha was her opposite, plump, stolid, bustling, comfortable—an altogether adorable housewife. She even accepted Sally as a friend, and they exchanged visits while they could, and afterwards letters.

It is a thousand pities that the correspondence of those two women across the form of George Washington should not have survived. Probably George wrote most of Martha's, as he wrote even her orders for clothes.

His courtship of her was business-like. A meeting, an all-night talk, probably mainly about real estate; a second meeting, an agreement to marry, and a long absence in the field.

But through it all, Washington must have thought mainly of Sally, when he had time to think of women, or realize that his overworked life included among its countless misfortunes a broken heart.

HE FINISHES WITH WAR

THE disaster of Grant's Hill left Washington grief-stricken for his lost men and his rejected advice. Gloomy as he might have been before, it seemed that fate was inexhaustibly versatile in inventing new pangs. "In the lowest deep a lower deep."

He had written Sally Fairfax that he would rather envy than regret such a death as that of his friend Lewis.

But when Bouquet humbled himself to send a flag of truce to Fort Du Quesne, it was learned that Lewis was alive and a prisoner with Grant, four officers and thirty-two men, all of whom had been sent at once to Montreal.

Washington wrote a report to Governor Fauquier blaming Grant for dividing his troops and praising the Virginians who alone were not panic-stricken. They and their commander Captain Bullet "were (in the hands of Providence) a means of preventing all of our people from sharing one common fate."

He scoffed at "the promoters of the new road" who believed "or would fain have it thought so," that the expedition might still succeed. But the road was not yet half opened, only twenty days' provision had been brought up, the frosts had "already changed the face of nature among these mountains." There was not more than a month's time left and horses could not subsist in a region stripped of its herbage, or "men half-naked live in Tents much longer." [1]

To add to the misery, the French returned Grant's visit,

attacked the camp at Loyalhannon and were not repulsed till they had destroyed a great number of the horses and cattle that were more needed than men.

Such horses and cattle as they had were, as usual, the dreadful evidences of corrupt practices among our forefathers, who had long since perfected the hateful custom of profiteering, which has distinguished all our wars and always comes as a fresh surprise.

The canny Quakers seem to have been no less unscrupulous than the other colonists. In the words of William Nelson:

"It is somewhat depressing to find that so long ago as 1747, while the colonies were voting men and money without stint for the purpose of defending the northern frontiers, and repelling the enemy, French and Indian, there were letters published in Parker's New York *Gazette* and *Weekly Post Boy,* boldly charging "graft" in the furnishing of antique and useless guns, and of malodorous beef, the same being defended by a correspondent who humorously explains that the guns of that description were supplied by the Quaker commissioners, in order that nobody should be hurt, and that the objectionable beef could be better carried at the cost of a whole colony than at the loss of the unfortunate owner." [2]

Washington's contempt for the Pennsylvanians was reflected in his officers, and William Ramsay wrote him at this time a budget of gossip against them:

"N. B.—The Pennsylvanians clear'd part of the road the Virginians were on, but it cost the Virginians three days labor to make the same passable—

"N. B.—By persons of undoubted veracity & in the imploy of Pensylvania, do publickly assert, that the new road from Shippys Town to the Camp, is worse than any part of the old road from Fort Cumberland to Fort Du Quesne—

"The Crown pays carriage of Provisions from Philadelp.ª
& I dare say costs Forty shillings per hundred—

"Soldiers here very Sickly & die fast—

"N. B.   I heard some Persons of Credit Publickly declare that the Waggons employ'd in the Kings Service in
Pennsylvania were Apprais'd upon an Average to £20 above
the intrinsic worth.

"They further said they knew Horses bought a few
days or hours before Appraisement, valued by the Appraisers
to £9 & £15 wch. only cost 50/ & 60/." ³

There was glorious news from the north in the taking of
Louisbourg, and Frontenac also fell to the arms of Colonel
Bradstreet, with an immense effect on the fortunes of Fort
Due Quesne, which was thus left helpless.   As Joseph Chew
wrote to Washington from New York:

"This is a Glorious stroak Cuts off all Communications
with their Western settlements & Forts & will I hope make
the Conquest of Duquesne Easie of which I impatiently Expect to hear.   Inclosed is a news paper to which I must
Refer you . . . my head something out of order having
Set up late last night and finished several Bottles to the
health of Colo. Broadstreet and his Army—our Worthy
friend Mr. Robinson his good Lady and Family are All well
and speak of you with great Affectation." ⁴

Later Chew wrote in great anguish of mind for his
younger brother, who was lost in Major Grant's defeat, and
added, "all his Letters have been full of Expressions of
Gratitude towards you . . ."

Every one seemed to speak of Washington with affection,
gratitude and admiration except the Pennsylvanians.   Even
Forbes wrote to him cordially, saying: "They tell me here
that you threaten us a visit soon, which I should be glad of
whenever it happens." ⁵

Governor Fauquier wrote of his "Zeal for the Service of

this Colony," and expressed a hope that Du Quesne might be reached soon, "otherwise I much fear whether the Ardor of this Colony has shewn to support the War will continue for another Year, the Flame being a little stifled by the inactivity of this Campaign. . . . The Treasury is exhausted . . . I hope your Men are not uneasy, but it was impossible to provide for their pay before." [6] In a later letter he warns Washington to provide his messengers with money for the journey, "for want of which Davis a Soldier of your Regiment (I think) who brought the Despatch to me, came almost dead having lain three nights in the Woods Almost without Sustenance. He having no Money, no House would receive him, or supply him with common necessaries of Life."

This is a vivid commentary on the humanity of the settlers.

In the meanwhile everything about the camp was as dismal as possible, and the new road seemed doomed to end in a sink of failure.

The rains came down now on the fresh clay and the horses began to founder and die as they slipped and broke their bones on the slimy surfaces. They could not drag across the two hundred miles of loathsome ooze enough food for themselves or the soldiers, who shivered and reeked and sickened in the unending deluge. If it was not rain it was snow.

The pain-griped body of Forbes had been brought up to Raystown and he confessed in a letter to Pitt that he "could not form any judgment how he was to extricate himself." He could get "not one scrape of a pen" from his commander-in-chief Abercrombie and he sighed, "It looks as if we were either forgot or left to our fate."

It was Abercrombie that was lost.

The gossip-bearers brought to Forbes word that Colonel

Stephen had written to Colonel Washington that everybody said the road could never be finished now. Forbes wrote of this to Bouquet and added:

"Col. Washington and my friend, Col. Byrd, would rather be glad this was true than otherways, seeing the other road (their favorite scheme) was not followed out. I told them plainly that, whatever they thought, yet I did aver that, in our prosecuting the present road, we had proceeded from the best intelligence that could be got for the good and convenience of the army, without any views to oblige any one province or another; and added that those two gentlemen were the only people that I had met with who had shewed their weakness in their attachment to the province they belong to, by declaring so publickly in favour of one road without their knowing anything of the other, having never heard from any Pennsylvania person one word about the road."

Later, he wrote to Bouquet to reconnoiter "Mr. Braddock's road in order to stop foolish mouths if it chances to prove anyways as good or practicable."

What a triumph it would have been for Washington if Forbes had yielded to his inclination to shift to the lower road!

In the meanwhile he asked all his colonels to give their opinions as to the best way to move an army through heavily wooded country so that the line of march might instantly be formed into an order of battle.

Washington sent him a letter with a beautifully drawn picture of such a plan. Aside from its tactical ingenuity it is noteworthy that he so arranges it that "every noncommissioned officer will have a party to command, under the eye of a subaltern, as the subalterns will have, under the direction of a captain, &c."

Remembering, perhaps, how at Braddock's Field the French, on encountering the English, had enveloped them

and taken cover at once, he directs that as soon as the vanguard is attacked, the first division is "to file off to the right
and left, and take to trees, gaining the enemy's flanks, and
surrounding them. . . . What Indians we have should be
ordered to get round, unperceived, and fall at the same time
upon the enemy's rear."

This, with his usual modesty, he "submitted to correction." [7]

From "Loyal Hanna" he wrote to Governor Fauquier re-
porting that Governor Sharpe in person had been left in
command at Fort Cumberland with a garrison of his own
militia, and "when the magazine was blown up had his store-
keeper included in the blast." He predicted that the expedition was bound to be given up.[8]

He received a letter from his Major Lewis whom he had
mourned as dead in Grant's catastrophe. Lewis wrote him
from Montreal, whither he had been sent, begging for
money.

"I have the hapiness of Aquanting you that I am in perfect helth—and tho I had the Misfortun of being made
prisoner the 14 Last month, ame as hapy and much more So,
than should have Expected under Such Sircomstances.
Nothing this Country Can afford but I have in plenty—with
the greatest Complesance—

"The time as well as mannar of my Being releved I ame a
Strangear to.—Cash I have non nither know I how to get a
Suply unless you be So good as to procure a Bill of Exchange
which may inable me to Draw my pay—Cloaths I must if
posable have, and Should any Gentleman in this place advance me Cash for that purpos I should be Sorry to leve
this Country with out paying him—

"I supos I shall be Soon Sent to Qubeck where I shall
have the pleasure of Seeing Capts. Stobo and Vanbram I
here they are in good helth—" [9]

It must have brought back gloomy memories to Wash-

ington to hear of Stobo and Van Braam, the two hostages he
had given to the French when they captured him at Fort
Necessity more than four years before. Dinwiddie having
refused to make Washington's promise good and release
the French prisoners taken in Jumonville's "assassination"
(as Van Braam had not translated it), Stobo and Van
Braam had languished in Canada ever since.

Washington must have felt that he himself was in little
better plight.

To add to the melancholy of the rain, and his dislike of
Pennsylvania, he had word from Williamsburg that ten
hogsheads of rum and three pipes of wine which had been
promised from Philadelphia could not be supplied; that the
Burgesses were in an ugly mood and his own First Virginia
Regiment "had like to have been broke by a Vote of the
House, but the Old and Judicious, carried it against the
Young Members by a Majority of five, however they have
so far prevail'd, that unless the Regim't return into this
Colony by the 1st of Dec'r next & guard our Frontiers, they
are to be no longer in the pay of this Colony. There is to
be no Lieut. Colo. Quarter Master, Adjutant nor Chaplain
& the yearly allowance for your Table is voted away." [10]

Thus every prospect was unpleasing and the weather was
vile.

Horrible as the roads were, General Forbes had his
wretched and failing frame brought up in a litter all the way
to Loyalhannon with the rest of the army and artillery. He
called a council of war and it was agreed that further boring
into this inferno of muck and ice would be useless until the
winter and the spring were over.

The army of six thousand drowned rats sat and moped
and regarded the disintegrating sky for a few days from
sheer inability to find the courage to take up the backward
march across that long canal of ice-edged glue.

They supposed that the heavily reinforced French were

laughing in their cosy fortress. But their commander, who
was now the same Ligneris who had been one of the captains who tore Braddock's host to shreds, was writing to his
governer, Vaudreuil, letters of abject helplessness. The
militia from the traders in Louisiana had dropped down the
Ohio, the militia from Illinois had just gone home. The
Indians from Detroit and the Wabash were folding their
blankets and loading up their squaws for the westerly trail.
The supplies and presents for the Indians that had been
prepared for Fort Du Quesne had been lost when the English army under Bradstreet captured Fort Frontenac on Lake
Ontario as well as the entire French fleet. Bradstreet's
Indian allies had begged him to turn his back while they
garnered a few scalps, but he refused.[11]

The French having also lost Louisbourg, their colonies
were split apart, though Abercrombie, the English commander-in-chief, had shattered his army of fifteen thousand
men in an attack on Ticonderoga defended by a third of the
number under Montcalm, who was now on his way to the
grand rendezvous at Quebec with Wolfe, for that immortal
duel in which both heroes died.

Few as the men were at Fort Du Quesne, they were more
than Ligneris could feed and he had to send most of them
away. He had no further hope of the Indian help that had
made the previous victories possible.

That love-feast at Easton had been attended by five
hundred Indians and had lasted from October 8th to the
26th. The governor of New Jersey and a Pennsylvania
delegation had greeted them. The Quakers had been free
with their liquor, but Croghan had won the Mohawks to his
side and finally the whole company agreed to a treaty of
eternal peace. The Indians promised to return their captives, and to persuade the Ohio Indians to the same terms.

Pennsylvania agreed to make no more settlements beyond

the Appalachian mountains without the Indian consent, and promised that Virginia and the other colonies would likewise abstain. This promise was kept like other brittle white promises, but, as Bouquet wrote, the treaty at Easton "knocked the French in the head." [12]

For the moment the dove was the bird that brooded over all. The missionary Post was sent out again beyond the Ohio and passed the good word to the troops at Loyalhannon as he hurried through. Croghan, Montour and other good woodsmen joined the army and Washington wrote to General Forbes that he was "much pleased to see the Indians up, and am very glad to hear that Mr. Croghan is so near at hand. The number with him is not mentioned. I wish they were in our front also." [13]

His feud with Croghan was over and would not begin again until they became rival speculators in gigantic land-deals long years afterward.[14]

Post went on past the Ohio and the Ohio Indians agreed to love the English and the ways of peace. Those who were at Fort Du Quesne bade the French a long farewell.

Of all this, the bedraggled crusaders of Forbes were dismally ignorant. And then one raw November day three prisoners were captured and brought in. They told the whole truth about the almost empty fortress.

This news was a Gabriel's trumpet of resurrection, and at once Forbes gave the order to advance with 2500 picked men, leaving behind the heavy artillery, wagons, and all baggage and tents. Washington was pushed ahead to cut a road. He sent back word, November 18th, that he had rested a day to slaughter some bullocks and dress provisions, but would march at three in the morning with a thousand men.

While he rested he had not delayed the road-work but "ordered out a working party, properly covered . . . to cut it forward till night should fall upon them, and then return back again." He asked for some "stilliards" so that he could weigh the meat fairly, since there had been complaint of injustice, though fifteen bullocks had been cut up and distributed.

He had built a chimney for the sick general's comfort and promised to put one up at the next post. He flattered himself that there need be no apprehensions of his being surprised by the enemy.[15]

Even now that he was hopeful of crossing the new road to the capture of the fortress in spite of him, Washington could not forbear one more good word for the old road. He wrote to Forbes on November 16th:

"The keeping Fort Duquesne (if we should be fortunate enough to take it) in its present situation, will be attended with great advantages to the middle colonies; and I do not know so effectual a way of doing it, as by the communication of Fort Cumberland and General Braddock's road, which is, in the first place, good, and in the next, fresh; affording good food if the weather keeps open, which is more than a road can do as much used as this has been." [16]

The groans or the curses that Forbes must have emitted when he read these lines are not in the record.

On November 28th, 1758, Washington was able to write to the governor of Virginia a message that he had longed for years to send:

TO GOVERNOR FAUQUIER.

"Camp, at Fort Duquesne, 28 November, 1758.
"Honble. Sir,
"I have the pleasure to inform you, that Fort Duquesne, or the ground rather on which it stood, was possessed by his Majesty's troops on the 25th instant. The enemy, after letting us get within a day's march of the place, burned the fort, and ran away (by the

light of it,) at night, going down the Ohio by water, to the number of about five hundred men, from our best information.   The possession of this fort has been matter of surprise to the whole army, and we cannot attribute it to more probable causes, than those of weakness, want of provisions, and desertion of their Indians.   Of these circumstances we were luckily informed by three prisoners, who providentially fell into our hands at Loyal Hanna, at a time when we despaired of proceeding. . . .

"The General purposes to wait here a few days to settle matters with the Indians, and then all the troops, (except a sufficient garrison which will I suppose be left here, to secure the possession,) will march to their respective governments.   I therefore give your Honor this early notice of it, that your directions relative to those of Virginia may meet me timely on the road.   I cannot help premising, in this place, the hardships the troops have undergone, and the naked condition they now are in, in order that you may judge if it is not necessary that they should have some little recess from fatigue, and time to provide themselves with necessaries, for at present they are destitute of every comfort of life.   If I do not get your orders to the contrary, I shall march the troops under my command directly to Winchester; from whence they may then be disposed of, as you shall afterwards direct. . . .

"This fortunate, and, indeed, unexpected success of our arms will be attended with happy effects." [17]

He urged the importance of securing the favor of the Delaware and other tribes by sending out goods at once and clinching the opportunity of "riveting them to our interest."

He did not ruin the good news by describing the horrors of the last three miles of the long march to Du Quesne. On the frosted ground lay the immarbled corpses of the Virginians and Highlanders frozen where they had fallen in Grant's exploit.

The Highlanders were maddened by one sight the Indians had prepared for them—Scots heads upheld on poles, and kilts wrapped round like petticoats to mock them for women.

There were still the bones of Braddock's men to find and inter.   The woods were full of them, scarred with the teeth of the forest animals that had feasted on the flesh. Four years of sodden autumn leaves were their shrouds.

A few Indians who had been in the battle guided the hunters. Washington's friend, Major Halkett, who had heard how his brother had fallen dead across his dying father, was led to the tree where they had perished and saw two skeletons with their bones immixed. He fainted across them.

Later the bones were wrapped in Highland plaid, and a squad of Pennsylvania soldiers fired a volley over their grave.

These were the only known relics, and the bones of the rest were collected and buried in a long trench.

General Forbes had lived to see his work accomplished. He turned back through the increasing chill, and snow-storms, and reached Philadelphia at last, where he lingered until his relief in March. He was buried in the chancel of Christ Church there.

Forbes had asked Washington to deliver in person the good tidings of the capture of Fort Du Quesne to the governor of Virginia. He made the effort, but could not find the horses to take him the two hundred miles between him and the supply-camp.

Provisions were so scarce that the army had to flee from its victory or starve in the ruins of the fort. The largest garrison he dared leave was two hundred, and he wrote the governor of the grave danger that even these men would have to "abandon the place or perish."

"To prevent . . . either of these events happening, I have . . . wrote a circular letter to the back inhabitants of Virginia, setting forth the great advantages of keeping that place." He mentioned, also, the good prices they would get for their provisions.

By spring the garrison must be reinforced or "inevitably

be lost, and then our frontiers will fall into the same distressed condition that they have been in for some time past."

He begged that steps be taken to secure trade with the Indians and "remove those bad impressions, that the Indians received from the conduct of a set of rascally fellows, divested of all faith and honor."

There was a good chance, too, of "getting a large share of the fur-trade, not only of the Ohio Indians, but, in time, of the numerous nations possessing the back country westward of it."

With an eye on those dear Pennsylvanians, he urged that commissioners be appointed from each of the colonies "to prevent this advantageous commerce from suffering in its infancy, by the sinister views of designing, selfish men of the different provinces," and "all the attempts of one colony undermining another, and thereby weakening and diminishing the general system."

He saves the worst news to the last. In spite of his opposition, the General had ordered him to make up the entire garrison from his unfortunate Virginians.

For the last time for a long while, his aching heart cried out in pity for his soldiers that they were "naked." His long business letter to the Governor ended with these words concerning his inability to move the General, who had never listened to him:

"I endeavored to show, that the King's troops ought to garrison it; but he told me, as he had no instructions from the ministry relative thereto, he could not order it, and our men that are left there, are in such a miserable situation, having hardly rags to cover their nakedness, exposed to the inclemency of the weather in this rigorous season, that, unless provision is made by the country for supplying them immediately, they must inevitably perish, and if the first Virginia regiment is to be kept up any longer, or any services are expected therefrom should forthwith be clothed as they are. By their present shameful nakedness, the advanced season, and the inconceivable fatigues of an uncommonly long and laborious campaign, rendered totally incapable of any kind of service; and sickness, death, and desertion must, if not speedily supplied, greatly reduce its numbers. To replace them with equally good men will, perhaps, be found impossible."

Fort Du Quesne was promptly rechristened Pittsburgh in honor of the statesman who had put new life into the dying empire. Washington rode south as soon as he could secure a mount, leaving his troops to follow in a triumphal return that was more like a rout.

Washington was utterly disgusted with war, and determined to resign and never return to the service. This was to be his seventh resignation in four years, but it would be his last.

The irony of the campaign was gall and wormwood. He was in the nauseating situation of a prophet who has cried out promise of disaster only to see good fortune result. He had registered innumerable announcements that the Pennsylvania road was impossible, and the use of it a result of chicanery.

Now it had led to an easy victory, in utter contrast with the annihilation of Braddock's army, which had used Washington's road as a result of alleged Virginian chicanery. Worse yet, Washington's regiment had been selected to garrison the fortress. This removed from his available forces an important element. Worst of all, the Virginia Assembly had decided to reduce and all but disband the little army he had toiled so hard to enlist, uniform, and whip into shape, flog into discipline.

From the sight of his ragged, unpaid, unfed, uncared-for men he fled in despair. All he wanted was to get himself married and back to the neglected farm.

After him his abandoned regiment reeled. His friend Captain Stewart described in letters to him the barbarous lack of shelter for the sick and wounded and the absence of surgeons and nurses. On the way from Raystown, "eight or nine had Parished with Cold." There was no clothing, no food, and the duty was such as to be "insupportable by at least 9/10th of the Human Species. . . . That Brave Corps equally Distinguish'd by their Discipline and Intrepidity before the Enemy will too probably dwindle to a Licentious Crowd."

In the latest attempt to parade them under arms, "the miserable and shameful appearance they made was really moving." [18]

Doctor Craik, Washington's devoted comrade since Fort Necessity days, wrote how the troops suffered from hunger and cold and sickness. "Great numbers are dayly flocking to the Hospital; and what is still more dreadfull not one medicine to give them."

But in all the hardships, nothing filled the regiments with so much dismay as the knowledge that their colonel was quitting the service.

All his life Washington had an uncanny gift for winning a profound admiration amounting often to awe. People were always afraid of him. Among all the letters sent to him, almost nobody seems to have addressed him as "George" except Captain Orme, Colonel Corbin and Speaker Robinson.

Correspondents of every sort and condition greeted him with ceremony. But then, he was never familiar or even democratic with other people.

He must have insisted upon the carriage of formal respect when it was not instinctively maintained. An example of this is seen in his manner of rebuking one of his officers, Captain Peter Hog, who made him two or three reports in which he neglected, perhaps through ignorance, to employ the usual deferential expressions. Washington's wrath was prompt and crushing.

Captain Hog had written that his men had grown riotous "because their Cloathes were not Sent along with their pay; Saying they were Imposed on. & cheated out of their 2ᵈ per day: that the sᵈ. arrears of 2ᵈ per day had run now almost 18 Months & for that time they had only Recᵈ one shirt a pᵣ of Stockᵍˢ & a pᵣ of Shoes: notwithstanding they were promised 2 of Each Last Spring at Winchestʳ. . . . In Short after they were Dismist from the parade their discontent was so great, & Vented in Such Speeches, that the Officers came and advised me to Send off a Messenger Express to quite the Men. . . .

"As I mentᵈ In both my Letters the tattered Condition of the Men Occasioned by the hard March & difficult paths on the Expedition It Surprises me you should overlook it. As the Opportunities are so Infrequent and the Conveyance of Letters so Indirect & Uncertain I could Wish you would be very particular In answering Every Paragraph." [19]

This clumsy bluntness made Washington wince, and he answered with a devastatingly imperious tone:

"I was very much surprized to find Corporal Smith here upon such an Errand—Your suffering such clamours among the men, argues very great remissness in *you:* I imagined your being put there over them was partly with an intent to keep them quiet and passive: but this Express sent purely to humour them, seems as if you were afraid to do your duty among them: and by the subject of your letter it appears to me you were much of the same way of thinking with them, and seem equally dissatisfied.

"Let me tell you in your own words that 'I was very much

surprized' at the contents of your letter, wrote in such a commanding style; and your demands so express and peremptory—that the *direction* was the only thing which gave me the least room even to suspect it could be wrote to any but John Roe, or some other of your menial Servants!—I shall always act for the good of the Service, and inform you [when I find it necessary] of my proceedings." [20]

Captain Hog's answer is not recorded.

Washington handled his men and his officers with severity. He tried to make them study the books as well as the Indian arts of bush fighting. In accordance with the cruel habit of his time he believed heartily in the lash and appealed to it incessantly. He punished his men with flogging for any number of offences, and put them to death for desertion, or cowardice, whenever he could get the authority. Being congenitally devoid of fear, he could not forgive it in others.

Yet he was just; he chastised his men only for the good of the service; he fought for them and with them; he was tireless in his efforts to secure them comfort and profit; he was apparently full of good cheer and amiability in the camp, and in battle he was the bravest of the brave. His men had reason to be proud of being Colonel Washington's men. His almost unbroken record of defeats did not destroy anybody's confidence in him. He was always spoken of as Virginia's foremost soldier.

His officers invariably speak in extravagant terms of his courtesy, his devotion to the cause, his eagerness to be of help to everybody deserving it. They eternally repeat the words "affection" and "gratitude."

The hard thing to keep in mind about him is that he was still only twenty-six years old. It is difficult to extend to him either the affection or the warm sympathy one feels for the young. As George William Fairfax said: "All Washingtons are born old."

Now that this young man planned to leave his regiment, the grief amounted to consternation. It was the loss of a father rather than a comrade. Doctor Craik wrote, "When the Regiment meets with that irreparable lose, of loseing you—The very thoughts of this lyes heavy on the whole when ever they think of it—and dread the consequence of your resigning. . . . I am resolved not to stay in the service when you quit it." [21]

Captain Stewart wrote: "If we must be so wretched as to loose you I cannot think of remaining in this Service—-That your highest expectations may be fully answer'd by a change of Life—that you continue the Darling of a grateful Country for the many eminent Services you have render'd her." [22]

Captain Mackenzie, eager for the favor of General Amherst, writes to him:

"Though I have as small a Title as any Person whatever to the least Share of your Esteem, yet, by often observing with what Pleasure you seize all Opportunities of using your good Offices for the Assistance of others, I dare to address you and to sollicit your Interest in an Affair of the greatest Importance to me, which from your Benevolence alone I hope to obtain."

And Washington writes back a letter in which the old-fashioned starch does not conceal a very exquisite tact, a sincere modesty and an eagerness to be of service:

"I am sorry you shoud think it necessary to introduce a request that is founded upon Reason and equity with an Apology, to me—had you claimd that as a Right, which you seem rather to ask as a favour I shoud have thought myself wanting in that justice which is the distinguishing Characteristick of an Honest Man to have with held it from you.—

"But how to answer your purposes and at the same time avoid the Imputation of Impertinence, I am I must confess, a little more at a loss to determine.—That Gen! Amherst may have heard of such a person as I am, is probable; And this I dare venture to say is the Ultimate knowledge he has of me; how then shoud I appear to him in an Epistalory way and to set down and write a Certificate of your behaviour carries an Air of formality that seems more adapted to the Soldiery than Officers. I must therefore beg the favour of you to make what use you please of this Letter.—[23]

He concludes with a testimonial in the highest terms.

Numberless examples of such appeals and such responses exist to show the overpowering influence of Washington upon his contemporaries.

Best of all was the tribute paid to him by his despondent fellow-soldiers, who drew up on December 31, 1758, at Fort Loudoun a last appeal, which they called "The humble Address of the officers of the Virginia Regiment":

"We your most obedient and affectionate Officers, beg leave to express our great Concern, at the disagreeable News we have received of your Determination to resign the Command of that Corps, in which we have under you long served.

"The happiness we have enjoy'd, and the Honor we have acquir'd, together with the mutual Regard that has always subsisted between you and your Officers, have implanted so sensible an Affection in the Minds of us all, that we cannot be silent on this critical Occasion.

"In our earliest Infancy you took us under your Tuition, train'd us up in the Practice of that Discipline, which alone can constitute good Troops, from the punctual Observance of which you never suffer'd the least Deviation.

"Your steady adherance to impartial Justice, your quick Discernment and invarable Regard to Merit, wisely intended to inculcate those genuine Sentiments, of true Honor and Passion for Glory, from which the great military Atcheivements have been deriv'd, first heighten'd our natural Emulation, and our Desire to excel. How much we improv'd by those Regulations, and your own Example, with what Alacrity we have hitherto discharg'd our Duty, with what Chearfulness we have encounter'd the several Toils, especially while under your particular Directions, we submit to yourself, and flatter ourselves, that we have in a great measure answer'd your Expectations.

"Judge then, how sensibly we must be Affected with the loss of such an excellent Commander, such a sincere Friend, and so affable a Companion. How rare is it to find those amable Qualifications blended together in one Man? How great the Loss of such a Man? Adieu to that Superiority, which the Enemy have granted us over other Troops, and which even the Regulars and Provincials have done us the Honor publicly to acknowledge. Adieu to that strict Discipline and order, which you have always maintain'd! Adieu to that happy Union and Harmony, which has been our principal Cement!

"It gives us an additional Sorrow, when we reflect, to find, our unhappy Country will receive a loss, no less irreparable, than ourselves. Where will it meet a Man so experienc'd in military Affairs? One so renown'd for Patriotism, Courage and Conduct? Who has so great knowledge of the Enemy we have to deal with? Who so well acquainted with their Situation & Strength? Who so much respected by the Soldiery? Who in short so able to support the military Character of Virginia?

"Your approv'd Love to your King and Country, and your uncommon Perseverance in promoting the Honor and true Interest of the Service, convince us, that the most cogent Reasons only could induce you to quit it, Yet we with the greatest Deference, presume to entreat you to suspend those Thoughts for another Year, and to lead us on to assist in compleating the Glorious Work of extirpating our Enemies, towards which so considerable Advances have been already made. In you we place the most implicit Confidence. Your Presence only will cause a steady Firmness and vigor to actuate in every Breast, despising the greatest Dangers, and thinking light of Toils and Hardships, while lead on by the Man we know and Love.

"But if we must be so unhappy as to part, if the Exigencies of your Affairs force you to abandon Us, we beg it as our last Request that you will recommend some Person most capable to command, whose Military Knowledge, whose Honor, whose Conduct, and whose disinterested Principles we may depend upon.

"Frankness, Sincerity, and a certain Openness of Soul, are the true Characteristics of an Officer, and we flatter ourselves that you do not think us capable of saying anything, contrary to the purest Dictates of our Minds. Fully persuaded of this, we beg Leave to assure you, that as you have hitherto been the actuating Soul of the whole Corps, we shall at all times pay the most invariable Regard to your Will and Pleasure, and will always be happy to demonstrate by our Actions, with how much Respect and Esteem we are, Sir. Your most affectionate & most obedt. humble Servants." [24]

Twenty-seven names are signed to it.

This is an epitaph to a military career that could not be surpassed. It was the sort of homage that Washington received all his life. He earned it and it should never be forgotten.

Such laurels are beautiful crowning the brow of a human being, fallible, defeated, heartbroken, tormented by a thousand frustrations, a man of laughter, chivalry, foppery, a man of business, a speculator, a farmer, a huntsman, a lover of good wines, good clothes, dances, games, races, fast horses, gossip, and fine women.

But the laurels wither into dried leaves when they are set on an effigy carved out of white stone and rivetted on a high pedestal with nothing stirring in the veins, the breast, or the huge limbs.

The soldier's heart in Washington must have ached as he read the *Ave atque Vale* of his soldiers, for there are few things on earth more touching than a tender word from the men whom one has abused, ridiculed, punished, reduced to military slavery, and led into every hardship and every peril, and from whom one yet receives gratitude and understanding.

But nothing could shake his decision to leave the tent in the wilderness, and he submitted his resignation as soon as he reached Williamsburg.

The war with France was still in doubt. It would rage on for five years more with the British Empire rocking on its foundations.

But George Washington had left old England to her own

devices. He was bent upon saving himself first. He was deep in debt. He was betrothed to a woman of great wealth. He was going to marry and settle down to the making of money. Which, after all, is one of the most important duties of any patriot.

XXIX

"DOMESTIC FELICITY"

THE men of greatest accomplishment are often men of feeble constitution, and Washington, for all his gigantic strength and lust for hardship, was the constant prey of illnesses. Camp dysentery was the torment of all soldiers then, and it was probably that that almost prostrated him again on his way to his wedding.

He was so sick a man when he rode into Winchester on December 9th, 1758, that he was not sure of being able to reach Williamsburg. He wrote Governor Fauquier from Winchester that he had to go to Mount Vernon for his papers in order to make "a full and final settlement with the country." He needed also, "almost every necessary for the journey," which doubtless referred to the clothes without which he would not care to visit the capital and his betrothed.

These things, he wrote, "oblige me to take my house in the way down." He promised, "If I easily get the better of my present disorder, I shall hope for the honor of seeing you about the 25th instant." [1]

He kept his promise, his accounts were accepted, with his resignation. On December 30th, 1758, he wrote to General Forbes, interceding for "Captain McNeill who commanded the first Virginia regiment in my absence" and who had rashly arrested a commissary. "This piece of rashness, I am told, is likely to bring McNeill into trouble. I therefore beg the favor of you, sir, as I am well convinced

McNeill had nothing in view but the welfare of his men, to interpose your kind offices to settle the difference. This will be doing a favor to Captain McNeill, as well as to myself."

He added good wishes that "a perfect return of good health has contributed to crown your successes." But it was death that crowned Forbes' success.

In Washington's collected writings the next letter to follow that plea for a military friend in trouble, is this very startling assumption of command in a new field:

TO ROBERT CARY AND COMPANY, MERCHANTS, LONDON.

"Williamsburg, 1 May, 1759.

"GENTLN.,

"The inclosed is the minister's certificate of my marriage with Mrs. Martha Custis, properly, as I am told, authenticated. You will, therefore for the future please to address all your letters, which relate to the affairs of the late Daniel Parke Custis, Esqr., to me, as by marriage I am entitled to a third part of that estate, and invested likewise with the care of the other two thirds by a decree of our General Court, which I obtained in order to strengthen the power I before had in consequence of my wife's administration.

"I have many letters of yours in my possession unanswered; but at present this serves only to advise you of the above change, and at the same time to acquaint you, that I shall continue to make you the same consignments of tobacco as usual, and will endeavor to increase it in proportion as I find myself and the estate benefitted thereby. . . .

"On the other side is an invoice of some goods, which I beg of you to send me by the first ship, bound either to Potomack or Rappahannock, as I am in immediate want of them. Let them be insured, and, in case of accident, re-shipped without delay. Direct for me at Mount Vernon, Potomack River, Virginia; the former is the name of my seat, the other of the river on which t' is situated. I am, &c."

Then follows the most astonishing list of things showing that the big soldier, the Indian-fighter and the farmer, was yet able to take delight in dainty things, in graceful furniture, the newest fabrics, the latest cut of clothes, for his wife, his children and himself. He believed in being in style and handsome, and he gave to fashion its rightful place in the world. He also ordered *A Speedy Way to Grow Rich:*

"1 Tester Bedstead 7½ feet pitch with fashionable bleu or blue and white curtains to suit a Room laid w yl Ireld. paper.—

"Window curtains of the same for two windows; with either Papier Mache Cornish to them, or Cornish covered with the Cloth.

"1 fine Bed Coverlid to match the Curtains. 4 Chair bottoms of the same; that is, as much covering suited to the above furniture as will go over the seats of 4 Chairs (which I have by me) in order to make the whole furniture of this Room uniformly handsome and genteel.

"1 Fashionable Sett of Desert Glasses and Stands for Sweet meats Jellys &c—together with Wash Glasses and a proper Stand for these also.—

"2 Setts of Chamber, or Bed Carpets—Wilton.

"4 Fashionable China Branches & Stands for Candles.

"2 pair of fashionable mixd. or Marble Cold. Silk Hose.

"6 pr of finest cotton Ditto.

"6 pr of finest thread Ditto.

"6 pr of midling Do. to cost abt 5/

"6 pr worsted Do of yl best Sorted—2 pr of wch. to be white.

"N.B. All the above Stockings to be long, and tolerably large.

"1 Suit of Cloaths of the finest Cloth & fashionable colour made by the Inclos'd measure.—

"The newest and most approvd Treatise of Agriculture—besides this, send me a Small piece in Octavo—called a New System of Agriculture, or a Speedy Way to grow Rich.

"Half a dozn pair of Men's neatest shoes, and Pumps, to be made by one Didsbury, on Colo. Baylor's Last—but a little larger than his—& to have high heels.—

"6 pr Mens riding Gloves—rather large than the middle size.

"Order from the best House in Madeira a Pipe of the best Old Wine, and let it be secured from Pilferers."

On the 6th of January he had married Martha Dandridge Custis, and according to the good old custom of the days when men were men and wives were nonentities, he had assumed the full control of Martha's property. By law he acquired for his own one-third of her dead husband's property, and he took pains to go to court and secure letters of administration for the other two-thirds. Martha Custis was indeed his. But he also took upon himself the full responsibility for her children, and a better stepfather never was, though he found himself baffled, as fathers have always been, by his inability to control the children even for their own good.

The wedding was, of course, according to the Church of England ritual. Nothing else was legal, but the colonists usually "insisted on holding their marriage ceremonies at home rather than in church, and no minister could move their determination." [2] The convivial ministers of that day probably made as feeble a struggle against this determination as they did against the cups that were offered them.

Even sermons were brought to the home of the well-to-do.

Bishop Meade points out that though it was against the old English canon for clergymen to preach at private houses, "no clergyman refused to preach a funeral sermon in a private house for forty shillings, and he preached [a regular sermon] for nothing." [3]

The gentry controlled the clergy and the poor were afraid even to ask "What must I do to be saved?" for "at that time people in the lower walks of life had not been accustomed to converse with clergymen, whom they supposed to stand in the rank of gentlemen and above the company and conversation of plebeians." [4]

It is small wonder that in an atmosphere where even religion lacked democracy, George Washington grew up to regard "the common run," as he called them, with a profound contempt that made it impossible for him in later years to act upon or even to understand the theory of another

Virginian, that "all men are created free and equal." Washington had bought too many white men and women to believe them essentially free.

The clergyman who officiated at the wedding was the Rev. David Mossom. Bishop Meade says that when he preached —usually to a congregation of the seven or eight very aged communicants who troubled to attend church in those days— Mr. Mossom preached "wholly from a written sermon, keeping his eyes continually fixed on the paper, and so near that what he said seemed rather addressed to the cushion than to the congregation." [5]

The state of morals and religion was very low in his parish and reflected little credit on Mr. Mossom, who came from Newburyport, Massachusetts, served at St. Peter's Church in New Kent county for forty years, and according to his epitaph, was the first of the Americans to be admitted to the office of presbyter in the Church of England.

He and his clerk had a bitter quarrel which they fought out in sermon and hymn. He had four wives and the last one made his life miserable.

He married Martha Dandridge twice—first to Daniel Parke Custis; second, to George Washington. The interval was an even ten years. Which does not compare with the record of the Rev. David Schuyler Bogart of the Dutch Reformed Church, who married Aaron Burr to Theodosia Prevost in 1782, and fifty-one years later married him to Betty Jumel.

There is dispute among the historians as to whether Washington's marriage took place in St. Peter's church or at Martha's home, "The White House," on the York River.[6] It was probably at the White House. Martha's first marriage had taken place at her father's home.

It was a time of brilliant weddings, and the little widow's wealth and the big soldier's fame brought a gorgeous company, including Governor Francis Fauquier in gold embroidered scarlet, bag wig and dress sword, with his lady in full uniform. English army and navy officers on colonial duty were there in glittering splendor. Several members of the Virginia legislature appeared to welcome the new burgess, among them Speaker Robinson, father of Beverley Robinson of New York. The aristocracy of the plantations crowded the home.

Not the least picturesque figure was the old soldier Bishop, in his British red uniform. There was, of course, a swarm of white and black servants. Among these was Cully, a negro who lived to be a hundred and then described the festival to G. W. P. Custis, who almost rivals Parson Weems in his dialogue. His negro dialect is especially remarkable:

" 'And so you remember when Colonel Washington came a courting of your mistress?' said the biographer to old Cully, in his hundredth year. 'Ay, master, that I do,' replied this ancient family servant, who had lived to see five generations; 'great times, sir, great times! Shall never see the like again!'—'And Washington looked something like a man, a proper man; hey, Cully?'—'Never see'd the like, sir; never the likes of him, tho' I have seen many in my day; so tall, so straight! and then he sat a horse and rode with such an air! Ah, sir; he was like no one else! Many of the grandest gentlemen, in their gold lace, were at the wedding, but none looked like the man himself!' Strong, indeed, must have been the impressions which the person and manner of Washington made upon the rude, 'untutored mind' of this poor negro, since the lapse of three quarters of a century had not sufficed to efface them." [7]

Martha naturally looked her best. According to Lossing, who had before him while he wrote, a piece of Mrs. Washington's wedding dress and a piece of her white satin ribbon brocaded with leaves, "the bride was attired in a white satin quilted petticoat, and a heavy, corded white silk overskirt; high-heeled shoes of white satin, with diamond buckles; rich point-lace ruffles; pearl necklace, ear-rings, and bracelet; and pearl ornaments in her hair. She was attended by three bridesmaids." [8]

"Her bodice was of plain satin, and the brocade was fastened on the bust with a stiff butterfly bow of the ribbon. Delicate lace finished the low, square neck. There were close elbow-sleeves revealing a puff and frill of lace. Strings of pearls were woven in and out of her powdered hair. Her high-heeled slippers were of white satin, with brilliant buckles." [9]

Mrs. Robins exclaims:

"Nothing ever could have been more elegant than his bride, who cast aside all traditions about the severity of a widow's wedding garb and decked herself in brave and becoming finery: . . . cascades of rich 'point' garnished her gown, and pearls glistened in her ears and around her throat and wrists." [10]

Charles Moore [11] says that her slippers of "purple satin trimmed with silver lace are still preserved at the home of her descendants, Tudor Place, in Washington," a city at that time unimagined and inconceivable.

The founder of this undreamed-of city towered over the little widow and had hung upon his six-foot-two of frame as much color as even he could venture with his love and practice of the fine art of costume.

He was in civilian dress of blue cloth, the coat lined with red silk, and trimmed with silver. Beneath was an embroidered white satin waistcoat. His knee breeches were fastened with buckles of gold. His stockings were of the finest. His huge feet were in shoes buckled with gold. He wore at his side a straight dress-sword. His hair was powdered. On his hands were white gloves that can still be seen in the Masonic Museum at Alexandria. They are monstrous.

The banks of the York River in January are not appropriate to the lawn revelries of June weddings, and the wedding was somewhat quieter than usual. But it did not lack for color, and Washington contributed his share.

He longed for aristocratic trappings as much as Shakespeare ever did, and he was at the opposite pole from that other Virginian, Jefferson, in his ideas of simplicity.

His attendants were as heraldic as he could make them. When he had made his thousand mile journey to Lake Erie and back in 1753, he had dressed in furs and carried a pack like a trader. When he made ready for his thousand-mile ride to Boston and back in 1756, he had written to London for the wardrobe of a great dandy. He also ordered "2 complete livery suits for servants, with a spare cloak and all other necessary trimmings for two suits more. I would have you choose the livery by our arms; only as the field is white, I think the clothes had better not be quite so, but nearly like the inclosed. The trimmings and facings of scarlet, and a scarlet waistcoat. If livery lace is not quite disused, I should be glad to have the cloaks laced. I like that fashion best, and two silver-laced hats for the above servants. 1 set of horse-furniture with livery lace, with the Washington crest on the housings, etc. The cloak to be of the same piece and color of the clothes, 3 gold and scarlet sword-knots, 3 silver and blue ditto, 1 fashionable gold-laced hat." [12]

If that was what his lackeys wore when he was a poor young colonial officer pleading for recognition, one may imagine his retinue when he rode south to his marriage.

Washington is constantly held up as the ideal example for the young and the ambitious. It is strange that this example is restricted to the fables about being unable to tell a lie and always obeying his mother.

The true moral, if any, to be drawn from his life, is that one should dress as magnificently as possible and indulge in every luxury available, including the dance, the theatre, the ballroom, hunting, fishing, racing, drinking and gambling, observing in all of them temperance, justice, honesty and pride, while avoiding excess and loss of dignity.

And a fine code it is.

There is every reason to believe that Washington saw to it that his guests made as merry as possible. He was always lavish in hospitality, and what must hospitality in Virginia have been when even the Philadelphia Quakers of that day were capable of wanton revelry?

"The wedding entertainments in olden times were very expensive and harassing to the wedded. The house of the parent would be filled with company to dine. The same company would stay to tea and supper both. For two days punch was dealt out in profusion. The gentlemen visited the groom on the first floor, and then ascended to the second floor to see the bride in the presence of her maids, &c. Then every gentleman, even to 150 in a day, severally took his kiss—even the plain Friends submitted to these doings. I have heard of rich families among them which had 120 persons to dine—the same who had signed their certificate of marriage at the monthly meeting—these also partook of tea and supper. As they formerly passed the meeting twice, the same entertainment was also repeated. Two days the male friends would call and take punch, and all would kiss the bride. Besides this, the married pair for two entire weeks saw large tea parties at their home; having in attendance every night the groomsmen and bridemaids. To avoid expense and trouble, Friends have since made it sufficient to pass but *one* meeting. When these marriage entertainments were made, it was expected also, that punch, cakes, and meats should be sent out generally in the neighbourhood, even to those who were not visitors in the family. Some of the aged now alive can remember such weddings." [13]

The honeymoon was spent at the home of the bride, where Washington lived for three months, before he took her to his own home at Mount Vernon.

It was not the custom then for married couples to dash away on the day of the ceremony, and instead of the simple "going-away gown," which the bridal fugitive of today dons soon after the ceremony, the new wife of those days, after her night in the decorated bridal chamber, was expected to appear before the company, or such of it as was able to be revived.

For this reappearance she wore what was known as "the second day's dress," of which Mrs. Robins writes: "Second-day dresses were adorable; rustling, shiny, flowered things opening on lace-ruffled white petticoats."

On the second day Martha rode to church in a coach with her husband galloping alongside on his horse. The departure and the return with a hilarious cavalcade made such a stir in the neighborhood that the legend arose of the church wedding.

After the first flurries of rapture, Washington took his wife up to her late husband's other home, the Six Chimney House in Williamsburg. The Burgesses were in session and he took his seat among them with a modesty repaid by appointment to the committee devoted to the diminution of the evils of stray hogs. For fifteen years he was regularly elected a member of the House of Burgesses, and he never forgot the value of conviviality on such occasions. Though a law had been passed, following his first election, forbidding the use of liquor at elections, Washington paid no heed to it, but went on dispensing fire-water, for Nicholas Creswell,[14] a young Englishman who travelled about young

America, describes in his Journal a visit to Alexandria, where he saw two sights, a dance and an election:

"Calm in the evening, the Captn. and I went ashore, to what they call a reaping frolic. This is a Harvest Feast. The people very merry, Dancing without either Shoes or Stockings and the Girls without stays, but I cannot partake of the diversion.

"Fair wind, got up to Colonel George Washington's, came to an Anchor in the Creek. Here is a small Insect which appears in the Night like sparks of Fire. Every time it extends its wings there is something of a luminous nature on the body, just under the wings, which is seen only when it extends them, only discernible in the night, and is called the Fire Fly. A great number of pleasant Houses along the River, both on the Virginia and Maryland side. All Tobacco Planters, some of them people of considerable property. This River parts the Province of Maryland and Colony of Virginia. *Saturday, July 9th, 1774.* Waiting for a load of Flour from Col. Washington's Mill.

"*Thursday, July 14th, 1774.* An Election for Burgesses in town (their Elections are annual). There were three Candidates, the Poll was over in about two hours and conducted with great order and regularity. The Members Col George Washington and Major Bedwater. The Candidates gave the populace a Hogshead of Toddy (what we call Punch in England). In the evening the returned Member gave a Ball to the Freeholders and Gentlemen of the town. This was conducted with great harmony. Coffee and Chocolate, but no tea. This Herb is in disgrace amongst them at present."

That was the sort of life Washington had hoped to lead for the rest of his mundane existence. Tea was not "in disgrace" in 1759, and he was inordinately fond of it while it was in good odor.

He was devoted to nuts, also, and sat eating them for hours at table. He even had them sent to him when he was at war, and while he was with General Forbes, one of his captains wrote him: "I have sent you Eight Doz'n eggs & 6 lb of Allmonds." [15]

Tobacco he could not endure to smoke. Custis says "he had the utmost abhorrence" of it. Even when it was necessary in conferences with Indians to take a whiff of the pipe of peace, he made a wry face and "drank" as little of the smoke as possible. [16]

Liquor of all kinds he loved and manufactured, imported, gave away and consumed in vast quantities. Where Charles Lamb won a bad name as a little sot because anything over a thimbleful went to his head, Washington was always drinking but never drunk.

His own writings give numberless proofs of this as well as the writings of other people. Thus John London of Wilmington says in his diary:

"Gen'l H[amilton] told us that Gen'l Washington, notwithstanding his perfect regularity and love of decorum, could bear to drink more wine than most people. He loved to make a procrastinated dinner—made it a rule to drink a glass of wine with every one at table and yet always drank 3-4 or more glasses of wine after dinner, according to his company—and every night took a pint of cream and toasted crust for supper." [17]

When the three months' honeymoon on the bride's property was finished, the couple went north to Mount Vernon, on whose enlargement Washington had been spending a great deal of money, though his absence in the field had compelled him to leave the direction of it to others, notably the Fairfaxes.

The arrival of Martha at Mount Vernon must have been another festival, for as Mrs. Pryor states:

"The 'infair,' the faring into the house of the bridegroom's parents, was quite as lengthy and important a function as the wedding. This great housewarming entertainment to celebrate the reception into the bridegroom's family was an ancient English custom, religiously observed in Virginia until the middle of the nineteenth century.

"The quantity of wedding-cake made in the Virginia kitchens was simply astounding! It was packed in baskets and sent all over the country to be eaten by the elders and 'dreamed on' by the maidens." [18]

Washington's mother, now fifty-two years old, was sincerely overjoyed by the wedding. She may have found some fault with the bride, as mothers-in-law have been known to do, but all Martha's faults were lost for the nonce in the virtue of her great deed. She had accomplished for George what his mother had always failed to do; she had made him leave the army. Mary wrote to her brother, Joseph Ball in London:

"There was no end to my troubles while George was in the army, but he has now given it up." [19]

It is well to rejoice when the mood is on, for it may not come again.

Sally Fairfax undoubtedly made the bride welcome.

It must have been an excruciating moment for everybody when the tall and lanky Washington first disclosed to the tall and very slender Mrs. Fairfax the plump and tiny Martha, while George William Fairfax stood in the background.

Her husband must have been either mercifully sheltered by the usual husband's blindfolds from any suspicion of his friend George's secret love-letters, or, if he knew, he must have been grateful to Martha for capturing and restraining this firebrand "darling of Virginia."

Martha must have learned all about Sally from the

gossips or from her own intuitions; but then, being a widow and the mother of four children, she could hardly demand a virgin soul from her husband.

What must George Washington have felt at that first encounter with Sally? If he had never been frightened before, he doubtless was terrified then. He could not have loved Sally any the less for making the best of it, for gathering the little wife into her friendship and increasing rather than diminishing the exchange of visits between Mount Vernon and Belvoir.

The Diaries show an incessant intercourse. The Fairfaxes were at Mount Vernon for dinner or for the night. The Washingtons were at Belvoir for the hunt or for dinner or for the night.

What, most of all, must Sally Fairfax have felt? Was she able to take it as a huge joke? or did she care so much for the Washington she had raised from a pupil to a lover, that she was glad of his next-best happiness, and resolved to do nothing to mar it, everything to enhance it?

What did she and George say to one another when they were alone by chance, as they must have been innumerable times? Did they fly to the protective presence of their wedded partners? Did they—but it is like fretting about what went on the other side of the moon a hundred and sixty odd years ago.

All we can be sure of is that Martha burned all of Washington's letters to her that she could find, and that Sally kept at least two till her dying day. Since they turned up a century and a quarter after the ink had dried upon them, the future may have further answers to the riddle, or mayhap further riddles.

Doubtless the bride and her children spent many exciting hours learning their way about and adjusting themselves to the new home. Doubtless they adjusted the new home to themselves.

There must have been a whirlwind of visits to make and visitations to receive. But as Martha took immense interest in all housewifely affairs, she must have enjoyed the giving of banquets and the making of guests comfortable. There were so many of them that as Washington afterward said, the home was like a tavern.

Early in the morning, before sunrise, Washington was up very betimes and riding about his farm, or setting out on a fox hunt. He drove his slaves hard, and Parkinson says, "It was the sense of all his neighbours that he treated them with more severity than any other man. He regularly delivered weekly to every working negro two or three pounds of pork, and some salt herrings, often badly cured, and a small portion of India corn. . . . A man unused to them and who is of a humane disposition, is unfit to employ negroes. I had rather do the work myself, than have continually to force others to do it." [20]

But then, Parkinson was an English visitor, not overly impressed by Washington, of whom he could say, "In his will, he valued himself, I think at ten times more than he was worth." Still, Parkinson was forced to admit that "General Washington managed his negroes better than any other man, he being brought up to the army, and by nature industrious beyond any description, and in regularity the same." Custis confirms him somewhat coldly:

"As a master of slaves, General Washington was consistent, as in every other relation of his meritorious life. They were comfortably lodged, fed, and clothed, required to do a full and fair share of duty; well cared for in sickness and old age, and kept in strict and proper discipline. These, we humbly conceive, comprise all the charities of slavery." [21]

Following his marriage he "bought largely," fourteen slaves in all, in 1759, for about six hundred pounds. Three years later he bought nine more, and so on until he had a considerable flock of blacks.

He kept a bibulous doctor named John Laurie to take care of them, at a salary of fifteen pounds a year.

Washington bought, also, many whites, including convicts, and once planned to import a large number of citizens from the Palatinate of the Rhine, but was warned that they were prejudiced against coming into Virginia, where the Established Church offered no hospitality to the Reformed Lutherans. They preferred to go to Pennsylvania, whose tolerant policy had won the envy of Lawrence Washington when the Ohio Company first began to open its lands. Thus Washington, who wanted the Palatinates for the very land coming to him as a soldier for the Ohio Company, learned a lesson in tolerance that made him afterwards speak with warm respect for the rights of Catholics, Baptists, Jews, even Mohammedans—even atheists.

He sold his slaves as reluctantly as he sold his land. He was for acquiring wealth in both. But when a man proved intractable, he would rid himself of him, selling him not "down the river," but to the West Indies, the hell below hell for all slaves. He sent one negro out with instructions to clean him up and trade him off for rum and sweet-meats.

The movement for emancipation had already begun to stir in Virginia as well as elsewhere. In time it influenced Washington, so that he was ashamed of keeping slaves and longed to be rid of them. By an odd coincidence, slave labor in tobacco fields grew less profitable as wheat began at last to earn the favor of the Virginians. Later, the cotton gin riveted the institution on the South.

Martha was a careful housewife and kept her own slaves

busy.   She enjoyed bookkeeping, the lending and the
management of money.

She took less pleasure in dancing than her husband did.
Perhaps she had too much of it on her honeymoon and was
dazed by her husband's insatiable appetite for it.   He was
one of those of whom the Presbyterian tutor, Fithian, wrote:
"Blow high, Blow Low, the Virginians are genuine blood—
they will Dance or die."   Dancing was so vital that even the
tutor regretted that his parents had not allowed him to learn
the necessary art.

One of the dancing teachers who gave lessons at times in
Mount Vernon found it necessary to rap the girls over the
shoulders and warn a lad that he was "insolent and wanton."
But in some of the games even the teacher "had several
Kisses of the Ladies."   One of the games was called "break
the Pope's neck." [22]

Washington made dancing teachers welcome and encouraged the stepchildren to all the graces.   He played
games with them and imported for them from London expensive toys, books, musical instruments and the most fashionable clothes.   When he had to lecture them, he never
took a pious or canting moralizing strain, but counselled them
with worldly wisdom and genuine affection.

It is a cruel irony that has to find comfort in such a statement as the ridiculously lauded epigram that "Providence
denied Washington children so that he might the better be
the Father of his Country."   It would be as sane to say that
Providence took away his teeth so that he should not be
tempted to bite his enemies.

For a time Washington had hopes of an heir, or at least
an heiress, for Martha wrote on June 1st, 1760, to her sister
Mrs. Nancy Bassett, one of the few letters of hers that she
did not manage to burn:

"DEAR SISTER: I have had the pleasure of receiving your very
welcome and affect'e Letters of the 10th of may intended to come

by Jack and the 23d by Mr. Bassett who I must acknowledge myself greatly obliged to for the favour of his last visit. I should not have suffered him to go without a letter to you had I not known of the opportunity that now offers and here I must do myself the pleasure of congratulating you very sincerely on your happy deliverance of, I wish I could say boy, as I know how much one of that sex was desired by you all. I am very sorry to hear my mamma's complaints of ill health and I feel the same uneasiness on that account that you doe but I hope Mr. S[co]tt's prescriptions will have the desired effect—the children are now very well and I think myself in a better state of helth than I have been in for a long time and don't dout but I shall present you a fine healthy girl again when I come down in the Fall which is as soon as Mr. W——ns business will suffer him to leave home. . . ." [23]

This presentation was never made, and no more children came to Martha. It was not until he wrote his will that Washington brought himself to say that "his expectation of having issue had ceased."

His heart was in nothing else so simple and unrestrained as in his devotion to children. Jacky and Patsy Custis had perfect love about them. Martha's own heart was all mother, and she wrote to her sister Nancy Bassett, of a visit to a Washington in Westmoreland, "whare I spent a weak very agreabley I carred my little patt with me and left Jackey at home for a trial to see how well I coud stay without him though we ware gon but won fortnight I was quite impatiant to get home. If I at aney time heard the doggs barke or a noise out, I thought thair was a person sent for me.

"I often fancied he was sick or some accident had happened to him so that I think it is impossible for me to leave him as long as Mr. Washington must stay when he comes down—If nothing happens I promise myself the pleasure of comeing down in the spring as it will be a healthy time of the year. I am very much obliged to you for your kind invatation and assure yourself nothing but my childrens interest should prevent me the sattisfaiton of seeing you and my good Friends I am always thinking of and wish it was possible for me to spend more of my time amongst. It gave me great sattisfaction to hear of your dear billy's recovery which I hope will be a lasting wone; you mentioned in your letter that Col More intended hear but we have seen nothing of him. We heard at Fredericksburg that he and my brother had been thaire but no higher. I should been very glad to seen them heare. We all injoy very good health at preasent, I think patty seems to be quite well now, Jackey is very thin but in good health, and learn thaire books very fast. I am sorry to hear you are unwell but hope your Complaint is slight. I have no news worth telling you."

Washington's hopes for release from his everlasting financial worry were no better realized than his hopes for children. Throughout his life he was forever borrowing or trying to borrow or to put off a loan.

Yet it was not selfishness or ambition for wealth that kept him in this plight. He was always lending as well as borrowing, always supporting some indigent relative or fortuitous dependent.

Nothing proves the goodness of his heart better than the confession he wrote to his old friend Captain Robert Stewart, who wanted to borrow four hundred pounds in order to buy himself out of a lowly commission into a higher.

"I wish, my dear Stewart, that the circumstances of my affairs would have permitted me to have given you an order upon any person, in the world, I might add—for £400 with as much ease & propriety as you seem to require it, or even for twice that sum if it would make you easy. But, alas! to show my inability in this respect, I enclose you a copy of Mr. Cary's last account current against me, which, upon my honor and the faith of a Christian, is a true one and transmitted to me with the additional aggravation of a hint at the largeness of it. Messrs. Hanbury's have also a ballance against me; and I have no other correspondents in England with whom I deal, unless it be with a namesake, for trifles such as cloaths; and for these I do not know whether the Ballance is for or against me.

"This, upon my soul, is a genuine account of my affairs in England. Here they are a little better, because I am not much in debt. I doubt not but you will be surprized at the badness of their condition unless you will consider under what terrible management and disadvantages I found my estate when I retired from the publick service of this Colony; and that besides some purchases of Lands and Negroes I was necessitated to make adjoining me (in order to support the expences of a large family), I had Provisions of all kinds to buy for the first two or three years; and my Plantation to stock in short with every thing;—buildings to make and other matters which swallowd up before I well knew where I was, all the money I got by marriage, nay more, brought me in debt, and I believe I may appeal to to your own knowledge of my circumstances before.

"I do not urge these things, my dear Sir, in order to lay open the distresses of my own affairs. On the contrary they should forever have remained profoundly secret to your knowledge, did it not appear necessary at this time to acquit myself in your esteem, and to evince my inability of exceeding £300, a sum I am now laboring to procure by getting money to purchase bills of that amount to remit to yourself; that Mr. Cary may have no knowledge of the transaction since he expected this himself, and for which my regard for you will disappoint him—a regard of that high nature that I could never see you uneasy without feeling a part and wishing to remove the cause; and therefore when you complained of the mortification of remaining a subaltern in a corps you had frequently commanded the subs of I wanted you out, and hoped it might be effected—but I shall have done on the subject, giving me leave to add only that in case you should not have a call for the money (and your letter speaks of this) you will then be so good as to pay it to Mr. Cary, to whom I believe it will be no disagreeable tender and advise me thereof. The inclosed will inform you of what I have wrote to him on this head, which letter you may deliver or destroy at pleasure. . . . I write in very great haste and know I may depend upon your Friend- ship to excuse any thing and every thing amiss in the Let- ter." [24]

The great man apologizes abjectly because he can squeeze out only three hundred pounds instead of the four hundred asked for! And to prove that he is not stingy, he lays all his cards on the table, asking only for confidence. Truly, as Charles Lamb wrote, it is the lenders that are humble in this world. One might write an inverted Beatitude, "Cursed are the creditors, for they shall be meek."

If ever a deception were graceful, Washington's was when he asked his friend not to let his creditor Cary know of the loan.

It was this same Stewart who had written to him shortly after his marriage:

"Be so good as to offer my Complements in the most re- spectful and obliging Terms to Your Lady (a new Stile in- deed) and tho' she has rob'd me and many others of the greatest satisfaction we ever had or can enjoy in this Service yet none can be more sollicitous of her happiness—

"The regret, dejection and grief your Resignation has occasion'd in the whole Corps is too melancholy a Subject to enter on at this Juncture will therefore wave it—" [25]

From Pittsburgh (where they were building "a very re- spectable Fort of Brick, to contain 4000 Men on Emergency, and capable of holding out against Shells"[26]) Captain Stewart had written:

"This Fort, which is yet but in embryo, will when finish'd, be the grandest that has yet been in this new world. . . . Those Nations [the Delawares and Shawanese] are greatly incens'd against you, who they call the Great Knife & look on you to be the Author of their greatest misfortunes."

Stewart noted that the Pennsylvanians were making fortunes from the Furr trade while "our Province remain dormant & inactive." Though he sighed "I'm already an old Fellow," he begged Washington to try to secure for him "the vacant Adjutancy of the Militia," seeking thereby to step into the rank with which young Washington began the military career he had now ended.

He added: "I am vastly oblig'd by your Lady's kind remembrance of me and your Joint Invitation to pass part of the Winter at Mount Vernon . . . tell her that our Freinds at Mount Vernon is a constant Toast in this Camp."[27]

At Pittsburgh sat Colonel George Mercer, and he wrote to Washington about the great dream that was to fill the Colonel's soul for years with plans of personal empire.

The Ohio Company had offered to all the soldiers who went out to defend their grant an immense bonus of land. Those soldiers had not redeemed the land but they had tried to and had suffered.

Washington began to press the claims and, when they were allowed, to buy up quietly at the lowest possible prices claims of such old soldiers as poverty compelled to accept what they could get.

He began to capture territory by money, not by arms, and became one of the great land speculators of his day.

XXX

THE DAILY ROUND

IF Washington's diaries had been published with his first biographies, they would have saved him and his fabricators and the public a vast amount of appalling falsehood of the loftiest sort.

A few historians had access to bits of them, and carefully selected morsels were published from time to time. But it was not until 1925 that Washington himself rose from his grave in the complete four-volume edition published for the Mount Vernon Ladies' Association of the Union.

When he rose he toppled over innumerable marble statues of himself in all sorts of pompous poses, and annulled no end of stilted portraits in oil and ink, not one of them representing him in his favorite postures of surveying, writing poetry of a sort, dancing, drinking toasts, hunting deer and pheasants with a gun, fishing with line and seine, hunting fox with hounds, playing Luther Burbank with his graftings and sowings and fertilizings, or riding about his plantations under a tall umbrella fastened to his saddle.

It is significant perhaps that it took an association of Virginia ladies to give the real Washington his resurrection in the *Diaries*, and that Mrs. Robins' story of Sally Fairfax and his other loves should have been written by the National Historian of the Colonial Dames of America and published under the auspices of the Virginia branch.

But then, Washington was so devoted always to the ladies that they really owed it to the gallant gentleman to do something for him.

The best thing they did was to permit the diaries to be published entire, transcribed with pious accuracy and edited with notes of profound research by John C. Fitzpatrick.

Aside from the accounts of special expeditions like his journey over the Blue Ridge, his voyage to Barbados, his expedition to the French commandant, and the captured records of the Fort Necessity fiasco, his journal really begins the year after his marriage.

The diaries are a sort of prose Bucolics. The things he noted are the index of his character. A simpler, more realistic, more comfortable, prosy, workaday man could not be imagined.

There is nothing less godlike than his summing-up of each day in this autobiography of his, beginning January 1, 1760:

"*Tuesday, 1.* Visited my Plantations and receivd an Instance of Mr. French's great love of Money in disappointing me of some Pork, because the price had risen to 22/6 after he had engaged to let me have it at 20/.

"Calld at Mr. Possey's in my way home and desird him to engage me 100 Bar'ls of Corn upon the best terms he could in Maryland.

"And found Mrs. Washington upon my arrival broke out with the Meazles.

"*Thursday, 3d.* The Weather continuing Bad and the same causes subsisting I confind myself to the House. Morris who went to work yesterday caught cold and was laid up bad again, and several of the Family were taken with the Measles, but no bad Symptoms seemd to attend any of them.

"Hauled the Sein and got some fish, but was near being disappointed of my Boat by means of an Oyster Man, who had lain at my landing and plagued me a good deal by his disorderly behaviour.

"*Saturday, 5th.* Mrs. Washington appeard to be something better. Mr. Green however came to see her at 11 oclock and in an hour Mrs. Fairfax arrivd. Mr. Green prescribd the needful, and just as we were going to Dinnr. Capt. Walter Stuart appeard with Doctr. Laurie.

"The Evening being very cold, and the wind high, Mrs. Fairfax went home in the Chariot. Soon afterwards Mulatto Jack arrivd from Fred[eric]k with 4 Beeves.

"*Sunday, 6th.* The Chariot not returng. time enough from Colo. Fairfax's we were prevented from Church.

"Mrs. Washington was a good deal better to day; but the Oyster Man still continuing his Disorderly behaviour at my Landing I was obliged in the most preemptory manner to order him and his compy. away, which he did not Incline to obey till next morning.

"*Tuesday, 8.* Directed an Indictment to be formd by Mr. Johnston against Jno. Ballendine for a fraud in some Iron he sold me.

"Got a little Butter from Mr. Dalton, and wrote to Colo. West for Pork.

"In the Evening 8 of Mr. French's Hogs from his Ravensworth Quarter came down, one being lost on the way—as the others might as well have been for their goodness.

"Nothing but the disappointments in this Article of Pork which he himself had causd and my necessities coud possibly have obliged me to take them.

"Carpenter Sam was taken with the Meazles.

"*Saturday, 12th.* Set out with Mrs. Bassett on her journey to Port Royal.

"Here I was informd that Colo. Cocke was disgusted at my House, and left because he see an old Negroe there resembling his own Image.

"*Sunday, 13th.* The Wind last Night chopd about from Southerly to the No. West blew extreame hard and made it excessive cold.

"We reached Mr. Seldon's abt. 3 o'clock and met with a certain Capt. Dives there, a Man who, as I have been informd, is pretty well known for some of his exploits, and suspected to be an Instrument in carrying Dickerson, whose Character and Memory are too well established to need any Commentaries.

"*Tuesday, 15th.* Several Gentlemen dind with us at Colo. Carter's (neighbour's of his), but we spent a very lonesome Evening at Colo. Champe's, not any Body favouring us with their Company but himself.

"*Wednesday, 16th.* I parted with Mr. Gibourne, leaving Colo. Champe's before the Family was stirring, and at 10 reached my Mother's, where I breakfasted and then went to Fredericksburg with my Brother Sam, who I found there.

"Abt. Noon it began snowing, the Wind at So. West, but not Cold; was disappointed of seeing my Sister Lewis and getting a few things which I wanted out of the Stores. Returnd in the Evening to Mother's—all alone with her.

"*Sunday, 20th.* My Wagon, after leaving 2 Hogsheads of Tobo. at Alexandria, arrivd here with 3 sides of sole Leather and 4 of upper Leather, 2 Kegs of Butter, one of which for Colo Fairfax and 15 Bushels of Salt which She took in at Alexandria.

"Visited at Belvoir to day, carrying Doctr. Craik with us, who spent the Evening there.

"*Friday, 25th.* Wrote to Doctr. Ross to purchase me a joiner, Bricklayer, and Gardner, if any Ship of Servants was in.

"Also wrote to my old Servt. Bishop to return to me again, if he was not otherwise engaged. Directed for him at Phila. but no certainty of his being there.

"*Monday, 28th.* Visited my Plantation. Severely reprimanded young Stephen's for his Indolence, and his father for suffering of it.

"Found the new Negroe Cupid ill. of a Pleurisy at Dogue Run Quarter and had him brot. home in a cart for better care of him.

"*Tuesday, 29th.* Darcus, daughter to Phillis, died, which makes 4 negroes lost this Winter; viz, 3 Dower Negroes namely—Beck,—appraisd to £50, Doll's Child born since, and Darcus—ap[praise]d at . . . , and Belinda, a Wench of mine, in Frederick.

"*Sunday, 3d.* Mrs. Possey went home and we to Church at Alexandria; dind at Colo. Carlyle's and returnd in the Evening.

"*Wednesday, 6th.* Colo. Fairfax and Mrs. Fairfax Dind here.

"*Friday, 15th.* A Small fine Rain froom No. Et. wet the Top of my Hay that had been landed last Night. It was all carted up however to the Barn and the wet and dry seperated.

"Went to a Ball at Alexandria, where Musick and Dancing was the chief Entertainment. However in a convenient Room detachd for the purpose abounded great plenty of Bread and Butter, some Biscuits with Tea, and Coffee which the Drinkers of coud not Distinguish from Hot water sweetened. Be it remembered that pocket-handkerchiefs servd the purposes of Table Cloths and Napkins and that no Apologies were made for either.

"The Proprietors of this Ball were Messrs. Carlyle, Laurie and Robt. Wilson, but the Doctr. not getting it conducted agreeable to his own taste woud claim no share of the merit of it.

"I shall therefore distinguish this Ball by the Stile and title of the Bread and Butter Ball.

"We lodgd at Colo. Carlyle's.

"*Saturday, 16th.* Returnd home, receiving an Invitation to Mrs. Chew's Ball on Monday night next, first.

"The Morning lowerd, and dript as yesterday but abt. 10 oclock the Wind So.'ly blew fresh, and cleard.

"*Sunday, 17th.* The Wind blew cold and fresh from the No. West. Went to Church and Dind at Belvoir.

"Sent 4 Yews and Lambs to the mill to be fatted.

"*Sunday, 24th.* Captn. Bullet dind here today also. So did Mr. Clifton, but the latter was able to give me no determinate answer in regard to his Land.

"Was unprovided for a demand of £90 made by Mr. Alligood in favour of Messrs. Atchison & Parker of Norfolk, my note of Hand to Sampson Darrel, but promisd the payment and Interest, at the April Court next.

"*Monday, 25th.* The Broken Legd horse fell out of his Sling and by that means and struggling together hurt himself so much that I orderd him to be killd.

"*Sunday, 2.* Mr. Clifton came here to day, and under pretence of his Wife not consenting to acknowledge her Right of Dower, wanted to disengage himself of the Bargain he had made with me for his Land on the 26th past and by his s[h]uffling behaviour on the occasion convinced me of his being the trifling body represented.

"*Wednesday, 19th.* Peter (my Smith) and I after several efforts to make a plow after a new model—partly of my own contriving—was feign to give it out, at least for the present.

"Snow but little dissolvd. Colo. Fairfax and Mrs. Fairfax came here in the Evening.

"*Thursday, 10th [April].* Mrs. Washington was blooded by Doctr. Laurie, who stayd all Night.

"*Sunday, 13th.* My Negroes askd the lent of the Sein today, but caught little or no Fish. Note the Wind blew upon the Shore today.

"*Sunday, 4th [May].* Warm and fine. Set out for Frederick to see my Negroes that lay ill of the Small Pox. Took Church in my way to Coleman's, where I arrivd about Sun setting.

"*Sunday, 11th.* Mrs. Washington went to Church.

"My black pacing Mare was twice Coverd.

"Proposd a purchase of some Lands which Col. F[airfa]x has at the Mouth of the Warm Spring Run join'g Barwick's bottom. He promisd me the preference if he shd. sell, but is not inclind to do it at prest."

His diaries are full of Rabelaisian details, the manure and realism of the stock-breeder's life, the amours of mares, the matings and misalliances of hounds whose pups he kills or saves.

His own diary gives the flattest possible contradiction to the effort to make him out a man of piety. It is said constantly and stoutly emphasized that Washington went unfailingly to church with a regularity that brooked no interruption from weather or company, however important.

His daily chronicles, beginning with January 1st, 1760, omit some Sundays from all reference; but of those that are recorded, it is perhaps interesting to note that on the first of all, January 6th, Mrs. Fairfax kept him home because she had not returned his borrowed chariot. On the next he was kept away by a business errand. On the next he had important deliveries to make and a call to pay at Belvoir. On the next it rained and froze. In other words, he did not go to church once in January, 1760.

On February 3rd he went to church at Alexandria and dined in town. On the 10th he missed church but discussed a real estate deal "obliqu'ly." On the 17th he went to church and dined at Belvoir and "sent 4 Yews and Lambs to the mill to be fatted." On the 24th he missed church and discussed real estate and put off paying a note he had given.

On March 2nd he did not get to church, but had another real estate wrangle. On the 9th and 16th he mentions only the bad weather. The 23rd had "Southerly Wind and Warm," but he did not get to church; no more did he on the 30th, when he did a good deal of grafting and planting of "Spanish pairs, Butter pears, Winter Boon Cherries, Bergamy Pears, New Town Pippin, and Maryland Red Strick." No wonder he missed the sermon.

On April 6th he was busy noting that his rye grass seed was coming up "pretty thick." On the 13th it rained and his slaves went fishing with poor luck. On the 19th he broke his chair and had a long walk to get it mended, but on Sunday the 20th he missed church. On the 27th he went to church.

On May 4th he went out to see his slaves sick with the smallpox, and "Took Church in my way to Coleman's" (a tavern). May 11th Mrs. Washington went to church and he stayed home to attend to the mating of his black pacing mare and to make a deal in real estate. On the 18th he set out on a journey.

Certain diaries are lost, or so fragmentary, that his church-going is not recorded again for many years, though he writes on November 20th, 1767: "Vestry in Truro Parish." He had been chosen a vestryman October 25, 1762, and attended one meeting that year, one the next, two in 1766, five in 1767; one in 1768; two in 1769; two in 1771; one in 1772; two in 1774. The post of vestryman was a strictly political one, of no religious significance.[1] The next reference to going to church is April 17th, 1768.

All of these business deals and journeys on the Sabbath, and, indeed, the staying away from church at all, were against the law, of course. He hunted, went to the theatre and received guests lavishly on Sunday, as he himself records.

All this would be unimportant and normal, if there were not such persistent statement by historians, biographers and others, that Washington kept the Sabbath holy with un-failing solemnity. By his own account, in the twenty Sundays of the first five months of 1760 he went to church three times. One looks in vain for a syllable about the text, the sermon, or even the minister's name.

Good Bishop Meade [2] devotes a chapter to the religious character of Washington, in which he refers to him as "the great high-priest of the nation," and quotes many testimonials to his intense devoutness, his incessant prayerfulness, his attendance at the church of which he was a member, and his taking of communion, all of which are disproved by Washington's own works.

He quotes the Reverend Lee Massey of Pohick church as saying, "I never knew so constant an attendant at church as Washington. . . . No company ever kept him from church."

He goes on to speak of him as "scarcely ever tasting ardent spirits or exceeding two glasses of wine"; and quotes his orders against the vices of gambling, drinking and profanity, as proofs that he never indulged in them himself.

He ridicules the attempt to "bring him down to the common level, by representing him as passionately fond, not merely of the chase and much addicted to it, but also of the dance, the ballroom, and the theatre."

The Bishop admits that when he was very young, Washington might have been decoyed into hunting now and then for a few months with Lord Fairfax. But after his marriage he was too busy. "What time, I ask, for the sports of the field? What do we find in his diary of dogs and kennels and the chase? We do not say that he may never have thus exercised himself . . . but how different must have been the pursuit with Washington from that of the idlers of his day?" He ridicules the thought that Washington could have hunted deer with a rifle.

The poor Bishop refers to the diaries, as orators do, serene in the hope that nobody else had read what he had not read. It was a noble bluff. He did not live to read the answer of the *Diaries*, of which the entries of 1768 are a fair example.

In January, 1768, the first entry is "Fox huntg. in my own Neck." Other entries are, "Started a Fox and run him 4 hours, took the Hounds off at Night," "At home all day at

Cards—it snowing," "Rid up to Toulston in order to Fox hunt it," "Fox hunting with Jacky Custis and L[un]d Washington. Catchd a fox after a 3 h'rs chase." "Never started a Fox but did a Deer." "Fishing for Sturgeon from Breakfast to Dinner but catchd none." "Went a ducking and Killd 2 Mallards and 5 bald faces."

In January he went hunting eleven days and not once to church. In February he hunted with hounds or gun on thirteen days, but went not once to church. In March he hunted seven days and was "much disordered by a Lax, Griping and violent straining" for eight days; no church. In April he went to church twice, hunting three times, once to a ball at Alexandria, and made a trip to Williamsburg. In May he went to the theatre once, church three times, and hunting or fishing seven times.

In September, besides giving and accepting many dinners, he went to church once, to one ball, to one meeting of the vestry, went fox hunting four times, twice to the theatre, and once "to a Purse Race at Accotinck," where he entered one of his pacing horses, and paid a jockey 12 shillings to ride him.

On December first he "Went to the Election for Burgesses for this County and was there, with Colo. West, chosen. Stayd all Night to a Ball wch. I had given." Later he went fox hunting. Eleven days and not once to church.

In January, 1769, he hunted twelve days and went to church once. And so the record goes on and on.

It is easy to answer the Bishop's query: "What do we find in his diary of dogs and kennels?" We find a great amount of the sort of thing entered on February 26, 1768:

"Much abt. this time a Hound Bitch Mopsey of Mr. R. Alexander's (now with me) was proud, and shut up chiefly with a black dog Tarter who lind her several times as did Tipler once, that is known of. The little Bitch Cloe in the House was also proud at the same time, but whether lined or not can not be known. See how long they go with Pup, and whether both the same time, being very difft. in size."

The result is reported May 3rd:

"The hound bitch Mopsey brought 8 Puppys—distinguished by the following Names, viz. Tarter, Jupiter, Trueman, and Tipler (being Dogs), and Truelove, June, Dutchess, and Lady, being the Bitches—in all eight.

"29. The bitch Chanter brought five Dog Puppies and 3 Bitch Ditto, which were named as follows, viz. Forrester, Sancho, Ringwood, Drunkard, and Sentwell, and Chanter, Singer and Busy."

On June 22nd he records an escapade by Musick, who was courted so "promiscuously by all the Dogs, intending to drown her Puppys."

"16 [September]. Anointed all my Hounds (as well as Puppies) which appeard to have the Mange with Hogs Lard and Brimstone."

In March 1769 there was a terrible wave of crime in the kennels:

"24. Returnd home from my journey to Frederick, etca., and found that the Hound Bitch Maiden had taken Dog promiscuously; That the Bitch Lady was in Heat and had also been promiscuously lind, and therefore I did not shut her up; That Dutchess was shut up, and had been lind twice by Drunkard, but was out one Night in her heat, and supposd to be lind by other Dogs; That Truelove was also in the House, as was Mopsy likewise (who had been seen lind to Pilot before she was shut up).

"26. The Bitch Musick brought five Puppies, one of which being thought not true was drownd immediately—the others, being somewhat like the Dog (Lockwood of Mr. Fairfax) which got them, were saved.

"27. The Hound Bitch Countess brought 7 Puppies and was with her Puppies carried away the next day by Alexr.

"31. To this time Mopsy had been lind several times by Lawlor as Truelove had been by Drunkard; but as this Bitch got out one Night during her Heat, it is presumable she was lind by other Dogs, especially Pilot the Master Dog and one who was seen lying down by her in the Morning."

Bishop Meade scoffs at the thought of Washington's stooping to the theatre:

"And as to his admiration of the theatre and his delighting in its ludicrous and indelicate exhibitions, does it seem probable that the grave and dignified Washington, with all the cares of the army and afterward of the state pressing upon him, should have found time for such entertainments?

"As to Washington's passionate fondness for the dance, if Cicero thought it an unbecoming exercise for any Roman citizen, as beneath the dignity of any who were admitted to the citizenship of that great republic, how unlikely that our great Washington—even if feeling no religious objection to this childish amusement—should be still a child and delight himself in such frivolous things!"

The usually careful and conscientious Bishop should have known better than to write such outrageous nonsense. There were innumerable instances of Washington's intense devotion to the theatre and the dance as commander-in-chief and as President. In these early days he was simply insatiable. He seems never to have missed the performance of a play in his vicinity, and he was forever giving dances and attending them. Though it is somewhat far in the future for this period, it is perhaps excusable to cite an instance from June, 1770, when he was at Williamsburg on most important business to the country's future. The "Club" he refers to was a group of friends who had a private table at a tavern, each man paying his own shot—what was later called a Dutch Treat Club.

He reached Williamsburg June 1st and left June 23rd.

He went to church on only one of the three Sundays. He rode into the country for a Sunday call and on Monday bought two slaves, at an auction. During his last week a theatrical troupe was in town and thus he answers Bishop Meade's indignant denial that he could have delighted in the theatre's "ludicrous and indelicate exhibitions:"

"16. Dined at the Club at Mrs. Campbell's and went to the Play in the Evening.

"17. Went to Church in the Forenoon, and from thence to Colo. Burwell's, where I dind and lodgd.

"18. Came into Williamsburg in the morning. Dined at the Club and went to the Play in the afternoon.

"19. Dined at the Club and went to the Play.

"20. Dined at the President's and went to the Play afterwards.

"21. Dined at the Club at Mrs. Campbell's at 8 Oclock and went to bed directly after.

"22. Dined at the Club and went to the Play, after meeting the Associates at the Capitol."

How fine a thing it was that Washington should have loved the theatre and treated actors and actresses with the courtesy they deserved! In return an actor gave perhaps the most delightful description of Washington in all the accounts. John Bernard [3] of England, travelling through the South, helped a tall farmer extricate two people from an overturned carriage. The farmer recognized the actor first, called him by name and was about to introduce himself when the actor gasped with belated realization that he was in the presence of a man already realized as one of time's masterpieces.

Washington took him home and entertained him at Mount Vernon with a grace and sweetness vividly shown in the actor's pages. How fortunate that the Father of His Country never allied himself with those bigots whose influence would have kept from this dismal world all that Greek tragedy, French, Spanish, English and American drama have meant to the world, the bigots who would have kept from this earth the very name of Shakespeare!

How well it was for America that the Father of His Country loved beauty, loved elegance, loved the dance, the convivial feast, stately ceremonial and romping hilarity!

For too long a time bigots disguised him as a grisly witch-burning morality-monger, a Cotton Mather, a Cromwell, whose very opposite he was. Another faction turned him into an equally false Sunday-school teacher's pet.

Mr. Philip Guedalla [4] is so much moved by these ironies as to exclaim: "Never, one feels, has a life of public service been worse rewarded by posterity. He saved, in a military sense he made, the Revolution, and its happy heirs have repaid him with a withered nosegay of schoolgirl virtues."

There are thousands of his letters that have not been published. Judging from the unscrupulous editing and selection of so many of those that have been printed, there are dazzling revelations awaiting their study by a human being.

Meanwhile, the *Diaries* have dealt a devastating blow to the Washington of tradition. It is pleasant to think that the wholesome iconoclasm was administered by his own hand.

There is nowhere in his writings any expression of skepticism, and he probably believed the essentials of the Established Church in a passive way, but his indifference was marked, and is in itself a contradiction of the furious allegations as to his fervor.

His wife, as often happens, furnished the religion for the family, said the prayers and read the Scriptures. His own great Bible looked as if it had never been opened.

He did not intefere with Martha's piety, nor with anybody's. His life with her seems to have satisfied him as well as he felt any one had a right to expect.

Mr. Meade Minnegerode [5] says:

"Martha was not George's first love, nor his third, nor yet his fifth; nor was she ever, perhaps, his real love."

Much virtue in a "perhaps." Much question about so vague a word as "love."

He adds: "That for long years George and Martha Washington shared each other's lives, in complete serenity and sympathy, and with ever increasing affection and devotion, remains perhaps his greatest and most admirable achievement, her most noteworthy accomplishment. For he never forgot Sally Fairfax."

Whether he loved Martha with the supreme passion or not, he certainly loved her with a devotion that satisfied him. They kept hoping for children of their own. Their home was full of the blissful agonies of illnesses and recoveries. They stood together round the bedside of the sick and the dying, and she saw him fall on his knees and sob over the cold body of her daughter whom he had worshipped as his own.

He called Martha "my dearest Patsy." She called him her "old man." And Custis, who should have known, says that he always wore around his neck a little chain with a miniature of Martha hanging on it. He sent for her to be with him when he went to war. He retired to solitude with her at every opportunity.

Eight months after his marriage he wrote to his London agent, Richard Washington, that though his brother had come home from a visit to England little benefitted, "the longing desire, which for many years I have had of visiting the great Matrapolis of that Kingdom is not in the least abated by his prejudices . . . but I am now tied by the Leg and must set Inclination aside.

"The Scale of Fortune in America is turned greatly in our favor, and success is become the boon Companion of our Fortunate Generals. Twould be folly in me to attempt particularizing their Actions since you receive accts. in a channel so much more direct than from hence. I am now I believe fixd at this seat with an agreable Consort for Life. And hope to find more happiness in retirement than I ever experienced amidst a wide and bustling World—I thank you heartily for your affectionate wishes—why wont you give me an occasion of Congratulating you in the same manner? None would do it with more cordiality and true sincerity." [6]

To Robert Cary and Company he wrote by the same ship:

"From this time it will be requisite, that you should raise three accounts; one for me, another for the estate, and a third for Miss Patty Custis; or, if you think it more eligible (and I believe it will be), make me debtor on my own account for John Parke Custis, and for Miss Martha Parke Custis, as each will have their part of the estate assigned them this fall, and the whole will remain under my management, whose particular care it shall be to distinguish always, either by letter or invoice, from whom tobaccos are shipped, and for whose use goods are imported, in order to prevent any mistakes arising."

He sends another of his lists of things to be shipped to him. It includes:

"A light Summer Suit made of Duroy by the measure; 2 best plain Beaver Hats, at 21s.; A Salmon-colored Tabby of the enclosed pattern, with satin flowers, to be made in a sack and coat; 1 Cap, Handkerchief, Tucker, and Ruffles, to be made of Brussels lace, or point, proper to wear with the above negliglee, to cost £20; 2 fine flowered Lawn Aprons; 1 pair woman's white Silk Hose; 6 pairs do, fine Cotton do; 4 pairs Thread do; 1 pair black, and 1 pair white Satin Shoes, of the smallest 5s; 1 dozen most fashionable Cambric Pocket Handkerchiefs; 6 m. Miniken Pins; 6 lbs. Perfumed Powder; 3 lbs. best Scotch Snuff; 25 lbs. Almonds in the shell; 1 hogshead best Porter; 2 dozen packs Playing Cards; 3 gallons of Rhenish in bottles; 8 Busts, according to the enclosed direction and measure.

"Directions for the Busts.

"4. One of Alexander the Great; another of Julius Cæsar; another of Charles XII. of Sweden; and a fourth of the King of Prussia. N. B. These are not to exceed fifteen inches in height, nor ten in width. 2 other Busts, of Prince Eugene and the Duke of Marlborough, somewhat smaller; 2 Wild Beasts, not to exceed twelve inches in height, nor eighteen in length. Sundry small ornaments for chimney-piece.

"For Master Custis, 6 years old.

"1 piece Irish Holland at 4s; 2 yards fine Cambric at 10s; 6 Pocket Handkerchiefs, small and fine; 6 pairs Gloves; 2 Laced Hats; 1 pair handsome silver Shoe and Knee Buckles; 10s worth of Toys; 6 little books for children beginning to read; 1 light duffel cloak with silver frogs.

"For Miss Custis, 4 years old.

"8 yards fine printed Linen at 3s. 6d.; 1 piece Irish Holland at 4s; 2 ells fine Holland at 10s; 8 pairs kid Mits; 4 pairs Gloves; 2 pair silk Shoes; 2 Caps, 2 pairs Ruffles, 2 Tuckers, Bibs, and Aprons, if fashionable; 2 Fans; 2 Masks; 2 Bonnets; 1 stiffened Coat of Fashionable silk, made to pack-thread stays; 1 fashionable-dressed baby 10s, and other Toys 10s; 6 Pocket Handkerchiefs."

This does not read like the requisition of a soldier, but it has the air of happiness and delight in the little graces of comfort.

He had achieved at twenty-eight what few men accomplish: he had dropped anchor in the harbor of his heart's desire. The world was at war, but he was at peace. He had attained the ideal he set himself as a lad when he transcribed into his copybook the following poem, still to be seen in the Library of Congress whence it is "copied after the clear boyish hand from the time-yellowed page":

"These are the things, which once possess'd
Will make a life that's truly bless'd
A good Estate on healthy Soil,
Not Got by Vice nor yet by toil;
Round a warm Fire, a pleasant Joke,
With Chimney ever free from Smoke:
A strength entire, a Sparkling Bowl,
A quiet Wife, a quiet Soul,
A Mind, as well as body, whole
Prudent Simplicity, constant Friend,
A Diet which no art Commends;
A Merry Night without much Drinking
A happy Thought without much Thinking;
Each Night by Quiet Sleep made Short
A Will to be but what thou art:
Possess'd of these, all else defy
And neither wish nor fear to Die
These are things, which once Possess'd
Will make a life that's truly bless'd." [7]

In 1760 Colonel George William Fairfax and his wife sailed for England for a brief visit. There was doubtless a farewell dinner. Doubtless Washington toasted each of his guests and perhaps when he stretched out his glass to Sally Fairfax, she followed a pretty custom of the day; perhaps her long slim fingers lifted one petal from a rose at her breast and let it fall into his brimming wine.

As he raised the glass and the petal smote his lips, his eyes upon her must have had much to say.

Sally, no doubt, smiled back triumphantly in her manner. She had conquered herself as well as him.

Martha watched them both no doubt, having learned from gossips or guessed from countless little clues many things that we cannot know. And she doubtless smiled, also. After all, she held Mr. Washington.

She probably liked Sally a little better for going abroad.

Then, no doubt, Washington rose to his full height, raised

his charged glass high and gave the toast that was going up all over the province:

"To the King and Queen, the Governor of Virginia and his Lady, and Success to American Trade and Commerce!"

XXXI

"INDEPENDENCY, AND WHAT NOT"

IN time, Washington began to add to his estate, not hundreds of acres, but tens of thousands of acres, and to cast his eyes westward with an enthusiasm that only later events of a revolutionary nature turned back to the north and east.

For the present he was an English squire on English soil, far from wars and the rumors of wars. The thought of a rebellion against his King, if it entered his brain, went out again at once as a silly fantasy.

There were anarchists and maniacs who had used the strange word, "independence." As early as 1738, it had been necessary for Mr. Joshua Gee [1] to prove how ridiculous the idea was. Even if the colonists grew so rich as to forget their loyalty, since they nearly all lived on navigable rivers and bays, the British navy could easily reach and subdue them.

In 1748, a Swedish botanist, Professor Peter Kalm [2] had prophesied that the colonies would some day outgrow dependence on little England. But then, he was only a Swede. How could he "peer and botanize" on American hearts?

Nobody could foresee what the capture of Fort Du Quesne and other successes of the brilliant Mr. Pitt were leading to, least of all the supposed savior of the empire, Mr. Pitt. As Professor Claude H. Van Tyne says:

"It was the strain which the Seven Years' War put upon the relations between Great Britain and her American colonies which forced into prominence every subject of controversy which for a hundred years had been setting by the ears the royal governor and the provincial assembly. Americans had never so clarified their ideas on constitutional questions, and, aided by the stress of war, had demanded everything nominated in the bond. What assistance had been secured by Pitt from the American colonies had been bought at an alarming price—concessions which deprived the governors of all but their pomp, and left the assemblies with every real power. Moreover, the utter want of any sense of loyalty to the empire on the part of individual colonists was shown in the extent to which illicit trade was carried on with the enemy. Not all the British naval activity could prevent colonial merchants from supplying French colonies with the provisions for want of which they must have capitulated. Fortunes were made in the trade, and so demoralized was public opinion that convictions on clear proof were not to be gotten from colonial juries." [3]

But Washington was no smuggler. Washington was loyal. Even when he quarreled with England it was as an Englishman jealous of the rights of an Englishman when a fool or a knave of a minister mismanaged the King's good will toward his devoted subjects overseas.

As late as 1775, in writing to George William Fairfax, then in England, he laid the blame for the battle of Lexington on "the ministerial troops (for we do not, nor can we yet prevail upon ourselves to call them the King's troops) . . . if the retreat had not been as precipitate as it was, and God knows it could not well have been more so, the ministerial troops must have surrendered. . . . Unhappy it is, though to reflect, that a brother's sword has been sheathed in a brother's breast."

He was pleading with the Fairfaxes to understand his feelings, and he signed himself, "with sincere regard and affectionate compliments to Mrs. Fairfax." [4]

If he could write so, after Lexington, and go on protesting his loyalty when he was once more a soldier and the commander-in-chief of a larger body of provincials, no wonder he wrote earlier, on October 9th, 1774, to persuade his old comrade and fellow-Virginian, Captain Robert Mackenzie, that he was "abused, grossly abused," by the strange people who were telling him "that the people of Massachusetts are rebellious, setting up for independency, and what not."

Since he wrote that letter from Philadelphia (when he was attending the first meeting of what was called a Continental Congress) he could and did assure Mackenzie, from his personal knowledge, "that it is not the wish or interest of that government, or any other upon this continent, separately or collectively, to set up for independence . . . no such thing is desired by any thinking man in all North America." [5]

But all that turmoil was a fortnight of years away from 1760, and everything was rosy.

In the very year after Washington's marriage, England received a new King, George III, a charming young twenty-two-year-old, of whom Walpole said: "He seems all good nature and wishing to satisfy everybody."

"The people rejoiced," says Mr. Frank Arthur Mumby,[6] "in again possessing a King who could speak their own language." He could not spell it—who could?—but he wrote in his maiden speech: "Born and educated in this country, I glory in the name of Britain, and the peculiar happiness of my life will ever consist in promoting the welfare of a people whose loyalty and affection I consider as the greatest and most permanent security of my Throne."

That "peculiar happiness" turned out to be very peculiar in the eyes of his subjects at home and abroad, but for the present he was a welcome substitute for his old father with the German dialect; who had doubtless called Washington "Vashinkton," when he scorned him years ago for writing to his brother that he loved to hear the bullets whistle.

But that was an echo from Washington's far-off youth of 1754. Now he was an old married man of eight and twenty. Now he loved to hear only the huntsman's horn, the whistle of the bullet flying after a deer or a "sprig tail" duck or a teal, the whistle of the boats that came up to the wharf for his tobacco.

He wrote no more letters imploring clothes and food for naked soldiers. He pleaded no longer for authority to punish the mutinous and the deserters. He was the monarch of all he surveyed.

Instead of writing war journals for the French to capture and garble, he kept a diary now, and never failed to note the ever-fascinating moods of the weather, the whims and mysteries of growing things, the names of visitors and visited, and all the matter-of-fact annals of a life that drifted on from day to day with nothing more troublesome than a sick child, a sick horse, a sick slave, a sick field, a lonely evening or a badly managed ball; nothing more admirable than a fine crop, a fine dinner, a fine hunt.

Though he had not yet had his lifelong wish to visit England, he could still hope; for it was still "home" to him. He used the word even when he wrote to his London agents:

"Mrs. Washington sends home a green sack to get cleaned, or fresh dyed of the same color; made up into a handsome sack again, would be her choice; but if the cloth won't afford that, then to be thrown into a genteel Night Gown."

He loved to keep Martha spruce and genteel. And he was calm when luck was bad:

"I am very sorry for the account of the Deliverance being lost. All the tobacco I had on board her was J. C., and I dare say would have disgraced no market whatever. But accidents of this nature are common, and ought not to be repined at." [7]

J. C. stood for "Jacky Custis's." But he was just as brave when "a continued series of rain for near four weeks has given a sad turn to our expectations . . . a great deal of the tobacco being drowned, and the rest spotting very fast."

Tobacco was no safer from drowning ashore than at sea. No wonder he longed for emancipation from it.

His only complaints against England were such as arose when the insurance was too high on the tobacco he shipped "per the Fair American," or when the *Charming Polly* brought to his dock goods "in bad order—the porter entirely drank out."

Or when the merchants and the tailors in London thought that they could palm off on "an infant, woody country, like ours," clothes of less than first quality and cut. Then he had to write such rebukes as this:

"And you may believe me when I tell you that, instead of getting things good and fashionable in their several kinds, we often have articles sent us that could only have been used by our forefathers in the days of yore."

Pretty soon the merchants who were ruling the empire would be sending over orders and regulations of the same sort.

AFTERWORD

To find out as far as possible and to report as faithfully as possible just what George Washington was, did, said, wrote, thought, and why and how—constitute the purpose of this work, and the excuse for adding another to the hundreds of his biographies. In 1889, in his *Bibliotheca Washingtoniana,* W. S. Baker had already listed five hundred and two. And practically every one of them was devoted to celebration rather than revelation.

"It is a platitude scarcely worth mentioning that all historical facts should be approached without any preconceived ideas as to their meaning," says Dr. George Louis Beer (in the preface to his *The Old Colonial System, 1660-1754*), justifying himself for giving so much importance to the economic factors which were almost completely neglected in the writing of American history until the present generation began to realize their vital importance.

But what he calls a platitude among conscientious historians is hardly yet the discovery of the biographers of Washington. The poor man has almost always been offered to his readers as a kind of angel, and the biographer as his high priest. It is perhaps perilous to try to tell the truth, the whole truth and nothing but the truth, but the try is worth the making. And while errors are inevitable and inevitably numerous, it is a comfort to know that none of them are intentional and that their correction is a service to the author as well as to the cause of truth.

No other man in history has suffered so much from malfeasance in office by historians. Nearly all of Washington's biographers have felt it their duty not only to correct his writings, but to blue-pencil, prettify and falsify his character. The Rev. Mason L. Weems began it by collecting and inventing sentimental anecdotes about him and turning his life into a Sunday-school book. The Rev. Jared Sparks followed by devoting enormous toil to the gathering of information which he proceeded to edit with sacrilegious ruthlessness—for it would seem to be sacrilege to tamper with the character and the expressions of a personage one pretends to revere. Washington Irving's humanity and geniality did not penetrate his characterization, but were devoted to his own style and the wreathing of bouquets which he laid at the feet of the icy statue he accepted from Sparks.

When, for example, Sparks deleted and Washington Irving omitted from an account of one of Washington's rages the "by God!" that made it thunder, they not only cheated the reader but ripped the guts from the living man. They helped to perpetuate as a devitalized deity one of the most eager, versatile, human men that ever lived. When Washington said he preferred to send out "scalping parties," and the biographers omitted the "scalping," they were false to the time, to Washington, and to his enemies. Hundreds of such perversions can be found in their works.

They carried their suppression so far that an English biographer, Cyrus R. Edmonds, was moved to the astounding statement:

"He was a man of whom it may almost be said that he had no private life."

In their fanatic zeal for denaturing this big, blundering, bewildered giant they have done a further injustice to all his contemporaries, of whom they have made either dwarfs or acolytes, and of his sincere adversaries demons of malice and envy.

It is poor patriotism, ridiculous idolatry, and rank dishonesty to rob the host of other strugglers for liberty and progress of their just deserts, and to perpetuate old slanders against his enemies at home and abroad in order to turn Washington into a god. As a god, Washington was a woeful failure; as a man he was tremendous. This is a study of the man.

We cannot do justice to our heroes or be fair to ourselves without being just and fair to the honest adversaries of our heroes and to the nations whom circumstances made at times our enemies, at times our allies.

In this book an earnest attempt is made to deal fairly with the French, the English, the colonists, with Braddock, Dinwiddie and all others who were at times Washington's warmest supporters, at times his most ardent opponents. To try to vilify them is not only caddish and contemptible, both as sportsmanship and as historicity, but it is a sneaking insult to Washington. A hero who cannot stand up under the clear light of truth without false props deserves to fall.

But the truth makes Washington real and lovable as well as admirable.

A further excuse for a new biography of Washington is the recent change in the whole spirit and knowledge of chronicle. As Professor Schlesinger says in his *New Viewpoints in American History*:

"Most adult Americans of today gained their knowledge of American history before the present generation of historians had made perceptible progress in their epoch-making work of reconstructing the story of our past in the light of their new studies and investigations. . . . Unfortunately, the product of the new school of American historians has, in very large part, been buried in the files of historical society journals, in the learned publications of the universities and in monographs privately printed at the expense of the authors. The new history was being written by historians for historians rather than for laymen; and the public generally has remained oblivious of the great revolution in our knowledge of American history wrought by the research specialists." Later in the same work he refers to "the witticism of a learned historian" who referred to the feelings of the ordinary American as "putting the 'hiss' into history."

My own research in the life and times of Washington goes back to the year 1900 when I began a four-year association with the construction of the *Historians' History of the World*. I worked in the British Museum, the Bibliothèque Nationale, and many American libraries, and was strongly impressed with the lack of international perspective and common justice in the histories of our country, as well as of all others.

I devoted a good deal of time to the study of Washington and his contemporaries and have never since ceased the hunt for the truth about him and them. I have written a number of stories concerned with the social, political and military history of our early periods, and have endeavored in all my fiction to document every statement thoroughly. For the purposes of this biography I have enjoyed the aid of every librarian to whom I have appealed and have added to my own collection everything available. I have tried to overlook nothing that has been unearthed or re-interpreted by the professional historians. A glance at the bibliography will show that university publications and monographs have been consulted with conscientious diligence. Privately printed works have been sought out wherever pertinent. Though it has been thought most considerate of the general reader to omit footnotes, index numbers are sprinkled throughout the text referring to the appendix, in which I have endeavored not only to give the authority for every important statement but to place before the reader views opposed to mine so that he may hear both sides and judge for himself where there is dispute.

The main effort, however, has been to let Washington tell his own story as fully as possible in his own words. This is, indeed, as nearly an autobiography as I can make it. To Sparks' edition of the *Writings*, and Worthington C. Ford's immense improvement upon them, have been added, as sources, the splendid edition of the *Diaries* by John C. Fitzpatrick, which the Mount Vernon Ladies' Association of the Union was patriotic enough to publish without expurgation or correction. Letters not included in Ford or Sparks have been studied when available and the curators of manuscript collections consulted frequently. S. M. Hamilton's compilation of letters addressed to Washington has been of vital help. For this volume I have made particularly heavy draughts on the *Dinwiddie Papers*, edited by R. A. Brock for the Virginia Historical Society. They give a most vivid picture of the confusion and conflict of a period almost altogether ignored by historians.

The text has been read by Mr. Willard O. Waters of the Henry E. Huntington Library at San Gabriel, California (where there is an almost unrivalled collection of Washingtoniana), and by a profound scholar in early Virginia history who prefers to be anonymous here.

In illustrating the book, I am indebted to the Henry E. Huntington Library, the New York Public Library, and the Library of Congress for photographs of documents; to the curator of the Jumel Mansion for the portrait of Mary Philipse; to the Parkman estate and the publishers, Little, Brown and Company, for the privilege of reproducing the Mackellar plan of Braddock's battlefield proving that the English were not ambushed; and to Mr. Albert H. Heusser, the curator of the Passaic County Historical Society, for giving me his exquisitely clear map of Washington's expeditions. For the Index I am indebted to Mr. O. S. Wadleigh.

The bulk of this volume is devoted to a Washington that is all but unmentioned in the largest biographies. The material is rich in human interest and it covers the important period of his life, the formative. His mysterious love for Sally Fairfax, one of the most poignant of romances, finds its proper place in his biography for the first time.

In order to give full play to the unsuspected and influential experiences of his early life, I have ended this volume with his marriage and his retirement into what he supposed to be a future of unbroken domestic felicity.

Of all the things in the world he least expected a rebellion against his King. Indeed, being human, he had to take things as they came. He saw a little further ahead and more clearly than most men; he had extraordinary courage, developed self-control, and was a patriot of unusual fire and purity; but he was no oracle and no prophet.

My incessant effort in this biography has been to see his life as he saw it. All other biographers have tacitly assumed that he knew the future and builded himself grandly for it. They have looked backward upon him through the dazzling aureole of his apotheosis. But that was not the way he saw the world. He had to grope for his path and he missed few of the pitfalls, the thorns and torments of the way. No more did he miss the primroses, the festivals, the dances and sports and romances.

In a future volume devoted to "George Washington, the Rebel and the Conservative," I hope to show the blind evolution of the most loyal of Englishmen into the leader of insurgents who, seeking only to reclaim their rights as Englishmen, made the surprising discovery that the insurrection was a great civil war, and that the unthinkable try for independence, instead of being impossible and undesirable, was inevitable.

It was realized at the time, though afterwards forgotten, that the Revolution was over before the Revolutionary War began. Washington's part in that war, his merits and demerits as a soldier and a general offer fascinating and dramatic riches by no means exhausted, and much that has been hardly touched—for example, the amazing disclosures of the Headquarters Papers of Sir Henry Clinton recently acquired by the William L. Clements Library at Ann Arbor.

During the long years of chaos before the Constitution was finally squeezed through as a compromise, Washington enjoyed himself hugely as a farmer, a tobacco-planter, a manager of slave and white labor, a fisherman, huntsman, stock-breeder, real-estate speculator, race-track enthusiast, indefatigable ballroom attendant, and country gentleman.

During his eight years as president, he was alternately the idol and the abomination of the people; from being a man above party he was forced into partisanship, and with the wrong party. From being a rebel he became a conservative, an old-school aristocrat in a republican nation pushing on toward heights of democracy that were beyond him.

This is not to be imputed to his discredit, for he had done more than could be expected of any man. Only a tidal wave can push all the way up the beach, and then with destruction.

After two administrations he retired, in a storm of conflicting eulogy and abuse, to the rural life he loved.

The influences of his times upon his character, and of his character upon his times, the true truth about his personal life, his mental and religious and financial and physical history—these and other phases in which the facts are so much more picturesque than the fables, await the telling in a throng.

The materials are only too abundant. The difficulty is in selecting and arranging them so that they do no injustice to him or his times. But the effort will still be, to illuminate his background with the wisdom and the researches of the most eminent scholars and, above all things, to treat him as the best authority concerning his own soul, and to let him speak for himself.

APPENDIX I

NOTES AND REFERENCES

CHAPTER I

1. *A Perfect Description of Virginia.* London, 1649, p. 12. A vivid account of the Virginia settlement is given by Prof. Charles M. Andrews, *The Colonial Background of the American Revolution.* Yale University Press. 1924, p. 3, 101: "Virginia was always more than a setting for the romantic adventures of John Smith, John Rolfe, and Pocahontas, more even than the birthplace in America of self-government and the cradle of a new republic. It was the beginning of a great experiment in the field of English colonization and overseas expansion, the starting point of a great world movement which to-day has spread to the farthermost parts of the earth. Our own country, which is a product of this movement, emerged from it as an independent national state, but only after one hundred and seventy-five years of membership in the British colonial family; and it is in the light of such membership, therefore, that the colonial period of our history must be approached. . . .

"The planting of a settlement in Virginia was a commercial enterprise, undertaken by certain private individuals for the purpose of enlarging the trade of the English kingdom and of bringing a profit both to themselves and to those who had invested money with them.

"Before 1750 the colonies exported more than they imported and received cash in return, but after 1755 their imports from Great Britain began to exceed their exports, until the balance in Great Britain's favor amounted to nearly two millions in 1760 and nearly three millions in 1770."

G. L. Beer, *The Old Colonial System, 1660-1794,* II, p. 104, gives a full history of tobacco, the rivalry between Virginia and the English counties wherein tobacco was raised, the prices, wars, etc. He quotes a report of 1661 concerning colonial tobacco: "It Smells well, and paies more Custome to his Ma'tie than the East Indies four times ouer."

2. Captain John Smith, *Generall Historie,* 1627, p. 126. J. C. Ballagh in his *History of Slavery in Virginia,* p. 8, note, clears up the controversy concerning the first nation guilty of landing the first negroes, and proves that it was a Dutch ship, not a Virginian. He also discusses the gradual origin of the theory of property in the slave, and tells much about the Indian slaves. R. A. Brock, in his Prefatory Note to "The Fourth Charter of the Royal African Company of England," in the *Virginia Historical Coll.,* 1887, Vol. VI, p. 8, also refutes the claim, by Neill, that it was the rapacious Argall, Deputy Governor of Virginia, who instituted negro slavery.

3. R. A. Brock, in Winsor's *Narrative and Critical History,* III, 139.

4. Charles A. and Mary R. Beard, *History of the United States,* 1921,

p. 13. The following reference to Bancroft is by James Davie Butler, *American Historical Review*, October, 1896, article "British Convicts Shipped to American Colonies." Charles A. Beard, *An Economic Interpretation of the Constitution of the United States*, New York, 1925, p. 2, quotes Bancroft's words, "Having a hand full, he opened his little finger," as a proof that Bancroft felt under no obligations to tell the whole truth. Nevertheless, Bancroft constantly recurs in his writings to that "higher power" which is operating in human affairs. . . . It appears to him to be the whole course of history. He is not the only one who was unable to see in Washington anything but an instrument of Providence.

5. John Bernard, *Retrospections of America*, New York, 1887, p. 162.

6. Thomas J. Wertenbaker, *The Planters of Colonial Virginia* (Princeton University Press, 1922), p. 137-9. An excellent account of the criminal stock-jobbing by which settlers were cheated into Virginia, and the various methods of transporting and managing indented servants and convicts, is given in James Curtis Ballagh's *White Servitude in the Colony of Virginia* (Johns Hopkins University Studies, 1895).

7. John Spencer Bassett in the *American Historical Association Annual Reports*, 1901, Vol. I, p. 552. The reference to Collinson is quoted by Mrs. Roger A. Pryor, *The Mother of Washington and Her Times*, 1903, p. 49.

8. *The Expedition of Major General Braddock. . . . Being Extracts of Letters from an Officer*, London, 1755, pp. 5, 6, 8, 9.

9. Marquis de Chastellux, *Voyages*, translated as *Travels in North America*, London, 1787.

10. W. W. Hening, *Statutes at Large*, New York, 1823, II, 517.

11. This table and the letter are given in Sparks' edition of Washington's *Writings*, I, 546, but not in the edition of Ford, who, however, gives the letter to the nephew, XIII, 444, and a very full history of the final disentanglement of the Washington genealogy, XIV, 319-431. The Sulgrave ancestry was long suspected and Washington Irving describes in his *Life*, Chapter I, a pious pilgrimage he made to Sulgrave, where he saw the Washington crest in colored glass in the ruins of the manor house and the brass effigies of Lawrence and his wife and their children in the church floor. But Irving believed the legend that traced Washington back to one of William the Conqueror's Normans, named William de Heartburn, who was granted an estate called Wessyngton and took his name from it. Still more remarkable were the fantastic researches of Albert Welles, who in 1879 published a "Pedigree and History of the Washington Family from Odin, B.C. 70, to General Washington." Odin was, of course, the Norse deity, and on his way back to him, Welles took in Thorfinn, who explored the coast of New England as early as 1107—according to the fables. It was Henry F. Waters who cleared up the matter to the almost perfect satisfaction of all doubts, in his *English Ancestry of George Washington* (*N. E. Hist. and Genealogical Register*, Oct., 1889), also published separately the same year. Waters says, p. 22, of John and Lawrence: "Supposing them to have been young men of only ordinary enterprise and ambition . . . what chance had they in England at that time, known as belonging to a royalist family? . . . No wonder their thoughts turned to Virginia, that transatlantic haven . . . for defeated royalists."

12. Henry F. Waters, *An Examination of the English Ancestry of George Washington*, p. 25.

13. John H. Latané, *The Early Relations Between Maryland and Virginia* (Johns Hopkins University Studies, 1895), p. 33. He gives a full account of this conflict, and the welcome the Puritans received in Maryland, to which neglected chapter in history a monograph is devoted in Daniel R. Randall's *A Puritan Colony in Maryland* (Johns Hopkins University Studies, 1886). On p. 47 he says, "As Roger Williams was driven from the mother commonwealth of Massachusetts for holding heretical doctrine, so Durand, the Puritan elder, was expelled from the mother colony of Virginia to seek a new home for religious toleration. Both leaders came to lands unoccupied save by Indians and invited their brethren to follow. Both called the land to which they came through Divine guidance, 'Providence.'"

14. See Bishop Meade, *Old Churches and Families of Virginia*, II, 167. The will is reproduced in full in Ford's *Writings*, XIV, 391-6.

15. Benson J. Lossing, *Mary and Martha, the Mother and the Wife of George Washington*, p. 5.

16. Mrs. Roger A. Pryor, op. cit., p. 11.

17. H. C. and M. W. Green, *Pioneer Mothers of America*, I, 463; Mrs. R. A. Pryor, op. cit., p. 32.

18. G. W. P. Custis, *Recollections*, op. cit., p. 141.

CHAPTER II

1. M. D. Conway, *George Washington and Mount Vernon* (Long Island Historical Society), Introduction, p. xxix.

2. "A fact which has hitherto escaped the notice of biographers." Mrs. Roger A. Pryor, *The Mother of Washington and Her Times*, p. 75.

3. Conway, op. cit., p. xxviii, denies the frequent statement that the house burned down soon after Washington's birth. He places the acreage at 400 instead of the thousand given by Marion Harland in her *Story of Martha Washington*. Bishop Meade, in his *Old Churches*, II, 169, describes a visit he paid to the spot when only a brick chimney remained of the mansion, and when the burial vault could not be viewed "without distress and even disgust," though it had been filled with earth to prevent visitors from carrying away the bones of the dead, as they had begun to.

4. *The Literary Diary of Ezra Stiles*, edited by F. B. Dexter, II, p. 324, on March 3, 1779: "Gen. Washington's Birthday celebrated 11th ult. at Milton. He was born in Virginia in Co. of Westmoreland, Feb. 11th, 1732. So now aet. 47."

5. J. C. Fitzpatrick, *The Diaries of George Washington*, IV, 271, 298.

6. Mrs. Pryor's *The Mother of Washington*, p. 82.

7. H. R. McIlwaine, *The Struggle of Protestant Dissenters for Religious Tolerance in Virginia*, Johns Hopkins Univ. Studies, p. 21. Bishop Meade, op. cit., II, p. 162, states positively that Washington was baptized at Pope's Creek Church, already decaying in 1812, and hardly to be traced in 1837. He felt sure that the Reverend Archibald Campbell was Washington's pastor

and perhaps schoolteacher, though this is elsewhere contradicted in his own book (II, 161 n.).

8. In 1705, absence from church, misconduct there, "gaming, or tippling or travel upon the road, except to and from church (cases of necessity and charity excepted)," or work in the field, were punished by a forfeit of five shillings or fifty pounds of tobacco for every such offence, or "on the bare back, ten lashes, well laid on." These laws are found in W. A. Blakely's *American State Papers*, Washington, D. C., 1911, pp. 33-36; also in Hening's *Statutes at Large*, I, 123, 203, Mercer's *Laws of Virginia*, 320. Thomas Jefferson in his *Notes on the State of Virginia*, Query XVII, speaking of the persecuting disposition and intolerance of the Anglican settlers, states that "several acts of the Virginia Assembly of 1659, 1662 and 1693, had made it penal in parents to refuse to have their children baptized." Washington ignored the ordinance against travel and toil on Sunday all his life. In 1789 and 1790, he wrote to Jews and Seventh Day Baptists his disapproval of any laws fettering conscience. Yet even while President, he was arrested in Connecticut for having missed his way on Saturday and making up a few miles on Sunday. The tithing-man let him go only on a promise to limit his ride to the next town. Alice Morse Earle, *The Sabbath in Puritan New England*, p. 75.

9. The lawful perquisites consisted of a monopoly of marriage and burial fees and the use of the glebes. This tobacco-subsidy was the occasion of the famous "Parsons' Cause," in which Patrick Henry won his first spurs, and in which the greed of the Virginia clergy was exhibited. When, in 1755, owing to a great tobacco shortage, the people could not pay their tobacco debts in kind, the House of Burgesses passed an act making it lawful for debtors to pay in money at a rate accepted by all creditors, except some of the clergy, who petitioned the King to annul the act. Henry's uncle, the Reverend Patrick Henry, was among them. Others of the clergy resolved to share the public misfortunes. Three years later there was another shortage, the law was passed again, and "the clergy were the only class that determined to resist its operation." They became exceedingly unpopular, but persuaded the King to veto the law. "The Assembly and the Church were in declared antagonism." The clergy were declared to be the only creditors who wished to oppress the debtors. They won their lawsuits, however, and young Patrick Henry was engaged to oppose them. In the course of a speech that made the listeners' "blood to run cold and their hair to rise on end," he cast aside the argument that the people who made their own laws were committing treason, and denounced the grasping churchmen of Virginia in these words:

"We have heard a great deal about the benevolence and holy zeal of our reverend clergy, but how is this manifested? Do they manifest their zeal in the cause of religion and humanity by practicing the mild and benevolent precepts of the Gospel of Jesus? Do they feed the hungry and clothe the naked? Oh, no, gentlemen! Instead of feeding the hungry and clothing the naked, these rapacious harpies would, were their powers equal to their will, snatch from the hearth of their honest parishioner his last hoe-cake, from the widow and her orphan children their last milch cow! the last bed, nay, the last blanket from the lying-in woman!"

The clergymen received one penny damages and said, "The ready road to popularity here is to trample under foot the interests of religion, the rights of the Church and the prerogative of the Crown." It was proposed to try Henry for treason, but the matter was allowed to lapse, and the clergy lost not only their cause, but "greatly weakened their hold upon the public. It was the prelude to the great contest." William Wirt Henry, *Patrick Henry*, I, 29-46. Meade, I, 216-225, takes the side of the clergy.

10. Meade, *Old Churches*, I, 15, 16, 18, 18 n., 19, 21 n., 52-4, 163, 383; II, 237, *et passim*. I have strung together a few of his phrases from the pages enumerated. The evidence of the dissoluteness of the clergymen is found on every hand. It is not to be forgotten that Parson Weems, who crystallizes a certain Washington in the gum-arabic of his style, used to play the fiddle at dances when he was not selling books or exhorting. (Meade, II, 234-5.) Delightful accounts of Weems are given in Beveridge's *Life of John Marshall*, to whom Weems gave quaint advice on writing for popularity. Senator Beveridge (III, 231) calls Weems "part Whitefield, part Villon."

11. Quoting Colonel Byrd of Virginia, who travelled in New England in 1733 and found the Puritan clergymen far better, Bishop Meade denies even this, and cites a clergyman in Andover who "was able to count nearly forty ministers of the Gospel, none of whom resided at a very great distance, who were either drunkards or addicted to intemperate drinking. . . . He mentions an ordination at which he was pained to see two aged ministers literally drunk and a third indecently excited by strong drink."

The Great Revival began in New England in 1734 under the ghastly terrorism of Jonathan Edwards and George Whitefield, who frightened throngs into hysterics, if not virtue; but though Whitefield visited Williamsburg in 1740, no such spirit stirred Virginia; and the effect in New England was gone in five years. There is a full account of this outburst, its utter futility and the reaction against it in Herbert L. Osgood's *The American Colonies in the Eighteenth Century*, Columbia University Press, 1924, III, 407-449. He says, p. 426: "The colonies south of Pennsylvania and the Lower Counties were only superficially affected." The growth of dissent, the persecution of dissenters, and the clerical greed and corruption in Virginia are also given much space in this splendid work (III, 451-490).

It was a Virginia clergyman who wrote to the Bishop of London in 1725, "The people here are very zealous for our Holy Church . . . and yet at the same time supinely ignorant in the very principles of religion, and very debauched in morals. . . . The great cause of all which I humbly conceive to be in the clergy, the sober part being slothful and negligent, and others so debauched that they are the foremost and most bent on all manner of vices." (Meade, I, 385.)

Bishop Meade set all the historians a noble example. His one aim was the telling of the truth "without unfaithfulness to the task undertaken. In consenting to engage in it, . . . it became my duty to present an honest exhibition of the subject, and not misrepresent by a suppression of the truth. . . . I have gone as far as conscience and judgment would allow in the way of omission even of things which have passed under my own eyes. . . . Let us seek the truth. It is not only mighty and will prevail, but will do good in the hands of the God of truth. Often and truly has it been said of the Church, in certain ages and countries where evil ministers have abounded, that but for God's faithful promise, those ministers would long since have destroyed it."

12. The boundaries of the counties were constantly shifted in those days, and Truro parish covered a region from which a portion was split off to make Fairfax County, from which Loudoun County was later taken. The 2,500 acre estate that came to be so well known as Mount Vernon was successively in the counties of Westmoreland, Stafford, Prince William, and finally Fairfax.

13. Jonathan Boucher, *Reminiscences of an American Loyalist* (privately printed), 1925, p. 49.

14. This sexton, William Grove, may have been nicknamed "Hobby" or there may have been another teacher named Hobby. M. D. Conway, in *Washington and Mount Vernon*, xxx, states that Reverend Dr. Philip Slaughter's researches led him to believe that Hobby was sexton at Falmouth, two miles above the Washington farm, and that the Washington children went to school there. Washington's most successful biographer, Parson Weems (Mason L. Weems, *Life*, 1837, p. 10), who could not always have been wrong, states that "the first place of education to which George was ever sent, was a little '*oldfield school*,' kept by one of his father's tenants, named Hobby; an honest poor old man, who acted in the double character of sexton and schoolmaster. . . . In his cups—for though a *sexton*, he would sometimes drink, particularly on the General's birthdays—he used to boast that *''Twas he, who, between his knees, had laid the foundation of George Washington's greatness.'* "

15. Byrd's account of his visit to Spotswood's home and iron mines is contained in the *Westover Manuscripts*, Petersburg, 1841, and in *The Writings of Col. William Byrd*. Edited by John Spencer Bassett, N. Y. 1901, p. 373.

16. When Byrd called Spotswood "the Tubal Cain of Virginia, he corrected me a little there, by assuring me he was . . . the first in North America who had erected a regular Furnace." (Bassett's *Byrd*, p. 358.) The cinders of some of the old ironworks are still traceable, but Captain Washington seems to have sunk his money in the Principio Company, for he died land-poor.

17. Homer C. Hockett, *Political and Social History of the U. S., 1492-1828*. N. Y. 1926, p. 42. A beautiful little book by Dora Chinn Jett, *In Tidewater Virginia*, describes this region and is richly illustrated (privately printed, 1924). Fredericksburg was named after the Prince of Wales, who was the father of George III. The town is almost exactly sixty miles due north of Richmond and almost the same distance south-south-west of Washington. The country rises terrace by terrace, and back of the town are those lofty places known as Marye's heights. On December 13th, 1862, the Union Army under Burnside, marching from its headquarters at Falmouth, where George Washington perhaps went to school, nearly annihilated itself in wave on wave against the troops commanded by Longstreet, Stonewall Jackson and Robert E. Lee. A little north of here was Chancellorsville, where so much blood would run, and close to the south lay the dense forests called the Wilderness where, in 1864, Americans slaughtered Americans for a

month, and eighty thousand fell 'n a duel of endurance in which each army
lost over forty per cent of its strength.

18. John Spencer Bassett, *The Writings of Colonel William Byrd*, p.
356.

19. Weems, loc. cit., p. 13. Weems says the anecdote is "too valuable to
be lost, and too true to be doubted." If he made it up, as alleged, its
original source has not been traced. Mrs. Roger A. Pryor, in *The Mother
of Washington*, p. 85, refused to give up the venerable anecdote and says
that Washington read Weems' *Life* and mildly commended it. According to
W. S. Baker's *Bibliotheca Washingtoniana*, p. 31, Weems' first edition was
printed in 1800 and dedicated to Martha Washington. Other editions were
sold rapidly, but in 1808 the edition known as the sixth "is really the First
of the popular Weems 'Washington' as the well-known 'curious anecdotes'
promised in the title-page, such as the hatchet story, the cabbage-seed story,
the dream of his mother, etc., etc., appear in this volume for the first time."
By that time Washington had been dead for eight years. In an article in the
Critic for February, 1904, p. 116, Joseph Rodman discusses the Cherry Tree
legend, refers to Weems' confession in a letter to a friend that he introduced
imaginary anecdotes for their good effect, and then makes the striking statement that R. T. H. Halsey, in a book on blue Staffordshire pottery, published
five years before, described a rough earthenware mug, apparently made in
Germany between 1770 and 1790, decorated with a quaint illustration of the
cherry tree story, a large hatchet, the letters G. W., and the numerals 1776.
Halsey insisted that the glaze was previous to 1790 and suggested that the
story might have been current long before Weems flourished, and been wafted
across the Atlantic during Revolutionary times. This evidence is, of course,
too involved to be conclusive.

20. *The Minstrel, by James Beattie, LL.D., to which are now added Miscellanies by James Hay Beattie, A.M., with an account of his Life and
Character, London, 1799.* In the second volume, the father gives a touching account of his gifted but short-lived son's earthly life; telling how he
taught the boy "to speak the truth and keep a secret." When the child was
five and knew his alphabet but no religion, his father went secretly to the
garden and "wrote in the mould with my finger the three initial letters of
his name, and sowing garden cresses in the furrows, covered up the seed."
Ten days after, the boy "came running to me and with astonishment on his
countenance, told me that his name was growing in the garden." The
father said it was mere chance. The boy would not have it so, and the
father drew from this a lesson, that his body and all things must have a
cause, and "told him the name of the Great Being who made him." From
this simple story Weems cooked up an elaborate drama of dialogue and dialect
and childish exclamation.

21. Toner, Dr. J. M., *Washington's Rules of Civility and Decent Behavior*, Washington, D. C., 1888. Dr. Toner, who edited the boyish manuscripts, believed them to have been mainly his own composition, but Conway
(*George Washington and Mount Vernon*, xxxv) finds a resemblance to
the work of the Jesuit Mussipontarius *Communis Vitae inter homines scita
urbanitas* of which a French translation was published in 1617, and notes
that Washington's teacher, the Huguenot, Reverend James Marye, may well

have possessed a copy. In his *George Was iington's Rules of Civility*, N. Y. 1890, Conway gives as the most probable source of Washington's inspiration a work called *Bienséance de la Conversation entre les Hommes* published in 1595 by the pensioners of the College of La Flèche and translated as *Youth's Behaviour or Decency in Conversation Amongst Men* . . . translated by Francis Hawkins, London, 1640. The maxims may have been inspired in part by Sir Matthew Hale's *Contemplations: Moral and Divine*, London, 1605, of which a copy bearing Mary Washington's name was found in the library of Mount Vernon.

22. Conway, op. cit., xxxv.
23. Weems, *Life*, p. 23.
24. G. W. P. Custis, *Recollections*, p. 132. Lodge, in his *Life of Washington*, I, 45, puts the anecdote aside as apocryphal because "Custis gives no authority for his minute account of a trivial event over a century old when he wrote"; yet he admits it as certain that Washington "rode and mastered many unbroken thoroughbred colts, and it is possible that one of them burst a blood-vessel . . . and died."
25. Dr. Lyon G. Tyler, *Williamsburg, The Old Colonial Capital*, p. 30. Jonathan Boucher, op. cit., p. 49.
26. Conway, op. cit., xxxiv.
27. Weems, *Life*, p. 28.
28. There is a picture of the knife in *The Memorial to Washington*, published at Alexandria. The letter to Joseph Ball is quoted in Meade's *Old Churches*, II, p. 128.
29. Weems, *Life*, p. 28.
30. S. Weir Mitchell, *The Youth of Washington*, p. 76.

CHAPTER III

1. *The Virginia Magazine of History and Biography*, April, 1925-January, 1926, contains a series of articles on "The Proprietors of the Northern Neck," by Fairfax Harrison. Lord Fairfax's great-great-grandfather Culpeper had been one of the adventurers named in the original grants of 1609 and 1610.
2. This earliest known of the lifelong series of diaries that Washington kept so indefatigably is given *verbatim et literatim* in the splendid four-volume edition of *The Diaries of George Washington*, 1925, which the Mount Vernon Ladies' Association of the Union was patriotic and conscientious enough to publish complete, under the masterly editorship of John C. Fitzpatrick, curator of manuscripts at the Library of Congress. This work, from which I shall quote freely by permission, places before all interested persons the real Washington in constant contrast to the fabulous.

It is interesting to compare Mr. Fitzpatrick's fidelity to the illiterate but lovable youngster's own words with the version of Sparks, who begins his nefarious prettifying at the beginning and omits, re-writes, re-spells, re-punctuates and corrects this Journal ruthlessly. Sparks expurgates the lice and fleas, omits the touch of wit in the reference to "y. Game we catched y. Night before"; the "Rum Punch in Plenty" and removes all the life as well as the inelegance from the account of the Indian dance.

There is something unpardonable in deliberately rewriting Washington's words: "Last Night was a blowing and Rainy night. Our Straw catch'd a Fire yt. we were laying upon and was luckily Preserv'd by one of our Mens awaking when it was in a . . . we run of four Lots this Day," so that they read thus: "a blowing, rainy night. Our straw, upon which we were lying, took fire, but I was luckily preserved by one of our men awaking when it was in a flame. We have run off four lots this day."

In Worthington C. Ford's edition, the spelling is fairly well followed, the use of capitals whimsically followed, but the careful insertion of commas, periods and apostrophes changes the whole picture.

Bernard C. Steiner, in his *Life and Correspondence of James McHenry*, p. 91 n., says of a certain letter, that both Sparks and Ford print it carelessly. "From a careful comparison of the original of the letters of Washington to McHenry, there seems little reason for Ford to be praised over Sparks as an editor. He is little more careful and often merely builds on Sparks's foundation." Nevertheless, without Ford's edition of the *Writings*, we should be all at sea on Washington documents.

3. Dr. L. G. Tyler, *Williamsburg*, pp. 143, 202. Rev. Jonathan Boucher, *Reminiscences of an American Loyalist*, p. 49, says that Washington "first set out in the world as Surveyor of Orange County, an appointment of about half the value of a Virginia Rectory, i.e. perhaps one hundred pounds a year."

4. Charles Moore, *The Family Life of Washington*, 1926, p. 34.

5. Sally Nelson Robins, *Love Stories of Famous Virginians*, p. 27.

6. Charles Moore, op. cit., p. 33.

7. This incredibly large estate of Lord Fairfax had a history worthy of its size. J. Franklin Jameson, in his *The American Revolution Considered as a Social Movement* (Princeton University Press, 1926), p. 53, includes it among the great American estates, and speaks of its final disappearance as an "example of Tory confiscation on the grand scale."

In Samuel Kercheval's *History of the Valley of Virginia*, published in 1833 and concerned with the very Shenandoah Valley property which Washington surveyed, there is an account of Lord Fairfax's management that is far from flattering.

He tells of the first sixteen families that cut a road through from Pennsylvania in 1732 (the year of Washington's birth), among them Joist Hite, of their failure to perfect their titles, and Lord Fairfax's unwillingness to make a fair settlement with them (p. 46):

"Instead of granting these lands upon the usual terms allowed to other settlers, he availed himself of the opportunity of laying off in mannors, fifty-five thousand acres, in what is called the South Branch manor, and nine thousand acres on Patterson's Creek.

"This was considered by the settlers an odious and oppressive act on the part of his lordship, and many of them left the country. These two great surveys were made in the year 1747. To such tenants as remained, his lordship granted leases for ninety-nine years, reserving an annual rent of twenty shillings sterling per hundred acres; whereas, for all other immigrants only two shillings per hundred was reserved, with a fee simple title to the tenant."

Fairfax himself had a great lawsuit in England to establish his claim to so much territory, and it was settled by compromise. In the meanwhile, Kercheval, who was writing in 1833, goes on (p. 158):

"The profligate manner of granting away lands in immense bodies was unquestionably founded in the most unwise and unjust policy. Instead of promoting the speedy settlement and improvement of the county, instead of holding out to the bulk of society every possible encouragement to make the most speedy settlement and improvement in the new country, monopolies in several instances were given, or pretended to be sold to a few favorites of the governing powers, whereby these favorites were enabled to amass vast estates, and to lord it over the great majority of their fellow men. Such are the blessings of kingly government. But the people of this free and happy republic have abundant cause to rejoice and bless their God that this wretched kind of policy and high-handed injustice is done away, in the freedom and wisdom of our institutions, and that we have no longer our ears assailed, nor our understandings outraged, with the disgusting, high-sounding title of 'My Lord!' applied to poor frail human beings.

"It appears that Lord Fairfax, among others, was an attentive officer in the time of the Indian wars. In truth it behooved his lordship to be active. He had more at stake, and the command of greater funds, than any other individual member of society.

"The State of Maryland has lately set up a claim to a considerable tract of territory on the northwest border of Virginia, including a part of the Northern Neck."

Kercheval tells many other interesting things about Lord Fairfax (many of them scandalous) and the estate which as late as 1832 had set Virginia and Maryland in dispute. John Marshall was the lawyer for Hite and for the other tenants and defeated Lord Fairfax's counsel.

Kercheval's views are of value for the spirit of their times, but they were tainted with the anti-British violence of almost all post-revolutionary writings. A more just and accurate statement of the case of Lord Fairfax is given by Fairfax Harrison in his articles on "The Proprietors of the Northern Neck" (*Virginia Magazine of History and Biography*, April, 1925–January, 1926).

CHAPTER IV

1. An interesting anthology of the poetry of our Presidents might be made. I quote all that is extant of Washington's. Carl Sandburg, in his Abraham Lincoln, *The Prairie Years* (1926), quotes numerous specimens, including an inscription in a copy-book (p. 53) contrasting characteristically with Washington's Latin warning:

> "Abraham Lincoln
> his hand and pen.
> he will be good but
> god knows When."

And also an early lament beginning:

> "Time! what an empty vapor 'tis!
> And days how swift they are:
> Swift as an Indian arrow—
> Fly on like a shooting star,
> The present moment is here
> Then slides away in haste,
> That we can never say they're ours,
> But only say they're past."

But he gives no love poetry such as Washington indited. Perhaps the only published example of President Wilson's muse is given in James Kerney's *The Political Education of Woodrow Wilson* (1926), p. 481:

> There was a young girl from Missouri
> Who took her case to the jury.
> She said, "Car Ninety-three
> Ran over my knee."
> But the jury said, "We're from Missouri."

Washington was the only one apparently who wrote amorous verse.

2. M. D. Conway, *George Washington and Mount Vernon*, xxxv.

3. W. B. McGroarty, in an article on "Elizabeth Washington of Hayfield" (*Virginia Magazine of History and Biography*, April, 1925, p. 154), says that Alice Strother married Robert, or Robin, Washington. In his will, George Washington mentions "the acquaintances and friends of my juvenile years, Lawrence Washington and Robert Washington of Chotank." In a letter from G. W. P. Custis, 1851, quoted in the Schroeder-Lossing letters, he speaks of two aged and highly estimable gentlemen, Lawrence and Robin Washington, who had been companions of the Chief in his juvenile days. They spoke of the fine manly youth; and of his gallant demeanor and daring exploits in horsemanship, and the athletic exercises of that remote period.

4. Conway, op. cit., p. xxxvi, thinks the acrostic might have been written "to some fair Fanny" of Alexandria, Virginia, near Mount Vernon. Paul Leicester Ford in *The True George Washington*, p. 87, assigns the acrostic to a member of the family of Alexanders, who had a plantation near Mount Vernon. There are frequent references to the Alexanders in the *Diaries* and in 1772 Washington speaks of a Miss Alexander who spent the night at Mount Vernon with four other women and two men. Ford assigns the acrostic to a later period than that of the Lowland Beauty, and says it "proves there was a 'midland' beauty as well." But Sally Nelson Robins, in her carefully studied *Love Affairs of Famous Virginians*, Richmond, 1925, page 17, calls her "his first recorded 'love.' She happened when he was fifteen. . . . Alas, we know only her name." She credits the discovery of the acrostic to Mary Newton Stanard, author of *Colonial Virginia*, and gives the next to the last line as "Xerxes wasn't free from Cupid's Dart."

5. General B. T. Johnson, in his *General Washington*, p. 67. He names five of Washington's sweethearts, with this sweeping addendum: "not to mention the hundred other girls from Boston to Annapolis with whom the

young Virginian colonel flirted and made love. . . . The Virginian way always has been to make love to every pretty girl with whom he was thrown. Young, handsome, with the second fortune in the province, and a family as good as any . . . with the first military reputation among the soldiers Virginia's wars against the French and Indians had trained—with the grave, decorous manners of his generation, no man in Virginia would naturally be received . . . with more cordial welcome than Colonel Washington. . . .

"What wonder, then, that he fell in love with every pretty girl and told her so? . . . Washington was a man all over—a man with strong appetites, fierce temper, positive, belligerent, and aggressive." But he does not explain why this dazzling hero could not get himself accepted.

6. Jared Sparks, Washington's *Writings*, II, appendix No. 1. Though he reproduced part of this one letter in an appendix in small type, he sacrilegiously and without warning corrected the spelling, punctuation and grammar. He managed, by slight changes, to give an appalling lifelessness to its bubbling spirit of boyish exuberance. "So little gone and so much away!"

The historians and biographers who have all suppressed or ignored the amorous side of Washington's character have succeeded in making him the most terrifying and the least beloved character in history.

Nearly every writer about Washington has bewailed the fact that he is an unknown man, and much in need of being realized as human; then has gone ahead and hoisted him a little higher into the skies, gilding even his feet of clay and setting them on a pedestal so lofty that his heart is lost in the clouds. The fault of all of them is that their chief ambition has been to make him strut—and to strut alongside him, *haud passibus aequis*.

It is small wonder that even the people who were interested enough to wade through many volumes of Washington's Writings thought him a fish-blooded precisian; for they saw him, as through a glass darkly, in the chill correctness of an editor who dared to turn an almost illiterate lad into a rival of Dr. Samuel Johnson at his worst.

As an example of Sparks' audacity, it seems worth while to set his version of Washington's rampant boyishness alongside Washington's own words. It need hardly be said that Washington is on the right:

"DEAR FRIEND ROBIN,

As it is the greatest mark of friendship and esteem, which absent friends can show each other, to write and often communicate their thoughts, I shall endeavour from time to time, and at all times, to acquaint you with my situation and employments in life, and I could wish you would take half the pains to send me a letter by any opportunity, as you may be well assured of its meeting with a very welcome reception.

"DEAR FRIEND ROBIN,

As it's the greatest mark of friendship and esteem, absent friends can shew each other, in writing and often communicating their thoughts, to his fellow companions, I make one endeavor to signalize myself in acquainting you, from time to time, and at all times, my situation and employments of life, and could wish you would take half the pains of contriving me a letter by any opportunity, as you may be well assured of its meeting with a very welcome reception.

My place of residence at present is at his Lordship's (Lord Fairfax's), where I might, were my heart disengaged, pass my time very pleasantly, as there is a very agreeable young lady in the same house, Colonel George Fairfax's wife's sister. But that only adds fuel to the fire, as being often and unavoidably in company with her revives my former passion for your Lowland beauty; whereas, were I to live more retired from young women, I might in some measure alleviate my sorrow, by burying that chaste and troublesome passion in oblivion; and I am very well assured, that this will be the only antidote or remedy."

My place of Residence is at present at His Lordships where I might was my heart disengag'd pass my time very pleasantly as theres a very agreeable Young Lady Lives in the same house (Colo George Fairfax's Wife's Sister) but as thats only adding Fuel to fire it makes me the more uneasy for by often and unavoidably being in Company with her revives my former Passion for your Low Land Beauty whereas was I to live more retired from young Women I might in some measure eliviate my sorrows by burying that chast and troublesome Passion in the grave of oblivion or etarnall forgetfulness for as I am very well assured thats the only antidote or remedy that I shall be releivd by or only recess that can administer any cure or help to me as I am well convinced was I ever to attempt any thing I should only get a denial which would be only adding grief to uneasiness."

There is something fundamentally dishonest as well as hypocritically canting in re-writing Washington thus and not even saying so. But that is all that Sparks cares about Washington's young loves! Yet he devotes nearly five solid pages to the copy-book maxims called the "Rules of Civility," and quotes fifty-seven of the hundred, picking only the pompous ones and carefully cleaning up all the solecisms, of course.

7. In the preface to his *Life of Washington,* Irving confesses to "frequent use" of Sparks' edition of the Writings, and professes that "a careful collation of many of them with the originals convinced me of the general correctness of the collection, and of the safety with which it may be relied upon for historical purposes." A careless collation of Irving's quotations from Washington convinces me that, if he discovered any discrepancies, which I doubt, he followed Sparks none the less slavishly.

John Marshall was a Virginian, of course, and wrote a five-volume biography of Washington; but even Senator Beveridge, his biographer, finds it a monstrosity that nobody could read, and nobody bought except the indignant subscribers in advance. Parson Weems, who expected to sell the book, wrote Marshall: "Give old Washington fair play and all will be well." Marshall could not even get Washington born until the second volume.

8. The first part of this letter is quoted from W. C. Ford's transcription, in *Writings,* I, 7. The portion in the text is from his brother, Paul Leicester Ford's version, which has at least the air of being more exact: *The True George Washington,* p. 85.

9. Conway, op. cit., xxxviii, says that this Sally may have been, according to a correspondent, Reverend Horace E. Hayden, "either of his young contemporaries and relatives, Sarah Ball, Sarah (Ball) Jones, or Sarah Conway (niece of Colonel Edwin Conway, who married Mary Ball's half-sister). The fair alluded to was probably that of June, though there was also an annual October fair in Fredericksburg."

10. In Paul Leicester Ford's *The True George Washington*, p. 86, this paragraph is quite differently transcribed: "I Pass the time of[f] much more agreeabler than what I imagined I should as there's a very agrewable Young Lady lives in the same house where I reside (Colo George Fairfax's Wife's Sister) that in a great Measure cheats my thoughts altogether from your Parts I could wish to be with you down there with all my heart but as it is a thing almost Impractakable shall rest myself where I am with hopes of shortly having some Minutes of your transactions in your Parts which will be very welcomely receiv'd."

11. General B. T. Johnson, op. cit., p. 67.

12. Sally Nelson Robins, *Love Stories of Famous Virginians*, p. 19.

13. In Meade's *Old Churches*, II, 480, is an account of the family history furnished by Dr. Henry Faunt Le Roy.

14. The portrait of Betsy is reproduced in *The Memorial to Washington* published by the Lodge at Alexandria, Va.

15. Quoted from a letter in E. J. Lee's, *Lee of Virginia*, Philadelphia, 1895, p. 288, written by Alice Lee of Stratford in 1722 to a kinsman in London who had threatened to retard her "success in the Matrimonial Way." She says: "I am little more than twelve years old. . . . And yet I pretend not to ridicule the holy sacred institution . . . you can't forbear a fling at femalities; believe me Curiosity is as imputable to the Sons as the Daughters of Eve. . . . The Annapolis Races Commence the 6th of October. The American Compy. of Players are there and said to be amazingly improved. I should like to see them, as I think Theatrical Entertainments a rational amusement."

The reference to girlish profanity as commonplace is from *The Journals and Letters of Philip Vickers Fithian*, edited by John Roger Williams, p. 84. According to Maud Wilder Goodwin's *The Colonial Cavalier*, p. 67, Jefferson wrote to Rebecca Burwell, Christmas, 1762: "Tell Miss Alice Corbin . . . the rats knew I was to win a pair of garters from her, or they never would have been so cruel as to carry mine away."

16. Meade's *Old Churches*, I, 108; II, 481. The story was contributed by Mary Cary's grandson, Edward Ambler, to Bishop Meade's book, but in the privately printed work, *Sally Cary*, by Captain Wilson Miles Cary, it is stated, p. 22, note, by the editor who had the family letters before him, that though they passed numerously between Belvoir and Hampton and are "profuse in all such matters," there are no suggestions that Washington was ever seriously interested in Mary Cary. This same editor denies that Washington could have proposed for Sally's hand, as has been suggested, since he was only sixteen when Sally married Fairfax.

17. Wilson Miles Cary, *Sally Cary*, p. 21.

18. Tyler's *Quarterly Historical and Genealogical Magazine*, Richmond, Va., Jan., 1926, p. 176.

CHAPTER V

1. The Journal is included entire in Fitzpatrick's edition of the *Diaries*, I, 17. It was first published by Dr. J. M. Toner in 1892 as *The Daily Journal of Major George Washington in 1751-2*. In his appendix is a very full account of Lawrence Washington's life and career.

2. Dr. Toner, in *The Daily Journal*, p. 53, notes that "blessings sometimes come in disguise," and the "immunity purchased by this sickness . . . was not an unmixed evil."

3. M. L. Weems, *Life*, p. 24.

4. In Meade's *Old Churches*, II, 480, Dr. Henry Faunt Le Roy, speaking of Betsy, says that she "became the wife of Mr. Adams, of James River, after having refused her hand to General Washington." The eldest of the sons, William and Moore, were "sent to Europe (home, as it was then called) to be educated." One of the other seven children was killed at the battle of Monmouth on his twenty-first birthday. Dr. Faunt Le Roy does not mention Betsy's first marriage to Bowler Cocke, the account of which I take from Mrs. Sally Nelson Robins' *Love Stories*, p. 18. In Miss Dora Chinn Jett's *In Tidewater Virginia*, p. 137, it is stated that the ruins of the old brick mansion at Naylor's Hole disappeared only a few years ago. There is a pretty legend that, a few years after Betsy jilted Washington, he rode through Williamsburg, not only a colonel of the colonial troops, but also the rich proprietor of Mount Vernon, which he had inherited; and that Betsy Fauntleroy, seeing him in all his majesty and realizing that she had married only a Mr. Adams, fainted. Perhaps she did, but the story is denied. Besides, it is told with even less plausibility of Mary Cary.

5. Marion Harland, *Some Colonial Homesteads*, pp. 94, 484.

6. The date of the marriage is given by Moncure D. Conway, in his *Washington and Mount Vernon* (xxxvi). In *The Virginia Magazine of History and Biography*, April, 1913, p. 196, is a partial list of Virginians who were educated in England. It includes Lawrence Washington and William Fauntleroy, 1760, but omits Edward Ambler. Mary Cary's grandson, Edward Ambler, contributed an account of her to Meade's *Old Churches*, I, 109, in which he tells the story of her father rejecting Washington's suit because Mary had her own carriage. The same story is told of Mary's elder sister Sally, who married George William Fairfax and won Washington's most serious and lasting love. Conway says that Sally's "legendary love affair with Washington is impossible before her marriage on December 17th, 1748" when Washington was only seventeen, but does not deny the possibility of it afterward. Mrs. Sally Cary Robins, however, in her *Love Stories of Famous Virginians*, p. 28, speaks of Mary Cary as one who was "thought to be Washington's sweetheart until the truth of Sally was revealed."

7. Meade's *Old Churches*, I, 109. In Edward Ambler's story of Mary Cary, he says that Colonel Cary's rebuff of "the stripling Washington produced the independence of the United States, and laid the foundation of the future fame of the first of heroes and the best of men—our immortal Washington; as it was more than probable that, had he obtained possession of the large fortune which it was known Miss Cary would carry to the

altar with her, he would have passed the remainder of his life in inglorious ease.

"It may be added, as a curious fact, that the lady General Washington afterward married resembled Miss Cary as much as one twin-sister ever did another."

8. Fitzpatrick, *Diaries*, I, p. 387 note.

9. Charles Moore, *The Family Life of Washington*, p. 39, "He was a devoted member of that order. He held office in the Alexandria Lodge, which still possesses the furniture of his day. Later he encouraged Masonry in the Continental Army, because of the fraternal feelings it promoted among soldiers and officers, and also because it served to mitigate rancor in the case of captives." Charles H. Callahan, of Alexandria, has written a privately printed work on *Washington the Man and the Mason*.

10. *Dinwiddie Papers*, I, 41.

11. All the historians state the pay as £150 a year, but Dinwiddie, in his accounts, puts it at £100. *Dinwiddie Papers*, I, 390.

CHAPTER VI

1. Randolph Greenfield Adams, *A History of the Foreign Policy of the United States*, New York 1926, p. 21. Clarence Walworth Alvord, *The Mississippi Valley in British Politics*, Cleveland, 1917, Vol. I, 85, 87. John H. Latané, *The Early Relations Between Virginia and Maryland* (Johns Hopkins University Studies, 13th Series, III, IV). There is an excellent clearing up of the boundary tangles in the monograph on *The Virginia Frontier*, 1754-1763, by Dr. Louis K. Koontz (Johns Hopkins University Studies, 1925). He believes (p. 61) that the grant of 1609 "gave Virginia a good title to the famous Forks of the Ohio."

2. Albert T. Volwiler, *George Croghan and the Western Movement* (Cleveland, 1926), p. 21. Edward Channing, *History of the United States* (1910), II, 555, says that the French leader Céloron "when he made his famous journey down the Ohio kept coming across English traders . . . the English influence was strong beyond the mountains . . . but it does not seem that there were any persons who can properly be called English settlers west of the mountains in 1750. The French, on the other hand, had established many permanent settlements."

3. Volwiler, op. cit., p. 24. Washington Irving, in his *Life*, Vol. I, Ch. V, tells the stories of Gist and Croghan with much recognition of the value of their services.

4. Volwiler, op. cit., p. 40, 45, 78.

5. Alvord, op. cit., I, p. 88, 89.

6. Sparks, *Writings*, II, p. 481. Perhaps it was the memory of the permanent ruin inflicted on Spanish prosperity by the Inquisition that led the King of Spain of a slightly later period to the desperate experiment of a hitherto intolerable tolerance, for in the *Literary Diary of Ezra Stiles*, President of Yale, III, p. 364-5, there is the following reference to an effort to attract settlers to the fur-trading post of St. Louis, in upper Louisiana:

"The King of Spain has this year begun a City on the West side of

Mississippi at the Mouth of Missouri. And published a Proclama. to invite Settlers . . . with great Immunities and Privileges—allows free Liby. of Conscience in Religion, gives 400 Acres to a Family & Cows & farmg. Utensils & ten years freedom from Taxes." Dr. Stiles prophesied prosperity and an influx of settlers, who would eventually rebel against Spain.

The financial danger of religious persecution is emphasized in H. C. Lea's, *A History of the Inquisition of Spain*, 1922, vol. II, p. 331. "It would be difficult to overestimate the wide-spread damage resulting when the accused were merchants . . . as in the immense confiscations in Mexico and Peru. . . . The hazards to which business was thus exposed was a factor, and by no means the least important in the decay of Spanish commerce, for no one could foresee at what moment the blow might fall." P. 386, "To it also is greatly attributable the stagnation of Spanish commerce and industry, for trade could not flourish when credit was impaired, and confidence could not exist when merchants and manufacturers of the highest standing might, at any moment, fall into the hands of the tribunal and all their assets be impounded. . . . The Inquisition came at a time when geographical discovery was revolutionizing the world's commerce . . . and the future belonged to the nations which should have fewest trammels in adapting themselves to the new developments. The position of Spain was such as to give it control of the illimitable possibilities of the future, but it blindly threw away all of its advantages into the laps of heretic Holland and England."

In Lea's *The Inquisition in the Spanish Dependencies*, he tells how all the colonies suffered steady deterioration. P. 512: "To this, the Inquisition contributed not only as a leading factor in internal misgovernment, but also by its hideous system under which the affluence of the tribunals depended upon the confiscations which they could levy."

7. Parkman, *Montcalm and Wolfe*, I, 48.

8. Volwiler, op. cit., 67, 69, 72, 76-77.

9. The founders of the company, in 1748, were thirteen Virginians and one Quaker merchant, Hanbury, in London. It was Hanbury who sent Braddock through Virginia for the sake of the Ohio Company. Thomas Lee and the Washington brothers, Lawrence and Augustine, were the chief magnates. Lee died and Lawrence Washington became the head of the company. Governor Dinwiddie and George Mason bought in. When Lawrence died, Dinwiddie took control (Brock, in *Dinwiddie Papers*, I, p. 17 n.). Channing, *History of the United States*, II, p. 557, notes that the royal grant was two hundred thousand acres "with a promise of 300,000 more if a hundred families were settled within seven years, and a fort built and maintained." This explains the discrepancy between historians, some of whom give the grant as 200,000 acres, and some as 500,000.

Robert Dinwiddie (1693-1770), a Scot, had been trained in a counting-house and, as a collector of customs in Bermuda, had exposed an elaborate system of fraud, and had been promoted to Inspector-General. In 1743 he detected enormous defalcation in the revenues from Barbados. Then he was appointed Lieutenant-Governor of Virginia. He was the acting governor from November 20th, 1751 (when he arrived with his wife and two daughters), till the end of 1757, when he retired broken in health and spirits (R. A. Brock, editor, in *Dinwiddie Papers*, I, viii-ix).

Dr. Louis K. Koontz, in his *The Virginia Frontier, 1754-1763* (Johns Hopkins University Studies, 1925), p. 36, tells of Dinwiddie's clashes with the Assembly. The home government complained that Virginia was paying her debts in a bad quality of tobacco. Dinwiddie, who was used to grafters, accused the Virginians of cheating and advised close inspection and the closing of many warehouses. This brought on such a crisis in tobacco that the frontier was neglected.

Dinwiddie made a further bad start by attempting to pick up a little graft on his own. When he arrived, he found waiting for him in his new office a thousand land patents to sign. Precedent justified him in asking a small fee for his seal. He wanted only a pistole per seal—about $3.50 in our money—but it meant thirty-five hundred dollars in his pocket. The House of Burgesses emitted a ferocious howl and though the Governor got his pistole fees, he lost his popularity and began a long war with the House, which refused him support money and supplies at critical moments out of sheer hostility. Great injustice has been done to him by historians, his good deeds in Washington's behalf are forgotten and his moments of impatience magnified. At all times he was better to Washington than the Virginians were and constantly intervened to protect him. His correspondence and other official records were published in two volumes by the Virginia Historical Society in 1883, splendidly edited by R. A. Brock with copious notes. This volume leans very heavily upon them in describing this formative period of Washington's life, which has been greatly neglected by other biographers.

10. Mrs. Roger A. Pryor, *The Mother of Washington*, p. 120.

11. The Journal is printed in Ford's *Writings*, I, 9, also in Fitzpatrick's *Diaries*, I, p. 43. But two copies of the original edition are known. Ford's transcription was made from the London edition of 1754.

12. Gist's *Journal* is published in the Collections of the Massachusetts Historical Society, Series 3, Vol. V.

13. Dinwiddie's letter and St. Pierre's answer are given in full in Hulbert's *Historic Highways*, III, p. 108.

14. Two years later St. Pierre was killed in battle on the Canadian border, leading a troop of Indians in "the bloody morning-scout" preceding the battle of Lake George where Dieskau was defeated and captured by William Johnson.

15. Professor Hulbert, op. cit., III, p. 114, calls this "a fit place for Joincare's assassin to lie in wait," but there is no justification whatever for charging him or the French with even a discourtesy, to say nothing of a diabolical plot, which, if devised, could have been carried out a hundred times with perfect certainty.

16. It is interesting to note that Jared Sparks, in his *Life of Washington* (1844), p. 32, fails to mention the rum. He says, "An apology, seconded by the more substantial token of a present, soothed her wounded dignity."

17. Jonathan Boucher, *Reminiscences of an American Loyalist* (1925), p. 49.

18. Herbert L. Osgood's *The American Colonies in the Eighteenth Century* (Columbia University Press, 1924), vol. III, ch. XVII, gives a brief review of the work of Logan, Conrad Weiser and many others who far anticipated Washington's performances and ideas. Winsor's *Narrative and*

Critical History is replete with references. Professor Frederic L. Paxson, in his *History of the American Frontier*, p. 65 note, states that when Archer Butler Hulbert was made professor at Marietta College, he came upon valuable manuscripts that led to many important works. In his *Washington and the West*, 1905, Hulbert published Washington's Diary of September, 1784, with a scholarly introduction. In his sixteen-volume *magnum opus* called *Historic Highways*, 1902, he has accumulated a vast amount of difficult information, eloquently emphasizing the vital importance of roads in our history. It is a work of high merit, but marred somewhat, perhaps, by too great a zeal to prove Washington's lonely grandeur as the father of the West, a great frontiersman and a prophet of amazing vision. In *Washington and the West* (p. 4), he exclaims: "Washington was our first expansionist, not for expansion's sake, truly, but for country's sake and duty's."

Surely, this is pure poetry. Aside from Franklin, there were thousands of American expansionists before Washington, and his ruling motive was no more for his country's good nor in the line of duty than theirs; nor was he less interested in the legitimate financial profits that might follow the sale or development of huge uninhabited tracts. As Professor Paxson says (p. 17), "The young George Washington . . . was already infected with the common virus of land desire." On page 10 of *Washington and the West*, Professor Hulbert tells how Washington, years later, "as ultimate commander of that expedition, became possessed of the lion's share [of the bounty lands], and he had shrewdly added to his holdings by purchasing other claims held by officers and soldiers under him who preferred ready money to a Colonial governor's promise. Washington bought the promises." Thus he gained patents for about 30,000 acres, and surveys for about 10,000 more. "Compared to some alleged private holdings, such as claimed by Richard Henderson and George Croghan, this was a small quantity; but it explains in full Washington's knowledge of the Western problem; it makes it very clear that when he wrote de Chastellux, 'Would to God we may have wisdom enough to improve the opportunity,' he knew full well the meaning of his ringing words."

This does not lack for ardor, but it would apply as well to a hundred men of Washington's time. The business of buying up for a song the claims of other soldiers has usually been given a rather ugly name when other people have done it, though their motives may have been as honorable as Washington's.

Dinwiddie is generally abused for a few controversies with Washington, and the fact is usually overlooked that he "discovered" the young man, gave him his chance, quarreled with him, but praised him, published his first journal and won him promotion, even asking a royal commission for him. As Dinwiddie was sixty-three years old at this time and a sufferer from paralysis, his energy was beyond praise.

Thomas E. Watson in his *Life and Times of Jefferson*, p. 150, says: "Prof. John Fiske falls into a flutter of wonder and admiration because Governor Dinwiddie selected so young a man as Washington to carry a message into the Ohio woods. Really there was no cause for the professor's excitement. The most casual enquiry into the facts clears up the mystery . . .

the two elder brothers of Washington were directors in the [Ohio] company; Gov. Dinwiddie was a member of the company; and Christopher Gist was the surveyor of the company."

Professor Hulbert is convinced that God himself selected Washington. In his *Historic Highways*, III, 87, he speaks amazingly of "the Indian, that race over which no man ever wielded a greater influence than Washington." Dr. Koontz, op. cit., p. 64, speaks of him as "one of those men whom the Indians both loved and feared and who appears never to have lost his influence over Indians who had once become attached to him."

This is astonishing, since at this time Washington could have had no influence at all on account of Indian respect for age, which was one thing Washington lacked. His own Journal shows his hopeless inability to sway the Indians. Furthermore, he was later ridiculed by the Half-King and called a slave-driver by other Indians. He never lost his influence, because he never gained any.

Professor Hulbert goes on: "He was to be, under Providence, a champion of that West worthy of its influence on human affairs. . . . No statesman of his day knew and believed in the West as Washington did. . . . The same divine Providence which directed this youth's steps into the Alleghenies, had brought him speedily to his next post of duty."

This may be maintained now, for it is easy to write history a hundred years after the event and distribute the rewards as fortune has done, but judging by the series of failures and catastrophes that hounded the young Washington at every step, there was little reason for satisfaction, not to say pious gratitude, at that time. And it is a perverted patriotism that robs dozens of brave and self-sacrificing Americans of their deserved encomiums in order to heap a mountain of them on the splendid youth who became George Washington. Nor is it quite decent to forget that other nations were doing as brilliant and courageous work: English, Irish, French, German, Dutch, Swiss. As for heroes, the woods were full of them.

Professor Hulbert speaks even of Washington's Journal in superlatives (*Highways*, III, 120): "No literary production of a youth of twenty-one ever electrified the world as did the publication of the *Journal* of this dauntless envoy of the Virginian governor." But the Journal told nothing that was not already well known; it merely described the delivery of a warning message and the return with the answer from the French, who refused to move, who, in fact, soon advanced and administered disastrous defeats.

19. Volwiler, op. cit., p. 66. As an offset to giving Washington a monopoly of the credit for the opening of the West, Volwiler's *George Croghan* is an invaluable work, fully documenting its immense research.

20. The *Dinwiddie Papers*, vol. I, contain the letters he wrote to the various governors and to England, enclosing Major Washington's Journal, also his honeyed letter to the various Indian chiefs. The reiteration of his frantic appeals for help becomes very eloquent in view of the cynicism with which his all-too-well-founded warnings were received. In reading these extremely human letters of this sick but indefatigable old gentleman, one grows very fond of him and resents the chill contempt with which most historians dismiss or belie him.

21. A comment in the Pennsylvania Archives, II, 238, quoted in Ford, *Writings*, I, p. 40 n.

22. *Dinwiddie Papers*, I, p. 74-5.

23. Dinwiddie, writing to Governor Hamilton of Pennsylvania, February 23, 1754, said, "As I am engag'd to meet the Chiefs of the several Tribes of Ind's at Winchester next May, w'ch the Cha[rge]s attending this Expedition to the Ohio makes our Assembly backward in loading the Country with more Expenses, therefore do not appoint any Comm[issione]rs for Albany." (*Dinwiddie Papers*, I, 81.)

24. James Truslow Adams, *Revolutionary New England, 1691-1776*, p. 214-215, 215 note. Channing, *History of the United States*, II, p. 569-571, says that Franklin "was not the only one to propose plans of union at that conference or Congress, as it is usually termed. Indeed, the idea of inter-colonial union seems to have been widespread at that time. Thomas Hutchinson of Massachusetts, Meshech Weare of New Hampshire, and the Reverend John Peters of Pennsylvania have also left plans of union in their own handwriting. The consideration of the subject at Albany seems to have been due to Governor Shirley of Massachusetts, but it is not clear that he acted on the initiative of the English Government." He describes another scheme prepared by Lords of Trade in August, 1754, providing for a military union, with a representative from each colony, to determine the quota of troops and money to be raised by each colony, the commander-in-chief to be appointed by the King. Though the failure of the Albany Plan to interest the colonies caused this plan to be dropped, the later appointment of Governor Shirley to be commander-in-chief of all the forces on the continent, "may be regarded as acting in conformity with the project of the Lords of Trade."

The suggestion that the colonies would inevitably unite and strike for independence had been discussed thoroughly by the Swedish botanist, Prof. Peter Kalm, who travelled in America in 1748 and published his observations. A translation of them published in 1771 is quoted in Hart's *American History told by Contemporaries*, II, 352.

Osgood, in *The American Colonies in the Eighteenth Century*, III, 578-580, emphasizes the great importance of Shirley in urging "colonial union under conditions that would not weaken imperial control." As early as 1748 Shirley had written of his fears that "a disunion of councils among His Majesty's colonies . . . would in the course of a long war prove destructive to the whole." He dreaded the "fatal infatuation" that would lead the colonies to be destroyed by a much inferior force for lack of co-operation at the point of attack. It was just this that led to the ruination of Dinwiddie's fine plans and the catastrophes that piled on Washington. Osgood says that "Franklin was the only colonist whose services in this direction were comparable with those of Shirley." Winsor, in his *Narrative and Critical History*, V, p. 611-3, gives much bibliographical information, and states that as early as 1752, "Dinwiddie had urged northern and southern confederacies." His cautious and unfavorable opinion of the Plan of Union is referred to in various letters (I, 157, 260, 283).

25. *Dinwiddie Papers*, I, p. 99.

26. *Dinwiddie Papers*, I, p. 170, 204, 205.

27. Louis K. Koontz, op. cit., p. 53. There is an interesting historical account of this and other Dinwiddie battles with the legislature in Dr. James Miller Leake's *The Virginia Committee System and the American Revolution* (Johns Hopkins University Studies, 1917), p. 47.

CHAPTER VII

1. Mrs. Pryor, *The Mother of Washington*, p. 118.
2. *Dinwiddie Papers*, I, 59.
3. Ignorant of the recently discovered fact that Washington was not commissioned until he was nearly twenty-two (see Chapter V, page 68), General H. B. Carrington, himself a great Indian fighter, in his *Washington the Soldier* (1899) p. 5, states that Washington, "at the age of nineteen was appointed Military Inspector, with the rank of Major. In 1752 he became the Adjutant-General of Virginia." But there were four Adjutants-General, and while their duties were "to inspect the militia at stated times in the manner prescribed by law" (*Dinwiddie Papers*, I, p. 49 n.), the stated times were far apart, and Washington could have had practically no chance to familiarize himself with the task of maneuvering troops, and must have had little or no experience, however much he may have learned of theory in what General Carrington describes as his preparation:

"As soon as Washington entered upon the duties of his office, he made a systematic organization of the militia his first duty. A plan was formulated, having special reference to frontier service. His journals and the old Colonial records indicate the minuteness with which this undertaking was carried into effect. His entire subsequent career is punctuated by characteristics drawn from this experience. Rifle practice, feats of horsmanship, signalling, restrictions of diet, adjustments for the transportation of troops and supplies with the least possible encumbrance; road and bridge building, the care of powder and the casting of bullets, were parts of this system. These were accompanied by regulations requiring an exact itinerary of every march, which were filed for reference, in order to secure the quickest access to every frontier post. The duties and responsibilities of scouts sent in advance of troops, were carefully defined. The passage of rivers, the felling of trees for breastworks, stockades, and block-houses, and methods of crossing swamps, by corduroy adjustments, entered into the instruction of the Virginia militia." Washington looked to all these points later, but not at this time.

4. Ford, *Writings*, I, p. 42; *Dinwiddie Papers*, I, p. 92.
5. Ford, *Writings*, I, 43, 44 n. The Reverend Jonathan Boucher, in his *Reminiscences of an American Loyalist*, p. 49, said of Washington, "When soon after a regiment was raised in Virginia, he had interest enough to be appointed the Lieutenant-Colonel of it, or rather, I believe, at first the Major only. A Colonel Jefferson [*sic*] who had formerly been grammar master at the College, commanded." Edward Channing, *History of the United States*, II, p. 559, puts it more gracefully when he says that Washington "was already favorably known to many influential persons. Of all men in history, not one so answers our expectations as Washington. Into whatever

part of his life the historian puts his probe, the result is always satisfactory." This again is epic poetry rather than cold chronicle.

6. *Dinwiddie Papers*, I, 106. The payroll is interesting; it is given on pp. 112-116, 172 as follows:

Colo. Joshua Fry	
Com'd'r in Chief	15 s. per day and £100 per ann. for his Table.
Geo. Washington, Esq'r,	
Lieut Colo.	12 shillings 6 pence
—— Muse, Major	10
Wm. Trent, Captain	8
Robert Stobo, do.	8
Jacob Vanbraam, Lieut.	4
—— Craick, Surgeon	4

The private men received 8 pence per day.

This Dr. James Craik, a Scotsman born a year before Washington, graduated at Edinburgh, served with him here, at Braddock's Field, and during the Revolution, when he helped unveil the conspiracy to remove Washington from command. Afterward, he settled near Mount Vernon where he took care of Washington's family and slaves, attended Washington's deathbed and lived on for fifteen years. His son, named George Washington Craik, was Washington's private secretary during his second administration.

7. Volwiler, *George Croghan and the Westward Movement*, p. 83 n.

8. Volwiler, op. cit., p. 84.

9. The English translation of the Journal is reproduced in Fitzpatrick's edition of the *Diaries*, I, p. 73. In Ford's *Writings*, I, p. 46, is a revision of his own, including some of Washington's letters.

10. Fitzpatrick, *Diaries*, I, p. 79; Ford, *Writings*, I, p. 53.

11. Ford, *Writings*, I, p. 54 n.

12. *Dinwiddie Papers*, I, p. 151.

13. *Dinwiddie Papers*, I, p. 170.

14. Volwiler, op. cit., p. 89.

15. *Dinwiddie Papers*, I, p. 120, 121.

16. This letter of May 18th, 1754, I must quote from Ford, *Writings*, I, p. 63, who quotes from Sparks' carefully edited version. The true flavor of the author comes out in his next letter, which is given *verbatim et literatim* in the Virginia Historical Society's edition of the *Dinwiddie Papers*, I, p. 171, 176. The *Dinwiddie Papers* contain (I, p. 169) a letter from Washington of May 18, 1754, but no complaints, yet on May 25th Dinwiddie (I, p. 171) answers his "complaints" of May 18th. Perhaps Sparks removed that portion from the files available to Brock, editor of the Dinwiddie papers.

17. The pay had been set by the Militia Law of 1748 at 50 pounds of tobacco a day for a colonel, 40 for a major, 15 for a private. In 1754 this was commuted to 15 shillings for a colonel, 12s. 6d. for a Lieutenant-Colonel, 10s. for a major, 8s. for a captain, and 8 pence for a private, besides his enlistment pistole. *Dinwiddie Papers*, I, p. 176; Ford, *Writings*, I, p. 77 n.

18. *Dinwiddie Papers*, I, p. 174.

19. *Dinwiddie Papers*, I, p. 175.

CHAPTER VIII

1. Reuben Gold Thwaites, *France in America*, p. 162-4.
2. Gen. B. T. Johnson, *General Washington*, p. 31.
3. *Dinwiddie Papers*, I, p. 179. The rest of this account is taken from Washington's letter of May 29, 1754, to Dinwiddie.
4. A. B. Hulbert, *Historic Highways*, III, p. 135.
5. *Dinwiddie Papers*, I, p. 179.
6. Washington rarely got a foreign name right. "Sprilldorph" was really Carolus de Splitdorph, who was later killed at Braddock's Defeat.
7. Peyronney, really William Chevalier de Peyronie, was a Huguenot who settled in Virginia. He has been referred to as a dancing-master. He was badly wounded at Fort Necessity and so poor as to have to ask the Assembly for money to buy new clothes. He received a vote of thanks and was promoted to captain in time to get killed at Braddock's Defeat. Exactly the same honors and death befell William Poulson. Ensign Waggener was also thanked by the Burgesses and died at Braddock's Defeat.
8. Quoted in Ford, *Writings*, I, p. 124. Weiser's report is included in *An Enquiry into the Causes of the Alienation of the Delaware and Shawanese Indians from the British Interests*, London, 1759.
9. *Dinwiddie Papers*, I, p. 186. Captain McKay's name is also spelled Mackay and Mackaye.
10. Ford, *Writings*, I, p. 89.
11. Horace Walpole, *Memoirs of George II*, I, p. 347. Sir George Trevelyan, in his famous work, *The American Revolution* (I, p. 53), makes a curiously blundering account of this whole affair, when, in lauding Washington, he says:

"At twenty-two he fought his first battle, with forty men against five and thirty, and won a victory, on its own small scale, as complete as that of Quebec. The leader of the French was killed, and all his party shot down or taken. It was an affair which, coming at one of the rare intervals when the world was at peace, made a noise as far off as Europe, and gained for the young officer in London circles a tribute of hearty praise, with its due accompaniment of envy and misrepresentation. Horace Walpole gravely records in his Memoirs of George the Second that Major Washington had concluded the letter announcing his success with the words: 'I heard the bullets whistle, and, believe me, there is something charming in the sound.' Of course there was nothing of the sort in the despatch, which in its businesslike simplicity might have been written by Wellington at six and forty. Many years afterwards a clergyman, braver even than Washington, asked him if the story was true. 'If I said so,' replied the General, 'it was when I was young.'"

But if Trevelyan had read Washington's letters or Irving's biography (I, Ch. XI) he would have learned that Washington actually did delight in the whistle of bullets and that his letter (which Walpole errs in calling a despatch) was published in the *London Magazine* the same year, as Irving discovered for himself a hundred years later, in 1855.

Professor Hulbert, *Historic Highways*, III, p. 138, says that "Washington was not the man to withdraw. Indeed, the celerity with which he precipitated

England and France into war made him the most criticized man on both continents." There can be no question of this, but his passion for making Washington superhuman in all things surely leads him astray when he says of the commonplace feat of leading 40 men through dark wet woods: "Beside this all-night march . . . Wolfe's ascent to the Plains of Abraham at Quebec was a pastime. . . . If a more difficult ten-hour march has been made in the history of warfare in America, who led it and where was it made?"

He gives a brilliantly vivid account of the battle at Fort Necessity and speaks of the capitulation as Washington's "first and last." His book includes minute descriptions and photographs of the scenes based on personal investigations.

Albert H. Heusser's *In the Footsteps of Washington* (Paterson, N. J., 1921), has many interesting photographs of these and other scenes, showing the grave of Jumonville with a cross over it (p. 100), the ledge of rock from which Washington fired on him (p. 99), the Great Meadows (p. 101), Fort Necessity (p. 103) and other points of historical importance.

Hulbert, like Parkman and others, makes much of the striking fact that Washington surrendered Fort Necessity on July fourth—a date that meant nothing but bitterness to him then. The Fourth of July played a curious part in his life: at twenty-two he surrendered to the French in his first real battle, July 4, 1754. Twenty-two years later, July 4, 1776, he was commander-in-chief of the colonials in rebellion against the English with French aid looming and independence declared. Twenty-two years later, July 4, 1798, as ex-president, his commission was signed making him commander-in-chief in a war against the French.

Before leaving this first battle of Washington's, it is interesting to note a statement quoted in Worthington C. Ford's *The Spurious Letters Attributed to Washington* (Privately Printed, Brooklyn, 1889, p. 149) from a letter written by "an old soldier" in 1778 (reprinted in the *Gentleman's Magazine*, 1778, p. 368, from *Lloyd's Evening Post*, August 17, 1778): "One circumstance, perhaps not so generally known, may be mentioned. The very first engagement in which he was ever concerned, was against his own countrymen. He unexpectedly fell in, in the woods, with a party of the other Virginia regiment in the night, and fifty men were killed before the mistake was found out. The blame was laid (and possibly with great justness) on the darkness of the night. It is remarkable, however, that the same misfortune befell him in his last action at Germantown; the blame was then also laid on a darkness occasioned by a thick fog."

If there is any evidence for this statement as to his first battle, it has not repaid a diligent search. If true, it would surely have been alluded to in Dinwiddie's papers somewhere.

CHAPTER IX

1. *Dinwiddie Papers*, I, p. 214.
2. *Dinwiddie Papers*, I, p. 216, June 20, 1754.
3. *Dinwiddie Papers*, I, p. 197, June 10, 1754.
4. *Dinwiddie Papers*, I, p. 218. Dinwiddie had previously written to Governor Sharpe of Maryland that he had made this arrangement, "To quell

the great Feud subsisting between the Independ't Compa's and our Forces in regard to rank" (I, 213). Nothing was wanting to perfect his perplexities. As he wrote the Secretary of State in England: "Every Gov't except No. Caro. has amus'd me with Expectations that have proved fruitless. . . . Virg'a alone is unable to support the whole Burthen." He proposed an act of Parliament "to oblige each Colony to raise by a Pole tax of 1s. st[erling] or otherways a proportionable Quota of a Gen'l sum, to be applied to the pres't Exigency . . . and if the King w'd be graciously pleased to send over a regiment at this Time, I am much perswaded that the Consequence w'd be little less than the Preservation of his Dom's in this Part of America" (I. 203, 204).

5. *Dinwiddie Papers,* I, p. 220.

6. *Dinwiddie Papers,* I, p. 221.

7. *Dinwiddie Papers,* I, p. 239. The frequent estimate of the French forces at 900 is undoubtedly excessive. Gen. B. T. Johnson in *General Washington,* p. 56 puts it at 900. Lodge, *Life,* I, 76, says the French outnumbered Washington "four to one." This would make them 1200—an army equal to Braddock's. The final report of Washington's losses from his "few more than 300 men" was: 13 killed, 53 wounded, 13 left lame on the road, 21 sick, 27 absent, leaving 165 for duty, a total of 292. The French account in the *Mémoire* puts the English at seven or eight hundred and states that Villiers' force was a "detachment" from the total force at the fort, which is set at five or six hundred. But Parkman, by searching the French archives, turned up reports omitted by the French from the *Mémoire* for various reasons, since it was mainly propaganda. In *Montcalm and Wolfe,* I, p. 161-167, Parkman quotes Villiers' story of the absolution by the footsore chaplain. He gives Villiers' account of his own distresses in the battle, his reasons for urging the capitulation, and an estimate that Washington had 350 men (probably an excessive estimate) and that Villiers had about 700, counting the Indians. The number 700 is supported by the Journal of Thomas Forbes, an Englishman in the French service who marched with Villiers. Villiers' instructions directed him to follow the English to their settlement, if they had retreated, and there inflict such destruction as should cause them to plead for peace. Fortunately for the settlers, the surrender of Washington satisfied the French. The Indians, however, wrecked the medicine chest, causing the wounded great agony in their retreat. Parkman says of Washington: "Perhaps this miserable morning was the darkest of his life. . . . His pride was humbled and his young ambition seemed blasted in the bud. It was the fourth of July. He could not foresee that he was to make that day forever glorious to a new-born nation hailing him as its father."

8. Dinwiddie wrote to Governor Hamilton of Pennsylvania: "The Article of Capitulation in regard to making no Settlem'ts for one Year, the Officers say it was only in regard to the Forces left with their Baggage and Sick; they gave no Parole for themselves and are now ready to proceed with the other Forces" (*Dinwiddie Papers,* I, p. 256).

On the same day he wrote to the Governor of Maryland: "Y't Article of not Settling in y't Part for a twelve mo' is conceiv'd only to restrain these Persons y't were left with the Baggage, so the Officers interpret it, tho' probably the French intended to extend it further."

No more outrageous evasion could be imagined than this way of ignoring a parole. The Sixth Article of the Capitulation says in so many words: "Since the English have almost no more horses or beeves, they shall be free to put their effects in hiding, to come and get them when they have regained their horses: they may to that end leave guards, in such number as they shall wish, on the condition that they shall give their word of honor to work no more on any establishment either in this vicinity or beyond the highlands."

The word "they" is used throughout to refer to all the English, and the agreement is signed by the two commanders, McKay and Washington.

The entire capitulation in French is given in Ford's *Writings*, I, p. 120.

Hulbert (*Historic Highways*, III, p. 166) charges Van Braam with misrepresenting this parole, and adds that "within sixty-three hours of a year, an English army, eight times as great as the party now capitulating, marched across the battlefield." He praises "the nice courtesy shown by the young colonel in allowing Captain McKay's name to take precedence over his own." Others comment on McKay's insolence in insisting on signing first.

The capitulation was perfectly well understood in England, where Horace Walpole wrote, "The French have tied up the hands of an excellent *fanfaron*, a Major Washington, whom they took and engaged not to serve for one year." (*Correspondence*, III, 73—quoted in Irving's *Life*, I, Ch. XII). With assassination and broken parole both charged against Washington, it is small wonder that his first appearance in French history was not handsome.

CHAPTER X

1. *Dinwiddie Papers*, II, p. 228.
2. *Dinwiddie Papers*, I, p. 225.
3. *Dinwiddie Papers*, I, p. 227.
4. *Dinwiddie Papers*, I, p. 251; 300. Washington's letter is in Sparks, *Writings*, II, p. 463.
5. The *Mémoire* has a footnote showing that the translator had guessed that the unknown word, "tamkanko," was really "casse-tête."
6. This I take from an article by J. W. Cruzat in the Louisiana Historical Society Publications, wherein the *Journal de la Campagne* de M. de Villiers, including Washington's capitulation, is given from a copy sent by Abbé Gosselin, archivist of the Seminary at Quebec.
7. Thomas Chapais, *Le Marquis de Montcalm* (Quebec, 1911).
8. Sparks, *Writings*, II, p. 447.
9. Robert Stobo, *Memoirs* (Pittsburgh, 1854).
10. P. L. Ford, *The True George Washington*, p. 307; Thomas E. Watson, *Life and Times of Jefferson*, p. 154.

CHAPTER XI

1. Quoting Voltaire as saying, "Such was the complication of political interests that a cannon-shot fired in America could give the signal that set Europe ablaze," Parkman objects: "It was not a cannon-shot, but a volley from the hunting-pieces of a few backwoodsmen, commanded by a Virginian

youth." (*Montcalm and Wolfe,* I, p. 1.)   In this same work (I, p. 155),
Parkman says that if Washington had passively waited the event, when the
French approached, he "would have exposed his small party to capture or
destruction. . . . It was inevitable that the killing of Jumonville should be
greeted in France by an outcry of real or assumed horror; but the Chevalier de
Lévis, second in command to Montcalm, probably expresses the true opinion
of Frenchmen best fitted to judge when he calls it 'a pretended assassination.'   Judge it as we may, this obscure skirmish began the war that set
the world on fire."   In a footnote he states that the Half-King boasted that
he had killed Jumonville with his hatchet.   Which adds a further tangle to
confusion already confounded.

Washington Irving, in his *Life,* I, Ch. XII, notes that the Half-King,
disgusted with both French and English, and dissatisfied with Washington,
carried his wife and children to a place of safety, and soon after fell
dangerously ill.   A medicine man said the French "had bewitched him in
revenge for the great blow he had struck them in the affair of Jumonville;
for the Indians gave him the whole credit of that success, he having sent
round the French scalps as trophies" (p. 125).   He died shortly after.

2. *Dinwiddie Papers,* I, p. 497.   This letter written by Dinwiddie Feb. 12,
1755, was in answer to one from the Earl dated Paris, Sept. 16.   The Earl
had died in Paris, Dec. 22, 1754.

3. S. M. Hamilton, *Letters to Washington,* I, p. 51.   Hulbert, *Historic
Highways,* III, p. 170, says that the record of the fort "should be enough—
though it is not—to silence all who, with gross ignorance of the facts, have
imputed to the young commander a lack of military skill in choosing the site.
. . . Criticisms of Washington on this score are ridiculous misrepresentations."   He describes various surveys and efforts at reconstruction of the fort.

General Bradley T. Johnson (*General Washington*) feels that Washington
was wise to take a chance, and adds (p. 34) : "Andrew Lewis afterward, with
a few Virginians, fought more Indians with success than the French force
that captured Fort Necessity; and George Rogers Clarke broke the Indian
power and occupied the Northwest for Virginia with no greater force."   He
might have added that, while Washington surrendered a fort containing 300
Virginians and Indians to Villiers with 700 French and Indians, the French
Captain Dumas, with 108 Frenchmen, 146 Canadians and 600 Indians, destroyed in the open Braddock's army of 1300.

4. *Dinwiddie Papers,* I, p. 57.   January, 1754.

5. *Dinwiddie Papers,* I, p. 393.

6. Monacatoocha was loyal to the English to the last, serving with them
at Braddock's Defeat, where his son was killed.

Lodge, and others, speak of the French as "bullying and cajoling the
Indians," as if the English did anything else.   The only difference was that
the French were more liberal minded, had less racial antipathy, treated the
Indians with more fairness, honesty, and tact.   Parkman (*Pontiac,* p. 175)
says: "The English . . . traders . . . cheated, cursed and plundered the
Indians and outraged their families; offering, when compared with the
French traders . . . a most unfavorable example of the character of their
nation."

7. Volwiler, *Croghan and the Westward Movement,* p. 87-8.

8. *Enquiry into the Causes of the Alienation of the Delaware and Sha-wanese Indians from the British Interest.* Written in Pennsylvania. London, 1759, p. 80.

9. S. M. Hamilton, *Letters to Washington*, I, p. 25. The Carlyle and Campbell letters are given in I, p. 4, 9, 15.

10. *Dinwiddie Papers*, I, p. 287.

11. *Dinwiddie Papers*, I, p. 270.

12. M. L. Weems, *Life of George Washington with Curious Anecdotes, etc.*, 1837, p. 189 (ch. xiv).

13. Meade, *Old Churches*, II, p. 165. On p. 253, Bishop Meade says: "Here was true greatness of soul. Here was the true courage of the Christian, breathed into the soul by the Spirit of God."

14. Ford, *Writings*, I, p. 131 (to William Fairfax).

15. *Dinwiddie Papers*, I, p. 289, August 21, 1754. Ford (*Writings*, I, p. 135) supposed the Mr. Wright to be William Wright, who was killed at Braddock's Defeat. This is supported by the reference to William Wright in Dinwiddie's letter, p. 316, and his inclusion as ensign in a list of commissions, p. 320. Peyroney's letter is given by Hamilton, op. cit., I, p. 39.

16. *Dinwiddie Papers*, I, p. 316.

17. *Dinwiddie Papers*, I, p. 313.

18. *Dinwiddie Papers*, I, p. 317.

19. *Dinwiddie Papers*, I, p. 308.

20. *Dinwiddie Papers*, I, p. 310.

21. *Dinwiddie Papers*, I, p. 339.

22. *Dinwiddie Papers*, I, p. 351.

23. *Dinwiddie Papers*, I, p. 359.

24. Lodge, *Life*, I, p. 80; M. L. Weems, *Life*, p. 38.

25. *Dinwiddie Papers*, I, p. 403 (to Sir Thomas Robinson, November 16, 1754): "An unhappy Difference subsists between the Officers of the Ind[ependen]t Compa's and those appointed by me; the former refuse to rank or do duty with the others. . . . Colo. Washington on y't Acc't has resign'd his Commiss'n; the other Officers, I have prevail'd to continue in Com'd till I hear from Home. I therefore entreat Y'r Applicat'n to His M'y, if he will graciously order out to me blank Commis's in the same Manner as was practic'd on the Carthagena Expedit'n, w'ch will bring the Officers on an Equality."

26. Ford, *Writings*, I, p. 138, November 15, 1754.

27. *Dinwiddie Papers*, I, p. 435.

28. *Dinwiddie Papers*, I, p. 498.

29. *Dinwiddie Papers*, I, p. 524 (a letter to William Allen of Philadelphia, March 10, 1755).

30. Dr. H. R. McIlwaine, in his *The Struggle of Protestant Dissenters for Religious Toleration in Virginia* (Johns Hopkins University Studies, 1894), pages 63-65, asserts that the outbreak of war with France put a temporary end to the war between the Established Church and the Dissenters, since "French victory probably meant annexation of the colonies by France, and the consequent loss by their inhabitants of the rights of free Englishmen. But possibly most alarming of all was the threatened Roman

Catholicism which it was thought would follow French occupation. . . . In the common fear of Popery, and the common danger, minor differences between regular Churchman and Dissenter began to be overlooked. Especially was this the case since the Dissenting population of the Valley bore the brunt of the Indian attacks, and their Dissenting brethren of Hanover county and vicinity heartily supported the government in its measures for prosecuting the war. Mr. Davies, by his sermons and addresses, fired the people as no other man could fire them. . . . The statement seems warranted that during the French and Indian War one phase of the struggle between the Dissenters and the Established Church came to an end." Mr. Davies, a Presbyterian, who preached for a few months in Virginia in 1747, had returned in 1748 and obtained a license, which was refused to his companion, Rev. John Rodgers. Mr. Davies broke the strict law freely, but finally won much toleration, considering the times. It was this same Mr. Davies who, preaching to one of Washington's companies after Braddock's Defeat, praised the courage of the Virginians and added: "As a remarkable instance of this, I may point out to the public that heroic youth, Colonel Washington, whom I cannot but hope Providence has hitherto preserved in so signal a manner for some important service." This famous utterance has been hailed as prophecy, but the same sort of thing has been said of innumerable heroes whom fate suppressed. It was Washington's patience and indomitable perseverance that lifted the preacher's words out of obscurity into fame, and made one a prophet who for many a long year must have felt his words mere rhetoric. In Samuel Kercheval's *History of the Valley of Virginia* (Winchester, Virginia, 1833), pp. 56-64, there is much fascinating matter concerning the religious practices of the time.

William Taylor Thom, in his *The Struggle for Religious Freedom in Virginia: The Baptists* (Johns Hopkins University Studies, 1900), p. 92, says that Puritanism never made itself a home in Virginia as in other colonies, Maryland, for instance. . . . Virginia felt but did not yield to the impulse of either Quaker or Presbyterian. Of the Baptists, though their power came later than this period, he says that they consolidated the "kind of religious anarchy" that arose, the "tremendous revolutionary impulse." And he notes in his first page the vital connection between the religious and the political developments:

"The struggle for Religious Freedom in Virginia was really a part of that greater struggle for political freedom with which it was so nearly coincident in time. Much the same causes led to each; the logic of both was the same; and there was no time at which the religious struggle was not largely political and not clearly seen to be so by the leaders of thought. The struggle for independence was against external coercion; the struggle for religious freedom was against that external coercion as represented within the colony itself. The failure of the struggle for independence meant the failure of the struggle for religious freedom; but the achievement of independence did not necessarily mean the attainment of religious freedom. Hence the religious struggle outlasted the political, and hence also it assumed towards the end a vindictiveness not pleasant to contemplate."

At no time did Washington seem to take any real interest in this seething unrest. He remained an Episcopalian in form, but was not at all concerned when the Established Church went to ruin for half a century after the outbreak of the Revolution.

CHAPTER XII

1. Mrs. Sally Nelson Robins, *Love Stories of Famous Virginians* (1925), p. 21.

2. Conway, *Washington and Mount Vernon*, p. xxxvi, gives the exact date as December 17, 1748. Fitzpatrick, *Diaries*, I, p. 108 n., gives it as December 12, 1748, and quotes as his authority the book, *Sally Cary, A Long Hidden Romance of Washington's Life*, by Wilson Miles Cary, with Notes by Another Hand. Privately printed, New York, 1916.

3. It is a pity that this beautifully written and annotated little volume is not available to the public, especially in view of the editor's statement on page 38 note: "The sneer which moved Captain Cary to the preparation of this paper is in P. L. Ford's *The True George Washington*." This refers doubtless to the following statement on page 91 of that book:

"It has been asserted that Washington loved the wife of his friend George William Fairfax, but the evidence has not been produced. On the contrary, though the two corresponded, it was in a purely platonic fashion, very different from the strain of lovers, and that the correspondence implied nothing is to be found in the fact that he and Sally Carlyle (another Fairfax daughter) also wrote each other quite as frequently and on the same friendly footing; indeed, Washington evidently classed them in the same category, when he stated that 'I have wrote to my two female correspondents.' Thus the claim seems due, like many another of Washington's mythical love-affairs, rather to the desire of descendants to link their family 'to a star' than to more substantial basis."

The letters from Washington to Sally Fairfax first turned up in a bundle of her old letters. Among the eighty-six were some in Washington's hand with his signature attached. They were first published in the New York *Herald* of March 30, 1877. In an article on Washington contributed by A. Everett to Appleton's *New American Encyclopædia*, the most fervid of them was described as addressed to Martha, but the letter itself makes such an ascription absurd. Dr. Neill, in his *Fairfaxes in England and America*, selected Mary Cary as the one addressed, but the proof of Washington's love for her is questionable; and besides, she was as much married as her sister Sally. Mary Cary married Edward Ambler in 1752, six years before this letter.

4. Fairfax Harrison, *Aris Sonis Focisque* (privately printed 1910), p. 194.

5. Dr. Elizabeth C. Cook, *Literary Influences in Colonial Newspapers*, 1704-1750 (Columbia University Press, 1912), pp. 247, 183.

6. Colonel William Byrd, *The Writings of*. Edited by John Spencer Bassett.

7. Lucinda Lee Dalrymple is not quite positively known as the author, but the work is always credited to her. Lucinda Lee Dalrymple, *Journal of a Young Lady of Virginia*, 1782, Baltimore, 1871.

8. Quoted in Alice Morse Earle's *Colonial Dames and Good Wives*, p. 210.

9. The letter is in the Pierpont Morgan collection. It is quoted in Eugene E. Prussing's *George Washington in Love and Otherwise*, Chicago, 1925, p. 8.

10. Quoted by Dr. Elizabeth C. Cook, op. cit., p. 192. On the same page is a reference to a fashion of women riding astride. On page 194 is the quotation from the *Monitor* concerning prudishness.

11. Ford, *Writings*, I, 154 and note. The letter was drawn up at Fort Cumberland, May 14th, 1755.

12. Archer Butler Hulbert, *Historic Highways*, IV, p. 34, a most excellent treatment of Braddock's campaign. This campaign has a whole literature devoted to it. Winthrop Sargent's *History of an Expedition Against Fort Du Quesne in 1755 under Major General Edward Braddock*, makes Number 5 of the *Pennsylvania Historical Society Memoirs*. The anecdote of Braddock's insolence is quoted by Sargent, p. 417, from the *Apology for the Life of George Anne Bellamy*, III, 55. Parkman devoted his great research and his opulent style to it twice, most completely in his *Montcalm and Wolfe*, I, ch. VII, and more briefly, earlier, in his *Conspiracy of Pontiac*, chapter IV, in which he deals very harshly with Braddock, of whom he says (p. 105), "A person worse fitted for the office could scarcely have been found. His experience had beeen ample, and none could doubt his courage; but he was profligate, arrogant, perverse, and a bigot to military rules." What his profligacy had to do with his fitness or how it affected his efficiency is not indicated. His arrogance was really the opposite, as Washington's experience proves. His perverseness was the perverseness of the colonials, and his bigotry to military rules has always been caricatured. It should also be noted that in the first chapter of his *Montcalm and Wolfe*, Parkman gives such a picture of colonial jealousy and blindness as Braddock wanted only the Parkmanian vocabulary to express; he had to resort to profanity. In ch. VII of that work, Parkman tells many anecdotes of Braddock's bad reputation as a rake, a man kept by a woman, a bankrupt gambler, a heartless brother of a gambling sister and in general a hopeless reprobate. But he alleges no bad conduct in America beyond ridicule of Americans. Governor Sharpe, Braddock's predecessor, criticized him fiercely for his conduct of the campaign, but Sharpe had also criticized Washington mercilessly, as has been indicated in an earlier chapter. John Fiske, in his *New France and New England*, ch. VIII, takes a comparatively favorable view of Braddock's character and skill: "It is not correct to say, as has often been said, that Braddock neglected all precaution and was drawn into an ambuscade. . . . Braddock made mistakes enough but he was not absolutely a fool" (p. 287).

13. *Dinwiddie Papers*, II, p. 3; I, p. 511.

14. *Dinwiddie Papers*, I, p. 509.

15. This summary of the strategic situation is condensed from Justin Winsor's condensed account in his *Narrative and Critical History*, V, p. 495.

16. *Dinwiddie Papers*, II, p. 30.

17. S. M. Hamilton, *Letters to Washington*, I, p. 57.

18. Ford, *Writings*, I, p. 141.

19. Mrs. Roger A. Pryor, *The Mother of Washington*, p. 118; B. J. Lossing, *Mary and Martha Washington*, p. 49.

20. Ford, *Writings*, I, p. 144.
21. Ford, *Writings*, I, p. 145 n.
22. Ford, *Writings*, I, p. 146.
23. Ford, *Writings*, I, p. 153.
24. Paul Leland Haworth, *George Washington, Country Gentleman* (Indianapolis, 1925), p. 9.
25. "This letter was never sent," Washington writes in his notebook. Since nothing but a photograph could do it justice, a reproduction is given of the copy in the Library of Congress.
26. Ford, *Writings*, I, 152, and note.

CHAPTER XIII

1. Ford, *Writings*, I, p. 155 (to John A. Washington, May 25, 1755).
2. Ford, *Writings*, I, p. 154.
3. W. H. Lowdermilk, *History of Cumberland* (Maryland), pp. 112-14, 135. General B. T. Johnson's *General Washington*, pp. 43-4, has also an account of Franklin's patriotic practical joke.
4. Ford, *Writings*, I, p. 157.
5. Ford, *Writings*, I, p. 161.
6. Ford, *Writings*, I, p. 152.
7. John F. Watson, *Annals of Philadelphia and Pennsylvania* (1857), II, p. 140.
8. Quoted from Channing's *History of the United States*, II, p. 572, note. Channing quotes from Boyd Crumrine's "excellent account of the Braddock expedition," in his *History of Washington County, Pennsylvania*, p. 52. And Crumrine quotes from Findley's letter in Niles's *Register*, XIV, p. 179. Channing comments, "In 1818, William Findley repeated in print the substance of what Washington, when President, had said to him as to Braddock's expedition. The recollection of one old man as a source of history is often deplorable—let alone that of what one old man averred that another old man had said years before. The statement attributed to Washington is so interesting, however, that it is here repeated for what it is worth." Channing's own opinion was that Braddock's "age of sixty years and his lack of tact are sufficient to account for his refusal to respect colonial conditions, but he also appears to have been deficient in administrative ability. . . . England has almost always suffered defeats in the beginnings of wars and has almost as invariably succeeded in the end; it was with the British as it was with Washington—failure was necessary to bring forth the highest effort."

But England has not "almost invariably" succeeeded in her wars, and it should be remembered of Braddock that he did not fail because of his unwillingness to fight in the colonial fashion. He failed because when he surprised the French and Indians, his vanguard was caught in an unlucky place where he could get them neither formed up nor withdrawn in an orderly manner. The colonials suffered as heavily as the regulars for all their legendary skill. Furthermore, Washington and his Virginians had been defeated by the same enemy before Braddock came, and he was as helpless when he got the command. The subsequent conquest of Fort Du Quesne under Forbes was a bloodless victory over an empty fort, due to victories in the North.

9. Ford, *Writings*, I, p. 162 (to William Fairfax from camp, June 7, 1755).

10. The quotations from Braddock are taken from Hulbert's *Historic Highways*, IV, 65-75. He quotes them from Braddock's Ms. Letters, Public Record Office, London: *America and West Indies, No. 82.* The phraseology of these letters differs from that of various historians who quote the English translation of the French translations of Braddock's letters, which were captured by the French and included in the *Mémoire* already referred to in earlier chapters, the *Mémoire* in which Washington's captured Journal was also published. Orme's *Journal* is reproduced in Sargent's *Expedition Against Fort Du Quesne*, pp. 297, 312, 330.

11. *The Expedition of Maj.-Gen'l Braddock* . . . being Extracts of Letters from an officer in one of those Regiments, London, 1755, p. 5. Winthrop Sargent, op. cit., calls it "a mere catch-penny production, made up perhaps of the reports of some ignorant camp-follower," and Winsor, *Narrative and Critical History*, V, 579, says that its untrustworthiness was exposed at the time. Nevertheless, it is exceedingly vivid and in no sense false to the situation.

12. Richard Peters, Secretary of the Pennsylvania Council, quoted in Volwiler's *Croghan and the Westward Movement*, p. 96. Here, as elsewhere, Volwiler, with well-documented proof, rescues Croghan's fame from the oblivion in which it was lost by the tendency to ascribe everything good to Washington. Hulbert repeats in his *Historic Highways*, IV, p. 66, the strange obsession of historians that Washington was responsible "for the faithfulness of these few" Indians who were loyal to Braddock. Volwiler makes the mistake of many historians when he speaks on page 97 of "the two chiefs, Scarroyady and Monacatootha." They were really the same man, as Brock points out in the *Dinwiddie Papers*, I, 57.

13. Sargent, op. cit., 393.

14. Hulbert, op. cit., p. 79, quotes this original work bodily, with a discussion of the mystery of its authorship. Sargent, in his *Braddock's Expedition*, had published an expanded version of it under the name, "The Morris Journal," from the name of its owner and editor. Professor Hulbert, comparing this version with the original, finds peculiar changes made by the Reverend Mr. Morris and decides that the work was really written by Engineer Harry Gordon of the 48th Artillery. It is often referred to as the Gordon Journal.

15. Hulbert, op. cit., p. 153.

16. Ford, *Writings*, I., p. 161 n. (to John A. Washington).

17. Ford, *Writings*, I., p. 157 (Winchester, May 25, 1755).

18. Quoted by Sargent, op. cit., p. 417, from the *Apology for the Life of George Anne Bellamy*, I, p. 194.

19. Dr. Louis K. Koontz, *The Virginia Frontier 1754-1763*, p. 68, accepts the familiar views of Braddock's self-confidence, bad temper, and autocracy, but states, "He at least saw the worth of two Americans, even if he did not always accept their advice. He at once called George Washington out of retirement, and made him one of his aides. He also saw in

Benjamin Franklin 'almost the only Instance of ability and honesty' he had found in all the colonies." In a footnote, p. 71, Dr. Koontz refers to "a remarkable, though depreciative, statement as to Braddock's fitness for leadership in this campaign," written by his military secretary, Governor Shirley's son, William, and addressed to Lt.-Gov. Morris of Pennsylvania. Young Shirley's letter is dated May 23, 1755 and was written before the battle in which both he and Braddock were killed. Included with it in Hamilton's *Letters to Washington*, I, 63, 83, is a letter in vindication of Braddock by Captain Orme to Washington written after the battle, Aug. 25, 1755. When Braddock's secretary and his chief aide disagreed as to his character, it is small wonder that posterity should be confused. According to Charles Moore's *The Family Life of Washington*, p. 43, Captain Orme was of a convivial disposition and spent his last night in London convivially at the home of an actress-friend with General Braddock. Moore adds, "Perhaps others of his contemporaries called Washington by his first name, but Orme is the only one whose pen naturally and easily writes the words 'dear George.'" Richard Corbin and Speaker Robinson are among the few who wrote "Dear George."

CHAPTER XIV

1. Professor Hulbert devotes volume IV of his *Historic Highways* to Braddock's Road, giving photographs of its still visible traces, and adding to a very full account of the expedition a whole chapter on Braddock's route from Neville B. Craig's account of it in *The Olden Time*, II, p. 465, 539, with Jared Sparks' account of his own investigations and T. C. Atkinson's story of his researches. General B. T. Johnson, in his *General Washington*, p. 46, ridicules the construction and selection of the road in unmeasured terms:

"The performances of that march, if they were not proved by absolutely indisputable proof, would be simply incredible. But Braddock's road is now (March, 1894) perfectly well defined, north of Cumberland. It looks as if intelligent purpose had exerted itself to waste time and labor. It is located without the slightest regard to grades or obstacles. Instead of blasting rocks—or, still better, avoiding them whenever possible—the engineers seem to have tried to leave monuments to their own stupidity. Great bowlders in the road, instead of being rolled or blasted out of the way, are carefully hewed down so as to present no obstruction. The third camp was only five miles from the first."

Professor Hulbert, however, is full of praise for it, IV, p. 191:

"The narrow swath of a road cut through the darkling Alleghenies by General Braddock has been worth all it cost in time and treasure. Throughout the latter half of the eighteenth century it was one of the main thoroughfares into the Ohio valley, and when, at the dawning of the nineteenth, the United States built our first and greatest public highway, the general alignment of Braddock's Road between Cumberland and the last range of the Alleghenies—Laurel Hill—was the course pursued. In certain localities this famed national boulevard, the Cumberland Road, was built upon the very bed of Braddock's Road, as Braddock's Road had been built partly upon the early Washington's Road which followed the path of Indian, buffalo, and mound-building aborigines. Nowhere in America can the evolution of road-building be studied to such advantage as between Cumberland, Maryland and Uniontown, Pennsylvania. . . .

"As the years passed Braddock's Road seems to have regained something of its early prestige, and throughout the Revolutionary period it was perhaps of equal consequence with any route toward the Ohio, especially because of Virginia's interest in and jealousy of the territory about Pittsburg. When, shortly after the close of the Revolution, the great flood of immigration swept westward, the current was divided into three streams near the Potomac; one went southward over the Virginian route through Cumberland Gap to Kentucky; the other two burst over Forbes's and Braddock's Roads. . . .

"It is difficult to say when Braddock's Road, as a route, ceased to be used since portions of it have never been deserted. . . .

"Braddock's Road broke the league the French had made with the Alleghenies; it showed that British grit could do as much in the interior of America as in India or Africa or Egypt; it was the first important material structure in this New West, so soon to be filled with the sons of those who had hewn it."

2. Hulbert, op. cit., p, 108, and others, say he marched June 7th, but Washington, on June 7th, writes: "To-morrow Sir Peter Halket (with the first brigade) is to begin their march." Ford, *Writings*, I., p. 163.

3. M. D. Conway, *Washington and Mount Vernon*, p. 42.

4. Ford, *Writings*, I., p. 161.

5. Fitzpatrick, *Diaries*, I., pp. 141 n, 296 n, 130 n, 133 n. Hannah Fairfax became in 1765 the second wife of Washington's first cousin, Warner Washington. Bryan Fairfax (1736-1802) joined the army, was converted to religion, jilted in love, resigned the service, took holy orders in 1789, resigned them in 1792, and in 1793 succeeded to the title of Lord Fairfax, which would have been George William's if he had lived a dozen years longer.

6. *Dinwiddie Papers*, II, p. 83, 84, 96.

7. *Dinwiddie Papers*, II, p. 112 (to Sir T. Robinson), 114 (to the Earl of Halifax.

8. Before this fact was noted, Jared Sparks received even more blame than he merited for his changes in Washington's texts. The letter to Mrs. Fairfax is quoted here from the transcript used by Eugene E. Prussing in his *George Washington in Love and Otherwise*, p. 9. It agrees save for a few details of spelling with the version used in Mrs. Robins' *Love Affairs of Famous Virginians*, p. 22. The version given by Ford, *Writings*, I, p. 163 n, is quite different, and runs as follows:

"When I had the pleasure to see you last you expressed a wish to be informed of my safe arrival at camp, with the charge that was entrusted to my care; but at the same time requested that it might be communicated in a letter to some friend of yours. Am I to consider the proposed mode of communication as a polite intimation of your wishes to withdraw your correspondence? To a certain degree it has that appearance; for I have not been honoured with a line from you since I parted with you at Belvoir. If this was your object, in what manner shall I apologize for my present disobedience? But on the contrary, if it was the effect of your delicacy, how easy is it to remove my suspicions, enliven dull hours, and make me happier than I am able to express, by honouring me with the correspondence you had given me the hope of."

9. Ford, *Writings*, I., p. 166 (Youghiogany, 28 June, 1755).

10. Hulbert, op. cit., p. 54, 211; R. G. Thwaites, *France in America*, p. 174. The Hon. J. W. Fortescue, *History of the British Army*, II, pp. 276-7. "A great initial blunder had been made by the military authorities in England in sending the troops to Virginia and ordering them to advance on the Ohio by the circuitous route from Will's Creek. This was, it is true, the line that had been taken by Washington; but Washington, like Shirley, was but an amateur, and a sounder military judgment would have shown that the suggestions of both were faulty. Disembarkation at Philadelphia, and a march directly westward from thence, would have saved not only distance and time but much trouble and expense; for Pennsylvania, unlike Maryland and Virginia, was a country rich in forage and in the means of carriage. . . . Nevertheless Braddock was too capable a man to blind himself to the merit of the ablest of his coadjutors; and it was in terms honourable to himself that he invited and obtained the services of Colonel George Washington upon his staff."

11. S. M. Hamilton, *Letters to Washington*, I, p. 66.

12. Ford, *Writings*, I, p. 170.

CHAPTER XV

1. *Dinwiddie Papers*, I, p. 151. Letter to Dinwiddie from Little Meadows, May 9, 1754. "I detach'd a party of 60 Men to make and amend the Road, which party, since ye 25th of Ap'l, and the main body since the 1st Inst't, have been laboriously employ'd and have got no further than these Meadows, ab't 20 Miles from the new Store" (the store-house established by the Ohio Company at Wills's Creek—Brock, note). "The great difficulty and labour that it requires to amend and alter the Roads, prevents our March'g above 2, 3 or 4 Miles a Day." Channing, *History of the U. S.*, II, p. 572, says: "In the conditions of ocean transport and wilderness road-cutting, Braddock made commendable speed."

2. Parkman, *The Conspiracy of Pontiac*, Ch. IV. "The difficulty was increased by the needless load of baggage which encumbered their march." He speaks later of Braddock's "insane confidence" and says that "there were flanking parties on either side, but no scouts to scour the woods in front." Croghan and his Indians and Gist, however, were with the advance party.

3. [Wm. Livingston] *A Review of the Military Operations in North America*, London, 1757.

4. A. B. Hulbert, *Historic Highways*, IV, p. 206.

5. Quoted by Hulbert, *Historic Highways*, IV, 100, from the Gordon (or Morris) Journal.

6. Volwiler, *Croghan and the Westward Movement*, p. 97. He bases his account on the report of James Burd, one of Braddock's road cutters

in the Penn. Colonial Records, VI, 435, 460, and on the Journal kept by Captain Orme. Battle histories are always steeped in confusion, none more so than Braddock's campaign; and it may be admitted once for all that, in compiling the story in this text, practically every detail maintained by one authority is disputed by another of equal worth. One can only select what seems most probable.

7. *The Gordon Journal,* quoted by Hulbert, op. cit., p. 101.

8. Gen. B. T. Johnson, *General Washington,* p. 48: "He intended to take Fort Du Quesne that day, and proposed that it should be done according to the rules and regulations of civilized war—by troops on dress parade, with colors flying, drums beating, and trumpets sounding." Parkman, *Pontiac,* Ch. IV, says: "It is said that at the outset Braddock showed signs of fear; but he soon recovered his wonted intrepidity." R. Mackenzie, *America,* II, ch. 3, says that Braddock was "so confident . . . that he refused to employ scouts and did not deign to inquire what enemy might be lurking near . . . Braddock, clinging to his old rules, strove to maintain his order of battle in the open ground . . . the poor pedantic man never got over his astonishment at a defeat so inconsistent with the established rules of war." But, as has been shown, he had all possible scouting done, he knew that the enemy's scouts followed his every movement, and he took the best advice he could get.

9. S. Weir Mitchell, *The Youth of Washington,* p. 247.

10. This story, and other stories of Bishop's, are given in Custis' *Recollections,* ch. XVIII, and may well be believed since Bishop afterwards became Washington's own body-servant, later an overseer, and when too old, a pensioner on Washington. He must have been a familiar figure to Custis.

11. Dumas in his report to the Ministry (Parkman, *Montcalm and Wolfe,* I, p. 218) claimed the credit for the idea, and in view of his magnificent conduct in the battle, his claim is worthy of acceptance. James Smith, an eighteen-year-old Colonial recently taken prisoner, was present in the fort and saw Beaujeu depart. He wrote *An Account of the Remarkable Occurrences, etc., in the life and travels of Col. James Smith* (Ohio Valley Historical Series No. V).

12. George Macaulay Trevelyan, *History of England,* New York, 1926, p. 542.

13. Channing, *History of the U. S.,* II, p. 573, note, quotes from a letter sent by Hermanns Alricks to the Governor of Penn. July 22, 1754, stating that "the French and Indians had cast an Intrenchment across the road before our Army which they Discover'd not Until they came Close up to it, from thence and both sides of the road the Enemy kept a Constant fireing on them, our Army being so confused, they could not fight." Lowdermilk, *History of Cumberland, Maryland,* p. 158, also mentions "a most singular ditch." But there are too many accounts, including the French, which flatly contradict any idea of a set intrenchment. In any such forest there are always abundant ravines to resemble trenches and furnish cover to those who are wise and cool enough to use them.

Parkman in his *Montcalm and Wolfe* makes use of French documents he found in the Archives of the Ministry. They reveal almost as much contradiction among the French reports as among the British. By some, including the chaplain at the fort, Beaujeu was said to have been in command at Du Quesne in place of Contrecoeur. But the governor of Canada and Contrecoeur's official report disprove that. Parkman, in Appendix D, gives Contrecoeur's report in the original French, saying that he sent out the troops—"je formai un party de tout ce que je pouvois mettre hors du fort pour aller à leur rencontre." He mentions Beaujeu's death at the first volley, the prompt flight of the Canadians, and Dumas' taking command. "Our French, full of courage, supported by the savages though they had no artillery, made the English recoil in their turn, though they fought in battle order and in good countenance. Seeing the ardor of our people who fought (*fonçoient*) with a infinite vigor, they were finally obliged to retreat (*plier*) altogether after four hours of heavy fire. Messieurs Dumas and Ligneris, who had with them no more than a score of French, did not attempt pursuit. They returned to the fort, since a majority of the Canadians, who unhappily were mere lads, had retreated at the first discharge."

Parkman gave out for the first time Dumas' letter asking for recognition. Since he gives it only in French and it is an important offset to the false legends, it is translated herewith:

"M. de Beaujeu marched out, and, under his orders, M. de Ligneris and I. He attacked with much audacity but with no order (*disposition*); our first volley was delivered out of range; the enemy delivered his nearer, and at the first moment of combat, a hundred militiamen who made up half of our French, shamefully took to their heels crying, 'Everybody for himself! (*Sauve qui peut!*)' Two cadets who have since been commissioned, authorized the flight by their example.

"This retreat encouraging the enemy, he made the welkin ring with cries of 'God save the King!' and advanced on us with energy. His artillery being put into play by this time, he commenced firing and frightened the savages so that they all took flight; the enemy's third volley of musketry slew M. de Beaujeu.

"Our rout presented itself to my eyes in the most wretched aspect, and lest I be charged with the bad management of others, I dreamed of nothing but letting myself be killed. It was then, sir, that I inspired with voice and gesture the few soldiers who remained, and advanced with the look that comes from despair.

"My platoon fired so vigorously that the enemy was astonished. The fire increased a little and the savages, seeing that my attack had silenced the shouts of the enemy, rallied around me. At once I sent M. le Chevalier Le Borgne and M. de Rocheblave to say to the officers who led the savages to take the enemy by the flank. The cannon that fired from the front favored my orders. The enemy, surrounded on all sides, fought with the most stubborn determination. Whole ranks fell at a time; almost all the officers perished, and the consequent disorder in the column threw it all into flight."

Parkman goes on to describe the important services of "the partisan chief," Charles Langlade, who was never mentioned in the reports, but whose grandson, as well as the traveller Anburey (a lieutenant with Burgoyne), and Burgoyne afterwards, gave him the credit for "leading the attack" and being "the author of Braddock's defeat." Though crosses of the Order of St. Louis were given to Contrecoeur, Dumas and Ligneris, Langlade received no honors. He was a French trader, a squaw-man, and led the successful attack on the Miamis at Pickawillany in 1752, where he won a great victory over the English traders and the Indian chief La Demoiselle whom his Indian allies boiled and ate alive. He also fought at Quebec in 1760. Langlade, in his memoirs, says that Beaujeu and his men arrived in time to see Braddock drilling his troops and giving them their dinner. His story is told in Tassé's *Notice sur Charles Langlade* (Revue Canadienne). According to Winsor's *Narrative and Critical History*, V, p. 568, he was the first to settle in Wisconsin.

In Hart's *American History Told by Contemporaries*, II, p. 365, is an anonymous French account coinciding largely with that of Dumas. It says "The detachment, before it could reach its place of destination, found itself in the presence of the enemy within three leagues of the fort. M. de Beaujeu, finding his ambush had failed, decided on an attack."

The Hon. J. W. Fortescue in his great *History of the British Army*, II, pp. 280-2, says:

"Braddock took every possible precaution against surprise.

"The regulars and such few of the Canadians as stood by them held their ground staunchly, and opened a fire of platoons which checked the ardour of Gage's men; while the Indians, yelling like demons but always invisible, streamed away through the forest along both flanks of the British, and there, from every coign of vantage that skilful bushmen could find, poured a deadly fire upon their hapless opponents. The cheering was silenced, for the red-coats began to fall fast. For a time they kept their ranks and swept the unheeding forest with volley after volley, which touched no enemy through the trees. They could see no foe, and yet the bullets rained continually and pitilessly upon them from front, flank, and rear, like a shower from a cloudless sky. The trial at last was greater than they could bear. They abandoned their guns, they broke their ranks, and huddling themselves together like a herd of fallow-deer they fell back in disorder, a mere helpless mass of terrified men."

The final disproof of the untenable theory of surprise and ambush is in the two plates (reproduced here from Parkman's *Montcalm and Wolfe*, I, p. 220) drawn by the chief engineer Pat. Mackellar, for Governor Shirley, and agreeing with a plan drawn by Captain Orme. The first plate shows the disposition of the British troops with guides and six light-horse ahead of the vanguard of the advance party, which was ahead of the working party. Flank guards are well out on both sides. At a considerable distance ahead of the scouts or guides is the body of French and Indians. At the right is the "Hill which the Indians did most of the Execution from." The hill is empty in the first plate.

The second plate shows "The whole Body of the British joined with little or no order but endeavouring to make Fronts toward ye Enemies Fire." The French and Indians "skulking behind Trees round the British." "The two Field Pieces of the advanced Party abandoned." A hollow way or ravine runs down to the river, but the British were well across it before the attack began. These plates, drawn by a participant and approved at the time, completely contradict the plate drawn in 1830 and reproduced in Sparks's *Life*, where the parallel ravines are shown at both sides of the road and filled with Indians. The ravines really ran the other way. Volwiler, *Croghan and the Westward Movement*, p. 98, quotes from a letter by Charles Swaine to Peters (Peters Mss, IV, 38, Aug. 5, 1755) in which he says that Croghan told him later that "he had a free sight of the Enemy as they approached . . . they were about three hundred, the French in shirts and the Indians naked . . . lead by three French officers with hats in their hands, and with which they gave a Signal for the firing." Gordon's Journal, p. 378 (quoted in Hulbert's *Historic Highways*, IV, p. 102, 105) says: "The advanc'd party was ¼ Mile before the Main Body, the Rear of which was just over the River, when the Front was attack'd. The 2 Granadier Comp'ys formed the Flank. The Piquets with the rest of the Men were sustaining the Carpenters while they were cutting the Roads. The first fire the Enemy gave was in Front & they likewise gaul'd the Piquets in Flank, so that in few Minutes the Granadiers were nearly cut to pieces and drove into the greatest Confusion as was Capt. Polsons Comp'y of Carpent'rs . . . Mr. Engineer Gordon was the first Man that saw the Enemy, being in the Front of the Carpenters, making & Picketing the Roads for them, and he declared where he first discover'd them, that they were on the Run, which plainly shews they were just come from *Fort Dec Quesne* and that their principal Intention was to secure the pass of the *Monongahela River* but the Officer who was their leader, dressed like an Indian w'th a Gorgeton, waved his Hatt by way of Signal to disperse to ye Right and left forming a half Moon."

It is noteworthy that nowhere in this Journal is Washington even mentioned. It is quite evident, therefore, that his importance in the retreat has been immensely exaggerated and that he acted throughout only as an aide, a messenger and a guide.

14. At Majuba Hill in 1881 the British were commanded by one of their best strategists, Sir George Colley (who contributed the article on Strategy to the Encyclopedia Britannica). Learning that the Boers occupied a camp overlooked by steep heights he brilliantly decided to plant artillery on a peak and shell them out. His men toiled all night and got the guns to the top. As Mark Twain put it in one of his writings, the Boers, realizing that their position was untenable, retreated,—up the hill. The British soldiers were practically annihilated and their general killed. They had not been trained to fire at individual men creeping up a mountainside, and the rifles of the dead were found with their sights fixed at 1000 yards! It is especially hard to fire with accuracy at objects beneath one. The Indians, by hugging the ground at Braddock's field, doubtless escaped many a bullet badly aimed.

15. Orme's *Journal*, in Winthrop Sargent's *Expedition Against Fort Du Quesne*, p. 353.

16. Watson, *Annals of Philadelphia*, II, 141, is the source of this and many other dubious yet plausible anecdotes taken from survivors and others. In I, 602, Watson says he knew Billy Brown when he was 93, and of clear memory. He had many adventures before he became Washington's slave.

17. There is no final reason for disbelieving this story, which was always believed when Tom Fawcett told it himself. General B. T. Johnson (*General Washington*, p. 53) finds it "merely incredible" since "no private soldier . . . ever, anywhere, could or ever did, in the heat of battle, with death looking right into his eyes, conceive of killing the superintending power which absolutely controlled his destiny." This is strong language, particularly in view of General Johnson's previous statements that the frenzied soldiers were firing into the air or into their own men, and had already destroyed two-thirds of the Virginian's relieving force, while Braddock was frantically demanding what was impossible, and was beating and cursing his men and manifestly no longer controlled anybody's destiny. General Johnson says "it was quite probable" that he had killed Fawcett's brother. It seems not at all unlikely, then, that an American bushfighter, seeing this bellowing foreigner kill his own brother, might have felt that he did the world a service in killing Braddock. But, of course, the story can neither be proved nor disproved. It was generally believed at the time, and the hostility to Braddock in Pennsylvania can be measured by the fact that Fawcett was permitted to boast of killing him and to live on to a ripe old age. Winsor's *Narrative and Critical History*, V, p. 501, gives the various theories concerning the act of Fossit, Fausett or Faucit, and the finding of Braddock's grave. Col. Dunbar stated that Braddock died of a wound in the abdomen. This was an error.

18. The soldier then received eight silver pennies a day or eight "sterlings." It took 252 to make a guinea; 15,120 to make 60 guineas. Dividing that by 8 to indicate the number of days, and by 365 to represent the years, the result is 5.1. The story is told in Volwiler, op. cit., p. 98, where it is also stated on Croghan's authority that Braddock attempted to seize Croghan's pistols to end his life.

19. James Smith, *Account of Remarkable Occurrences*, p. 9. The Hon. J. W. Fortescue, in his *History of the British Army*, II, pp. 284, 286, writes eloquently of Braddock's last hours, and his services:

"But there was little speech now left in the rough, bullying martinet, whose mouth had once been so full of oaths, and whose voice had been the terror of every soldier. It was not only that his lungs were shot through and through, but that his heart was broken. Throughout the first day's march he lay white and silent, with his life's blood bubbling up through his lips; nor was it until evening that his misery found vent in the almost feminine ejaculation, 'Who would have thought it?' Again through the following day he remained silent, until towards sunset, as if to sum up repentance for past failure and good hope for the future, he murmured gently, 'Another time we shall know better how to deal with them.' And so, having learned his lesson he lay still, and a few minutes later he was dead.

"With all his faults this rude indomitable spirit appeals irresistibly to our sympathy.

"Nevertheless, though Braddock's ideal of a British officer may have been mistaken, it cannot be called low. In rout and ruin and disgrace, with the hand of death gripping tightly at his throat, his stubborn resolution never wavered and his untamable spirit was never broken. He kept his head and did his work to the last, and thought of his duty while thought was left in him. . . . But the lesson which he had learned too late was not lost on his successors, and it may truly be said that it was over the bones of Braddock that the British advanced again to the conquest of Canada."

20. Albert H. Heusser, *In the Footsteps of Washington*, p. 117, 119, 121, gives photographs of Braddock's Field as it is in Braddock, Pa., of Col. Dunbar's camp near Jumonville, Pa., and of the monument to Braddock which was dedicated in 1913 by Secretary of State Knox, and General Codrington of the Coldstream Guards, Braddock's old regiment.

21. The statement was made that Braddock's military chest contained 75,000 pounds, which is strange in view of Washington's hasty journey to collect 4000 pounds; but it is given in a letter of Col. James Byrd, July 25, 1755, written after a talk with Col. Dunbar. The whole letter is quoted in Watson's *Annals of Philadelphia and Pennsylvania*, II, 138. The Gordon *Journal* gives the loss as £1000 which Sargent, op. cit., p. 389, thinks a clerical error for £10,000.

22. Ford, *Writings*, I, p. 173. (To Governor Dinwiddie from Fort Cumberland, July 18, 1755.)

23. Ford, *Writings*, I, p. 177 (to Robert Jackson, Aug. 2, 1755.)

24. Gen. B. T. Johnson, *General Washington*, p. 57.

25. Ford, *Writings*, I, p. 175 (July 18, 1755).

26. Sparks, *Writings*, II, p. 86.

CHAPTER XVI

1. Dr. Louis K. Koontz, *The Virginia Frontier, 1754-1763*, p. 26, quotes this from the quotation of it in C. J. H. Hayes' *A Political and Social History of Modern Europe*, I, p. 307. Dr. Koontz calls the defeat of Braddock "a blessing in disguise, as it served to arouse the colonies to something of concerted action." He explains the persisting apathy and jealousy among the colonies as largely due to religious factions. Congregational New England had been afraid of Dinwiddie as a Scotch Presbyterian who "would respect that Church." New England abhorred Catholicism so that, as Koontz says, "It is not going too far to say that this term ["Papists"] had about the same effect on the earlier New Englander that the word 'fire' would produce on persons living in the vicinity of a powder mill." The New Englanders dreaded the Church of England for its lingering Catholicism. To aid England was to aid the Anglican church. In New York the excuse was that the French had invaded none of His Majesty's dominions. New Jersey was "a slice of New York." Maryland was largely Catholic; Virginia strongly Anglican; North Carolina torn between Establishment and dissent; South Carolina was thinking it over; Pennsylvania, like Maryland, was a proprietary colony with two masters. The Quakers were at odds with everybody except the Indians. Aside from the religious feuds and suspicions, the governors were everywhere at odds with the assemblies. *The Johns Hopkins University Studies*, in which Dr. Koontz' monograph is included, devote a number of invaluable publications to phases of this immensely important religious matter. It is hard to resist the temptation to quote copiously from such a scholarly and picturesque work as Dr. H. R.

McIlwaine's *The Struggle of Protestant Dissenters for Religious Toleration in Virginia*. He quotes (p. 63) Commissary Dawson's address to the convention of the clergy held at Williamsburg, October 30th, 1754, "It would be needless to inform you in what condition the Church of Virginia at present is, attacked by the blind zeal of fanaticism on the one hand, and the furious malice of popery on the other." In March, 1756, the General Assembly passed an act for disarming Papists and "reputed Papists," who refused to take the oaths to the government. Even the poor Acadians who had found their way to Virginia were ordered transported to England. The neglected influence of the Puritans remaining in Virginia is discussed in John H. Latané's *The Early Relations between Maryland and Virginia*. They had little political influence but kept the Anglican ritual simpler, so that surplices were not worn in Virginia till well on in the 19th Century (p. 64). Dr. S. B. Weeks, in *Church and State in North Carolina*, points out the bad quality of the missionaries, who were scoundrels or weaklings, debauched or drunkards (p. 15, 16) and seem to have rivalled the Virginia clergy in dissipation. The Baptists of North Carolina "were the most prosperous body of Baptist Christians in the world" (p. 29). The struggle there was to establish the Established Church and it was bitterly contested. In Herbert L. Osgood's *The American Colonies in the Eighteenth Century*, almost all of volume III is devoted to the religious ferment.

2. *Dinwiddie Papers*, II, p. 94. The following citations are from pages 99, 101, 108, 116, 118, 120, 178, 189.

3. *Dinwiddie Papers*, II, p. 122, July 26, 1755.

4. *Dinwiddie Papers* II, p. 135, 142, 168, 177.

5. S. M. Hamilton, *Letters to Washington*, I, p. 73.

6. Mrs. Sally Nelson Robins, *Love Stories of Famous Virginians*, p. 28.

7. James Truslow Adams, *New England in the Republic*, p. 6.

8. Parkman, *Montcalm and Wolfe*, I, p. 341, from which is quoted Dumas' report to the ministry and the letter of the priest, Reverend C. G. Cocquard, S. J. See also T. J. Chapman, *The French in the Allegheny Valley*, p. 71-3.

9. Hulbert, *Historic Highways*, IV, p. 135. The belief that Christ was French is quoted from Count Zinzendorf's *Journal* by Parkman, *Montcalm and Wolfe*, I, p. 58.

10. Volwiler, *Croghan and the Westward Movement*, p. 100, 101-5.

11. Volwiler, op. cit., p. 103, 106, 128.

12. Samuel Kercheval's *History of the Valley of Virginia*, p. 78, a treasure-chest of dramatic and pitiful stories of these terrible times, mostly taken from the lips of survivors or relatives, as were the incidents related in the text.

13. Koontz, *The Virginia Frontier*, 1754-1763, p. 72.

14. Ford, *Writings*, I, p. 178.

15. Sparks, *Writings*, II, p. 93; Ford, *Writings*, I, p. 180.

16. Ford, *Writings*, I, p. 182.

17. *Dinwiddie Papers*, II, p. 146, 184, 200.

18. *Dinwiddie Papers*, II, p. 236; Ford, *Writings*, I, p. 501.

19. *Dinwiddie Papers*, II, p. 474. J. C. Ballagh, in his *History of Slavery* (Johns Hopkins Press) says, p. 11, "Projected insurrections of negroes in

1710, 1722, and 1730 bear witness to their alarming increase, and by the middle of the century the blacks were almost as numerous as the whites." Pp. 78-9 he tells of the various laws enacted because of this fear. In 1701, "Billy," a slave, terrorized three counties. On other occasions militia was kept in readiness. People went to church under arms. (P. 89) "No actual insurrection worthy of the name occurred until the nineteenth century," the worst being that of "a well-educated and well-treated negro preacher in 1831" (p. 93).

20. *Dinwiddie Papers*, II, p. 102, 114.
21. *Dinwiddie Papers*, II, p. 239.
22. *Dinwiddie Papers*, II, p. 240.
23. *Dinwiddie Papers*, II, p. 243. Dinwiddie's letter to Fairfax is given in full, II, p. 249.
24. *Journal of Captain Charles Lewis*, Virginia Historical Collections, vol. XI, pp. 205-218.
25. *Dinwiddie Papers*, II, p. 273.
26. Ford, *Writings*, I, p. 227.
27. *Dinwiddie Papers*, II, p. 318, 325, 331, 338.
28. Ford, *Writings*, I, p. 227.
29. Ford, *Writings*, I, p. 219.

CHAPTER XVII

1. Bolton, *History of Westchester County*, N. Y., 1881, II, p. 633: "In the Manor Hall [in Yonkers] July 3, 1730, was born Mary Philipse, daughter of the Hon. Frederick Philipse, speaker of the House of Assembly, and lord of the Manor of Philipsborough. From this lady's character, Fenimore Cooper formed the heroine of *The Spy*, under the name of 'France.' "
2. W. H. Shelton, *The Jumel Mansion*, p. 13. This volume by the curator of the Jumel Mansion in New York is invaluable for its Washington material and the history of the Philipses and Morrises. The Mansion, built by Capt. Morris for Mary Philipse, was briefly occupied by Washington as headquarters during the Revolutionary War, when the Morrises were attainted of Toryism, and was occupied by various other generals during the struggle.
3. James Grant Wilson, *Memorial History of New York*, III, p. 369. The history of Mary Philipse is given fully in this and other New York histories. In Mrs. Lambs' *History of the City of New York*, Ch. XXVII, there is a good account of Beverly Robinson's distinguished family and of the Philipse dynasty, with mention also of a log cabin near Lake Mahopac where Mary Philipse lived when she visited her tenants. "Morris's log-house was more than once occupied by Washington and was the scene of many tragic events."
4. Ford, *Writings*, I, p. 232. Ford gives here also Washington's list of expenses and extracts from the *Pennsylvania Gazette* mentioning his various arrivals.
5. Justin Winsor, *Memorial History of Boston*, II, p. 127. In his *Narrative and Critical History of America*, VII, p. 563, this portrait and its authenticity are discussed. Washington Irving published it in the first edition of his *Life of Washington*.

6. Parkman, *Montcalm and Wolfe*, I, p. 336, quotes these letters and gives a very full account of Shirley's activities. H. L. Osgood, in *The American Colonies in the XVIIIth Century* (III, p. 579), devotes a whole chapter to Shirley. He emphasizes Shirley's great work for colonial union. "This all served to stimulate the sentiment of national pride which lies at the root of imperialism and to fan these emotions till they led to aggressive action and finally to war. . . . Franklin was the only colonist whose services in this direction were comparable with those of Shirley."

7. Dr. Charles Henry Lincoln, *The Correspondence of William Shirley* (1912), II, p. 412.

8. Lincoln, op. cit., II, p. 448.

9. S. M. Hamilton, *Letters to Washington*, I, p. 179.

CHAPTER XVIII

1. Dr. Koontz, *The Virginia Frontier, 1754-1763*, p. 98. "The English nation has always been strong in defence. . . . Governor Dinwiddie . . . saw from the very first that the extended frontier of the colony must be fortified at strategic points. He outlined a plan which finally resulted in a cordon of forts, stockades, and block-houses which stretched along the entire frontier of Virginia joining the colonies to the North and to the South, thus fortifying the outposts of the English settlements from Crown Point, New York, to the borders of Georgia. The mind of Dinwiddie and the hand of Washington manifested themselves in the fact that the Virginia Frontier was literally dotted with these fortifications, while the frontiers of the other colonies North and South were meagerly defended. There was some difference of opinion between Governor Dinwiddie and Washington as to the number of forts, but . . . the governor left that matter largely to Washington."

Dr. Koontz gives the plan for a cordon as drawn up by a council of war July 27, 1756, and the independent plan drawn up by Washington later. There were great difficulties in getting the forts built and keeping them manned, and Captain Dagworthy's name appears in 1757 in a letter from Fort Cumberland warning Washington that "a large Body of French and Indians with a train of artillery, were actually marched from Fort Du Quesne with a design, as they conceived, to make an attempt on Fort Cumberland." With infinite research Dr. Koontz has prepared a list and description of 81 forts on the Virginia frontier, giving a description and history of each (op. cit., Appendix I).

Hulbert, *Historic Highways*, vol. V, devotes chapter II to the forts of Pennsylvania and Virginia under the title "A Blood-Red Frontier." He asks (p. 43): "Is the splendid lesson of these years clear? By Providential dispensation these colonies were a miniature of the America of 1775 suddenly thrown upon its own resources and in war. The divine hand is not more clearly seen in our national development than in the struggle of the colonies between 1745 and 1763."

The divine hand was certainly well hidden from the eyes of the colonists who believed that a redder hand was at work everywhere. And it should not be forgotten that Washington opposed the chain of forts with such vehemence that he was sharply rebuked.

2. Ford, *Writings*, I, p. 238.

3. Ford, *Writings*, I, p. 238 note.

4. *Dinwiddie Papers*, II, p. 653.

5. Ford, *Writings*, I, p. 239.

6. Ford, *Writings*, I, p. 241 note.

7. *Dinwiddie Papers*, II, p. 383.

8. *Dinwiddie Papers*, II, p. 388.

9. *Dinwiddie Papers*, II, p. 407.

10. *Dinwiddie Papers*, II, p. 381.

11. Ford, *Writings*, I, p. 245, 255, note.

12. Ford, *Writings*, I, p. 249, 252.

13. Ford, *Writings*, I, p. 265. The letters of Washington are packed with wretchedness throughout this period.

14. Ford, *Writings*, II, p. 289, 298, 303 note.

15. *Dinwiddie Papers*, II, p. 523, 655; Ford, *Writings*, I, p. 350.

16. Albert Jay Nock, *Jefferson* (N. Y., 1926), p. 5.

17. *Dinwiddie Papers*, II, p. 695-7.

18. Ford, *Writings*, I, p. 321, 332, 364. See also Koontz, *The Virginia Frontier*, p. 116.

19. *Dinwiddie Papers*, II, p. 485.

20. Ford, *Writings*, I, p. 335.

21. Ford, *Writings*, I, p. 296-7, note.

CHAPTER XIX

1. Worthington C. Ford hunted for years for a copy of this issue of the *Virginia Gazette* without finding it, but eventually came across a number of the *Pennsylvania Journal* for November 4, 1756 (published by William Bradford), in which it was copied. Ford published it (with a foreword and an article in defense of the troops, probably by Richard Bland) in the *Pennsylvania Magazine of History and Biography*, Jan., 1899.

2. It is odd that the motto which Washington put on his seal in later years bore this motto in the original Latin from Ovid's *Heroides:* EXITUS ACTA PROBAT. It was not on the silver seal of his which was lost on Braddock's Field and found there in 1842 by Daniel Boone Logan. (Conway, *Washington and Mount Vernon*, p. xv.)

CHAPTER XX

1. Quoted by Sparks, *Life*, chapter IV. Sparks makes a ferocious attack on Dinwiddie and is responsible largely for the subsequent injustice toward Washington's best friend of the period. It is a pleasure to find one's own high opinion of Dinwiddie authenticated by such a scholar as Dr. Koontz who, in *The Virginia Frontier, 1754-1763*, pp. 76-84, makes an ardent defense of him and incidentally lays his finger on the fundamental error of Washington's unreasonable idolaters:

"The pith of much of this criticism of Dinwiddie's blunt candor in his letters to Washington comes from reading his letters in the light of what we now know of Washington, and the reverence we have for his character. Historians and biographers have thought and written of Dinwiddie as though they demanded that he span the half century in which he was living, see Washington first as the successful leader of the American colonial troops, then as first president of the new Republic, and finally as one idealized to such an extent that an early biographer of Washington's felt that he dare not publish Washington's letters without 'doctoring' them to suit his own taste (Jared Sparks). Surely, to expect Dinwiddie to know all of this was expecting too much of even a shrewd Scotchman! To Dinwiddie, at this time, Washington was an officer of 'great Merit and Resolution,' who owed his opportunities and commissions to the very man who wrote so frankly to him. And we know that Governor Dinwiddie exacted of Washington nothing more than he exacted of himself."

2. *Dinwiddie Papers*, II, p. 425 (May 28, 1756, to Maj.-Gen. Abercrombie).

3. *Dinwiddie Papers*, II, p. 552

4. Ford, *Writings*, I, p. 384.

5. Ford, *Writings*, I, p. 388, note.

6. Ford, *Writings*, I, p. 389.

7. Ford, *Writings*, I, p. 393, 411.

8. Ford, *Writings*, I, p. 404.

9. Ford, *Writings*, I, p. 400.

10. Ford, *Writings*, I, p. 406.

11. Ford, *Writings*, I, p. 409.

12. Ford, *Writings*, I, p. 414.

13. *Dinwiddie Papers*, II, p. 540 (to Henry Fox).

14. Ford, *Writings*, I, p. 430 n.

15. Ford, *Writings*, I, p. 431 n.

16. *Dinwiddie Papers*, II, p. 606.

17. Ford, *Writings*, I, p. 431.

18. Ford, *Writings*, I, p. 451 note.

19. Ford, *Writings*, I, p. 441.

20. Victor Hugo Paltsits, *Washington's Note Book*. Selections from a newly discovered manuscript written by him while a Virginia Colonel in 1757. Bulletin of the New York Public Library, Vol. 24, No. 8, Aug., 1920.

21. Ford, *Writings*, I, p. 438.

22. Ford, *Writings*, I, p. 463.

23. Ford, *Writings*, I, p. 471 and note.

CHAPTER XXI

1. *Dinwiddie Papers*, II, p. 595.

2. S. M. Hamilton, *Letters to Washington*, II, p. 49 (March 14, 1757), 137, 168.

3. W. H. Shelton, *The Jumel Mansion*, pp. 14-15. He quotes the article by Mrs. Amherst Morris from the *Herefordshire Magazine*, November, 1907.

4. Bolton's *History of Westchester County*, New York, II, p. 633, has an account of the exceedingly brilliant wedding and the mysterious Indian.

CHAPTER XXII

1. Ford, *Writings*, I, p. 158.
2. S. M. Hamilton, *Letters to Washington*, I, p. 158, 162.
3. The fact that Washington ran for office in 1757 was either ignored or disputed by many historians. It is proved, however, in R. T. Barton's *The First Election of Washington to the House of Burgesses* (Collections of the Virginia Historical Society, new series, XI, 1892), p. 115. Barton says, p. 118: "Of Hugh West no record remains except that he was thus connected with the name of Washington." But the facts in the text concerning him are given in Fitzpatrick's note to the *Diaries*, I, p. 110.
4. *Dinwiddie Papers*, II, p. 353.
5. P. L. Haworth, *George Washington, Country Gentleman*, pp. 192 n., 218.
6. J. M. Leake, *The Virginia Committee System and the American Revolution* (Johns Hopkins University Studies, 1917), pp. 22, 81. Beard, *American Government and Politics*, p. 455, says: "In Virginia the voter had to be a freeholder of an estate of at least fifty acres of land, if there was no house on it; or twenty-five acres with a house twelve feet square; or, if a dweller in a city or town, he had to own a lot or part of a lot with a house twelve feet square." Leake, op. cit., pp. 81-2, gives the exact terms or various enactments concerning the qualifications for suffrage.
7. R. T. Barton, op. cit., p. 123.
8. R. T. Barton, op. cit., p. 116
9. Ford, *Writings*, I, p. 501.
10. Wilson Miles Cary, *Sally Cary*, p. 27, note.

CHAPTER XXIII

1. Ford, *Writings*, I, p. 487, 483 n.
2. Ford, *Writings*, I, p. 43-4.
3. S. M. Hamilton, *Letters to Washington*, II, p. 181.
4. Ford, *Writings*, I, p. 485.
5. Ford, *Writings*, I, p. 487.
6. *Dinwiddie Papers*, II, p. 703.
7. Ford, *Writings*, I, p. 494.
8. *Dinwiddie Papers*, II, p. 707.
9. *Dinwiddie Papers*, II, p. 720, 721. Capt. Stewart's letter is in S. M. Hamilton, *Letters to Washington*, II, p. 231, Dinwiddie's reply in II, p. 239.
10. *Dinwiddie Papers*, II, p. 705.
11. *Dinwiddie Papers*, II, p. 608.
12. *Dinwiddie Papers*, II, p. 235.
13. *Dinwiddie Papers*, I, p. 30.
14. Ford, *Writings*, II, p. 86, Sept. 1, 1758.

15. *Dinwiddie Papers*, I, p. 524—the letter to William Allan, Mar. 10, 1755, already quoted.

The editor of his papers, Mr. R. A. Brock, says of him (*Dinwiddie Papers*, I, p. xiii) : "The administration of Governor Dinwiddie had been a peculiarly trying one. His disputes with the Assembly, and his difficulties with Washington, have, through the prejudiced representations of some writers, left an unpleasant impression of his character on the American mind, which has been allowed to veil virtues which would otherwise have commanded undivided esteem and regard. An attempt has been made to blacken his memory with the crime of dishonesty, in the charge of misappropriation, to his own use, of funds, entrusted to him for the public service—a calumny which rests alone upon the unsupported statements of his enemies."

This eulogy contrasts strangely with Sparks' contemptuous farewell to him. Sparks, *Writings*, II, p. 270, note, and *Life*, Chapter V.

16. Ford, *Writings*, II, p. 2, note.

17. Ford, *Writings*, II, p. 4.

CHAPTER XXIV

1. G. W. P. Custis, *Recollections*, p. 499. "The lady was fair to behold, of fascinating manners and splendidly endowed with worldly benefits. The hero fresh from his early fields, redolent of fame, and with a form on which 'every god did seem to set his seal, to give the world assurance of a man.' "

Charles Moore, *The Family Life of George Washington*, gives the date as February, 1758, on p. 52, and as May, 1758, on p. 229.

2. Ford, *Writings*, II, p. 26.

3. Anne Hollingsworth Wharton *Martha Washington*, gives Martha's birthday as June 21, 1731, on p. 3, but on p. 30 says she was "three months younger than her lover although she has so often been spoken of as the elder of the two." Custis, op. cit., p. 495, gives her birth date as May, 1732. Wilson Miles Cary, in *The William and Mary College Quarterly*, July, 1896, states that the family Bible gives the date as June 2, 1731. Others say, June 21; but the month and year seem indisputable.

4. Meade, *Old Churches*, I, p. 194.

5. Mrs. Wharton, op. cit., p. 17. B. J. Lossing, *Mary and Martha Washington*, pp. 86, 91.

6. Mrs. Wharton, op. cit., p. 27.

7. Dora Chinn Jett, *In Tidewater Virginia*, p. 56.

8. Woodrow Wilson, *George Washington*, p. 101.

9. So her grandson, Edward Ambler, declared—Meade, *Old Churches*, I, p. 108. But Wilson Miles Cary, *Sally Cary*, denies that Washington was ever in love with Mary or proposed for either her or her sister, to Colonel Cary.

10. Mrs. Wharton, op. cit., p. 25. G. W. P. Custis, *Recollections*, p. 497.

11. Marion Harland, *Some Colonial Homesteads*, p. 489. "The great chieftain is a trifle more human to our apprehension for the rift in the granitic formation that grants us a glimpse of fire in the heart of the boulder."

12. Mrs. Wharton, op. cit., p. 35, where she calls attention to the fact that

Thackeray used this story in *The Virginians* with some license as to facts and dates.

13. Lossing, op. cit., p. 99. Martha's early portraits are in dispute. The one familiarly published, M. D. Conway declares (*Washington and Mount Vernon*, p. li.), to be that of Washington's sister, Betty Lewis, who bore such a resemblance to him that in a uniform she might have been taken for him. He says, "It is inconceivable that any one could discover a resemblance between" this portrait and Martha. He reproduces Col. Lewis W. Washington's comments in agreement with him. Yet Mrs. Wharton, op. cit., p. 31 n., quotes in opposition to Conway and L. W. Washington, Prof. G. W. Brown and Charles W. Hart, who insist that Custis would never have published the portrait as of his grandmother in his *Recollections*, p. 495, nor permitted Sparks and Irving to publish it, if it had not been hers.

CHAPTER XXV

1. Ford, *Writings*, II, p. 5. Nicholas' letter is in S. M. Hamilton, *Letters to Washington*, II, p. 251 (Feb. 6, 1758).
2. George M. Trevelyan, *History of England*, N. Y., 1926, p. 542.
3. Ford, *Writings*, II, pp. 8, 11.
4. Ford, *Writings*, II, p. 24.
5. S. M. Hamilton, *Letters to Washington*, II, p. 343, 349.
6. R. T. Barton, *The First Election of Washington* (Virginia Hist. Coll., vol. XI), p. 117. He speaks of Washington's recent engagement to the widow Custis, and adds, "That this contemplated marriage had something to do with our hero's so quickly repeated candidacy is a surmise that is not far to seek."
7. S. M. Hamilton, *Letters to Washington*, II, p. 397; Ford, *Writings*, II, p. 53. Needless to say, Sparks does not mention the liquor bill, but only the tributes of praise for Washington (*Life*, p. 99). Lodge, *Life*, I, 102, says merely, "While away on his last campaign he had been elected a member of the House of Burgesses" and tells the story of his modest inability to utter a word when he took his seat and was greeted with a eulogy.
8. R. T. Barton, op. cit., p. 123.
9. Ford, *Writings*, II, p. 59.
10. R. T. Barton, *op. cit.*, p. 124.
11. Ford, *Writings*, II, p. 53.
12. Dr. J. M. Leake, *The Virginia Committee System and the American Revolution* (Johns Hopkins University Studies, 1917), pp. 79-84.
13. William Wirt, *Sketches of the Life of Patrick Henry*, p. 45. It is noteworthy that William Wirt Henry, who developed the sketch into a three-volume work, omits the story of Washington's confusion.

Gen. B. T. Johnson, *George Washington*, p. 73, scouts the tale, saying: "Like many of the demigod myths and fables of Washington, this story smacks of the incredible. In the first place, those people at that time, as now, were not inclined or partial to dramatic performances by themselves. . . . When, therefore, the Speaker by order of the House presented its thanks to Colonel Washington, the dignified and becoming thing for

Colonel Washington to do was to rise in his place, bow to the Speaker, and take his seat as he did. The idea of his attempting to 'answer back' originated in another latitude—never among Virginians."

14. P. L. Ford, *The True George Washington*, p. 298.

CHAPTER XXVI

1. Parkman, *Montcalm and Wolfe*, II, pp. 41, 42. George Louis Beer in his *British Colonial Policy, 1754-1765*, has written a splendid treatise on this period. He gives, p. 65, note, the exact number of troops called in from each colony and notes "the considerable discrepancy between these numbers and those actually in the field."

2. Hulbert, *Historic Highways*, V, p. 82, says that Forbes had originally planned to march by Braddock's Road and proves his point from Forbes' letter to the Governor of Pennsylvania (Penn. Records, N, p. 206). It was St. Clair who won him over to the new route. Hulbert (p. 88) calls St. Clair "a vacillating know-nothing" and remarks on Bouquet's unhappy situation with such a quartermaster-general and a commander-in-chief who could not come to the front.

3. G. L. Beer, op. cit., p. 62 note, quoting letters from Forbes to Pitt, in the *Pitt Correspondence*, I, 342, 372.

4. Parkman, op. cit., II, p. 144, who persists in calling Colonel Byrd "Burd" and St. Clair "Sinclair." He wrote with copies of the printed letters and manuscript letters of Forbes before him. They are in the *Additional Manuscripts* in the British Museum, the 21,641st volume! Winsor, *Narrative and Critical History*, spells St. Clair's name both ways, but prefers St. Clair.

5. Ford, *Writings*, II, p. 6.

6. Ford, *Writings*, II, p. 51.

7. Ford, *Writings*, II, p. 12 n.

8. Ford, *Writings*, II, p. 49.

9. Sparks, *Writings*, II, 294; Irving, *Life*, ch. xxiv.

10. Ford, *Writings*, II, p. 50 note.

11. Ford, *Writings*, II, p. 23.

12. Ford, *Writings*, II, p. 32.

13. Ford, *Writings*, II, p. 50.

14. Ford, *Writings*, II, p. 65.

15. Ford, *Writings*, II, p. 72.

16. Ford, *Writings*, II, p. 73.

17. Hulbert, op. cit., V, pp. 84, 91, 95, 106.

18. Hulbert, op. cit., p. 113. In the fifth volume of his *Historic Highways*, Prof. Hulbert quite loses the awe he had expressed for Washington in his fourth volume. There everything that Washington did was under the direct guidance of Providence. In this volume, however, he criticizes Washington with great severity, though he does full justice to his honesty and even to his wisdom, which might have been demonstrated if factors other than military had not brought about the success of Forbes' expedition. Aside from the early reference already quoted from his forty-third page, concerning the Providential dispensation that threw the colonies on their own resources

and the clearly seen "divine hand" that prepared them thus for 1775, there is no allusion to Providence except his quotation on p. 159, of Bouquet's fervent tribute to Forbes, "After God, the success of this expedition is entirely due to the General." To which Prof. Hulbert adds, "His last campaign must be considered one of the most heroic in the annals of America" and quotes Parkman's praise in *Montcalm and Wolfe*, II, p. 169: "Its solid value was above price. . . . From southern New York to North Carolina, the frontier populations had cause to bless the memory of the steadfast and all-enduring soldier."

Prof. Hulbert gives the final credit rather to Pitt than to Providence. As for Washington, on reviewing his dismal exile from important service, Prof. Hulbert must have felt, as Washington did, that Providence had abandoned him entirely, after having previously shown its love mainly by its chastisement.

19. Volwiler's *Croghan and the Westward Movement* is rich in evidences of the activity of these traders and other civilian toilers and shabby diplomats. At one time Croghan entertained two hundred Indians at his house and kept them sober lest they steal away before the conference (p. 132). "During the year 1757 Croghan had held three major and many minor Indian conferences in Pennsylvania" (p. 136). He made Johnson Hall his headquarters for nearly a year and assisted Sir William Johnson in conferences. "In the spring of 1758 Croghan was on the frontier in the Mohawk valley. . . . In July, Johnson and Croghan led about four hundred Iroquois warriors to assist the new commander-in-chief Abercromby, in his ill-advised attack on Ticonderoga." Abercromby sent Croghan back to help Forbes. "Few men did more to hasten this decision than Christian Frederick Post." (p. 137).

20. Ford, *Writings*, II, p. 75.

21. These letters from Forbes and Bouquet are quoted by Parkman and Hulbert from the Forbes-Bouquet correspondence. Hulbert, V, p. 135.

22. Ford, *Writings*, II, p. 58, assigns this to Gabriel Jones with a query. In October, 1757, Washington had appealed to Gabriel Jones for help against the "absurd, irregular and illegal practices" of the magistrates who were releasing the captured deserters as fast as they were brought to trial; and many of the men, immediately after getting drunk, deserted for fear Washington would have them flogged. See Ford, *Writings*, I, p. 501.

23. Hulbert, op. cit., V, pp. 137-141.

24. Volwiler, *Croghan*, p. 138.

25. Volwiler, *Croghan*, p. 137. Parkman in his *Montcalm and Wolfe*, II, pp. 150, 157, writes some of his finest pages concerning Post's glorious services.

26. Hulbert, op. cit., V., p. 142.

27. Hulbert, op. cit., V, p. 148.

28. Ford, *Writings*, II, pp. 84, 85.

29. S. M. Hamilton, *Letter to Washington*, III, p. 50.

30. Ford, *Writings*, II, p. 91.

31. See John Robinson's letter to Washington, Ford, *Writings*, II, p. 94. See also Hamilton, *Letters to Washington*, III, p. 94.

32. "As is true of so many great Western routes, so of this path—the bold Christopher Gist was the first white man of importance to leave reliable

record of it" (Hulbert, op. cit., V, p. 16). He had travelled it on his outward way to the Forks of the Ohio when he went out in 1750 for the Ohio Company. Leaving Col. Cresap's near Fort Cumberland he had come upon "an old, old Indian Path" eleven miles northeast. It led him along the Great Warrior Mountain, through the Flintstone district of Alleghany County, Maryland. The path ran onward into Bedford County, Pennsylvania, through Warrior's Gap to the Juniata River. Here it joined the "Old Trading Path." Eight miles further on near the present town of Bedford it turned northwest to Venango. Laurel-hanne, "signifying the middle stream in the Delaware tongue" is halfway between the Juniata at Bedford and the Ohio at Pittsburgh.

33. Parkman, *Montcalm and Wolfe*, II, p. 148, quotes Vaudreuil's letters to the Ministry.

34. Volwiler, *Croghan*, p. 138.

35. Quoted in Parkman's brilliant account of the battle, in *Montcalm and Wolfe*, II, p. 160.

36. Ford, *Writings*, II, p. 101. In this letter Washington prematurely mourns as dead Major Lewis, who was taken prisoner, as he learned three days later.

CHAPTER XXVII

1. *Dinwiddie Papers*, II., p. 674. In a letter to Colonel Stephen, July 22nd, 1757: "I can't tell how to reconcile this, unless contrary to Orders, You carri'd more Women than I directed; the No. to a Company in all the Regulars are only 6 to a Comp'y, and You promis'd me to carry no more."

2. S. M. Hamilton, *Letters to Washington*, I., p. 184.

3. S. M. Hamilton, *Letters to Washington*, II., p. 205.

4. Winthrop Sargent, *Braddock's Expedition*, p. 257.

5. S. M. Hamilton, *Letters to Washington*, II., p. 173.

6. S. M. Hamilton, *Letters to Washington*, II., p. 180.

7. S. M. Hamilton, *Letters to Washington*, III., 51.

8. Wilson Miles Cary, *Sally Cary*, p. 37 note: "Mrs. Spotswood was probably Mary Dandridge, widow of John Spotswood, who was son of the Governor of that ilk. She became Mrs. Spotswood in 1745, a widow in 1757, and subsequently gave her hand *en secondes noces* to one John Campbell, Gent."

9. Wilson Miles Cary, *Sally Cary*, p. 40 note: "The original, like the others quoted, came back to America from Bath among Sally's personal papers."

10. S. M. Hamilton, *Letters to Washington*, II., p. 67.

11. The letter and the one following are printed in Ford's *Writings*, II., p. 95, 98, and elsewhere. Mrs. Burton (Constance Cary) Harrison's article was printed in *Scribner's Monthly*, July, 1876.

12. Wilson Miles Cary, *Sally Cary*, p. 33.

13. Sally Nelson Robins, *Love Stories of Famous Virginians*, p. 23.

14. Ford, *Writings*, II., p. 101.

15. Wilson Miles Cary, *op. cit.*, p. 35 note.

16. Ford, *Writings*, II., p. 53.

CHAPTER XXVIII

1. Ford, *Writings*, II., p. 104.
2. William Nelson, *The American Newspapers of the 18th Century as Sources of History*, American Historical Association, Annual Reports, 1908, vol. I., p. 217.
3. S. M. Hamilton, *Letters to Washington*, III., p. 60.
4. S. M. Hamilton, *Letters to Washington*, III., p. 92, 114.
5. S. M. Hamilton, *Letters to Washington*, III., p. 103.
6. S. M. Hamilton, *Letters to Washington*, III., p. 103, 111.
7. Ford, *Writings*, II., p. 105.
8. Ford, *Writings*, II, p. 108.
9. S. M. Hamilton, *Letters to Washington*, III., p. 124.
10. S. M. Hamilton, *Letters to Washington*, III., p. 117 (from Wm. Ramsay).
11. Parkman, *Montcalm and Wolfe*, II., p. 162, 134.
12. Volwiler, *Croghan and the Westward Movement*, p. 137-9.
13. Ford, *Writings*, II, p. 113.
14. Volwiler, *op. cit.*, p. 234, 335, 289-294.
15. Ford, *Writings*, II., p. 113.
16. Ford, *Writings*, II., p. 110 note.
17. Ford, *Writings*, II., p. 116-124. On p. 118 note, is a long account of the French versions of the abandonment of the fort. Ligneris still hoped to strike the English a telling return-blow. The French accounts are taken from the Pennsylvania Archives, Second Series, vol. VI.
18. Hamilton, *op. cit.*, III., p. 133-138.
19. Hamilton, *op. cit.*, I., p. 286.
20. Hamilton, *op. cit.*, I., p. 289. This letter is not given in Ford or Sparks.
21. Hamilton, *op. cit.*, III., p. 138.
22. Hamilton, *op. cit.*, III., p. 149-50.
23. Hamilton, *op. cit.*, III., p. 193, 194 note. See also Ford, *Writings*, II., p. 177, where the text is somewhat different as well as the spelling.
24. Hamilton, *op. cit.*, III., p. 143, also in Sparks, *Writings*, II., Appendix V.

CHAPTER XXIX

1. Sparks, *Writings*, II., p. 325. Ford omits this letter but gives those to Forbes and Cary, II, p. 124, 126.
2. Maud Wilder Goodwin, *The Colonial Cavalier*, p. 73.
3. Bishop Meade, *Old Churches*, I., p. 472.
4. The Rev. Devereux Jarratt quoted by Bishop Meade, I., p. 471.
5. Meade, *op. cit.*, I., 470, 472, 386; II., 460. Bishop Meade says that his epitaph calls him a native American, but his own quotation of it gives Mossom's birthplace as London, and states that he was an alumnus of St. John's College, Cambridge:

"Reverendus David Mossom prope Jacet,
Collegii St. Joannis Cantabrigiæ olim Alumnus,
Hujus Parochiæ Rector Annos Quadraginta.
Omnibus Ecclesiæ Anglicanæ Presbyteriis.
Inter Americanos Ordine Presbyteratus Primus;
Literatura Paucis Secundus. . . .
$\left\{\begin{array}{l}\text{Londini Natus 25 Martii 1690} \\ \text{Obiit 4° Jan}^{ii}\text{ 1767.''}\end{array}\right.$

6. Bishop Meade, I., 386, says it was at the White House, as do Washington Irving, ch. XXIV., Mrs. Wharton, *Martha Washington*, p. 46; Charles Moore, *The Family Life of Washington*, p. 56; Haworth, *George Washington, Country Gentleman*, p. 13. Sparks and Custis do not say where. Lossing, *Mary and Martha Washington*, p. 101, describes the church wedding and is followed by Lodge, I., p. 101; Woodrow Wilson, p. 102; Thayer, p. 35, and Ford, *Writings*, II., p. 125 n. Moore says that the married couple rode to church the next day and that this "gave rise to the impression that there was a church wedding." Mrs. Pryor, *The Mother of Washington*, p. 123. Custis, *Recollections*, p. 502, recounts his vain efforts to find the date and quotes Sparks' method of discovering it from a statement made by Washington in 1779 to Benjamin Franklin's daughter. But Washington, in his reply to Sir Isaac Heard's request for genealogical information, definitely writes the date as January 6th, 1759. Sparks, *Writings*, I., p. 549.

7. G. W. P. Custis, *Recollections*, p. 501.

8. Lossing, *op. cit.*, p. 101.

9. Mrs. Roger A. Pryor, *The Mother of Washington*, p. 108.

10. Mrs. Sally Nelson Robins, *Love Stories of Famous Virginians*, p. 39.

11. Moore, *op. cit.*, p. 56.

12. Maude Wilder Goodwin, *op. cit.*, p. 84.

13. John F. Watson, *Annals of Philadelphia and Pennsylvania*, I., p. 503, 178.

14. *The Journal of Nicholas Creswell, 1774-1777*, N. Y., 1924, p. 26.

15. S. M. Hamilton, *Letters to Washington*, III., p. 86. It was the Marquis de Chastellux who, in his *Travels in North America*, I., p. 112, said that after "the cloth was taken off, and apples and a great quantity of nuts were served, which General Washington usually continues eating for two hours, *toasting* and conversing all the time. These nuts are small and dry, and have so hard a shell (hickory nuts) that they can only be broken by the hammer; they are served half open, and the company are never done picking and eating them."

16. G. W. P. Custis, *Recollections*, p. 303.

17. Quoted in Charles M. Andrews, *Colonial Folkways*, p. 108, 116.

18. Mrs. Pryor, *op. cit.*, p. 110.

19. Quoted by Conway, *George Washington and Mount Vernon*, p. xliii, dated July 26, 1759.

20. Richard Parkinson, *A Tour in America in 1798, 1799, and 1800* (London, 1805), vol. II, p. 419, 427, 436.

21. G. W. P. Custis, *op. cit.*, p 157. The whole subject is taken up with much documentation in a pamphlet called "Washington as an Employer and

Importer of Labor," privately printed and anonymously, but with an introduction signed by Worthington C. Ford.

22. Mrs. Pryor, *op. cit.*, 203, 204. She quotes *The Journal of Philip Vickers Fithian*, edited by John Roger Williams.

23. From the Dreer Collection in the Pennsylvania Historical Society. First reprinted in *Harper's Magazine*, April, 1889. Martha's second letter is quoted from the same source.

24. Ford, *Writings*, II., p. 189.

25. Hamilton, *op. cit.*, III., p. 151.

26. Hamilton, *op. cit.*, III., p. 160, in a letter from Colonel George Mercer.

27. Hamilton, *op. cit.*, III., p. 163.

CHAPTER XXX

1. Fitzpatrick, *Diaries*, I., p. 240 note, where the editor gives a list of attendances from the Pohick Vestry Book. The other references to the *Diaries* are found under their dates.

2. Meade, *Old Churches*, II., p. 242-255.

3. John Bernard, *Retrospections of America*, edited from the manuscript by Mrs. Bayle Bernard. New York, 1887, p. 85. This passage is also quoted in Allan Nevins, *American Social History as Recorded by British Travellers*, p. 28.

4. Philip Guedalla, *Fathers of the Revolution*, p. 196.

5. Meade Minnegerode, *Some American Ladies*, p. 9. He states that Washington proposed to Colonel Cary for Sally Fairfax's hand. This has been shown to have been impossible.

6. Ford, *Writings*, II., p. 130-132.

7. Paul Leland Haworth, *George Washington, Country Gentleman*, p. 5.

CHAPTER XXXI

1. Joshua Gee, *Trade and Navigation of Great Britain Considered*, 6th ed., p. 71. London, 1738. Cited by Professor Claude H. Van Tyne in *The Causes of the War of Independence*, Boston, 1922, p. 75.

2. Peter Kalm, *Beschreibung der Reise*, etc. Göttingen, 1734. Translated by J. R. Forster as *Travels into North America*, 3 vols., 1770-71. Quoted in Hart's *American History told by Contemporaries*, II., p. 352.

3. Van Tyne, *op. cit.*, p. 83.

4. Ford, *Writings*, II., p. 474.

5. Ford, *Writings*, II., p. 441.

6. Frank Arthur Mumby, *George III and the American Revolution*, Boston, 1925; p. 3.

7. Ford, *Writings*, II., p. 173-175.

APPENDIX II

THE SPURIOUS PRAYERS

In 1891, there appeared at an auction in Philadelphia, among a mass of relics offered for sale by Washington's descendants, a little manuscript book found at Mount Vernon and promptly assumed to be in his autograph. It was also decided that he wrote it when he was about twenty.

Save for one newspaper at the time, nobody seems to have questioned its authenticity and no protest has been made against enshrining it as "without exception the most hallowed of all his writings." [1] Yet there is really every reason to cast this document out as not only the work of some other hand than Washington's, but as a writing that could hardly have been written by anybody during his lifetime.

The Reverend W. Herbert Burk, in a privately printed edition of the manuscript, describes it as a confirmation of the story of Washington's prayer at Valley Forge, which is "woven into the web and woof of the historic tapestry of the school-child mind."

Unfortunately, both web and woof of that school-child mind are largely of the same yarn from which the histories of the roof-rider, Santa Claus, Cinderella, Little Red Riding Hood and other characters are woven— immortal characters that can never die because they have never lived, yet

---

[1] See W. Herbert Burk, *Washington's Prayers*, 1907. This was read before the clerical brotherhood of the diocese of Pennsylvania, May 13th, 1907. Five hundred copies of it were printed for the benefit of the Washington Memorial chapel the same year. It includes a fac-simile of the alleged prayers as first published by Stan V. Henkels, Philadelphia, under the title, "Fac-simile of Manuscript Prayer-Book written by George Washington." On the reverse of the title page of this work is a fac-simile in the autograph of Lawrence Washington, saying that the original MS was "found among the papers which descended to me by inheritance from Genl. George Washington; and was declared by such experts as the late Dr. J. M. Toner, Simon Gratz, and Ferdinand J. Dreer, to be in the handwriting of Genl. Washington."

In his *George Washington the Christian*, William J. Johnson collects all the available evidence to prove his thesis. He says of this manuscript, p. 277, "Experts in Washington City, Philadelphia and New York are satisfied that it is Washington's handwriting without a doubt." The expression, "without a doubt" is always used to conceal a very strong dubiety.

552

persist the more for all that in an affectionate imagination more precious to many people than the cold truth.[1]

Though Henry Brueckner made a familiar painting of Washington on his knees at Valley Forge, and there is a bronze bas-relief of it on a public building in New York, no conscientious historian of today believes for a moment that Washington ever went out in the woods and prayed so noisily that his landlord, the Quaker Isaac Potts, hearing a man crying aloud, went near and discovered the agonized wrestler in the snow to be none other than the Commander-in-chief of the American army.

Potts in his dotage told the story, but if every senile reminiscence is to be believed, history might as well surrender its office to the creators of nursery rhymes and fairy stories.

The proof of the story has always rested upon the statement that Washington occupied as his headquarters at that time the house then owned by Isaac Potts, and still called by his name.

There could be no more startling example of the unreliability of such traditions than the utter collapse of the Isaac Potts story on investigation. In Washington's own handwriting, in his religiously kept account books, is the absolute destruction of the Potts house legend.

The facts are succinctly stated by one of the greatest of Washington authorities, the editor of Washington's complete *Diaries,* and the curator of his manuscripts at the Library of Congress, John C. Fitzpatrick, in whose volume of historical essays, *The Spirit of the Revolution,* the evidence is disclosed.

After pointing out that Washington, with his unfailing devotion to his soldiers, lived in a "canvas tent on a freezing hillside" while his soldiers were unhoused, and "did not move under a roof at Valley Forge until the log huts were finished and his troops were able to abandon their tents," Mr. Fitzpatrick writes:

"On Christmas Day the Commander-in-Chief moved from his tent near the Artillery Park, over the crest of the rise and down into the real valley to the house of Deborah Hewes, near the mouth of Valley Creek. Up to now the Valley Forge Headquarters has been known as the Isaac Potts House, but this is an undeserved honor. Despite the cheap sentimentality of the prayer story, proof is lacking that Isaac Potts was at Valley Forge that winter, and proof is lacking that he owned, in 1777-78, the house now pointed out as Headquarters. The accounts show that Deborah Hewes was paid by Washington for the use of her house and furniture at Valley Forge, and it is an injustice to Mistress Hewes that she, up to now, has been ignored. Isaac Potts only came into possession of the house near the end of the war, and not until forty years afterwards was the place pointed out as Washington's Headquarters. By then Potts's long residence had fixed it in the

[1] Apropos of Mr. Burk's tender reference to the "school-child mind," Henry C. Lea in an address on "Ethical Values in History" (published in the *American Historical Review,* January, 1904) said:

"History is not to be written as a Sunday-school tale for children of larger growth. It is, or should be, a serious attempt to ascertain the severest truth as to the past and to set it forth without fear or favor. It may, and it generally will, convey a moral, but that moral should educe itself from the facts."

minds of the country folk as the Potts House. Rightfully it should be known as the Hewes House, and Mistress Deborah's name should be recalled instead of the Quaker Isaac's." [1]

Valley Forge is a long way off in the chronicles of Washington, but since the story of his prayer there is used to support the story of the prayers he is said to have written at the age of twenty, it has importance.

Mr. Burk quotes some verses on "Christmas Day," copied by Washington when he was thirteen years old, beginning:

> "Assist me, Muse divine, to sing the morn,
> On which the Saviour of mankind was born."

Aside from such an instance and one reference to "the Divine author of our blessed religion" in 1783, there is no direct allusion to Christ, and the word Christ has been found in none of Washington's almost countless autographs.

His refusal to take communion was admitted by his own clergyman, William White, Bishop of the Episcopal Church in America from 1787 to 1836. Colonel Mercer had written to ask if General Washington "occasionally went to the communion," or "if he ever did at all." Bishop White answered:

"Truth requires me to say that General Washington never received the communion in the churches of which I am parochial minister. Mrs. Washington was an habitual communicant. . . . I have been written to by several on the point of your inquiry; and have been obliged to answer them as I now do you." Bishop White had previously written the same Colonel Mercer, in 1832: "As your letter seems to intend an inquiry on the point of kneeling during the service, I owe it to truth to declare that I never saw him in the said attitude." [2]

Another clergyman of Washington's, Reverend Dr. James Abercrombie, described how Washington always walked out of church before communion, "always leaving Mrs. Washington with the other communicants, she invariably being one." Dr. Abercrombie felt it his duty to rebuke this custom, and Washington "never afterwards came on the morning of sacramental Sunday" at all. He was, indeed, heard to say that he had "never been a communicant." [3]

Jefferson said that Washington was a Deist. [4]

This would seem to be the truth. In his time the word "deist" was a term of fierce reproach, almost worse than atheist, though a deist believed in an all-wise deity who cared for the world and provided a future reward

[1] John C. Fitzpatrick, *The Spirit of the Revolution, New Light from Some of the Original Sources of American History*, pp. 47, 88.

[2] Bird Wilson, D.D., *Memoir of the Life of the Right Reverend William White, D.D.* (Philadelphia, 1839), pp. 197, 189.

[3] Sprague, Wm. B., *Annals of the American Pulpit*; Life of Reverend James Abercrombie.

[4] Dr. M. D. Conway's monograph, "The Religion of George Washington." *The Open Court*, Oct. 24, 1889, p. 1895. Dr. Conway was born in Virginia.

for the good. This deity was not, however, the Israelitic Jehovah and was not the father of Christ, who was considered a wise and virtuous man, but not of divine origin.

Such was probably Washington's opinion on the subject, though there is little evidence either way. In spite of his incessant allusions to providence, Washington was persistently silent as to his dogmatic beliefs.

The fanatically abused "atheist," Jefferson, was far more religious than Washington, and intensely interested in Jesus, whom he revered this side of divinity. Franklin wrote President Stiles that he doubted the divinity of Christ (*Literary Diary*, III, p. 387). The greatly reviled Thomas Paine believed in God as a loving father, though he denounced the Bible as not His word. So many of the founders of the Republic were deists that the whole revolutionary movement was branded as infidel, though many ardently religious men were heroically for independence.

Strangely enough, nothing is heard of Benedict Arnold's warm adherence to the faith. He was brought up as a church member, filled his proclamations with piety, and joined the church anew shortly before he betrayed the United States. And in his statement "To the Inhabitants of America," proclaiming his reasons for reverting to the King, he gave the principal place to his dread that the alliance with France, "the Enemy of the Protestant Faith," would turn the country over to the papacy—a fear that was one of the chief forces in stimulating the colonies to the French and Indian War.[1]

The Reverend Doctor Moncure D. Conway makes a statement that is impressive in view of the emphasis unjustifiably laid on the imaginary doctrine that Washington was brought up in an atmosphere of intense religion:

"In his many letters to his adopted nephew and young relatives, he admonishes them about their morals, but in no case have I been able to discover any suggestion that they should read the Bible, keep the Sabbath, go to church, or any warning against Infidelity.

"Washington had in his library the writings of Paine, Priestley, Voltaire, Frederick the Great, and other heretical works."

Dr. Conway, speaking of Washington's Diaries, notes "his pretty regular attendance at church but never any remark on the sermons." [2]

If Washington were, indeed, so fervent a Christian as to deserve the name of "a soldier of the cross," often given to him by the clergy, it is puzzling that there should be such difficulty in finding a number of fervent proofs of his ardor.

Because of the utter dearth of such documents, the manuscript prayers were given an extraordinary welcome. Their first publisher, Stan V. Henkels, said of the little memorandum book, "This gem is all in the handwriting of George Washington, when about twenty years old, and is, without exception, the most hallowed of all the writings. It is neatly written on twenty-four pages of a little book about the size of the ordinary pocket memorandum." [3]

[1] See this proclamation and another to the army, given in full in Isaac N. Arnold's, *The Life of Benedict Arnold*, p. 330-4.

[2] M. D. Conway, *Washington and Mount Vernon*, p. lxix.

[3] Burk, op. cit., p. 13, 14, 17.

Mr. Burk describes their discovery:

"By the merest accident Mr. Henkels discovered this document. While making arrangements for the sale, he came across a dilapidated trunk, which Mr. Washington assured him contained only papers of no value, papers which had been rejected by the authorities of the Smithsonian Institute when offered for exhibition. In looking them over he came across this document and recognized at once what he considered the penmanship of Washington. His judgment was substantiated by other experts, to whom the manuscript was submitted.

"Mr. W. E. Benjamin, the well-known New York dealer, purchased the manuscript for twelve hundred and fifty dollars, and by him it was sold to the late Reverend Charles Frederick Hoffman, D.D. Naturally the discovery and sale of such an important manuscript of Washington attracted considerable attention and in the columns of the *New York Evening Post* the authenticity of the manuscript was challenged. It is not my purpose to revive that controversy. Where experts disagree a layman's opinion counts for little. Able experts declare the prayers were written by Washington. One says they were written by a Washington. Another, they are 'written in the unformed hand of the great patriot. It is a well-known fact that Washington between the years 1755 and 1763 changed his hand from the angular to the round formation.'

"The ultimate judgment must be based on the chirography, for there are no *a priori* arguments to prove that Washington did not write them.

"What disposition Dr. Hoffman made of the manuscript I have been unable to discover. In Dr. Potter's *Washington a Model in his Library and Life* is the following statement: 'The Rev. Dr. Chas. F. Hoffman has lately purchased "Washington's Prayers," the MSS. containing morning and evening prayers for various days of the week. He has under consideration, for the benefit of young men and others, a division of this very valuable manuscript, forming a sermon every page, for deposit in the fire-proof libraries of St. Stephen's College, Hobart College, Trinity College, and the University of the South, each institution to have also a complete free circulation of the whole work.'

"An analysis of the first prayer shows that it is made up almost entirely of sentences from the Prayer Book, and the other prayers are drawn largely from the same source. Almost every part of the Prayer Book has been laid under contribution, showing that the author was very familiar with its entire contents.

"While the Prayer Book is undoubtedly the source of the prayers, the question of their authorship is not determined. Dr. Lyman Abbott and Prof. Upham attributed them to Washington.

"No proof can be given that these prayers were composed by Washington, but, on the other hand, no proof has been produced to show that they were not his work. Professor Lucien M. Robinson is of the opinion that they are taken from some collection of prayers, but has not yet been able to confirm his opinion. I think this is very probable, and have endeavored to discover their source, but so far the search has been in vain. At present, the question is an open one, and its settlement will depend on the discovery of the originals, or upon the demonstration that they are the work of Washington."

These being the arguments in favor of the prayers, the arguments against them may be considered, without dwelling over much on their discovery in a neglected old trunk ·whose contents, as Mr. Henkels confesses, "had been rejected by the authorities of the Smithsonian Institute when offered for exhibition."

The rejection of the manuscript neither implies nor excuses any suggestion of fraud in their connection. Sincerity is granted to the believers in it. Forgery is not to be considered since a forger would have given at least an imitation of Washington's penmanship. And of this there is no trace.

The little memorandum-book contains twenty-four pages of handwriting consisting of a series of daily prayers headed "The Daily Sacrifice." There is a prayer for each morning and evening, beginning Sunday morning and ending abruptly in the middle of a sentence under Thursday morning.

The fervor of the prayers could not be exceeded, nor the sense of grovelling wickedness and need of forgiveness. Nothing, indeed, could be imagined more passionately religious, or more ecclesiastical in language.

To one who has read at all widely in what Washington has written, the tone is as foreign as if they were written in Greek. There is not a misspelled word, not a touch of incorrect grammar, not a capitalized noun or other emphatic word except the titles of the deity. In the final two entries of his Diary for December 12 and 13, 1799, Washington spells the following words with a capital: "Cloudy, Mercury, Moon, Night, Hail, Rain, Snowing, O'clock." The punctuation is precise and faultless.

This is not the place for a theological or bibliological treatise, but one who will read such a work as Rev. Dr. John Wright on *Early Prayer Books of America*[1] will find it hard to believe that either Washington or anybody else could have written this manuscript until the early part of the Nineteenth Century. Washington died in 1799.

Mount Vernon was occupied variously after his death, and some member of the household—probably a woman—may easily have begun a transcript of phrases from the Prayer Book and given it up before the work was done.

The impossibility of the work being in Washington's hand should be apparent to the most casual comparison. The writer of the Prayers, for instance, always crosses his final "t's," and all his "t's" are squatty and fat. Washington always wrote a tall thin "t," and usually ended it with a mere sidewise uplift. Little words like "and," "the," "this," and "most" are utterly unlike Washington's other examples, early or late. The capital "I" is not like his, nor the familiar "G," nor the "L," nor the "D," nor any of the capitals. The same is true of the small letters, their joinings and angles. The dates and days of the week are not in the least like his. Never in his life could Washington have written the sentences as they run. The

---

[1] Rev. John Wright, D.D., *Early Prayer Books of America* (Privately printed), St. Paul, Minn., 1896. He does not commit himself as to the authenticity of the *Daily Sacrifice*, merely saying "It may be of interest to call attention to a collection of manuscript prayers found among the effects of George Washington."

"round hand" he practiced for a time has no resemblance to this specimen. The tracings herewith may be compared with the facsimiles from Washington's Note Books of 1757 which were written in the so-called "round hand" he used for ten years.

Mr. Milton Carlson, one of America's most competent handwriting experts, with legal standing in the highest courts, having examined the text and many examples of Washington's known writings, agrees fully with the above contentions.

He finds it incredible that Washington could have either composed or copied the *Daily Sacrifice*. The writing, he says, shows a deliberation and feebleness that at no time characterized Washington's style of penmanship, which was remarkable for delicacy, slenderness, vigor, and speed. The

Tracings from the Prayers (left hand column) alleged to be in Washington's hand, and from the Report to the Earl of Loudoun, 1757, known to be in his hand. The "Sunday" and "Monday" are from Washington's Journal of 1748.

chirography of the text is round, slow and fat. In the spacing of the words, the weak terminals of the letters, the general slant, and relation of the letters in height, angle, and width; in fact, in all the qualities that determine an authentic autograph, this *Daily Sacrifice* is completely unlike anything of Washington's.

Of course, the Prayers have been useful for certain purposes, and religious people have never been over-cautious about ascribing texts to convenient authors; but it is rank dishonesty to continue the pretence that this work is Washington's.

It has infinitely less resemblance than those forged letters which were published in England during Washington's warfare with the British, admitted by him to contain many ingenious imitations of the truth, but none the less unquestionably spurious.

In denying his authorship of *The Daily Sacrifice*, there is no suggestion that at this time and for most of his life he was a skeptic or a rebel against the creed of the church which he served as a vestryman; though proof has never been given that he was ever a communicant, and certain ministers closely associated with him were puzzled by his refusal to take communion.

While it seems ridiculous to impute *The Daily Sacrifice* to Washington at any time of his life, it seems peculiarly impossible that the mood of those prayers should have been his in his twentieth year. For at that time Washington was not only dallying with love promiscuously, but was devoting his days to the study of the art of war and the practice of fencing under two foreign soldiers.

These men had been hired by Lawrence Washington before his death for the express purpose of turning the young man, not into a Puritan preacher or a curate, but into a skilful drillmaster and leader of soldiers against the French and Indians, who were trespassing on the great real estate venture called the Ohio Company.

APPENDIX III

A FRENCH POEM INSPIRED BY WASHINGTON

Five years after Washington slew Jumonville, the French were still so bitter that the crime was celebrated in a brief epic poem describing his crime as one that should "enrage eternity," and calling on posterity to punish what France could not.

The twenty-two-year-old backwoodsman had certainly burst into fame.

Perhaps this poem is picturesque enough to deserve a little space, especially as it is nowhere described at length in English. The Congressional Library copy of the volume has this pencilled note:

"Excessively rare volume and historically valuable. The assassination of Jumonville by Washington, as claimed by the French, gave rise to the Declaration of War by France against England, and by which it lost Canada."

Antoine Léonard Thomas was born in 1732 and died in 1785. His *Jumonville Poème* is the first in a volume of *Poésies Diverses*, Paris, 1763. At the head of the poem, Washington's execrable deed is branded in Latin from Vergil:

> Quod genus hoc hominum? Quaere hunc tam barbara morem
> Permittit Patria.

There is a prose preface briefly sketching the history of French and English disputes following the peace of Aix-la-Chapelle in 1748 and accusing the British of deception while preparing the conquest of Canada. At length the English invaded French territory and built a fort on the river "Oyo." The poet tells the story of Jumonville's "assassination" and the capture of the Fort de la Nécessité. "While the English, by the greatest of crimes, were stained with the blood of a French envoy, the French respected the blood even of assassins" in order to "avoid all that might cause a rupture between the two crowns."

After its capture, they destroyed the fort, that frightful monument, both of the unjust usurpation of the English and of the crime they had committed to assure their possession.

The poet then discusses the difference between true poetry and true history. Since this is a poem of vengeance, Contrecoeur's mere dismissal of the English was neither complete enough nor startling enough. So "the Poet takes nature for his guide and not the arrangements of politics."

Though Jumonville was only a humble officer, he is a fit subject for a poem since he is "no longer a simple individual, but a man clothed with a sacred character, who, in his quality of envoy, represents the august body of his nation.

"I dare to say that this death ought to interest, not only the French, but all the nations of the world except that which has been able to commit such a crime. . . . The assassination of Jumonville is a monument of perfidy that ought to enrage eternity.

"Since, unluckily for the human race, there is no tribunal where one can cite guilty nations, at least let posterity do that office and let the fear of infamy at least restrain them."

Save for the free versions in this chapter, there is perhaps no translation of the poem, and not likely to be. It begins with all the booming personification of the Eighteenth Century, including a statement that "the Thames in fury bellows in her reeds. To fight the Seine she arms her waves."

"Haughty English, of France implacable rivals, it is little to have forged the glave of war, to scatter your gold for the evils of the earth! Your sacrilegious hands have committed crimes that the veils of time will never cover, pirates, assassins, usurpers, perjurers, what a horrible picture for future races!

"Could I, O Jumonville, eternalizing thy glory in immortal chants, consecrate thy memory, and, painting the fury of thy assassins, impress upon their names an eternal horror!"

He describes English ferocity in contrast to the benevolent work of the lily of France. In a manner that would have surprised that poor but honest stream, the Ohio River, he describes it—or him—as reposing in deep grottos, feeling his waves shiver under his urn, and fleeing in fright from his humid palace.

> "L'Oyo qui reposoit dans ses grottes profondes,
> Tout-à-coup sous son urne entend frémir ses ondes."

Ohio, seeing the English covering his waves with battalions, hastens to Neptune in terror. The English build a fort in the woods.

> "With the French troops are two illustrious mortals:
> Issued from the same blood, born of the same mother,
> Their lips made use of the tender name of brother."

Their mother, seeing them sail away had cried, "O God, arbiter of mankind, attend my cries, a mother's!" But the jealous winds scatter her prayers.

Jumonville is sent to the English, and goes in noble confidence, never dreaming of ambush. The poet makes the surprising announcement that "The Frenchman is too great to suspect crime."

When he is surrounded, Jumonville addresses the English as follows:

> "Illustrious enemies, supports of England,
> Citizens in peace, heroes in war,
> May heaven make us kings of these realms.
> I come not here, as minister of war,
> In a generous blood to drench my cruel hands
> And rouse new discords with my steel."

He points out that nature has set the boundaries for the two nations. They have fought long enough. " 'Equal by nature, equal in our sufferings, let us live as friends, fellow-citizens, brothers. Let virtue bind us and not treaties. And in the calm bliss of an eternal peace, let both peoples'—at these words dictated by his zeal, by a homicidal bullet outrageously pierced, at the feet of his butchers he falls backward. Thrice he lifts his heavy eyelids. Thrice his dimming eye closes upon the light. The tender memory of France comes to charm, as he dies, his great soul at his last sigh. He dies. Trodden under the feet of an inhuman pack, his shattered members throb on the sand."

The poet asks of the Indians if they have ever seen such a people, or such a crime. He bids them carve on the rocks of their deserts the frightful scene; and calls upon the winds to carry the murder to foreign climes. "The Englishman is never only halfway cruel or perjurous (*L'Anglois n'est ni cruel ni perjure à demi*)."

So now the English promptly shoot eight other defenceless Frenchmen down while the Supreme Genius of the Law of Nations takes flight, shuddering, from the impious soil.

One Frenchman, an American (or as we would say, a Canadian), takes flight, mortally wounded but sustained by the desire to escape the tigers and carry the word of their atrocities.

He flees like a stag pierced with an arrow. He reaches the French and thrice essays to speak, thrice fails, then seeing Villiers,—

"O mon Père,[1] dit-il, avec des longs sanglots, Jumonville! il expire, en prononçant ces mots."

The horrified French rush to arms and Villiers is sent to lead them. The commander embraces the hero, bathed in tears:

> "O virtuous warrior, O brother unfortunate,"
> Said he, "Go and in the blood of a people of perjuries
> Efface the insults to thy King whom they outrage.
> But you, O sacred names that the worlds adore,
> O Nature! O Justice! A virtue that I implore,
> Thou passion of the sage, love of humankind,
> I can raise to heaven an innocent hand;
> I have not first blood-stained the land;
> I have not set the torch of war aflame.
> If Europe fights, the English are to blame."

The troops march off and the ghost of Jumonville appears to his brother, who holds out his arms to the shade:

> "O toi, s'écria-t-il, ombre terrible & chère
> Triste & fatal objet de tendresse & d'effroi
> Hélas! c'est donc ainsi qu' tu t'offres à moi!"

The spectre thrice shrieks "Vengeance!" till the woods and rocks resound. The soldiers proceed in growing fury till they reach the scene of the

[1] *Author's Note:* "Les Sauvages appellent les François leurs Pères."

murder, where Villiers, weeping, gathers in his arms the disfigured body of his brother and, of course, delivers an appropriate oration concerning their past, their mother, "who with her cries fatigues the altars, but cries in vain." He wonders how he can face her and confess that he was far from his brother at the time of his death, and his body, robbed of burial, was food for vultures.

> "And I was far from you at that hideous time!
> And my dying hand did not close thine eyes!
> I could not embrace thee! on thy plaintive lips
> I could not gather (*recueillir*) thy fleeting soul."

The French weep. Even the Indians are touched. Then Villiers calls for war.

The curious thing about it is that there seems to be never anywhere any mention of what became of Jumonville's body except in this highly unhistorical poem. His brother, in his report, quoted in the *Mémoire*, had merely stated:

"I stopped at the place where my brother had been assassinated and saw there yet some bodies (J'arrestay au lieu où mon frère avoit été assassiné et j'y vis encore quelques cadavres.")

Washington says that the Indians took some scalps, even from the wounded, and sent them about among the tribes. But no one seems to tell what became of Jumonville.

The poem carries the French to the strong fort, in which the English cower, terribly chilled by Jumonville's ghost. They are speedily crushed by the French.

> "O Malheureux Anglois! Peuple foible & superbe
> Impuissants dans la guerre, assassins dans la paix."

The fort is destroyed. "Bradhoc's" disaster is mentioned and general woe is promised to England, that ambitious people who should learn to fear the arms of mortals and the thunder of the gods.

And this is the poem for which Washington was to blame. Nothing could be less inspired or more lacking in realism. The realism came in the prolonged and devastating war in which England apparently won the victory, but really schooled her own children to turn against her.

BOOKS CONSULTED AND QUOTED

Adams, James Truslow, Revolutionary New England 1691-1776, Boston, 1923.

Adams, James Truslow, New England in the Republic, Boston, 1926.

Adams, Randolph Greenfield, A History of the Foreign Policy of the United States, N. Y., 1926.

Alvord, Clarence Walworth, The Mississippi Valley in British Politics, 2 volumes, Cleveland, 1917.

American Historical Review.

American Nation Series, The. See Hart, A. B.

Andrews, Charles M., The Colonial Background of the American Revolution, (Yale University Press) New Haven, 1924.

Andrews, Charles M., Colonial Folkways, The Chronicles of America, vol. IX, (Yale University Press) New Haven, 1921.

Anonymous [Charles Thomson?], An Enquiry into the Causes of the Alienation of the Delaware and Shawanese Indians from the British Interests, London, 1759.

Anonymous, The Expedition of Major-General Braddock to Virginia. Being Extracts of Letters from an Officer, etc. London, 1755.

Arnold, Isaac N., The Life of Benedict Arnold, Chicago, 1880.

Baker, W. S., Bibliotheca Washingtoniana, A Descriptive List of the Biographies and Biographical Sketches of George Washington, Philadelphia, 1889.

Ballagh, James Curtis, A History of Slavery in Virginia (Johns Hopkins University Press), Baltimore, 1902.

Ballagh, James Curtis, White Servitude in the Colony of Virginia (Johns Hopkins University Studies), Baltimore, 1895.

Barton, R. T., The First Election of Washington to the House of Burgesses. (Collections of the Virginia Historical Society, new series XI.) Richmond, 1892.

Bassett, John Spencer. See Byrd.

Bassett, John Spencer, The Virginia Planter and the London Merchant (American Historical Association Reports, 1901, I).

Beard, Charles A., American Government and Politics, New York, 1925.

Beard, Charles A. and Mary R., History of the United States, New York, 1921.

Beard, Charles A. and William C. Bagley, The History of the American People, New York, 1923.

Beattie, James, The Minstrel, to which are now added Miscellanies by James Hay Beattie, with an account of his Life and Character, London, 1799.

Beer, George Louis, The Origins of the British Colonial System, 1578-1660, N. Y., 1922.

Beer, George Louis, The Old Colonial System, 1660-1754, 2 volumes, New York, 1912.

Beer, George Louis, British Colonial Policy, 1754-1765, New York, 1922.

Bernard, John, Retrospections of America, 1797-1811, Edited from the Manuscript by Mrs. Bayle Bernard. New York, 1887.

Beveridge, Albert J., Life of John Marshall, 3 volumes, New York, 1916.

Blakely, W. A., American State Papers, Washington, D. C., 1911.

Bolton, Rev. Robert, History of Westchester County, 2 volumes, New York, 1881.

Boucher, Jonathan, Reminiscences of an American Loyalist 1738-1789, Boston, 1925.

Brock, R. A., See Dinwiddie Papers. Also Article on Virginia in Winsor's Narrative and Critical History.

Burk, W. Herbert, Washington's Prayers, Published for the benefit of the Washington Memorial Chapel, Norristown, Pa., 1907.

Butler, James Davie, British Convicts Shipped to American Colonies, published in The American Historical Review, October, 1896.

Byrd, Colonel William, The Writings of, Edited by John Spencer Bassett, New York, 1901.

Callahan, Charles H., The Memorial to Washington, An Historic Souvenir, Washington, 1923.

Callahan, Charles H., The Lodge of George Washington and His Masonic Neighbors, Washington, 1920.

Callahan, Charles H., Washington the Man and the Mason, Published under the Auspices of the G. W. National Memorial Assn., Washington, D. C., 1913.

Carrington, General Henry B., Washington the Soldier, New York, 1899.

Cary, Wilson Miles, Sally Cary, a Long Hidden Romance of Washington's Life, with Notes by Another Hand (privately printed), New York, 1916.

Channing, Edward, A History of the United States, 6 volumes, New York, 1909-1926.

Channing, Edward, and Albert Bushnell Hart, Guide to the Study of American History, Boston, 1897.

Chapais, Thomas, Le Marquis de Montcalm, Quebec, 1911.

Chastellux, Marquis de, Voyages, translated as Travels in North America, London 1787.

Chronicles of America, See Johnson, Allen.

Clements, William L., The William L. Clements Library of Americana at the University of Michigan (Published by the University), Ann Arbor, 1923.

Conkling, Margaret C., Memoirs of the Mother and Wife of Washington, New Edition. Auburn, N. Y., 1853.

Conway, M. D., George Washington and Mount Vernon (Long Island Historical Society), Brooklyn, 1889.

Conway, Moncure D., George Washington's Rules of Civility, N. Y., 1890.

Conway, Moncure D., The Religion of George Washington, The Open Court, October 24, 1889.

Cook, Dr. Elizabeth C., Literary Influence in Colonial Newspapers 1704-1750 (Columbia University Press), New York, 1912.

Cooke, John Esten, Virginia, A History of the People, Boston, 1903.
Craig, Neville B., The Olden Time, a magazine, 2 volumes, Pittsburgh, 1846-1848.
Creswell, Nicholas, Journal, 1774-1777, N. Y., 1924.
Crumrine, Boyd, History of Washington County, Philadelphia, 1882.
Cruzat, J. W., Journal de la Campagne de M. de Villiers (Louisiana Historical Society Publications).
Custis, George Washington Parke, Recollections and Private Memoirs of Washington, New York, 1860.

Dexter, F. B., see Stiles.
Dinwiddie Papers, 2 volumes, Edited by R. A. Brock (Virginia Historical Collections), Richmond, 1883.

Earle, Alice Morse, The Sabbath in Puritan New England, New York, 1892.
Earle, Alice Morse, Colonial Dames and Good Wives, New York, 1924.
Edmonds, Cyrus R., The Life and Times of General Washington, London, 1838.

Fiske, John, New France and New England, Boston and New York, 1902.
Fithian, Philip Vickers, Journal, Edited by John Roger Williams, Princeton, 1900.
Fitzpatrick, John C., Diaries of George Washington, Published for the Mount Vernon Ladies' Association of the Union, 4 volumes, Boston and New York, 1925.
Fitzpatrick, John C., The Spirit of the Revolution, New Light from some of the Original Sources of American History, Boston, 1924.
Ford, Paul Leicester, The True George Washington, Philadelphia, 1896.
Ford, Worthington C., Life of George Washington, Boston, 1899.
Ford, Worthington C., The Spurious Letters Attributed to Washington (Privately Printed), Brooklyn, 1889.
Ford, Worthington C., The Writings of George Washington, 14 volumes, New York, 1889-93.
Ford, Worthington C., Washington and "Centinel X," Reprinted from the Pennsylvania Magazine of History and Biography, January, 1899.
Ford, Worthington C., Washington as an Employer and Importer of Labor, Privately printed, Brooklyn, 1889.
Fortescue, the Hon. J. W., A History of the British Army, 11 volumes, London, 1910-1923.

Gist, Christopher, Journal, Published in the Collections of the Massachusetts Historical Society, Series III, volume V.
Goodwin, Maud Wilder, The Colonial Cavalier, Boston, 1895.
Green, H. C. and M. W., Pioneer Mothers of America, 3 volumes, New York, 1912.
Guedalla, Philip, Fathers of the Revolution, New York 1926.

Hale, Sir Matthew, Contemplations: Moral and Divine, London, 1605.
Hamilton, Stanislaus Murray, Letters to Washington and Accompanying

Papers, Published by the Society of the Colonial Dames of America, 5 volumes, Boston, 1898.

Hapgood, Norman, George Washington, New York, 1901.

Harland, Marion, Some Colonial Homesteads and their Stories, New York, 1897.

Harland, Mrs. Marion, More Colonial Homesteads and their Stories, New York, 1899.

Harrison, Fairfax, Aris Sonis Focisque, A Memoir of the Harrisons of Skimino, edited by Fairfax Harrison from material collected by Francis Burton Harrison. Privately printed, 1910.

Harrison, Fairfax, The Proprietors of the Northern Neck (Virginia Magazine of History and Biography, April, 1925–January, 1926), Richmond, Va.

Hart, Albert Bushnell, American History told by Contemporaries, 4 volumes, New York, 1910.

Hart, Albert B., Editor, The American Nation, 28 volumes, New York, 1905.

Haworth, Paul Leland, George Washington, Country Gentleman, Indianapolis, 1925.

Hellman, George S., New Letters of Washington, Harper's Magazine, January, 1907.

Hening, W. W., Statutes at Large, 13 volumes, New York, 1823.

(Henkels, Stan V.)   Fac-simile of Manuscript Prayer Book written by George Washington, Philadelphia, 1891.

Henry, William Wirt, Life, Correspondence and Speeches of Patrick Henry, 3 volumes, New York, 1891.

Heusser, Albert H., In the Footsteps of Washington, Paterson, N. J., 1921.

Hockett, Homer C., Political and Social History of the United States, 1492–1828. New York, 1926.

Holliday, Carl, Woman's Life in Colonial Days, Boston, 1922.

Hulbert, Archer Butler, Washington and the West, Cleveland, 1911.

Hulbert, Archer Butler, Historic Highways of America, 16 volumes, Cleveland, 1902-1905.

Irving, Washington, Life of George Washington, 5 volumes, New York, 1856.

Jameson, J. Franklin, The American Revolution Considered as a Social Movement, Princeton University Press, 1926.

Jefferson, Thomas, Notes on the State of Virginia, Newark, N. J., 1801.

Jett, Dora Chinn, In Tidewater Virginia, Richmond, 1924.

Johnson, Allen, Editor, The Chronicles of America, 50 vols. (Yale University Press), New Haven, 1921.

Johnson, Allen, The Historian and Historical Evidence, New York, 1926.

Johnson, General Bradley T., General Washington, New York, 1897.

Johnson, William J., George Washington the Christian, New York and Cincinnati, 1919.

Kercheval, Samuel, A History of the Valley of Virginia, Winchester, Virginia, 1833, Woodstock, Virginia, 1902.

Kerney, James, The Political Education of Woodrow Wilson, New York, 1926.

Koontz, Dr. Louis K., The Virginia Frontier, 1754-1763 (Johns Hopkins University Studies), Baltimore, 1925.

Lamb, Mrs. Martha J. and Mrs. Burton Harrison, History of the City of New York, 3 volumes, New York, 1877.
Latané, John H., The Early Relations between Virginia and Maryland (Johns Hopkins University Studies), Baltimore, 1895.
Lea, H. C., A History of the Inquisition of Spain, 4 volumes, New York, 1922.
Lea, H. C., Ethical Values in History, An Address to the American Historical Association (American Historical Review. January, 1904).
Lea, H. C., The Inquisition in the Spanish Dependencies, New York, 1922.
Leake, Dr. James Miller, The Virginia Committee System and the American Revolution (Johns Hopkins University Studies), Baltimore, 1917.
Lee, E. J., Lee of Virginia, Philadelphia, 1895.
Lewis, Captain Charles, Journal, 1755 (Virginia Historical Collections, vol. XI), Richmond, 1892.
Lincoln, Charles Henry, Correspondence of William Shirley, 2 volumes, New York, 1912.
Livingston, William, A Review of the Military Operations in North America, London, 1757.
Lodge, Henry C., The Life of George Washington, 2 volumes, Boston and New York, 1920.
Lossing, Benson J., Mary and Martha, the Mother and Wife of George Washington, New York, 1886.
Lowdermilk, W. H., History of Cumberland, Maryland, Washington, D. C., 1878.

Marshall, John, The Life of George Washington, 5 vols. Philadelphia, 1804-1807. Reprinted Fredericksburg, Virginia, 1926.
McGroarty, William Buckner, Elizabeth Washington of Hayfield (Virginia Magazine of History and Biography, April, 1925), Richmond, Virginia.
McIlwaine, Dr. H. R., The Struggle of Protestant Dissenters for Religious Toleration in Virginia (Johns Hopkins University Studies), Baltimore, 1894.
Meade, Bishop, Old Churches, Ministers and Families of Virginia, 2 volumes, Philadelphia, 1897.
Mémoire contenant le Précis des Faits, avex leurs Pièces justificatives, Paris, 1756 [probably written by J. N. Moreau].
Minnigerode, Meade, Some American Ladies, Seven Informal Biographies, New York, 1926.
Mitchell, S. Weir, The Youth of Washington, New York, 1904.
Moore, Charles, The Family Life of George Washington, Boston, 1926.
Mumby, Frank Arthur, George III and the American Revolution, Boston, 1925.

Nelson, William, The American Newspapers of the 18th Century as Sources of History. (American Historical Association, Annual Reports, 1908, I.)
Nevins, Allan, The American States during and after the Revolution. New York, 1924.

Nevins, Allan, American Social History as recorded by British Travellers, New York, 1923.
Nock, Albert Jay, Jefferson, New York, 1926.

Osgood, Herbert L., The American Colonies in the 18th Century (Columbia University Press), four volumes, New York, 1924.

Paltsits, Victor Hugo, Washington's Note Book, Selections from a Newly Discovered MS. written by him while a Virginia Colonel, in 1757. Bulletin of New York Public Library, vol. 24, No. 8, August, 1920.
Parkinson, Richard, A Tour in America in 1798, 1799, and 1800. 2 vols., London, 1805.
Parkman, Francis, The Conspiracy of Pontiac, and the Indian War after the Conquest of Canada, Boston, 1913.
Parkman, Francis, Montcalm and Wolfe, 2 volumes, Boston, 1925.
Paxson, Frederic L., History of the American Frontier 1763-1893, Boston, 1924.
Penniman, James Hosmer, George Washington as Man of Letters (Privately printed), Washington, D. C., 1918.
Pennsylvania Magazine of History and Biography.
Perfect Description of Virginia, A, London, 1649.
Prussing, Eugene E., George Washington in Love and Otherwise, Chicago, 1925.
Pryor, Mrs. Roger A., The Mother of Washington and Her Times, New York, 1903.

Randall, Daniel R., A Puritan Colony in Maryland (Johns Hopkins University Studies), Baltimore, 1886.
Remsburg, John E., Six Historic Americans, New York, 1906.
Robins, Sally Nelson, Love Stories of Famous Virginians, Published under the Auspices of the National Society, Colonial Dames of America in the State of Virginia, Richmond, 1925.
Rodman, Joseph, The Cherry Tree Legend, The Critic, February 1904, New York.

Sandburg, Carl, Abraham Lincoln, The Prairie Years, 2 volumes, New York, 1926.
Sargent, Winthrop, The History of an Expedition Against Fort Du Quesne in 1755 under Major-General Edward Braddock (No. 5 of the Pennsylvania Historical Society Memoirs), Philadelphia, 1856.
Schlesinger, Arthur Meier, New Viewpoints in American History, New York, 1925.
Shelton, W. H., The Jumel Mansion, Boston, 1916.
Smith, Captain John, Generall Historie, London, 1627. Richmond, Va., 1819 (also in Arber's Reprints).
Sparks, Jared, The Writings of George Washington, 12 volumes, Boston, 1834.
Sparks, Jared, The Life of George Washington, Boston, 1844.
Steiner, Bernard C., The Life and Correspondence of James McHenry, Cleveland, 1907.

Stiles, Ezra, The Literary Diary of (Edited by F. B. Dexter), 3 volumes, New York, 1901.

Stobo, Robert, Memoirs, Pittsburgh, 1854.

Thayer, William Roscoe, George Washington, Boston, 1922.

Thom, William Taylor, The Struggle for Religious Freedom in Virginia: The Baptists (Johns Hopkins University Studies), Baltimore, 1900.

Thomas, Antoine Léonard, Poésies Diverses, Jumonville, Paris, 1763.

Thomson, Charles. See Anonymous.

Thwaites, Reuben Gold, France in America, 1497-1673, The American Nation series vol. VII, New York, 1905.

Toner, Dr. J. M., Washington's Rules of Civility and Decent Behavior, Washington, D. C., 1888.

Toner, Dr. J. M., Index to Names of Persons and Churches in Bishop Meade's Old Churches, etc., Revised by Hugh A. Morrison (Publications of the Southern History Association), Washington, D. C., 1898.

Toner, Dr. J. M., The Daily Journal of Major George Washington in 1751-52, Albany, 1892.

Trevelyan, George Macaulay, History of England, New York, 1926.

Trevelyan, Sir George Otto, The American Revolution, 3 volumes, New York, 1908.

Turner, Frederick Jackson, The Frontier in American History, New York, 1921.

Tyler, Lyon Gardiner, England in America. The American Nation series vol. IV, New York, 1905.

Tyler, Lyon Gardiner, Narratives of Early Virginia, 1606-1625, New York, 1907.

Tyler, Lyon Gardiner, Williamsburg: The Old Colonial Capital, Richmond, Va., 1907.

Tyler's Quarterly Historical and Genealogical Magazine, Edited by Lyon G. Tyler. Holdcroft, Virginia.

Van Tyne, Claude H., The Causes of the War of Independence, Boston, 1922.

Villiers, M. de, See Cruzat, J. W.

Virginia Historical Collections, Richmond, Virginia.

Virginia Magazine of History and Biography. Published Quarterly by the Virginia Historical Society, Richmond, Virginia.

Volwiler, Albert T., George Croghan and the Westward Movement, 1741-1782, Cleveland, 1926.

Walpole, Horace, Memoirs of the Last Ten Years of the Reign of George II., Edited by Lord Holland, London, 1847.

Walter, James, Memorials of Washington and of Mary, his Mother, and Martha, his Wife from Letters and Papers of Robert Cary and James Sharpless. New York, 1887.

Washington, George, Writings. See Conway, Ford, Hulbert, Sparks, Toner.

Waters, Henry F., An Examination of the English Ancestry of George Washington, Boston, 1889.

Watson, John F., Annals of Philadelphia and Pennsylvania in the Olden Time, 2 volumes, Philadelphia, 1857.

Watson, Thomas E., Life and Times of Thomas Jefferson, New York, 1903.

Weeks, Dr. S. B., Church and State in North Carolina (Johns Hopkins University Studies), Baltimore, 1893.

Weems, Mason L., The Life of George Washington, Philadelphia, 1837.

Wertenbaker, Thomas J., The Planters of Colonial Virginia (Princeton University Press), 1922.

Wilson, Bird, Memoir of the Life of the Right Reverend William White, D.D., Philadelphia, 1839.

Wilson, James Grant, Memorial History of the City of New York, 4 volumes, New York, 1892.

Winsor, Justin, Memorial History of Boston, 4 volumes, Boston, 1880.

Winsor, Justin, Narrative and Critical History of America, 8 volumes, Boston, 1889.

Wister, Owen, The Seven Ages of Washington, a Biography, New York, 1922.

Wright, Reverend John, Early Prayer Books of America (Privately printed), St. Paul, Minn., 1896.

INDEX